MW00844907

ASP.NET Core 5 and Angular

Fourth Edition

Full-stack web development with .NET 5 and Angular 11

Valerio De Sanctis

Packt

BIRMINGHAM - MUMBAI

ASP.NET Core 5 and Angular

Fourth Edition

Producer: Caitlin Meadows
Acquisition Editor – Peer Reviews: Saby Dsilva
Content Development Editor: Lucy Wan
Technical Editor: Aniket Shetty
Project Editor: Parvathy Nair
Copy Editor: Safis Editing
Proofreader: Safis Editing
Indexer: Pratik Shirodkar
Presentation Designer: Ganesh Bhadwalkar

First published: October 2016
Second edition: November 2017
Third edition: February 2020
Fourth edition: January 2021

Production reference: 1270121

Published by Packt Publishing Ltd.
Livery Place
35 Livery Street
Birmingham B3 2PB, UK.

ISBN 978-1-80056-033-8

`www.packt.com`

Contributors

About the author

Valerio De Sanctis is a skilled IT professional with more than 20 years of experience in lead programming, web-based development, and project management using ASP.NET, PHP, and Java. He has held senior positions at a range of financial and insurance companies, most recently serving as Chief Technology Officer, Chief Security Officer, and Chief Operating Officer at a leading after-sales and IT service provider for multiple top-tier life and non-life insurance groups. He's also a **Microsoft Most Valuable Professional** (**MVP**) for Developer Technologies and Cloud and Datacenter Management.

He has written various books on web development, many of which have become best-sellers on Amazon, with tens of thousands of copies sold worldwide.

I would like to thank those who supported me in writing this book: my beloved and beautiful wife, Carla, for her awesome encouragement and invaluable support; my children, Viola and Daniele, as well as my parents and my sister. Last but not least, I would like to thank you, the reader, for picking up this book. I really hope you will enjoy it!

About the reviewer

Wouter Huysentruit is a seasoned software developer and architect with 20 years of experience in many different fields. He strives for solutions that are easy to understand and maintain. His current interest is in developing user-friendly web applications based on Microsoft technologies and Angular, in addition to working on many open-source projects for which he also received the Microsoft MVP award.

Wouter works for the Belgian company Noest as a .NET software architect. Next to his day job, Wouter also runs his own small company, Cup of Tea, with a focus on open-source software.

A big thanks goes out to my wife and kids for supporting me during the review of this book.

Table of Contents

Preface xiii

Chapter 1: Getting Ready 1

Technical requirements 2
Two players, one goal 2
The ASP.NET Core revolution 3
ASP.NET Core 1.x 3
ASP.NET Core 2.x 4
ASP.NET Core 3.x 6
.NET 5 7
What's new in Angular? 10
GetAngular 10
AngularJS 11
Angular 2 12
Angular 4 13
Angular 5 14
Angular 6 14
Angular 7 15
Angular 8 16
Angular 9 17
Angular 10 18
Angular 11 19
Reasons for choosing .NET and Angular 19
A full-stack approach 21
MPAs, SPAs, PWAs, and NWAs 21
Multi-page applications 22
Single-page applications 22
Progressive web applications 23
Native web applications 25
Product owner expectations 25
A sample SPA project 27
Not your usual Hello World! 28
Preparing the workspace 28
Disclaimer – do (not) try this at home 29
The broken code myth 29
Stay hungry, stay foolish, yet be responsible as well 30
Setting up the project 31
Installing the .NET 5 SDK 31
Checking the SDK version 32
Creating the .NET and Angular project 32

Opening the new project in Visual Studio 32
Performing a test run 34
Summary **36**
Suggested topics **36**
References **37**

Chapter 2: Looking Around **39**

Technical requirements **40**
Solution overview **40**
The ASP.NET back-end **41**
Razor Pages 41
Advantages of using Razor Pages 42
Controllers 42
Advantages of using Controllers 42
WeatherForecastController 43
Configuration files 43
Program.cs 44
Startup.cs 46
appsettings.json 52
The Angular front-end **53**
Workspace 54
angular.json 54
package.json 55
tsconfig.json 61
Other workspace-level files 62
The /ClientApp/src/ folder 63
The /app/ folder 64
Testing the app 67
HomeComponent 67
NavMenuComponent 68
CounterComponent 69
Our first app test 71
Creating a new app with the Angular CLI **72**
Installing the Angular CLI 73
Creating a new Angular app 73
Comparing the Angular apps 75
Updating the Startup.cs file 76
Testing the NG Angular app 77
Getting to work **78**
Static file caching 78
How the HTTP cache works 80
Improving our caching strategy 82
Client app cleanup 86
Trimming down the component list 86
The AppModule source code 89
Adding the AppRoutingModule 89
Updating the NavMenu 91
Summary **94**
Suggested topics **95**

References 95

Chapter 3: Front-End and Back-End Interactions 97

Technical requirements 98

Introducing ASP.NET Core health checks 98

Adding the HealthChecks middleware 98

Adding an Internet Control Message Protocol (ICMP) check 100

Possible outcomes 101

Creating an ICMPHealthCheck class 101

Adding the ICMPHealthCheck to the pipeline 103

Improving the ICMPHealthCheck class 104

Adding parameters and response messages 104

Updating the middleware setup 106

Implementing a custom output message 107

Configuring the output message 109

Health checks in Angular 110

Creating the Angular component 110

Creating components using the Angular CLI 110

health-check.component.ts 111

health-check.component.html 121

health-check.component.css 122

Adding the component to the Angular app 124

AppModule 124

AppRoutingModule 125

NavMenuComponent 125

Testing it out 126

Summary 127

Suggested topics 128

References 128

Chapter 4: Data Model with Entity Framework Core 131

Technical requirements 132

The WorldCities web app 132

Styling and CSS basics 134

Reasons to use a data server 137

The data source 138

The data model 140

Introducing Entity Framework Core 140

Installing Entity Framework Core 141

The SQL Server Data Provider 142

DBMS licensing models 143

What about Linux? 143

SQL Server alternatives 144

Data modeling approaches 144

Code-First 144

Database-First 145

Making a choice 147

Creating the entities 147

Defining the entities 148

The City entity 149

The Country entity 152
Defining relationships 155
Adding the Country property to the City entity class 155
Adding the Cities property to the Country entity class 156
Defining the database table names 158
Getting a SQL Server instance **159**
Installing SQL Server 2019 159
Creating a SQL Database on Azure 162
Setting up a SQL Database 163
Configuring the instance 166
Configuring the database 169
Creating the WorldCities database 170
Adding the WorldCities login 171
Mapping the login to the database 172
Creating the database using Code-First **173**
Setting up the DbContext 173
Entity type configuration methods 174
Data Annotations 174
Fluent API 175
EntityTypeConfiguration classes 176
Making a choice 177
Database initialization strategies 178
Updating the appsettings.json file 179
Securing the connection string 179
Introducing Secrets Storage 181
Adding the secrets.json file 181
Working with the secrets.json file 184
Creating the database 184
Updating Startup.cs 184
Adding the initial migration 186
Using the dotnet CLI 186
Using the Package Manager Console 190
Understanding migrations 190
Populating the database **191**
Implementing SeedController 192
Importing the Excel file 193
Entity controllers **200**
CitiesController 201
CountriesController 204
Testing it out 204
Summary **206**
Suggested topics **206**
References **207**
Chapter 5: Fetching and Displaying Data **209**
Technical requirements **209**
Fetching data **210**
Requests and responses 210
JSON conventions and defaults 210

A (very) long list 212
city.ts 212
cities.component.ts 213
cities.component.html 214
cities.component.css 216
app.module.ts 216
app-routing.module.ts 217
nav-component.html 218
Serving data with Angular Material 219
MatTableModule 221
Adding pagination with MatPaginatorModule 225
Client-side paging 226
Server-side paging 229
Adding sorting with MatSortModule 240
Extending ApiResult 240
Installing System.Linq.Dynamic.Core 244
Updating CitiesController 249
Updating the Angular app 249
Adding filtering 254
Extending ApiResult (again) 255
CitiesController 261
CitiesComponent 262
CitiesComponent template (HTML) file 264
CitiesComponent style (CSS) file 264
AngularMaterialModule 265
Performance considerations 267
Adding the countries to the loop 267
ASP.NET 267
CountriesController 267
Angular 270
country.ts 271
countries.component.ts 271
countries.component.html 273
countries.component.css 274
AppModule 275
AppRoutingModule 275
NavComponent 276
Testing CountriesComponent 277
Summary 278
Suggested topics 278
ASP.NET 278
Angular 278
References 279
Chapter 6: Forms and Data Validation 281
Technical requirements 282
Exploring Angular forms 282
Forms in Angular 282
Reasons to use forms 284
Template-Driven Forms 285
The pros 286

The cons 286
Model-Driven/Reactive Forms 287
Building our first Reactive Form 290
ReactiveFormsModule 290
CityEditComponent 291
city-edit.component.ts 293
city-edit.component.html 296
city-edit.component.css 297
Adding the navigation link 297
app.module.ts 298
app-routing.module.ts 299
cities.component.html 299
Adding a new city 301
Extending the CityEditComponent 302
Adding the "Add a new City" button 306
Adding a new route 306
HTML select 308
Angular Material select (MatSelectModule) 314
Understanding data validation 316
Template-driven validation 317
The Safe Navigation Operator 318
Model-driven validation 319
Our first validators 319
Server-side validation 326
DupeCityValidator 328
Introducing the FormBuilder 333
Creating the CountryEditComponent 334
country-edit.component.ts 334
The IsDupeField server-side API 339
country-edit.component.html 341
country-edit.component.css 343
AppModule 344
AppRoutingModule 345
countries.component.html 346
Testing the CountryEditComponent 347
Improving the filter behavior 350
Throttling and debouncing 351
Definitions 351
Why would we want to throttle or debounce our code? 351
Debouncing calls to the back-end 352
Updating the CitiesComponent 352
Updating the CountriesComponent 354
What about throttling? 355
Summary 355
Suggested topics 356
References 356
Chapter 7: Code Tweaks and Data Services 359
Technical requirements 360

Optimizations and tweaks **360**
Template improvements 360
Form validation shortcuts 360
Class inheritance 362
Implementing a BaseFormComponent 362
Extending CityEditComponent 364
Extending CountryEditComponent 365
Bug fixes and improvements **366**
Validating lat and lon 366
city-edit.component.ts 366
city-edit.component.html 368
Adding the number of cities 369
CountriesController 370
Creating the CountryDTO class 372
Angular front-end updates 373
DTO classes – should we really use them? 377
Separation of concerns 377
Security considerations 377
DTO classes versus anonymous types 378
Securing entities 379
Final thoughts 382
Adding the country name 383
CitiesController 383
Angular front-end updates 384
Data services **388**
XMLHttpRequest versus Fetch (versus HttpClient) 388
XMLHttpRequest 388
Fetch 390
HttpClient 391
Building a data service 393
Creating the BaseService 394
Adding the common interface methods 395
Creating the CityService 397
Implementing the CityService 399
Creating the CountryService 406
Summary **413**
Suggested topics **414**
References **414**
Chapter 8: Back-End and Front-End Debugging **417**
Technical requirements **418**
Back-end debugging **418**
Windows or Linux? 419
The basics 419
Conditional breakpoints 420
Conditions 421
Actions 421
Testing the conditional breakpoint 422
The Output window 423
Configuring the Output window 424

Debugging EF Core 425
The GetCountries() SQL query 426
Front-end debugging **432**
Visual Studio JavaScript debugging 433
JavaScript source maps 434
Browser developer tools 435
Angular form debugging 439
A look at the Form Model 440
The pipe operator 442
Reacting to changes 442
The activity log 443
Client-side debugging 447
Unsubscribing the Observables 447
The unsubscribe() method 448
The takeUntil() operator 449
Other viable alternatives 451
Should we always unsubscribe? 453
Application logging **453**
Introducing ASP.NET Core logging 455
DBMS structured logging with Serilog 455
Installing the NuGet packages 455
Configuring Serilog 456
Logging HTTP requests 458
Accessing the logs 458
Summary **461**
Suggested topics **461**
References **462**
Chapter 9: ASP.NET Core and Angular Unit Testing **463**
Technical requirements **464**
ASP.NET Core unit tests **464**
Creating the WorldCities.Test project 464
Moq 466
Microsoft.EntityFramework.InMemory 467
Adding the WorldCities dependency reference 468
Our first test 468
Arrange 470
Act 471
Assert 472
Executing the test 472
Debugging tests 474
Test-driven development 476
Behavior-driven development 478
Angular unit tests **479**
General concepts 480
Introducing the TestBed interface 481
Testing with Jasmine 481
Our first Angular test suite 482
The import section 482
The describe and beforeEach sections 483

Adding a mock CityService 484
Implementing the mock CityService 485
Configuring the fixture and the component 488
Creating the title test 489
Creating the cities tests 489
Running the test suite 491
Summary **493**
Suggested topics **494**
References **494**
Chapter 10: Authentication and Authorization **495**
Technical requirements **496**
To auth, or not to auth **496**
Authentication 497
Third-party authentication 498
Authorization 499
Third-party authorization 499
Proprietary versus third-party 500
Proprietary auth with .NET Core **501**
The ASP.NET Core Identity model 503
Entity types 503
Setting up ASP.NET Core Identity 504
Adding the NuGet packages 505
Creating ApplicationUser 505
Extending ApplicationDbContext 506
Adjusting our unit tests 507
Configuring the ASP.NET Core Identity middleware 508
Configuring IdentityServer 511
Revising SeedController 513
A word on async tasks, awaits, and deadlocks 523
Updating the database **524**
Adding identity migration 525
Applying the migration 525
Updating the existing data model 526
Dropping and recreating the data model from scratch 527
Seeding the data 528
Authentication methods **529**
Sessions 530
Tokens 531
Signatures 532
Two-factor 533
Conclusions 533
Implementing authentication in Angular **534**
Creating the AuthSample project 534
Troubleshooting the AuthSample project 535
Exploring the Angular authorization APIs 537
Route Guards 539
HttpInterceptor 544
The authorization components 546

Testing registration and login 552
Implementing the auth API in the WorldCities app 553
Importing the front-end authorization APIs 554
api-authorization.constants 554
AppModule 554
AppRoutingModule 555
NavMenuComponent 556
Adjusting the back-end code 557
Installing the ASP.NET Core Identity UI package 558
Mapping Razor Pages to EndpointMiddleware 559
Securing the back-end action methods 559
Testing login and registration 561
Adding an email sending service 563
Transactional email API using SendGrid 564
Create a SendGrid account 564
Get the Web API key 566
Install the SendGrid NuGet package 568
Verify the integration 568
Implement the IEmailSender interface 571
Scaffold the Identity pages 575
Disable link-based account verification 578
Test the email-based account verification 579
External SMTP server using MailKit 582
Install the MailKit NuGet package 582
Set up the SMTP settings 583
Implement the IEmailSender interface 583
Startup class 586
Summary 587
Suggested topics 588
References 588
Chapter 11: Progressive Web Apps 591
Technical requirements 592
PWA – distinctive features 592
Secure origin 593
Offline loading and Web App Manifest 594
Service workers versus HttpInterceptors 595
Introducing @angular/service-worker 595
The ASP.NET Core PWA middleware alternative 596
Implementing the PWA requirements 597
Manual installation 597
Adding the @angular/service-worker npm package 598
Updating the angular.json file 598
Importing ServiceWorkerModule 599
Updating the index.html file 600
Adding the Web App Manifest file 601
Adding the favicon 605
Adding the ngsw-config.json file 606
Automatic installation 607
The Angular PNG icon set 608
Handling the offline status 609

Option 1 – the window's ononline/onoffline event 609
Option 2 – the Navigator.onLine property 609
Downsides of the JavaScript approaches 610
Option 3 – the ng-connection-service npm package 610
Installing ng-connection-service 611
Updating the app.component.ts file 612
Removing the isOnline.txt static file from the cache 613
Installing the ng-connection-service via npm (alternate route) 614
Updating the app.component.html file 615
Cross-Origin Resource Sharing 616
Testing the PWA capabilities **618**
Compiling the app with the Angular CLI 618
Updating the Startup.cs file 618
Compiling the app with Visual Studio 619
Creating a publish profile 620
Copying the CLI-generated files 622
Updating the Startup.cs file 623
Testing out our PWAs 623
Installing the PWA 626
Alternative testing methods 628
Serving our PWA using http-server 628
Summary **629**
Suggested topics **629**
References **630**
Chapter 12: Windows, Linux, and Azure Deployment **631**
Technical requirements **632**
Getting ready for production **632**
ASP.NET Core deployment tips 632
The launchSettings.json file 633
Development, staging, and production environments 634
Rule(s) of thumb 636
Setting the environment in production 637
.NET 5 deployment modes 638
Angular deployment tips 640
ng serve, ng build, and the package.json file 641
Differential loading 642
The angular.json configuration file 644
Automatic deployment 644
CORS policy 644
Windows deployment **645**
Creating a Windows Server VM on MS Azure 645
Accessing the MS Azure portal 646
Adding and configuring a new VM 646
Configuring a DNS name label 649
Setting the inbound security rules 650
Configuring the VM 652
Adding the IIS web server 652
Installing the ASP.NET Core Windows hosting bundle 654
Publishing and deploying the HealthCheck app 655

Folder publish profile 655
FTP publish profile 656
Azure Virtual Machine publish profile 657
Alternative method using the IIS Web Deploy Publishing feature 659
Configuring IIS 661
Adding an SSL certificate 661
Adding a new IIS website entry 663
Configuring the IIS application pool 665
Testing the HealthCheck web application 666
Updating the testing machine's HOSTS files 667
Testing the app 667
Linux deployment **669**
Creating a Linux CentOS VM on MS Azure 669
Add and configure the Linux CentOS VM 670
Configuring a DNS name label 671
Setting the inbound security rules 671
Configuring the Linux VM 672
Connecting to the VM 672
Installing the ASP.NET Core runtime 673
Installing Nginx 674
Opening the 80 and 443 TCP ports 676
Adapting the WorldCities app 678
Adding the forwarded headers middleware 678
Checking the database connection string 679
Creating the appsettings.Production.json file 680
Publishing and deploying the WorldCities app 681
Creating the /var/www folder 682
Adding permissions 682
Copying the WorldCities publish folder 683
Configuring Kestrel and Nginx 685
Creating the self-signed SSL certificate 686
Configuring the Kestrel service 687
Configuring the Nginx reverse proxy 690
Testing the WorldCities application 692
Update the testing machine's HOSTS files 693
Testing the app 693
Troubleshooting 695
Azure App Service deployment **696**
Creating the Web App instance 696
Publishing the Web App 699
Summary **701**
Suggested topics **702**
References **703**
Other Books You May Enjoy **705**
Index **707**

Preface

ASP.NET Core is a free and open source modular web framework developed by Microsoft that runs on top of the full .NET Framework (Windows) or .NET Core (cross-platform). It has been made specifically for building efficient HTTP services that can be reached and consumed by a massive range of clients, including web browsers, mobile devices, smart TVs, web-based home automation tools, and more.

Angular is the successor to AngularJS, a world-renowned development framework born with the aim of providing the coder with the toolbox that is needed to build reactive and cross-platform web-based apps that are optimized for desktop and mobile. It features a structure-rich template approach based upon a natural, easy-to-write, and readable syntax.

Technically, these two frameworks have little or nothing in common: ASP.NET Core is mostly focused on the server-side part of the web development stack, while Angular is dedicated to covering all the client-side aspects of web applications, such as the **User Interface** (**UI**) and **User Experience** (**UX**). However, both of them came into being because of a common vision shared by their respective creators: the HTTP protocol is not limited to serving web pages; it can also be used as a viable platform upon which to build web-based APIs to effectively send and receive data. This is the notion that slowly made its way through the first 20 years of the World Wide Web's life and is now an undeniable, widely acknowledged statement and also a fundamental pillar of almost every modern web development approach.

As for the reasons behind this perspective switch, there are plenty of good ones, the most important of them being related to the intrinsic characteristics of the HTTP protocol: it's rather simple to use, and flexible enough to match most of the development needs of the ever-changing environment that the World Wide Web happens to be in. This is not to mention how universal it has become nowadays: almost any platform that we can think of has an HTTP library, so HTTP services can reach a broad range of clients, including desktop and mobile browsers, IoT devices, desktop applications, video games, and so on.

The main purpose of this book is to bring together the latest versions of ASP.NET Core and Angular within a single development stack to demonstrate how they can be used to create high-performance web applications and services that can be used seamlessly by any clients.

Who this book is for

This book is for intermediate and experienced developers who already know about ASP.NET Core and Angular and are looking to learn more about them and understand how to use them together to create a production-ready **Single-Page Application** (**SPA**) or **Progressive Web Application** (**PWA**) using SQL Server and Entity Framework Core.

However, the fully documented code samples (also available on GitHub) and the step-by-step implementation tutorials make this book easy to understand even for beginners and developers who are just getting started.

What this book covers

Chapter 1, Getting Ready, introduces some of the basic concepts of the frameworks that we are going to use throughout the book, as well as the various kinds of web applications that can be created (SPAs, PWAs, native web apps, and more).

Chapter 2, Looking Around, is a detailed overview of the various back-end and front-end elements provided by the .NET Core and Angular template shipped with Visual Studio 2019, backed up with some high-level explanations of how they can work together in a typical HTTP request-response cycle.

Chapter 3, Front-End and Back-End Interactions, provides a comprehensive tutorial for building a sample ASP.NET Core and Angular app that provides diagnostic info to the end user by querying health check middleware using a Bootstrap-based Angular client.

Chapter 4, Data Model with Entity Framework Core, constitutes a journey through Entity Framework Core and its capabilities as an **Object-Relational Mapping** (**ORM**) framework, from SQL database deployment (cloud-based and/or local instance) to data model design, including various techniques to read and write data from back-end controllers.

Chapter 5, Fetching and Displaying Data, covers how to expose Entity Framework Core data using the ASP.NET Core back-end web API, consume that data with Angular, and then show it to end users using the front-end UI.

Chapter 6, Forms and Data Validation, details how to implement the HTTP PUT and POST methods in back-end web APIs in order to perform insert and update operations with Angular, along with server-side and client-side data validation.

Chapter 7, Code Tweaks and Data Services, explores some useful refactoring and improvements to strengthen your app's source code and includes an in-depth analysis of Angular's data services to understand why and how to use them.

Chapter 8, Back-End and Front-End Debugging, looks at how to properly debug the back-end and front-end stacks of a typical web application using the various debugging tools provided by Visual Studio to their full extent.

Chapter 9, ASP.NET Core and Angular Unit Testing, comprises a detailed review of the **Test-Driven Development** (**TDD**) and **Behavior-Driven Development** (**BDD**) development practices and goes into how to define, implement, and perform back-end and front-end unit tests using xUnit, Jasmine, and Karma.

Chapter 10, Authentication and Authorization, gives you a high-level introduction to the concepts of authentication and authorization and presents a narrow lineup of some of the various techniques, methodologies, and approaches to properly implementing proprietary or third-party user identity systems. A practical example of a working ASP.NET Core and Angular authentication mechanism based upon ASP.NET Identity and IdentityServer4 is included.

Chapter 11, Progressive Web Apps, delves into how to convert an existing SPA into a PWA using service workers, manifest files, and offline caching features.

Chapter 12, Windows, Linux, and Azure Deployment, teaches you how to deploy the ASP.NET and Angular apps created in the previous chapters and publish them in a cloud-based environment using a Windows Server 2019 or Linux CentOS virtual machine, as well as Azure App Service deployment.

To get the most out of this book

These are the software packages (and relevant version numbers) used to write this book and test the source code:

- Visual Studio 2019 Community Edition 16.8.2 with the optional ASP.NET and web development workload (it can be selected from the *Workloads* section within the Visual Studio installer app)
- Microsoft .NET 5 SDK 5.0.100
- TypeScript 4.0.5
- NuGet package manager 5.7.0
- Node.js 14.15.0 (we strongly suggest installing it using the **Node Version Manager**, also known as **NVM**)
- Angular 11.0.1

For deployment on **Windows**:

- **Internet Information Services** (**IIS**) (Windows Server)
- **ASP.NET Core Runtime 5 and Windows Hosting Bundle Installer for Win64** (ASP.NET official website)

For deployment on **Linux**:

- **ASP.NET Core Runtime 5 for Linux** (YUM package manager)
- **.NET 5 CLR for Linux** (YUM package manager)
- **Nginx HTTP Server** (YUM package manager)

If you're on Windows, I strongly suggest installing Node.js using NVM for Windows, a neat Node.js version manager for the Windows system. You can download it from the following URL:

`https://github.com/coreybutler/nvm-windows/releases`

We strongly suggest using the same version used within this book - or newer, but at your own risk! Jokes aside, if you prefer to use a different version, that's perfectly fine, as long as you are aware that, in that case, you may need to make some manual changes and adjustments to the source code.

Download the example code files

The code bundle for the book is hosted on GitHub at `https://github.com/PacktPublishing/ASP.NET-Core-5-and-Angular`. We also have other code bundles from our rich catalog of books and videos available at `https://github.com/PacktPublishing/`. Check them out!

Download the color images

We also provide a PDF file that has color images of the screenshots/diagrams used in this book. You can download it here: `https://static.packt-cdn.com/downloads/9781800560338_ColorImages.pdf`.

Conventions used

There are a number of text conventions used throughout this book.

`CodeInText`: Indicates code words in text, database table names, folder names, filenames, file extensions, pathnames, dummy URLs, user input, and Twitter handles. For example: "Navigate to the `/ClientApp/src/app/cities` folder."

A block of code is set as follows:

```
<mat-form-field [hidden]="!cities">
<input matInput (keyup)="loadData($event.target.value)"
placeholder="Filter by name (or part of it)...">
</mat-form-field>
```

When we wish to draw your attention to a particular part of a code block, the relevant lines or items are **`set in bold`**:

```
import { FormGroup, FormControl } from '@angular/forms';

class ModelFormComponent implements OnInit {
    form: FormGroup;

    ngOnInit() {
```

```
            this.form = new FormGroup({
                title: new FormControl()
            });
        }
    }
```

Any command-line input or output is written as follows:

```
> dotnet new angular -o HealthCheck
```

Bold: Indicates a new term, an important word, or words that you see on the screen, for example, in menus or dialog boxes, also appear in the text like this. For example: "A simple **Add a new City** button will fix both these issues at once."

Warnings or important notes appear like this.

Tips and tricks appear like this.

Get in touch

Feedback from our readers is always welcome.

General feedback: Email `feedback@packtpub.com`, and mention the book's title in the subject of your message. If you have questions about any aspect of this book, please email us at `questions@packtpub.com`.

Errata: Although we have taken every care to ensure the accuracy of our content, mistakes do happen. If you have found a mistake in this book we would be grateful if you would report this to us. Please visit `http://www.packtpub.com/submit-errata`, selecting your book, clicking on the Errata Submission Form link, and entering the details.

Piracy: If you come across any illegal copies of our works in any form on the Internet, we would be grateful if you would provide us with the location address or website name. Please contact us at `copyright@packtpub.com` with a link to the material.

If you are interested in becoming an author: If there is a topic that you have expertise in and you are interested in either writing or contributing to a book, please visit `http://authors.packtpub.com`.

Reviews

Please leave a review. Once you have read and used this book, why not leave a review on the site that you purchased it from? Potential readers can then see and use your unbiased opinion to make purchase decisions, we at Packt can understand what you think about our products, and our authors can see your feedback on their book. Thank you!

For more information about Packt, please visit `packtpub.com`.

1

Getting Ready

In this chapter, we'll build the basics of our ASP.NET and Angular journey by mixing theoretical coverage of their most relevant features with a practical approach. More specifically, in the first part of this chapter, we'll briefly review the recent history of ASP.NET/ .NET Core and Angular frameworks, while in the latter part, we'll learn how to configure our local development environment so we can assemble, build, and test a sample web application boilerplate.

By the end of this chapter, you'll have gained knowledge of the path taken by ASP.NET and Angular to improve web development in the last few years and learned how to properly set up an ASP.NET and Angular web application.

Here are the main topics that we are going to cover:

- **The ASP.NET Core revolution**: A brief history of ASP.NET Core and Angular's most recent achievements
- **A full-stack approach**: The importance of being able to learn how to design, assemble, and deliver a complete product
- **Multi-Page Applications** (**MPAs**), **Single-Page Applications** (**SPAs**), **Native Web Applications** (**NWAs**), **and Progressive Web Applications** (**PWAs**): Key features of and the most important differences between the various types of web applications, as well as how well ASP.NET and Angular could relate to each one of them
- **A sample SPA project**: What we're going to do throughout this book
- **Preparing the workspace**: How to set up our workstation to achieve our first goal – implementing a simple Hello World boilerplate that will be further extended in the following chapters

Technical requirements

These are the software packages (and relevant version numbers) used to write this book and test the source code:

- Visual Studio 2019 Community edition 16.8.2 with the optional *ASP.NET and web development* workload (it can be selected from the Workloads section within the Visual Studio installer app)
- Microsoft .NET 5 SDK 5.0.100
- TypeScript 4.0.5
- NuGet package manager 5.7.0
- Node.js 14.15.0 (we strongly suggest installing it using **Node Version Manager**, also known as **nvm**)
- Angular 11.0.1

> If you're on Windows, we strongly suggest installing Node.js using `nvm` for Windows – a neat Node.js version manager for the Windows system. You can download it from the following URL: `https://github.com/coreybutler/nvm-windows/releases`

We strongly suggest using the same version used within this book – or newer, but at your own risk! Jokes aside, if you prefer to use a different version, that's perfectly fine, as long as you are aware that, in that case, *you may need to make some manual changes and adjustments to the source code.*

The code files for this chapter can be found here: `https://github.com/PacktPublishing/ASP.NET-Core-5-and-Angular`

Two players, one goal

From the perspective of a fully functional web-based application, we can say that the Web API interface provided with the ASP.NET framework is a programmatic set of server-side handlers used by the server to expose a number of hooks and/or endpoints to a defined request-response message system. This is typically expressed in structured markup languages (XML), language-independent data formats (JSON), or query languages for APIs (GraphQL). As we've already said, this is achieved by exposing **application programming interfaces** (**APIs**) through HTTP and/or HTTPS protocols via a publicly available web server such as IIS, Node.js, Apache, NGINX, and so on.

Similarly, Angular can be described as a modern, feature-rich, client-side framework that pushes the HTML and ECMAScript's most advanced features, along with the modern browser's capabilities, to their full extent by binding the input and/or output parts of an HTML web page into a flexible, reusable, and easily testable model.

Can we combine the *back-end* strengths of ASP.NET and the *front-end* capabilities of Angular in order to build a modern, feature-rich, and highly versatile web application?

The answer, in short, is yes. In the following chapters, we'll see how we can do that by analyzing all the fundamental aspects of a well-written, properly designed, web-based product, and how the latest versions of ASP.NET and/or Angular can be used to handle each one of them. However, before doing all that, it might be very useful to backtrack a bit and spend some valuable time recollecting what's happened in the last 6 years in the development history of the two frameworks we're going to use. It will be very useful to understand the main reasons why we're still giving them full credit, despite the valuable efforts of their ever-growing competitors.

The ASP.NET Core revolution

To summarize what has happened in the ASP.NET world within the last 6 years is not an easy task; in short, we can say that we've undoubtedly witnessed the most important series of changes in .NET Framework since the year it came to life. This was a revolution that changed the whole Microsoft approach to software development in almost every way. To properly understand what happened in those years, it would be useful to identify some distinctive key frames within a slow, yet constant, journey that allowed a company known (and somewhat loathed) for its proprietary software, licenses, and patents to become a driving force for open source development worldwide.

The first relevant step, at least in my humble opinion, was taken on April 3, 2014 at the annual Microsoft Build conference, which took place at the Moscone Center (West) in San Francisco. It was there, during a memorable keynote speech, that Anders Hejlsberg – father of Delphi and lead architect of C# – publicly released the first version of the .NET Compiler Platform, known as Roslyn, as an open source project. It was also there that Scott Guthrie, executive vice president of the Microsoft Cloud and AI group, announced the official launch of the .NET Foundation, a non-profit organization aimed at improving open source software development and collaborative work within the .NET ecosystem.

From that pivotal day, the .NET development team published a constant flow of Microsoft open source projects on the GitHub platform, including Entity Framework Core (May 2014), TypeScript (October 2014), .NET Core (October 2014), CoreFX (November 2014), CoreCLR and RyuJIT (January 2015), MSBuild (March 2015), the .NET Core CLI (October 2015), Visual Studio Code (November 2015), .NET Standard (September 2016), and so on.

ASP.NET Core 1.x

The most important achievement brought by these efforts toward open source development was the public release of ASP.NET Core 1.0, which came out in Q3 2016. It was a complete reimplementation of the ASP.NET framework that we had known since January 2002 and that had evolved, without significant changes in its core architecture, up to version 4.6.2 (August 2016). The brand new framework united all the previous web application technologies, such as MVC, Web API, and web pages, into a single programming module, formerly known as MVC6. The new framework introduced a fully featured, cross-platform component, also known as .NET Core, shipped with the whole set of open source tools mentioned previously, namely, a compiler platform (Roslyn), a cross-platform runtime (CoreCLR), and an improved x64 Just-In-Time compiler (RyuJIT).

> Some of you might remember that ASP.NET Core was originally called ASP.NET 5. As a matter of fact, ASP.NET 5 was no less than the original name of ASP.NET Core until mid-2016, when the Microsoft developer team chose to rename it to emphasize the fact that it was a complete rewrite. The reasons for that, along with the Microsoft vision about the new product, are further explained in the following Scott Hanselman blog post that anticipated the changes on January 16, 2016: `http://www.hanselman.com/blog/ASPNET5IsDeadIntroducingASPNETCore10AndNETCore10.aspx`
>
> Scott's 2016 words might sound a bit ironic nowadays, as Microsoft recently decided to bring the ASP.NET 5 name back to the fore and ditch the "Core" term: we'll talk more about that in a while.
>
> For those who don't know, Scott Hanselman has been the outreach and community manager for .NET/ASP.NET/IIS/Azure and Visual Studio since 2007. Additional information regarding the perspective switch is also available in the following article by Jeffrey T. Fritz, program manager for Microsoft and a NuGet team leader: `https://blogs.msdn.microsoft.com/webdev/2016/02/01/an-update-on-asp-net-core-and-net-core/`
>
> As for Web API 2, it was a dedicated framework for building HTTP services that returned pure JSON or XML data instead of web pages. Initially born as an alternative to the MVC platform, it has been merged with the latter into the new, general-purpose web application framework known as MVC6, which is now shipped as a separate module of ASP.NET Core.

The 1.0 final release was shortly followed by ASP.NET Core 1.1 (Q4 2016), which brought some new features and performance enhancements, and also addressed many bugs and compatibility issues affecting the earlier release. These new features include the ability to configure middleware as filters (by adding them to the MVC pipeline rather than the HTTP request pipeline); a built-in, host-independent URL rewrite module, made available through the dedicated `Microsoft.AspNetCore.Rewrite` NuGet package; view components as tag helpers; view compilation at runtime instead of on demand; .NET native compression and caching middleware modules; and so on.

> For a detailed list of all the new features, improvements, and bug fixes of ASP.NET Core 1.1, check out the following links.
>
> **Release notes**: `https://github.com/aspnet/AspNetCore/releases/1.1.0`
>
> **Commits list**: `https://github.com/dotnet/core/blob/master/release-notes/1.1/1.1-commits.md`

ASP.NET Core 2.x

Another major step was taken with ASP.NET Core 2.0, which came out in Q2 2017 as a preview and then in Q3 2017 for the final release. The new version featured a wide number of significant interface improvements, mostly aimed at standardizing the shared APIs among .NET Framework, .NET Core, and .NET Standard to make them backward-compatible with .NET Framework.

Thanks to these efforts, moving existing .NET Framework projects to .NET Core and/or .NET Standard became a lot easier than before, giving many traditional developers a chance to try and adapt to the new paradigm without losing their existing know-how.

Again, the major version was shortly followed by an improved and refined one: ASP.NET Core 2.1. This was officially released on May 30, 2018 and introduced a series of additional security and performance improvements, as well as a bunch of new features, including SignalR, an open source library that simplifies adding real-time web functionality to .NET Core apps; Razor class libraries; a significant improvement in the Razor SDK that allows developers to build views and pages into reusable class libraries, and/or library projects that could be shipped as NuGet packages; the Identity UI library and scaffolding, to add identity to any app and customize it to meet your needs; HTTPS support enabled by default; built-in **General Data Protection Regulation** (**GDPR**) support using privacy-oriented APIs and templates that give users control over their personal data and cookie consent; updated SPA templates for Angular and ReactJS client-side frameworks; and much more.

> For a detailed list of all the new features, improvements, and bug fixes of ASP.NET Core 2.1, check out the following links.
>
> **Release notes**: `https://docs.microsoft.com/en-US/aspnet/core/release-notes/aspnetcore-2.1`
>
> **Commits list**: `https://github.com/dotnet/core/blob/master/release-notes/2.1/2.1.0-commit.md`

Wait a minute: did we just say Angular? Yeah, that's right. As a matter of fact, since its initial release, ASP.NET Core has been specifically designed to seamlessly integrate with popular client-side frameworks such as ReactJS and Angular. It is precisely for this reason that books such as this exist. The major difference introduced in ASP.NET Core 2.1 is that the default Angular and ReactJS templates have been updated to use the standard project structures and build systems for each framework (the Angular CLI and NPX's `create-react-app` command) instead of relying on task runners such as Grunt or Gulp, module builders such as webpack, or toolchains such as Babel, which were widely used in the past, although they were quite difficult to install and configure.

> Being able to eliminate the need for these tools was a major achievement, which has played a decisive role in revamping the .NET Core usage and growth rate among the developer communities since 2017. If you take a look at the two previous installments of this book – *ASP.NET Core and Angular 2*, published in mid-2016, and *ASP.NET Core 2 and Angular 5*, out in late 2017 – and compare their first chapter with this one, you will see the huge difference between having to manually use Gulp, Grunt, or webpack and relying on the integrated framework-native tools. This is a substantial reduction in complexity that would greatly benefit any developer, especially those less accustomed to working with those tools.

Six months after the release of the 2.1 version, the .NET Foundation came out with a further improvement: ASP.NET Core 2.2 was released on December 4, 2018 with several fixes and new features, such as an improved endpoint routing system for better dispatching of requests, updated templates featuring Bootstrap 4 and Angular 6 support, a new health checks service to monitor the status of deployment environments and their underlying infrastructures, including container orchestration systems such as Kubernetes, built-in HTTP/2 support in Kestrel, a new SignalR Java client to ease the usage of SignalR within Android apps, and so on.

> For a detailed list of all the new features, improvements, and bug fixes of ASP.NET Core 2.2, check out the following links.
>
> **Release notes**: `https://docs.microsoft.com/en-US/aspnet/core/release-notes/aspnetcore-2.2`
>
> **Commits list**: `https://github.com/dotnet/core/blob/master/release-notes/2.2/2.2.0/2.2.0-commits.md`

ASP.NET Core 3.x

ASP.NET Core 3 was released in September 2019 and came with another bunch of performance and security improvements and new features, such as Windows desktop application support (Windows only) with advanced importing capabilities for Windows Forms and **Windows Presentation Foundation** (**WPF**) applications; C# 8 support; .NET Platform-Dependent Intrinsic access through a new set of built-in APIs that could bring significant performance improvements in certain scenarios; single-file executables support via the `dotnet publish` command using the <PublishSingleFile> XML element in project configuration or through the `/p:PublishSingleFile` command-line parameter; new built-in JSON support featuring high performance and low allocation that's arguably two to three times faster than the JSON.NET third-party library (which became a de facto standard in most ASP.NET web projects); TLS 1.3 and OpenSSL 1.1.1 support in Linux; some important security improvements in the `System.Security.Cryptography` namespace, including AES-GCM and AES-CCM ciphers support; and so on.

A lot of work has also been done to improve the performance and reliability of the framework when used in a containerized environment. The ASP.NET Core development team put a lot of effort into improving the .NET Core Docker experience on .NET Core 3.0. More specifically, this is the first release featuring substantive runtime changes to make CoreCLR more efficient, honor Docker resource limits better (such as memory and CPU) by default, and offer more configuration tweaks. Among the various improvements, we could mention improved memory and GC heap usage by default, and PowerShell Core, a cross-platform version of the famous automation and configuration tool, which is now shipped with the .NET Core SDK Docker container images.

.NET Core 3 also introduced Blazor, a free and open source web framework that enables developers to create web apps using C# and HTML.

Last but not least, it's worth noting that the new .NET Core SDK is much smaller than the previous installments, mostly thanks to the fact that the development team removed a huge set of unnecessary artifacts included in the various NuGet packages that were used to assemble the previous SDKs (including ASP.NET Core 2.2) from the final build. The size improvements are huge for Linux and macOS versions, while less noticeable on Windows because that SDK also contains the new WPF and Windows Forms set of platform-specific libraries.

> For a detailed list of all the new features, improvements, and bug fixes of ASP.NET Core 3.0, check out the following links.
>
> **Release notes**: `https://docs.microsoft.com/en-us/dotnet/core/whats-new/dotnet-core-3-0`
>
> **ASP.NET Core 3.0 releases page**: `https://github.com/dotnet/core/tree/master/release-notes/3.0`

ASP.NET Core 3.1, which is the most recent stable version at the time of writing, was released on December 3, 2019. The changes in the latest version are mostly focused on Windows desktop development, with the definitive removal of a number of legacy Windows Forms controls (*DataGrid*, *ToolBar*, *ContextMenu*, *Menu*, *MainMenu*, and *MenuItem*) and added support for creating C++/CLI components (on Windows only).

Most of the ASP.NET Core updates were fixes related to Blazor, such as preventing default actions for events and stopping event propagation in Blazor apps, partial class support for Razor components, additional *Tag Helper Component* features, and so on; however, much like the other *.1* releases, the primary goal of .NET Core 3.1 was to refine and improve the features already delivered in the previous version, with more than 150 performance and stability issues fixed.

> A detailed list of the new features, improvements, and bug fixes introduced with ASP.NET Core 3.1 is available at the following URL.
>
> **Release notes**: `https://docs.microsoft.com/en-us/dotnet/core/whats-new/dotnet-core-3-1`

.NET 5

Just when everyone thought that Microsoft had finally taken a clear path with the naming convention of its upcoming frameworks, the MS developer community was shaken again on May 6, 2019 by the following post by Richard Lander, Program Manager of the .NET team, which appeared on the Microsoft Developer Blog: `https://devblogs.microsoft.com/dotnet/introducing-net-5/`

The post got an immediate backup from another article that came out the same day written by Scott Hunter, Program Management Director of the .NET ecosystem: `https://devblogs.microsoft.com/dotnet/net-core-is-the-future-of-net/`

The two posts were meant to share the same big news to the readers: .NET Framework 4.x and .NET Core 3.x would converge in the next major installment of .NET Core, which would skip a major version number to properly encapsulate both installments.

The new unified platform would be called .NET 5 and would include everything that had been released so far with uniform capabilities and behaviors: .NET Runtime, JIT, AOT, GC, BCL (Base Class Library), C#, VB.NET, F#, ASP.NET, Entity Framework, ML.NET, WinForms, WPF, and Xamarin.

> Microsoft said they wanted to eventually drop the term "Core" from the framework name because .NET 5 would be the main implementation of .NET going forward, thus replacing .NET Framework and .NET Core; however, for the time being, the ASP.NET Core ecosystem is still retaining the name "Core" to avoid confusing it with ASP.NET MVC 5; Entity Framework Core will also keep the name "Core" to avoid confusing it with Entity Framework 5 and 6. For all of these reasons, in this book, we'll keep using "ASP.NET Core" (or .NET Core) and "Entity Framework Core" (or "EF Core") as well.

From Microsoft's point of view, the reasons behind this bold choice are rather obvious:

- Produce a single .NET runtime and framework that can be used everywhere and that has uniform runtime behaviors and developer experiences
- Expand the capabilities of .NET by taking the best of .NET Core, .NET Framework, Xamarin, and Mono
- Build that product out of a single code base that internal (Microsoft) and external (community) developers can work on and expand together and that improves all scenarios

> The new name could reasonably generate some confusion among those developers who still remember the short timeframe (early to mid 2016) in which ASP.NET Core v1 was still called ASP.NET 5 before its final release. Luckily enough, that "working title" was ditched by the MS developer team and the .NET community before it could leave noticeable traces on the web.

.NET 5 was released on General Availability in November 2020, a couple of months after its first Release Candidate, thus respecting the updated .NET schedule that aims to ship a new major version of .NET once a year, every November:

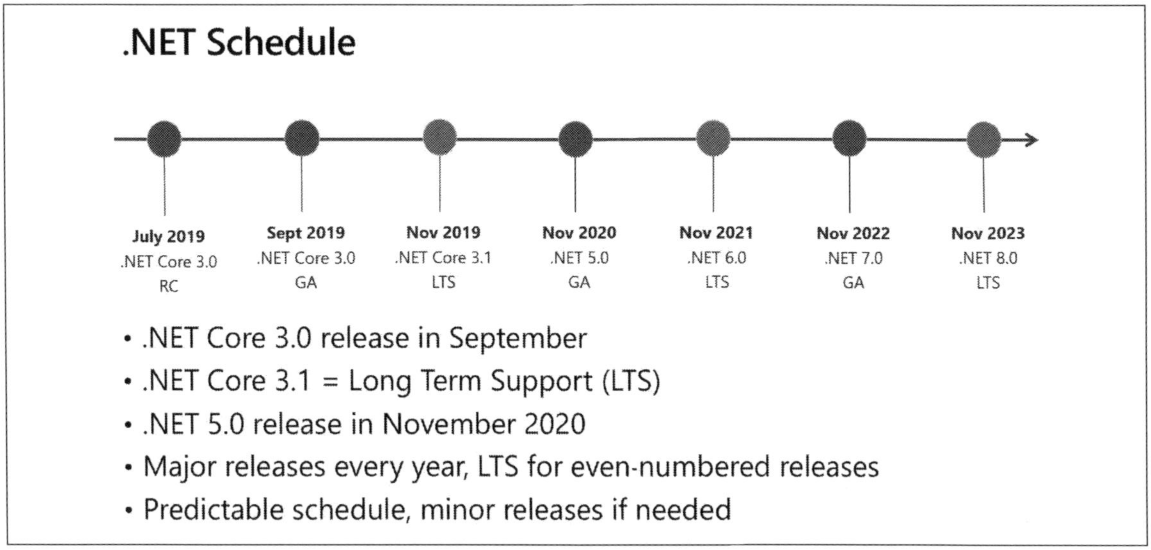

Figure 1.1: .NET schedule

In addition to the new name, the latest version of .NET brings a lot of interesting changes, such as:

- *Performance improvements and measurement tools*, summarized in this great analysis performed by Stephen Toub (.NET Partner Software Engineer) using the new Benchmark.NET tools: `https://devblogs.microsoft.com/dotnet/performance-improvements-in-net-5/`
- *Half Type*, a binary floating-point that occupies only 16 bits and that can help to save a good amount of storage space where the computed result does not need to be stored with full precision. For additional info, take a look at this post by Prashanth Govindarajan (Senior Engineering Manager at LinkedIn): `https://devblogs.microsoft.com/dotnet/introducing-the-half-type/`
- *Assembly trimming*, a compiler-level option to trim unused assemblies as part of publishing self-contained applications when using the self-contained deployment option, as explained by Sam Spencer (.NET Core team Program Manager) in this post: `https://devblogs.microsoft.com/dotnet/app-trimming-in-net-5/`
- *Various improvements to the new System.Text.Json API*, including the ability to ignore default values for value-type properties when serializing (for better serialization performance) and to better deal with circular references.
- *C# 9 and F# 5* language support, with a bunch of new features such as *Init Only Setters* (that allows the creation of *immutable* objects), *function pointers, static anonymous functions, target-typed conditional expressions, covariant return types, module initializers*, and so on.

And a lot of other new features and improvements.

A detailed list of the new features and improvements and a comprehensive explanation of the reasons behind the release of ASP.NET 5 is available at the following URL.

Release notes: `https://docs.microsoft.com/en-us/dotnet/core/dotnet-five`

For additional info about the C# 9.0 new features, take a look at the following URL: `https://docs.microsoft.com/en-us/dotnet/csharp/whats-new/csharp-9`

This concludes our journey through the recent history of ASP.NET. In the next section, we'll move our focus to the Angular ecosystem, which experienced a rather similar turn of events.

What's new in Angular?

If following in the footsteps of Microsoft and the .NET Foundation in recent years has not been an easy task, things were not going to get any better when we turned our eyes to the client-side web framework known as Angular. In order to understand what happened there, we have to go back 10 years, to when JavaScript libraries such as jQuery and MooTools were dominating the client-side scene; the first client-side frameworks, such as Dojo, Backbone.js, and Knockout.js, were struggling to gain popularity and reach wide adoption; and stuff such as React and Vue.js didn't even exist.

Truth be told, jQuery is still dominating the scene to a huge extent, at least according to BuiltWith (`https://trends.builtwith.com/javascript/javascript-library`) and w3Techs (`https://w3techs.com/technologies/overview/javascript_library/all`). However, despite being used by 74.1% of all websites, it's definitely an option chosen less often by web developers than it was 10 years ago.

GetAngular

The story of AngularJS started in 2009 when Miško Hevery (now senior computer scientist and Agile coach at Google) and Adam Abrons (now director of engineering at Grand Rounds) were working on their side project, an **end-to-end** (**E2E**) web development tool that would have offered an online JSON storage service and also a client-side library to build web applications depending on it. To publish their project, they took the `GetAngular.com` hostname.

During that time, Hevery, who was already working at Google, was assigned to the Google Feedback project with two other developers. Together, they wrote more than 17,000 lines of code in 6 months, slowly sinking into a frustrating scenario of code bloat and testing issues. Given the situation, Hevery asked his manager to rewrite the application using GetAngular (the side project mentioned previously), betting that he could do that alone within 2 weeks. His manager accepted and Hevery lost the bet shortly thereafter, as the whole thing took him 3 weeks instead of 2; however, the new application had only 1,500 lines of code instead of 17,000. This was more than enough to get Google's interest in the new framework, which was given the name AngularJS shortly thereafter.

> To listen to the full story, take a look at the following Miško Hevery keynote speech at ng-conf 2014: `https://www.youtube.com/watch?v=r1A1VR0ibIQ`

AngularJS

The first stable release of AngularJS (version 0.9.0, also known as dragon-breath) was released on GitHub in October 2010 under an MIT license; when AngularJS 1.0.0 (also known as temporal domination) came out in June 2012, the framework had already achieved huge popularity within the web development communities worldwide.

The reasons for such extraordinary success can hardly be summarized in a few words, but I'll try to do that nonetheless by emphasizing some key selling points:

- **Dependency injection**: AngularJS was the first client-side framework to implement it. This was undeniably a huge advantage over the competitors, including DOM-manipulating libraries such as jQuery. With AngularJS, developers could write loosely coupled and easily testable components, leaving the framework with the task of creating them, resolving their dependencies, and passing them to other components when requested.
- **Directives**: These can be described as markers on specific DOM items such as elements, attributes, styles, and so on: a powerful feature that could be used to specify custom and reusable HTML-like elements and attributes that define data bindings and/or other specific behaviors of presentation components.
- **Two-way data binding**: The automatic synchronization of data between model and view components. When data in a model changes, the view reflects the change; when data in the view changes, the model is updated as well. This happens immediately and automatically, which makes sure that the model and the view are updated at all times.
- **Single-page approach**: AngularJS was the first framework to completely remove the need for page reloads. This provided great benefits at both the server-side (fewer and smaller network requests) and client-side level (smoother transitions, a more responsive experience), and paved the way for the Single-Page Application pattern that would be also adopted by React, Vue.js, and the other runner-up frameworks later on.
- **Cache-friendly**: All the AngularJS magic was meant to happen on the client side, without any server-side effort to generate the UI/UX parts. For this very reason, all AngularJS websites could be cached anywhere and/or made available through a CDN.

> For a detailed list of AngularJS features, improvements, and bug fixes from 0.9.0 through 1.7.8, check out the following link.
>
> **AngularJS 1.x Changelog**: `https://github.com/angular/angular.js/blob/master/CHANGELOG.md`

Angular 2

The new release of AngularJS, released on September 14, 2016 and known as Angular 2, was a complete rewrite of the previous one, entirely based upon the new ECMAScript version 6 (officially ECMAScript 2015) specifications. Just like the ASP.NET Core rewrite, the revolution brought such a number of breaking changes at the architectural level and for HTTP pipeline handling, app life cycle, and state management that porting the old code to the new one was nearly impossible. Despite keeping its former name, the new Angular version was a brand new framework with little or nothing in common with the previous one.

The choice to not make Angular 2 backward-compatible with AngularJS clearly demonstrated the intention of the author's team to adopt a completely new approach: not only in the code syntax but also in their way of thinking and designing the client app. The new Angular was highly modular, component-based, and came with a new and improved dependency injection model and a whole lot of programming patterns its older cousin had never heard of.

Here's a brief list of the most important improvements introduced with Angular 2:

- **Semantic versioning**: Angular 2 is the first release to use semantic versioning, also known as SemVer: a universal way of versioning the various software releases to help developers track down what's going on without having to dig into the changelog details. SemVer is based on three numbers - *X.Y.Z* - where *X* stands for a *major* version, *Y* stands for a *minor* version, and *Z* stands for a *patch* release. More specifically, the *X* number, representing the *major* version, gets incremented when incompatible API changes are made to stable APIs; the *Y* number, representing the *minor* version, gets incremented when backward-compatible functionality is added; and the *Z* number, representing a *patch* release, gets incremented when a backward-compatible bug is fixed. Such improvements can be easily underestimated, yet it's a must-have for most modern software development scenarios where **Continuous Delivery** (**CD**) is paramount and new versions are released with great frequency.
- **TypeScript**: Seasoned developers will probably already know what TypeScript is. Those who don't won't need to worry, since we're going to use it a lot during the Angular-related chapters of this book. For now, let's just say that TypeScript is a Microsoft-made superset of JavaScript that allows the use of all ES2015 features (such as Default-Rest-Spread Parameters, Template Literals, Arrow Functions, Promises, and more) and adds powerful type-checking and object-oriented features during development (such as class and type declarations). The TypeScript source code can be transpiled into standard JavaScript code that all browsers can understand.
- **Server-side rendering** (**SSR**): Angular 2 comes with Angular Universal, an open source technology that allows a *back-end* server to run Angular applications and serve only the resulting static HTML files to the client. In a nutshell, the server will render a first pass of the page for faster delivery to the client, then immediately refresh it with client code. SSR has its caveats, such as requiring Node.js to be installed on the host machine to execute the necessary pre-rendering steps, as well as having the whole `node_modules` folder there, but can greatly increase the app's response time for a typical internet browser, thus mitigating a known AngularJS performance issue.

- **Angular Mobile Toolkit** (**AMT**): A set of tools specifically designed for building high-performance mobile apps.
- **Command-line interface** (**CLI**): The new CLI introduced with Angular 2 can be used by developers to generate components, routes, services, and pipes via console/Terminal commands, together with simple test shells.
- **Components**: These are the main building blocks of Angular 2, entirely replacing the controllers and scopes of AngularJS, and also taking on most of the tasks previously covered by the former directives. Application data, business logic, templating, and the styling of an Angular 2 app can all be done using components.

> I did my best to explore most of these features in my first book, *ASP.NET Core and Angular 2*, which was published in October 2016, right after the final release of the two frameworks: `https://www.packtpub.com/product/asp-net-core-and-angular-2/9781786465689`

Angular 4

On March 23, 2017, Google released Angular 4: the number 3 version was skipped entirely in order to unify all the major versions of the many Angular components that had been developed separately before that date, such as Angular Router, which already was at version 3.x at the time. Starting with Angular 4, the entire Angular framework was then unified into the same MAJOR.MINOR.PATCH SemVer pattern.

The new major version brought a limited number of breaking changes, such as a new and improved routing system, TypeScript 2.1+ support (and a requirement), and some deprecated interfaces and tags. There were also a good number of improvements, including:

- **Ahead-of-time** (**AOT**) **compilation**: Angular 4 compiles the templates during the build phase and generates JavaScript code accordingly. That's a huge architectural improvement over the JIT mode used by AngularJS and Angular 2 where the app was compiled at runtime. For example, when the application starts, not only is the app faster since the client doesn't have to compile anything, but it throws/breaks at build time instead of during runtime for most component errors, thus leading to more secure and stable deployments.
- **Animations npm package**: All the existing UI animations and effects - as well as new ones - were moved to the `@angular/animations` dedicated package instead of being part of `@angular/core`. This was a smart move to give non-animated apps the chance to drop that part of code, thus being much smaller and arguably faster.

Other notable improvements included: a new form validator to check for valid email addresses, a new paramMap interface for URL parameters in the HTTP routing module, better internalization support, and so on.

Angular 5

Released on November 1, 2017, Angular 5 featured TypeScript 2.3 support, another small set of breaking changes, many performance and stability improvements, and a few new features, such as the following:

- **New HTTP Client API**: Starting from Angular 4.3, the `@angular/http` module was put aside in favor of a new `@angular/common/http` package with better JSON support, interceptors, and immutable request/response objects, and other stuff. The switch was completed in Angular 5 with the previous module being deprecated and the new one recommended for use in all apps.
- **State Transfer API**: A new feature that gives the developer the ability to transfer the state of the application between the server and the client.
- **A new set of router events for more granular control over the HTTP life cycle**: `ActivationStart`, `ActivationEnd`, `ChildActivationStart`, `ChildActivationEnd`, `GuardsCheckStart`, `GuardsCheckEnd`, `ResolveStart`, and `ResolveEnd`.

> November 2017 was also the release month of my *ASP.NET Core 2 and Angular 5* book, which covers most of the aforementioned improvements: `https://www.packtpub.com/product/asp-net-core-2-and-angular-5/9781788293600`
>
> In June 2018, that book was made available as a video course: `https://www.packtpub.com/product/asp-net-core-2-and-angular-5-video/9781789531442`

Angular 6

Released in April 2018, Angular 6 was mostly a maintenance release, more focused on improving the overall consistency of the framework and its toolchain than adding new features. Therefore, there were no major breaking changes. RxJS 6 supports a new way to register providers, the new `providedIn` injectable decorator, improved Angular Material support (a component specifically made to implement material design in the Angular client-side UI), more CLI commands/updates, and so on.

Another improvement worth mentioning was the new CLI `ng add` command, which uses the package manager to download new dependencies and invoke an installation script to update our project with configuration changes, add additional dependencies, and/or scaffold package-specific initialization code.

Last, but not least, the Angular team introduced Ivy, a next-generation Angular rendering engine that aims to increase the speed and decrease the size of the application.

Angular 7

Angular 7 came out in October 2018 and it definitely was a major update, as we can easily guess by reading the words written by Stephen Fluin, developer relations lead at Google and prominent Angular spokesman, on the official Angular development blog upon the official release:

> *"This is a major release spanning the entire platform, including the core framework, Angular Material, and the CLI with synchronized major versions. This release contains new features for our toolchain and has enabled several major partner launches."*

Here's a list of the new features:

- **Easy upgrade**: Thanks to the groundwork laid by version 6, the Angular team was able to reduce the steps that need to be done to upgrade an existing Angular app from an older version to the most recent one. The detailed procedure can be viewed by visiting `https://update.angular.io`, an incredibly useful Angular upgrade interactive guide that can be used to quickly recover the required steps, such as CLI commands, package updates, and so on.
- **CLI update**: A new command that attempts to automatically upgrade the Angular application and its dependencies by following the procedure mentioned previously.
- **CLI prompts**: The Angular command-line interface has been modified to prompt users when running common commands such as `ng new` or `ng add @angular/material` to help developers discover built-in features such as routing, SCSS support, and so on.
- **Angular Material and CDK**: Additional UI elements such as virtual scrolling; a component that loads and unloads elements from the DOM based on the visible parts of a list, making it possible to build very fast experiences for users with very large scrollable lists; CDK-native drag-and-drop support; improved drop-down list elements; and more.
- **Partner launches**: Improved compatibility with a number of third-party community projects such as Angular Console, a downloadable console for starting and running Angular projects on your local machine; `AngularFire`, the official Angular package for Firebase integration; Angular for NativeScript, integration between Angular and NativeScript – a framework for building native iOS and Android apps using JavaScript and/or JS-based client frameworks; some interesting new Angular-specific features for StackBlitz, an online IDE that can be used to create Angular and React projects, such as a tabbed editor and integration with the Angular Language Service; and so on.
- **Updated dependencies**: Added support for TypeScript 3.1, RxJS 6.3, and Node 10, although the previous versions can still be used for backward compatibility.

> The Angular Language Service is a way to get completions, errors, hints, and navigation inside Angular templates: think about it as a virtuous mix between a syntax highlighter, IntelliSense, and a real-time syntax error checker. Before Angular 7, which added the support for StackBlitz, such a feature was only available for Visual Studio Code and WebStorm.
>
> For additional information about the Angular Language Service, take a look at the following URL: `https://angular.io/guide/language-service`

Angular 8

Angular 7 was quickly followed by Angular 8, which was released on May 29, 2018. The new release is mostly about Ivy, the long-awaited new compiler/runtime of Angular: despite being an ongoing project since Angular 5, version 8 was the first one to officially offer a runtime switch to actually opt into using Ivy, which would become the default runtime starting from Angular 9.

> In order to enable Ivy on Angular 8, the developers had to add an `"enableIvy": true` property to the `angularCompilerOptions` section within the app's `tsconfig.json` file.
>
> Those who want to know more about Ivy are encouraged to have an extensive look at the following post by Cédric Exbrayat, cofounder and trainer of the Ninja Squad website and now part of the Angular developer team: `https://blog.ninja-squad.com/2019/05/07/what-is-angular-ivy/`

Other notable improvements and new features included:

- **Bazel support**: Angular 8 was the first version to support Bazel, a free software tool developed and used by Google for the automation of building and testing software. It can be very useful for developers aiming to automate their delivery pipeline as it allows incremental builds and tests, and even the possibility to configure remote builds (and caches) on a build farm.
- **Routing**: A new syntax was introduced to declare the lazy-loading routes using the `import()` syntax from TypeScript 2.4+ instead of relying on a string literal. The old syntax was kept for backward compatibility but may be dropped soon.
- **Service workers**: A new registration strategy was introduced to allow developers to choose when to register their workers instead of doing it automatically at the end of the app's startup life cycle. It's also possible to bypass a service worker for a specific HTTP request using the new `ngsw-bypass` header.
- **Workspace API**: A new and more convenient way to read and modify the Angular workspace configuration instead of manually modifying the `angular.json` file.

> In client-side development, a service worker is a script that the browser runs in the background to do any kind of stuff that doesn't require either a user interface or any user interaction. If you're new to the concept, don't worry - we'll extensively talk about them in *Chapter 11, Progressive Web Apps*, where we'll build our very own service worker.

The new version also introduced some notable breaking changes - mostly due to Ivy - and removed some long-time deprecated packages such as `@angular/http`, which was replaced by `@angular/common/http` in Angular 4.3 and then officially deprecated in 5.0.

> A comprehensive list of all the deprecated APIs can be found in the official Angular deprecations guide at the following URL: `https://angular.io/guide/deprecations`

Angular 9

Angular 9 was released in February 2020 after a long streak of release candidates through 2019 Q4 and was the most recent version for only 4 months before being replaced by its successor (Angular 10).

The new release brought the following new features:

- **JavaScript bundles and performance**: An attempt to fix the very large bundle files, one of the most cumbersome issues of the previous versions of Angular, which drastically increased the download time and brought down the overall performance.
- **Ivy compiler**: The new Angular build and render pipeline, shipped with Angular 8 as an opt-in preview, is now the default rendering engine.
- **Selector-less bindings**: A useful feature that was available to the previous rendering engine, but missing from the Angular 8 Ivy preview, is now available to Ivy as well.
- **Internationalization**: Another Ivy enhancement that makes use of the Angular CLI to generate most of the standard code necessary to create files for translators and to publish an Angular app in multiple languages, thanks to the new `i18n` attribute.

> The new `i18n` attribute is a numeronym, which is often used as an alias for internationalization. The number 18 stands for the number of letters between the first *i* and the last *n* in the word internationalization. The term seems to have been coined by the **Digital Equipment Corporation** (**DEC**) around the 1970s or 1980s, together with `l10n` for localization, due to the excessive length of the two words.

The long-awaited Ivy compiler deserves a couple more words, being a very important feature for the future of Angular.

As the average Angular developer already knows, the rendering engine plays a major role in the overall performance of any *front-end* framework since it's the tool that translates the actions and intents laid out by the presentation logic (in Angular components and templates) into the instructions that will update the DOM. If the renderer is more efficient, it will arguably require fewer instructions, thus increasing the overall performance while decreasing the amount of required JavaScript code at the same time. Since the JavaScript bundles produced by Ivy are much smaller than the previous rendering engine, Angular 9's overall improvement is relevant in terms of both performance and size.

> February 2020 was also the release month of my *ASP.NET Core 3 and Angular 9* book, featuring a whole new set of source code snippets and project samples that can also be found in this book: `https://www.packtpub.com/product/asp-net-core-3-and-angular-9-third-edition/9781789612165`

Angular 10

Angular 10 was released on June 24, 2020, just a few months after Angular 9. The short timeframe between Angular 9 and 10 was explained by the Angular development team as an attempt to get the framework back on its regular schedule, since Angular 9 got delayed by a few weeks.

The new release was mostly focused on fixing issues: more than 700 issues were fixed and over 2,000 were touched on in the process. However, there were still quite a few important updates to be aware of:

- *Upgrade to TypeScript 3.9*, as well as TSLib 2.0, and TS Lint v6. It's worth noting that earlier versions of TypeScript are no longer supported because they are not compatible with some potentially breaking changes in the `tsconfig.json` file structure (see below).
- *Angular Material improvements*, including a new date range picker.
- *Additional warnings when using CommonJS imports*, as they can result in both larger and slower applications.
- *Optional stricter settings*: developers are now able to create new projects with a *strict* flag that enables stricter listing rules and bundle sizes, thus resulting in more efficient tree-shaking (a term commonly used in JavaScript contexts for dead-code elimination using the `import` and `export` module syntax).

> For additional info about the improved `tsconfig.json` file structure (namely "*Solution Style*" *tsconfig.json files*), take a look at the following paragraph from the TypeScript 3.9 release notes: `https://www.typescriptlang.org/docs/handbook/release-notes/typescript-3-9.html#support-for-solution-style-tsconfigjson-files`
>
> To know more about the meaning of the term "tree-shaking," check out the following guide: `https://developer.mozilla.org/en-US/docs/Glossary/Tree_shaking`

Angular 11

Last, but not least, we come to Angular 11, which was released on November 11, 2020 and is currently the most recent version.

The new release adds these new features:

- *Component Test Harnesses*, a set of classes that lets a test interact with a component via a supported API. By using the Harness API, a test insulates itself against updates to the internals of a component, such as changing its DOM structure: such an idea comes from the `PageObject` pattern, which is commonly used for integration testing.
- *Updated Hot Module Replacement Support*: HMR is a mechanism that allows modules to be replaced without a full browser refresh; configuring HMR in Angular 11 is a lot easier, and they also introduced a new `--hmr` CLI command to enable it.
- *TypeScript 4.0 Support*, while TypeScript 3.9 (and lower) support has been dropped, this important upgrade allows Angular 11 apps to build much faster than previous versions.
- *Webpack 5 support*, although still experimental since the new version has only been released recently and might still not be entirely stable.
- *TSLint to ESLint migration*: This is one of the most important changes of this version, since TSLint and Codelyzer have been officially deprecated and they will likely get removed in the next release. To help developers to deal with such an update, the Angular team has introduced a three-step method that can be used to seamlessly migrate from TSLint to ESLint using the CLI.
- *Dropped support for Internet Explorer 9 and 10*, as well as IE mobile.

Other new features include: updated Language Service Preview, new automated migrations and schematics, some service worker improvements, lazy loading support for named outlets, resolve guard generation via the Angular CLI, stricter types for built in pipes, and ISO 8601 week-numbering year format support in the `formatDate` function.

This concludes our brief review of the recent history of the ASP.NET Core and Angular ecosystems. In the next sections, we'll summarize the most important reasons that led us to choose them in 2021.

Reasons for choosing .NET and Angular

As we have seen, both frameworks have gone through many intense years of changes. This led to a whole refoundation of their core and, right after that, a constant strain to get back on top - or at least not lose ground against most modern frameworks that came out after their now-departed golden age. These frameworks are eager to dominate the development scene: Python, Go, and Rust for the server-side part and React, Vue.js, and Ember.js for the client-side part, not to mention the Node.js and Express ecosystem, and most of the old competitors from the 1990s and 2000s, such as Java, Ruby, and PHP, which are still alive and kicking.

That said, here's a list of good reasons for picking ASP.NET Core in 2020-2021:

- **Performance**: The new .NET web stack is considerably fast, especially since .NET Core 3.1, with further improvements in .NET 5.
- **Integration:** It supports most, if not all, modern client-side frameworks, including Angular, React, and Vue.js.
- **Cross-platform approach**: .NET Core web applications can run on Windows, macOS, and Linux in an almost seamless way.
- **Hosting**: .NET web applications can be hosted almost anywhere: from a Windows machine with IIS to a Linux appliance with Apache or Nginx, from Docker containers to edge-case, self-hosting scenarios using the Kestrel and WebListener HTTP servers.
- **Dependency injection**: The framework supports a built-in dependency injection design pattern that provides a huge number of advantages during development, such as reduced dependencies, code reusability, readability, and testing.
- **Modular HTTP pipeline**: ASP.NET middleware grants developers granular control over the HTTP pipeline, which can be reduced to its core (for ultra-lightweight tasks) or enriched with powerful, highly configurable features such as internationalization, third-party authentication/authorization, caching, routing, seamless integration with industry-standard APIs, interfaces, and tools such as *SignalR*, *GraphQL*, *Swagger*, *Webhooks*, *JWT*, and so on.
- **Open source**: The whole .NET stack has been released as open source and is entirely focused on strong community support, thus being reviewed and improved by thousands of developers every day.
- **Side-by-side execution**: It supports the simultaneous running of multiple versions of an application or component on the same machine. This basically means that it's possible to have multiple versions of the common language runtime, and multiple versions of applications and components that use a version of the runtime, on the same computer at the same time. This is great for most real-life development scenarios as it gives the development team more control over which versions of a component an application binds to, and more control over which version of the runtime an application uses.

As for the Angular framework, the most important reason we're picking it over other excellent JS libraries such as React, Vue.js, and Ember.js is the fact that it already comes with a huge pack of features out of the box, making it the most suitable choice, although maybe not as simple to use as other frameworks/libraries. If we combine that with the consistency benefits brought by the TypeScript language, we can say that Angular, from its 2016 rebirth up to the present day, has embraced the framework approach more convincingly than the others. This has been consistently confirmed in the last few years, with the project undergoing six major versions and gaining a lot in terms of stability, performance, and features, without losing much in terms of backward compatibility, best practices, and overall approach. All these reasons are solid enough to invest in it, hoping it will continue to keep up with these compelling premises.

Now that we have acknowledged the reasons to use these frameworks, let's ask ourselves the best way to find out more about them: the next sections should give us the answers we need.

A full-stack approach

Learning to use ASP.NET Core and Angular together means being able to work with both the *front-end* (client side) and *back-end* (server side) of a web application; to put it in other words, it means being able to design, assemble, and deliver a complete product.

Eventually, in order to do that, we'll need to dig through the following:

- *Back-end* programming
- *Front-end* programming
- UI styling and UX design
- Database design, modeling, configuration, and administration
- Web server configuration and administration
- Web application deployment

At first glance, it can seem that this kind of approach goes against common sense; a single developer should not be allowed to do everything by themselves. Every developer knows that the *back-end* and the *front-end* require entirely different skills and experience, so why in the world should we do that?

Before answering this question, we should understand what we really mean when we say *being able to*. We don't have to become experts on every single layer of the stack; no one expects us to. When we choose to embrace the full-stack approach, what we really need to do is raise our awareness level throughout the whole stack we're working on; this means that we need to know how the *back-end* works, and how it can and will be connected to the *front-end*. We need to know how the data will be stored, retrieved, and then served through the client. We need to acknowledge the interactions we will need to layer out between the various components that our web application is made from, and we need to be aware of security concerns, authentication mechanisms, optimization strategies, load balancing techniques, and so on.

This doesn't necessarily mean that we have to have strong skills in all these areas; as a matter of fact, we hardly ever will. Nonetheless, if we want to pursue a full-stack approach, we need to understand the meaning, role, and scope of all of them. Furthermore, we should be able to work our way through any of these fields whenever we need to.

MPAs, SPAs, PWAs, and NWAs

In order to demonstrate how ASP.NET and Angular can work together to their full extent, we couldn't think of anything better than building some small SPA projects with most, if not all, Progressive Web Application features. The reason for such a choice is quite obvious: there is no better approach to demonstrate some of the best features they have to offer nowadays. We'll have the chance to work with modern interfaces and patterns such as the HTML5 pushState API, webhooks, data transport-based requests, dynamic web components, UI data bindings, and a stateless, AJAX-driven architecture capable of flawlessly encompassing all of these. We'll also make good use of some distinctive PWA features such as service workers, web manifest files, and so on.

If you don't know the meaning of these definitions and acronyms, don't worry, we are going to explore these concepts in the next couple of sections, which are dedicated to enumerating the most relevant features of the following types of web applications: MPAs, SPAs, PWAs, and NWAs. While we're there, we'll also try to figure out the most common product owner's expectations for a typical web-based project.

Multi-page applications

Multi-Page Applications, also known as MPAs, are those web applications that work in a traditional way: each time the user asks for (or submits) data to the server, they render a new page that is sent back to the browser.

This is how all websites used to work during the first 20 years of the World Wide Web, and is still the most used approach nowadays due to a number of advantages that MPAs can still provide: excellent SEO performance, a fast and steady learning curve to serve, the ability to manage and customize static and dynamic content, and a lot of great **content management systems** (**CMSes**), frameworks, and UI themes - such as WordPress, Joomla, and the like - that can be used to build them from the ground up in a few minutes.

However, MPAs also come with some significant cons: the required server-side roundtrips tend to make them quite expensive in terms of bandwidth; moreover, front-end and back-end development are often tightly coupled, thus making them harder to maintain and update. Luckily enough, most of these issues have been mitigated throughout the years, thanks to various browser features and technology improvements such as CDN, server-side caching, AJAX requests, and so on. At the same time, such techniques add more complexity to the development and deployment phases; that is, unless we choose to rely upon one of the CMS platforms that we talked about early on, thus giving up on most of the coding aspects - with all that that implies.

Single-page applications

To put it briefly, an SPA is a web-based application that tries to provide the same user experience as a desktop application. If we consider the fact that all SPAs are still served through a web server and thus accessed by web browsers just like any other standard website, we can easily understand how that desired outcome can only be achieved by changing some of the default patterns commonly used in web development, such as resource loading, DOM management, and UI navigation. In a good SPA, both content and resources - HTML, JavaScript, CSS, and so on - are either retrieved within a single page load or are dynamically fetched when needed. This also means that the page doesn't reload or refresh; it just changes and adapts in response to user actions, performing the required server-side calls behind the scenes.

These are some of the key features provided by a competitive SPA nowadays:

- **No server-side round trips**: A competitive SPA can redraw any part of the client UI without requiring a full server-side round trip to retrieve a full HTML page. This is mostly achieved by implementing a **separation of concerns** (**SOC**) design principle, which means that the data source, the business logic, and the presentation layer will be separated.

- **Efficient routing**: A competitive SPA is able to keep track of the user's current state and location during its whole navigation experience using organized, JavaScript-based routers. We'll talk more about that in the upcoming chapters when we introduce the concepts of server-side and client-side routing.
- **Performance and flexibility**: A competitive SPA usually transfers all of its UI to the client, thanks to its JavaScript SDK of choice (Angular, jQuery, Bootstrap, and so on). This is often good for network performance as increasing client-side rendering and offline processing reduces the UI impact over the network. However, the real deal brought by this approach is the flexibility granted to the UI as the developer will be able to completely rewrite the application *front-end* with little or no impact on the server, aside from a few of the static resource files.

This list can easily grow, as these are only some of the major advantages of a properly designed, competitive SPA. These aspects play a major role nowadays, as many business websites and services are switching from their traditional **Multi-Page Application** (**MPA**) mindset to fully committed or hybrid SPA-based approaches.

Progressive web applications

In 2015, another web development pattern pushed its way into the light when Frances Berriman (a British freelance designer) and Alex Russel (a Google Chrome engineer) used the term PWAs for the first time to refer to those web applications that could take advantage of a couple of new important features supported by modern browsers: service workers and web manifest files. These two important improvements could be successfully used to deliver some functionalities usually only available on mobile apps – push notifications, offline mode, permission-based hardware access, and so on – using standard web-based development tools such as HTML, CSS, and JavaScript.

The rise of Progressive Web Apps began in March 19, 2018, when Apple implemented support for service workers in Safari 11.1. Since that date, PWAs have been widely adopted throughout the industry thanks to their undeniable advantages over their "non-progressive" counterparts: faster load times, smaller application sizes, higher audience engagement, and so on.

Here are the main technical features of a Progressive Web App (according to Google):

- **Progressive**: Works for every user, regardless of browser choice, using progressive enhancement principles
- **Responsive**: Fits any form factor: desktop, mobile, tablet, or forms yet to emerge
- **Connectivity independent**: Service workers allow offline use, or on low-quality networks
- **App-like**: Feels like an app to the user with app-style interactions and navigation
- **Fresh**: Always up to date due to the service worker update process
- **Safe**: Served via HTTPS to prevent snooping and ensure content hasn't been tampered with

- **Discoverable**: Identifiable as an application by a web manifest (`manifest.json`) file, and a registered service worker, and discoverable by search engines
- **Re-engageable**: The ability to use push notifications to maintain engagement with the user
- **Installable**: Provides home screen icons without the use of an app store
- **Linkable**: Can easily be shared via a URL and does not require complex installation

However, their technical baseline criteria can be restricted to the following subset:

- **HTTPS**: They must be served from a secure origin, which means over TLS with green padlock displays (no active mixed content)
- **Minimal offline mode**: They must be able to start even if the device is not connected to the web, with limited functions or at least displaying a custom offline page
- **Service workers**: They have to register a service worker with a fetch event handler (which is required for minimal offline support, as explained previously)
- **Web manifest file**: They need to reference a valid `manifest.json` file with at least four key properties (`name`, `short_name`, `start_url`, and `display`) and a minimum set of required icons

> For those interested in reading about this directly from the source, here's the original link from the Google Developers website: `https://developers.google.com/web/progressive-web-apps/`
>
> In addition, here are two follow-up posts from Alex Russell's Infrequently Noted blog: `https://infrequently.org/2015/06/progressive-apps-escaping-tabs-without-losing-our-soul/`
>
> `https://infrequently.org/2016/09/what-exactly-makes-something-a-progressive-web-app/`
>
> For those who don't know, Alex Russell has worked as a senior staff software engineer at Google since December 2008.

Although they have some similarities, PWAs and SPAs are two different concepts, have different requirements, and differ in many important aspects. As we can see, none of the PWA requirements mentioned previously refer to Single-Page Applications or server-side round trips. A Progressive Web App *can* work within a single HTML page and AJAX-based requests (thus also being an SPA), but it *could* also request other server-rendered (or static) pages and/or perform standard HTTP GET or POST requests, much like an MPA. It's also the opposite: any SPA can implement any single PWA technical criteria, depending on the product owner's requirements (more on that later), the server-side and client-side frameworks adopted, and the developer's ultimate goal.

Native web applications

The first good definition of Native Web Applications (also known as NWAs) available on the web can arguably be found in Sam Johnston's blog post written on January 16, 2009, which went like this:

> *A Native Web Application (NWA) is a web application which is 100% supported out of the box by recent standards-compliant web browsers.*

A similar approach was used 6 years later (January 22, 2015) by Henrik Joreteg to describe the defining feature of NWAs:

> *The thing these apps all have in common is that they all depend on the native web technologies: HTML, CSS, and JavaScript (arguably, you could add WebGL to that list).*

These definitions help us to understand that we're dealing with a rather generic term that encompasses SPAs, MPAs, and even PWAs - since they all depend on native web technologies that are supported out of the box by all recent browsers; however, due to the emphasis given to the *recent* keyword and the existence of the more specific web application types, the NWA term is mostly used to identify those web applications that, although being built using modern web-based technologies, cannot be classified as MPA, SPA or PWA because they tend to adopt a *hybrid* approach.

Since we're going to use Angular, which is all about developing Single-Page Applications, and has also shipped with a strong and steady service worker implementation since version 5, we are fully entitled to take advantage of the best of both worlds. For this very reason, we're going to use service workers - along with the benefits of increased reliability and performance they provide - whenever we need to, all while keeping a solid SPA approach. Furthermore, we're definitely going to implement some strategic HTTP round trips (and/or other redirect-based techniques) whenever we can profitably use a microservice to lift off some workload from our app, just like any good Native Web Application is meant to do.

Are all these features able to respond to modern market needs? Let's try to find it out.

Product owner expectations

One of the most interesting, yet underrated, concepts brought out by many modern Agile software development frameworks, such as Scrum, is the importance given to the meanings and definitions of roles. Among these, there's nothing as important as the product owner, also known as the customer in Extreme Programming methodology, or customer representative elsewhere. They're the ones who bring to the development table the expectations we'll struggle to satisfy.

They will tell us what's most important to deliver and when they will prioritize our work based on its manifest business value rather than its underlying architectural value. They'll be entitled by management to make decisions and make tough calls, which is sometimes great, sometimes not; this will often have a big impact on our development schedule. To cut it short, they're the ones in charge of the project; that's why, in order to deliver a web application matching their expectations, we'll need to understand their vision and feel it as if it were our own.

This is always true, even if the project's product owner is our dad, wife, or best friend: that's how it works.

Now that we have made that clear, let's take a look at some of the most common product owner's expectations for a typical web-based SPA project. We ought to see whether the choice of using ASP.NET and Angular will be good enough to fulfill each one of them, as follows:

- **Early release(s)**: No matter what we're selling, the customer will always want to see what they're buying. For example, if we plan to use an Agile development framework such as Scrum, we'll have to release a potentially shippable product at the end of each sprint. If we are looking to adopt a Waterfall-based approach, we're going to have milestones, and so on. One thing is for sure, the best thing we can do in order to efficiently organize our development efforts will be to adopt an iterative and/or modular-oriented approach. ASP.NET and Angular, along with the strong separation of concerns granted by their underlying MVC- or MVVM-based patterns, will gracefully push us into the mindset needed to do just that.
- **GUI over back-end**: We'll often be asked to work on the GUI and *front-end* functionalities because that will be the only really viewable and measurable thing for the customer. This basically means that we'll have to mock the data model and start working on the *front-end* as soon as possible, delaying the back-end implementation as much (and as long) as we can. Note that this kind of approach is not necessarily bad; we just won't do that just to satisfy the product owner's expectations.

  On the contrary, the choice of using ASP.NET along with Angular will grant us the chance to easily decouple the presentation layer and the data layer, implementing the first and mocking the latter, which is a great thing to do. We'll be able to see where we're going before wasting valuable time or being forced to make potentially wrong decisions. ASP.NET's Web API interface will provide the proper tools to do that by allowing us to create a sample web application skeleton in a matter of seconds using the controller templates available within Visual Studio and in-memory data contexts powered by Entity Framework Core, which we'll be able to access using Entity models and code first. As soon as we do that, we'll be able to switch to GUI design using the Angular presentation layer toolbox as much as we want until we reach the desired results. Once we're satisfied, we'll just need to properly implement the Web API controller interfaces and hook up the actual data.

- **Fast completion**: None of the preceding things will work unless we also manage to get everything done in a reasonable time span. This is one of the key reasons to choose to adopt a server-side framework and a client-side framework that work together with ease. ASP.NET and Angular are the tools of choice, not only because they're both built on solid, consistent ground, but also because they're meant to do precisely that - get the job done on their respective sides and provide a usable interface to the other partner.
- **Adaptability**: As stated by the Agile Manifesto, being able to respond to change requests is more important than following a plan. This is especially true in software development where we can even claim that anything that cannot handle change is a failed project. That's another great reason to embrace the separation of concerns enforced by our two frameworks of choice, as this grants the developer the ability to manage—and even welcome, to some extent—most of the layout or structural changes that will be expected during the development phase.

> A few lines ago, we mentioned Scrum, which is one of the most popular Agile software development frameworks out there. Those who don't know it yet should definitely take a look at what it can offer to any results-driven team leader and/or project manager. Here's a good place to start: `https://en.wikipedia.org/wiki/Scrum_(software_development)`
>
> For those who are curious about the Waterfall model, here's a good place to learn more about it: `https://en.wikipedia.org/wiki/Waterfall_model`

That's about it. Note that we didn't cover everything here as it would be impossible without the context of an actual assignment. We just tried to give an extensive answer to the following general question: if we were to build an SPA and/or a PWA, would ASP.NET and Angular be an appropriate choice? The answer is undoubtedly yes, especially when used together.

Does this mean that we're done already? Not a chance, as we have no intention of taking this assumption for granted. Conversely, it's time for us to demonstrate this by ceasing to speak in general terms and starting to put things in motion. That's precisely what we're going to do in the next section: prepare, build, and test a sample Single-Page Application project.

A sample SPA project

What we need now is to conceive a suitable test case scenario similar to the ones we will eventually have to deal with - a sample SPA project with all the core aspects we would expect from a potentially shippable product.

In order to do this, the first thing we need to do is to become our own customer for a minute and come up with an idea, a vision to share with our other self. We'll then be able to put our developer shoes back on and split our abstract plan into a list of items we'll need to implement; these will be the core requirements of our project. Finally, we'll set up our workstation by getting the required packages, adding the resource files, and configuring both the ASP.NET and Angular frameworks in the Visual Studio IDE.

Not your usual Hello World!

The code we're going to write within this book won't be just a shallow demonstration of full-stack development concepts; we won't throw some working code here and there and expect you to connect the dots. Our objective is to create solid, realistic web applications - with server-side web APIs and client-side UIs - using the frameworks we've chosen, and we're also going to do that following the current development best practices.

Each chapter will be dedicated to a single core aspect. If you feel like you already know your way there, feel free to skip to the next one. Conversely, if you're willing to follow us through the whole loop, you'll have a great journey through the most useful aspects of ASP.NET and Angular, as well as how they can work together to deliver the most common and useful web-development tasks, from the most trivial ones to the more complex beasts. It's an investment that will pay dividends as it will leave you with a maintainable, extensible, and well-structured project, plus the knowledge needed to build your own. The following chapters will guide us through such a journey. During that trip, we'll also learn how to take care of some important high-level aspects such as SEO, security, performance issues, best coding practices, and deployment, as they will become very important if/when our applications are eventually published in a production environment.

To avoid making things too boring, we'll try to pick enjoyable themes and scenarios that will also have some usefulness in the real world: to better understand what we mean - no spoilers here - you'll just have to keep reading.

Preparing the workspace

The first thing we have to do is set up our workstation; it won't be difficult because we only need a small set of essential tools. These include Visual Studio 2019, an updated Node.js runtime, a development web server (such as the built-in IIS Express), and a decent source code control system such as Git. We will take the latter for granted as we most likely already have it up and running.

> In the unlikely case you don't, you should really make amends before moving on! Stop reading, go to `www.github.com`, `www.bitbucket.com`, or whichever online SCM service you like the most, create a free account, and spend some time learning how to effectively use these tools; you won't regret it, that's for sure.

In the next sections, we'll set up the web application project, install or upgrade the packages and libraries, and build and eventually test the result of our work. However, before doing that, we're going to spend a couple of minutes understanding a very important concept that is required to properly use this book without getting (emotionally) hurt - at least in my opinion.

Disclaimer – do (not) try this at home

There's something very important that we need to understand before proceeding. If you're a seasoned web developer, you will most likely know about it already; however, since this book is for (almost) everyone, I feel like it's very important to deal with this matter as soon as possible.

This book will make extensive use of a number of different programming tools, external components, third-party libraries, and so on. Most of them, such as TypeScript, NPM, NuGet, most .NET frameworks/packages/runtimes, and so on, are shipped together with Visual Studio 2019, while others, such as Angular, its required JS dependencies, and other third-party server-side and client-side packages, will be fetched from their official repositories. These things are meant to work together in a 100% compatible fashion; however, they are all subject to changes and updates during the inevitable course of time. As time passes by, the chance that these updates might affect the way they interact with each other and the project's health will increase.

The broken code myth

In an attempt to minimize the chances of this occurring, this book will always work with fixed versions/builds of any third-party component that can be handled using the configuration files. However, some of them, such as Visual Studio and/or .NET SDK updates, might be out of that scope and might bring havoc to the project. The source code might cease to work, or Visual Studio could suddenly be unable to properly compile it.

When something like that happens, a less-experienced person will always be tempted to put the blame on the book itself. Some of them may even start thinking something like this: *There are a lot of compile errors, hence the source code must be broken!*

Alternatively, they may think like this: *The code sample doesn't work: the author must have rushed things here and there and forgot to test what he was writing.*

It goes without saying that such hypotheses are rarely true, especially considering the amount of time that the authors, editors, and technical reviewers of these books spend in writing, testing, and refining the source code before building it up, making it available on GitHub, and often even publishing working instances of the resulting applications to worldwide public websites.

> The GitHub repository for this book can be found here: `https://github.com/PacktPublishing/ASP.NET-Core-5-and-Angular`
>
> It contains a Visual Studio solution file for each chapter (`Chapter_01.sln`, `Chapter_02.sln` and so on), as well as an additional solution file (`All_Chapters.sln`) containing the source code for all the chapters.

Any experienced developer will easily understand that most of these things couldn't even be done if there was some broken code somewhere; there's no way this book could even attempt to hit the shelves without coming with a 100% working source code, except for a few possible minor typos that will quickly be reported to the publisher and thus fixed within the GitHub repository in a short while. In the unlikely case that it looks like it doesn't, such as raising unexpected compile errors, the novice developer should spend a reasonable amount of time trying to understand the root cause.

Here's a list of questions they should try to answer before anything else:

- Am I using the same development framework, third-party libraries, versions, and builds adopted by the book?
- If I updated something because I felt like I needed to, am I aware of the changes that might affect the source code? Did I read the relevant changelogs? Have I spent a reasonable amount of time looking around for breaking changes and/or known issues that could have had an impact on the source code?
- Is the book's GitHub repository also affected by this issue? Did I try to compare it with my own code, possibly replacing mine?

If the answer to any of these questions is *No*, then there's a good chance that the problem is not ascribable to this book.

Stay hungry, stay foolish, yet be responsible as well

Don't get me wrong: if you want to use a newer version of Visual Studio, update your TypeScript compiler, or upgrade any third-party library, you are definitely encouraged to do that. This is nothing less than the main scope of this book – making you fully aware of what you're doing and capable of, way beyond the given code samples.

However, if you feel you're ready to do that, you will also have to adapt the code accordingly; most of the time, we're talking about trivial stuff, especially these days when you can Google the issue and/or get the solution on Stack Overflow. Have they changed the name of a property or method? Then you need to load the new typings. Have they moved the class somewhere else? Then you need to find the new namespace and change it accordingly, and so on.

That's about it – nothing more, nothing less. The code reflects the passage of time; the developer just needs to keep up with the flow, performing minimum changes to it when required. You can't possibly get lost and blame someone other than yourself if you update your environment and fail to acknowledge that you have to change a bunch of code lines to make it work again.

Am I implying that the author is not responsible for the source code of this book? It's the exact opposite; the author is always responsible. They're supposed to do their best to fix all the reported compatibility issues while keeping the GitHub repository updated. However, you should also have your own level of responsibility; more specifically, you should understand how things work for *any* development book and the inevitable impact of the passage of time on any given source code.

No matter how hard the author works to maintain it, the patches will never be fast or comprehensive enough to make these lines of code always work in any given scenario. That's why the most important thing you need to understand - even before the book's topics - is the most valuable concept in modern software development: being able to efficiently deal with the inevitable changes that *will* always occur. Whoever refuses to understand that is doomed; there's no way around it.

Now that we've clarified these aspects, let's get back to work.

Setting up the project

Assuming that we have already installed Visual Studio 2019 and Node.js, here's what we need to do:

1. Download and install the .NET 5 SDK
2. Check that the .NET CLI will use that SDK version
3. Create a new .NET and Angular project
4. Check out the newly created project within Visual Studio
5. Update all the packages and libraries to our chosen versions

Let's get to work.

Installing the .NET 5 SDK

The .NET 5 SDK can be downloaded from either the official Microsoft URL (`https://dotnet.microsoft.com/download/dotnet/5.0`) or from the GitHub official release page (`https://github.com/dotnet/core/tree/master/release-notes/5.0`).

The installation is very straightforward – just follow the wizard until the end to get the job done, as follows:

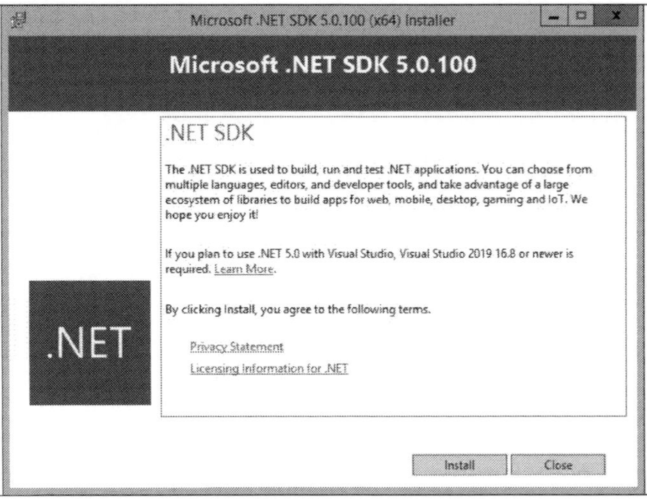

Figure 1.2: .NET SDK 5.0.100 installer

The whole installation process shouldn't take more than a couple of minutes.

Checking the SDK version

Once the .NET SDK has been installed, we need to confirm that the new SDK PATH has been properly set and/or that the .NET CLI will actually use it. The fastest way to check that is by opening a Command Prompt and typing the following:

```
> dotnet --help
```

Be sure that the .NET CLI executes without issue and that the given version number is the same as we installed a moment ago.

> If the prompt is unable to execute the command, go to **Control Panel** | **System** | **Advanced System Settings** | **Environment Variables** and check that the `C:\Program Files\dotnet\` folder is present within the `PATH` environment variable; manually add it if needed.

Creating the .NET and Angular project

The next thing we have to do is create our first .NET and Angular project – in other words, our first app. We'll do that using the Angular project template shipped with the .NET SDK as it provides a convenient starting point by adding all the required files and also a general-purpose configuration that we'll be able to customize later on to better suit our needs.

From the command line, create a root folder that will contain all our projects and get inside it.

> In this book, we're going to use `\Projects\` as our root folder: non-experienced developers are strongly advised to use the same folder to avoid possible path errors and/or issues related to path names being too long (Windows 10 has a 260-character limit that can create some issues with some deeply nested NPM packages).

Once there, type the following command to create the Angular app:

```
> dotnet new angular -o HealthCheck
```

This command will create our first Angular app in the `C:\Projects\HealthCheck\` folder. As we can easily guess, its name will be `HealthCheck`: there's a good reason for such a name, as we're going to see in a short while (no spoilers, remember?).

Opening the new project in Visual Studio

It's now time to launch Visual Studio 2019 and perform a quick checkup of our newly created project. This can be done by either double-clicking on the `HealthCheck.csproj` file or through the VS2019 main menu (**File** | **Open** | **Project/Solution**).

Once done, we should be able to see our project's source tree in all its lightweight glory, as shown in the following screenshot:

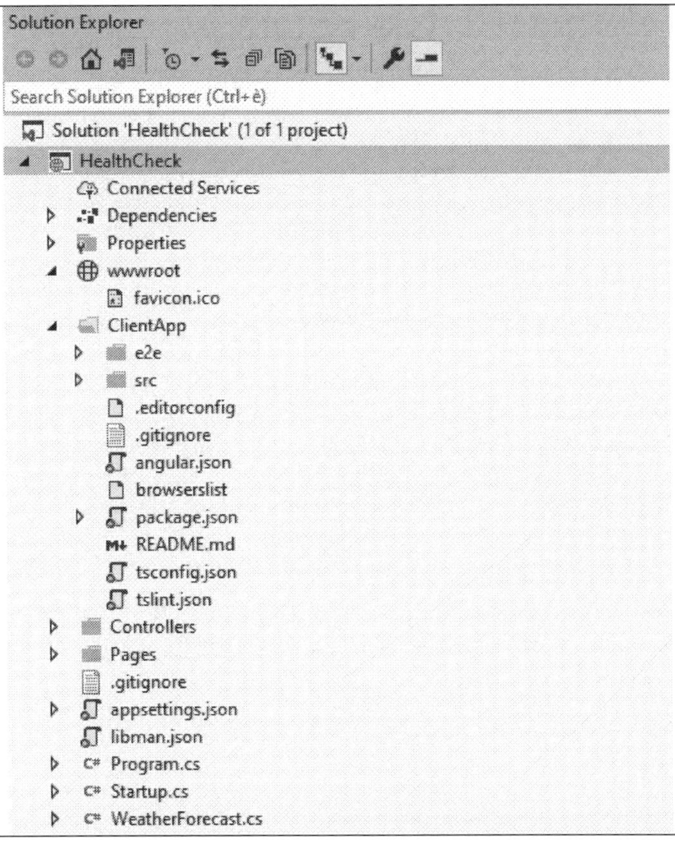

Figure 1.3: Examining our project's source tree

As we can see from the previous screenshot, it's a rather compact boilerplate that only contains the required .NET and Angular configuration files, resources, and dependencies: just what we need to start coding!

However, before doing that, let's continue our brief review. As we can see by looking at the various folders, the working environment contains the following:

- The default ASP.NET MVC `/Controllers/` and `/Pages/` folders, both containing some working samples.
- The `/ClientApp/src/` folder with some TypeScript files containing the source code of a sample Angular app.
- The `/ClientApp/e2e/` folder containing some sample E2E tests built with the Protractor testing framework.
- The `/wwwroot/` folder, which will be used by Visual Studio to build an optimized version of the client-side code whenever we need to execute it locally or have it published elsewhere. That folder is initially empty, but it will be populated upon the project's first run.

If we spend some time browsing through these folders and taking a look at their content, we will see how the .NET developers did a tremendous job in easing the .NET experience with the Angular project setup process. If we compare this boilerplate with the built-in Angular 2.x/5.x templates shipped with Visual Studio 2015/2017, we will see a huge improvement in terms of readability and code cleanliness, as well as a better file and folder structure. Also, those who fought with task runners such as Grunt or Gulp and/or client-side building tools such as webpack in the recent past will most likely appreciate the fact that this template is nothing like that: all the packaging, building, and compiling tasks are entirely handled by Visual Studio via the underlying .NET and Angular CLIs, with specific loading strategies for development and production.

> It's worth noting that the Visual Studio and Angular sample template that we're going to use throughout this book hosts the back-end (the .NET APIs) and the front-end (the Angular app) within a single project; such an approach can be very useful and will greatly ease the learning and development phase, but it's not the only way to do it. For example, we might opt for an alternative approach that involves splitting the server-side and the client-side parts into two separate projects: doing this will enforce decoupling, which is paramount when building microservice-based architectures. However, it will also create additional work and potential issues (versioning, deploying, CORS issues, etc.), which might be hard to overcome even for expert developers.
>
> Considering the pros and cons of such a choice, we can definitely say that being able to work with the back-end and the front-end within the same project is a good approach for learning, thus making these templates an ideal approach for the purpose of a programming book - and that's why we're always going to use them.

Before moving on, we should definitely perform a quick test run to ensure that our project is working properly. This is what the next section is all about.

Performing a test run

Luckily enough, performing a test run at this point is just as easy as hitting the **Run** button or the *F5* key:

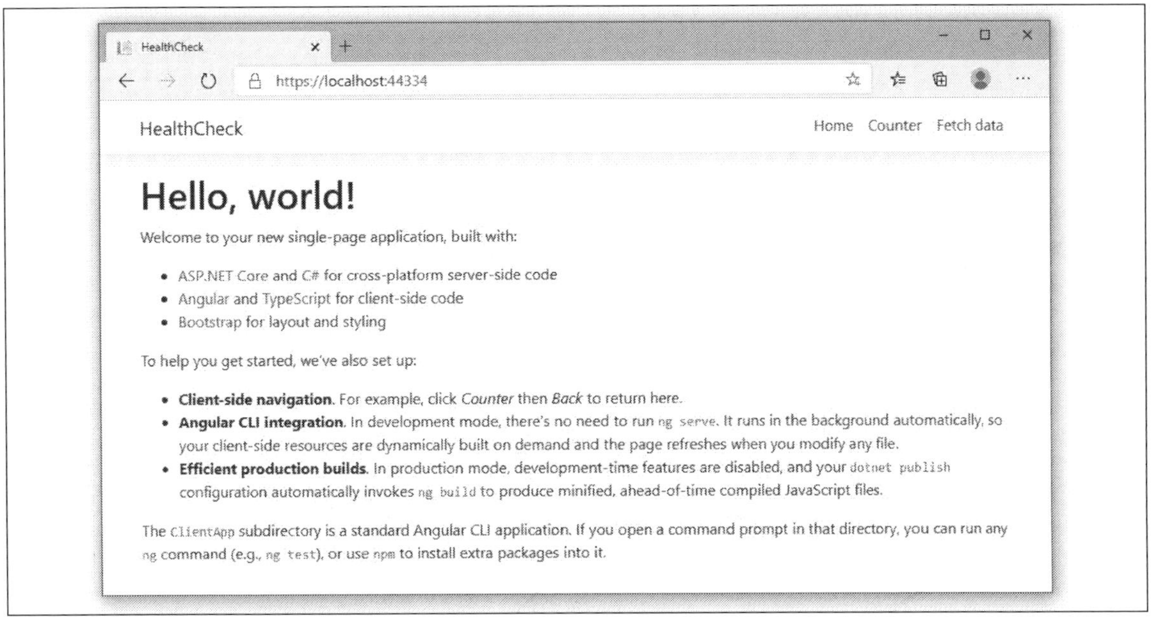
HealthCheck
https://localhost:44334
HealthCheck
Home Counter Fetch data
Hello, world!
Welcome to your new single-page application, built with:
ASP.NET Core and C# for cross-platform server-side code
Angular and TypeScript for client-side code
Bootstrap for layout and styling
To help you get started, we've also set up:
Client-side navigation. For example, click Counter then Back to return here.
Angular CLI integration. In development mode, there's no need to run ng serve. It runs in the background automatically, so your client-side resources are dynamically built on demand and the page refreshes when you modify any file.
Efficient production builds. In production mode, development-time features are disabled, and your dotnet publish configuration automatically invokes ng build to produce minified, ahead-of-time compiled JavaScript files.
The ClientApp subdirectory is a standard Angular CLI application. If you open a command prompt in that directory, you can run any ng command (e.g., ng test), or use npm to install extra packages into it.

Figure 1.4: Performing a test run of our web app

This is an excellent consistency check to ensure that our development system is properly configured. If we see the sample Angular SPA up and running, as shown in the preceding screenshot, it means that we're good to go; if we don't, it probably means that we're either missing something or that we've got some conflicting software preventing Visual Studio and/or the underlying .NET and Angular CLIs from properly compiling the project.

In order to fix that, we can try to do the following:

- Uninstall/reinstall Node.js, as we possibly have an outdated version installed.
- Uninstall/reinstall Visual Studio 2019, as our current installation might be broken or corrupted. The .NET SDK should come shipped with it already; however, we can try reinstalling it as well.

If everything still fails, we can try to install VS2019 and the previously mentioned packages in a clean environment (be it either a physical system or a VM) to overcome any possible issues related to our current operating system configuration.

> If none of these work, the best thing we can do is to ask for specific support on the .NET community forums at: `https://forums.asp.net/default.aspx/7?General+ASP+NET`

If we manage to successfully perform the test run, it means that the sample app is working: we're ready to move on.

Summary

So far, so good; we've just set up a working skeleton of what's about to come. Before moving on, let's do a quick recap of what we just did (and learned) in this chapter.

We briefly described our platforms of choice – ASP.NET and Angular – and acknowledged their combined potential in the process of building a modern web application. We spent some valuable time recalling what's happened in these last few years and summarizing the efforts of both development teams to reboot and improve their respective frameworks. These recaps were very useful to enumerate and understand the main reasons why we're still using them over their ever-growing competitors.

Right after that, we did our best to understand the differences between the various approaches that can be adopted to create web apps nowadays: SPAs, MPAs, and PWAs. We also explained that, since we'll be using .NET and Angular, we'll stick to the SPA approach, but we'll also implement most PWA features, such as service workers and web manifest files. In an attempt to reproduce a realistic production-case scenario, we also went through the most common SPA features, first from a technical point of view, and then putting ourselves in the shoes of a typical product owner while trying to enumerate their expectations.

Last, but not least, we learned how to properly set up our development environment; we chose to do that using the latest Angular SPA template shipped with the .NET SDK, thus adopting the standard ASP.NET Core/.NET 5 approach. We created our app using the .NET CLI and then tested it on Visual Studio to ensure it was working properly.

In the next chapter, we'll take an extensive look at the sample app we just created in order to properly understand how the .NET *back-end* and the Angular *front-end* perform their respective tasks and what they can do together.

Suggested topics

Agile development, Scrum, Extreme Programming, MVC and MVVM architectural patterns, ASP.NET Core, .NET Core, .NET 5, Roslyn, CoreCLR, RyuJIT, Single-Page Application (SPA), Progressive Web Application (PWA), Native Web Application (NWA), Multi-Page Application (MPA), NuGet, NPM, ECMAScript 6, JavaScript, TypeScript, webpack, SystemJS, RxJS, Cache-Control, HTTP Headers, .NET middleware, Angular Universal, server-side rendering (SSR), Ahead-of-Time (AOT) compiler, service workers, web manifest files, tsconfig.json.

References

- *Native Web Apps, Henrik Joreteg, 2015*: `https://blog.andyet.com/2015/01/22/native-web-apps/`
- *Manifesto for Agile Software Development, Kent Beck, Mike Beedle, and many others, 2001*: `https://agilemanifesto.org/`
- *ASP.NET 5 is dead – Introducing ASP.NET Core 1.0 and .NET Core 1.0*: `http://www.hanselman.com/blog/ASPNET5IsDeadIntroducingASPNETCore10AndNETCore10.aspx`
- *An Update on ASP.NET Core and .NET Core*: `https://blogs.msdn.microsoft.com/webdev/2016/02/01/an-update-on-asp-net-core-and-net-core/`
- *ASP.NET Core 1.1.0 release notes*: `https://github.com/aspnet/AspNetCore/releases/1.1.0`
- *ASP.NET Core 1.1.0 Commits list*: `https://github.com/dotnet/core/blob/master/release-notes/1.1/1.1-commits.md`
- *ASP.NET Core 2.1.0 release notes*: `https://docs.microsoft.com/en-US/aspnet/core/release-notes/aspnetcore-2.1`
- *ASP.NET Core 2.1.0 Commits list*: `https://github.com/dotnet/core/blob/master/release-notes/2.1/2.1.0-commit.md`
- *ASP.NET Core 2.2.0 release notes*: `https://docs.microsoft.com/en-US/aspnet/core/release-notes/aspnetcore-2.2`
- *ASP.NET Core 2.2.0 Commits list*: `https://github.com/dotnet/core/blob/master/release-notes/2.2/2.2.0/2.2.0-commits.md`
- *ASP.NET Core 3.0.0 release notes*: `https://docs.microsoft.com/en-us/dotnet/core/whats-new/dotnet-core-3-0`
- *ASP.NET Core 3.0 releases page*: `https://github.com/dotnet/core/tree/master/release-notes/3.0`
- *ASP.NET Core 3.1.0 release notes*: `https://docs.microsoft.com/en-us/dotnet/core/whats-new/dotnet-core-3-1`
- *.NET Core is the future of .NET*: `https://devblogs.microsoft.com/dotnet/net-core-is-the-future-of-net/`
- *The Evolution from .NET Core to .NET 5*: `https://docs.microsoft.com/en-us/dotnet/core/dotnet-five`
- *Introducing .NET 5*: `https://devblogs.microsoft.com/dotnet/introducing-net-5/`
- *Performance improvements in .NET 5*: `https://devblogs.microsoft.com/dotnet/performance-improvements-in-net-5/`
- *Introducing the Half Type*: `https://devblogs.microsoft.com/dotnet/introducing-the-half-type/`
- *App Trimming in .NET 5*: `https://devblogs.microsoft.com/dotnet/app-trimming-in-net-5/`

- *What's new in C# 9.0*: `https://docs.microsoft.com/en-us/dotnet/csharp/whats-new/csharp-9`
- *BuiltWith: JavaScript Library Usage Distribution*: `https://trends.builtwith.com/javascript/javascript-library`
- *Usage of JavaScript libraries for websites*: `https://w3techs.com/technologies/overview/javascript_library/all`
- *Miško Hevery and Brad Green - Keynote - NG-Conf 2014*: `https://www.youtube.com/watch?v=r1A1VR0ibIQ`
- *AngularJS 1.7.9 Changelog*: `https://github.com/angular/angular.js/blob/master/CHANGELOG.md`
- *ASP.NET Core and Angular 2*: `https://www.packtpub.com/application-development/aspnet-core-and-angular-2`
- *ASP.NET Core 2 and Angular 5*: `https://www.packtpub.com/application-development/aspnet-core-2-and-angular-5`
- *ASP.NET Core 2 and Angular 5 - Video Course*: `https://www.packtpub.com/web-development/asp-net-core-2-and-angular-5-video`
- *Angular Update Guide*: `https://update.angular.io`
- *Angular Language Service*: `https://angular.io/guide/language-service`
- *Angular Deprecated APIs and Features*: `https://angular.io/guide/deprecations`
- *What is Angular Ivy?*: `https://blog.ninja-squad.com/2019/05/07/what-is-angular-ivy/`
- *Solution Style tsconfig.json files*: `https://www.typescriptlang.org/docs/handbook/release-notes/typescript-3-9.html#support-for-solution-style-tsconfigjson-files`
- *Tree Shaking*: `https://developer.mozilla.org/en-US/docs/Glossary/Tree_shaking`
- *Progressive Web Apps*: `https://developers.google.com/web/progressive-web-apps/`
- *Progressive Web Apps: Escaping Tabs Without Losing Our Soul*: `https://infrequently.org/2015/06/progressive-apps-escaping-tabs-without-losing-our-soul/`
- *What, Exactly, Makes Something A Progressive Web App?*: `https://infrequently.org/2016/09/what-exactly-makes-something-a-progressive-web-app/`
- *Scrum (software development)*: `https://en.wikipedia.org/wiki/Scrum_(software_development)`
- *Waterfall model*: `https://en.wikipedia.org/wiki/Waterfall_model`
- *ASP.NET Community Forums*: `https://forums.asp.net/default.aspx/7?General+ASP+NET`

2

Looking Around

Now that our project has been created, it's time to take a quick look around and try to understand some of the hard work that the .NET and Angular SPA template has done to make it work.

...Hey, wait a minute! Shouldn't we skip all these setup technicalities and just jump into coding?

As a matter of fact, yes, we'll definitely be doing that in a little while. However, before doing that, it's wise to highlight a couple of aspects of the code that have been put in place already so that we'll know how to move effectively within our project in advance: where to find the *server-side* and *client-side* code, where to put new content, how to change our initialization parameters, and so on. It will also be a good chance to review our basic knowledge of the Visual Studio environment and the packages we will need.

That's precisely what we're going to do in this chapter. More precisely, the following are the main topics we're going to cover:

- **Solution overview**: A high-level summary of what we'll be dealing with
- **The ASP.NET back-end**: Razor Pages, controllers, configuration files, and so on
- **The Angular front-end**: The workspace, the `ClientApp` folder, the Angular initialization cycle, and so on
- **Creating a new app with the Angular CLI**: Installation, creation, and testing
- **Getting to work**: Caching concepts, removing some .NET controllers and Angular components that we no longer require, and so on

IMPORTANT! The sample code we're reviewing here is the code that comes with the default Angular SPA Visual Studio template shipped by .NET 5 SDK at the time of writing—the one created with the `dotnet new angular` command. In the (likely) event that this sample code is updated in future releases, ensure you get the former source code from the web using this book's official GitHub repository and use it to replace the contents of your project folder.

Caution: failing to do this could result in you working with different sample code from the code featured in this book.

Technical requirements

In this chapter, all of the previous technical requirements listed in *Chapter 1*, *Getting Ready*, will apply, with no additional resources, libraries, or packages.

The code files for this chapter can be found here: `https://github.com/PacktPublishing/ASP.NET-Core-5-and-Angular/tree/main/Chapter_02/`

Solution overview

The first thing that catches the eye is that, as we've already mentioned, the layout of a standard ASP.NET Core solution is quite different from what it used to be in ASP.NET 4 and earlier versions. However, provided that we already have some ASP.NET MVC experience, we should be able to distinguish the ASP.NET *back-end* part from the Angular *front-end* part, and also figure out how these two aspects can interact.

The ASP.NET *back-end* stack is contained in the following folders:

- The `Dependencies` virtual folder, which basically replaces the old `References` folder and contains all the internal, external, and third-party references required to build and run our project. All the references to the NuGet packages that we'll add to our project will also be put there.
- The `/Controllers/` folder, which has been shipped with any MVC-based ASP.NET application since the preceding release of the MVC framework.
- The `/Pages/` folder, which contains a single Razor Page—`Error.cshtml`—to handle runtime and/or server errors (more on that later on).
- The root-level files—`Program.cs`, `Startup.cs`, and `appsettings.json`—which will determine our web application's configuration, including the modules and middlewares, compilation settings, and publishing rules; we'll address them all in a while.

As for the Angular *front-end*, it comprises the following folders:

- The `/wwwroot/` folder, which will contain the compiled, *ready-to-publish* contents of our application: HTML, JS, and CSS files, along with fonts, images, and everything else we want our users to have access to in terms of **static files**.

- The `/ClientApp/` root folder, which hosts the Angular (and package manager) configuration files, as well as a couple of important sub-folders of which we're about to give an overview.
- The `/ClientApp/src/` folder, which contains the Angular app source code files. If we look at them, we can see that they all have a `.ts` extension, which means we'll be using the **TypeScript** programming language (we'll say more about this in a bit).
- The `/ClientApp/e2e/` folder, containing some sample **end-to-end** (E2E) tests built with the *Protractor* testing framework.

Let's quickly review the most important parts of this structure.

The ASP.NET back-end

If you hail from the ASP.NET MVC framework(s), you might want to know why this template doesn't contain a `/Views/` folder: where did our Razor views go?

As a matter of fact, this template doesn't make use of views. If we think about it, the reason is quite obvious: a **Single-Page Application** (**SPA**) might as well get rid of them since they are meant to operate within a single HTML page that gets served only once. In this template, such a page is the `/ClientApp/src/folder/index.html` file—and, as we can clearly see, it's also a static page. The only *server-side*-rendered HTML page provided by this template is the `/Pages/Error.cshtml` Razor Page, which is used to handle runtime and/or server errors that could happen *before* the Angular bootstrap phase.

Razor Pages

Those who have never heard of Razor Pages should spend 5-10 minutes taking a look at the following guide, which explains what they are and how they work: `https://docs.microsoft.com/en-us/aspnet/core/razor-pages/`

In a nutshell, Razor Pages were introduced in .NET Core 2.0 and represent an alternative way to implement the ASP.NET Core MVC pattern. A Razor Page is rather similar to a Razor view, with the same syntax and functionality, but it also contains the controller source code—which is placed in a separate file: such files share the same name as the page with an additional `.cs` extension.

To better show the *dependence* between the `.cshtml` and the `.cshtml.cs` files of a Razor Page, Visual Studio conveniently nests the latter within the former, as we can see from the following screenshot:

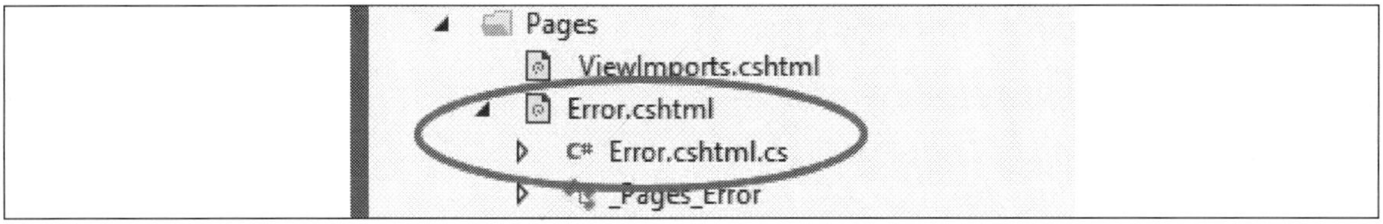

Figure 2.1: Examining .cshtml and .cshtml.cs files

...Hey, wait a minute: where have I seen this movie before?

Yes, this definitely rings a bell: being a slimmer version of the standard MVC *Controller* + *view* approach, a Razor Page is pretty similar to an old `.aspx` + `.aspx.cs` ASP.NET Web Form.

Advantages of using Razor Pages

As a matter of fact, one of the most important benefits of Razor Pages is the fact that they implement the *Single Responsibility Principle* in a seamless and effective way: each Razor Page is *self-contained*, as its view and controller are intertwined and organized together.

> The **Single Responsibility Principle** (also known as **SRP**) is a computer programming good practice which advises that every module, class, or function should have responsibility for a single part of the functionality provided by the software and that this responsibility should also be entirely encapsulated by that class.

The approach enforced by Razor Pages is definitely easier to understand for a novice developer than the "standard" MVC model, which relies on the intertwined work of Controllers and Views; this also means that Razor Pages will be easier to develop, update, document, and test.

Controllers

If Razor Pages are so great, why we do still have a `/Controller/` folder? Wouldn't it be better to just drop such a concept and switch to them from now on?

Well, it's not that simple: not all controllers are meant to serve *server-rendered* HTML pages (or views). For example, they can output a JSON output (REST APIs), XML-based response (SOAP web services), a static or dynamically created resource (JPG, JS, and CSS files), or even a simple HTTP response (such as an HTTP 301 redirect) without the content body. This basically means that Controllers still have a very important role, especially in web applications that strongly depend upon server-side JSON content coming from a REST API like those we're about to build.

Advantages of using Controllers

Among the many benefits of using Controllers, there's the fact that they allow a *decoupling* between what is meant to serve standard HTML content, which we usually call *pages* or *views*, and the rest of the HTTP response, which can be loosely defined as *service APIs*.

Such division enforces a **separation of concerns** between how we load the *server-side* pages (1%) and how we serve our *server-side* APIs (99%). The percentages shown are valid for our specific scenario: we're going to follow the SPA approach, which is all about serving and calling web APIs.

That's why we'll mostly deal with Controllers, whereas Razor Pages would mostly shine in a multi-page application scenario.

WeatherForecastController

By acknowledging all this, we can already infer that the single sample `WeatherForecastController` contained in the `/Controllers/` folder is there to expose a bunch of web APIs that will be used by the Angular *front-end*. To quickly check it out, hit *F5* to launch the project in *debug* mode and execute the default route by typing the following URL: `https://localhost:44334/WeatherForecast`.

> The actual port number may vary, depending on the project configuration file: to set a different port for debug sessions, change the `iisSettings | iisExpress | applicationUrl` and/or `iisSettings | iisExpress | sslPort` values in the `Properties/launchSettings.json` file.

This will execute the `Get()` method defined in the `WeatherForecastController.cs` file. As we can see by looking at the source code, such a method has an `IEnumerable<WeatherForecast>` return value, meaning that it will return multiple objects of the `WeatherForecast` type.

If you copy the preceding URL into the browser and execute it, you should see a JSON array of randomly generated data, as shown in the following screenshot:

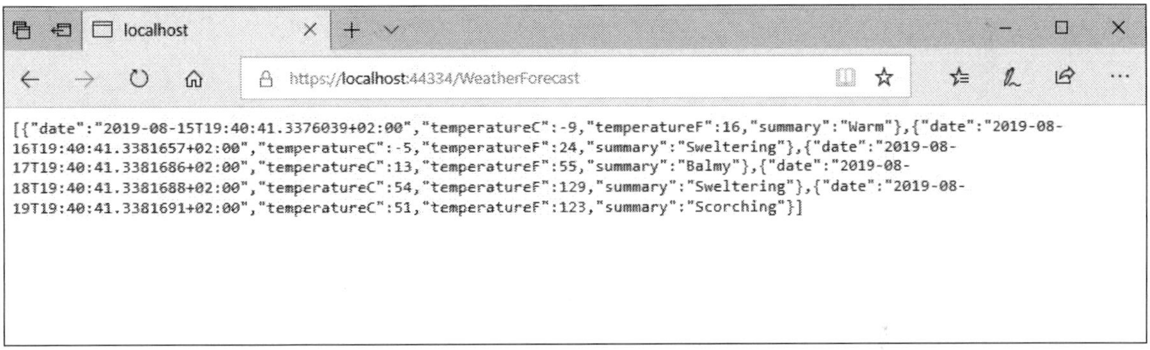

Figure 2.2: JSON array of weather data

It's not difficult to imagine who'll be asking for these values.

Configuration files

Let's now take a look at root-level configuration files and their purpose: `Program.cs`, `Startup.cs`, and `appsettings.json`. These files contain our web application's configuration, including the modules and middlewares, as well as environment-specific settings and rules.

The `WeatherForecast.cs` file contains a strongly typed class designed to be returned from the `Get` method of the `WeatherForecastController`: this model can be seen as a View Model, as it will be serialized into JSON by the ASP.NET Core Framework. In our humble opinion, the template authors should have put it within the `/ViewModel/` folder (or something like that) instead of leaving it at the root level. Anyway, let's just ignore it for now, since it's not a configuration file, and focus on the rest.

Program.cs

The `Program.cs` file will most likely intrigue most seasoned ASP.NET programmers, as it's not something we usually see in a web application project. First introduced in ASP.NET Core 1.0, the `Program.cs` file's main purpose is to create a `HostBuilder`, an object that will be used by the .NET Core runtime to set up and build the `IHost`, and which will host our web application.

IHost versus web server

That's great to know, but what is a *host*? In just a few words, it is the execution context of any ASP.NET Core app. In a web-based application, the host must implement the `IHost` interface, which exposes a collection of web-related features and services and also a `Start` method. The web host references the server that will handle requests.

The preceding statement can lead to the assumption that the web host and the web server are the same thing. However, it's very important to understand that they're not, as they serve very different purposes. Simply put, the host is responsible for application startup and lifetime management, while the server is responsible for accepting HTTP requests. Part of the host's responsibility includes ensuring that the application's services and the server are available and properly configured.

We can think of the host as being a wrapper around the server: the host is configured to use a particular server, while the server is unaware of its host.

> For further info regarding the `IHost` interface, the `HostBuilder` class, and the purpose of the `Setup.cs` file, take a look at the following guide: `https://docs.microsoft.com/en-us/aspnet/core/fundamentals/`

If we open the `Program.cs` file and take a look at the code, we can easily see that the `HostBuilder` is built in an extremely straightforward manner, as follows:

```
using Microsoft.AspNetCore.Hosting;
using Microsoft.Extensions.Configuration;
using Microsoft.Extensions.Hosting;
using Microsoft.Extensions.Logging;
using System;
using System.Collections.Generic;
using System.Linq;
using System.Threading.Tasks;

namespace HealthCheck
{
    public class Program
    {
        public static void Main(string[] args)
```

```
        {
            CreateHostBuilder(args).Build().Run();
        }

        public static IHostBuilder CreateHostBuilder(string[] args) =>
            Host.CreateDefaultBuilder(args)
                .ConfigureWebHostDefaults(webBuilder =>
                {
                    webBuilder.UseStartup<Startup>();
                });
    }
}
```

The `CreateDefaultBuilder(args)` method was introduced in ASP.NET Core 2.1 and is a great improvement on its 1.x counterpart, as it simplifies the amount of source code required to set up basic use cases, thus making it easier to get started with a new project.

To understand this better, let's take a look at the sample `Program.cs` equivalent, like it was in ASP.NET Core 1.x:

```
public class Program
{
    public static void Main(string[] args)
    {
        var host = new WebHostBuilder()
            .UseKestrel()
            .UseContentRoot(Directory.GetCurrentDirectory())
            .UseIISIntegration()
            .UseStartup<Startup>()
            .UseApplicationInsights()
            .Build();

        host.Run();
    }
}
```

The preceding code was intended to perform the following steps:

1. Setting up the `Kestrel` web server
2. Setting up the content `root` folder, that is, where to look for the `appsettings.json` file and other configuration files
3. Setting up `IIS integration`
4. Defining the `Startup` class to use (usually defined in the `Startup.cs` file)
5. Finally, executing **Build** and **Run** on the now configured `IWebHost`

In ASP.NET Core 1.x, all these steps must be called explicitly here and also manually configured within the Startup.cs file; although such an "explicit" approach is still supported in ASP.NET Core 2.x, .NET Core 3.x, and .NET 5, using the CreateDefaultBuilder() method is almost always a better way as it takes care of most of the job, and also lets us change the defaults whenever we want.

> If you're curious about this method, you can even take a peek at the source code on GitHub: https://github.com/aspnet/MetaPackages/blob/master/src/Microsoft.AspNetCore/WebHost.cs
>
> At the time of writing, the WebHost.CreateDefaultBuilder() method implementation starts at line #148.

As we can see, the CreateHostBuilder method ends with a chained call to UseStartup<Startup>() to specify the startup type that will be used by the web host. That type is defined in the Startup.cs file, which is what we're going to talk about.

Startup.cs

If you're a seasoned .NET developer, you might already be familiar with the Startup.cs file since it was first introduced in OWIN-based applications to replace most of the tasks previously handled by the good old Global.asax file.

> **Open Web Interface for .NET** (**OWIN**) comes as part of project **Katana**, a flexible set of components released by Microsoft back in 2013 for building and hosting OWIN-based web applications. For additional info, refer to the following link: https://www.asp.net/aspnet/overview/owin-and-katana

However, the similarities end here; the class has been completely rewritten to be as pluggable and lightweight as possible, which means that it will include and load only what's strictly necessary to fulfill our application's tasks.

More specifically, in .NET 5, the Startup.cs file is the place where we can do the following:

- Add and configure services and Dependency Injection, in the ConfigureServices() method
- Configure an HTTP request pipeline by adding the required *middleware*, in the Configure() method

To better understand this, let's take a look at the following lines taken from the Startup.cs source code shipped with the project template we chose:

```
using Microsoft.AspNetCore.Builder;
using Microsoft.AspNetCore.Hosting;
using Microsoft.AspNetCore.HttpsPolicy;
using Microsoft.AspNetCore.SpaServices.AngularCli;
using Microsoft.Extensions.Configuration;
```

```
using Microsoft.Extensions.DependencyInjection;
using Microsoft.Extensions.Hosting;

namespace HealthCheck
{
    public class Startup
    {
        public Startup(IConfiguration configuration)
        {
            Configuration = configuration;
        }

        public IConfiguration Configuration { get; }

        // This method gets called by the runtime.
        // Use this method to add services to the container.
        public void ConfigureServices(IServiceCollection services)
        {
            services.AddControllersWithViews();
            // In production, the Angular files will
            // be served from this directory
            services.AddSpaStaticFiles(configuration =>
            {
                configuration.RootPath = "ClientApp/dist";
            });
        }

        // This method gets called by the runtime.
        // Use this method to configure the HTTP request pipeline.
        public void Configure(IApplicationBuilder app, IWebHostEnvironment env)
        {
            if (env.IsDevelopment())
            {
                app.UseDeveloperExceptionPage();
            }
            else
            {
                app.UseExceptionHandler("/Error");
                // The default HSTS value is 30 days.
                // You may want to change this for production scenarios,
                // see https://aka.ms/aspnetcore-hsts.
                app.UseHsts();
            }

            app.UseHttpsRedirection();
```

```
            app.UseStaticFiles();
            if (!env.IsDevelopment())
            {
                app.UseSpaStaticFiles();
            }

            app.UseRouting();

            app.UseEndpoints(endpoints =>
            {
                endpoints.MapControllerRoute(
                    name: "default",
                    pattern: "{controller}/{action=Index}/{id?}");
            });

            app.UseSpa(spa =>
            {
                // To learn more about options for serving an Angular SPA
                // from ASP.NET Core,
                // see https://go.microsoft.com/fwlink/?linkid=864501

                spa.Options.SourcePath = "ClientApp";

                if (env.IsDevelopment())
                {
                    spa.UseAngularCliServer(npmScript: "start");
                }
            });
        }
    }
}
```

The `Startup` class contains the `Configure()` method implementation, where, as we just said, we can set up and configure the HTTP request pipeline.

The code is very readable, so we can easily understand what happens here:

- The first bunch of lines features an `if-then-else` statement that implements two different behaviors to handle runtime exceptions in development and production, throwing the exception in the former case and showing an opaque error page to the end user in the latter; that's a neat way to handle runtime exceptions in very few lines of code.

- Right after that, we can see the first block of middlewares: `HttpsRedirection`, to handle HTTP-to-HTTPS redirects; `StaticFiles`, to serve static files placed under the `/wwwroot/` folder; and `SpaStaticFiles`, to serve static files in the `/ClientApp/src/assets/` folder (the `assets` folder of our Angular app). Without these last two middlewares, we won't be able to serve locally hosted assets such as JS, CSS, and images; this is the reason they are in a pipeline. Also, note how these methods are called with no parameters: this just means that their default settings are more than enough for us, so there's nothing to configure or override here.
- After the three-pack, there's a call to the `EndpointRoutingMiddleware`, which adds route matching to the middleware pipeline. This middleware looks at the set of endpoints defined in the app and selects the best match based on each incoming HTTP request.
- The `EndpointRoutingMiddleware` is followed by the `EndpointsMiddleware`, which will add the required routing rule(s) to map certain HTTP requests to our web API controllers. We'll extensively talk about that in upcoming chapters, when we'll deal with *server-side* routing aspects; for now, let's just understand that there's an active mapping rule that will *catch* all HTTP requests resembling a *controller* name (and/or an optional *action* name, and/or an optional ID `GET` parameter) and route them to that controller. That's precisely why we were able to call the `WeatherForecastController.Get()` method from our web browser and receive a result.
- Last but not least comes the `UseSpa` middleware, which gets added to the HTTP pipeline with two configuration settings:
    - The first one is pretty easy to understand: it's just the source path of the Angular app's root folder. In this template's scenario, it's the `/ClientApp/` folder. Let's keep a mental note of this folder's literal definition, because we'll come back to it later on.
    - The second one, which will only be executed in development scenarios, is way more complex. To explain it in a few words, the `UseAngularCliServer()` method tells .NET 5 to pass through all the requests addressed to the Angular app to an instance of the Angular CLI server: this is great for development scenarios because our app will always serve up-to-date CLI-built resources without having to run the Angular CLI server manually each time. At the same time, it's not ideal for production scenarios because of the additional overhead and an obvious performance impact.

> It's worth noting that middlewares added to the HTTP pipeline will process incoming requests in registration order, from top to bottom. This means that the `StaticFile` middleware will take priority over the `Endpoint` middleware, which will take place before the `Spa` middleware, and so on. Such behavior is very important and could cause unexpected results if taken lightly, as shown in the following Stack Overflow thread: `https://stackoverflow.com/questions/52768852/`

Let's perform a quick test to ensure that we properly understand how these middlewares work:

1. From Visual Studio's Solution Explorer, go to the `/wwwroot/` folder and add a new `test.html` page to our project.
2. Once done, fill it with the following contents:

```
<!DOCTYPE html>
<html>
<head>
  <meta charset="utf-8" />
  <title>Time for a test!</title>
</head>
<body>
  Hello there!
  <br /><br />
  This is a test to see if the StaticFiles middleware is
  working properly.
</body>
</html>
```

Now, let's launch the application in *debug* mode—using the **Run** button or the *F5* keyboard key—and point the address bar to the following URL: `https://localhost:44334/test.html`.

> Again, the TCP/IP port number may vary. Edit the `Properties/launchSettings.json` file if you want to change it.

We should be able to see our `test.html` file in all its glory, as shown in the following screenshot:

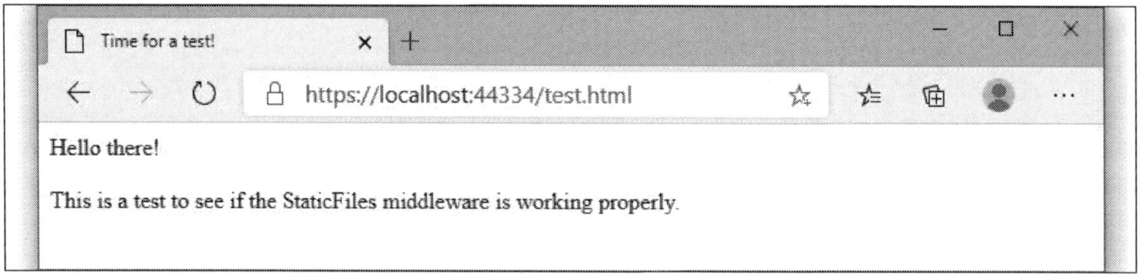

Figure 2.3: Viewing test.html

Based on what we learned a moment ago, we know that this file is being served thanks to the `StaticFiles` middleware. Let's now go back to our `Startup.cs` file and comment out the `app.UseStaticFiles()` call to prevent the `StaticFiles` middleware from being loaded:

```
app.UseHttpsRedirection();
// app.UseStaticFiles();
if (!env.IsDevelopment())
{
    app.UseSpaStaticFiles();
}
```

Once done, run the application again and try to go back to the previous URL, as shown in the following screenshot:

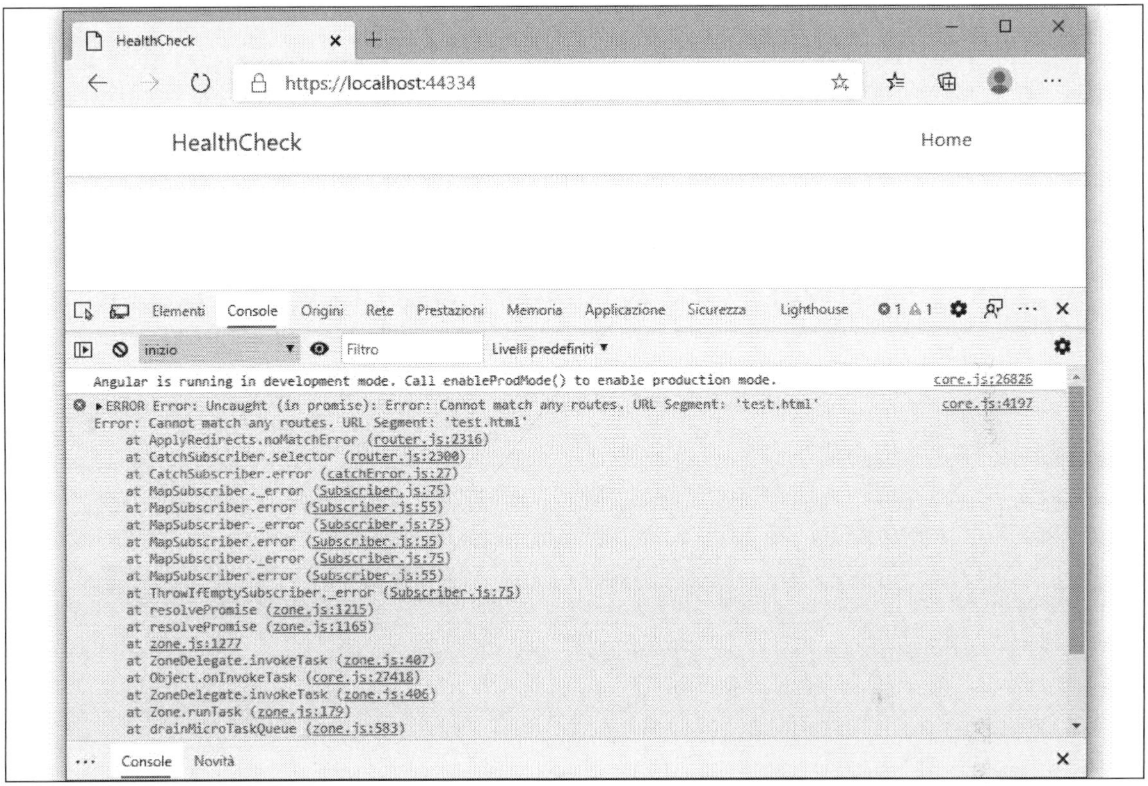

Figure 2.4: Trying to view test.html

As expected, the `test.html` static file isn't served anymore. The file is still there, but the `StaticFile` middleware is not registered and cannot handle it. Therefore, the now-unhandled HTTP request goes all the way through the HTTP pipeline until it reaches the `Spa` middleware, which acts as a catch-all and tosses it to the *client-side* Angular app. However, since there is no *client-side* routing rule that matches the `test.html` pattern, the request is eventually redirected to the app's starting page.

The last part of the story is fully documented in the browser's **Console** log, as shown in the preceding screenshot. The `Cannot match any routes` error message comes from Angular, meaning that our request passed through the whole ASP.NET Core *back-end* stack.

Now that we've proved our point, we can bring the `StaticFiles` middleware back in place by removing the comments and moving on.

> For additional information regarding the `StaticFiles` middleware and static file handling in .NET Core, visit the following URL: `https://docs.microsoft.com/en-us/aspnet/core/fundamentals/static-files`.

All in all, since the `Startup.cs` file shipped with the Angular SPA template already has everything we need, we can leave it as it is for now.

Thanks to this brief overview, we should now be fully aware of how the HTTP request received by our web application will be handled. Let's try to wrap everything up:

1. Each request will be received by the **ASP.NET Core back-end**, which will try to handle it at the *server-side* level by checking the various middlewares registered in the HTTP pipeline (in registration order). In our specific scenario, we'll first check the static files in the `/wwwroot/` folder, then the static files in the `/ClientApp/src/assets/` folder, and then those in the routes mapped to our web API controllers/endpoints.
2. If one of the aforementioned middlewares is able to match and handle the request, the **ASP.NET Core back-end** will take care of it. Conversely, the `Spa` middleware will pass the request through to the Angular *client-side* app, which will handle it using its *client-side* routing rules (more on them later on).

appsettings.json

The `appsettings.json` file is just a replacement for the good old `Web.config` file; the XML syntax has been replaced by the more readable and considerably less verbose JSON format. Moreover, the new configuration model is based upon key/value settings that can be retrieved from a wide variety of sources, including, but not limited to, JSON files, using a centralized interface.

Once retrieved, they can be easily accessed within our code using **Dependency Injection** via literal strings (using the `IConfiguration` interface):

```
public SampleController(IConfiguration configuration)
{
    var myValue = configuration["Logging:IncludeScopes"];
}
```

Alternatively, we can achieve the same result with a *strongly typed* approach using a custom `POCO` class (we'll get to that later on).

It's worth noting that there's also an `appsettings.Development.json` file nested below the main one. Such a file serves the same purpose as the old `Web.Debug.config` file, which was widely used during the ASP.NET 4.x period. In a nutshell, these additional files can be used to specify additional configuration key/value pairs (and/or override existing ones) for specific environments.

To better understand the concept, let's take a look at the two files' contents.

The following is the `appsettings.json` file:

```
{
  "Logging": {
      "LogLevel": {
        "Default": "Warning"
      }
    },
  "AllowedHosts": "*"
}
```

And here's the `appsettings.Development.json` file:

```
{
  "Logging": {
    "LogLevel": {
      "Default": "Debug",
      "System": "Information",
      "Microsoft": "Information"
    }
  }
}
```

As we can see, the `Logging.LogLevel.Default` value for our app is set to `Warning` in the first file. However, whenever our app runs in *development* mode, the second file will overwrite the value, setting it to `Debug`, and add the `System` and `Microsoft` log levels, setting them both to `Information`.

> Back in .NET Core 1.x, this overriding behavior had to be specified manually within the `Startup.cs` file. In .NET Core 2, the `Host.CreateDefaultBuilder()` method within the `Program.cs` file takes care of that automatically, by assuming that you can rely on this default naming pattern and don't need to add another custom `.json` configuration file.

Assuming that we understood everything here, we're done inspecting the ASP.NET Core *back-end* part; it's time to move on to the Angular *front-end* folders and files.

The Angular front-end

The *front-end* part of the template will probably be seen as more complex to understand, because Angular—just like most *client-side* frameworks—has evolved at a dramatic pace, thus experiencing many breaking changes in its core architecture, toolchain management, coding syntax, template, and setup.

For this very reason, it's very important to take our time understanding the role of the various files shipped with the template. This brief overview will start with root-level configuration files, which will also be updated with the latest versions of the Angular packages (and their dependencies) that we'll need to use.

Workspace

The Angular workspace is the filesystem place containing the Angular files: a collection of application files, libraries, assets, and so on. In our template, as in most ASP.NET Core and Angular projects, the workspace is located within the `/ClientApp/` folder, which is defined as the workspace root.

The workspace is usually created and initialized by the CLI command used to create the app. Do you remember the `dotnet new` command we used in *Chapter 1*, *Getting Ready*? That's what we're talking about: the Angular part of the template was created by that command. We could achieve that same result with the Angular CLI, using the `ng new` command.

Any CLI commands operating on the app and/or their libraries (such as adding or updating new packages) will be executed from within the workspace folder.

angular.json

The most important role within the workspace is played by the `angular.json` file, created by the CLI in the workspace root. This is the workspace configuration file and contains workspace-wide and project-specific configuration defaults for all build and development tools provided by the Angular CLI.

> It's worth noting that all the paths defined within this file are meant to be relative to the workspace root folder; in our scenario, for example, `src/main.ts` will resolve to `/ClientApp/src/main.ts`.

The first few properties at the top of the file define the workspace and project configuration options:

- `version`: The configuration file version.
- `newProjectRoot`: The path where new projects are created, relative to the workspace root folder. We can see that this value is set to the *projects* folder, which doesn't even exist. That's perfectly normal since our workspace is meant to contain two Angular projects in two already defined folders: our HealthCheck Angular app, located in the `/ClientApp/src/` folder, and *end-to-end* tests, located in the `/ClientApp/e2e/` folder. Therefore, there is no need to define a `newProjectRoot`—and it's also important to not use an existing folder to avoid the risk of overwriting some existing stuff.
- `projects`: A container item that hosts a sub-section for each project in the workspace, containing project-specific configuration options.

- `defaultProject`: The default project name—any CLI command that doesn't specify a project name will be executed on this project.

> It's worth noting that the `angular.json` file follows a standard generic-to-specific cascading rule. All configuration values set at the workspace level will be the default values for any project and can be overridden by those set at the project level. These, in turn, can be overridden by command-line values available when using the CLI.
>
> It's also worth mentioning that, before **Angular 8**, manually modifying the `angular.json` file was the only way to make changes to the workspace config.

That's all we need to know, at least for the time being. All the configuration values are already good enough for our scenario, hence, we'll just leave them as they are for now.

> Up to **Angular 7**, manually modifying the `angular.json` file was the only way to make changes to the workspace config. This changed with **Angular 8** with the introduction of the **workspace API**, which now allows us to read and modify these configurations much more conveniently. For additional info regarding this new feature, we suggest taking a look at the following page: `https://github.com/angular/angular-cli/blob/master/packages/angular_devkit/core/README.md#workspaces`

package.json

The `package.json` file is the **Node Package Manager** (**npm**) **configuration file**. It basically contains a list of **npm packages** that the developer wants to be restored before the project starts. Those who already know what npm is and how it works can skip to the next section, while those who don't should definitely keep reading.

npm started its life as the default package manager for the JavaScript runtime environment known as **Node.js**. During recent years, though, it has also been used to host a number of independent JavaScript projects, libraries, and frameworks of any kind, including *Angular*. Eventually, it became the *de facto* package manager for JavaScript frameworks and tooling. Those who have never used it can think of it as the *NuGet* for the JavaScript world.

Although npm is mostly a *command-line* tool, the easiest way to use it from Visual Studio is to properly configure a `package.json` file containing all the npm packages we want to get, restore, and keep up-to-date later on. These packages get downloaded in the `/node_modules/` folder within our project directory, which is hidden by default within Visual Studio; however, all retrieved packages can be seen from the npm virtual folder. As soon as we add, delete, or update the `package.json` file, Visual Studio will automatically update that folder accordingly.

In the Angular SPA template we've been using, the shipped `package.json` file contains a huge number of packages—all **Angular** packages—plus a good bunch of dependencies, tools, and third-party utilities such as **Karma** (a great test runner for JavaScript/TypeScript).

Before moving ahead, let's take a further look at our `package.json` file and try to get the most out of it. We can see how all packages are listed within a standard JSON object entirely made up of *key-value* pairs. The package name is the *key*, while the *value* is used to specify the version number. We can either input precise build numbers or use the standard **npmJS** syntax to specify *auto-update rules* bound to custom version ranges using supported prefixes, such as the following:

- **The Tilde** (~): A value of `"~1.1.4"` will match all 1.1.x versions, excluding 1.2.0, 1.0.x, and so on.
- **The Caret** (^): A value of `"^1.1.4"` will match everything above 1.1.4, excluding 2.0.0 and above.

This is another scenario where *IntelliSense* comes in handy, as it will also visually explain the actual meaning of these prefixes.

> For an extensive list of available npmJS commands and prefixes, it's advisable to check out the official npmJS documentation at: `https://docs.npmjs.com/files/package.json`

Upgrading (or downgrading) Angular

As we can see, the Angular SPA template uses fixed version numbers for all Angular-related packages; this is definitely a wise choice since we have no guarantees that newer versions will seamlessly integrate with our existing code without raising some potentially breaking changes and/or compiler errors. Needless to say, the version number will naturally increase with the passage of time, because template developers will definitely try to keep their good work up to date.

That said, here are the most important Angular packages and releases that will be used throughout this book (not including a small bunch of additional packages that will be added later on):

```
"@angular/animations": "11.0.1",
"@angular/common": "11.0.1",
"@angular/compiler": "11.0.1",
"@angular/core": "11.0.1",
"@angular/forms": "11.0.1",
"@angular/platform-browser": "11.0.1",
"@angular/platform-browser-dynamic": "11.0.1",
"@angular/platform-server": "11.0.1",
"@angular/router": "11.0.1",

"@angular-devkit/build-angular": "0.1100.1",
"@angular/cli": "11.0.1",
"@angular/compiler-cli": "11.0.1",
"@angular/language-service": "11.0.1"
```

The former group can be found in the `dependencies` section, while the latter is part of the `devDependencies` section. As we can see, the version number is mostly the same for all packages and corresponds to the latest Angular final release available at the time of writing.

> The version of Angular that we use in this book was released a few weeks before this book hit the shelves. We did our best to use the latest available (non-beta, non-rc) version to give the reader the best possible experience with the most recent technology available. That said, that freshness will eventually decrease over time and this book's code will start to become obsolete. When this happens, try not to blame us for that!

If we want to ensure the highest possible level of compatibility between our project and this book's source code, we should definitely adopt that same release, which, at the time of writing, also corresponds to the latest stable one. We can easily perform the upgrade—or downgrade—by changing the version numbers; as soon as we save the file, Visual Studio *should* automatically fetch new versions through **npm**. In the unlikely scenario that it doesn't, manually deleting the old packages and issuing a full rebuild should be enough to fix the issue.

As always, we're free to overwrite such behavior and get newer (or older) versions of these packages, assuming that we properly understand the consequences and according to the **Disclaimer** in *Chapter 1, Getting Ready*.

> If you encounter problems while updating your `package.json` file, such as conflicting packages or broken code, ensure that you download the full source code from the official GitHub repository of this book, which includes the same `package.json` file that has been used to write, review, and test this book. It will definitely ensure a great level of compatibility with the source code you'll find here.

Upgrading (or downgrading) the other packages

As we might expect, if we upgrade (or downgrade) Angular to 11.0.1, we also need to take care of a series of other npm packages that might need to be updated (or downgraded).

Here's the full package list (including the Angular packages) we'll be using in our `package.json` file throughout the book, split into `dependencies`, `devDependencies`, and `optionalDependencies` sections. The relevant packages are summarized in the following snippet—be sure to triple-check them!

```
{
  "name": "healthcheck",
  "version": "0.0.0",
  "scripts": {
    "ng": "ng",
    "start": "ng serve",
```

```
    "build": "ng build",
    "build:ssr": "ng run HealthCheck:server:dev",
    "test": "ng test",
    "lint": "ng lint",
    "e2e": "ng e2e"
  },
  "private": true,
  "dependencies": {
    "@angular/animations": "11.0.1",
    "@angular/common": "11.0.1",
    "@angular/compiler": "11.0.1",
    "@angular/core": "11.0.1",
    "@angular/forms": "11.0.1",
    "@angular/platform-browser": "11.0.1",
    "@angular/platform-browser-dynamic": "11.0.1",
    "@angular/platform-server": "11.0.1",
    "@angular/router": "11.0.1",
    "aspnet-prerendering": "3.0.1",
    "bootstrap": "4.5.3",
    "core-js": "3.8.0",
    "jquery": "3.5.1",
    "oidc-client": "1.10.1",
    "popper.js": "1.16.1",
    "rxjs": "6.6.3",
    "zone.js": "0.10.3"
  },
  "devDependencies": {
    "@angular-devkit/build-angular": "0.1100.1",
    "@angular/cli": "11.0.1",
    "@angular/compiler-cli": "11.0.1",
    "@angular/language-service": "11.0.1",
    "@types/jasmine": "3.6.2",
    "@types/jasminewd2": "2.0.8",
    "@types/node": "14.14.10",
    "codelyzer": "6.0.1",
    "jasmine-core": "3.6.0",
    "jasmine-spec-reporter": "5.0.2",
    "karma": "5.2.3",
    "karma-chrome-launcher": "3.1.0",
```

```
        "karma-coverage-istanbul-reporter": "3.0.3",
        "karma-jasmine": "4.0.1",
        "karma-jasmine-html-reporter": "1.5.4",
        "typescript": "4.0.5"
    },
    "optionalDependencies": {
        "node-sass": "4.14.1",
        "postcss": "8.1.10",
        "protractor": "7.0.0",
        "ts-node": "9.0.0",
        "tslint": "6.1.3"
    }
}
```

It's advisable to perform a manual command-line `npm install` followed by an `npm update` from the project's root folder right after applying these changes to the `package.json` file in order to trigger a batch update of all the project's npm packages. Sometimes, Visual Studio doesn't update the packages automatically and doing that using the GUI can be tricky.

For this very reason, a convenient `update-npm.bat` batch file has been added to this book's source code repository on GitHub (inside the `/ClientApp/` folder) to handle that without having to type the preceding command manually. Such a batch file can be launched either by opening a command prompt or by installing the **Open Command Line** Visual Studio extension by Mads Kristensen. This extension adds a neat "Execute File" command in the Visual Studio contextual menu that opens when we right-click to a file from the **Solution Explorer**.

Those who run into **npm** and/or **ngcc** compilation issues after the `npm update` command can also try to delete the `/node_modules/` folder and then perform an `npm install` from scratch.

Upgrading the Angular code

It's worth noting that our updated `package.json` file doesn't include some of the packages that were present in the Visual Studio default ASP.NET and Angular SPA project template. The reason for that is quite simple: those packages are either deprecated, obsolete, or not required by the code samples we'll be working with from now on.

At the same time, since we're upgrading an existing (albeit minimalistic) Angular app, excluding some of them might lead to compiler errors and a broken source code. As a matter of fact, if we try to run our project now that we're changed our `package.json` file (and updated the `/node_modules/` folders accordingly using `npm`), we'll definitely get some TypeScript errors coming from the `/ClientApp/src/app/app.server.module.ts` file, as shown in the following screenshot:

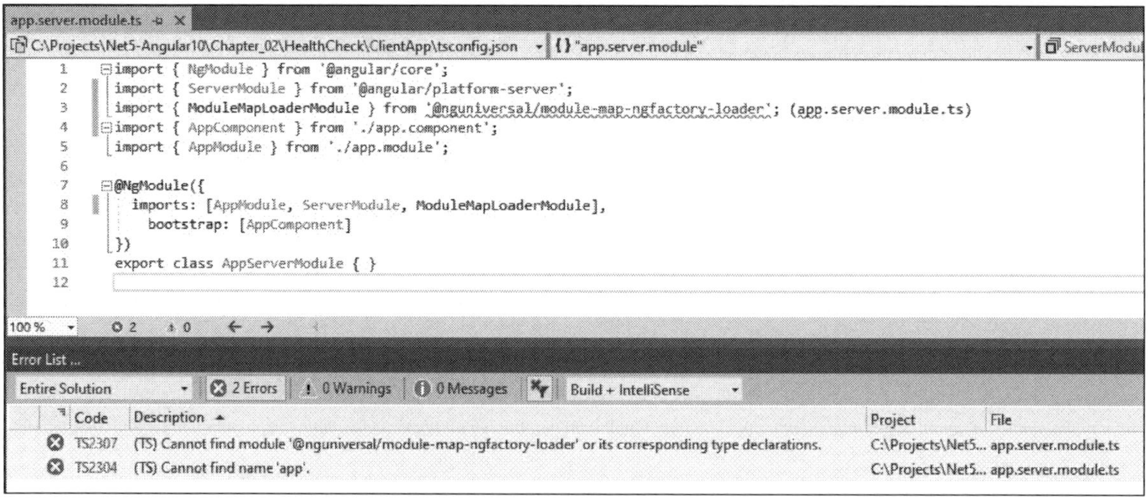

Figure 2.5: Errors after trying to run our project

These errors are due to the fact that we've removed the `@nguniversal/module-map-ngfactory-loader` JS library, which has been obsolete since Angular 9. In order to fix them, we need to perform the following updates to the `app.server.module.ts` file:

- Remove the whole line starting with `import { ModuleMapLoaderModule }` (line 3)
- Remove `ModuleMapLoaderModule` from the imports array (line 8)

Here is the `/ClientApp/src/app/app.server.module.ts` file's updated source code:

```
import { NgModule } from '@angular/core';
import { ServerModule } from '@angular/platform-server';
import { AppComponent } from './app.component';
import { AppModule } from './app.module';

@NgModule({
  imports: [AppModule, ServerModule],
    bootstrap: [AppComponent]
})
export class AppServerModule { }
```

Once done, we need to perform another minor, yet necessary, change to upgrade our existing project structure to the new naming conventions introduced by Angular 10 and 11:

- Locate the `/ClientApp/browserlist` file
- Rename it to `/ClientApp/.browserlistrc` (don't forget the starting dot!)

> For additional information regarding these changes, refer to this section of the Angular 9 to 10 official migration guide at the following URL: `https://update.angular.io/?l=3&v=9.0-10.0`

For further reference and/or future updates, please also check the updated source code in this book's official GitHub repository, which will always contain the latest improvements, bug fixes, compatibility fixes, and so on.

tsconfig.json

The `tsconfig.json` file is the TypeScript configuration file. Again, those who already know what TypeScript is won't need to read all this, although those who don't should.

In fewer than 100 words, TypeScript is a free, open source programming language developed and maintained by Microsoft that acts as a JavaScript superset; this means that any JavaScript program is also a valid TypeScript program. TypeScript also compiles to JavaScript, so it can seamlessly work on any JavaScript-compatible browser without external components. The main reason to use it is to overcome JavaScript's syntax limitations and overall shortcomings when developing large-scale applications or complex projects. Simply put, it makes the developer's life easier when they are forced to deal with non-trivial JavaScript code.

In this project, we will definitely use TypeScript for a number of good reasons; the most important ones are as follows:

- TypeScript has a number of features over JavaScript, such as static typing, classes, and interfaces. Using it in Visual Studio also gives us the chance to benefit from the *built-in* IntelliSense, which is a great benefit and often leads to a remarkable productivity boost.
- For a large *client-side* project, TypeScript will allow us to produce more robust code, which will also be fully deployable anywhere a plain JavaScript file would run.

Not to mention the fact that the Angular SPA template we chose already uses TypeScript. Hence, we can say that we already have a foot in the water!

Jokes aside, we're not the only ones praising TypeScript; this has been acknowledged by the Angular team itself, considering the fact that *the Angular source code has been written using TypeScript since Angular 2*, as was proudly announced by Microsoft in the following MDSN blog post in March 2015: `https://devblogs.microsoft.com/typescript/angular-2-built-on-typescript/`

This was further emphasized in this great post by *Victor Savkin* (cofounder of Narwhal Technologies and acknowledged Angular consultant) on his personal blog in October 2016: `https://vsavkin.com/writing-angular-2-in-typescript-1fa77c78d8e8`

Getting back to the `tsconfig.json` file, there's not much to say; the option values used by the Angular SPA template are more or less what we need to configure both Visual Studio and the **TypeScript compiler** (**TSC**) to properly transpile the TypeScript code files included in the `/ClientApp/` folder.

> For additional info about the `tsconfig.json` file and all the available options, visit the following URL: `https://angular.io/config/tsconfig`

Other workspace-level files

There are also other notable files created by the CLI in the workspace root. Since we'll not be changing them, we'll just briefly mention them in the following list:

- `.editorconfig`: Workspace-specific configuration for code editors.
- `.gitignore`: A text file that tells Git—a version-control system you most likely know quite well—which files or folders to ignore in the workspace. These are intentionally untracked files that shouldn't be added to the version control repository.
- `README.md`: Introductory documentation for the workspace. The `.md` extension stands for **Markdown**, a lightweight markup language created by *John Gruber* and *Aaron Swartz* in 2004.
- `package-lock.json`: Provides version information for all packages installed in the `/node_modules/` folder by the **npm** client. If you plan to replace **npm** with **Yarn**, you can safely delete this file (the `yarn.lock` file will be created instead).

> **Yarn** is a package manager for the JavaScript programming language developed and released by Facebook in October 2016 to address some of the limitations that **npm** had at the time, and is meant to be a drop-in replacement for **npm**. For further info, read here: `https://yarnpkg.com/`

- `/node_modules/`: A folder containing all the **npm** packages for the entire workspace. This folder will be populated with packages defined in the `package.json` file located on the workspace root, which will be visible to all projects.
- `tslint.json`: Default **TSLint** configuration options for all projects in the workspace. These general rules will be integrated and/or overwritten with the project-specific `tslint.json` file included in the project root folder.

> **TSLint** is an extensible static analysis tool that checks TypeScript code for readability, maintainability, and functionality errors; it's very similar to **JSLint**, which performs the same tasks for JavaScript code. The tool is widely supported across modern editors and build systems and can be customized with your own linting rules, configurations, and formatters.
>
> For additional info, check out the following URL: `https://palantir.github.io/tslint/`

The /ClientApp/src/ folder

It's now time to pay a visit to our sample Angular app and see how it works. Rest assured, we won't stay for long; we just want to get a glimpse of what's under the hood.

By expanding the `/ClientApp/src/` directory, we can see that there are the following sub-folders:

- The `/ClientApp/src/app/` folder, along with all its subfolders, contains all the TypeScript files related to our Angular app; in other words, the whole *client-side* application source code is meant to be put here.
- The `/ClientApp/src/assets/` folder is meant to store all the application's images and other asset files. These files will be copied and/or updated *as-is* in the `/wwwroot/` folder whenever the application is built.
- The `/ClientApp/src/environment/` folder contains build configuration options that target specific environments; this template, just like any Angular new project default, includes an `environment.ts` file (for development) and an `environment.prod.ts` file (for production).

There is also a bunch of root-level files:

- `browserslistrc`: Configures the sharing of target browsers and Node.js versions among various *front-end* tools.
- `index.html`: The main HTML page that is served when someone visits your site. The CLI automatically adds all JavaScript and CSS files when building your app, so you typically don't need to add any `<script>` or `<link>` tags here manually.
- `karma.conf.js`: Application-specific *Karma* configuration. Karma is a tool used to run *Jasmine*-based tests. We can safely ignore the whole topic for now, as we'll get to it later on.

- `main.ts`: The main entry point for your application. Compiles the application with the JIT compiler and bootstraps the application's *root module* (`AppModule`) to run in the browser. You can also use the AOT compiler without changing any code by appending the `--aot` flag to CLI build and serve commands.
- `polyfills.ts`: Provides polyfill scripts for improving browser support.
- `styles.css`: A list of CSS files that supply styles for a project.
- `test.ts`: The main entry point for the project's unit tests.
- `tsconfig.*.json`: Project-specific configuration options for various aspects of our app: `.app.json` for *application-level*, `.server.json` for *server-level*, and `.spec.json` for *tests*. These options will override those set in the generic `tsconfig.json` file in the workspace root.
- `tslint.json`: The **TSLint** configuration for the current project.

The /app/ folder

Our template's `/ClientApp/src/app/` folder follows Angular folder structure best practices and contains our project's logic and data, thus including all Angular *modules*, *services*, and *components*, as well as *templates* and *styles*. It's also the only sub-folder worth investigating, at least for the time being.

AppModule

As we briefly anticipated in *Chapter 1, Getting Ready*, the basic building blocks of an Angular application are **NgModules**, which provide a compilation context for components. The role of NgModules is to collect related code into functional sets. Therefore, the whole Angular app is defined by a set of one or more NgModules.

An Angular app requires a *root module*—conventionally called `AppModule`—that tells Angular how to assemble the application, thus enabling bootstrapping and starting the initialization life cycle (see the diagram that follows). The remaining modules are known as **feature modules** and serve a different purpose. The *root module* also contains a reference list of all available components.

The following is a schema of the standard **Angular Initialization Cycle**, which will help us better visualize how it works:

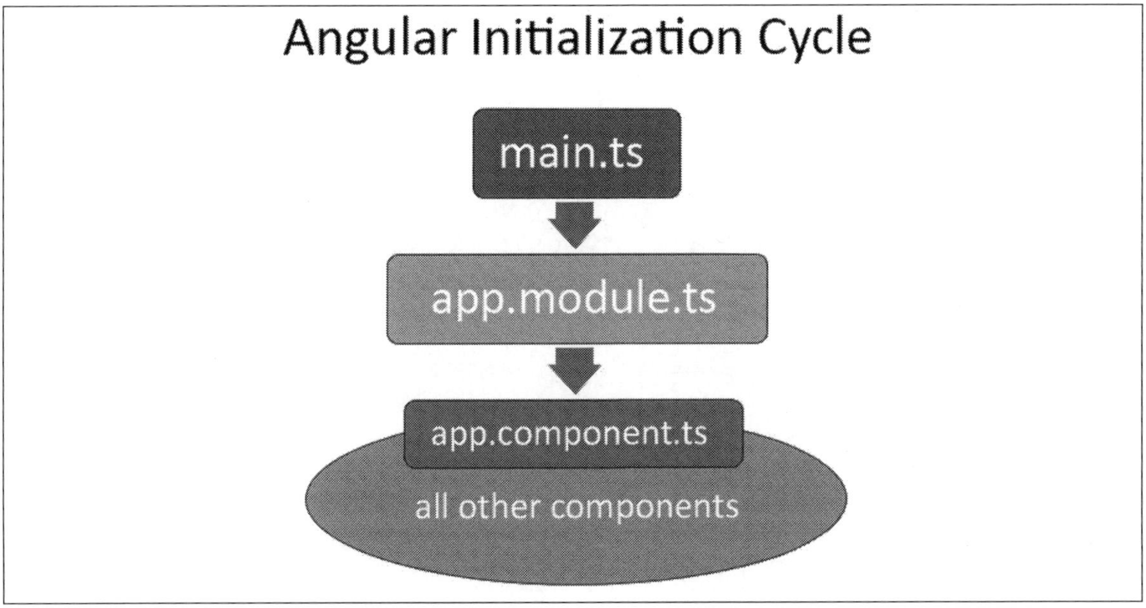

Figure 2.6: The Angular initialization cycle

As we can see, the `main.ts` file bootstraps `app.module.ts` (`AppModule`), which then loads the `app.component.ts` file (`AppComponent`); the latter, as we'll see in a short while, will then load all the other components whenever the application needs them.

The *root module* of the sample Angular app created by our template can be found in the `/ClientApp/src/app/` folder and is defined within the `app.module.ts` file. If we take a look at the source code, we can see that it contains a bunch of `import` statements and some arrays referencing *components*, other *modules*, *providers*, and so on. This should be no mystery since we just said that the *root module* is basically a reference file.

Server-side AppModule for SSR

As we can see, the `/ClientApp/src/app/` folder also contains an `app.server.module.ts` file, which will be used to enable the **Angular Universal Server-Side Rendering (SSR)**—a technology that renders Angular applications on the server, provided that the *back-end* framework supports it. The template generated this file because .NET natively supports such convenient features.

The following is the improved Angular initialization schema when using SSR:

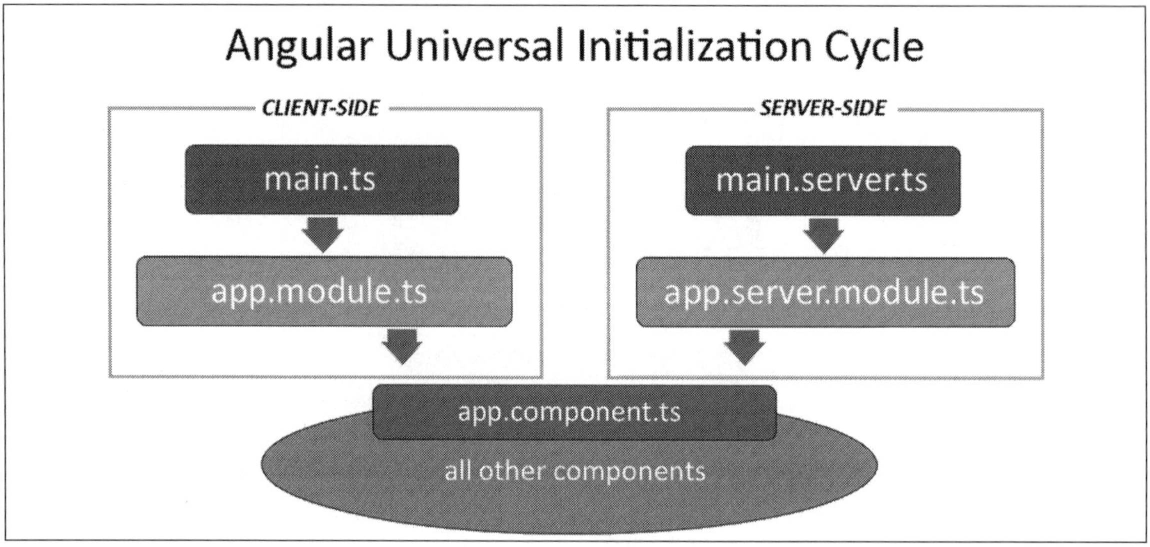

Figure 2.7: The Angular universal initialization cycle

That's about it, at least for now. If you feel like you're still missing something here, don't worry—we'll come back to this soon enough to help you understand all of this better.

> To avoid losing too much time on the theoretical aspects of ASP.NET Core and Angular, we won't enter into the details of SSR. For a more detailed look at different techniques and concepts surrounding **Angular Universal** and SSR, we suggest checking out the following article: `https://developers.google.com/web/updates/2019/02/rendering-on-the-web`

AppComponent

If NgModules are Angular building blocks, **Components** can be defined as the bricks used to put the app together, to the extent that we can say that an Angular app is basically a tree of components working together.

Components define **views**, which are sets of screen elements that Angular can choose between and modify according to your program logic and data, and use **services**, which provide specific functionality not directly related to views. **Service providers** can also be injected into components as *dependencies*, thus making the app code modular, reusable, and efficient.

The cornerstone of these components is conventionally called `AppComponent`, which is also the only component that—according to Angular folder structure conventions—should be placed in the `/app/` root folder. All other components should be put in a sub-folder, which will act as a dedicated *namespace*.

As we can see, our sample AppComponent consists of two files:

- app.component.ts: Defines the component logic, that is, the component class source code.
- app.component.html: Defines the HTML template associated with the AppComponent. Any Angular component can have an optional HTML file containing its UI layout structure instead of defining it within the component file itself. This is almost always a good practice unless the component comes with a very minimal UI.

Since the AppComponent is often lightweight, it doesn't have other optional files that could be found in other components, such as:

- <*>.component.css: Defines the base CSS style sheet for a component. Just like the .html file, this file is optional and should always be used unless the component doesn't require UI styling.
- <*>.component.spec.ts: Defines a unit test for the component.

Other components

Other than AppComponent, our template contains four more components, each one in a dedicated folder, as follows:

- CounterComponent: Placed in the counter subfolder
- FetchDataComponent: Placed in the fetch-data subfolder
- HomeComponent: Placed in the home subfolder
- NavMenuComponent: Placed in the nav-menu subfolder

As we can see by looking at the source files within their respective subfolders, only one of them has some defined tests: CounterComponent, which comes with a counter.component.spec.ts file containing two tests. It might be useful to run them to see whether the *Karma* + *Jasmine* testing framework that has been set up by our template actually works. However, before doing that, it might be wise to take a look at these components to see how they are meant to function within the Angular app.

In the next sections, we'll take care of both of these tasks.

Testing the app

Let's start by taking a look at these components to see how they are meant to work.

HomeComponent

As soon as we hit *F5* to run the app in *debug* mode, we'll be greeted by HomeComponent, as seen in the following screenshot:

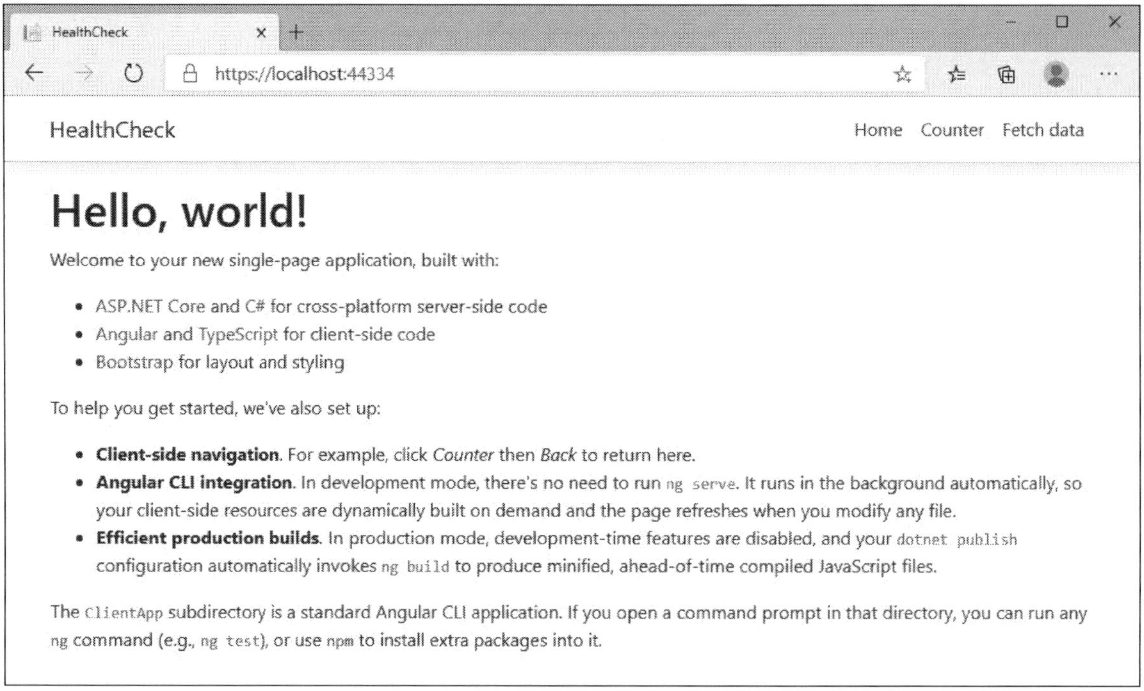
HealthCheck
https://localhost:44334
HealthCheck
Home Counter Fetch data
Hello, world!
Welcome to your new single-page application, built with:
ASP.NET Core and C# for cross-platform server-side code
Angular and TypeScript for client-side code
Bootstrap for layout and styling
To help you get started, we've also set up:
Client-side navigation. For example, click Counter then Back to return here.
Angular CLI integration. In development mode, there's no need to run ng serve. It runs in the background automatically, so your client-side resources are dynamically built on demand and the page refreshes when you modify any file.
Efficient production builds. In production mode, development-time features are disabled, and your dotnet publish configuration automatically invokes ng build to produce minified, ahead-of-time compiled JavaScript files.
The ClientApp subdirectory is a standard Angular CLI application. If you open a command prompt in that directory, you can run any ng command (e.g., ng test), or use npm to install extra packages into it.

Figure 2.8: Viewing HomeComponent

As the name clearly suggests, the `HomeComponent` could be considered the *home page* of our app; however, since the *page* concept might be rather misleading when dealing with *single-page apps*, we'll call them views instead of *pages* throughout the book. The word view basically refers to the combined HTML template generated by the Angular component (including all sub-components) that corresponds to a given navigation *route*.

NavMenuComponent

Do we have sub-components already? Yes, we do. The `NavMenuComponent` is a perfect example of that, since it doesn't have a dedicated *route* for itself, but is rendered as part of other components within their corresponding view.

More precisely, it's the top portion of each view, as we can see from the following screenshot:

HealthCheck
Home Counter Fetch data

Figure 2.9: Examining the NavMenuComponent subcomponent

The main purpose of the NavMenuComponent is to let users navigate through the main views of the app. In other words, it's where we implement all **first-level** *navigation routes* defined in AppModule, all pointing to a given Angular component.

First-level navigation routes are those that we want our users to reach with a single click, that is, without having to navigate through other components first. In the sample app we're reviewing now, there are three of them:

- /: Pointing to the HomeComponent
- /counter: Pointing to the CounterComponent
- /fetch-data: Pointing to the FetchDataComponent

As we can see, these *navigation routes* have been implemented in the NavMenuComponent by using anchor links placed within a single unordered list; a bunch of <a> elements placed inside a <ul> / <li> structure, which is rendered on the right-hand side of the component, and at the top-right corner of any component containing it.

Let's now review the design to handle the two remaining *first-level navigation routes*: CounterComponent and FetchDataComponent.

CounterComponent

The CounterComponent shows an incrementing counter that we can increase by pressing an **Increment** button:

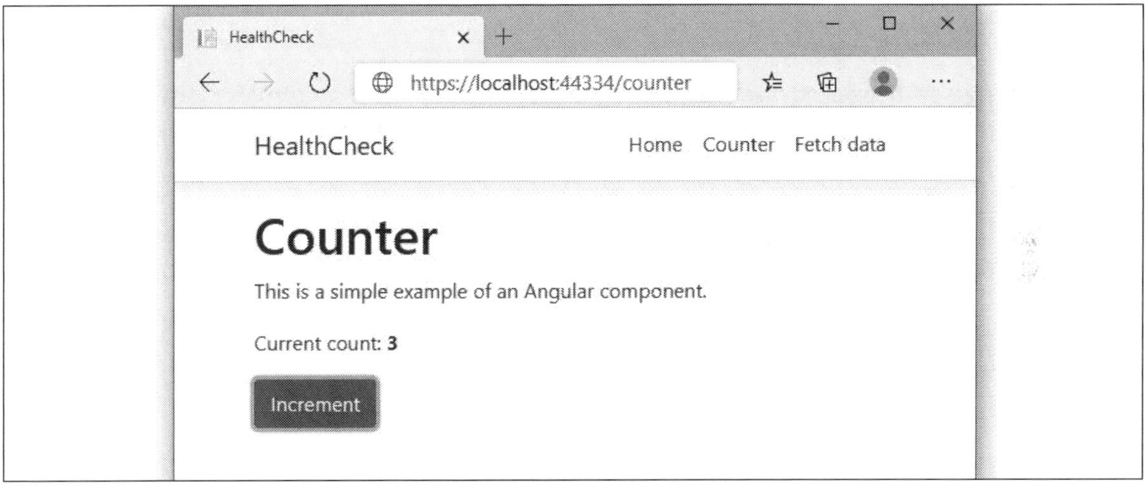

Figure 2.10: Viewing CounterComponent

The `FetchDataComponent` is an interactive table populated with the JSON array generated by the *server-side* web API via `WeatherForecastController`, which we saw a while ago when we were examining the *back-end* part of our project:

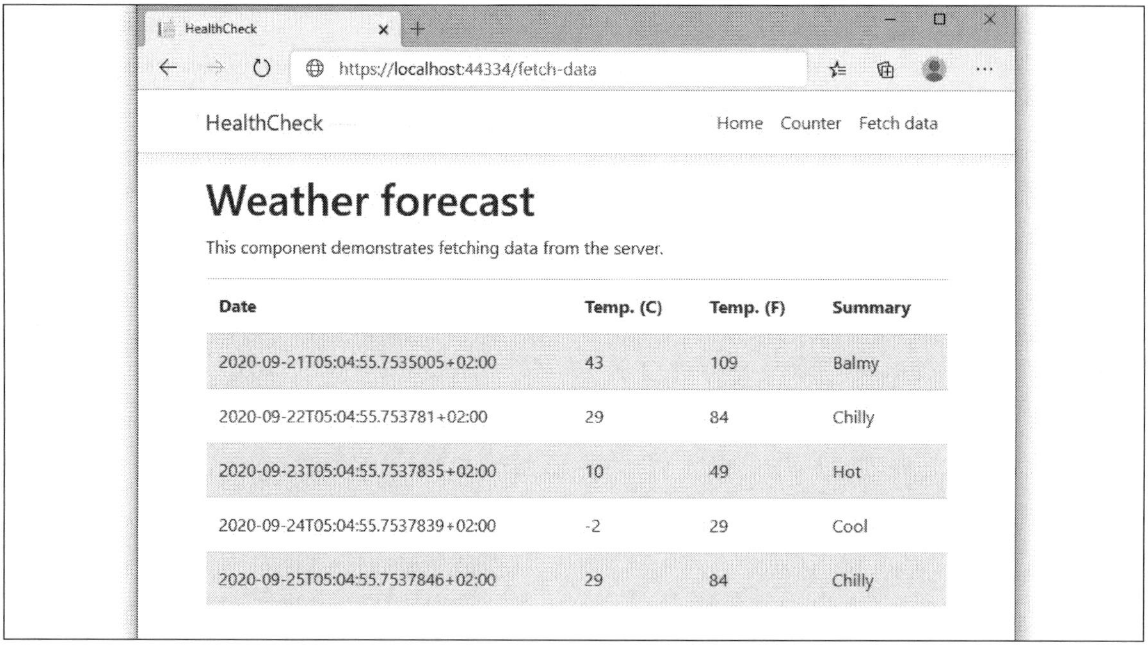

Figure 2.11: Viewing FetchDataComponent

The spec.ts file(s)

If we take a look at the source files within the preceding component's subfolders, we can see that the `CounterComponent` comes with a `counter.component.spec.ts` file. Those files, as per the Angular naming convention, are meant to contain **unit tests** for the `counter.component.ts` source file and are run using the *Jasmine* JavaScript test framework through the *Karma* test runner.

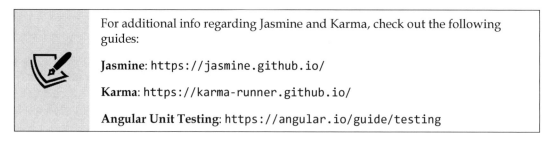

> For additional info regarding Jasmine and Karma, check out the following guides:
>
> **Jasmine**: `https://jasmine.github.io/`
>
> **Karma**: `https://karma-runner.github.io/`
>
> **Angular Unit Testing**: `https://angular.io/guide/testing`

While we're there, it could be useful to give them a run to see whether the *Jasmine* + *Karma* testing framework that has been set up by our template actually works.

Our first app test

Before running the test, it may be useful to understand a little more about *Jasmine* and *Karma*. If you don't know anything about them, don't worry—you will soon. For now, just know that **Jasmine** is an open source testing framework for JavaScript that can be used to define *tests*, while **Karma** is a test runner tool that automatically spawns a web server that will execute JavaScript source code against Jasmine-made *tests* and output their respective (and combined) results on a command line.

In this quick test, we'll basically launch **Karma** to execute the source code of our sample Angular app against the **Jasmine** *tests* defined by the template in the `counter.component.spec.ts` file; this is actually a much easier task than it might seem.

Open Command Prompt, navigate to the `<project>/ClientApp/` folder, and then execute the following command:

```
> npm run ng test
```

This will call the Angular CLI using **npm**.

> **IMPORTANT**: Chrome needs to be installed, otherwise the test won't work.

Alternatively, we can install the Angular CLI globally using the following command:

```
> npm install -g @angular/cli
```

Once done, we'll be able to directly call it in the following way:

```
> ng test
```

> In the unlikely event that the `npm` command returns a `program not found` error, check that the `Node.js/npm` binary folder is properly set within the `PATH` variable. If it's not there, be sure to add it, and then close and re-open the command-line window and try again.

Right after we hit *Enter*, a new browser window should open with the Karma console and a list of results for the Jasmine tests, as shown in the following screenshot:

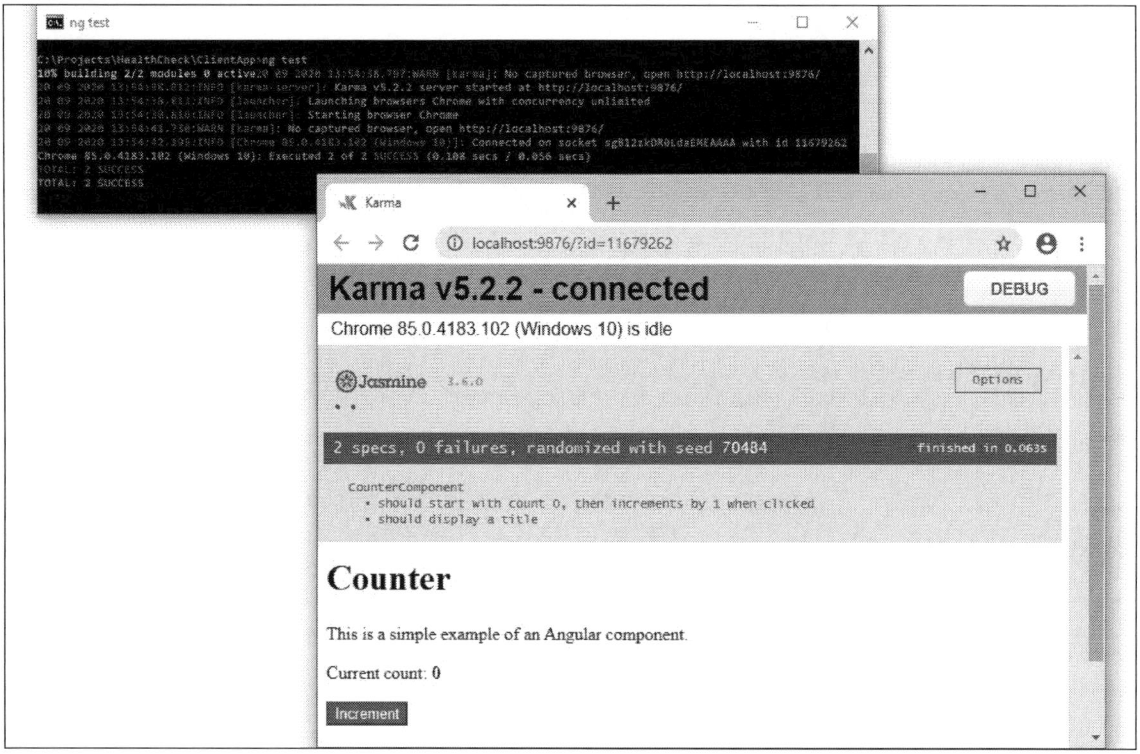

Figure 2.12: Results of the Jasmine test

As we can see, both tests have been completed successfully—that's everything we need to do for now. There's no need to peek at the `counter.component.spec.ts` source code since we're going to ditch it—together with all the template components—and create new ones (with their own tests).

> For the sake of simplicity, we're going to stop here with Angular app tests for the time being; we'll discuss them in far greater depth in *Chapter 9, ASP.NET Core and Angular Unit Testing*.

Creating a new app with the Angular CLI

In the previous sections, we've spent a good amount of time reviewing and learning the structure of the sample Angular app created by Visual Studio's ASP.NET and Angular default template. However, there are other - and arguably even better - ways to create a sample Angular app from scratch; as a matter of fact, the approach recommended by the Angular development team is entirely based on creating the app through the *Angular Command-Line Interface*, better known as the **Angular CLI**.

> For reasons of space, we'll only scratch the surface of the Angular CLI throughout the whole book, limiting its usage to what we need here and there. Those who want to know more about this powerful tool can take a look at the following URL: `https://cli.angular.io/`

In this paragraph, we'll see how to take this alternative route, so that we can compare the resulting apps and highlight their similarities and differences. More specifically, here's what we're going to do:

- Install the Angular CLI (unless we've done that already)
- Create a new Angular app using the `ng create` command
- Compare the Angular CLI generated source code files with those generated by Visual Studio
- Modify the .NET's `Startup.cs` file so that we can choose which Angular app to run
- Take a look at the alternative Angular app

Are we ready? Let's do this!

Installing the Angular CLI

If we haven't installed the Angular CLI yet, we can do so using the following command:

```
> npm install -g @angular/cli@11.0.1
```

The `-g` option will ensure that the CLI is installed globally, which will allow us to run the `ng` command-line tool in any folder; the `@11.0.1` at the end will force npm to install the specific version used by this book.

> Those who are bold enough to use the latest version can do that by running the following command:
>
> ```
> npm install -g @angular/cli@latest
> ```
>
> However, since we'll use the CLI to create a new Angular app that we'll mostly use for code review, it's strongly advisable to install the specific version used by this book.

Creating a new Angular app

When the Angular CLI has been installed, open a command prompt and navigate to the root-level folder of our existing HealthCheck app, such as `/Projects/HealthCheck/`.

Once there, issue the following command:

```
> ng new HealthCheck
```

This command will start a terminal wizard that will ask you the following questions:

> *Do you want to enforce stricter type checking and stricter bundle budgets in the workspace? This setting helps improve maintainability and catch bugs ahead of time. For more information, see* `https://angular.io/strict`.

Answer NO by typing the *N* key.

> *Would you like to add Angular routing?*

Answer YES by typing the *Y* key.

> *Which stylesheet format would you like to use? (use the arrow keys)*

Select **SCSS** using the keyboard's arrow keys.

Right after that, the code generation process will start, with all the required npm packages being downloaded and installed accordingly:

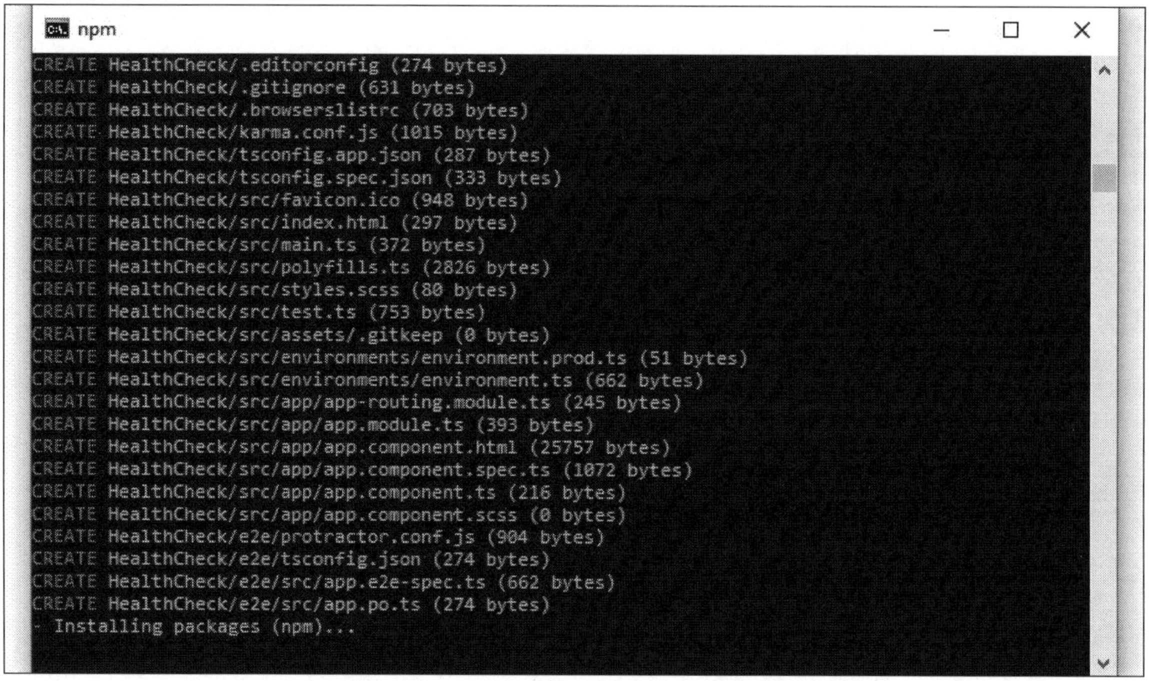

Figure 2.13: Creating a new Angular app

Wait for the tool to complete the task, and then do the following:

- Type `cd HealthCheck` to enter the newly created folder
- Execute the `npm install` and `npm update` commands to update the npm packages

At the end of these tasks, reload your Visual Studio project and include the new `/HealthCheck/` folder so that you'll be able to access it from the VS GUI, as shown in the following screenshot:

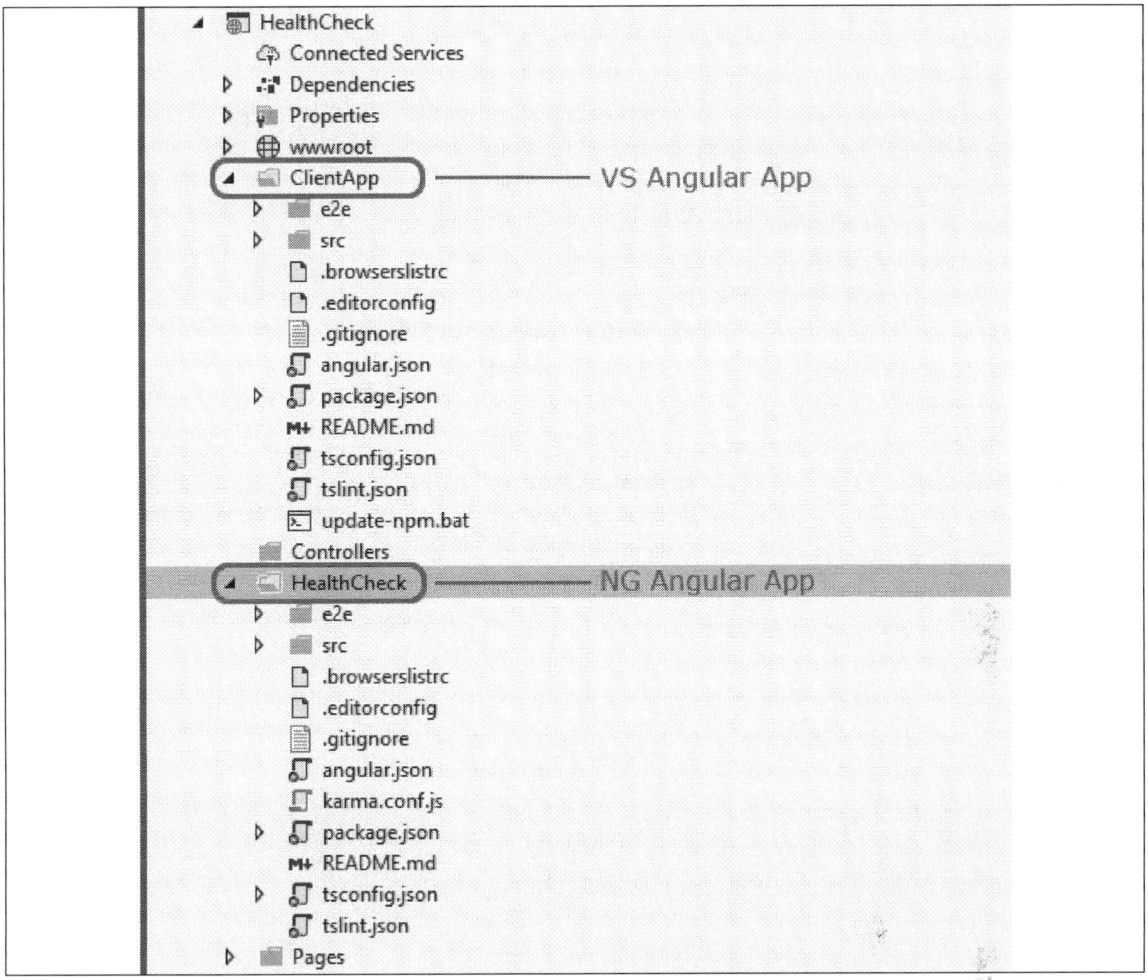

Figure 2.14: Examining our VS and NG Angular app folders

Now we have two differently generated Angular apps that we can compare; for the sake of convenience, we'll call them the **VS app** (Visual Studio app) and the **NG app** (Angular CLI app) from now on.

Comparing the Angular apps

If we take a look at the filesystem structure, we'll immediately be able to see a lot of similarities between the two apps: both of them feature roughly the same set of configuration files, with some minor differences related to the folder nesting level. For example, the NG app has the `karma.conf.js` file and all the various `tsconfig.json` files in the root folder, while the VS app has them within the `/src/` folder, and so on. However, for the most part, the two apps seem very similar in terms of overall structure: this is definitely a good thing, because it means that our *front-end* code review is still valid!

If we take a closer look and start to compare the various file contents, we'll see that the major differences are in the following files:

- `package.json`, which will potentially contain different package versions (the Angular CLI command will always use the latest Angular version available)
- `tsconfig.json`, which will definitely contain some small differences in terms of TypeScript configuration and won't likely have the `angularCompilerOptions` section that we've added early on
- All the files contained in the `/app/` folder, due to the fact that the two sample apps have a very different look and feature set
- The NG app features a separate `app-routing.module.ts` file (`AppRoutingModule`) that contains Angular's `RouterModule`, while the VS app implements the routing patterns within the main `app.module.ts` file (`AppModule`).

> Loading and configuring the router in a separate, top-level module dedicated to routing and imported by the root `AppModule` has been an Angular best practice since Angular 10. Hence, we can definitely say that the NG app has a better approach; we'll use it to our advantage later on.

Luckily enough, none of these differences will prevent our project from running, as we'll be able to see in a short while.

Updating the Startup.cs file

If we want to launch the NG app instead of the VS app, we need to perform some changes to the `Startup.cs` file, which, as we know, is responsible for loading the front-end.

Open that file, scroll down to the `ConfigureServices` method, and change the following line (line 27 or so):

```
configuration.RootPath = "ClientApp/dist";
```

in the following way:

```
configuration.RootPath = "HealthCheck/dist";
```

Right after that, scroll down to the `Configure` method and do the same with the following line (line 66 or so):

```
spa.Options.SourcePath = "ClientApp";
```

Change it as follows:

```
spa.Options.SourcePath = "HealthCheck";
```

Alternatively, you can declare a new `ClientApp` read-only variable at the top of the file:

```
public class Startup
{
    /// <summary>
    /// The name of the folder that hosts the Angular app
    /// </summary>
    public static readonly string ClientApp = "HealthCheck";

[...]
```

And then change the above literals into more convenient references in the following way:

```
configuration.RootPath = string.Format("{0}/dist", ClientApp);

[...]

spa.Options.SourcePath = ClientApp;
```

Both of these approaches achieve what we want: they tell ASP.NET to run the NG app instead of the VS app.

Testing the NG Angular app

Let's now take a look at the NG app by hitting *F5* to issue a debug run. If we've done everything properly, we should be greeted by the following welcome screen:

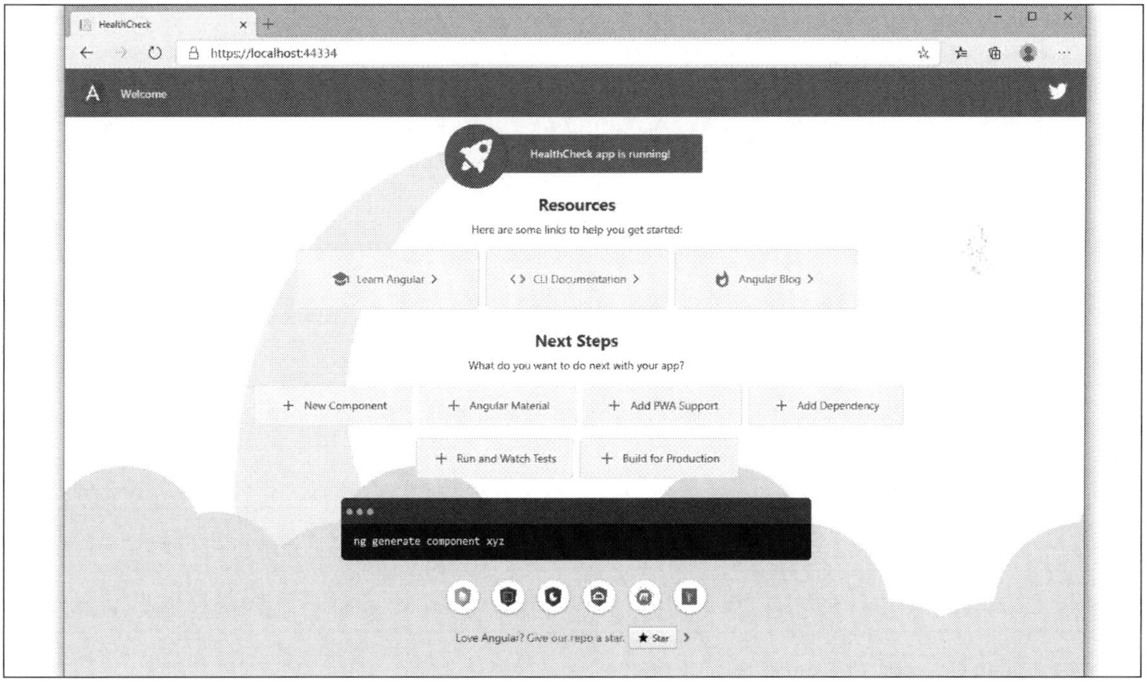

Figure 2.15: Testing the Angular app

Here we go: truth be told, the app created by the Angular CLI looks much prettier than the Visual Studio sample!

However, for the sake of simplicity, we'll just revert the changes that we just made to the `Startup.cs` file and switch back to the `/ClientApp/`, which will also be the app that we'll be using in the next chapters.

> Those who want to keep using the new NG app are free to do that. All the code samples, updates and exercises that we'll encounter throughout the whole book are fully compatible with both apps… after all, we've just seen that they're basically the same thing! The only real difference will involve some minor path-related differences, which shouldn't be an issue for most readers. That said, the choice is yours: if you don't mind such additional work and a minor risk of headaches, you might as well stay with the NG app and keep your `Startup.cs` file as it is, otherwise switch back to the `ClientApp` literal before going further.

Getting to work

Now that we've got a general picture of our new project, it's time to do something. Let's start with two simple exercises that will also come in handy in the future. The first of these will involve the *server-side* aspects of our application, while the second will be performed on the *client side*. Both will help us discover whether we have really understood everything there is to know before proceeding to subsequent chapters.

Static file caching

Let's start with the *server-side* task. Do you remember the `/wwwroot/test.html` file we added when we wanted to check how the `StaticFiles` middleware works? We will use it to do a quick demonstration of how our application will internally cache static files.

The first thing we have to do is to run the application in *debug* mode (by clicking on the **Run** button or pressing the *F5* key). When the app is fully loaded, press *CTRL+SHIFT+J* to open the *Developer tools* bar and navigate to the **Network** tab, which will show the browser's network activity.

Once done, put the following URL in the address line to load the `test.html` page: `http://localhost:<port>/test.html`

If we did everything properly, we should be able to identify the HTML page's response in the **Network** tab's bottom-most table:

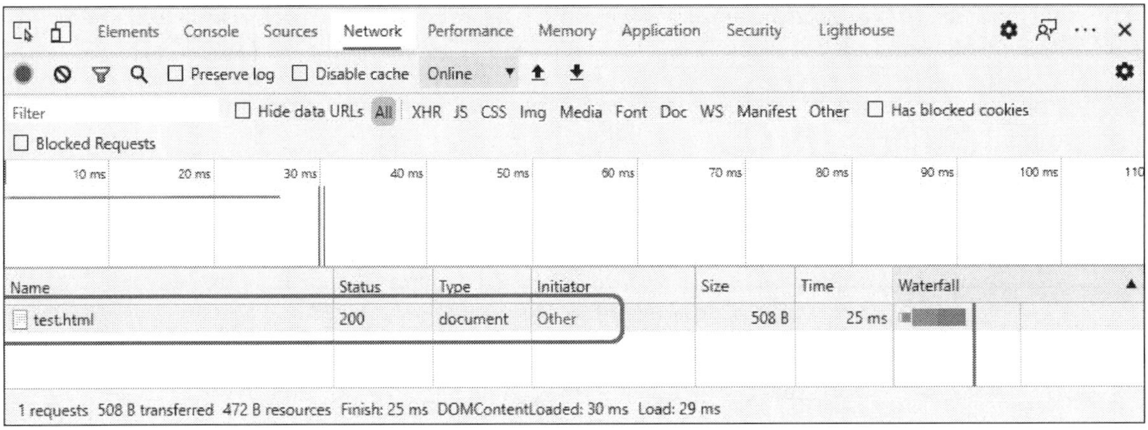

Figure 2.16: Examining the HTML page's response

Click to that row and a new tab panel will open to the right part of the screen.

Go to the **Headers** tab, where we'll be able to see the HTTP headers of the response that brought us that static page:

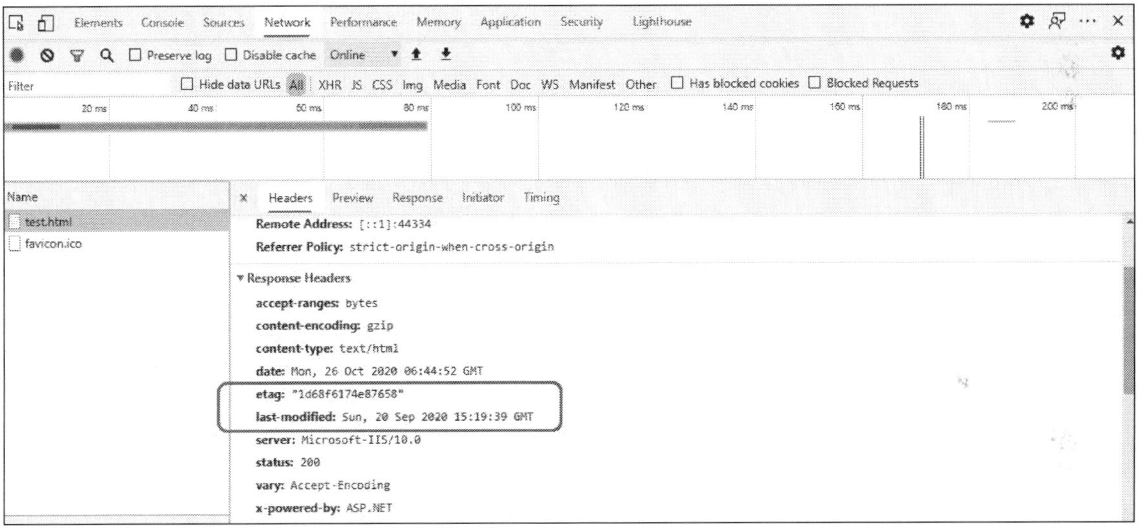

Figure 2.17: Examining the response headers

As we can see, the HTTP request doesn't have many cache-related headers; it definitely seems that the default settings of `StaticFilesMiddleware` only add the `etag` and `last-modified` header values to the requested static resources.

Are these headers good enough to prevent our browser from fully downloading that static HTML file upon each request, even if its content doesn't change? Let's find out.

While keeping the **Network** tab open, click to the browser address bar and press *Enter* again to issue another HTTP request to the `test.html` file.

> Ensure that you don't use *F5* or the *Refresh* button, as doing so would force a page refresh on the server through an explicit request header added by the browser, which is not what we want.

The **Network** table will get refreshed as well and will eventually show the new response result for the `test.html` file:

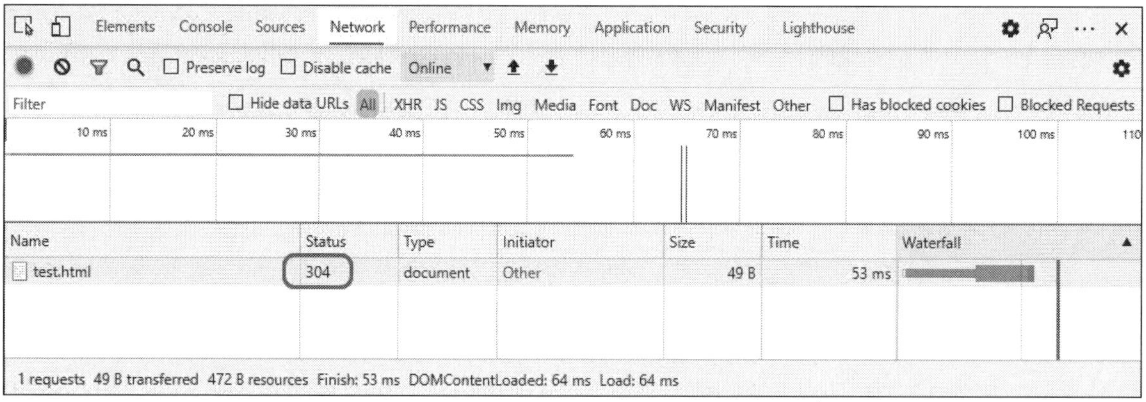

Figure 2.18: The new response result for test.html

As we can see, the HTTP status code is not `200 OK`, like it was on our first attempt. It has changed to `304 Not Modified`, which means that the browser got it from its cache instead of re-downloading it.

That's precisely what the `ETag` header is there for. For those who have never heard of it, let's try to explain how it works. However, before doing that, it could be useful to spend a couple of minutes performing a brief recap of the whole HTTP cache request-response cycle.

How the HTTP cache works

When we use a browser client to surf the World Wide Web, we basically instruct it to connect to a server (typically a web server or a reverse proxy) and retrieve the content that we want. This retrieval process is performed through one or more HTTP *requests* ("please give me that resource") that get answered by the service using one or more corresponding HTTP *responses* ("here it is"). Both the request and the response are equipped with a set of metadata, known as **headers**, that contains contextual information regarding the request and returned content. As we can easily guess, the request's headers are set by the browser, while the response's headers are added by the server.

One of the many purposes of such headers is to control the browser's cache, which is a temporary internal storage where it stores the requested resources (HTML pages, JS/CSS files, images, videos, and so on) according to the caching rules determined by the headers.

As a matter of fact, all the requests issued by the browser are first directed to its cache to check whether there's a *valid* cached response that can fulfill each request without having to re-download it from the server. In case there's a match, the requested resource is read from the cache, thus eliminating the need for a file transfer and dramatically reducing its overall latency and bandwidth costs.

The browser's cache's behavior is determined by a combination of these request and response headers, which in turn depend on how their actors (browser and server) have been configured; however, unless we change the browser's default *cache-handling* configuration - which is something that 99.9% of average internet users won't ever do – the part that matters the most is the response headers set by the server. The browser will just act accordingly using its default behavior, which is almost always good enough, and what a typical web developer should reasonably expect.

The `ETag` and `last-modified` *response headers* are two of them; let's see how their presence will influence our browser's caching behavior.

The ETag response header

The `ETag` response header is calculated by the server using collision-resistant hash functions of the requested resource's content, in order to uniquely identify it and then add it to the response header with the sole purpose of getting stored (together with the resource) in the browser's cache.

When the browser requests that resource a second time, if the `ETag` response header is present and the other cache-related headers are not present (or expired), it adds its value (using an `If-None-Match` request header) to the request that will immediately be issued to the server to fetch that resource again.

When the server receives such a request, it will check the received `ETag` value against the requested file. If the file has changed, it will serve it from scratch, otherwise it will send a `304 Not Modified` response, thus instructing the browser to use the cached data instead.

> For further information about the `ETag` response header, check out the following URL: `https://developer.mozilla.org/en-US/docs/Web/HTTP/Headers/ETag`

The Last-Modified response header

The `Last-Modified` response header works in a similar way to `ETag`. However, instead of relying on a content-based strategy to determine whether a resource has changed, it uses the resource's last modified time.

The workflow is also very similar: instead of the `If-None-Match` request header used by the `ETag`, the browser sets its value to an `If-Modified-Since` header to allow the server to perform the check.

> For further information about the `Last-Modified` response header, check out the following URL: `https://developer.mozilla.org/en-US/docs/Web/HTTP/Headers/Last-Modified`

Improving our caching strategy

As we've seen a short while ago, both the `ETag` and the `Last-Modified` tags are being set by default by the `StaticFileMiddleware`. Now, we know why we got a `304 Not Modified` response on our second request.

Being able to rely on these response headers is indeed a great way to make our user's HTTP request much more efficient, and we get it for free since it's a built-in feature: yay!

However, it's very important to understand that when the `ETag` and/or `Last-Modified` headers come into action, the browser is still sending an HTTP request to your server, albeit very small: this means that it will need to wait for the server's response, even if it's a mere `304 Not Modified` response. There could be many scenarios where such a downside is non-trivial, such as when we have high latency connections (mobile devices, bad WI-FI signal, and so on).

In order to properly deal with such circumstances, we should find a way to make the browser assume that the file is the same for a certain amount of time without performing a check (and hence a request) to the server; this is precisely what the `Cache-Control` header is for.

The Cache-Control header

The `Cache-Control` HTTP header holds a series of *directives* that instruct the browser about how to handle the caching for that given resource.

Here's the standard set of `Cache-Control` directives that can be used in an HTTP response:

- Cache-Control: must-revalidate
- Cache-Control: no-cache
- Cache-Control: no-store
- Cache-Control: no-transform
- Cache-Control: public
- Cache-Control: private
- Cache-Control: proxy-revalidate
- Cache-Control: max-age=<seconds>
- Cache-Control: s-maxage=<seconds>

As we can see by looking at the directives' names, this header can be used to specify *if*, *how*, and *for how long* the browser (and/or other intermediate parties, such as proxies) should cache the response before having to perform a request to the server, including the one to check for the ETag and/or Last-Modified value changes.

That's precisely what we need! However, the StaticFilesMiddleware doesn't natively add such headers to our server-side responses. Let's see how we can implement it.

> For further information about the Cache-Control header and its set of directives, check out the following URL: https://developer.mozilla.org/it/docs/Web/HTTP/Headers/Cache-Control

A blast from the past

Back in ASP.NET 4.x (and earlier versions), we could easily implement the Cache-Control header by adding some lines to our main application's Web.config file, such as the following:

```
<caching enabled="false" />
<staticContent>
    <clientCache cacheControlMode="DisableCache" />
</staticContent>
<httpProtocol>
    <customHeaders>
        <add name="Cache-Control" value="no-cache, no-store" />
    </customHeaders>
</httpProtocol>
```

We could even restrict such behavior to the *debug* environment by adding these lines to the Web.debug.config file.

However, we can't use the same approach in .NET Core, as the configuration system has been redesigned from scratch and is now quite different from the previous versions. As we said earlier, the Web.config and Web.debug.config files have been replaced by the appsettings.json and appsettings.Development.json files, which also work in a completely different way.

Back to the future

Now that we understand the basics, let's see whether we can solve that caching issue by taking advantage of the new configuration model.

The first thing to do is to understand how we can modify default HTTP headers for static files. As a matter of fact, we can do that by adding a custom set of configuration options to the app.UseStaticFiles() method call in the Startup.cs file that adds the StaticFiles middleware to the HTTP request pipeline.

In order to do that, open `Startup.cs`, scroll down to the `Configure` method, and replace that single line with the following code (new/modified parts are highlighted):

```
app.UseStaticFiles(new StaticFileOptions()
{
    OnPrepareResponse = (context) =>
    {
        // Disable caching for all static files.
        context.Context.Response.Headers["Cache-Control"] =
            "max-age=3600";
    }
});
```

That wasn't hard at all; we just added some additional configuration values to the method call, wrapping them all within a dedicated `StaticFileOptions` object instance.

> As we can see, we've used the `max-age` directive, which is a great way to set a fixed amount of time: the value is expressed in seconds, meaning that our static content will be cached for 1 hour.

However, we're not done yet; now that we've learned how to change the default behavior, we just need to change these static values with some convenient references pointing to the `appsettings.json` file.

To do that, we can add the following *key/value* section to the `appsettings.json` file in the following way (new lines highlighted):

```
{
  "Logging": {
    "LogLevel": {
      "Default": "Warning"
    }
  },
  "AllowedHosts": "*",
  "StaticFiles": {
    "Headers": {
      "Cache-Control": "max-age=3600"
    }
  }
}
```

Then, change the preceding `Startup.cs` code accordingly (modified lines are highlighted):

```
app.UseStaticFiles(new StaticFileOptions()
{
    OnPrepareResponse = (context) =>
```

```
    {
        // Retrieve cache configuration from appsettings.json
        context.Context.Response.Headers["Cache-Control"] =
            Configuration["StaticFiles:Headers:Cache-Control"];
    }
});
```

Now that we've set a caching policy to the generic `appsettings.json` file, it might be wise to selectively overwrite that rule for the *development* environment, where we don't need any cache.

In order to do that, open the `appsettings.Development.json` file and define a different `Cache-Control` directive in the following way (new lines highlighted):

```
{
  "Logging": {
    "LogLevel": {
      "Default": "Debug",
      "System": "Information",
      "Microsoft": "Information"
    }
  },
  "StaticFiles": {
    "Headers": {
      "Cache-Control": "no-cache"
    }
  }
}
```

That's it. As we can see, we've used the `no-cache` directive, which tells the browser to always validate the stored resource with the server before using it. This would be perfect for our development environment, since we don't want to cache any static resource unless the server confirms that the content has not been changed (using `ETag` and/or `Last-Modified` checks).

Now that we've performed these changes, we're going to have those static files cached for an hour in our production environment without the risk of creating refresh issues during the development phase. Learning how to properly use this pattern is strongly advisable, as it's a great and effective way to properly configure our application's settings.

The strongly typed approach(es)

The approach that we chose to retrieve the `appsettings.json` configuration values makes use of the generic `IConfiguration` object, which can be queried using the preceding string-based syntax. This approach is rather practical; however, if we want to retrieve this data in a more robust way, for example, in a *strongly typed* fashion, we can—and *should*—implement something better. Although we won't cover this in more depth in this book, we suggest you read the following great articles, showing three different approaches for achieving this result:

The first one, written by *Rick Strahl*, explains how to do that using the `IOptions<T>` provider interface: `https://weblog.west-wind.com/posts/2016/may/23/strongly-typed-configuration-settings-in-aspnet-core`

The second, by *Filip W*, explains how to do that with a simple `POCO` class, thus avoiding the `IOptions<T>` interface and the extra dependencies required by the preceding approach: `https://www.strathweb.com/2016/09/strongly-typed-configuration-in-asp-net-core-without-ioptionst/`

The third, by *Khalid Abuhakmeh*, shows an alternative way to use a standard `POCO` class and directly register it as a `Singleton` with the `ServicesCollection`, while also (optionally) shielding it from unwanted modifications due to development mistakes: `https://rimdev.io/strongly-typed-configuration-settings-in-asp-net-core-part-ii/`

All of these approaches were originally meant to work with .NET Core 1.x; however, they can still be used with .NET 5 (at the time of writing). That said, if we were to choose, we would probably go with the final option, as we find it to be the cleanest and cleverest.

Client app cleanup

Now that our *server-side* journey has come to an end, it's time to challenge ourselves with a quick *client-side* exercise. Don't worry—it will just be a rather simple demonstration of how we can update the Angular source code that lies within the `/ClientApp/` folder to better suit our needs. More specifically, we will remove all the stuff we don't need from the sample Angular app shipped with our chosen Angular SPA template and replace it with our own content.

> We can never say it enough, so it's worth repeating again: the sample source code explained in the following sections is taken from the **ASP.NET Core with Angular (C#)** project template originally shipped with the .NET 5 SDK, as explained in the following URL: `https://docs.microsoft.com/en-US/aspnet/core/client-side/spa/angular?view=aspnetcore-5.0&tabs=visual-studio`
>
> This project template might be updated in the future and become different from what we've seen in this chapter; for this very reason, it's important to check it against the code published in this book's GitHub repo. If you find relevant differences between the book's code and yours, feel free to get the one from the repository and use that instead.

Trimming down the component list

The first thing we have to do is delete Angular components that we don't want to use.

Go to the `/ClientApp/src/app/` folder and delete the `counter` and the `fetch-data` folders, together with all the files they contain.

> Although they can still be used as valuable code samples, keeping these components within our client code will eventually confuse us, hence it's better to delete them in order to prevent the Visual Studio TypeScript compiler from messing with the `.ts` files contained there. Don't worry; we'll still be able to check them out via the book's GitHub project.

As soon as we do that, the Visual Studio **Error List** view will immediately raise two blocking TypeScript-based issues:

```
Error TS2307 (TS) Cannot find module './counter/counter.component'.
Error TS2307 (TS) Cannot find module './fetch-data/fetch-data.component'.
```

All of these errors will point to the `app.module.ts` file, which, as we already know, contains the references of all the TypeScript files used by our Angular application. If we open the file, we'll immediately be able to see the issues:

```
import { BrowserModule } from '@angular/platform-browser';
import { NgModule } from '@angular/core';
import { FormsModule } from '@angular/forms';
import { HttpClientModule, HTTP_INTERCEPTORS } from '@angular/common/http';
import { RouterModule } from '@angular/router';

import { AppComponent } from './app.component';
import { NavMenuComponent } from './nav-menu/nav-menu.component';
import { HomeComponent } from './home/home.component';
import { CounterComponent } from './counter/counter.component';
import { FetchDataComponent } from './fetch-data/fetch-data.component';

@NgModule({
  declarations: [
    AppComponent,
    NavMenuComponent,
    HomeComponent,
    CounterComponent,
    FetchDataComponent
  ],
  imports: [
    BrowserModule.withServerTransition({ appId: 'ng-cli-universal' }),
    HttpClientModule,
    FormsModule,
    RouterModule.forRoot([
      { path: '', component: HomeComponent, pathMatch: 'full' },
      { path: 'counter', component: CounterComponent },
      { path: 'fetch-data', component: FetchDataComponent },
    ])
  ],
  providers: [],
  bootstrap: [AppComponent]
})
export class AppModule { }
```

Figure 2.19: Examining the app.module.ts file

In order to fix them, we need to remove the two offending `import` references (lines 10-11). Right after that, two more errors will appear:

```
Error TS2304 (TS) Cannot find name 'CounterComponent'.
Error TS2304 (TS) Cannot find name 'FetchDataComponent'.
```

This can be fixed by removing the two offending component names from the `declarations` array (lines 18-19, which became 16-17 after the previous deletion) and from the `RouterModule` configuration (lines 27-28, or 23-24 after the deletion).

Once done, our updated `app.module.ts` file should look like this:

```
import { BrowserModule } from '@angular/platform-browser';
import { NgModule } from '@angular/core';
import { FormsModule } from '@angular/forms';
import { HttpClientModule, HTTP_INTERCEPTORS } from '@angular/common/http';
import { RouterModule } from '@angular/router';

import { AppComponent } from './app.component';
import { NavMenuComponent } from './nav-menu/nav-menu.component';
import { HomeComponent } from './home/home.component';

@NgModule({
  declarations: [
    AppComponent,
    NavMenuComponent,
    HomeComponent
  ],
  imports: [
    BrowserModule.withServerTransition({ appId: 'ng-cli-universal' }),
    HttpClientModule,
    FormsModule,
    RouterModule.forRoot([
      { path: '', component: HomeComponent, pathMatch: 'full' }
    ])
  ],
  providers: [],
  bootstrap: [AppComponent]
})
export class AppModule { }
```

Since we're here, those who don't know how Angular works should spend a couple of minutes to better understand how an `AppModule` class actually works.

The AppModule source code

Angular **modules**, also known as **NgModules**, were introduced in Angular 2 RC5 and are a great, powerful way to organize and bootstrap any Angular application; they help developers consolidate their own set of **components**, **directives**, and **pipes** into *reusable* blocks. As we said previously, every Angular application since v2 RC5 must have at least one module, which is conventionally called a **root module** and is thus given the `AppModule` class name.

`AppModule` is usually split into two main code blocks:

- A list of **import** statements, pointing to all the references (in the form of TypeScript files) required by the application.
- The root `NgModule` block, which, as we can see, is basically a collection of named arrays, each one containing a set of Angular objects that serve a common purpose: **directives**, **components**, **pipes**, **modules**, **providers**, and so on. The last one contains the component we want to bootstrap, which, in most scenarios—including ours—is the main application component, the `AppComponent`.

Adding the AppRoutingModule

Now that we know the gist of how `AppModule` actually works, we can better understand why dealing with routing in a separate, top-level module is considered a best practice. Since we're cleansing our app's workspace, let's take the chance to "steal" such neat behavior from the NG app and embrace such best practice as well.

From **Solution Explorer**, navigate to the `/ClientApp/src/app/` folder and create a new TypeScript file, calling it `app-routing.module.ts`. Once done, fill it with the following content:

```
import { NgModule } from '@angular/core';
import { Routes, RouterModule } from '@angular/router';
import { HomeComponent } from './home/home.component';

const routes: Routes = [
  { path: '', component: HomeComponent, pathMatch: 'full' }
];

@NgModule({
  imports: [RouterModule.forRoot(routes)],
  exports: [RouterModule]
})
export class AppRoutingModule { }
```

Once done, open the `app.module.ts` file and replace the following `import` statement (around line 5):

```
import { RouterModule } from '@angular/router';
```

with this one:

```
import { AppRoutingModule } from './app-routing.module';
```

Right after that, scroll down to lines 21-23 and replace the entire `RouterModule` configuration block:

```
imports: [
  BrowserModule.withServerTransition({ appId: 'ng-cli-universal' }),
  HttpClientModule,
  FormsModule,
  RouterModule.forRoot([
    { path: '', component: HomeComponent, pathMatch: 'full' },
  ])
],
```

With a single reference to the newly created `AppRoutingModule`:

```
imports: [
  BrowserModule.withServerTransition({ appId: 'ng-cli-universal' }),
  HttpClientModule,
  FormsModule,
  AppRoutingModule
],
```

Here's the full `app.module.ts` source code after the trimming:

```
import { BrowserModule } from '@angular/platform-browser';
import { NgModule } from '@angular/core';
import { FormsModule } from '@angular/forms';
import { HttpClientModule, HTTP_INTERCEPTORS } from '@angular/common/http';

import { AppRoutingModule } from './app-routing.module';

import { AppComponent } from './app.component';
import { NavMenuComponent } from './nav-menu/nav-menu.component';
import { HomeComponent } from './home/home.component';

@NgModule({
  declarations: [
    AppComponent,
    NavMenuComponent,
```

```
    HomeComponent
  ],
  imports: [
    BrowserModule.withServerTransition({ appId: 'ng-cli-universal' }),
    HttpClientModule,
    FormsModule,
    AppRoutingModule
  ],
  providers: [],
  bootstrap: [AppComponent]
})
export class AppModule { }
```

What we did should be quite straightforward. We've removed the Angular's `RouterModule` references and configuration from the `AppModule` and replaced them with a single reference to our brand-new `AppRoutingModule`, which will take care of routing from now on.

Reasons for using a dedicated routing module

We've repeated many times that using a separate, dedicated routing module is considered an Angular best practice, but we still don't know the reasons. What are the benefits that will compensate the additional work required to reference/import all the components twice, like we've just done with `HomeComponent`?

As a matter of fact, there are no real benefits for small and/or sample apps. When that's the case, most developers will probably choose to skip the routing module and merge the routing configuration directly into the `AppModule` itself, just like the sample VS app did in the first place.

However, such an approach is only convenient when the app's configuration is minimal. When the app starts to grow, its routing logic will eventually become much more complex, thanks to some advanced features (such as *specialized guard* and *resolver* services) that, sooner or later, we'll want (or have) to implement. When something like this happens, a dedicated routing module will help us to keep the source code clean, simplify and streamline the testing activities, and increase the overall consistency of our app.

Updating the NavMenu

Let's go back to what we were doing. If we run our project in *debug* mode, we can see that our recent code changes – the deletion of `CounterComponent` and `FetchDataComponent` and the creation of the `AppRoutingModule` – do not prevent the client app from booting properly. We didn't break it this time – yay!

However, if we try to use the navigation menu to go to the `Counter` and/or `Fetch data` by clicking the links from the main view, nothing will happen. This is hardly a surprise since we've moved these components out of the way. To avoid confusion, let's remove these links from the menu as well.

Open the `/ClientApp/app/nav-menu/nav-menu.component.html` file, which is the UI template for the `NavMenuComponent`. As we can see, it does contain a standard HTML structure containing the header part of our app's main page, including the main menu.

It shouldn't be difficult to locate the HTML part we need to delete in order to remove the links to `CounterComponent` and `FetchDataComponent`—both of them are contained within a dedicated HTML `<li>` element:

```
[...]

<li class="nav-item" [routerLinkActive]="['link-active']">
  <a class="nav-link text-dark" [routerLink]="['/counter']"
    >Counter</a
  >
</li>
<li class="nav-item" [routerLinkActive]="['link-active']">
  <a class="nav-link text-dark" [routerLink]="['/fetch-data']"
    >Fetch data</a
  >
</li>

[...]
```

Delete the two `<li>` elements and save the file.

Once done, the updated HTML structure of the `NavMenuComponent` code should look as follows:

```
<header>
  <nav
    class="navbar navbar-expand-sm navbar-toggleable-sm navbar-light bg-white
border-bottom box-shadow mb-3"
  >
    <div class="container">
      <a class="navbar-brand" [routerLink]="['/']">HealthCheck</a>
      <button
        class="navbar-toggler"
        type="button"
        data-toggle="collapse"
        data-target=".navbar-collapse"
        aria-label="Toggle navigation"
        [attr.aria-expanded]="isExpanded"
        (click)="toggle()"
      >
        <span class="navbar-toggler-icon"></span>
      </button>
```

```
      <div
        class="navbar-collapse collapse d-sm-inline-flex flex-sm-row-reverse"
        [ngClass]="{ show: isExpanded }"
      >
        <ul class="navbar-nav flex-grow">
          <li
            class="nav-item"
            [routerLinkActive]="['link-active']"
            [routerLinkActiveOptions]="{ exact: true }"
          >
            <a class="nav-link text-dark" [routerLink]="['/']">Home</a>
          </li>
        </ul>
      </div>
    </div>
  </nav>
</header>
```

While we're here, let's take the chance to get rid of something else. Do you remember the `Hello, World!` introductory text shown by the browser when we first ran the project? Let's replace it with our own content.

Open the `/ClientApp/src/app/home/home.component.html` file and replace its entire contents with the following:

```
<h1>Greetings, stranger!</h1>

<p>This is what you get for messing up with ASP.NET and Angular.</p>
```

Save, run the project in *debug* mode, and get ready to see the following:

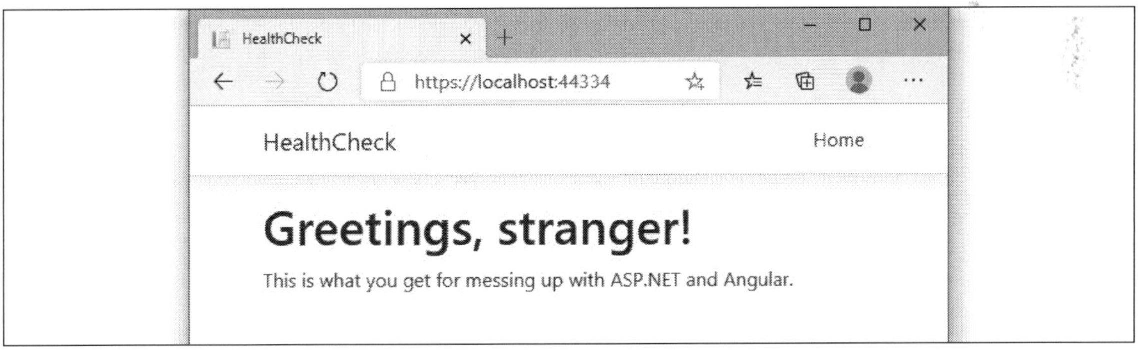

Figure 2.20: Looking at our home view

The `Counter` and `Fetch data` menu links are gone, and our `Home View` welcome text couldn't be sleeker.

Now that we've removed any references from the *front-end*, we can do the same with the following *back-end* files, which we don't need anymore:

- `WeatherForecast.cs`
- `Controllers/WeatherForecastController.cs`

Locate these two files using Visual Studio's Solution Explorer and delete them.

> It's worth noting that, once we do that, we will no longer have any .NET controllers available in our web application. That's perfectly fine since we don't have Angular components that need to fetch data either. Don't worry, though—we're going to add them back in upcoming chapters!

That's about it for now. Rest assured, we can easily do the same with other components and completely rewrite their text, including the navigation menu. We'll do that in the following chapters, where we'll also update the UI layout, add new components, and so on. For the time being, understanding how easy it is to change the content—and also how rapidly Visual Studio, ASP.NET, and Angular will react to our modifications—is good enough.

Summary

In this second chapter, we spent some valuable time exploring and understanding our sample project's core components, how they work together, and their distinctive roles. For the sake of simplicity, we split the analysis into two parts: the .NET *back-end* ecosystem and the Angular *front-end* architecture, each with its own configuration files, folder structure, naming conventions, and overall scope.

At the end of the day, we can definitely say that we met the end goal of this chapter and learned a fair number of useful things: we know the location and purpose of both *server-side* and *client-side* source code files, we are able to remove existing content and insert new stuff, we are aware of the caching system and other setup parameters, and so on.

A relevant part of the chapter was dedicated to the Angular CLI: we've spent a good amount of time learning how to create a sample app using the `ng new` command and to understand the similarities and the differences between a "canonical" Angular app and the sample app provided by the Visual Studio Angular SPA project template. Such time was very well spent, since now we know how to set up a new ASP.NET Core and Angular project without having to rely on the default templates created by Microsoft.

Last but not least, we also took the time to perform some quick tests to see whether we're ready to hold our ground against what's coming in upcoming chapters: setting up an improved request-response cycle, building our own controllers, defining additional routing strategies, and more.

Suggested topics

Razor Pages, separation of concerns, the single responsibility principle, JSON, web hosts, Kestrel, ASP.NET middlewares, Dependency Injection, the Angular workspace, Jasmine, Karma, unit tests, Server-Side Rendering (**SSR**), TypeScript, Angular architecture, the Angular initialization cycle, browser cache, and client cache.

References

- *Introduction to ASP.NET Core*: `https://docs.microsoft.com/en-us/aspnet/core/`
- *Angular: Setting Up the Local Environment and Workspace*: `https://angular.io/guide/setup-local`
- *Angular Architecture Overview*: `https://angular.io/guide/architecture`
- *Angular Upgrade Guide*: `https://update.angular.io/`
- *npmJS*: `https://docs.npmjs.com/files/package.json`
- *Yarn Package Manager*: `https://yarnpkg.com/`
- *TypeScript – Modules*: `https://www.typescriptlang.org/docs/handbook/modules.html`
- *TypeScript – Module Resolution*: `https://www.typescriptlang.org/docs/handbook/module-resolution.html`
- *TypeScript Configuration*: `https://angular.io/config/tsconfig`
- *TSLint*: `https://palantir.github.io/tslint/`
- *Angular AoT Compiler*: `https://angular.io/guide/aot-compiler`
- *Karma*: `https://karma-runner.github.io/`
- *Jasmine*: `https://jasmine.github.io/`
- *Angular – Testing*: `https://angular.io/guide/testing`
- *ETag HTTP Header*: `https://developer.mozilla.org/en-US/docs/Web/HTTP/Headers/ETag`
- *Last-Modified HTTP Header*: `https://developer.mozilla.org/en-US/docs/Web/HTTP/Headers/Last-Modified`
- *Cache-Control HTTP Header*: `https://developer.mozilla.org/en-US/docs/Web/HTTP/Headers/Cache-Control`
- *Strongly Typed Configuration Settings in ASP.NET Core*: `https://weblog.west-wind.com/posts/2016/may/23/strongly-typed-configuration-settings-in-aspnet-core`
- *Strongly Typed Configuration Settings in ASP.NET Core without IOptions<T>*: `https://www.strathweb.com/2016/09/strongly-typed-configuration-in-asp-net-core-without-ioptionst/`
- *Strongly Typed Configuration Settings in ASP.NET Core Part II*: `https://rimdev.io/strongly-typed-configuration-settings-in-asp-net-core-part-ii/`

3
Front-End and Back-End Interactions

Now that we have a minimalistic—yet fully working—ASP.NET Core and Angular web app up and running, we can definitely start to build some stuff. In this chapter, we're going to learn the basics of client-side and server-side interactions: in other words, how the *front-end* (Angular) can fetch some relevant data from the *back-end* (ASP.NET Core) and display it on-screen, in a readable fashion.

Wait a minute... as a matter of fact, we should've already got the gist of how it works, right? We saw this in *Chapter 2*, *Looking Around*, before getting rid of Angular's `FetchDataComponent` and ASP.NET Core's `WeatherForecastController.cs` classes and files. The Angular component (*front-end*) pulls data from the ASP.NET controller (*back-end*) and then puts it on the browser screen (UI) for display.

Such a statement is absolutely correct. However, controllers aren't the only way for our ASP.NET Core *back-end* to serve data to the *front-end*: it can also serve static files, Razor Pages, and any other middleware designed to handle requests and output a response stream or content of some sort, as long as we add it into our application pipeline. Such a highly modular approach is one of the most relevant concepts of ASP.NET Core. In this chapter, we'll make use of that by introducing (and playing with) a built-in middleware that has little or nothing to do with .NET controllers, although it is able to deal with requests and responses just like they do: `HealthChecksMiddleware`.

Here's a quick breakdown of what we're going to achieve:

- **Introducing ASP.NET Core health checks**: What they are and how we can use them to learn some useful concepts about ASP.NET Core and Angular interactions
- **HealthCheckMiddleware**: How to properly implement it within our ASP.NET Core *back-end*, configure it within our web application's pipeline, and output a JSON-structured message that can be used by our Angular app

- **HealthCheckComponent**: How to build an Angular component to fetch the `HealthCheck` structured data from the ASP.NET Core *back-end* and bring it all to the *front-end* in a human-readable fashion

Are you ready? Let's do this!

Technical requirements

In this chapter, we're going to need all the technical requirements listed in the previous chapters, with no additional resources, libraries, or packages.

The code files for this chapter can be found here: `https://github.com/PacktPublishing/ASP.NET-Core-5-and-Angular/tree/main/Chapter_03/`

Introducing ASP.NET Core health checks

We called our first project `HealthCheck` for a reason: the web app we're about to build will act as a monitoring and reporting service that will check the *health* status of a target server—and/or its infrastructure—and show it on-screen in real time.

In order to do that, we're going to make good use of the `Microsoft.AspNetCore.Diagnostics.HealthChecks` package, a built-in feature of the ASP.NET Core framework first introduced in 2.2, refined and improved for the ASP.NET Core 3 release and then made available for .NET 5 as well. This package is meant to be used to allow a monitoring service to check the status of another running service—for example, another web server, which is precisely what we're about to do.

> For additional information about ASP.NET Core health checks, we strongly suggest reading the official MS documentation at the following URL: `https://docs.microsoft.com/en-us/aspnet/core/host-and-deploy/health-checks?view=aspnetcore-5.0`

Adding the HealthChecks middleware

The first thing we need to do is to add the `HealthChecks` middleware to our web app. This can be done in the following way:

1. Open the `Startup.cs` file
2. Add the following lines to the `ConfigureServices` method:

```
public void ConfigureServices(IServiceCollection services)
{
    services.AddControllersWithViews();
```

```
    // In production, the Angular files will be served
    // from this directory
    services.AddSpaStaticFiles(configuration =>
    {
        configuration.RootPath = "ClientApp/dist";
    });

    services.AddHealthChecks();
}
```

3. And the following lines to the `Configure` method:

```
public void Configure(IApplicationBuilder app, IWebHostEnvironment env)
{
    // ...existing code...

    app.UseRouting();

    app.UseEndpoints(endpoints =>
    {

        endpoints.MapHealthChecks("/hc");
        endpoints.MapControllerRoute(
            name: "default",
            pattern: "{controller}/{action=Index}/{id?}");
    });

    // ...existing code...
}
```

> The `// ...existing code...` comment is just a way to tell us to leave the already-existing code as it is, without altering it. We're going to use that keyword whenever we need to add a few lines of code to an existing block instead of rewriting the unmodified lines—thus saving some valuable space!

The `/hc` parameters we passed to the `UseHealthChecks` middleware will create a server-side route for the health checks. It's also worth noting that we added that middleware right before `UseEndpoints` so that our new route won't be overridden by the general-purpose controller route pattern specified there.

We can immediately check out the new route by doing the following:

1. Press *F5* so that our web application will run in *debug* mode.
2. Manually type `/hc` at the end of the starting URL and hit *Enter*.

As soon as we do that, we should be able to see something like this:

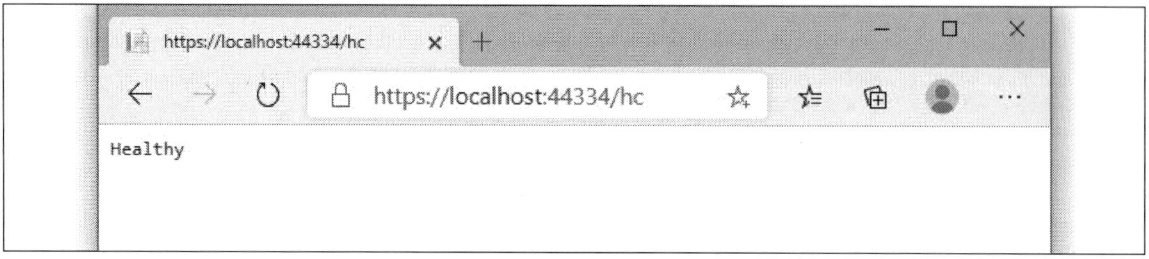

Figure 3.1: Checking our health check

As we can see, our system is `Healthy`: that's rather obvious since we have no checks defined yet.

How about adding one? That's what we're going to do in the next section.

Adding an Internet Control Message Protocol (ICMP) check

The first check we're going to implement is one of the most popular ones: an **Internet Control Message Protocol** (**ICMP**) request check to an external host, also known as **PING**.

As we most likely already know, a PING request is a rather basic way to check the presence—and therefore the availability—of a server that we know we should be able to reach within a **local area network** (**LAN**) or **wide area network** (**WAN**) connection. In a nutshell, it works in the following way: the machine that performs the PING sends one or more ICMP echo request packets to the target host and waits for a reply; if it receives one, it reports the round-trip time of the whole task; otherwise, it times out and reports a `host not reachable` error.

The `host not reachable` error can be due to a number of possible scenarios, as listed here:

- The target host is **not available**
- The target host is **available, but actively refuses TCP/IP communications** of any kind
- The target host is **available and accepts incoming connections, but it has been configured to explicitly refuse ICMP requests** and/or not send ICMP echo replies back
- The target host is **available and properly configured to accept ICMP requests and send echo replies back, but the connection is very slow or hindered** by unknown reasons (performance, heavy load, and so on), so the round-trip time takes too long—or even times out

As we can see, this is an ideal scenario for a health check: if we properly configure the target host to accept the PING and always answer it, we can definitely use it to determine whether the host is in a healthy status or not.

Possible outcomes

Now that we know the common scenarios behind a PING test request, we can put down a list of possible outcomes, as follows:

- `Healthy`: We can consider the host `Healthy` whenever the PING succeeds with no errors or timeouts.
- `Degraded`: We can consider the host `Degraded` whenever the PING succeeds, but the round-trip takes too long.
- `Unhealthy`: We can consider the host `Unhealthy` whenever the PING fails—that is, the check times out before any reply.

Now that we've identified these three *statuses*, we just need to properly implement them within our health check.

Creating an ICMPHealthCheck class

The first thing we have to do is create a new `ICMPHealthCheck.cs` class in our project's root folder.

Once done, fill it with the following content:

```
using Microsoft.Extensions.Diagnostics.HealthChecks;
using System;
using System.Net.NetworkInformation;
using System.Threading;
using System.Threading.Tasks;

namespace HealthCheck
{
    public class ICMPHealthCheck : IHealthCheck
    {
        private readonly string Host = "www.does-not-exist.com";
        private readonly int HealthyRoundtripTime = 300;

        public async Task<HealthCheckResult> CheckHealthAsync(
            HealthCheckContext context,
            CancellationToken cancellationToken = default)
        {
            try
            {
                using var ping = new Ping();
                var reply = await ping.SendPingAsync(Host);
```

```
                switch (reply.Status)
                {
                    case IPStatus.Success:
                        return (reply.RoundtripTime > HealthyRoundtripTime)
                            ? HealthCheckResult.Degraded()
                            : HealthCheckResult.Healthy();

                    default:
                        return HealthCheckResult.Unhealthy();
                }
            }
            catch (Exception e)
            {
                return HealthCheckResult.Unhealthy();
            }
        }
    }
}
```

As we can see, we implemented the `IHealthCheck` interface since it's the official .NET way to deal with health checks: such an interface requires a single `async` method—`CheckHealthAsync`—which we used to determine if the ICMP request was successful or not.

> In the preceding code, the `ping` variable has been declared with the `using` keyword: this technique is called *using declaration* and was introduced in C# version 8 as a convenient replacement for the `using` statements/blocks to reduce nesting and produce more readable code.
>
> For further info regarding the *using declaration* feature, take a look at the following URL:
>
> `https://docs.microsoft.com/en-us/dotnet/csharp/language-reference/proposals/csharp-8.0/using`
>
> Those who want to use them are strongly advised to also read this great post by Steve Gordon (Microsoft MVP) to better understand how they work under the hood:
>
> `https://www.stevejgordon.co.uk/csharp-8-understanding-using-declarations`

The code is very easy to understand and handles the three possible scenarios we defined in the previous section. Let's go over what the host can be considered to be:

- `Healthy`, if the PING request gets a successful reply with a round-trip time of 300 ms or less
- `Degraded`, if the PING request gets a successful reply with a round-trip time greater than 300 ms

- `Unhealthy`, if the PING request fails or an `Exception` is thrown

> Notice that the host is hardcoded to a non-existing name, which is rather awkward! Don't worry! We did that for demonstration purposes so that we'll be able to simulate an unhealthy scenario: we're going to change it later on.

That's pretty much it. Our health check is ready to be tested—we just need to find a way to *load* it into our web application's pipeline.

Adding the ICMPHealthCheck to the pipeline

In order to load our ICMP health check into the web application pipeline, we need to add it to the `HealthChecks` middleware. To do that, open the `Startup.cs` class again and change the line we previously added to the `ConfigureServices` method in the following way:

```
public void ConfigureServices(IServiceCollection services)
{
    /// ...existing code...

    services.AddHealthChecks()
        .AddCheck<ICMPHealthCheck>("ICMP");
}
```

That's it: now, we can hit *F5* and try it out. Here's what we should be able to see:

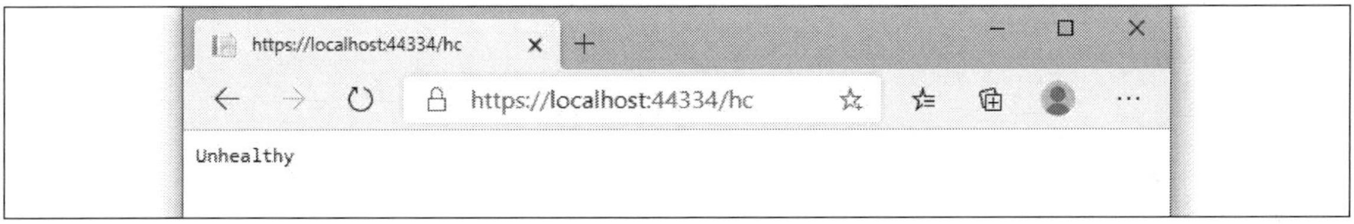

Figure 3.2: Checking our health check

That's great, right?

Well, actually, it's not that great. Our health check does indeed work, but comes with the following three major flaws:

- **Hardcoded values**: The `Host` and `HealthyRoundtripTime` variables should be passed as parameters so that we can set them programmatically.
- **Uninformative response**: `Healthy` and `Unhealthy` are not that great—we should find a way to have a custom (and better) output message instead.
- **Untyped output**: The current response is being sent in plain text—if we want to fetch it with Angular, a JSON content type would definitely be better (and way more usable, as we'll see in the *Health checks in Angular* section later on).

Let's fix these issues, one at a time.

Improving the ICMPHealthCheck class

In this section, we'll improve our `ICMPHealthCheck` class by adding the `host` and `healthyRoundtripTime` parameters, a custom outcome message for each possible status, and a JSON-structured output.

Adding parameters and response messages

Open the `ICMPHealthCheck.cs` class file and perform the following changes (added/modified lines are highlighted):

```
using Microsoft.Extensions.Diagnostics.HealthChecks;
using System;
using System.Net.NetworkInformation;
using System.Threading;
using System.Threading.Tasks;

namespace HealthCheck
{
    public class ICMPHealthCheck : IHealthCheck
    {
        private readonly string Host;
        private readonly int HealthyRoundtripTime;

        public ICMPHealthCheck(string host, int healthyRoundtripTime)
        {
            Host = host;
            HealthyRoundtripTime = healthyRoundtripTime;
        }

        public async Task<HealthCheckResult> CheckHealthAsync(
            HealthCheckContext context,
            CancellationToken cancellationToken = default)
        {
            try
            {
                using var ping = new Ping();
                var reply = await ping.SendPingAsync(Host);

                switch (reply.Status)
                {
                    case IPStatus.Success:
```

```
                        var msg =
                            $"ICMP to {Host} took {reply.RoundtripTime} ms.";

                        return (reply.RoundtripTime > HealthyRoundtripTime)
                            ? HealthCheckResult.Degraded(msg)
                            : HealthCheckResult.Healthy(msg);

                    default:
                        var err =
                            $"ICMP to {Host} failed: {reply.Status}";
                        return HealthCheckResult.Unhealthy(err);
                }
            }
            catch (Exception e)
            {
                var err =
                    $"ICMP to {Host} failed: {e.Message}";
                return HealthCheckResult.Unhealthy(err);
            }
        }
    }
}
```

As we can see, we changed a couple of things, as follows:

- We added a constructor accepting the two parameters we'd like to set programmatically: `host` and `healthyRoundtripTime`. The old *hardcoded* variables are now set by the constructor upon initialization and then used within the class afterward (such as within the main method).
- We created various different *outcome messages* containing the target host, the ping outcome, and the round-trip duration (or the runtime error), and added them as parameters to the `HealthCheckResult` return objects.

> In the preceding code, we've used *string interpolation*, a powerful text formatting feature released in C# version 6 to replace the previous `string.Format` approach. For further info regarding this feature, go to the following URL:
>
> `https://docs.microsoft.com/en-us/dotnet/csharp/tutorials/string-interpolation`

That's pretty much about it. Now, we just need to set the `host` name and `healthyRoundtripTime` programmatically since the old *hardcoded defaults* are now gone. In order to do that, we have to update our middleware setup in the `Startup.cs` file.

Updating the middleware setup

Open the `Startup.cs` file again and change the middleware initialization code within the `ConfigureServices` method in the following way:

```
public void ConfigureServices(IServiceCollection services)
{
    /// ...existing code...

    services.AddHealthChecks()
        .AddCheck("ICMP_01",
            new ICMPHealthCheck("www.ryadel.com",
            100))
        .AddCheck("ICMP_02",
            new ICMPHealthCheck("www.google.com",
            100))
        .AddCheck("ICMP_03",
            new ICMPHealthCheck("www.does-not-exist.com",
            100));
}
```

Here we go: as we can see, another advantage of being able to programmatically configure the host is that we can add the ICMP health check multiple times—one for each host we'd like to actually check. In the preceding example, we're taking the chance to test three different hosts: `www.ryadel.com`, `www.google.com`, and the same non-existing host we used before, which allows us to emulate an `Unhealthy` status as well as the `Healthy` ones.

Now, we could be tempted to hit *F5* and try it out... However, if we were to do that, we would face a rather disappointing outcome, as shown in the following screenshot:

Figure 3.3: Checking our health check

The reason for this is quite obvious: even if we're running multiple checks, we're still relying on the default outcome message... which is nothing more than a Boolean sum of the statuses returned by all the checked hosts. For that very reason, if at least one of them is `Unhealthy`, the whole check will be flagged as `Unhealthy` as well.

Luckily enough, we can avoid that sum—and get a much more granular output—by dealing with the third flaw of our `ICMPHealthCheck`: implementing a custom, JSON-structured output message.

Implementing a custom output message

To implement a custom output message, we need to override the `HealthCheckOptions` class. To do that, add a new `CustomHealthCheckOptions.cs` file to the project's root folder and fill it with the following contents:

```
using Microsoft.AspNetCore.Diagnostics.HealthChecks;
using Microsoft.AspNetCore.Http;
using System.Linq;
using System.Net.Mime;
using System.Text.Json;

namespace HealthCheck
{
    public class CustomHealthCheckOptions : HealthCheckOptions
    {
        public CustomHealthCheckOptions() : base()
        {
            var jsonSerializerOptions = new JsonSerializerOptions()
            {
                WriteIndented = true
            };

            ResponseWriter = async (c, r) =>
            {
                c.Response.ContentType =
                 MediaTypeNames.Application.Json;
                c.Response.StatusCode = StatusCodes.Status200OK;

                var result = JsonSerializer.Serialize(new
                   {
                      checks = r.Entries.Select(e => new
                         {
                            name = e.Key,

                            responseTime =
                             e.Value.Duration.TotalMilliseconds,
                            status = e.Value.Status.ToString(),
                            description = e.Value.Description
                         }),
                      totalStatus = r.Status,
                      totalResponseTime =
                       r.TotalDuration.TotalMilliseconds,
                   }, jsonSerializerOptions);
                await c.Response.WriteAsync(result);
```

```
                };
            }
        }
    }
```

The code is quite self-explanatory: we override the standard class—the one that outputs the one-word output we want to change—with our own custom class so that we can change its `ResponseWriter` property, in order to make it output whatever we want.

More specifically, we want to output a custom JSON-structured message containing a lot of useful stuff from each of our checks, listed here:

- `name`: The identifying string we provided while adding it to the pipeline within the `ConfigureServices` method of the `Startup.cs` file: `"ICMP_01"`, `"ICMP_02"`, and so on
- `responseTime`: The whole duration of that single check
- `status`: Not to be confused with the status of the whole `HealthCheck`— that is, the Boolean sum of all the inner checks statuses
- `description`: The custom informative message we configured earlier on when we refined the `ICMPHealthCheck` class

All these values will be properties of the array items contained in the JSON output: one for each check. It's worth noting that the JSON file, in addition to that array, will also contain the following two additional properties:

- `totalStatus`: The Boolean sum of all the inner checks statuses — `Unhealthy` if there's at least an `Unhealthy` host, `Degraded` if there's at least a `Degraded` host, and `Healthy` otherwise
- `totalResponseTime`: The whole duration of all the checks

That's a lot of useful information, right? We just have to configure our middleware to output them, instead of those one-word responses we've seen before.

About health check responses and HTTP status codes

Before going further, it's worth noting that—in the preceding `CustomHealthCheckOptions` class—we did set the *ResponseWriter*'s HTTP status code to a fixed `StatusCodes.Status200OK`. Is there a reason behind that?

As a matter of fact, there is, and it's also quite an important one. The `HealthChecks` middleware's default behavior returns either an HTTP status code 200 if all the checks are OK (`Healthy`) or an HTTP status code 503 if one or more checks are KO (`Unhealthy`). Since we've switched to a JSON-structured output, we don't need the 503 code anymore, as it would most likely break our *front-end* client UI logic—unless properly handled. Therefore, for the sake of simplicity, we just forced an HTTP 200 response, regardless of the end result. We'll find a way to properly emphasize the errors within the upcoming Angular UI.

Configuring the output message

Open the `Startup.cs` file, scroll down to the `Configure` method, and change the following lines accordingly (the updated code is highlighted):

```
app.UseEndpoints(endpoints =>
{
    endpoints.MapHealthChecks("/hc", new CustomHealthCheckOptions());
    endpoints.MapControllerRoute(
        name: "default",
        pattern: "{controller}/{action=Index}/{id?}");
});
```

Once done, we can finally hit *F5* and properly test it out. This time, we won't be disappointed by the outcome, as shown in the following screenshot:

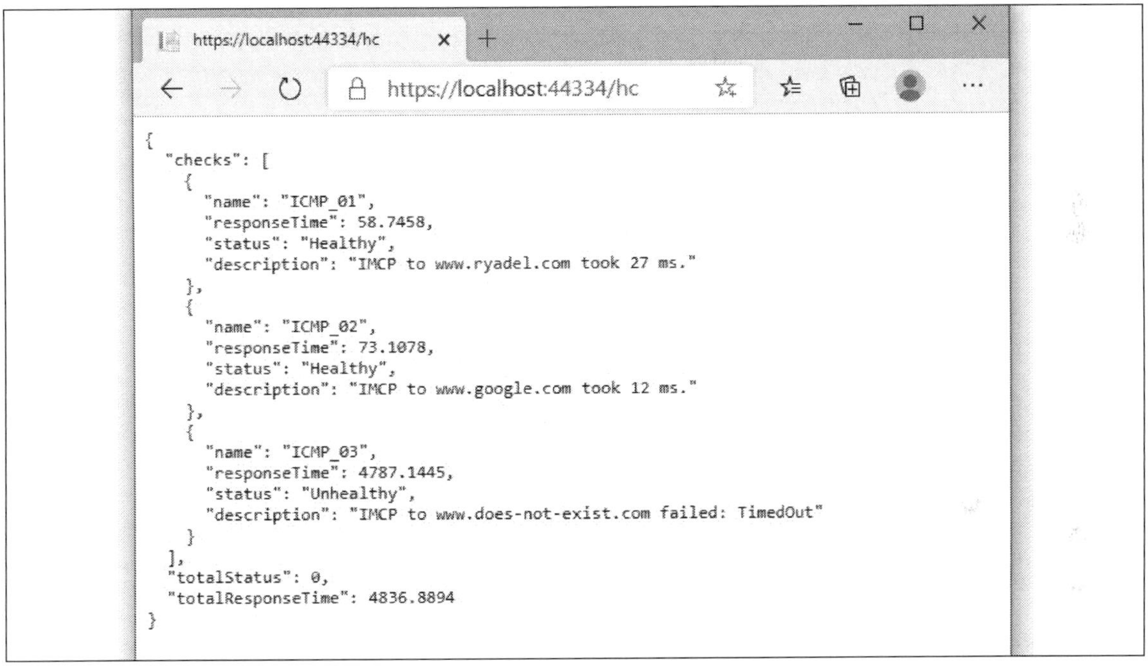

Figure 3.4: A more detailed health check output message

That's a pretty nice response, isn't it?

Now, each and every check is properly documented, as well as the *total* outcome data, in a structured JSON object. This is just what we need to feed some Angular components that we can show on-screen in a human-readable (and fashionable) way, which we're just about to do, starting with the next section.

Health checks in Angular

It's now time to build an **Angular component** that is capable of fetching and displaying the structured JSON data we managed to pull off in the previous sections.

As we know from *Chapter 2, Looking Around*, an Angular component is commonly made of three separate files, as follows:

- The **component** (`.ts`) file, written in TypeScript and containing the `component` class, together with all the module references, functions, variables, and so on
- The **template** (`.html`) file, written in HTML extended with the *Angular template syntax*, which defines the UI layout architecture
- The **style** (`.css`) file, written in CSS and containing the Cascading Style Sheets rules and definitions for drawing the UI

> Although the aforementioned three-files approach is arguably the most practical one, the only required file is the component one, as both the template and the style files could also be embedded as inline elements within the component file. The choice between using separate files or going inline is a matter of taste; however, we strongly suggest adopting the three-files approach because it enforces the separation of concerns embodied within the component/template duality featured by Angular.
>
> If we're used to the **model-view-controller** (**MVC**) and **model-view-viewmodel** (**MVVM**) patterns, we can say that, in Angular, the component is the controller/viewmodel and the template represents the view.

In the next section, we'll implement them all.

Creating the Angular component

From Solution Explorer, navigate through the `/ClientApp/src/app` folder and create a new `health-check` folder.

Once inside, create the following `.ts`, `.html`, and `.css` files:

- `health-check.component.ts`
- `health-check.component.html`
- `health-check.component.css`

Once done, fill them with the following content.

Creating components using the Angular CLI

If you don't want to manually create the `.ts`, `.html`, and `.css` component files, you can generate them using the Angular CLI in the following way:

```
> ng generate component <name> [options]
```

More precisely, here's the relevant command for the preceding scenario:

```
> ng generate component health-check --skipTests=true
```

The `--skipTests` switch will prevent the Angular CLI from creating the `spec.ts` file for the unit tests, which we've already encountered back in *Chapter 2*, *Looking Around*: for the sake of simplicity, we'll not consider them until *Chapter 9*, *ASP.NET Core and Angular Unit Testing*, when we talk about client-side and server-side testing.

> From now on, we'll always create component files manually throughout the rest of the book to ensure that the source code won't change with the Angular versions that will be released in the future: that said, using the Angular CLI is the most suitable way to add new components to our apps in real development scenarios.

health-check.component.ts

Here's the `/ClientApp/src/app/health-check/health-check.component.ts` source code:

```
import { Component, Inject, OnInit } from '@angular/core';
import { HttpClient } from '@angular/common/http';

@Component({
    selector: 'app-health-check',
    templateUrl: './health-check.component.html',
    styleUrls: ['./health-check.component.css']
})
export class HealthCheckComponent implements OnInit {
  public result: Result;

  constructor(
    private http: HttpClient,
    @Inject('BASE_URL') private baseUrl: string) {
  }

  ngOnInit() {
    this.http.get<Result>(this.baseUrl + 'hc').subscribe(result => {
      this.result = result;
    }, error => console.error(error));
  }
}

interface Result {
    checks: Check[];
```

```
    totalStatus: string;
    totalResponseTime: number;
}

interface Check {
    name: string;
    status: string;
    responseTime: number;
}
```

If you're curious about what we did there, here's a breakdown of the most relevant stuff:

- At the start of the file, we made sure to `import` all the Angular *directives*, *pipes*, *services*, and *components*—in one word, *modules*—that we need throughout the whole class.
- In the class declaration, we've explicitly implemented the `OnInit` interface by adding the `implements OnInit` instruction to add type-safety: this way we won't risk typing or spelling mistakes within the `ngOnInit` lifecycle hook.
- In the component's constructor, we instantiated an `HttpClient` service and a `baseUrl` variable using **dependency injection** (**DI**); the `baseUrl` value is being set by making use of the `BASE_URL` provider, defined in the `/ClientApp/src/main.ts` file, which we briefly introduced in *Chapter 2, Looking Around*. As we can see by looking at that file's source code, it will resolve to our application's root URL: such a value is required by the `HttpClient` service, to build the URL that will be used to fetch the data from the server with an HTTP GET request to the .NET `HealthChecks` middleware that we set up earlier on (see the `'hc'` string).
- Last but not least, we defined two interfaces to deal with the JSON request we're expecting to receive from the `HealthChecks` middleware: `Result` and `Check`, which we designed to host the whole JSON resulting object and each element of the internal array, respectively.

Before going further, it could be useful to spend some valuable time expanding on some very important topics we've just met by implementing the preceding code, as follows:

- **Imports and modules**
- **Dependency injection**
- **ngOnInit** (and other lifecycle hooks)
- **Constructor**
- **HttpClient**
- **Observables**
- **Interfaces**

Since we're going to see them all throughout this book, it's definitely advisable to review them now.

Imports and modules

The static `import` statement that we used multiple times in the preceding `HealthCheckComponent` is used to import bindings that are exported by other JavaScript modules.

The concept of working with *modules* started with ECMAScript 2015 and has been thoroughly adopted by TypeScript and, therefore, Angular. A *module* is basically a collection of variables, functions, classes, and so on, grouped within a class: each *module* is executed within its own scope, not in the global scope, meaning that all the elements declared within it are not visible from the outside unless they are explicitly *exported* using the `export` statement. Conversely, to consume a variable, function, class, interface, and so on contained (and *exported*) within a *module*, that *module* has to be imported using the `import` statement. This is quite similar to what we do with *namespaces* in most programming languages (C# has `using` statements, for example).

As a matter of fact, all the Angular *directives*, *pipes*, *services*, and *components* are also packed into collections of *JavaScript modules*, which we have to *import* into any TypeScript class whenever we want to use them. These collections are basically libraries of modules: we can easily recognize them since their name begins with the `@angular` prefix. Our `/ClientApp/packages.json` file (the NPM package file), which we've seen in previous chapters, contains most of them.

> To know more about ECMAScript modules and better understand the module resolution strategy in TypeScript, check out the following URLs:
>
> **TypeScript modules**: `https://www.typescriptlang.org/docs/handbook/modules.html`
>
> **Module resolution**: `https://www.typescriptlang.org/docs/handbook/module-resolution.html`

IMPORTANT: *JavaScript modules* should not be confused with Angular's own modularity system, which is based upon the `@NgModule` decorator. As we already know from *Chapter 1, Getting Ready*, and *Chapter 2, Looking Around*, Angular's *NgModules* are *building blocks*—that is, containers for a cohesive block of code dedicated to an application domain, a workflow, or a common feature set. We know from the aforementioned chapters that each Angular app has at least one `NgModule` class, called the root module, which is conventionally named `AppModule` and resides in the `app.module.ts` file in the application root; additional NgModules will be added in the upcoming chapters.

Unfortunately, the *JavaScript module system* and the *Angular NgModule system* use a rather similar vocabulary (*import* versus *imports*, *export* versus *exports*) that might lead to confusion—especially considering that *Angular apps require the developer to use both of them at the same time* (and often in the same class file). Luckily enough, although being forced to intertwine these two systems might be a bit tricky at first, eventually, we'll become familiar with the different contexts in which they are used.

Here's a sample screenshot, taken from our `HealthCheck` app's `AppModule` class file, which should help you distinguish between the two different systems:

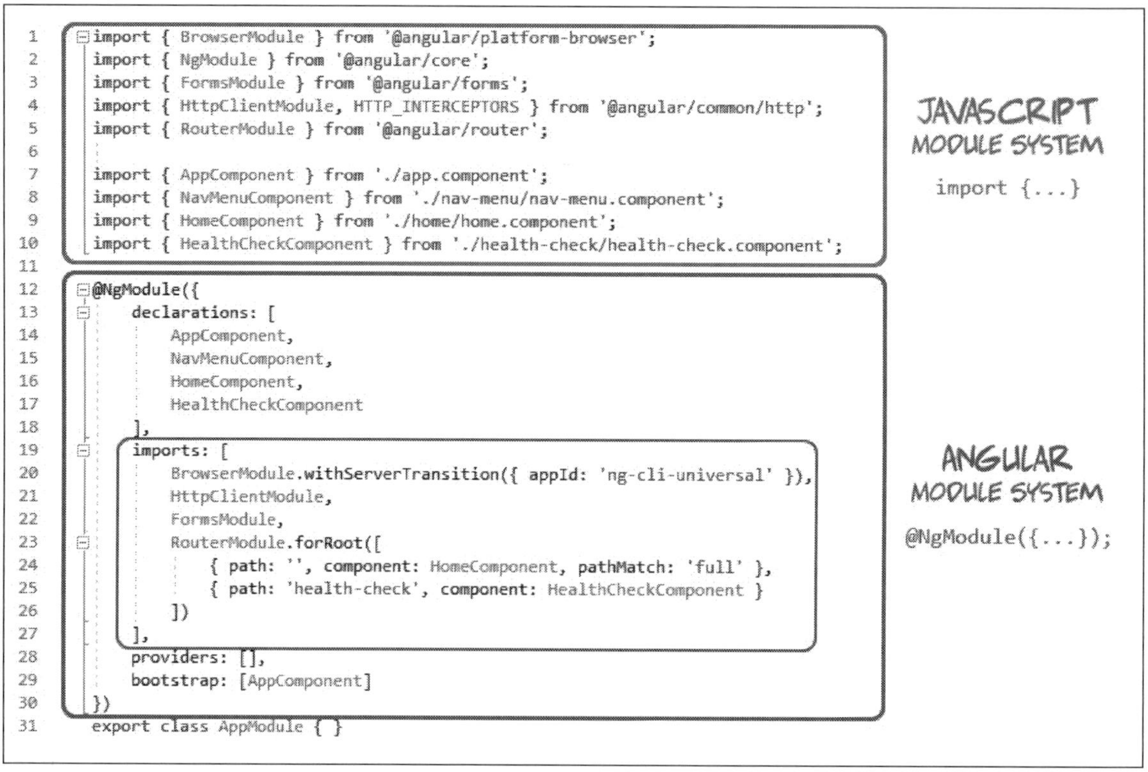

import { BrowserModule } from '@angular/platform-browser';
import { NgModule } from '@angular/core';
import { FormsModule } from '@angular/forms';
import { HttpClientModule, HTTP_INTERCEPTORS } from '@angular/common/http';
import { RouterModule } from '@angular/router';
import { AppComponent } from './app.component';
import { NavMenuComponent } from './nav-menu/nav-menu.component';
import { HomeComponent } from './home/home.component';
import { HealthCheckComponent } from './health-check/health-check.component';
@NgModule({
declarations: [
AppComponent,
NavMenuComponent,
HomeComponent,
HealthCheckComponent
],
imports: [
BrowserModule.withServerTransition({ appId: 'ng-cli-universal' }),
HttpClientModule,
FormsModule,
RouterModule.forRoot([
{ path: '', component: HomeComponent, pathMatch: 'full' },
{ path: 'health-check', component: HealthCheckComponent }
])
],
providers: [],
bootstrap: [AppComponent]
})
export class AppModule { }
JAVASCRIPT
MODULE SYSTEM
import {...}
ANGULAR
MODULE SYSTEM
@NgModule({...});

Figure 3.5: Inspecting the AppModule class file

> For additional information regarding the Angular module system and the `NgModule` decorator, check out the following URLs:
>
> **NgModule**: `https://angular.io/guide/ngmodules`
>
> **Angular architecture: NgModules and JavaScript modules**: `https://angular.io/guide/architecture-modules#ngmodules-and-javascript-modules`

Dependency injection (DI)

We've talked about DI a number of times already, and with good reason, because it's an important application design pattern for both ASP.NET Core and Angular, with both frameworks making extensive use of it to increase their efficiency and modularity.

To explain what DI actually is, we must first talk about what *dependencies* are in a class: these can be defined as *services* or *objects* that a class needs to *instantiate* into *variables* or *properties*, in order to perform one or more tasks.

In a *classic* coding pattern, those dependencies are instantiated *on the fly* within the class itself—for example, during its initialization phase, such as within the constructor method. Here's a typical example of that:

```
public MyClass() {
    var myElement = new Element();
    myElement.doStuff();
}
```

In the preceding example, the `myElement` variable is an object instance of the `Element` type, and also a (local) *dependency* of `MyClass`: as we can see, it gets instantiated in the constructor because we most likely need to use it there. From there, we can either use it as a local variable (and let it *die* at the end of the constructor's *scope*) or assign it to a class property to further extend its *life span* and *scope*.

DI is an alternative software design pattern, in which a class asks for dependencies *from external sources* rather than creating them itself. To better understand this concept, let's try to rewrite the same code as before with a *DI* approach, like this:

```
public MyClass(Element myElement) {
    myElement.doStuff();
}
```

As we can see, there's no need to instantiate the `myElement` variable because this task is already handled by the **dependency injector**—external code that is responsible for creating the *injectable* objects and *injecting* them into the classes.

The whole DI coding pattern is based upon the concept of **Inversion of Control** (**IoC**), to resolve dependencies. Such a concept revolves around the basic idea that, formally, if `ObjectA` depends on `ObjectB`, then `ObjectA` must not create or import `ObjectB` directly, but provide a way to *inject* `ObjectB` instead. In the preceding code block example, `ObjectA` is obviously `MyClass`, while `ObjectB` is the `myElement` instance.

> For additional information about the DI software design pattern, check out the following links:
>
> **DI in ASP.NET Core**: `https://docs.microsoft.com/en-us/aspnet/core/fundamentals/dependency-injection`
>
> **DI in Angular**: `https://angular.io/guide/dependency-injection`

In Angular, the DI framework provides declared dependencies to a class when that class is instantiated.

In the preceding `HealthCheckComponent` class, we used DI in the component's constructor method to inject an `HttpClient` service instance and a `baseUrl` instance; as we can see, we also took the chance to assign the `private` *access modifier* to both of them. Thanks to that modifier, those variables will be accessible through the whole component class.

> As per Angular conventions, a parameter injected without an access modifier can only be accessed within the constructor; conversely, if it gets an access modifier such as `private` or `public`, it will be defined as a class member, hence changing its scope to the class. Such a technique is called **variable scoping**, and we're going to use it a lot in our Angular components from now on.

ngOnInit (and other lifecycle hooks)

The `ngOnInit` method that we used in the `HealthCheckComponent` class is one of the component's *lifecycle hook methods*: in this section, we'll try to shed some light on them, since we're going to use them a lot throughout this book.

Each Angular component has a *lifecycle*, which is managed by Angular. Each time a user visits a view within our app, the Angular framework creates and renders the required *components* (and *directives*) along with their children, reacts to their changes whenever the user interacts with them, and eventually destroys and removes them from the **Document Object Model** (**DOM**) when the user navigates elsewhere. All these "key moments" trigger some *lifecycle hook methods* that Angular exposes to the developers so that they can perform something when each one of them actually occurs.

Here's a list of the available hooks, in order of execution (when possible, since some of them are called multiple times during the component's lifecycle):

- `ngOnChanges()`: Responds when Angular (re)sets data-bound input properties. The method receives a `SimpleChanges` object of current and previous property values. Called before `ngOnInit()`, and whenever one or more data-bound input properties changes.
- `ngOnInit()`: Initializes the directive/component after Angular first displays the data-bound properties and sets the directive/component's input properties. Called once, after the first `ngOnChanges()` method.
- `ngDoCheck()`: Detects and acts upon changes that Angular can't, or won't, detect on its own. Called during every change detection run, immediately after `ngOnChanges()` and `ngOnInit()`.
- `ngAfterContentInit()`: Responds after Angular projects external content into the component's view/the view that a directive is in. Called once after the first `ngDoCheck()` method.
- `ngAfterContentChecked()`: Responds after Angular checks the content projected into the directive/component. Called after the `ngAfterContentInit()` method and every subsequent `ngDoCheck()` method.
- `ngAfterViewInit()`: Responds after Angular initializes the component's views and child views/the view that a directive is in. Called once after the first `ngAfterContentChecked()` method.
- `ngAfterViewChecked()`: Responds after Angular checks the component's views and child views/the view that a directive is in. Called after the `ngAfterViewInit()` method and every subsequent `ngAfterContentChecked()` method.

- `ngOnDestroy()`: Cleans up just before Angular destroys the directive/component. Unsubscribes `Observables` and detaches the event.
- Handlers to avoid memory leaks: Called just before Angular destroys the directive/component.

The preceding **lifecycle hook methods** are available for all Angular *components* and *directives*. To make use of them, we can just add them to our component class—which is precisely what we did in the preceding `HealthCheckComponent`.

Now that we have understood the role of `ngOnInit()`, we should take a moment to explain why we put the `HttpClient` source code in the `ngOnInit()` lifecycle hook method instead of using the component's `constructor()` method: shouldn't we have used that instead?

The next section should greatly help us to understand the reason for such a choice.

Constructor

As we most likely already know, all TypeScript classes have a `constructor()` method that will be called whenever we create an instance of that class: since TypeScript is, by all means, a superset of JavaScript, any TypeScript `constructor()` method will be transpiled into a JavaScript `constructor()` function.

The following code block shows an example of a TypeScript class:

```
class MyClass() {
  constructor() {
    console.log("MyClass has been instantiated");
  }
}
```

This will be transpiled into the following JavaScript function:

```
function MyClass() {
  console.log("MyClass has been instantiated");
}
```

If we omit the constructor in TypeScript, the JavaScript transpiled function will be empty; however, whenever the framework needs to instantiate it, it will still call it in the following way, regardless of whether it has the constructor or not:

```
var myClassInstance = new MyClass();
```

Understanding this is very important because it greatly helps us to understand the difference between the component's `constructor()` method and its `ngOnInit()` lifecycle hook, and it's a huge difference, at least from the perspective of the component initialization phase.

The whole Angular Bootstrap process can be split into two major (and subsequent) stages:

- **Instantiating the components**
- **Performing change detection**

As we can easily guess, the `constructor()` method is called during the former phase, while all the lifecycle hooks—including the `ngOnInit()` method—are called throughout the latter.

If we look at these methods from this perspective, it's pretty easy to understand the following key concepts:

- If we need to create or *inject* some *dependencies* into an Angular component, we should use the `constructor()` method; as a matter of fact, this is also the only way we can do that since the constructor is the only method that gets called in the context of the Angular injector.
- Conversely, whenever we need to perform any component *initialization* and/or *update* task—such as performing an HTTP request, updating the DOM, and so on—we should definitely do that by using one of the *lifecycle hooks*.

The `ngOnInit()` method, as its name implies, is often a great choice for the component's initialization tasks, since it happens right after the directive's and/or component's input properties are set. That's why we have used this to implement our HTTP request, using the Angular built-in `HttpClient` service.

HttpClient

Being able to efficiently send and receive JSON data from our ASP.NET Core controllers is probably the most important requirement for our **single-page application** (**SPA**). We chose to do that using the Angular `HttpClient` service, first introduced in Angular 4.3.0-RC.0, which is among one of the best answers the framework can give to get the job done. For this very reason, we will use it a lot throughout this book; however, before doing that, it might be advisable to properly understand what it is, why is it better than the former implementation, and how to properly implement it.

The new `HttpClient` service was introduced in July 2017 as an improved version of the former Angular HTTP client API, also known as `@angular/http`, or, simply, `HTTP`. Instead of replacing the old version in the `@angular/http` package, the Angular development team has put the new classes in a separate package—`@angular/common/http`. They chose to do that to preserve the *backward compatibility* with the existing code bases, and also to ensure a slow, yet steady, migration to the new API.

Those who used the old Angular HTTP service class at least once will most likely remember its main limitations, listed here:

- **JSON was not enabled by default**, forcing the developers to explicitly set it within the request *headers*—and `JSON.parse` / `JSON.stringify` the data—when working with RESTful APIs.
- **There was no easy way to access the HTTP request/response pipeline**, thus preventing the developer from intercepting or altering the *request* and/or *response* calls after they were issued or received by using some ugly and pattern-breaking hacks. As a matter of fact, extensions and wrapper classes were basically the only way to customize the service, at least on a global scope.

- **There was no native strong-typing for request and response objects**, although that could be addressed by casting JSON-as-interfaces as a workaround.

The great news is that the new `HttpClient` does all of this and much more; other features include testability support and better error handling via APIs entirely based on `Observables`.

> It's worth noting that putting the `HttpClient` service within the component itself is not good practice because it will often lead to unnecessary code repetition among the various components that need to perform HTTP calls and handle their results. This is a known issue that greatly affects production-level apps, which will likely require post-processing of the received data, handling errors, adding retry logic to deal with intermittent connectivity, and so on.
>
> To better deal with those scenarios, it's strongly advisable to separate the data access logic and the data presentation role by encapsulating the former in a separate service, which can then be injected into all the components that require it, in a standardized and centralized way. We'll talk more about that in *Chapter 7, Code Tweaks and Data Services*, where we'll eventually replace multiple `HttpClient` implementations and centralize their source code within a couple of data services.

Observables

Observables are a powerful feature for managing async data; they are the backbone of the **ReactiveX JavaScript** (**RxJS**) library, which is one of the Angular required dependencies. Those who are familiar with ES6 *Promises* can think of them as an improved version of that approach.

An *observable* can be configured to send literal values, structured values, messages, and events, either *synchronously* or *asynchronously*: the values can be received by subscribing to the *observable* itself using the `subscribe` method hook, meaning that the whole data flow is handled within it—until we programmatically choose to *unsubscribe*. The great thing about this approach is that, regardless of the chosen approach (*sync* or *async*), streaming *frequency*, and *data type*, the programming interface for listening to values and stopping listening is the same.

The great advantages of *observables* are the reason why Angular makes extensive use of them when dealing with data. If we take a good look at our `HealthCheckComponent` source code, we can see how we use them as well when our `HttpClient` service fetches the data from the server and stores the result in the `this.result` local variable. Such a task is performed by calling two consecutive methods: `get<Result>()` and `subscribe()`.

Let's try to summarize what they do, as follows:

- `get<Result>()`: As the name suggests, this method issues a standard HTTP request to our ASP.NET Core `HealthChecks` middleware to fetch the *Result* JSON response object. This method needs a URL parameter, which we create on the fly by adding the `hc` literal string (the same string that we set early on, within the `Configure` method of the `Startup.cs` file) to the Angular app's `BASE_URL`.

- `subscribe()`: This method invokes the *observable* returned by the get call, which will execute two very different actions right after a result and/or in case of an error. Needless to say, all this will be done *asynchronously*, meaning that it will run in a separate thread (or scheduled for later execution) while the rest of the code continues to execute.

> Those who want to get additional information can take a look at the following URLs, taken from the RxJS official documentation:
>
> **ReactiveX Library—Observables guide**: `http://reactivex.io/rxjs/class/es6/Observable.js~Observable.html`
>
> **Angular.io—Observables guide**: `https://angular.io/guide/observables`

It's very important to understand that we're only scratching the surface of what an *observable* can do. However, this is all we need for now: we'll have the chance to talk more about them later on.

Interfaces

Now that we know how the Angular `HttpClient` service works, we have every right to ask ourselves a couple of questions: why are we even using these **interfaces**? Can't we just use the raw JSON data sent by the ASP.NET Core `HealthChecks` middleware that we defined early on, consuming them as anonymous JavaScript objects?

Theoretically speaking, we can, just as we can output raw JSON from the controllers, instead of creating all the ViewModel classes like we did instead. In a well-written app, though, we should always resist the temptation to handle raw JSON data and/or to use anonymous objects for a number of good reasons:

- **We have chosen TypeScript over JavaScript because we want to work with type definitions**: Anonymous objects and properties are the exact opposite; they lead to the JavaScript way of doing things, which is something we wanted to avoid in the first place
- **Anonymous objects (and their properties) are not easy to validate**: We don't want our data items to be error-prone or forced to deal with missing properties
- **Anonymous objects are hardly reusable**, and won't benefit from many handy Angular features —such as *object mapping*—that require our objects to be actual instances of an interface and/or a type

The first two arguments are very important, especially if we're aiming for a production-ready application; no matter how easy our development task might seem at first, we should never think that we can afford to lose that level of control over our application's source code.

The third reason is also crucial, as long as we want to use Angular to its full extent. If that's the case, using an undefined array of properties—such as raw JSON data—is basically out of the question; conversely, using a structured TypeScript interface is arguably the most lightweight way to work with structured JSON data in a *strongly typed* fashion.

> It's worth noting that we've not added the `export` statement to our interface: we did that on purpose since we're only going to use this within the `HealthCheckComponent` class. Should we need to change this behavior in the future—for example, to create an external data service—we'll have to add this statement (and, arguably, move each one of them into a separate file) to enable us to `import` them into other classes.

health-check.component.html

Here's the `/ClientApp/src/app/health-check/health-check.component.html` source code:

```
<h1>Health Check</h1>

<p>Here are the results of our health check:</p>

<p *ngIf="!result"><em>Loading...</em></p>

<table class='table table-striped' aria-labelledby="tableLabel" *ngIf="result">
  <thead>
    <tr>
      <th>Name</th>
      <th>Response Time</th>
      <th>Status</th>
      <th>Description</th>
    </tr>
  </thead>
  <tbody>
    <tr *ngFor="let check of result.checks">
      <td>{{ check.name }}</td>
      <td>{{ check.responseTime }}</td>
      <td class="status {{ check.status }}">{{ check.status }}</td>
      <td>{{ check.description }}</td>
    </tr>
  </tbody>
</table>
```

As we can see, the *template* part of our Angular component is basically an HTML page, containing a table with some Angular directive. Before moving on, let's have a closer look, as follows:

- `ngIf`: This is a *structural directive* that conditionally includes the container HTML element, based on the Boolean expression value specified after the equals (=) sign: when such an expression evaluates to *true*, Angular renders the element; otherwise, it doesn't. It can be chained with an `else` block that—if present—will be shown when the expression evaluates to *false* or *null*. In the preceding code block, we use it within the <table> element so that it only appears when the `result` internal variable (which we defined in the **component** class earlier on) stops being *null*, which will happen after the data has been fetched from the server.

- ngFor: Another *structural directive* that renders a template for each item contained in a given collection. The directive is placed on an element, which becomes the parent of the cloned templates. In the preceding code block, we use it inside the main <table> element to create and show a <tr> element (a row) for each check item within the result.checks array.
- {{ check.name }}, {{ check.responseTime }}, and so on: These are called *interpolations* and can be used to incorporate calculated strings into the text between HTML element tags and/or within attribute assignments. In other words, we can use them as placeholders for our class variables' property values. As we can see, the *interpolation* default delimiters are the double curly braces, {{ and }}.

> To understand more about ngIf, ngFor, interpolations, and other Angular UI fundamentals, we strongly suggest taking a look at the official documentation:
>
> **Displaying data**: https://angular.io/guide/displaying-data
>
> **Template syntax**: https://angular.io/guide/template-syntax
>
> **Structural directives**: https://angular.io/guide/structural-directives

health-check.component.css

Here's the /ClientApp/src/app/health-check/health-check.component.css source code:

```
.status {
  font-weight: bold;
}

.Healthy {
  color: green;
}

.Degraded {
  color: orange;
}

.Unhealthy {
  color: red;
}
```

There's not much to say here; just some vanilla CSS to style out the component template. Notice how we played a bit with the styling of the table cell, which will contain the *status* of the various checks. It's strongly advisable to highlight them as much as we can, so we made them bold and with a color matching the status type: green for Healthy, orange for Degraded, and red for Unhealthy.

> Due to space limitations, we won't be able to talk much about CSS styling in this book: we will just take it for granted that the average web programmer knows how to handle the simple definitions, selectors, and styling rules we will use in our examples.
>
> Those who want (or need) to understand more about CSS and CSS3 are encouraged to take a look at this great online tutorial: `https://developer.mozilla.org/en-US/docs/Web/CSS`

A word on Angular component styling

As a matter of fact, Angular gives us at least two ways to define custom CSS rules for our components:

- Setting them within a `styles` property in the component metadata
- Loading styles from external CSS files by adding a `styleUrls` property in the component metadata

Both of the preceding approaches rely upon properties that need to be added to the component's `@Component` decorator; the latter is the one used by the default template we reviewed back in *Chapter 2, Looking Around*, and is preferable in most cases, since it allows us to separate the HTML structure from the CSS styling.

If we wanted to migrate to the former, here's how we should set the `styles` property instead:

```
@Component({
  selector: 'app-health-check',
  templateUrl: './health-check.component.html',
  styles: ['
    .status { font-weight:bold; }
    .Healthy { color: green; }
    .Degraded { color: orange; }
    .Unhealthy { color: red; }
  ']
})
```

The only real advantage of such an approach is that it doesn't need the addition of a separate CSS file, which could make it viable enough for small and lightweight components that require little styling: that said, in the vast majority of cases, the `styleUrls` property is definitely the way to go.

> It goes without saying that we've only scratched the surface of a huge and complex topic; however, for obvious reasons of space, we won't go much further than this for the rest of the book.
>
> Those who want to know more about *component styling* are strongly encouraged to take a look at the Angular official guide: `https://angular.io/guide/component-styles`

Now that our *component* is ready, we need to properly add it to our Angular app.

Adding the component to the Angular app

In order to add our new component to our Angular app, we need to make some minimal changes to the following files:

- `app.module.ts`
- `app-routing.module.ts`
- `nav-menu.component.ts`
- `nav-menu.component.html`

Let's get this done.

AppModule

As we know from *Chapter 2, Looking Around,* each new *component* must be referenced in the `AppModule` so that it can be registered within our app.

Open the `/ClientApp/src/app/app.module.ts` file and add the following highlighted lines:

```
import { BrowserModule } from '@angular/platform-browser';
import { NgModule } from '@angular/core';
import { FormsModule } from '@angular/forms';
import { HttpClientModule, HTTP_INTERCEPTORS } from '@angular/common/http';
import { RouterModule } from '@angular/router';

import { AppRoutingModule } from './app-routing.module';

import { AppComponent } from './app.component';
import { NavMenuComponent } from './nav-menu/nav-menu.component';
import { HomeComponent } from './home/home.component';
import { HealthCheckComponent } from './health-check/health-check.component';

@NgModule({
  declarations: [
    AppComponent,
    NavMenuComponent,
    HomeComponent,
    HealthCheckComponent
  ],
  imports: [
    BrowserModule.withServerTransition({ appId: 'ng-cli-universal' }),
    HttpClientModule,
    FormsModule,
    AppRoutingModule
  ],
```

```
  providers: [],
  bootstrap: [AppComponent]
})
export class AppModule { }
```

Mission accomplished: let's move on.

AppRoutingModule

Since we've created a dedicated `AppRoutingModule` to handle routing, we also need to update it by adding the new routing entry, so that our users will be able to navigate to that page.

Open the `/ClientApp/src/app/app-routing.module.ts` file and add the following highlighted lines:

```
import { NgModule } from '@angular/core';
import { Routes, RouterModule } from '@angular/router';
import { HomeComponent } from './home/home.component';
import { HealthCheckComponent } from './health-check/health-check.component';

const routes: Routes = [
  { path: '', component: HomeComponent, pathMatch: 'full' },
  { path: 'health-check', component: HealthCheckComponent }
];

@NgModule({
  imports: [RouterModule.forRoot(routes)],
  exports: [RouterModule]
})
export class AppRoutingModule { }
```

Once done, we can move further.

NavMenuComponent

Adding our new *component* navigation path to `RoutingModule` is a required step to make sure our users are able to reach it; however, we also need to add a link for our users to click on. Since `NavMenuComponent` is the component that handles the navigation user interface, we need to perform some stuff there as well.

Open the `ClientApp/src/app/nav-menu/nav-menu.component.html` file and add the following highlighted lines:

```
// ... existing code...

<ul class="navbar-nav flex-grow">
  <li
```

```
      class="nav-item"
      [routerLinkActive]="['link-active']"
      [routerLinkActiveOptions]="{ exact: true }"
    >
      <a class="nav-link text-dark" [routerLink]="['/']">Home</a>
    </li>
    <li class="nav-item" [routerLinkActive]="['link-active']">
      <a class="nav-link text-dark" [routerLink]="['/health-check']"
        >Health Check</a
      >
    </li>
  </ul>

// ... existing code...
```

Now that our new *component* has been added to our Angular app, we just need to test it out.

Testing it out

To see our new `HealthCheckComponent` in all of its glory, we just need to do the following:

- Hit *F5* to launch the project in *debug* mode
- When the home view is done loading, click on the new **Health Check** link in the top-right corner

If we did everything correctly, the browser should load the new **Health Check** view, which should look just like the following screenshot:

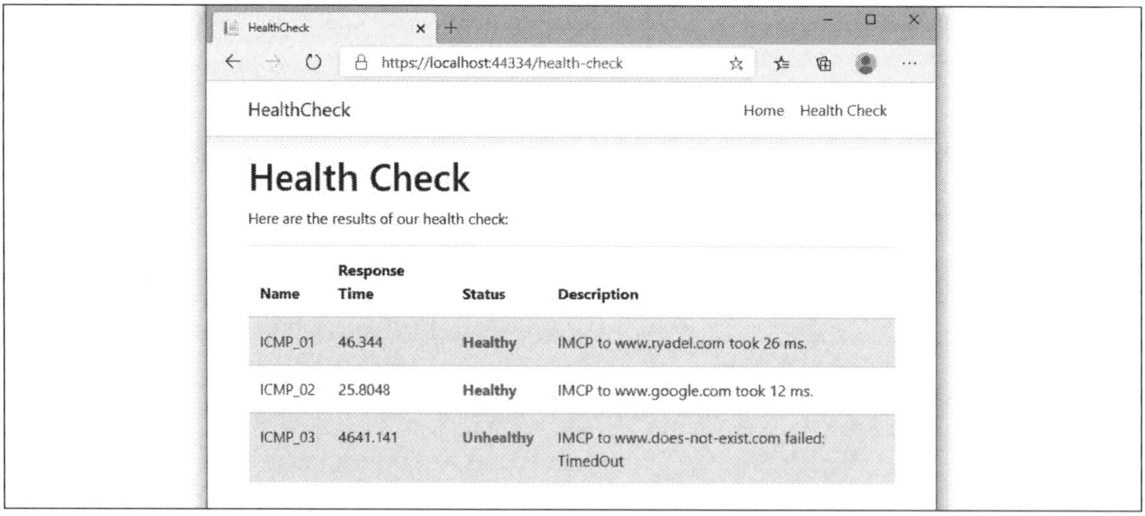

Figure 3.6: Our new HealthCheckComponent

It definitely seems like we did it!

Our health check is up and running, proudly showing us the results of the three ICMP requests we set up within our ASP.NET Core's `HealthChecksMiddleware`.

Now that we've learned the basics, we'll move on to a completely different topic. However, the reader should already be able (and is strongly encouraged) to further expand this sample project with more sophisticated use case scenarios, such as:

- Create additional checks using the same approach that we've adopted for the `ICMPHealthCheck` class: a DBMS connection check, read/write permissions on UNC folders or resources, presence/absence of watchdog files, internet connectivity, CPU/memory/bandwidth usage, and so on.
- Proactively handle the different states in our application depending on the various health check results: show a message to our users in case the application is not working properly, disable the components of the application that are not working, switch to a fallback alternative, send alert email notifications to the administrators, and so on.
- Extend the `HealthChecksMiddleware` capabilities with **LiteXHealthChecks**, a lightweight yet powerful NuGet package with a number of modular add-ons that allows us to check the status of a component in the application, such as a backend service, database, or some internal state.

... and more.

Summary

Let's spend a minute briefly recapping what we learned in this chapter. First of all, we acknowledged that *.NET controllers* are not the only tool in the shed: as a matter of fact, any middleware is virtually able to deal with the HTTP *request* and *response* cycle—as long as it is in our application's pipeline.

In order to demonstrate such a concept, we introduced `HealthChecksMiddleware`, a neat ASP.NET Core built-in feature that can be used to implement status monitor services.... and that's basically what we did throughout this chapter. We started with the ASP.NET Core *back-end*, refining our work until we were able to create a JSON-structured output; then, we switched to Angular, where we learned how to properly fetch it with a *component* and show it on-screen through the browser's HTML-based UI. Eventually, the final outcome was good enough to reward us for our hard work.

That's enough for health checks, at least for the time being: starting from the next chapter, we'll bring back the standard .NET *controllers* pattern and see how we can leverage it to learn something new.

Suggested topics

Health Monitoring, Health Checks, HealthChecksMiddleware, HealthCheckOptions, HTTP Requests, HTTP Responses, ICMP, PING, ResponseWriter, JSON, JsonSerializerOptions. Components, Routing, Modules, AppModule, HttpClient, ngIf, ngFor, Directives, Structural Directives, Interpolations, NgModule, Angular module system, JavaScript module system (import/export).

References

- *Health checks in ASP.NET Core*: `https://docs.microsoft.com/en-US/aspnet/core/host-and-deploy/health-checks`
- *Request and response operations in ASP.NET Core*: `https://docs.microsoft.com/en-us/aspnet/core/fundamentals/middleware/request-response`
- *ASP.NET Core health monitoring*: `https://docs.microsoft.com/en-us/dotnet/architecture/microservices/implement-resilient-applications/monitor-app-health`
- *"pattern-based using" and "using declarations"*: `https://docs.microsoft.com/en-us/dotnet/csharp/language-reference/proposals/csharp-8.0/using`
- *C# 8.0: Understanding Using Declarations*: `https://www.stevejgordon.co.uk/csharp-8-understanding-using-declarations`
- *String Interpolation in C#*: `https://docs.microsoft.com/en-us/dotnet/csharp/tutorials/string-interpolation`
- *TypeScript modules*: `https://www.typescriptlang.org/docs/handbook/modules.html`
- *Module Resolution*: `https://www.typescriptlang.org/docs/handbook/module-resolution.html`
- *Dependency Injection in ASP.NET Core*: `https://docs.microsoft.com/en-us/aspnet/core/fundamentals/dependency-injection`
- *Angular.io – Dependency Injection*: `https://angular.io/guide/dependency-injection`
- *Angular – Lifecycle Hooks*: `https://angular.io/guide/lifecycle-hooks`
- *ReactiveX Library – Observables*: `http://reactivex.io/rxjs/class/es6/Observable.js~Observable.html`
- *Angular.io – Observables guide*: `https://angular.io/guide/observables`
- *JavaScript – Import statement*: `https://developer.mozilla.org/en-US/docs/Web/JavaScript/Reference/Statements/import`
- *JavaScript – Export statement*: `https://developer.mozilla.org/en-US/docs/Web/JavaScript/Reference/Statements/export`
- *Angular – HttpClient*: `https://angular.io/guide/http#httpclient`
- *Angular – NgModules*: `https://angular.io/guide/ngmodules`

- *Angular – NgModules and JavaScript modules*: `https://angular.io/guide/architecture-modules#ngmodules-and-javascript-modules`
- *Angular – Displaying Data*: `https://angular.io/guide/displaying-data`
- *Angular – Template Syntax*: `https://angular.io/guide/template-syntax`
- *Angular – Structural Directives*: `https://angular.io/guide/structural-directives`
- *CSS – Cascading Style Sheets*: `https://developer.mozilla.org/en-US/docs/Web/CSSs`

4

Data Model with Entity Framework Core

The `HealthCheck` sample app that we've been playing with since *Chapter 1, Getting Ready*, is working fine, yet it lacks some important features we would likely make use of in a typical web application; among the most important of them is the ability to read and write data from a **Database Management System** (**DBMS**) since this is an essential requirement for almost any web-related task: content management, knowledge sharing, instant communication, data storage and/or mining, tracking and statistics, user authentication, system logging, and so on.

Truth be told, even our `HealthCheck` app could definitely use some of these tasks: tracking the host statuses over time could be a nice feature; user authentication should be a must-have, especially if we plan to publicly release it to the web; system logging is always great to have; and so on. However, since we prefer to keep our projects as simple as possible, we're going to create a new one and grant some DBMS capabilities to it.

Here's what we're going to do in this chapter:

- **Create a brand-new .NET and Angular web application project** called *WorldCities*: a database of cities from all over the world
- **Choose a suitable data source** to fetch a reasonable amount of *real* data to play with
- **Define and implement a data model** using Entity Framework Core
- **Configure and deploy a DBMS engine** that will be used by our project
- **Create the database** using Entity Framework Core's Data Migrations feature
- **Implement a data seeding strategy** to load the data source to the database
- **Read and write data with .NET** using the **Object-Relational Mapping** (**ORM**) techniques provided by Entity Framework Core

Are you ready to get started?

Technical requirements

In this chapter, we're going to need all of the technical requirements that were listed in the previous chapters, plus the following external libraries:

- `Microsoft.EntityFrameworkCore` NuGet package
- `Microsoft.EntityFrameworkCore.Tools` NuGet package
- `Microsoft.EntityFrameworkCore.SqlServer` NuGet package
- **SQL Server 2019** (if we opt for the local SQL instance route)
- **MS Azure subscription** (if we opt for the cloud database hosting route)

As always, it's advisable to avoid installing these straight away. We're going to bring them in during this chapter so that we can contextualize their purpose within our project.

The code files for this chapter can be found at: `https://github.com/PacktPublishing/ASP.NET-Core-5-and-Angular/tree/main/Chapter_04`

The WorldCities web app

The first thing we're going to do is create a new .NET and Angular web application project. Remember what we did during the second part of *Chapter 1, Getting Ready*? We can either do the same (and make all of the relevant changes to the sample project that we made in *Chapter 2, Looking Around*) or take our existing `HealthCheck` project, copy it to another folder, rename all of the references to `HealthCheck` (source code *and* filesystem), and undo everything we did in *Chapter 2, Looking Around*, and *Chapter 3, Front-End and Back-End Interactions*.

Although both approaches are fine, the former option would arguably be more practical, not to mention that it's a great chance to put into practice what we've learned until now and ensure we've understood each relevant step.

Let's briefly recap what we need to do:

1. Create a new project with the `dotnet new angular -o WorldCities` command
2. Edit or delete the following .NET *back-end* files:
    - `Startup.cs` (edit – if we want to use our improved Cache-Control strategy)
    - `appsettings.json` (edit – for the Cache-Control production settings)
    - `appsettings.Development.json` (edit – for the Cache-Control dev settings)
    - `WeatherForecast.cs` (delete)
    - `/Controllers/WeatherForecastController.cs` (delete)
3. Edit or delete the following Angular *front-end* files (as we did in *Chapter 3, Front-End and Back-End Interactions*):
    - `/ClientApp/package.json` (edit)
    - `/ClientApp/src/app/app.module.ts` (edit)

- `/ClientApp/src/app/nav-menu/nav-menu.component.html` (edit)
- `/ClientApp/src/app/counter/` (delete – whole folder)
- `/ClientApp/src/app/fetch-data/` (delete – whole folder)

4. Perform the required code updates to update the Angular version featured in the Visual Studio template to the latest Angular version, such as removing the `ModuleMapLoaderModule` from the `app.server.module.ts` file (see *Chapter 2, Looking Around* for details)
5. Add the `AppRoutingModule` in a dedicated `app-routing.module.ts` file and update the `AppModule` accordingly (see *Chapter 3, Front-End and Back-End Interactions* for details)

> In the unlikely case that we choose to copy and paste the `HealthCheck` project, which we don't recommend, we would need to remove the `HealthChecks` middleware references from the `Startup.cs` file and the Angular components references within the various Angular configuration files. We would also have to delete the related .NET and Angular class files (`ICMPHealthCheck`, `CustomHealthCheckOptions`, the `/ClientApp/src/app/HealthCheck/` folder, and so on).
>
> As we can see, cloning a project would mean that we would have to perform a lot of undo and/or rename activities: this is precisely why starting from scratch is generally a better approach.

After making all these changes, we can check that everything is working by pressing *F5* and inspecting the outcome. If everything has been done properly, we should be able to see the following screen:

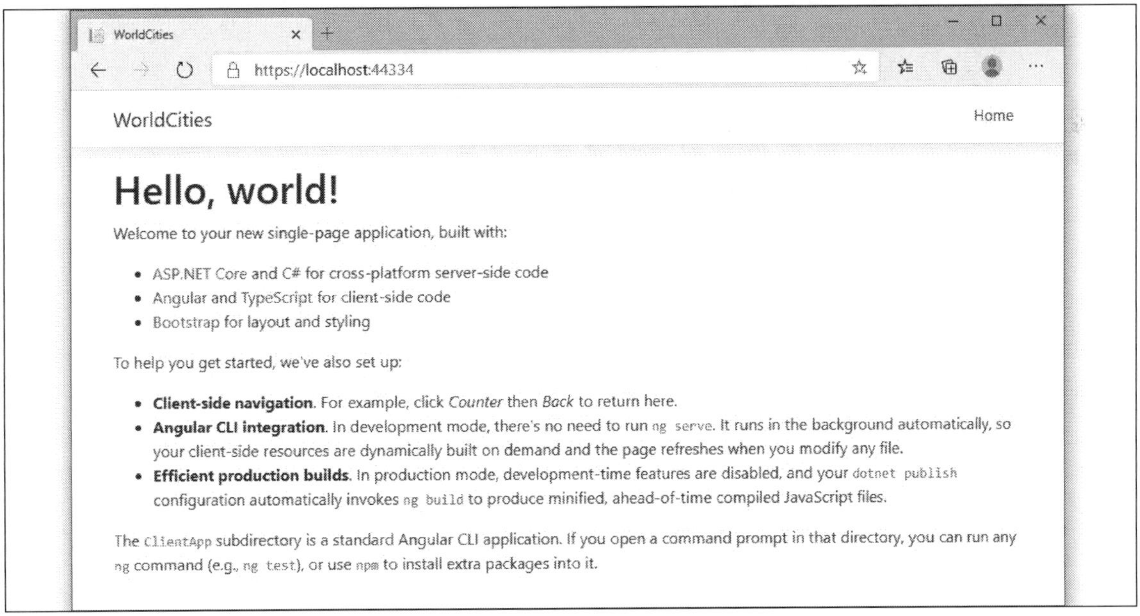
WorldCities
https://localhost:44334
WorldCities
Home
Hello, world!
Welcome to your new single-page application, built with:
ASP.NET Core and C# for cross-platform server-side code
Angular and TypeScript for client-side code
Bootstrap for layout and styling
To help you get started, we've also set up:
Client-side navigation. For example, click Counter then Back to return here.
Angular CLI integration. In development mode, there's no need to run ng serve. It runs in the background automatically, so your client-side resources are dynamically built on demand and the page refreshes when you modify any file.
Efficient production builds. In production mode, development-time features are disabled, and your dotnet publish configuration automatically invokes ng build to produce minified, ahead-of-time compiled JavaScript files.
The ClientApp subdirectory is a standard Angular CLI application. If you open a command prompt in that directory, you can run any ng command (e.g., ng test), or use npm to install extra packages into it.

Figure 4.1: Inspecting our WorldCities web app

> If we want to be sure that we've correctly applied all the preceding steps, we can compare our new `WorldCities` project against the one present in the GitHub repository (the `/Chapter_04/` folder).

Since we don't want to read that "Hello, world!" phrase for the rest of this book, let's spend 2 more minutes of our time slightly personalizing our new app's home page: while doing this, we'll take the chance to introduce some basic styling concepts that will help us to improve the look and feel of our Angular components using **Cascading Style Sheets** (**CSS**).

Styling and CSS basics

Open the web browser and go to `www.pexels.com`, a neat website that offers free stock photos and videos shared by talented creators from all over the world: type `world map` in the search bar and pick a suitable cover image, possibly with landscape proportions.

Here's a good one, taken from the following URL: `https://www.pexels.com/photo/close-up-of-globe-335393/`:

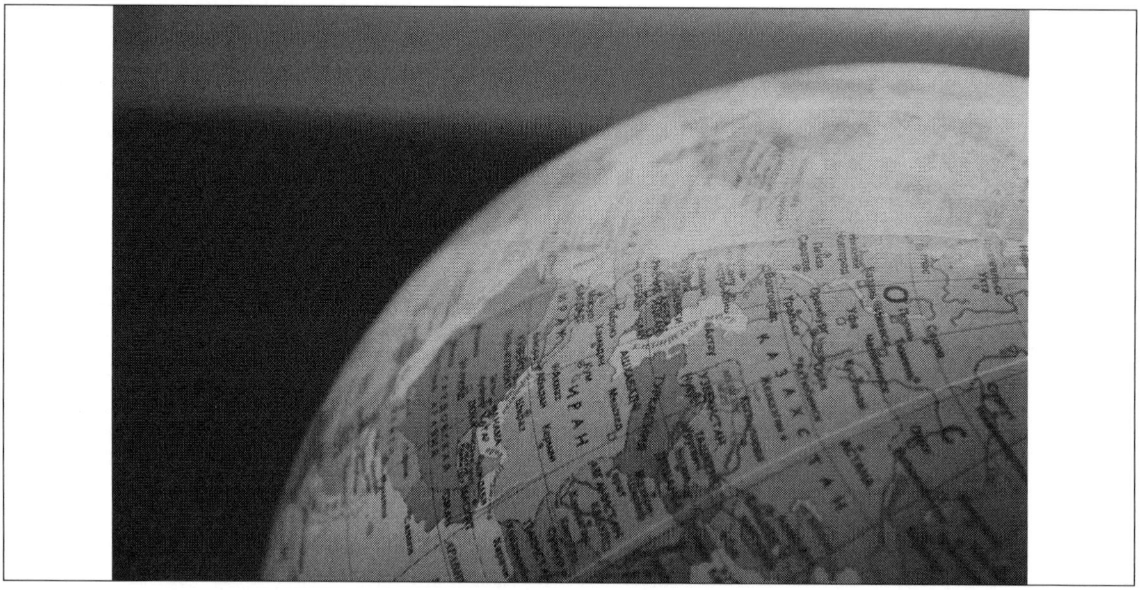

Figure 4.2: World map for our cover image

> Many thanks to **NastyaSensei** for making the preceding image available under Pexel's *free to use* license: `https://www.pexels.com/license/`
>
> You can check out more of her photos here: `https://www.pexels.com/@nastyasensei-66707`

Download the photo using the lowest possible resolution available (640x426) and save it in our **WorldCities** app using the following path and name:

```
/wwwroot/img/home.jpg
```

In order to do this, we'll have to create the `/img/` folder, because it isn't there yet.

Now that we have our own home cover image, let's update the home view to show it in a proper way; open the `/ClientApp/src/app/home/home.component.html` file and change its contents in the following way:

```
<p>
  A sample web application to demonstrate
  how to interact with ASP.NET, Angular,
  Entity Framework Core and a SQL Database.
</p>

<img src="/img/home.jpg" alt="WorldCities"
     class="home-cover" />
```

As we can see from the preceding code, we plan to show our new image using an `<img>` element that also features a `class` attribute: this means that now we need to implement that `home-cover` CSS class using one of the styling component approaches supported by Angular.

As we know from *Chapter 3, Front-End and Back-End Interactions*, we could do that by either adding a `styles` property to the component's metadata by updating the `/ClientApp/src/app/home/home-component.ts` TypeScript file...

```
@Component({
  selector: 'app-home',
  templateUrl: './home.component.html',
  styles: ['.home-cover { display:block; margin:auto; max-width:100%; }']
})
```

... or we could create a separate CSS file, implement the class there, and then reference it from within the component using the `styleUrls` property. We've also learned that this latter approach is arguably better, as it will allow us to separate the HTML structure from the CSS styling without messing up the component code: let's do this.

From **Solution Explorer**, right-click on the `/ClientApp/src/app/home/` folder and add a new `home.component.css` file. Once done, fill its contents with the following code:

```
.home-cover {
  display:block;
  margin: auto;
  max-width:100%;
}
```

Right after saving the new file, add a reference to it within the component's `/ClientApp/src/app/home/home-component.ts` file in the following way:

```
@Component({
  selector: 'app-home',
  templateUrl: './home.component.html',
  styleUrls: ['./home.component.css']
})
```

Now that we've implemented the new CSS file, let's look at the style sheet rules that we've put in the `home-cover` class: as we can see, we've applied some minimal CSS styling to center the image and make it automatically resize so that its base width (640 px) won't be a hindrance for mobile phones.

Let's now press *F5* and see what our new home view looks like:

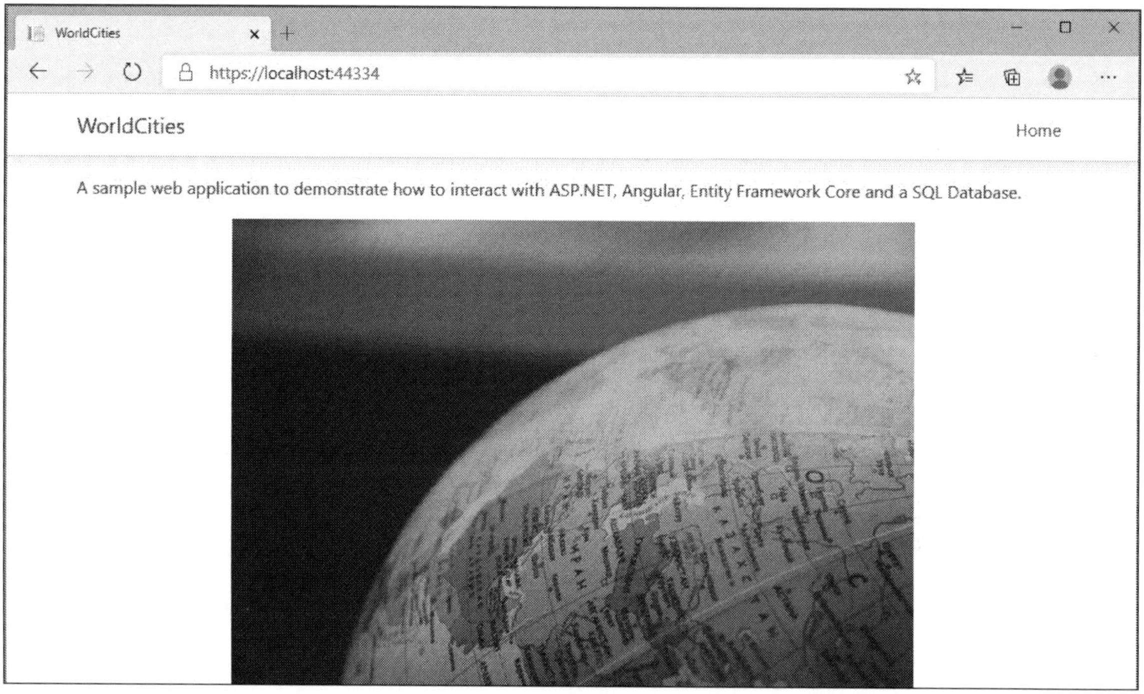

Figure 4.3: Inspecting our cover image

We will never win an award for this layout, but that's OK for our purposes.

If we reduce our browser width to the minimum amount, we can also see how it would look on mobile devices:

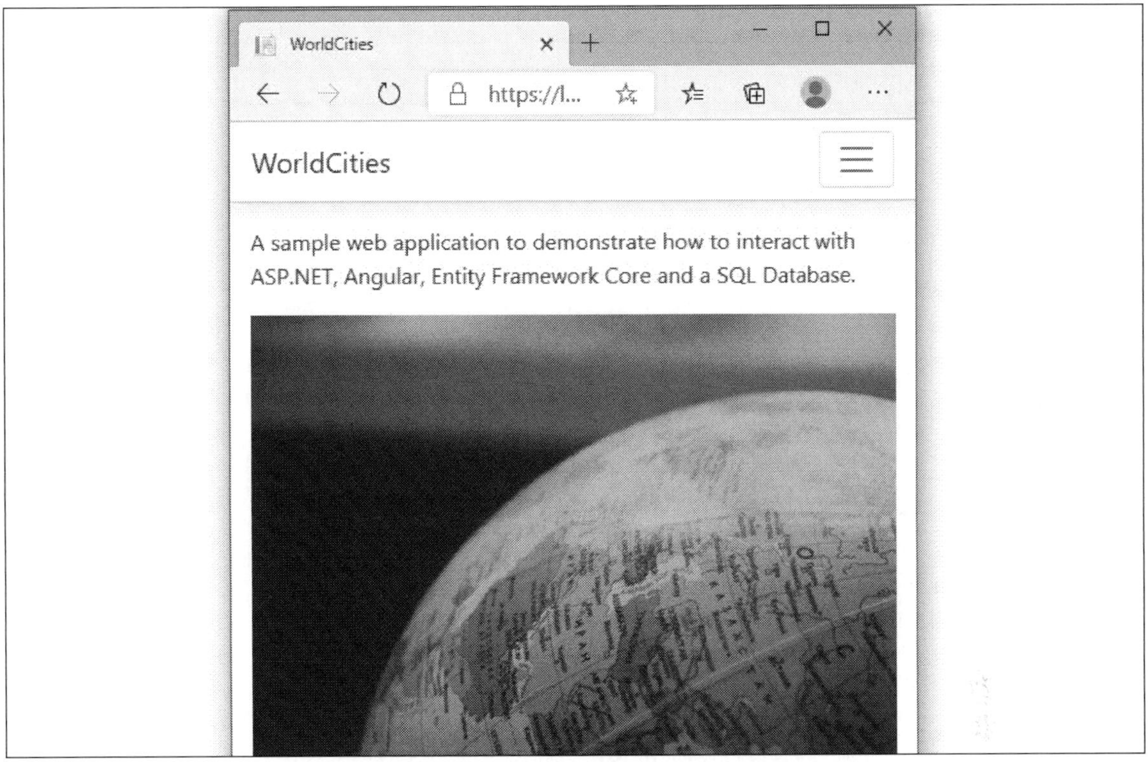

Figure 4.4: Mobile devices view of our cover page

Not that bad, is it?

That's about it: now we have a brand-new .NET and Angular web application to play with. We just need a data source and a data model that can be accessed through a *back-end Web API* to retrieve some data from: in other words, a data server.

Reasons to use a data server

Before we move on, it would be wise to spend a couple of minutes answering the following question: *do we really need a real data server?* Can't we just emulate one somehow? We're only running code samples, after all.

As a matter of fact, we could definitely avoid doing that and skip this entire chapter: Angular provides a neat **in-memory Web API** package that replaces the `HttpClient` module's `HttpBackend` and emulates **CRUD** operations over a RESTful API; the emulation is performed by intercepting the Angular HTTP requests and redirecting them to an in-memory data store under our control.

This package is great and works really well for most test case scenarios, such as the following:

- To simulate operations against data collections that haven't been implemented on our dev/test server
- To write unit test apps that read and write data without having to intercept multiple HTTP calls and manufacturing sequences of responses
- To perform end-to-end tests without messing with the real database, which is great for **Continuous Integration** (CI) builds

The *in-memory* Web API service works so well that the entire Angular documentation at `https://angular.io/` relies upon it. However, we're not going to use it for now, for a simple (and rather obvious) reason: this book's focus is not on Angular, but the **client/server interoperability between Angular and .NET**; for that very reason, developing a *real* Web API and connecting it to a real data source through a real data model is part of the game.

We don't want to simulate the behavior of a RESTful *back-end* because we need to understand what's going on there and how to implement it properly: we want to implement it, along with the DBMS that will host and provide the data.

That's precisely what we're going to do, starting from the next section.

> Those who want to get additional information about the Angular in-memory Web API service can visit the `in-memory-web-api` GitHub project page at: `https://github.com/angular/in-memory-web-api/`

The data source

What kind of data will our *WorldCities* web application need? We already know the answer: a database of cities from all over the world. Does such a repository even exist yet?

As a matter of fact, there are several alternatives we can use to populate our database and then make it available to our end users.

The following is the free world cities database by DSpace-CRIS:

- **URL**: `https://dspace-cris.4science.it/handle/123456789/31`
- **Format**: CSV
- **License**: Free to use

The following is GeoDataSource's world cities database (free edition):

- **URL**: `http://www.geodatasource.com/world-cities-database/free`
- **Format**: CSV
- **License**: Free to use (registration required)

The following is the world cities database by simplemaps.com:

- **URL**: `https://simplemaps.com/data/world-cities`
- **Format**: CSV, XLSX
- **License**: Free to use (CC BY 4.0, `https://creativecommons.org/licenses/by/4.0/`)

All of these alternatives are good enough to suit our needs: we'll go with simplemaps.com since it requires no registration and provides a human-readable spreadsheet format.

Open your favorite browser, type in or copy the above URL, and look for the **Basic** column of the **World Cities Database** section:

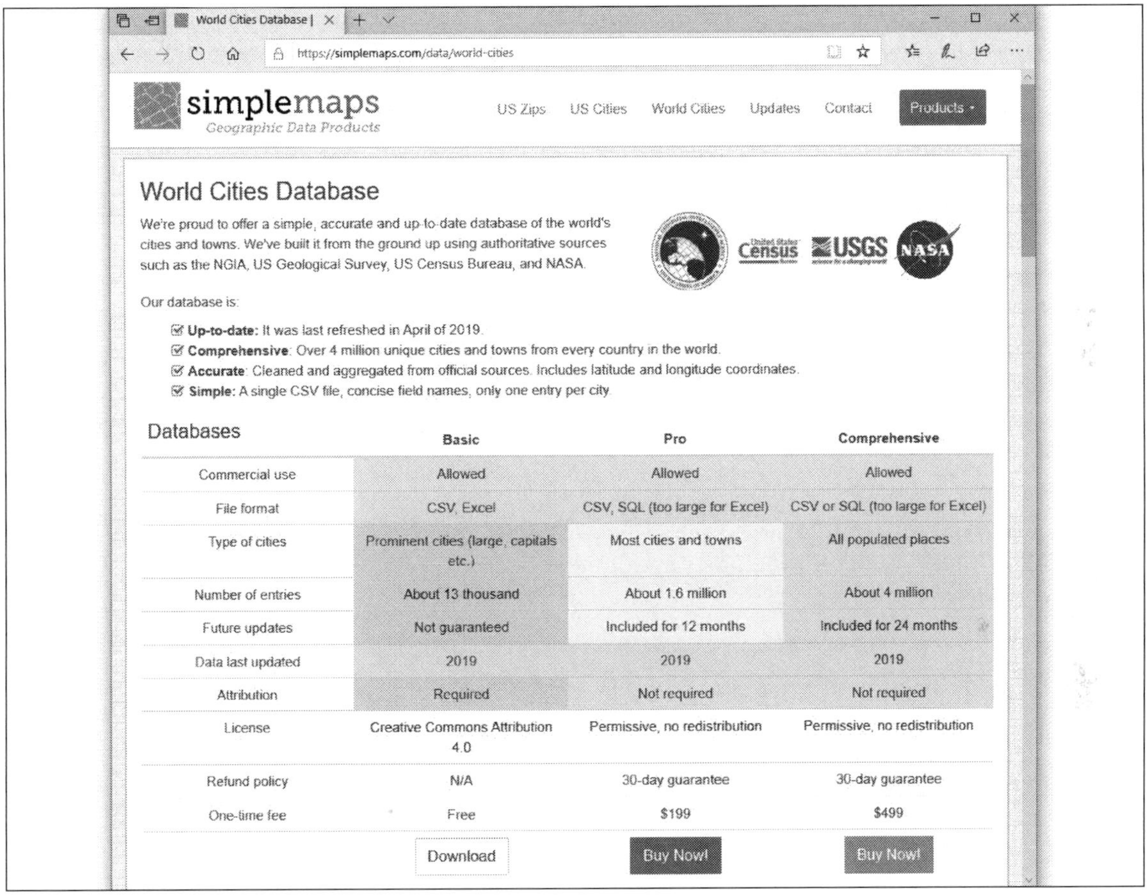

Figure 4.5: Downloading a world cities database from simplemaps.com

Click the **Download** button to retrieve the (huge) ZIP file containing both the `.csv` and `.xlsx` files and save it somewhere. That's it for now; we'll deal with these later on.

Starting with the next section, we'll start the building process of our data model: it's going to be a long, but also very rewarding, journey.

The data model

Now that we have our raw data source, we need to find a way to make it available to our web application so that our users will be able to retrieve (and maybe alter) the actual data.

For the sake of simplicity, we won't waste our precious time by introducing the whole data model concept, as well as the various meanings of these two words. Those of you who are experienced, as well as seasoned developers, will probably be aware of all of the relevant stuff. We'll just say that when we are talking about a data model, we don't mean anything more or anything less than a lightweight, definitely typed set of entity classes representing persistent, code-driven data structures that we can use as resources within our Web API code.

The word persistent has been used for a reason; we want our data structure to be stored in a database. That's rather obvious for any application based on data. The brand-new web application we're about to create won't be an exception since we want it to act as a collection—or a repository—of records so that we can read, create, delete, and/or modify according to our needs.

As we can easily guess, all of these tasks will be performed by some *back-end* business logic (.NET controllers) that's triggered by a *front-end* UI (Angular components).

Introducing Entity Framework Core

We will create our database with the help of **Entity Framework Core** (also known as **EF Core**), the well-known, open source **object relational mapper** (**ORM**) for **ADO.NET** that's developed by Microsoft. The reasons for such a choice are as follows:

- Seamless integration with the Visual Studio IDE
- A conceptual model based upon entity classes (**Entity Data Model** (**EDM**)), which will allow us to work with data using domain-specific objects without the need to write data-access code, which is precisely what we're looking for
- Easy to deploy, use, and maintain in development and production phases
- Compatible with all of the major open source and commercial SQL engines, including **MSSQL**, **SQLite**, **Azure Cosmos DB**, **PostgreSQL**, **MySQL/MariaDB**, **MyCAT**, **Firebird**, **Db2/Informix**, **Oracle DB**, and more, thanks to the official and/or third-party providers and/or connectors available via NuGet.

> It's worth mentioning that **Entity Framework Core** was previously known as **Entity Framework 7** until its latest RC release. The name change follows the ASP.NET 5/ASP.NET Core perspective switch we already talked about as it also emphasizes the Entity Framework Core major rewrite/redesign if we compare it to the previous installments.

You might be wondering why we're choosing to adopt a SQL-based approach instead of going for a NoSQL alternative; there are many good NoSQL products such as MongoDB, RavenDB, and CouchDB that happen to have a C# connector library. What about using one of them instead?

The answer is rather simple: despite being available as third-party providers, they haven't been included in the official **Entity Framework Core Database provider list** (see the link in the following information box). For that very reason, we're going to stick to the relational database, which may also be a more convenient approach for the simple database schemas we're going to design within this book.

> For those who want to know more about the upcoming release and/or feel bold enough to use it anyway—maybe with a NoSQL DB as well—we strongly suggest that you take a look at the following links and docs:
>
> **Project roadmap**: `https://github.com/aspnet/EntityFramework/wiki/Roadmap`
>
> **Source code on GitHub**: `https://github.com/aspnet/EntityFramework`
>
> **Official documentation**: `https://docs.efproject.net/en/latest/`
>
> **Official Entity Framework Core Database provider list**: `https://docs.microsoft.com/en-us/ef/core/providers/?tabs=dotnet-core-cli`

Installing Entity Framework Core

To install Entity Framework Core, we need to add the relevant packages to the dependencies section of our project file. We can easily do this using the visual GUI in the following way:

- Right-click on the `WorldCities` project
- Select **Manage NuGet Packages**
- Ensure that the **Package source** drop-down list is set to **All**
- Go to the **Browse** tab and search for the packages containing the `Microsoft.EntityFrameworkCore` keyword:

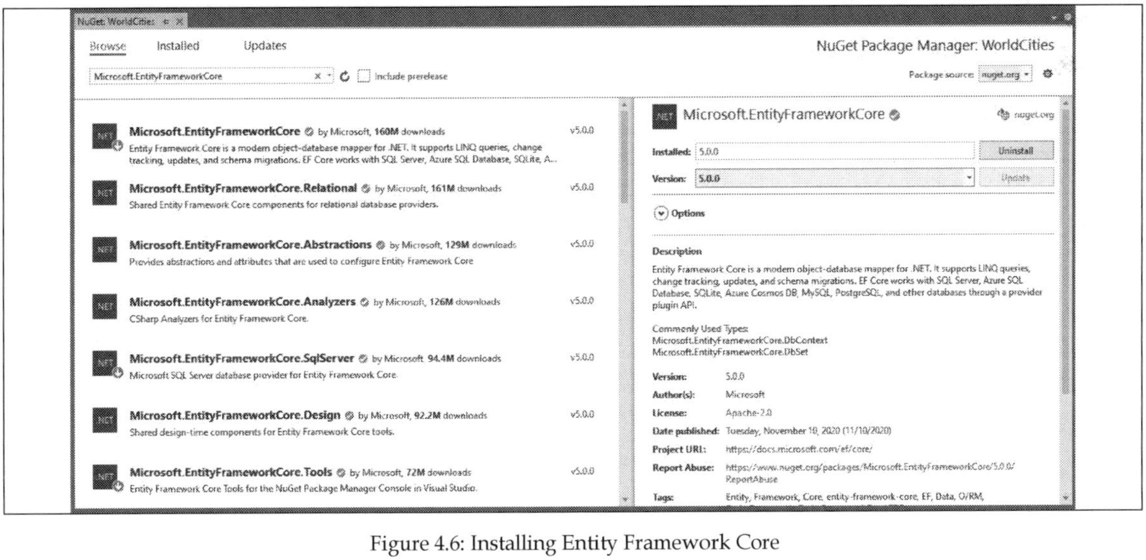

Figure 4.6: Installing Entity Framework Core

Once there, select and install the following packages (the latest at the time of writing):

- `Microsoft.EntityFrameworkCore` version 5.0.0
- `Microsoft.EntityFrameworkCore.Tools` version 5.0.0
- `Microsoft.EntityFrameworkCore.SqlServer` version 5.0.0

All of these packages will also bring some required dependencies, which we'll need to install as well:

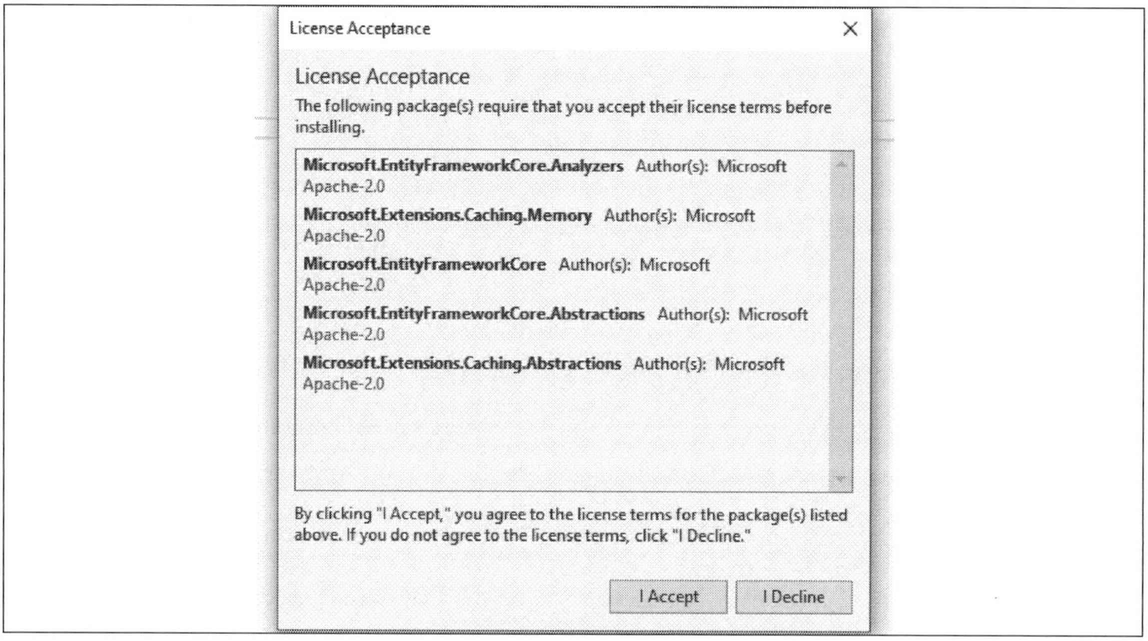

Figure 4.7: Accepting the license

If we prefer to do this using the NuGet package manager command line, we can input the following:

```
PM> Install-Package Microsoft.EntityFrameworkCore -Version 5.0.0
PM> Install-Package Microsoft.EntityFrameworkCore.Tools -Version 5.0.0
PM> Install-Package Microsoft.EntityFrameworkCore.SqlServer -Version 5.0.0
```

It's worth noting that the version number, which is the one that's the most recent at the time of writing, might be subject to change: be sure to triple-check it in this book's GitHub repository as well!

The SQL Server Data Provider

Among the installed namespaces, it's worth noting the presence of `Microsoft.EntityFrameworkCore.SqlServer`, which is the **Microsoft SQL Database Provider** for Entity Framework Core. This highly versatile connector provides an interface for the whole Microsoft SQL Server database family, including the latest SQL Server 2019.

DBMS licensing models

Despite having a rather expensive (to say the least) licensing model, there are at least three Microsoft SQL editions that can be used for free, as long as certain requirements are met:

- **Evaluation Edition** is free, but comes with no production use rights, meaning that we can only use it on development servers. Additionally, it can only be used for 180 days. After that, we'll have to either buy a license or uninstall it (and migrate to a different edition).
- **Developer Edition** is also free and comes with no production use rights. However, it can be used without limitations, providing that we only use it for development and/or testing scenarios.
- **Express Edition** is free and can be used in any environment, meaning that we can use it on development and production servers. However, it has some major performance and size limitations that could hinder the performance of a complex and/or high-traffic web application.

> For additional information regarding the various SQL Server editions, including the commercial ones that do require a paid licensing model, check out the following links:
>
> `https://www.microsoft.com/en-us/sql-server/sql-server-2019`
>
> `https://www.microsoft.com/en-us/sql-server/sql-server-2019-comparison`

As we can easily see, both the **Developer** and **Express** editions can be a great deal for small web applications like those we're playing with in this book.

What about Linux?

SQL Server 2019 is also available for Linux and officially supported for the following distributions:

- **Red Hat Enterprise Linux** (RHEL)
- **SUSE Enterprise Server**
- **Ubuntu**

Other than that, it can also be set to run on Docker and even provisioned as a virtual machine on Azure, which can often be a great alternative if we don't want to install a local DMBS instance and save our precious hardware resources.

As for the licensing model, all SQL Server products are licensed the same way for all of these environments: this basically means that we can use our license (including the free ones) on the platform of our choice.

SQL Server alternatives

If you don't feel like using Microsoft SQL Server, you're 100% free to pick another DBMS engine, such as MySQL, PostgreSQL, or any other product, as long as it has some kind of Entity Framework Core official (or third-party) support.

Should we make this decision now? This entirely depends on the data modeling approach we want to adopt; for the time being, and for the sake of simplicity, we're going to stick to the Microsoft SQL Server family, which allows us to install a decent DBMS for free on either our local machine (development and/or production) or Azure (thanks to its €200 cost and 12-month free trial): don't worry about this for now—we'll get there later on.

Data modeling approaches

Now that we have Entity Framework Core installed and we know—more or less—which DBMS we are going to use, we have to choose between one of the two available approaches to model the data structure: **Code-First** or **Database-First**. Each one comes with its fair number of advantages and disadvantages, as those of you with experience and those of you who are seasoned .NET developers will almost certainly know. Although we won't dig too much into these, it would be useful to briefly summarize each before making a choice.

Code-First

This is Entity Framework's flagship approach since version 4 and also the recommended one: an elegant, highly efficient data model development workflow. The appeal of this approach can be easily found in its premise; the Code-First approach allows developers to define model objects using only standard classes, without the need for any design tool, XML mapping files, or cumbersome piles of autogenerated code.

To summarize, we can say that going Code-First means *writing the data model entity classes we'll be using within our project and letting Entity Framework generate the database accordingly*:

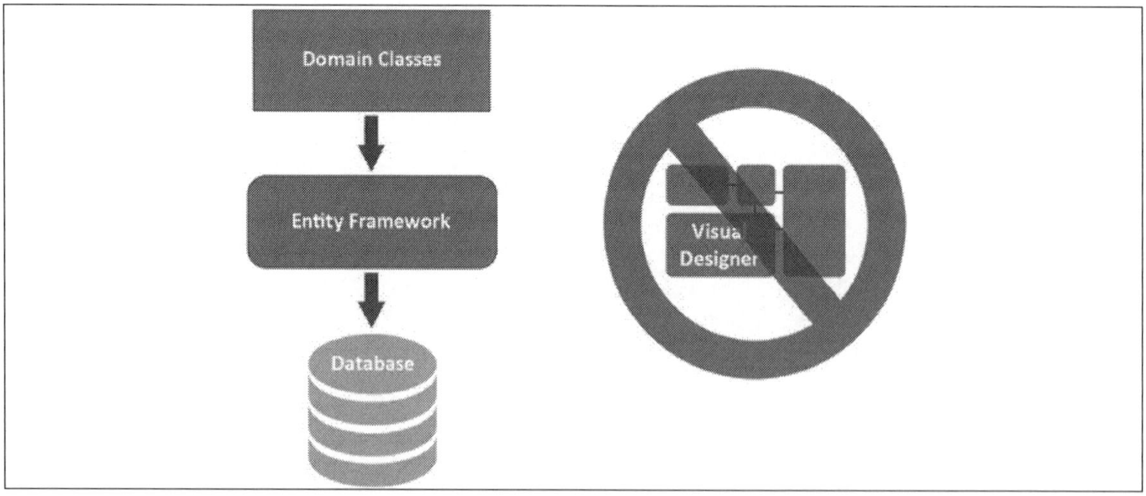

Figure 4.8: The Code-First approach

The pros and cons are explained in the following sections.

Pros

- There is no need for diagrams and visual tools whatsoever, which can be great for small-to-medium-sized projects as it will save a lot of time.
- It has a fluent code API that allows the developer to follow a convention-over-configuration approach so that it can handle the most common scenarios, while also giving them the chance to switch to a custom, attribute-based implementation that overrides the need to customize the database mapping.

Cons

- Good knowledge of C# and updated EF conventions is required.
- Maintaining the database can often be tricky, as well as handling updates without suffering data loss. Migration support, which was added in 4.3 to overcome this issue and has been continuously updated since then, greatly mitigates the problem although it also affects the learning curve in a negative way.

Database-First

If we either have an existing database already or don't mind building it beforehand, we could consider an alternative approach that goes the other way around: instead of letting EF Core automatically build the database using the SQL commands generated from the model objects, we generate these objects from an existing database using the `dotnet ef` command-line tool. This code generation technique is known as *model scaffolding* and relies upon the following command:

```
> dotnet ef dbcontext scaffold
```

For additional info about EF model scaffolding and Database-First, visit the following URL:

`https://docs.microsoft.com/en-us/ef/core/miscellaneous/cli/dotnet#dotnet-ef-dbcontext-scaffold`

We can summarize this by saying that going Database-First will mean *building the database and letting Entity Framework create/update the rest accordingly*:

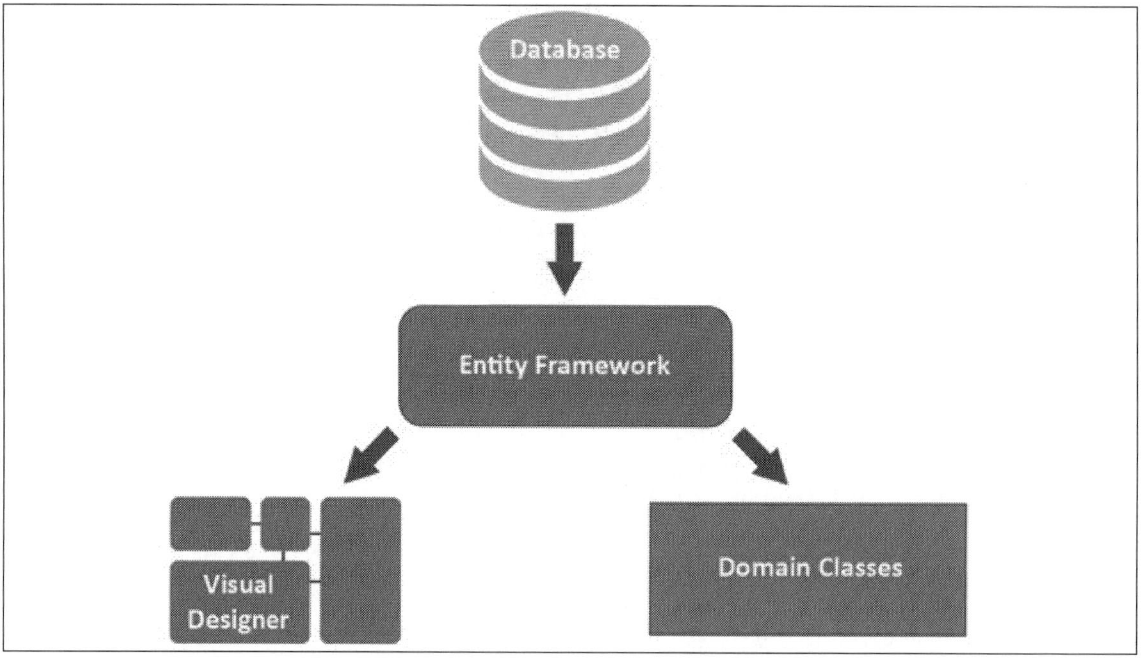

Figure 4.9: The Database-First approach

The pros and cons are explained in the following sections.

Pros

- If we have an already-existing database in place, this will probably be the way to go as it will spare us the need to recreate it.
- The risk of data loss will be kept to a minimum because any structural change or database model update will always be performed on the database itself.

Cons

- Manually updating the database can be tricky if we're dealing with clusters, multiple instances, or several development/testing/production environments as we will have to manually keep them in sync instead of relying on code-driven updates/migrations or autogenerated SQL scripts.
- We will have less control over the auto-generated model classes, therefore managing associations, foreign keys and constraints will be more difficult.

Making a choice

By taking the advantages and disadvantages of these two options into account, there is no such thing as an overall *better* or *best* approach; conversely, we can say that each project scenario will likely have a best-suited approach. That said, considering that Code-First is the recommended approach for Entity Framework Core, especially for new applications and/or whenever the database doesn't exist yet, we have little to no doubt that adopting it will be our best choice.

> Truth be told, the Database-First approach has become less and less popular in recent years, and the framework support for this technique dropped as well: as a matter of fact, such an approach is rarely used nowadays, unless there's an already-existing database structure that can't be easily updated or needs to be preserved the way it already is because other apps and/or services are already accessing it.

Now that we've made our choice, we'll need to create some entities and find a suitable DBMS to store our data: this is precisely what we're going to do in the following sections.

Creating the entities

Now that we have a data source, we can leverage one of the major advantages of the *Code-First* approach we talked about earlier and start writing our **entity** classes early on, without worrying too much about what database engine we'll eventually use.

> Truth be told, we already know something about what we'll eventually use. We won't be adopting a NoSQL solution as they aren't officially supported by Entity Framework Core yet; we also don't want to commit ourselves to purchasing expensive license plans, so the commercial editions of Oracle and SQL Server are probably out of the picture as well.
>
> This leaves us with relatively few choices: SQL Server Developer (or Express) Edition, MySQL/MariaDB, the community edition of Oracle (known as Oracle XE), or other less well-known solutions such as PostgreSQL. Furthermore, we are still not 100% sure about installing a local DBMS instance on our development machine (and/or on our production server) or relying on a cloud-hosted solution such as Azure.
>
> That being said, adopting Code-First will give us the chance to postpone the call until our data model is ready.

However, to create the entity classes, we need to know what kind of data they are going to contain and how to structure it: that strongly depends on the data source and the database tables that we eventually want to create using Code-First.

In the following sections, we're going to learn how we can deal with these tasks.

Defining the entities

In Entity Framework Core, as well as in most ORM frameworks, an **entity** is a class that maps to a given database table. The main purpose of entities is to make us able to work with data in an object-oriented fashion while using strongly-typed properties to access table columns (and data relations) for each row. We're going to use entities to fetch data from the database and serialize them to JSON for the *front-end*. We will also do the opposite, that is, deserializing them back whenever the *front-end* issues POST or PUT requests that will require the back-end to perform some permanent changes to the database, such as adding new rows or updating existing ones.

If we try to enlarge our focus and look at the general picture, we will be able to see how the entities play a central role among the whole bi-directional data flow between the DBMS, the *back-end*, and the *front-end* parts of our web application.

To understand such a concept, let's take a look at the following diagram:

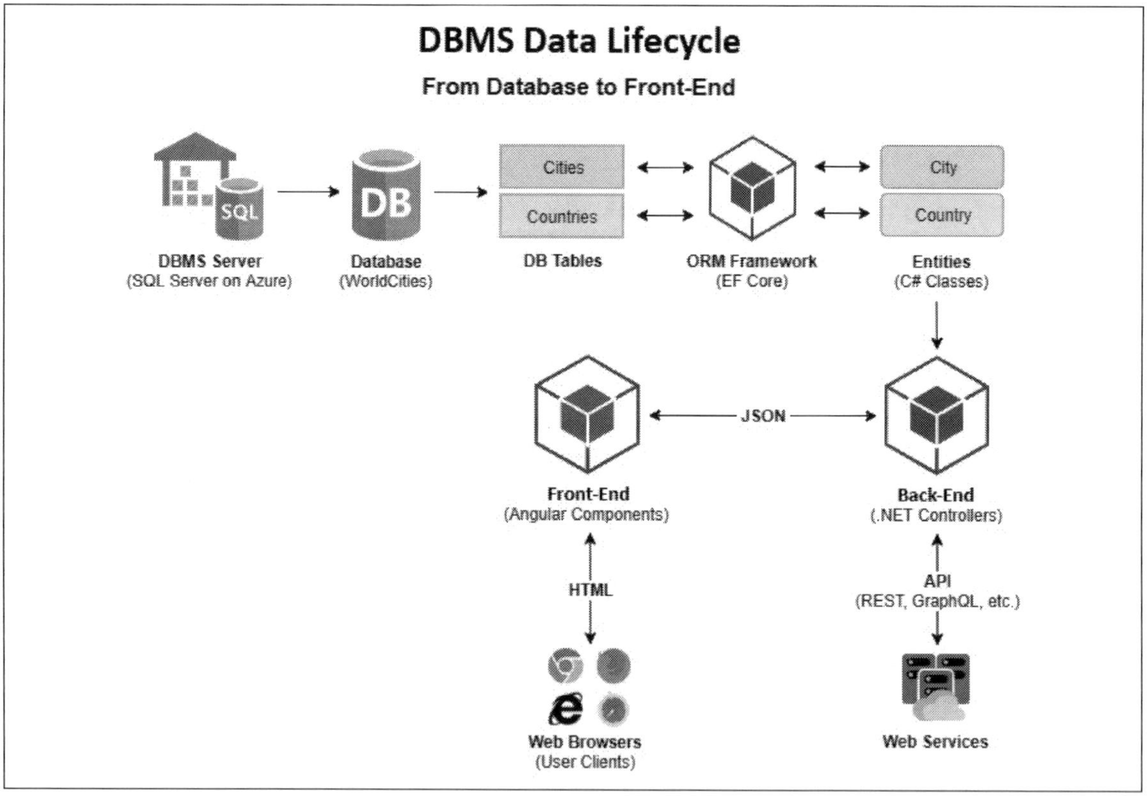

Figure 4.10: The DBMS data lifecycle

As we can clearly see, the main purpose of **Entity Framework Core** is to map the database tables to entity classes: that's precisely what we need to do now.

Unzip the world cities compressed file we downloaded a while ago and open the `worldcities.xlsx` file: if you don't have MS Excel, you can import it on Google Drive using Google Sheets, as shown at the following URL: `http://bit.ly/worldcities-xlsx`

> Right after importing it, I also took the chance to make some small readability improvements to that file: bolding column names, resizing the columns, changing the background color and freezing on the first row, and so on.

If we open the preceding URL, we will see what the imported spreadsheet looks like:

	A	B	C	D	E	F	G	H	I	J	K
1	**city**	**city_ascii**	**lat**	**lng**	**country**	**iso2**	**iso3**	**admin_name**	**capital**	**population**	**id**
2	Malishevë	Malisheve	42.4822	20.7458	Kosovo	XK	XKS	Malishevë	admin		1901597212
3	Prizren	Prizren	42.2139	20.7397	Kosovo	XK	XKS	Prizren	admin		1901360309
4	Zubin Potok	Zubin Potok	42.9144	20.6897	Kosovo	XK	XKS	Zubin Potok	admin		1901608808
5	Kamenicë	Kamenice	42.5781	21.5803	Kosovo	XK	XKS	Kamenicë	admin		1901851592
6	Viti	Viti	42.3214	21.3583	Kosovo	XK	XKS	Viti	admin		1901328795
7	Shtërpcë	Shterpce	42.2394	21.0272	Kosovo	XK	XKS	Shtërpcë	admin		1901828239
8	Shtime	Shtime	42.4331	21.0397	Kosovo	XK	XKS	Shtime	admin		1901598505
9	Vushtrri	Vushtrri	42.8231	20.9675	Kosovo	XK	XKS	Vushtrri	admin		1901107642
10	Dragash	Dragash	42.0265	20.6533	Kosovo	XK	XKS	Dragash	admin		1901112530
11	Podujevë	Podujeve	42.9111	21.1899	Kosovo	XK	XKS	Podujevë	admin		1901550082
12	Fushë Kosovë	Fushe Kosove	42.6639	21.0961	Kosovo	XK	XKS	Fushë Kosovë	admin		1901134407
13	Kaçanik	Kacanik	42.2319	21.2594	Kosovo	XK	XKS	Kaçanik	admin		1901200321
14	Klinë	Kline	42.6217	20.5778	Kosovo	XK	XKS	Klinë	admin		1901230162
15	Leposaviq	Leposaviq	43.1039	20.8028	Kosovo	XK	XKS	Leposaviq	admin		1901974597
16	Pejë	Peje	42.66	20.2922	Kosovo	XK	XKS	Pejë	admin		1901339694
17	Rahovec	Rahovec	42.3994	20.6547	Kosovo	XK	XKS	Rahovec	admin		1901336358
18	Gjilan	Gjilan	42.4689	21.4633	Kosovo	XK	XKS	Gjilan	admin		1901235642
19	Lipjan	Lipjan	42.5217	21.1258	Kosovo	XK	XKS	Lipjan	admin		1901682048
20	Obiliq	Obiliq	42.6869	21.0703	Kosovo	XK	XKS	Obiliq	admin		1901102771
21	Gjakovë	Gjakove	42.3803	20.4308	Kosovo	XK	XKS	Gjakovë	admin		1901089874
22	Pristina	Pristina	42.6666	21.1724	Kosovo	XK	XKS	Prishtinë	primary		1901760068

Figure 4.11: Inspecting the worldcities.xlsx file

By looking at the spreadsheet headers, we can infer at least two database tables we're going to need:

- **Cities**: For columns *A*, *B*, *C*, and *D* (and arguably *K*, if we want to keep those unique IDs)
- **Countries**: For columns *E*, *F*, and *G*

This seems to be the most convenient choice in terms of common sense. Alternatively, we could put everything into a single `Cities` table, but we're going to have a lot of redundant content, which is something we would arguably want to avoid.

If we're going to deal with two database tables, this means that we need two entities to map them on and to create them in the first place, since we plan to adopt the Code-First approach.

The City entity

Let's start with the `City` entity.

From the project's **Solution Explorer**, do the following:

1. Create a new `/Data/` folder at the root level of the `WorldCities` project; this will be where all of our Entity Framework-related classes will reside.

2. Create a `/Data/Models/` folder.
3. Add a new **ASP.NET** | **Code** | **Class** file, name it `City.cs`, and replace the sample code with the following:

```
using System;
using System.Collections.Generic;
using System.ComponentModel.DataAnnotations;
using System.ComponentModel.DataAnnotations.Schema;
using System.Linq;
using System.Threading.Tasks;

namespace WorldCities.Data.Models
{
    public class City
    {
        #region Constructor
        public City()
        {

        }
        #endregion

        #region Properties
        /// <summary>
        /// The unique id and primary key for this City
        /// </summary>
        [Key]
        [Required]
        public int Id { get; set; }

        /// <summary>
        /// City name (in UTF8 format)
        /// </summary>
        public string Name { get; set; }

        /// <summary>
        /// City name (in ASCII format)
        /// </summary>
        public string Name_ASCII { get; set; }

        /// <summary>
        /// City Latitude
        /// </summary>
        public decimal Lat { get; set; }
```

```
        /// <summary>
        /// City Longitude
        /// </summary>
        public decimal Lon { get; set; }
        #endregion

        /// <summary>
        /// Country Id (foreign key)
        /// </summary>
        public int CountryId { get; set; }
    }
}
```

As we can see, we added a dedicated property for each of the spreadsheet columns we identified early on; we also included a `CountryId` property, which we're going to use to map the *foreign key* for the `Country` related to the city (more on that later on). We also tried to improve the overall readability of the entity class source code by providing each property with some useful comments that will definitely help us to remember what they are meant for.

Last but not least, it's worth noting that we took the chance to decorate our entity class using some **Data Annotations** attributes as they are the most convenient way to override the default Code-First conventions. More specifically, we used the following annotations:

- `[Required]`: This defines the property as a *required* (non-nullable) field.
- `[Key]`: This means that the property hosts the *primary key* of the database table.

Additional data annotations attributes will be added later on.

Those of you who have some experience with Entity Framework (and relational databases) will most likely understand what those data annotations are there for: they are a convenient way to instruct Entity Framework on how to properly build our database when using the Code-First approach. There's nothing complex here; we're just telling Entity Framework that the database columns that were created to host these properties should be set as required and that the primary key should be bound in a one-to-many relationship to other *foreign* columns in different tables.

In order to use the data annotations, we have to add a reference to one or both of the following namespaces, depending on the attributes we're going to use:

```
System.ComponentModel.DataAnnotations
System.ComponentModel.DataAnnotations.Schema
```

If we take a look at the preceding code, we will see that both of these namespaces have been referenced with a `using` statement for convenience, even if the attributes we've used so far (`[Key]` and `[Required]`) only require the first one.

> We'll definitely talk more about Data Annotations in this chapter later on. If you want to find out more about Data Annotations in Entity Framework Core, we strongly suggest reading the official documentation, which can be found at the following URL: `https://docs.microsoft.com/en-us/ef/core/modeling/`

The Country entity

The next entity will be the one for identifying the countries, which will have a one-to-many relationship with `Cities`.

> This is hardly a surprise: we're definitely going to expect a single `Country` for each `City` and multiple `Cities` for each given `Country`: this is what one-to-many relationships are for.

Right-click on the `/Data/Models/` folder, add a `Country.cs` class file, and fill it with the following code:

```
using System;
using System.Collections.Generic;
using System.ComponentModel.DataAnnotations;
using System.ComponentModel.DataAnnotations.Schema;
using System.Linq;
using System.Threading.Tasks;

namespace WorldCities.Data.Models
{
    public class Country
    {
        #region Constructor
        public Country()
        {

        }
        #endregion

        #region Properties
        /// <summary>
        /// The unique id and primary key for this Country
        /// </summary>
        [Key]
        [Required]
        public int Id { get; set; }
```

```
        /// <summary>
        /// Country name (in UTF8 format)
        /// </summary>
        public string Name { get; set; }

        /// <summary>
        /// Country code (in ISO 3166-1 ALPHA-2 format)
        /// </summary>
        public string ISO2 { get; set; }

        /// <summary>
        /// Country code (in ISO 3166-1 ALPHA-3 format)
        /// </summary>
        public string ISO3 { get; set; }
        #endregion
    }
}
```

Again, there's a property for each spreadsheet column with the relevant Data Annotations and comments.

> **ISO 3166** is a standard that was published by the **International Organization for Standardization** (**ISO**) that's used to define unique codes for the names of countries, dependent territories, provinces, and states. For additional information, check out the following URLs:
>
> `https://en.wikipedia.org/wiki/ISO_3166`
>
> `https://www.iso.org/iso-3166-country-codes.html`
>
> The part that describes the country codes is the first one (ISO 3166-1), which defines three possible formats: **ISO 3166-1 alpha-2** (two-letter country codes), **ISO 3166-1 alpha-3** (three-letter country codes), and **ISO 3166-1 numeric** (three-digit country codes). For additional information about the ISO 3166-1 ALPHA-2 and ISO 3166-1 ALPHA-3 formats, which are the ones that are used in our data source and therefore in this book, check out the following URLs:
>
> `https://en.wikipedia.org/wiki/ISO_3166-1_alpha-2`
>
> `https://en.wikipedia.org/wiki/ISO_3166-1_alpha-3`

Should we (still) use #regions?

If we look at the code samples of the two entity classes we've just added, we can see that we've used some `#region` directives: let's spend a minute talking about them.

As most C# developers already know, regions are preprocessor directives that let the developer specify a block of code that can be expanded or collapsed when using the outlining feature of the code editor.

> For additional info about C# regions and common usage samples, read this guide:
>
> `https://docs.microsoft.com/en-us/dotnet/csharp/language-reference/preprocessor-directives/preprocessor-region`

Regions were introduced with the first versions of C# and were praised during the language's early years because they were seen as a viable technique to improve the code readability, especially in long and complex classes. However, they can also lure the developer into adopting a number of bad practices, such as shoving "unoptimized" or repeating code to hide it from view instead of refactoring it; dividing a complex method (or class) into multiple "tasks" instead of splitting it into multiple methods (or classes); embedding redundant code instead of making it less redundant; and so on.

Since the potential disadvantages of regions vastly exceed their supposed advantages, regions are now considered a bad practice by most C# developers and their usage has declined. This opinion has been enforced by **StyleCop**, a great open-source static code analysis tool from Microsoft that checks C# code for conformance to the recommended coding styles and design guidelines, which summarizes its judgment regarding regions in its SA1124 rule:

> *TYPE: SA1124DoNotUseRegions*
>
> *CAUSE: The C# code contains a region.*
>
> *DESCRIPTION: A violation of this rule occurs whenever a region is placed anywhere within the code. In many editors, including Visual Studio, the region will appear collapsed by default, hiding the code within the region. It is generally a bad practice to hide code, as this can lead to bad decisions as the code is maintained over time.*
>
> *HOW TO FIX: To fix a violation of this rule, remove the region from the code.*

This kind of settles it: we should never use regions, period.

> Those who want to know more about the `#regions` debate within the C# developer community and the reasons why they are discouraged nowadays might enjoy reading this Stack Overflow thread, which pretty much summarizes it:
>
> `https://softwareengineering.stackexchange.com/questions/53086/are-regions-an-antipattern-or-code-smell`

Although I generally agree with this rule, I still think that using `#regions` to group together fields, properties, and so on can still be useful in some edge-case scenarios, such as code samples and tutorials (like the classes we're creating and reviewing in this book), because it allows us to distinguish between different parts of code: for example, we're going to use them to help the reader tell apart *standard properties* versus *navigation properties* within an entity type.

This is why in this book we're still using them here and there, even if we're fully aware that a good, StyleCop-compliant code won't need them—not even to group together fields, properties, private methods, constructors, and so on: at the same time, I also recommend not using them (or limiting their usage to a minimum amount) in your actual code.

Defining relationships

Now that we have built our main `City` and `Country` entity skeleton, we need to enforce the relationship we know exists between them. We want to be able to do stuff such as retrieve a `Country` and then browse all of its related `Cities`, possibly in a strongly typed fashion.

To do this, we have to add a couple of new entity-related properties, one for each entity class. More specifically, we will be adding the following:

- A `Country` property in our `City` entity class, which will contain a single country related to that city (the *parent*)
- A `Cities` property in our `Country` entity class, which will contain a collection of the cities related to that country (the *children*)

If we take a deeper look and try to visualize the relationship between those entities, we will be able to see how the former property identifies the *parent* (from each child perspective), while the latter will contain the *children* (from the parent perspective): such a pattern is precisely what we can expect for a *one-to-many relationship* like the one we're dealing with.

In the following sections, we'll learn how we can implement these two *navigation* properties.

Adding the Country property to the City entity class

Add the following code lines near the end of the file, near the end of the *Properties* region (new lines are highlighted):

```
using System.ComponentModel.DataAnnotations.Schema;

// ...existing code...

/// <summary>
/// Country Id (foreign key)
/// </summary>
[ForeignKey(nameof(Country))]
public int CountryId { get; set; }
#endregion

#region Navigation Properties
/// <summary>
/// The country related to this city.
```

```
/// </summary>
public virtual Country Country { get; set; }
#endregion

// ...existing code...
```

As we can see, other than adding the new `Country` property, we also decorated the already-existing `CountryId` property with a new `[ForeignKey(nameof(Country))]` Data Annotation. Thanks to that annotation, Entity Framework will know that such a property will host a primary key of a foreign table and that the `Country` navigation property will be used to host the *parent* entity.

> It's worth noting that the binding that's declared using that `[ForeignKey]` data annotation will also be formally enforced by creating a constraint, as long as the database engine supports such a feature.

It's also worth noting that we used `nameof(Country)` instead of a mere `"Country"` literal string: we did that to increase the type safety of our code, thus making it less prone to typing errors.

As we can see by looking at the first line of the preceding source code, in order to use the `[ForeignKey]` data annotation we have to add a reference to the `System.ComponentModel.DataAnnotations.Schema` namespace at the beginning of the class in case we didn't already.

Adding the Cities property to the Country entity class

Again, add the following at the end of the *Properties* region (the new lines are highlighted):

```
// ...existing code...

#region Navigation Properties
/// <summary>
/// A list containing all the cities related to this country.
/// </summary>
public virtual List<City> Cities { get; set; }
#endregion

// ...existing code...
```

That's it. As we can see, no *foreign key properties* have been defined for this entity since *one-to-many* relationships don't need them from the *parent* side: therefore, there's no need to add a `[ForeignKey]` data annotation and/or its required namespace.

Entity Framework Core loading pattern

Now that we have a `Cities` property in the `Country` entity and a corresponding `[ForeignKey]` data annotation in the `City` entity, you may be wondering how we can use these navigation properties to load the related entities. To put this another way: **how are we going to populate the Cities property within the Country entity whenever we need to?**

Such a question gives us the chance to spend a couple of minutes enumerating the three ORM patterns supported by Entity Framework Core to load these kinds of related data:

- **Eager loading**: The related data is loaded from the database as part of the initial query.
- **Explicit loading**: The related data is explicitly loaded from the database at a later time.
- **Lazy loading**: The related data is transparently loaded from the database when the entity navigation property is accessed for the first time. This is the most complex pattern among the three and might suffer some serious performance impacts when not implemented properly.

It's important to understand that, whenever we want to load an entity's *related data*, we need to activate (or implement) one of these patterns. This means that, in our specific scenario, our `Country` entity's `Cities` property will be set to `NULL` whenever we fetch one or more countries from the database, **unless we explicitly tell Entity Framework Core to load the cities as well**. This is a very important aspect to consider when dealing with Web APIs because it will definitely impact how our .NET *back-end* will serve their JSON structured data responses to our *front-end* Angular client.

To understand what we mean, let's take a look at a couple of examples.

The following is a standard Entity Framework Core query that's used to retrieve `Country` from a given `Id` with the EF Core default behavior (no loading pattern defined or implemented):

```
var country = await _context.Countries
    .FindAsync(id);

return country; // country.Cities is still set to NULL
```

As we can see, the `country` variable is returned to the caller with the `Cities` property set to NULL, simply because we didn't ask for it: for that very reason, if we convert that variable into a JSON object and return it to the client, the JSON object would contain no cities either.

The following is an Entity Framework Core query that retrieves `country` from a given `id` using **eager loading**:

```
var country = await _context.Countries
    .Include(c => C.Cities)
    .FindAsync(id);

return country; // country.Cities is (eagerly) loaded
```

Let's try to understand what is happening here:

- The `Include()` method that was specified at the start of the query tells Entity Framework Core to activate the eager loading data retrieval pattern.
- As for the new pattern, the EF query will fetch the `country` as well as all of the corresponding cities in a single query.
- For all of these reasons, the returned `country` variable will have the `Cities` property filled with all the `cities` related to `country` (that is, the `CountryId` value will be equal to that *country's* `id` value).

> For the sake of simplicity, we're only going to use **eager loading** through this book, using the `Include()` method whenever we need it; for additional information regarding **lazy loading** and **explicit loading**, we strongly suggest that you take a look at the following URL: `https://docs.microsoft.com/en-US/ef/core/querying/related-data`.

Defining the database table names

The SQL script generated by EF Core using the Code-First approach, as per its default settings, will create a database table for each entity using the entity's class name: this basically means that we're going to have a `City` table containing all the cities and a `Country` table for the countries. Although there's nothing wrong with these names, we might as well change this default setting to create the tables in plural form for consistency reasons: `Cities` for the cities, `Countries` for the countries.

To "force" a database table name of our choice for each individual entity, we can add the `[Table]` data annotation attribute to the entity class in the following way.

For the `City` entity (the `/Data/Models/City.cs` file):

```
[Table("Cities")]
public class City
```

For the `Country` entity (the `/Data/Models/Country.cs` file):

```
[Table("Countries")]
public class Country
```

Before going further, let's perform this simple update to our classes in order to demonstrate how easy it is to achieve additional control over the auto-generated database.

With this, we're done with the entities, at least for the time being. Now, we just need to get ourselves a DBMS so that we can actually create our database.

Getting a SQL Server instance

Let's close this gap once and for all and provide ourselves with a SQL Server instance. As we already mentioned, there are two major routes we can take:

- **Install a local SQL Server instance** (Express or Developer Edition) on our development machine.
- **Set up a SQL Database (and/or Server) on Azure** using one of the several options available on that platform.

The former option embodies the classic, cloudless approach that software and web developers have been using since the dawn of time: a local instance is easy to pull off and will provide everything we're going to need in development and production environments... as long as we don't care about data redundancy, heavy infrastructure load and possible performance impacts (in the case of high-traffic websites), scaling, and other bottlenecks due to the fact that our server is a single physical entity.

In Azure, things work in a different way: putting our DBMS there gives us the chance to have our SQL Server workloads running as either a hosted infrastructure (**Infrastructure as a Service**, also known as **IaaS**) or a hosted service (**Platform as a Service**, also known as **PaaS**): the first option is great if we want to handle the database maintenance tasks by ourselves, such as applying patches and taking backups; the second option is preferable if we want to delegate these operations to Azure. However, regardless of the path we choose, we're going to have a scalable database service with full redundancy and *no single point of failure* guarantees, plus a lot of other performance and data security benefits. The downsides, as we can easily guess, are as follows: the additional cost and the fact that we're going to have our data located elsewhere, which can be a major issue in terms of privacy and data protection in certain scenarios.

In the following section, we'll quickly summarize how to pull off both of these approaches so that we can make the most convenient choice.

Installing SQL Server 2019

If we want to avoid the cloud and stick to an "old-school" approach, we can choose to install a **SQL Server Express** (or Developer) on-premises instance on our development (and later, on our production) machine.

To do that, perform the following steps:

1. **Download the SQL Server 2019 on-premises installation package** (we're going to use the Windows build here, but the Linux installer is also available) from the following URL: `https://www.microsoft.com/en-us/sql-server/sql-server-downloads`.
2. **Double-click on the executable file** to start the installation process. When prompted for the installation type, select the **BASIC** option (unless we need to configure some advanced options to accommodate specific needs, provided that we know what we're doing).

The installation package will then start downloading the required files. When it's done, we'll just have to click **New SQL Server stand-alone installation** (the first available option starting from the top, as shown in the following screenshot) to start the actual installation process:

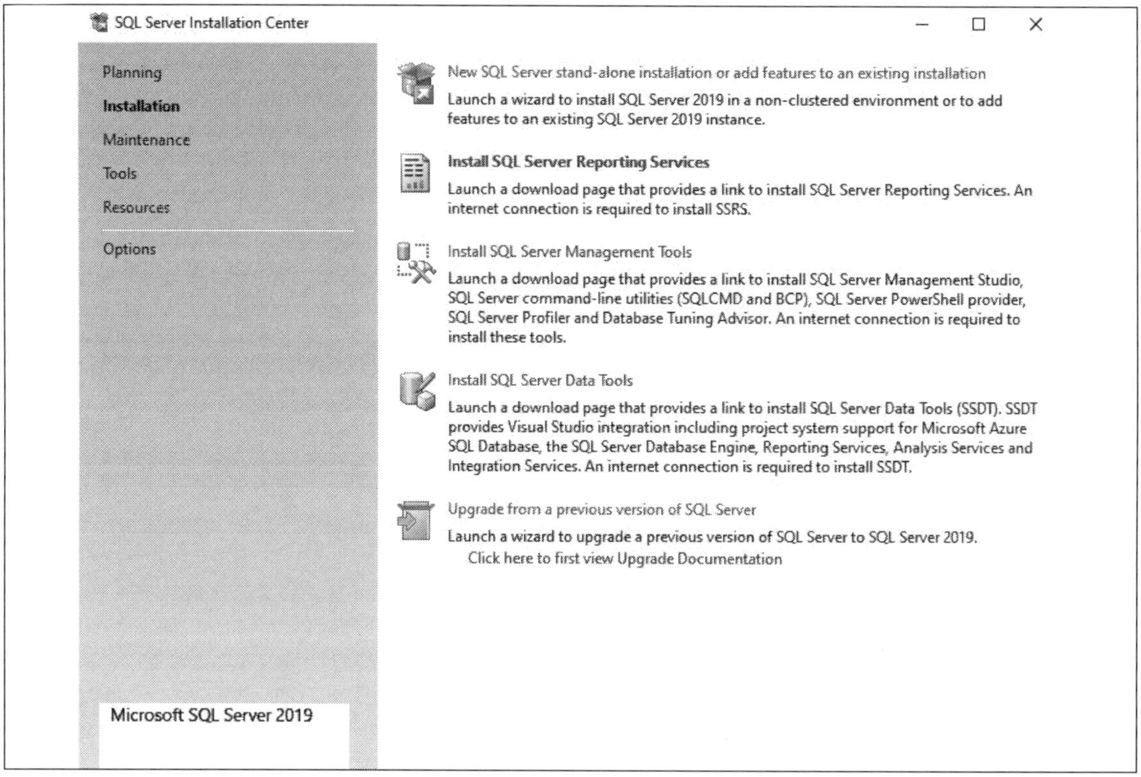

Figure 4.12: Installing SQL Server 2019

Accept the license terms and go ahead, keeping all of the default options and performing the required operations (such as opening the **Windows Firewall**) when asked to.

> If we want to keep our disk space consumption to a minimum amount, we can safely remove the SQL Replication and Machine Learning services from the **Feature Selection** section and save roughly 500 MB.

Set the **Instance Name** to `SQLExpress` and the **Instance ID** to `SQLEXPRESS`. Remember that choice: we're going to need it when we have to write down our connection string.

When we're asked to choose an **Authentication Mode** (as we can see in the following screenshot), choose one of the following options:

- **Windows authentication mode**, if we want to be able to have unrestricted access to the database engine only from the local machine (using our Windows credentials)
- **Mixed Mode**, to enable the SQL Server system administrator (the `sa` user) and set a password for it

These two options can be seen in the following screenshot:

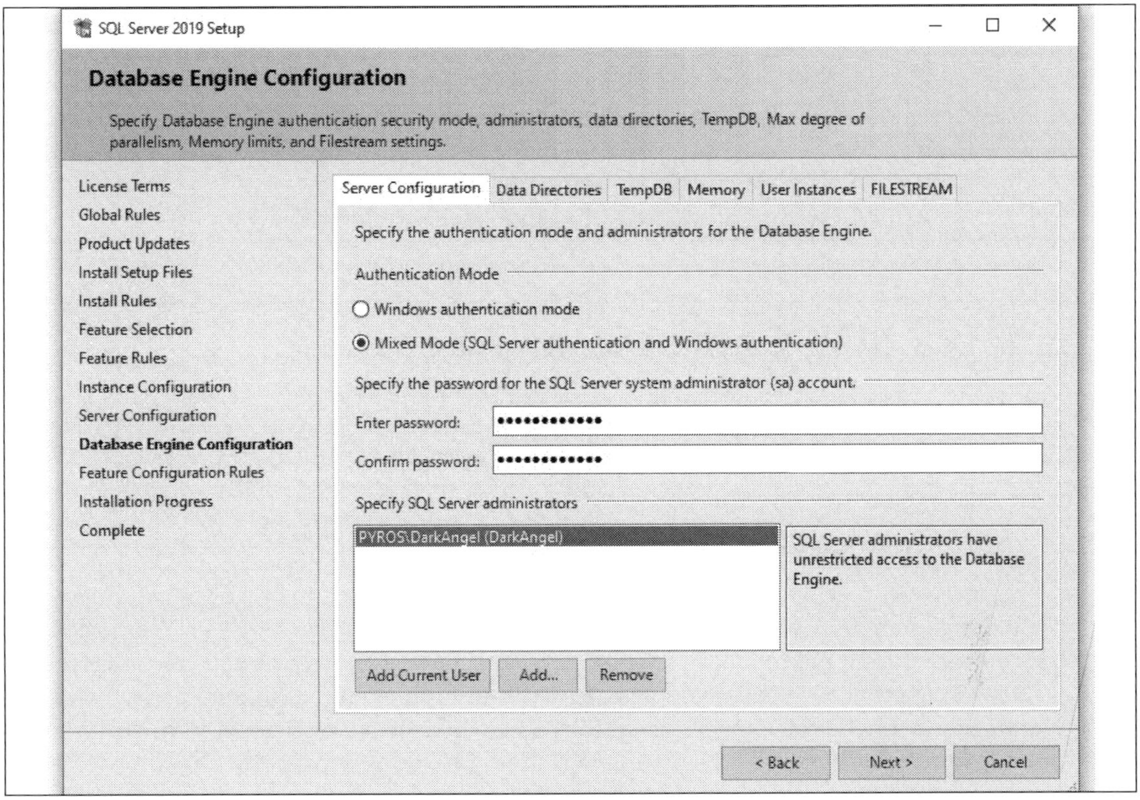

Figure 4.13: Server configuration

The former option is great for security, while the latter is much more versatile—especially if we're going to administer the SQL server remotely using the SQL Server built-in administrative interface, which is the tool we're going to use to create our database.

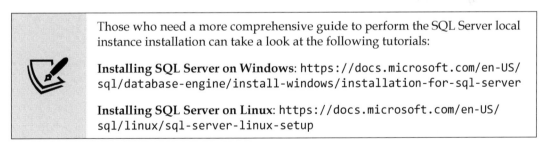

> Those who need a more comprehensive guide to perform the SQL Server local instance installation can take a look at the following tutorials:
>
> **Installing SQL Server on Windows**: `https://docs.microsoft.com/en-US/sql/database-engine/install-windows/installation-for-sql-server`
>
> **Installing SQL Server on Linux**: `https://docs.microsoft.com/en-US/sql/linux/sql-server-linux-setup`

After the SQL Server installation is complete, we should also install the **SQL Server Management tools**—a bunch of useful tools that can be used to manage any SQL instance available locally and/or remotely, as long as the server is reachable and has been configured to allow remote access. More specifically, the tool we're going to need is **SQL Server Management Studio** (**SSMS**), which is basically a GUI interface that can be used to create databases, tables, stored procedures, and so on, as well as manipulate data.

> Although being available from the SQL Server installation and setup tool, SSMS is a separate product and is available (free of charge) at the following URL:
>
> `https://docs.microsoft.com/en-us/sql/ssms/download-sql-server-management-studio-ssms`

However, before using it, we're going to spend some valuable time talking about the Azure path.

Creating a SQL Database on Azure

If you want to get over the DBMS local instances and embrace the *cloudful* **Azure** route, our to-do list entirely depends on which of the main approaches provided by the Azure platform we're going to choose from. Here are the three main options available to end users, from the least to the most expensive. They are as follows:

- **SQL Database**: This is a fully-managed SQL Database engine based on SQL Server Enterprise Edition. This option allows us to set up and manage one or more single relational databases hosted in the Azure cloud with a **Platform-as-a-Service** (**PaaS**) usage and billing model: more specifically, we can define it as a **Database-as-a-Service** (**DBaaS**) approach. This option provides built-in high availability, intelligence, and management, which means it's great for those who want a versatile solution without the hassle of having to configure, manage, and pay for a whole server host.
- **SQL Managed Instance**: This is a dedicated SQL managed instance on Azure. This is a scalable database service that provides near 100% compatibility with a standard SQL Server instance and features an IaaS usage and billing model. This option provides all of the PaaS benefits of the previous one (SQL Database) but adds some additional infrastructure-related capabilities, such as a native **Virtual Network** (**VNet**), custom private IP addresses, multiple databases with shared resources, and so on.
- **SQL virtual machine**: This is a fully managed SQL Server consisting of a Windows or Linux virtual machine with a SQL Server instance installed on top of it. This approach, which also adopts an IaaS usage and billing model, offers full administrative control over the whole SQL Server instance and the underlying OS, hence being the most complex and customizable one. The most significant difference from the other two options (SQL Database and SQL Managed Instance) is that SQL Server virtual machines also allow full control over the database engine: we can choose when to start maintenance/patching, change the recovery model, pause/start the service, and so on.

For more information regarding the pros and cons of the Azure options described here, we strongly suggest that you read the following guide: `https://docs.microsoft.com/en-US/azure/sql-database/sql-database-paas-vs-sql-server-iaas`

All of these options are good and, although very different in terms of overall costs, can be activated free of charge: **SQL Database** is arguably the cheapest one because it's free for 12 months, thanks to the trial subscription plan offered by Azure, as long as we keep its size under 250 GB; both **SQL Managed Instance** and **SQL Virtual Machine** are rather expensive, since they both provide a virtualized IaaS, but they can be activated for free (at least for a few weeks) with the €200 provided by that same Azure trial subscription plan.

In the following sections, we're going to learn how to set up a SQL Database since it is the less expensive approach in the long term: the only downside is that we'll have to keep its size under 250 GB... which is definitely not an issue, considering that our world cities data source file is less than 1 GB in size.

In case we want to opt for an Azure SQL Managed Instance (option #2), here's a great guide explaining how to do that: `https://docs.microsoft.com/en-us/azure/sql-database/sql-database-managed-instance-get-started`

If you wish to set up a SQL Server installed on a virtual machine (option #3), here's a tutorial covering that topic: `https://docs.microsoft.com/en-US/azure/virtual-machines/windows/sql/quickstart-sql-vm-create-portal`

Setting up a SQL Database

Let's start by visiting the following URL: `https://azure.microsoft.com/en-us/free/services/sql-database/`

This will bring us to the following web page, which allows us to create an Azure SQL managed instance:

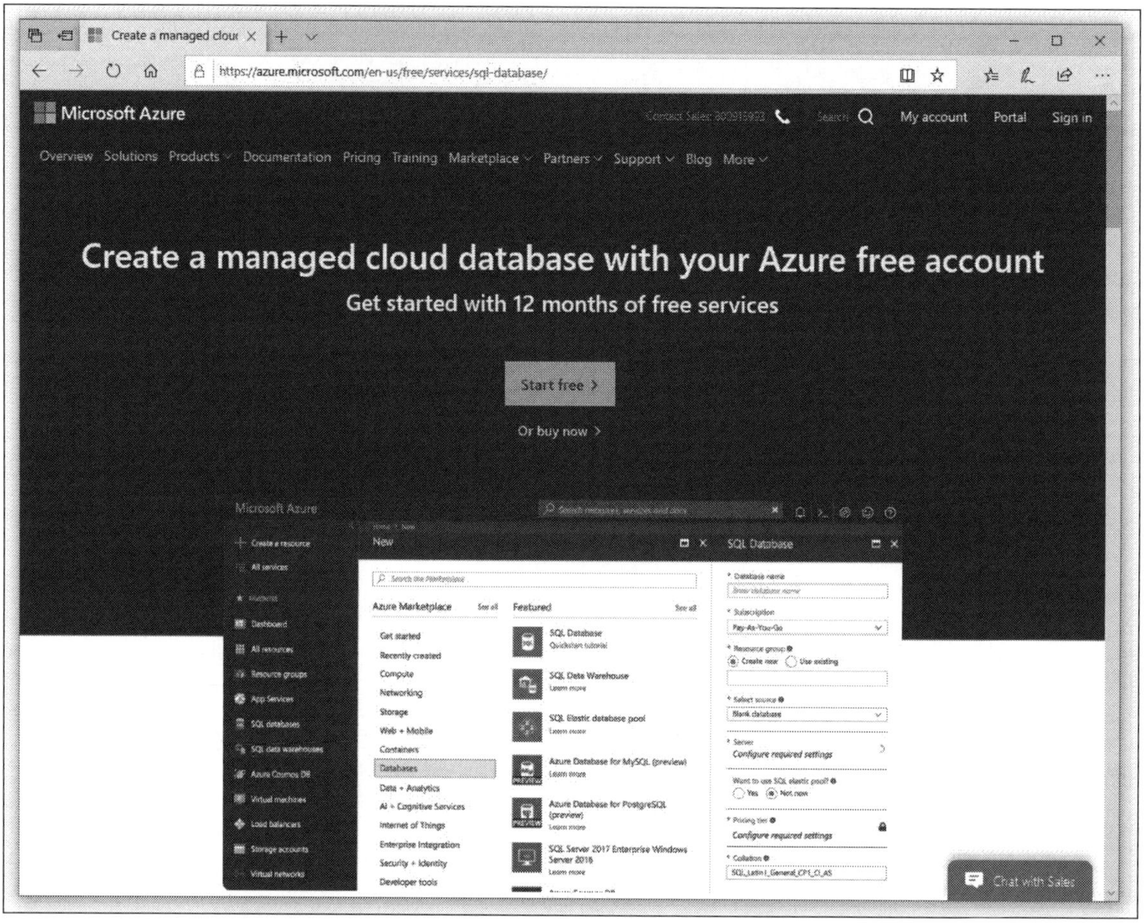

Figure 4.14: Creating a new Azure free account

Click the **Start free** button and create a new account.

> If you already have a valid MS account, you can definitely use it; however, you should only do that if you're sure that you want to use the free Azure trial on it: if that's not the case, consider creating a new one.

After a brief registration form (and/or login phase), we'll be redirected to the Azure portal.

It goes without saying that if the account we've logged in with has already used up its free period or has an active paid subscription plan, we'll be gracefully bounced back:

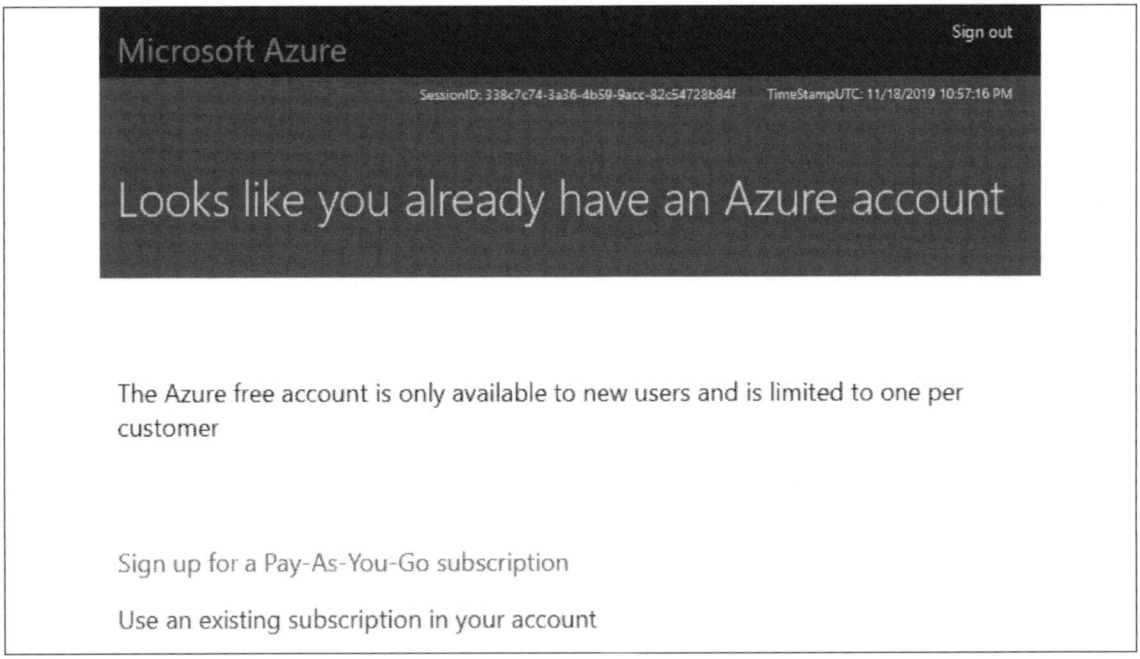

Figure 4.15: View for users who aren't new

Eventually, after we've sorted everything out, we should be able to access the Azure portal (`https://portal.azure.com`) in all of its glory:

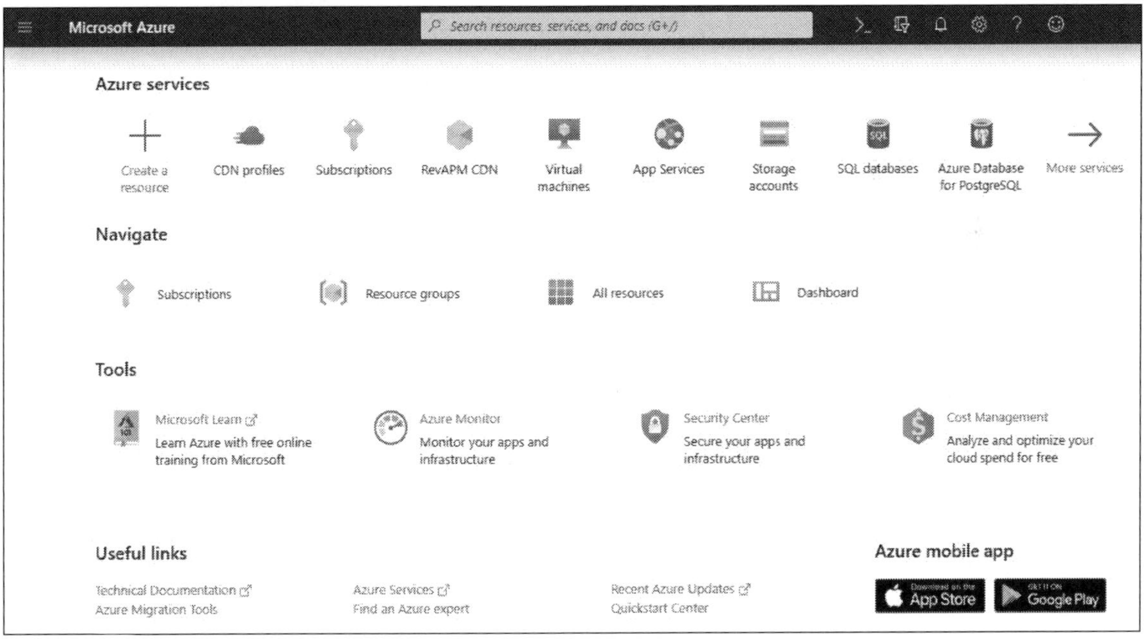

Figure 4.16: The Azure portal

Once there, do the following:

1. Click the **Create a resource** button to access the **Azure Marketplace**.
2. Search for an entry called **Azure SQL**.
3. Click **Create** to access the selection page shown in the following screenshot:

> **IMPORTANT**: Be careful that you don't pick the **SQL managed instances** entry instead, which is the one for creating the SQL Server virtual machine—this is option #2 that we talked about earlier.

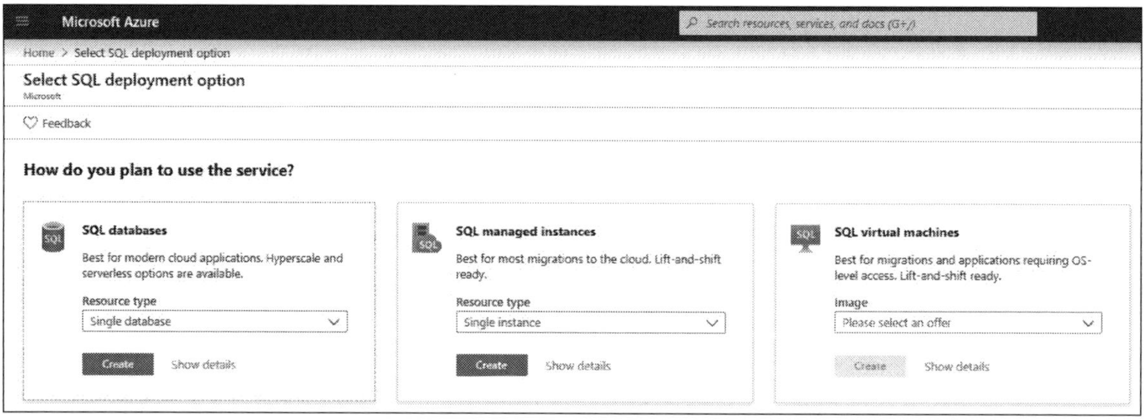

Figure 4.17: Selecting an SQL deployment option

From the preceding selection screen, do the following:

1. Select the first option (**SQL databases**).
2. Set the **Resource type** drop-down list to **Single database**.
3. Click the **Create** button to start the **main setup** wizard.

During this process, we'll be also asked to create our very first **Azure Tenant** (unless we already have one). This is a virtual organization that owns and manages a specific set of Microsoft cloud services. Tenants are identified by unique URLs in the following format: <TenantName>.onmicrosoft.com. Just give it a suitable name and go ahead.

Configuring the instance

As soon as we click the **Create** button, we'll be asked to configure our SQL Database with a wizard-like interface split into the following tabs:

- **Basics**: Subscription type, instance name, admin username and password, and so on
- **Networking**: Network connectivity method and firewall rules

- **Additional settings**: Collation and time zone
- **Tags**: A set of name/value pairs that can be applied to logically organize Azure resources into functional categories or groups sharing a common scope (such as Production and Test)
- **Review + Create**: Review and confirm all of the preceding

In the **Basics** tab, we have to insert the database details, such as the database name and the server we would like to use. If this is our first time coming here, we're not going to have any available servers. Due to this, we'll have to create our first one by clicking on the **Create new** link and filling in the pop-over form that will slide to the rightmost side of the screen. Be sure to set a non-trivial **Server admin login** and a complex **Password** as we will need those credentials for our upcoming connection string.

The following screenshot shows an example of how to configure this part of the wizard:

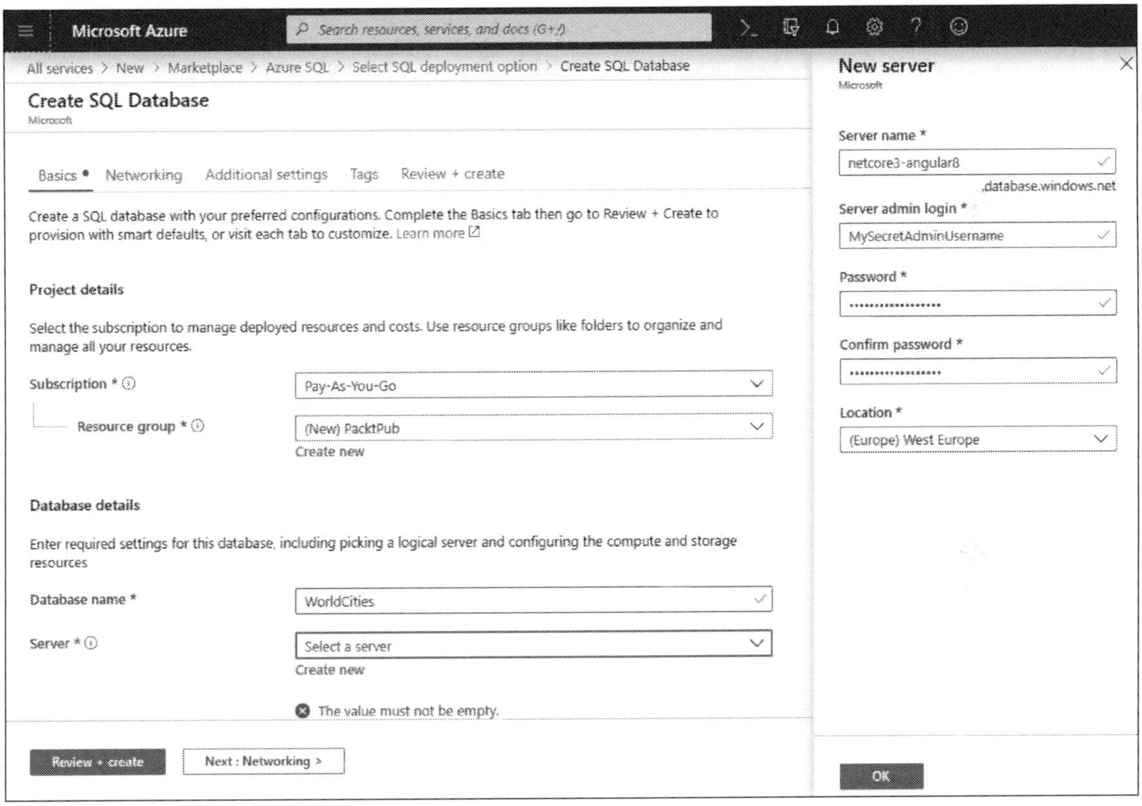

Figure 4.18: Configuring our SQL Database

The last option in the **Basics** tab will ask us for the **Compute + storage** type: for this specific project, we can definitely choose the minimum possible tier—a **Basic** storage type with 2 GB maximum space (see the following screenshot):

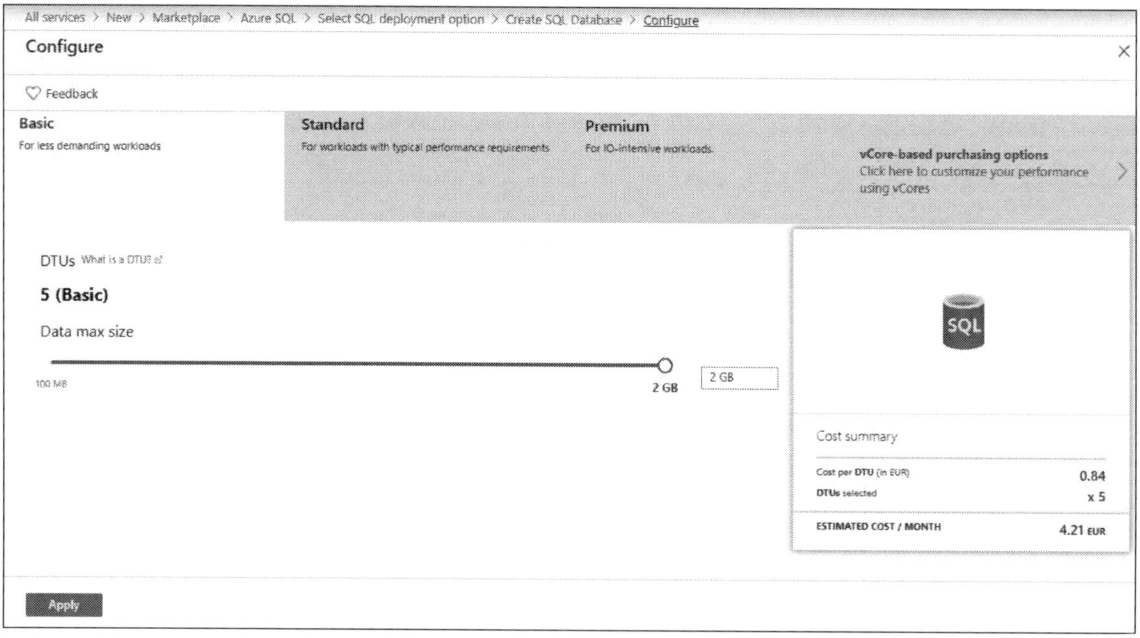

Figure 4.19: Choosing the compute and storage type

However, if we're feeling bold, we can go for a **Standard** type with 250 GB storage instead since it would still be free for 12 months.

In the **Networking** tab, be sure to choose a **public endpoint** to enable external access from the internet so that we'll be able to connect to our database from all of our environments. We should also set both the firewall rules to **Yes** to *allow Azure services and resources to access the server* and *add our current IP address* to the allowed IPs whitelist.

> Wait a minute: isn't that a major security issue? What if our databases contain personal or sensitive data?
>
> As a matter of fact, it is: allowing public access from the internet is something we should always avoid unless we're playing with open data for testing, demonstrative, or tutorial purposes... which is precisely what we're doing right now.

The **Additional Settings** and **Tags** tabs are OK with their default settings: we should only change them if we need to alter some options (such as the collation and the time zone that is most suitable to our language and country) or to activate specific stuff such as the *advanced data security*—which is completely unnecessary for our current needs.

In the **Review + Create** tab, we'll have our last chance to review and change our settings (as shown in the following screenshot): if we're not sure about them, we have the chance to go back and change them. When we're 100% sure, we can hit the **Create** button and have our SQL Database deployed in a few seconds:

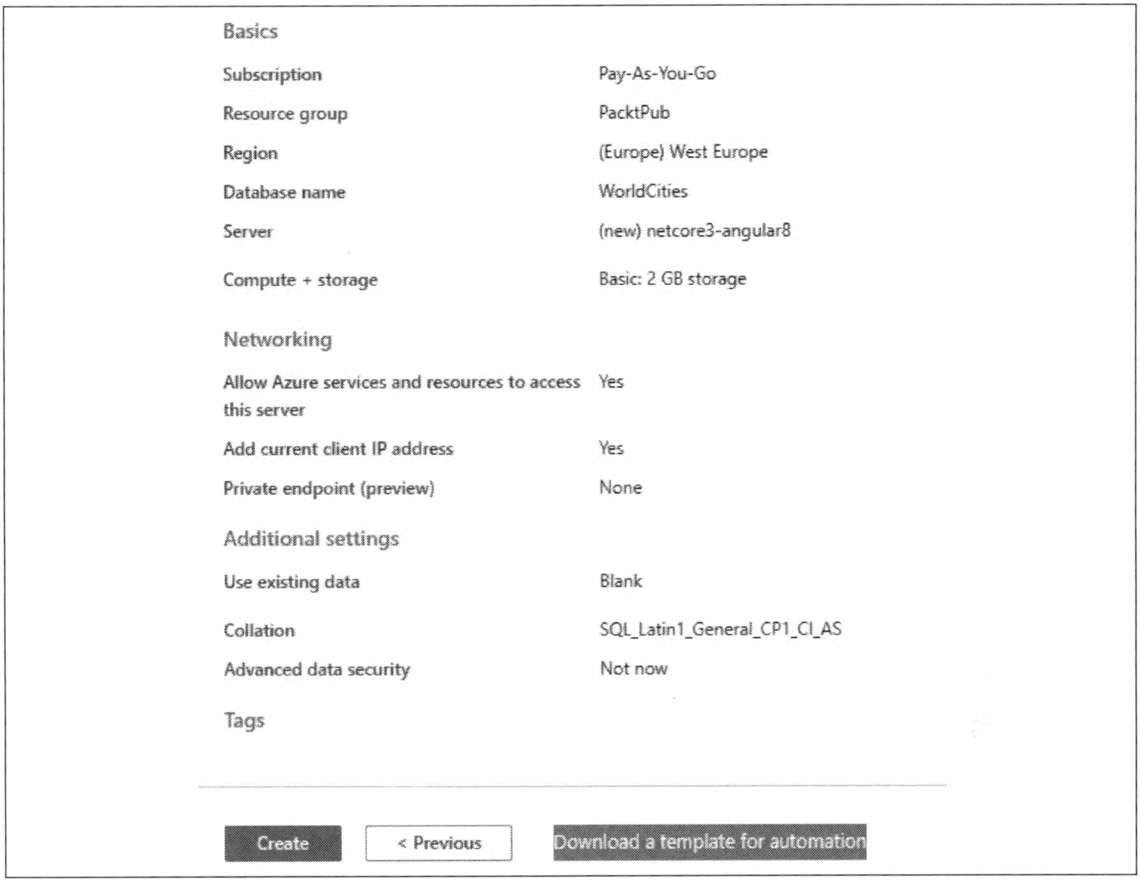

Figure 4.20: Reviewing our chosen settings

> It's worth noticing that we can also download a template for automation in case we want to save these settings to create additional SQL Databases in the future.

That's it: now, we can focus on configuring our database.

Configuring the database

Regardless of the path we take—a local instance or Azure—we should be ready to manage our newly-created Azure SQL Database.

The most practical way to do that is using SSMS, the free SQL Server Management GUI, which we can download for free by following the instructions we explained a while ago (see the *Installing SQL Server 2019* section). In case we don't have installed it yet, we can do that right after we've downloaded it.

Once done, we just have to select **SQL Server Authentication** and then type in the **Server name**, **Login**, and **Password** we chose when we installed our local SQL Server instance or created the SQL Database on Azure. This can be seen in the following screenshot:

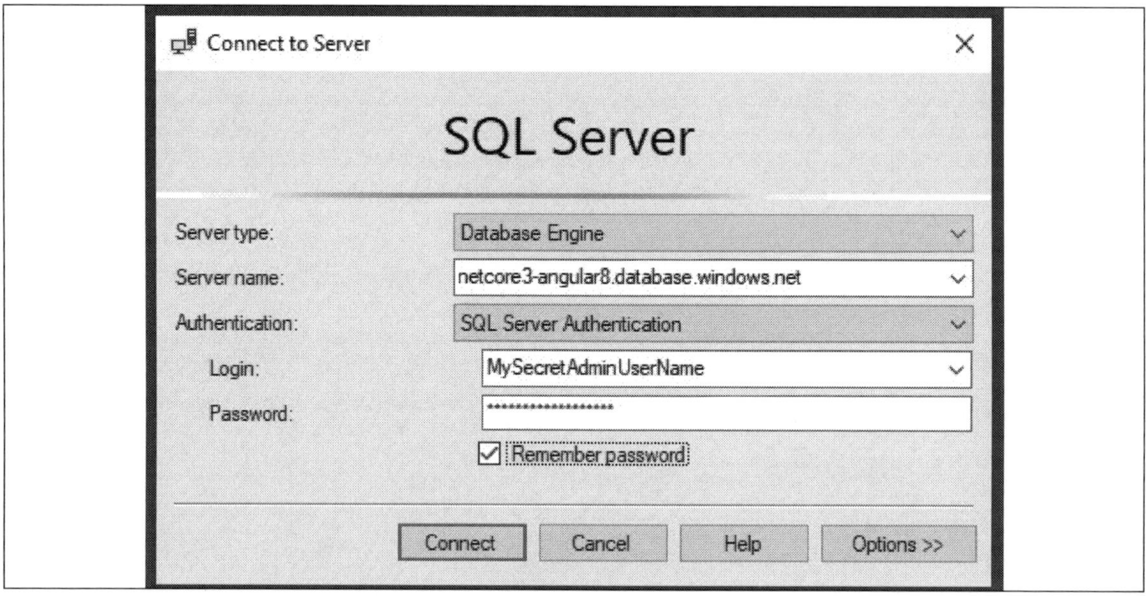

Figure 4.21: Connecting to the SQL Server

As we can see by looking at the URL that we wrote in the **Server name** field, in the preceding screenshot we're connecting to a typical Azure SQL Database instance: in order to connect to a locally installed SQL Server, we would use **localhost\SQLEXPRESS**, **127.0.0.1\SQLEXPRESS** or something like that, depending on the instance name that we've chosen during the installation process.

By clicking the **Connect** button, we should be able to log in to our database server. As soon as SSMS connects to the SQL Database server, a **Server Explorer** window will appear, containing a tree view representing the structure of our SQL Server instance. This is the interface we'll use to create our database, as well as the user/password that our application will use to access it.

Creating the WorldCities database

If we took the Azure SQL Database route, we should already be able to see the `WorldCities` database in the `Databases` folder of the **Object Explorer** tree to the left:

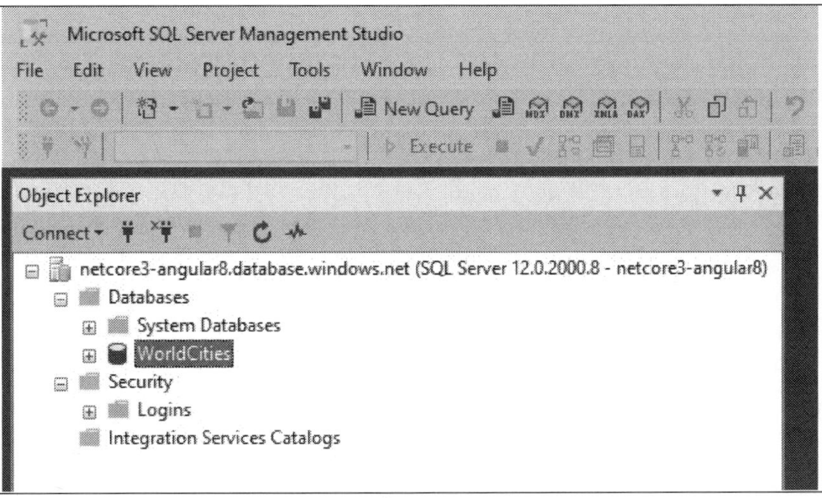

Figure 4.22: Inspecting the WorldCities folder in the Object Explorer

Alternatively, if we installed our local *SQL Server Express* or *Development* instance, we'll have to manually create it by doing the following:

1. Right-click on the `Databases` folder
2. Choose **Add Database** from the **contextual** menu
3. Type in the **WorldCities** name, then click on **OK** to create it

Once the database has been created, we'll get the chance to expand its tree node by clicking on the plus (+) sign to the left and visually interact with all its child objects—*tables, stored procedures, users*, and so on—through the SSMS GUI. It goes without saying that if we do that now, we would find no tables because we haven't created them yet: that's something that Entity Framework Core will do for us later on. However, before doing that, we're going to add a **login** account to make our web application able to connect.

Adding the WorldCities login

From the SSMS Object Explorer, go back to the top root folder and expand the `Security` folder, which should be just below it. Once there, do the following:

- Right-click on the `Logins` subfolder and choose **New Login**
- In the modal window that appears, set the login name to `WorldCities`
- From the radio button list below the login name, select **SQL Server Authentication** and set a suitable password with decent strength (such as **MyVeryOwn$721**—we're going to use this one for the code samples and screenshots from now on)
- Be sure to disable the **User must change the password at next login** option (which is *checked* by default); otherwise, Entity Framework Core will be unable to perform the login later on

- Set the user's default database to `WorldCities`
- Review all of the options, then click on **OK** to create the `WorldCities` account

> If we want a simpler password, such as `WorldCities` or `Password`, we might have to disable the **enforce password policy** option. However, we strongly advise against doing that: choosing a weak password is never a wise choice, especially if we do that in a production-ready environment. We suggest that you always use a strong password, even in testing and development environments. Just be sure not to forget it, as we're going to need it later on.

Mapping the login to the database

The next thing we need to do is properly map this login to the `WorldCities` database we added earlier. Here's how to do that:

1. Double-click the `WorldCities` login name from the `Security` folder to open the same model we used just a few seconds ago.
2. From the navigation menu to the left, switch to the **User Mapping** tab.
3. Click on the checkbox to the left of the `WorldCities` database: the **User** cell should be automatically filled with the `WorldCities` value. In case it doesn't, we'll need to manually type `WorldCities` into it.
4. In the **Database role membership for** box in the bottom-right panel, assign the `db_owner` membership role.

All of the preceding steps are depicted in the following screenshot:

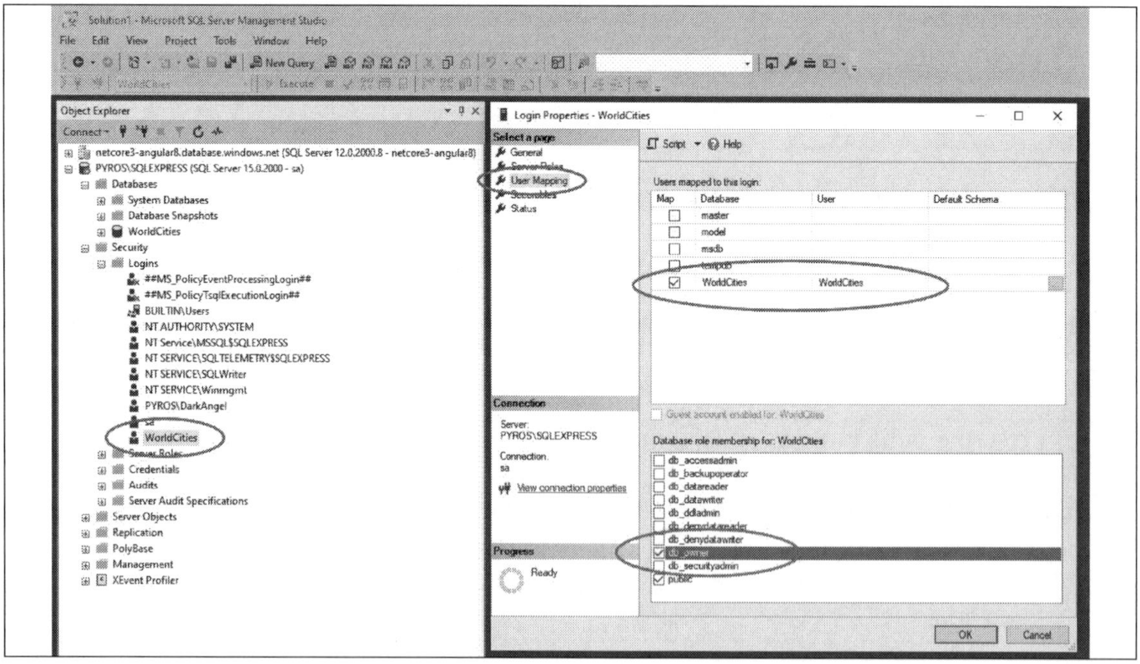

Figure 4.23: Mapping the login to the WorldCities database

That's it! Now, we can go back to our web application project, add the connection string, and create our tables (and data) using the Entity Framework Code-First approach.

Creating the database using Code-First

Before going further, let's do a quick checklist:

- Are we done with our entities? **Yes**
- Do we have a DBMS and a `WorldCities` database available? **Yes**
- Have we gone through all of the required steps we need to complete to actually create and fill in the aforementioned database using Code-First? **No**

As a matter of fact, we need to take care of two more things:

- Set up an appropriate **Database Context**
- Enable **Code-First Data Migrations support** within our project.

Within the following sections, we're going to fill all of these gaps and eventually fill our `WorldCities` database.

Setting up the DbContext

To interact with data as objects/entity classes, Entity Framework Core uses the `Microsoft.EntityFrameworkCore.DbContext` class, also called `DbContext` or simply **Context**. This class is in charge of all of the entity objects during runtime, including populating them with data from the database, keeping track of changes, and persisting them to the database during CRUD operations.

We can easily create our very own `DbContext` class for our project—which we will call `ApplicationDbContext`—by doing the following:

1. From **Solution Explorer**, right-click on the `/Data/` folder we created a while ago and add a new `ApplicationDbContext.cs` class file.
2. Fill it with the following code:

```
using Microsoft.EntityFrameworkCore;
using WorldCities.Data.Models;

namespace WorldCities.Data
{
    public class ApplicationDbContext : DbContext
    {

        public ApplicationDbContext() : base()
        {
        }
```

```
        public ApplicationDbContext(DbContextOptions options)
         : base(options)
        {
        }


        public DbSet<City> Cities { get; set; }
        public DbSet<Country> Countries { get; set; }

    }
}
```

As we can see, we took the chance to add a `DbSet<T>` property for each of our entities so that we can easily access them later on.

Entity type configuration methods

Since we chose to adopt the Code-First data modeling approach, we need to make sure that our entities are properly configured from within the code, so that the SQL scripts generated by Entity Framework Core will create the database using the names, database types, definitions, and rules that we want.

EF Core provides three available methods for configuring various aspects of your model:

- **Data Annotations**, through attributes applied directly on the entity types
- **Fluent API** (also known as *ModelBuilder API*), via custom rules applied by overriding the `OnModelCreating` method in `DbContext`
- **EntityTypeConfiguration classes**, via custom rules applied to separate configuration classes referenced in the `DbContext` `OnModelCreating` override method (by all means an alternative take on the **Fluent API** approach)

All of them are viable enough for most scenarios: however, in a real project, it is highly advisable to avoid mixing them and just pick one for the sake of consistency.

Let's briefly review all of them before choosing our pick.

Data Annotations

Data annotations are dedicated attributes that can be applied to entity classes and properties to override the default Code-First conventions and/or to define new rules. The major advantage of Data Annotations is that they allow the developer to manage the data definition within the class code, which is great for code readability and maintainability.

As a matter of fact, we already used Data Annotations in our existing entity classes when we added the `[Key]`, `[Required]`, and `[ForeignKey]` attributes to their database-relevant properties. This means that, if we want to switch to another configuration method, we'll need to perform some minor refactoring on our code.

Data Annotations are great for applying simple configuration changes, which often makes them ideal for small projects; however, they don't support the whole set of configuration options made available by EF Core; whenever we need to gain more control over our entity type settings we might easily feel the urge to switch to a more powerful method.

Fluent API

In order to use the Fluent API, we need to override the `OnModelCreating` method in our derived context and use the `ModelBuilder` API to configure our model.

A great way to understand how we can use the Fluent API might be to see how we can convert our existing Data Annotations into `ModelBuilder` settings. Here's how we can do that:

```
[...]

protected override void OnModelCreating(ModelBuilder modelBuilder)
{
    base.OnModelCreating(modelBuilder);

    modelBuilder.Entity<City>().ToTable("Cities");
    modelBuilder.Entity<City>()
        .HasKey(x => x.Id);
    modelBuilder.Entity<City>()
        .Property(x => x.Id).IsRequired();

    modelBuilder.Entity<City>().ToTable("Countries");
    modelBuilder.Entity<Country>()
        .HasKey(x => x.Id);
    modelBuilder.Entity<Country>()
        .Property(x => x.Id).IsRequired();
    modelBuilder.Entity<City>()
        .HasOne(x => x.Country)
        .WithMany(y => y.Cities)
        .HasForeignKey(x => x.CountryId);
}

[...]
```

The preceding `override` method should be added to the `ApplicationDbContext` class right after the constructors: refer to the source code in the GitHub repository for details.

As we can see, for each data annotation that we've used so far there's a corresponding Fluent API method: `ToTable()` for `[Table]`, `HasKey()` for `[Key]`, `IsRequired()` for `[Required]`, and so on.

The major advantage of the Fluent API is that such a method allows us to specify the entity configuration without modifying our entity classes; furthermore, Fluent API configurations have the highest precedence, meaning that they will override any existing EF Core convention and/or data annotation applied to entity classes and properties.

Their only real downside is that, despite being "fluid" they are quite verbose; in big projects and/or complex entity configuration scenarios, which is also when they really shine, the amount of code they require easily increases a lot as the required settings pile up, thus making the `DbContext` source code quite hard to read and maintain.

EntityTypeConfiguration classes

`EntityTypeConfiguration` classes are the pivotal aspect of an advanced coding pattern that aims to overcome the major issue of the Fluent API while retaining all their advantages.

In a nutshell, this technique leverages the `ApplyConfigurationsFromAssembly` Fluent API method, which allows the definition of external rules within separated configuration files, thus removing the need to stack up all of them within `DbContext`'s `OnModelCreating` override method and reduces the required amount of code to a single line.

Again, the best way to understand how this method works is to explain how we could convert our existing data annotation rules into configuration classes.

This time, we would need to create two additional files. The first one would be called `/Data/Models/CityEntityTypeConfiguration.cs`:

```
using Microsoft.EntityFrameworkCore;
using Microsoft.EntityFrameworkCore.Metadata.Builders;

namespace WorldCities.Data.Models
{
    public class CityEntityTypeConfiguration
        : IEntityTypeConfiguration<City>
    {
        public void Configure(EntityTypeBuilder<City> builder)
        {
            builder.ToTable("Cities");
            builder.HasKey(x => x.Id);
            builder.Property(x => x.Id).IsRequired();
            builder
                .HasOne(x => x.Country)
                .WithMany(x => x.Cities)
                .HasForeignKey(x => x.CountryId);
        }
```

```
    }
}
```

And the second one would be called `/Data/Models/CountryEntityTypeConfiguration.cs`:

```
using Microsoft.EntityFrameworkCore;
using Microsoft.EntityFrameworkCore.Metadata.Builders;

namespace WorldCities.Data.Models
{
    public class CountryEntityTypeConfiguration
        : IEntityTypeConfiguration<Country>
    {
        public void Configure(EntityTypeBuilder<Country> builder)
        {
            builder.ToTable("Countries");
            builder.HasKey(x => x.Id);
            builder.Property(x => x.Id).IsRequired();
        }
    }
}
```

Adding these configuration classes to our `ApplicationDbContext` would be as easy as adding this single line within the `OnModelCreating` method, which we added early on:

```
protected override void OnModelCreating(ModelBuilder modelBuilder)
{
    base.OnModelCreating(modelBuilder);

    // add the EntityTypeConfiguration classes
    modelBuilder.ApplyConfigurationsFromAssembly(
        typeof(ApplicationDbContext).Assembly
        );
}
```

Not bad, right?

Making a choice

Now that we've explored the three alternative ways to configure our entities offered by EF Core, we need to choose which one we use from now on.

It goes without saying that the `EntityTypeConfiguration` classes method is easily the most preferred approach for large projects because it gives us the chance to organize our settings in a consistent, structured, and readable way: however, since we'll be dealing with very simple database models that will require a minimal number of configuration settings throughout this book, we'll keep using the data annotation approach.

> The basic implementation of the other two methods that we've discussed in this section early on is also available in *Chapter 4*'s source code in the GitHub repository, so that readers who want to adopt a different approach can still review them. Both the `ApplicationDbContext`'s `OnModelCreating` method and the `EntityTypeConfiguration` classes have been documented with a `<summary>` explaining that this code is a redundant override of the data annotation rules and meant for educational purposes only: such redundant code will be removed in *Chapter 5, Fetching and Displaying Data*, and in the subsequent chapters, which will only feature the Data Annotations.

Database initialization strategies

Creating the database for the first time isn't the only thing we need to worry about; for example, how can we keep track of the changes that will definitely occur for our data model?

In previous, non-core versions of EF (up to 6.x), we could choose one of the database management patterns (known as **database initializers** or **DbInitializers**) offered by the *Code-First* approach, that is, by picking the appropriate database initialization strategy for our specific needs, out of:

- `CreateDatabaseIfNotExists`
- `DropCreateDatabaseIfModelChanges`
- `DropCreateDatabaseAlways`
- `MigrateDatabaseToLatestVersion`

Additionally, should we need to address specific requirements, we can also set up our own custom initializer by extending one of the preceding ones and overriding their core methods.

The major flaw of DbInitializers was them not being immediate and streamlined enough for the average developer. They were viable, yet difficult to handle without extensive knowledge of Entity Framework's logic.

In Entity Framework Core, this pattern has been greatly simplified; there are no DbInitializers, and automatic data migrations have also been removed. The database initialization aspect is now entirely handled through PowerShell commands, with the sole exception of a small set of commands that can be placed directly on the `DbContext` implementation constructor to partially automatize the process; they are as follows:

- `Database.EnsureCreated()`
- `Database.EnsureDeleted()`
- `Database.Migrate()`

There's currently no way to create data migrations programmatically; they must be added via PowerShell, as we will see shortly.

Updating the appsettings.json file

From Solution Explorer, open the `appsettings.json` file and add a new `"ConnectionStrings"` JSON key section right below the `"Logging"` one with the following value (new lines are highlighted):

```
{
  "Logging": {
    "LogLevel": {
      "Default": "Warning"
    }
  },
  "AllowedHosts": "*",
  "ConnectionStrings": {
    "DefaultConnection": "Server=localhost\\SQLEXPRESS;
    Database=WorldCities;
    User Id=WorldCities;Password=MyVeryOwn$721;
    Integrated Security=False;MultipleActiveResultSets=True"
  }
}
```

> Unfortunately, JSON doesn't support LF/CR, so we'll need to put the `DefaultConnection` value on a single line. If you copy and paste the preceding text, ensure that Visual Studio doesn't automatically add additional double quotes and/or escape characters to these lines; otherwise, your connection string won't work.

This is the connection string we'll be referencing in our project's `Startup.cs` file later on.

IMPORTANT: As we can see, now our `appsettings.json` file contains our database `User Id` and `Password` in clear text, thus posing a non-trivial security issue. While this file currently resides solely on our development machine, it is possible that sooner or later it will be "accidentally" shared or published elsewhere, for example in a GitHub repository. For that very reason, do not check-in your project until you've read the next paragraph.

Securing the connection string

Being able to securely store the database password and API keys in web applications while maintaining full efficiency in terms of debugging and testing has always been a challenge for all developers.

Back in the ASP.NET pre-Core days, most ASP.NET developers used to store them in the `<connectionStrings>` and/or `<appSettings>` sections of their project's `Web.config` file in the following way:

```
<connectionStrings>
  <add name="DefaultConnection" connectionString="[MY CONNECTION STRING]"/>
</connectionStrings>
<appSettings>
  <add key="Google_ApiKey" value="[MY API KEY]"/>
  <add key="Facebook_Secret" value="[MY FB SECRET]"/>
</appSettings>
```

This practice is still in use nowadays, with the `Web.config` file being replaced by the `appsettings.json` file.

In terms of pure functionality, this behavior works very well, because when we launch our web applications, they will automatically fetch the required credentials whenever they need them even if we run them in *Debug* mode, just like they would do in a production environment.

This practice has always been very convenient because it also leverages the fact that ASP.NET allows us to define multiple files for different environments. More specifically:

- **The Web.config approach** can rely on multiple configuration files (`Web.Debug.config`, `Web.Release.config`, and so on) that could be easily "merged" during the publishing phase using a highly configurable XSD transformation feature
- **The appsettings.json approach** supports multiple configuration files as well (`appsettings.Development.json`, `appsettings.Production.json`, and so on) that can be used to add or override the default settings for specific runtime environments using a cascade logic

Unfortunately, none of these places are safe or secure: if we get used to putting our valuable credentials in those plain text files, there's a high risk that we'll end up "accidentally" pushing them in a GitHub repository, with all the other developers being able to see and use them. For that very reason, such a habit is widely considered a bad practice and—if we're still using it—we should definitely take the chance to get rid of it and start to handle our valuable secrets in a much better (and safer) way.

The question is: how we can do that without losing the effectiveness provided by the "good old" (and insecure) approach?

Introducing Secrets Storage

Starting with .NET Core 2.x and Visual Studio 2019, Microsoft provided their developers with a new feature that can be used to store any secret (database passwords, API keys, and so on) in a secure and effective way: this feature is called *Secrets Storage* and is well documented in Microsoft's *Safe storage of app secrets in development in ASP.NET Core* official guide, available at the following URL: `https://docs.microsoft.com/en-us/aspnet/core/security/app-secrets`

In a nutshell, the new feature creates a `secrets.json` file in the development machine's user folder (in a typical Windows environment, the `\Users\UserName\AppData\Roaming\Microsoft\UserSecrets` directory), which can be used to add to or override elements of the standard `appsettings.json` files using the same syntax they already have.

This is good for a number of reasons, including:

- The `secrets.json` file cannot be accessed by remote users, such as those who could get the project from a GitHub repository, because it will be created in a local folder
- The `secrets.json` file cannot be accessed by local users, because it will be created in the developer's very own personal folder (which is inaccessible to other local users)
- The `secrets.json` file will work right out of the box, basically extending the `appsettings.json` file without forcing us to write any secrets there

Such a feature is a great alternative to the *environment variables* approach, which is another workaround suggested by Microsoft in the preceding guide that I personally don't like as much (at least for development environments) because it is much less flexible and straightforward.

Now that we've chosen our path, let's see how we can implement it.

Adding the secrets.json file

Among the greatest aspects of the *Secrets Storage* feature is the fact that it can be used from within the Visual Studio GUI, which is arguably the best way to do it.

All we need to do is to right-click the project's root folder from Solution Explorer and select the **Manage User Secrets** options, as shown in the following screenshot:

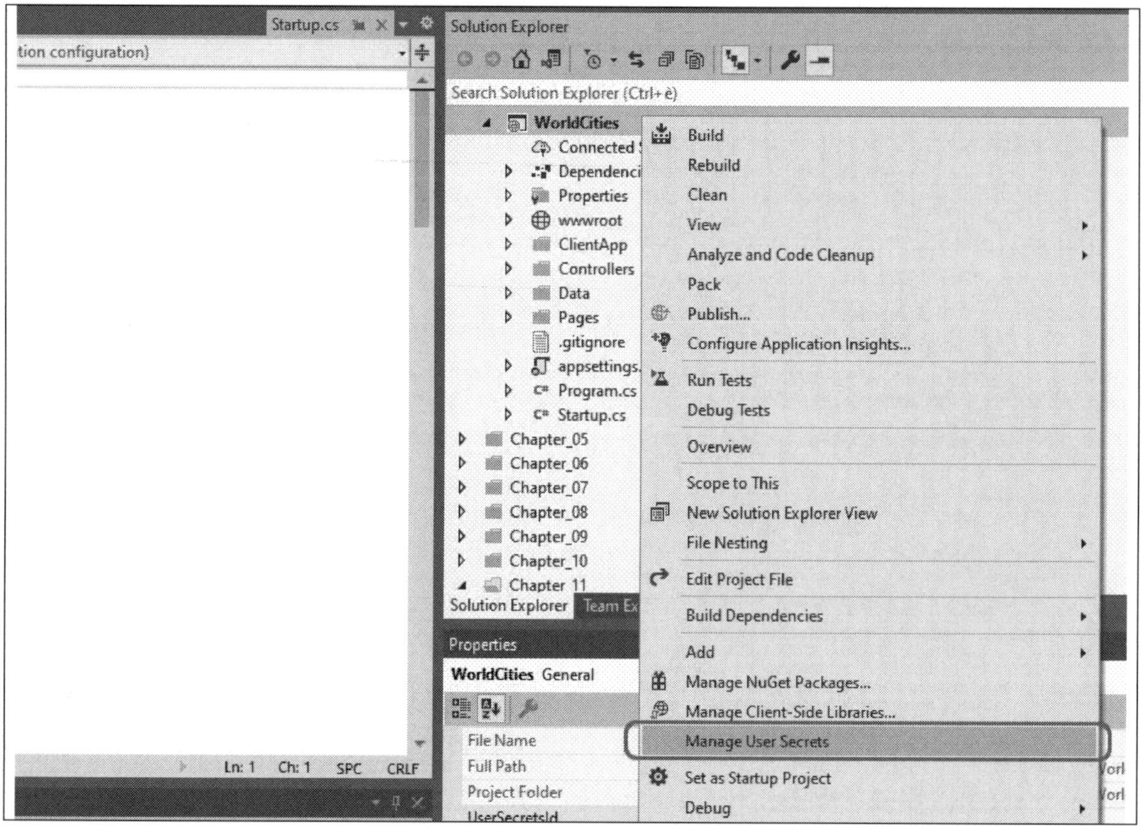

Figure 4.24: Adding the secrets.json file

As soon as we select that option, Visual Studio will add a `UserSecretsId` element within a `PropertyGroup` of the project's `.csproj` file, assigning a random GUID value to it:

```
<PropertyGroup>
  <TargetFramework>net5.0</TargetFramework>

  [...]

  <UserSecretsId>9430de8f-8575-4a47-9d22-a98e491af64c</UserSecretsId>
</PropertyGroup>
```

Such a random `UserSecretsId` value is then used by Visual Studio to generate an empty `secrets.json` file in the following folder:

```
\Users\UserName\AppData\Roaming\Microsoft\UserSecrets\
```

Right after that, Visual Studio will open that `secrets.json` file within the GUI in edit mode, so that we can use it to store our secrets.

Sharing the secrets.json file between multiple projects

By default, the inner text of `UserSecretsId` is a randomly generated GUID; however, such a value is arbitrary and can be changed: using a (random) unique identifier will prevent different projects from having the same `secrets.json` file; at the same time, choosing the same identifier can be useful if we want to "share" the same secrets between multiple projects.

In this book's GitHub repository, we've taken advantage of this behavior by defining an arbitrary `UserSecretsId` for each different project—one for **HealthCheck**, another one for **WorldCities**, and so on—and "recycling" it through all the instances of these projects within the various chapters' folders. For example, here's the `UserSecretsId` value that we've used for all the instances of the current project:

```
<UserSecretsId>WorldCities</UserSecretsId>
```

In order to manually set that value, we can use the **Edit Project File** option available from the Visual Studio GUI, which is accessible by right-clicking on Solutions Explorer's project root folder:

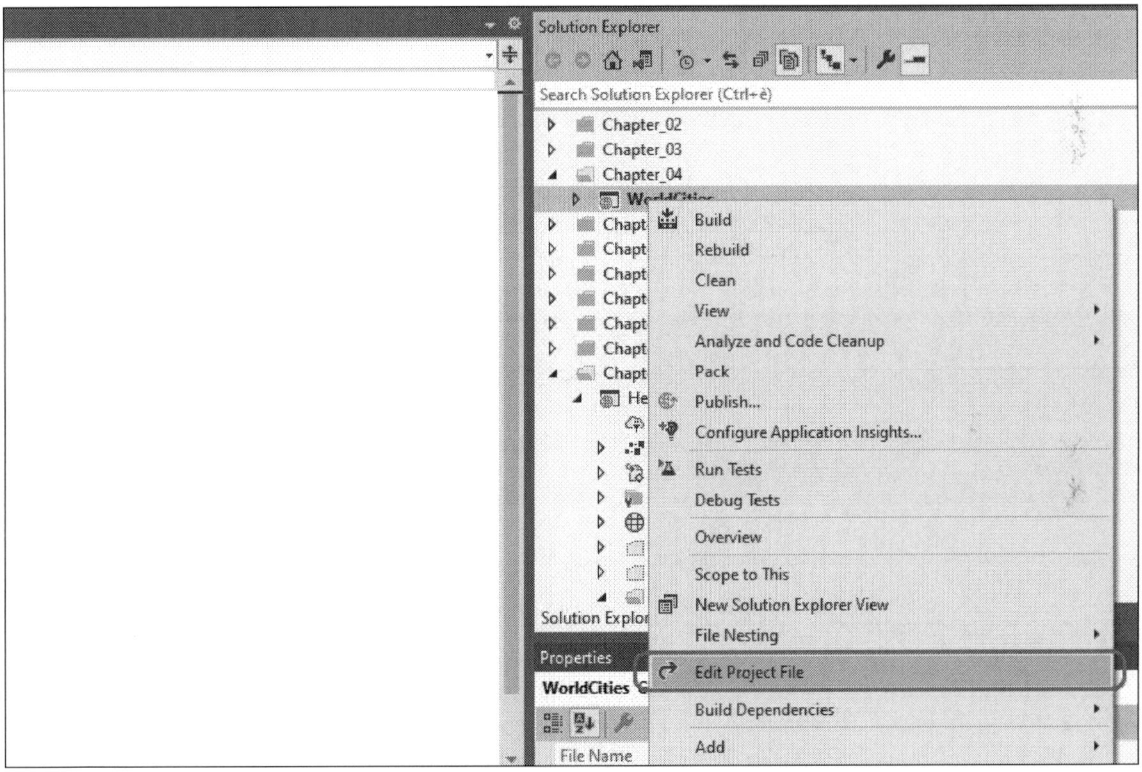

Figure 4.25: Manually setting the UserSecretsId value

Alternatively, we can also edit the `WorldCities.csproj` file in the project's root folder using a text editor of our choice (including the Windows **Notepad**) and find the relevant line/value to change.

Working with the secrets.json file

Now that we've created our `secrets.json` file, let's use it: open the `appsettings.json` file and cut out the whole `ConnectionStrings` block:

```
{
  "Logging": {
    "LogLevel": {
      "Default": "Warning"
    }
  },
  "AllowedHosts": "*"
}
```

And paste it within the `secrets.json` file in the following way:

```
{
  "ConnectionStrings": {
    "DefaultConnection": "Server=localhost\\SQLEXPRESS;
    Database=WorldCities;
    User Id=WorldCities;Password=MyVeryOwn$721;
    Integrated Security=False;MultipleActiveResultSets=True"
  }
}
```

That's basically it: the JSON keys defined in the `secrets.json` file will be added to those already present in the `appsettings.json` file (replacing them if already present) in a seamless and transparent way, without us having to do anything else.

In the next section, we'll get a good chance to make use of such a handy feature.

Creating the database

Now that we have set up our own `DbContext` and defined a valid connection string pointing to our `WorldCities` database, we can easily add the initial migration and create our database.

Updating Startup.cs

The first thing we have to do is add the `EntityFramework` support and our `ApplicationDbContext` implementation to our application startup class. Open the `Startup.cs` file and update the `ConfigureServices` method in the following way (the new lines are highlighted):

```
// ...existing code...

public void ConfigureServices(IServiceCollection services)
{
    services.AddControllersWithViews();
    // In production, the Angular files will be served
    // from this directory
    services.AddSpaStaticFiles(configuration =>
    {
        configuration.RootPath = "ClientApp/dist";
    });

    // Add ApplicationDbContext and SQL Server support
    services.AddDbContext<ApplicationDbContext>(options =>
        options.UseSqlServer(
            Configuration.GetConnectionString("DefaultConnection")
            )
    );
}

// ...existing code...
```

The new code will also require the following namespace references:

```
using Microsoft.EntityFrameworkCore;
using WorldCities.Data;
```

As we can see, we've used the `GetConnectionString("DefaultConnection")` extension method—provided by the `Microsoft.Extensions.Configuration` namespace for the `IConfiguration` interface—which can be used to retrieve the `ConnectionStrings:DefaultConnection` JSON key from the `appsettings.json` file.

However, in our specific scenario, this value will be fetched from the `secrets.json` file, since we moved the whole `ConnectionStrings` block there a short while ago.

> The `GetConnectionString("DefaultConnection")` method is basically a shortcut for the `Configuration["ConnectionStrings:DefaultConnection"]` command: both of them will return the same JSON key value, as long as those keys exist, from the `appsettings.json` and/or `secrets.json` files.

Adding the initial migration

To add the initial migration we can either use the dotnet CLI (from the command line) or the Package Manager Console (from within the Visual Studio GUI).

> Based on reader feedback, the CLI has proven to be quite unstable in some specific configuration scenarios, while the Package Manager Console seems to be slightly more reliable: at the same time, if your development environment went through a number of.NET Core SDK subsequent updates, the Package Manager Console might pick the wrong tooling and fail. With that in mind, I suggest trying the CLI first, then switch to the Package Manager Console in case of issues: if both approaches fail, it might be advisable to uninstall some of the old .NET Core SDKs and try again.

Using the dotnet CLI

Open PowerShell Command Prompt and navigate through the project's root folder, which is as follows in our example:

```
C:\ThisBook\Chapter_04\WorldCities\
```

Once there, type the following command to globally install the `dotnet-ef` command-line tool:

```
dotnet tool install --global dotnet-ef
```

Wait until the installation is complete. When we receive the *green* message output, type in the following command to add the first migration:

```
dotnet ef migrations add "Initial" -o "Data/Migrations"
```

> The optional `-o` parameter can be used to change the location where the migration code-generated files will be created; if we don't specify it, a root-level `/Migrations/` folder will be created and used by default. Since we put all of the `EntityFrameworkCore` classes into the `/Data/` folder, it's advisable to store migrations there as well.

The preceding command will produce the following output:

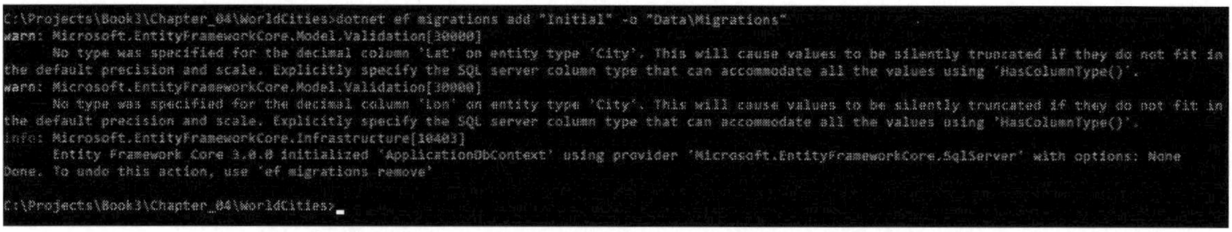

C:\Projects\Book3\Chapter_04\WorldCities>dotnet ef migrations add "Initial" -o "Data\Migrations"
warn: Microsoft.EntityFrameworkCore.Model.Validation[30000]
No type was specified for the decimal column 'Lat' on entity type 'City'. This will cause values to be silently truncated if they do not fit in the default precision and scale. Explicitly specify the SQL server column type that can accommodate all the values using 'HasColumnType()'.
warn: Microsoft.EntityFrameworkCore.Model.Validation[30000]
No type was specified for the decimal column 'Lon' on entity type 'City'. This will cause values to be silently truncated if they do not fit in the default precision and scale. Explicitly specify the SQL server column type that can accommodate all the values using 'HasColumnType()'.
info: Microsoft.EntityFrameworkCore.Infrastructure[10403]
Entity Framework Core 3.0.0 initialized 'ApplicationDbContext' using provider 'Microsoft.EntityFrameworkCore.SqlServer' with options: None
Done. To undo this action, use 'ef migrations remove'
C:\Projects\Book3\Chapter_04\WorldCities>

Figure 4.26: Command-line output after trying to add the first migration

Hey, wait a second: what are those yellow warning messages?

Let's spend a handful of seconds carefully reading them and acknowledging the issue they are pointing to. It seems that the Lat/Lon properties within the `City` entity (both of decimal type) are both missing an explicit precision value: if we don't provide this information, Entity Framework won't know which precision to set for the database table columns it will create for those properties and will fall back to its default values. That fallback could result in a loss of precision if our actual data has a greater number of decimals.

Even if we couldn't care less about the precision of these Lat/Lon coordinates in our specific scenario, since we're just playing with data, it's advisable to fix these kinds of issues as soon as we see them. Luckily, this can easily be done by adding some Data Annotations to these properties.

Open the `/Data/Models/City.cs` file and change the following code accordingly (the modified lines are highlighted):

```
// ...existing code...

/// <summary>
/// City Latitude
/// </summary>
[Column(TypeName = "decimal(7,4)")]
public decimal Lat { get; set; }

/// <summary>
/// City Longitude
/// </summary>
[Column(TypeName = "decimal(7,4)")]
public decimal Lon { get; set; }

// ...existing code...
```

For the sake of convenience, those two new attributes have also been implemented via Fluent API and the `EntityTypeConfiguration` classes in the *Chapter 4* source code on GitHub, together with the other Data Annotations overrides.

Once done, delete the `/Data/Models/Migration` folder (along with all files within it) and launch the `dotnet-ef` command again:

```
dotnet ef migrations add "Initial" -o "Data/Migrations"
```

This time, the migration should be created without *yellow* warning issues, as shown in the following screenshot:

C:\Projects\Book3\Chapter_04\WorldCities>dotnet ef migrations add "Initial" -o "Data\Migrations"
info: Microsoft.EntityFrameworkCore.Infrastructure[10403]
Entity Framework Core 3.0.0 initialized 'ApplicationDbContext' using provider 'Microsoft.EntityFrameworkCore.SqlServer' with options: None
Done. To undo this action, use 'ef migrations remove'
C:\Projects\Book3\Chapter_04\WorldCities>

Figure 4.27: Command-line output without any issues

This means that we finally have the *green light* to apply it.

> If we go back to Visual Studio and take a look at our project's **Solution Explorer**, we will see that there's a new `/Data/Migrations/` folder containing a bunch of code-generated files. Those files contain the actual low-level SQL commands that will be used by Entity Framework Core to create and/or update the database schema.

Updating the database

Applying a data migration basically means creating (or updating) the database in order to synchronize its contents (tables structure, constraints, and so on) with the rules that are defined by the overall patterns and definitions within the `DbContext`, and by the data annotations within the various Entity classes. More specifically, the first data migration creates the whole database from scratch, while the subsequent ones will update it (creating tables, adding/modifying/removing table fields, and so on).

In our specific scenario, we're about to execute our first migration. Here's the one-liner we need to type from the command line (within the project root folder, just like before) to do that:

```
dotnet ef database update
```

Once we hit *Enter*, a bunch of SQL statements will fill the output of our command-line Terminal window. When done, if everything is looking good, we can go back to the SSMS tool, refresh the **Server Object Explorer** tree view, and verify that the `WorldCities` database has been created, along with all of the relevant tables:

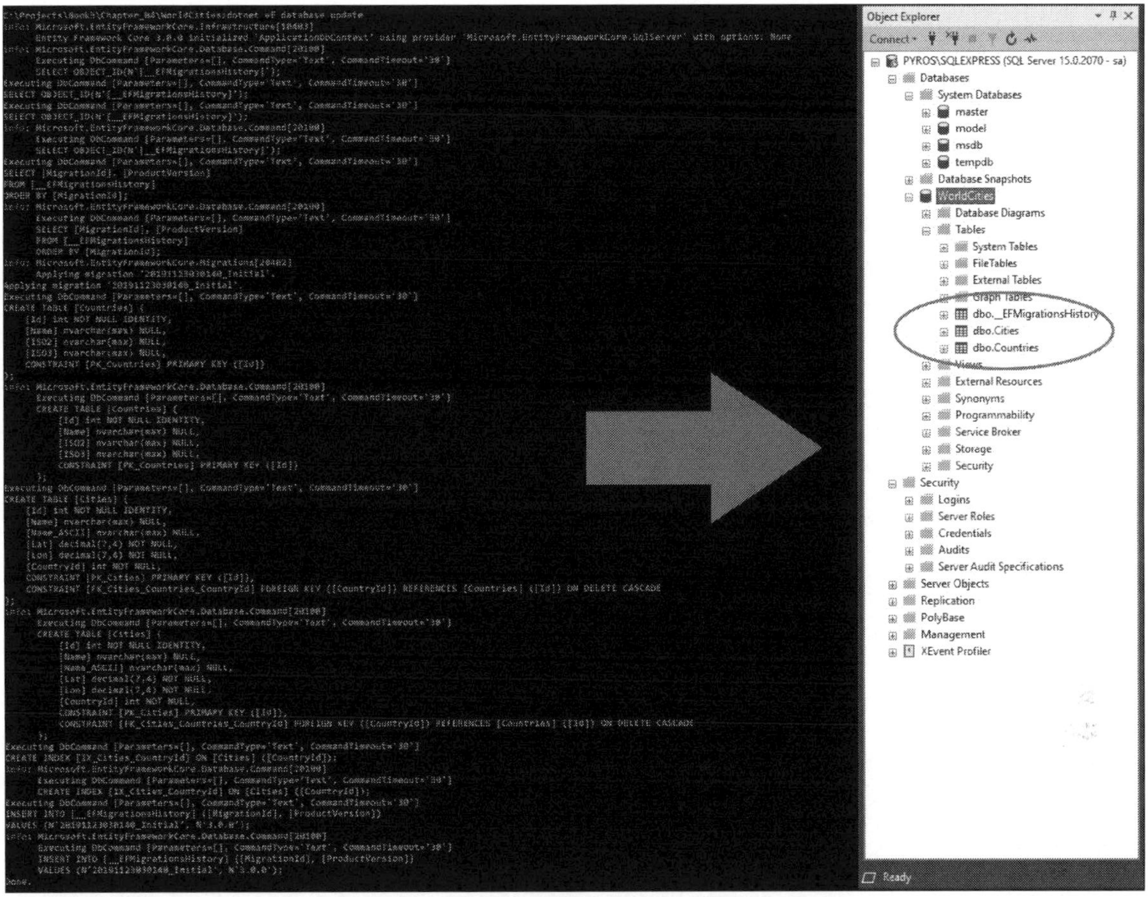

Figure 4.28: Checking the Object Explorer

The "No executable found matching command dotnet-ef" error

At the time of writing, there's a nasty issue affecting most .NET-based Visual Studio projects that can prevent the `dotnet ef` command from working properly. More specifically, we may be prompted by the following error message when trying to execute any `dotnet ef`-based command:

```
No executable found matching command "dotnet-ef"
```

If we happen to experience this issue, we can try to check out the following:

- Double-check that we added the `Microsoft.EntityFrameworkCore.Tools` package library (as explained earlier) properly, as it's required for the command to work.
- Ensure that we're issuing the `dotnet ef` command in the project's root folder—the same one that also contains the `<ProjectName>.csproj` file; it won't work anywhere else.

> A lot more can be said regarding this issue but doing so is outside the scope of this book. Those of you who want to know more can take a look at this article I wrote about it while working on my *ASP.NET Core 2 and Angular 5* book at: `https://goo.gl/Ki6mdb`

Using the Package Manager Console

In case we get issues while using the dotnet CLI, we can often avoid nasty headaches by switching to the Package Manager Console provided by the Visual Studio GUI. To activate it, select **View** > **Other Windows** > **Package Manager Console** from Visual Studio's main topmost menu.

Here's the full set of PMC commands that can be used to replace the previously mentioned `dotnet ef` ones:

```
Add-Migration Initial -OutputDir "Data/Migrations"
Update-Database
```

> To know more about the dotnet CLI commands and their corresponding Package Manager Console alternatives, check out the following official guides:
>
> **EF Core .NET CLI reference:** `https://docs.microsoft.com/en-us/ef/core/miscellaneous/cli/dotnet`
>
> **EF Core PMC / PowerShell reference:** `https://docs.microsoft.com/en-us/ef/core/miscellaneous/cli/powershell`

Understanding migrations

Before we move on, it would be useful to say a few words explaining what Code-First migrations actually are and the advantages we gain by using them.

Whenever we're developing an application and defining a data model, we can be sure that it will change a number of times for many good reasons: new requirements from the product owner, optimization processes, consolidation phases, and so on. A bunch of properties will be added, deleted, or have their types changed. Chances are, sooner or later, we'll be adding new entities as well and/or changing their relation pattern according to our ever-changing needs.

Each time we do something like that, we'll also put our data model out of sync with its underlying, Code-First-generated database. This won't be a problem when we're debugging our app within a development environment because that scenario usually allows us to recreate the database from scratch whenever the project changes.

Upon deploying the application into production, we'll be facing a whole different story: as long as we're handling real data, dropping and recreating our database won't be an option anymore. This is what the Code-First migrations feature is meant to address: giving the developer a chance to alter the database schema without having to drop/recreate the whole thing.

> We won't dig deeper into this topic; Entity Framework Core is a world of its own and addressing it in detail is out of the scope of this book. If you want to learn more, we suggest that you start with the official Entity Framework Core MS documentation at the following link:
>
> `https://docs.microsoft.com/en-us/ef/core/`

Is data migration required?

Data migration can be very useful, but it's not a required feature and we are definitely not forced to use it if we don't want to. As a matter of fact, it can be quite a difficult concept to understand for a lot of developers, especially for those who aren't much into DBMS design and/or scripting. It can also be very complex to manage in most scenarios, such as in companies where the DBA role is covered by someone who is below the IT development team (such as an external IT consultant or specialist).

Whenever we don't want to use data migration from the beginning—or we get to a point where we don't want to use it anymore—we can switch to a Database-First approach and start to manually design, create, and/or modify our tables: Entity Framework Core will work great, as long as the property types that are defined in the entities 100% match the corresponding database table fields. This can definitely be done, including when we put the project samples presented in this book into practice (this also applies to the `WorldCities` project), as long as we feel that data migration is not needed.

Alternatively, we can give it a try and see how it goes. The choice, as always, is yours.

Populating the database

Now that we have a SQL Database available and a `DbContext` that we can use to read from and write to it, we are finally ready to populate those tables with our world cities data.

To do that, we need to implement a **data seeding** strategy. We can do this using one of the various Entity Framework Core-supported approaches:

- **Model data seed**
- **Manual migration customization**
- **Custom initialization logic**

These three methods are well-explained in the following article, along with their very own sets of pros and cons: `https://docs.microsoft.com/en-us/ef/core/modeling/data-seeding`

Since we have to handle a relatively big Excel file, we're going to adopt the most customizable pattern we can make use of: some *custom initialization logic* relying upon a dedicated .NET controller that we can execute—manually or even automatically—whenever we need to seed our database.

Implementing SeedController

Our *custom initialization logic* implementation will rely upon a brand-new dedicated controller, which will be called `SeedController`.

From our project's **Solution Explorer**, do the following:

1. Right-click on the `/Controllers/` folder.
2. Click on **Add** | **Controller**.
3. Choose the **API Controller - Empty** option (the third from the top, at the time of writing).
4. Give the controller the `SeedController` name and click **Add** to create it.

Once done, open the newly created `/Controllers/SeedController.cs` file and take a look at the source code: you'll see that there's just an empty class, just as expected for an empty controller! This is great since we need to understand some key concepts and—most importantly—learn how to properly translate them into source code.

Do you remember when we added our `ApplicationDbContext` class to the `Startup.cs` file? As we should already know from *Chapter 2, Looking Around,* this means that we added the Entity Framework Core middleware to our application's pipeline. This means that we can now leverage the dependency injection loading feature provided by the .NET architecture to inject an instance of that `DbContext` class within our controllers.

Here's how we can translate such a concept into source code (the new lines are highlighted):

```
using System;
using System.Collections.Generic;
using System.Linq;
using System.Threading.Tasks;
using Microsoft.AspNetCore.Http;
using Microsoft.AspNetCore.Mvc;
using WorldCities.Data;

namespace WorldCities.Controllers
{
```

```
    [Route("api/[controller]")]
    [ApiController]
    public class SeedController : ControllerBase
    {
        private readonly ApplicationDbContext _context;

        public SeedController(ApplicationDbContext context)
        {
            _context = context;
        }
    }
}
```

As we can see, we've added a `_context` private variable and used it to store an object instance of the `ApplicationDbContext` class within the constructor. Such an instance will be provided by the framework—through its dependency injection feature—within the constructor method of `SeedController`.

Before making good use of that `DbContext` instance to insert a bunch of entities into our database, we need to find a way to read those world cities values from the Excel file. How can we do that?

Importing the Excel file

Luckily enough, there's a great third-party library that does precisely what we need: reading (and even writing!) Excel files using the Office Open XML format (`xlsx`), hence making their content available within any .NET-based application.

The name of this great tool is `EPPlus`. Its author, Jan Källman, made it freely available on GitHub and NuGet at the following URLs:

- **GitHub (source code)**: `https://github.com/JanKallman/EPPlus`
- **NuGet (.NET Package)**: `https://www.nuget.org/packages/EPPlus`

As we can see, the project recently changed its licensing model:

- Until version 4.x it was licensed under the GNU **Library General Public License (LGPL)** v3.0, meaning that we were allowed to integrate it into our software without limitations, as long as we didn't modify it
- From version 5.x and below it uses a *PolyForm Noncommercial* and *Commercial* dual license, which basically means that we can use it only for non-commercial purposes

  For that very reason, in order to avoid any possible license infringement, we're going to use EPPlus v4.5.3.3, it being the latest GNU-LGPL version available.

> For additional info about the new EPPlus *PolyForm Noncommercial* license, check out the following URL:
>
> `https://polyformproject.org/licenses/noncommercial/1.0.0/`
>
> To find out more about the EPPlus licensing change, read this: `https://www.epplussoftware.com/Home/LgplToPolyform`

The best way to install `EPPlus` in our `WorldCities` project is to add the NuGet package using the NuGet package manager GUI:

1. From the project's Solution Explorer, right-click on the `WorldCities` project
2. Select **Manage NuGet Packages...**
3. Use the **Browse** tab to search for the `EPPlus` package, choose the version you want to install (4.5.3.3 in our case), and then initiate the task by clicking the **Install** button at the top right:

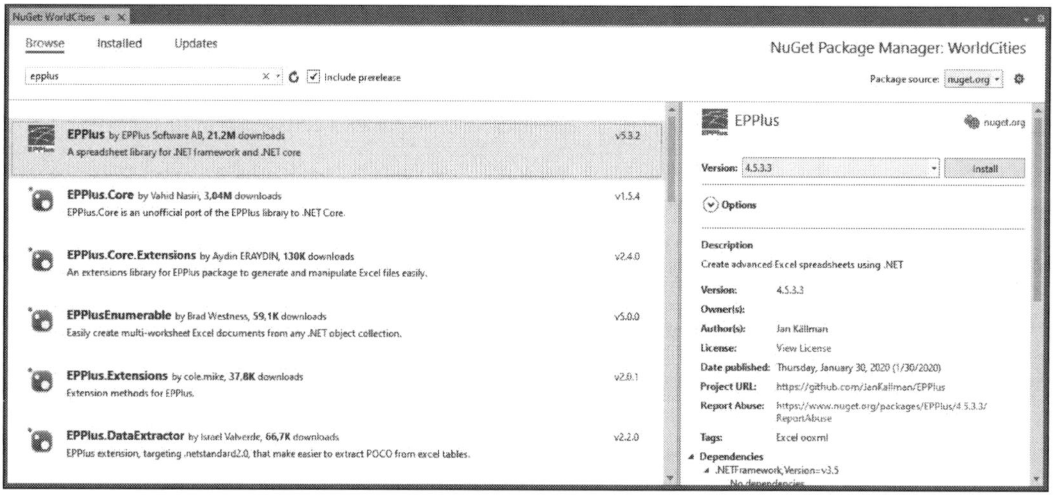

Figure 4.29: Adding the NuGet package using the NuGet Package Manager

Alternatively, type the following command from Visual Studio's Package Manager Console:

```
> Install-Package EPPlus -Version 4.5.3.3
```

Once done, we can go back to the `SeedController.cs` file and use the awesome features of `EPPlus` to read the `worldcities.xlsx` Excel file.

However, before doing that, it could be wise to move that file so that it's within our sample project's `/Data/` folder so that we'll be able to read it using the .NET filesystem capabilities provided by the `System.IO` namespace. While we're there, let's create a `/Data/Source/` subfolder and put it there to separate it from the other Entity Framework Core files:

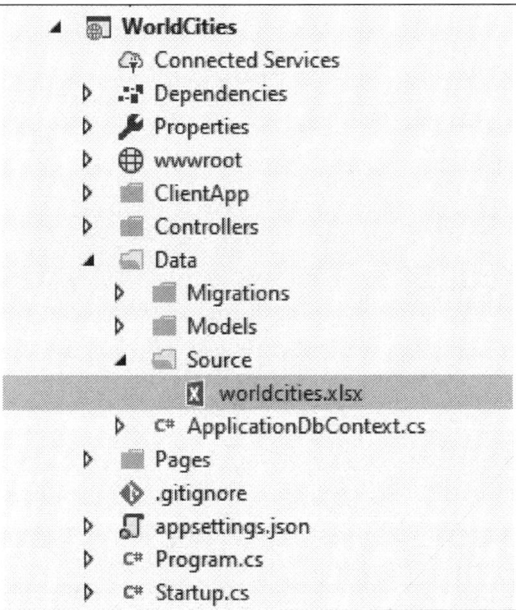

Figure 4.30: Creating a separate Source subfolder for the worldcities.xlsx file

Here's the source code that we need to add to our `SeedController.cs` file to read the `worldcities.xlsx` file and store all of the rows in a list of `City` entities:

```
using System;
using System.Linq;
using System.Threading.Tasks;
using Microsoft.AspNetCore.Mvc;
using WorldCities.Data;
using OfficeOpenXml;
using System.IO;
using Microsoft.AspNetCore.Hosting;
using WorldCities.Data.Models;
using Microsoft.EntityFrameworkCore;
using Microsoft.Extensions.Hosting;
using System.Security;

namespace WorldCities.Controllers
{
    [Route("api/[controller]/[action]")]
    [ApiController]
    public class SeedController : ControllerBase
    {
        private readonly ApplicationDbContext _context;
        private readonly IWebHostEnvironment _env;
```

```
public SeedController(
    ApplicationDbContext context,
    IWebHostEnvironment env)
{
    _context = context;
    _env = env;
}

[HttpGet]
public async Task<ActionResult> Import()
{
    // prevents non-development environments from running this method
    if (!_env.IsDevelopment())
            throw new SecurityException("Not allowed");

    var path = Path.Combine(
        _env.ContentRootPath,
        "Data/Source/worldcities.xlsx");

    using var stream = System.IO.File.OpenRead(path);
    using var excelPackage = new ExcelPackage(stream);

    // get the first worksheet
    var worksheet = excelPackage.Workbook.Worksheets[0];

    // define how many rows we want to process
    var nEndRow = worksheet.Dimension.End.Row;

    // initialize the record counters
    var numberOfCountriesAdded = 0;
    var numberOfCitiesAdded = 0;

    // create a lookup dictionary
    // containing all the countries already existing
    // into the Database (it will be empty on first run).
    var countriesByName = _context.Countries
        .AsNoTracking()
        .ToDictionary(x => x.Name, StringComparer.OrdinalIgnoreCase);

    // iterates through all rows, skipping the first one
    for (int nRow = 2; nRow <= nEndRow; nRow++)
    {
        var row = worksheet.Cells[
            nRow, 1, nRow, worksheet.Dimension.End.Column];

        var countryName = row[nRow, 5].GetValue<string>();
```

```
        var iso2 = row[nRow, 6].GetValue<string>();
        var iso3 = row[nRow, 7].GetValue<string>();

        // skip this country if it already exists in the database
        if (countriesByName.ContainsKey(countryName))
            continue;

        // create the Country entity and fill it with xlsx data
        var country = new Country
        {
            Name = countryName,
            ISO2 = iso2,
            ISO3 = iso3
        };

        // add the new country to the DB context
        await _context.Countries.AddAsync(country);

        // store the country in our lookup to retrieve its Id later on
        countriesByName.Add(countryName, country);

        // increment the counter
        numberOfCountriesAdded++;
    }

    // save all the countries into the Database
    if (numberOfCountriesAdded > 0)
        await _context.SaveChangesAsync();

    // create a lookup dictionary
    // containing all the cities already existing
    // into the Database (it will be empty on first run).
    var cities = _context.Cities
        .AsNoTracking()
        .ToDictionary(x => (
            Name: x.Name,
            Lat: x.Lat,
            Lon: x.Lon,
            CountryId: x.CountryId));

    // iterates through all rows, skipping the first one
    for (int nRow = 2; nRow <= nEndRow; nRow++)
    {
        var row = worksheet.Cells[
            nRow, 1, nRow, worksheet.Dimension.End.Column];
```

```
                var name = row[nRow, 1].GetValue<string>();
                var nameAscii = row[nRow, 2].GetValue<string>();
                var lat = row[nRow, 3].GetValue<decimal>();
                var lon = row[nRow, 4].GetValue<decimal>();
                var countryName = row[nRow, 5].GetValue<string>();

                // retrieve country Id by countryName
                var countryId = countriesByName[countryName].Id;

                // skip this city if it already exists in the database
                if (cities.ContainsKey((
                    Name: name,
                    Lat: lat,
                    Lon: lon,
                    CountryId: countryId)))
                    continue;

                // create the City entity and fill it with xlsx data
                var city = new City
                {
                    Name = name,
                    Name_ASCII = nameAscii,
                    Lat = lat,
                    Lon = lon,
                    CountryId = countryId
                };

                // add the new city to the DB context
                _context.Cities.Add(city);

                // increment the counter
                numberOfCitiesAdded++;
            }

            // save all the cities into the Database
            if (numberOfCitiesAdded > 0)
                await _context.SaveChangesAsync();

            return new JsonResult(new
            {
                Cities = numberOfCitiesAdded,
                Countries = numberOfCountriesAdded
            });
        }
    }
}
```

As we can see, we're doing a lot of interesting things here. The preceding code features a lot of comments and should be very readable; however, it could be useful to briefly enumerate the most relevant parts:

- We injected an `IHostEnvironment` instance through dependency injection, just like we did for `ApplicationDbContext`, so that we can retrieve the web application path and be able to read the Excel file.
- We added an `Import` action method that will use `ApplicationDbContext` and the `EPPlus` package to read the Excel file and add `Countries` and `Cities`.
- At the start of the `Import` method's implementation, we used the `IHostEnvironment` instance to determine if we're running in a development environment or not: in case we aren't, the code will throw a `SecurityException`. By acting that way we'll prevent anyone—including our users—from calling this method in production, thus restricting the whole importing task to developers only.
- `Countries` are imported first because the `City` entities require the `CountryId` foreign key value, which will be returned when the corresponding `Country` is created in the database as a new record.
- We defined a `Dictionary` container object to store all existing countries (plus each new `Country` right after we create it) so that we can query that list using LINQ to retrieve the `CountryId` instead of performing a lot of `SELECT` queries: this logic will also prevent the method from inserting the same country multiple times, should we happen to execute it more than once.
- We defined another `Dictionary` container object to prevent the insertion of duplicate cities as well.
- Last but not least, we created a JSON object to show the overall results on the screen.

> It's worth noting that we've issued our queries using EF Core's `AsNoTracking` extension method, which returns a new query where the entities returned will not be cached in the `DbContext` or `ObjectContext` in case they are modified within the code: this basically means that less data will be cached and tracked, with obvious benefits in terms of memory usage.
>
> For additional info on the `AsNoTracking` extension method, read the following URL:
>
> `https://docs.microsoft.com/en-us/dotnet/api/system.data.entity.dbextensions.asnotracking`

If we want to get a closer look at how the whole importing procedure works, we can put some breakpoints inside the `if` loops to check it out while it's running.

To execute the action method, hit *F5* to launch the web application in debug mode and then type the following URL to the browser's address bar: `https://localhost:44334/api/Seed/Import`

Be aware that the `Import` method is designed to import 230+ countries and 12,000+ cities, so this task will likely require some time—between about 10 and 30 seconds on an average development machine, depending on the amount of available RAM, CPU performance, and database connection speed. It's definitely a major data seed! We're kind of stressing out the framework here.

> In case we don't want to wait, we can always give the `nEndRow` internal variable a fixed value, such as 1,000, to limit the total number of cities (and countries) that will be read and therefore loaded into the database.

Eventually, we should be able to see the following response in our browser window:

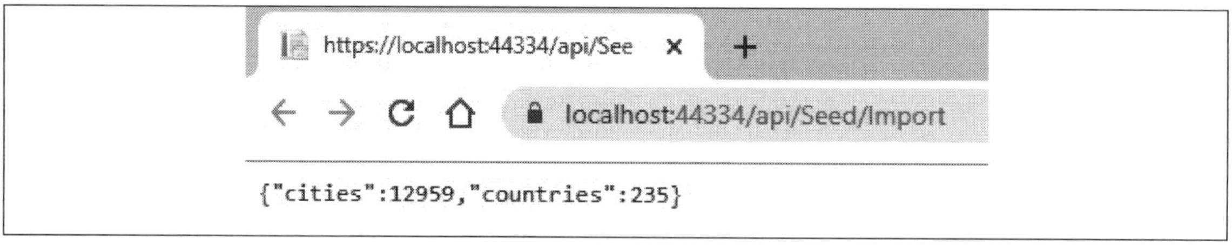
https://localhost:44334/api/See
localhost:44334/api/Seed/Import
{"cities":12959,"countries":235}

Figure 4.31: Inspecting the data import

The preceding output means that the import has been performed successfully: we did it! Our database is now filled with `12959` cities and `235` countries for us to play with.

> Those numbers might slightly change depending on the *WorldCities* database version: at the time of writing we're using v1.5, which was updated on April 11, 2019, but any subsequent version should work as well—as long as the MS Excel file structure doesn't change. If you want to use the same exact MS Excel file that was used to write this book, you can find it in the GitHub project's `/Data/Source/` folder.

In the next section, we're going to learn how we can read this data as well so that we'll be able to bring Angular into the loop.

Entity controllers

Now that we have thousands of cities and hundreds of countries in our database, we need to find a way to bring this data to Angular and vice versa. As we already know from *Chapter 2, Looking Around*, this role is played by the .NET controllers, so we're going to create two of them:

- `CitiesController`, to serve (and receive) the cities' data
- `CountriesController`, to do the same with the countries

Let's get started.

CitiesController

Let's start with the cities. Remember what we did when we created `SeedController`? What we're going to do now is rather similar, but this time we'll make good use of Visual Studio's code-generation features.

From our project's **Solution Explorer**, follow these steps:

1. Right-click on the `/Controllers/` folder.
2. Click on **Add** | **Controller**.
3. Choose the **Add API Controller with actions, using Entity Framework** option (the last one from the top, at the time of writing).
4. In the model window that appears, choose the `City` model class and the `ApplicationDbContext` data context class, as shown in the following screenshot. Name the controller `CitiesController` and click **Add** to create it:

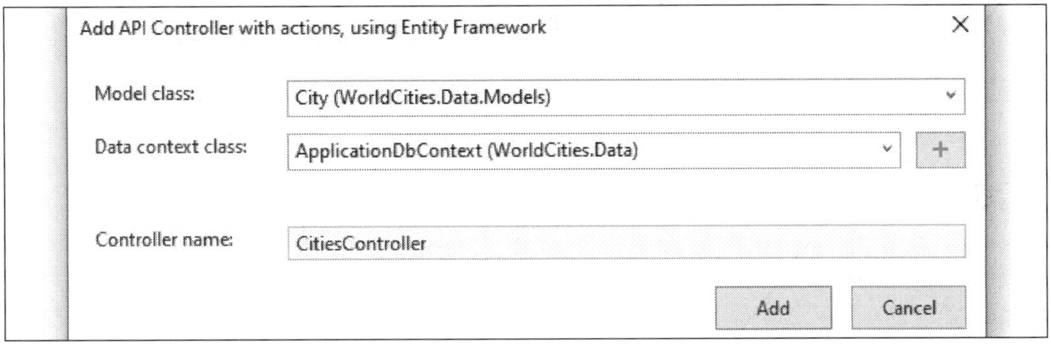

Figure 4.32: Creating CitiesController

The settings we specified during this phase will be used by Visual Studio to analyze our entities (and our `DbContext`) and auto-generate a whole API controller stuffed with useful methods.

Here's the source code that we're getting for free:

```
using System;
using System.Collections.Generic;
using System.Linq;
using System.Threading.Tasks;
using Microsoft.AspNetCore.Http;
using Microsoft.AspNetCore.Mvc;
using Microsoft.EntityFrameworkCore;
using WorldCities.Data;
using WorldCities.Data.Models;
```

```
namespace WorldCities.Controllers
{
    [Route("api/[controller]")]
    [ApiController]
    public class CitiesController : ControllerBase
    {
        private readonly ApplicationDbContext _context;

        public CitiesController(ApplicationDbContext context)
        {
            _context = context;
        }

        // GET: api/Cities
        [HttpGet]
        public async Task<ActionResult<IEnumerable<City>>> GetCities()
        {
            return await _context.Cities.ToListAsync();
        }

        // GET: api/Cities/5
        [HttpGet("{id}")]
        public async Task<ActionResult<City>> GetCity(int id)
        {
            var city = await _context.Cities.FindAsync(id);

            if (city == null)
            {
                return NotFound();
            }

            return city;
        }

        // PUT: api/Cities/5
        // To protect from overposting attacks, see https://go.microsoft.com/
fwlink/?linkid=2123754
        [HttpPut("{id}")]
        public async Task<IActionResult> PutCity(int id, City city)
        {
            if (id != city.Id)
            {
                return BadRequest();
            }

            _context.Entry(city).State = EntityState.Modified;
```

```
            try
            {
                await _context.SaveChangesAsync();
            }
            catch (DbUpdateConcurrencyException)
            {
                if (!CityExists(id))
                {
                    return NotFound();
                }
                else
                {
                    throw;
                }
            }

            return NoContent();
        }

        // POST: api/Cities
        // To protect from overposting attacks, see https://go.microsoft.com/
fwlink/?linkid=2123754
        [HttpPost]
        public async Task<ActionResult<City>> PostCity(City city)
        {
            _context.Cities.Add(city);
            await _context.SaveChangesAsync();

            return CreatedAtAction("GetCity", new { id = city.Id },
             city);
        }

        // DELETE: api/Cities/5
        [HttpDelete("{id}")]
        public async Task<ActionResult<City>> DeleteCity(int id)
        {
            var city = await _context.Cities.FindAsync(id);
            if (city == null)
            {
                return NotFound();
            }

            _context.Cities.Remove(city);
            await _context.SaveChangesAsync();
```

```
            return NoContent();
        }

        private bool CityExists(int id)
        {
            return _context.Cities.Any(e => e.Id == id);
        }
    }
}
```

As we can see, the code generator did a lot of useful work while sticking to a pattern that's similar to the one we followed for our `SeedController` class. Here's a breakdown of the relevant methods, in order of appearance:

- `GetCities()` returns a JSON array containing all of the cities in the database
- `GetCity(id)` returns a JSON object containing a single `City`
- `PutCity(id, city)` allows us to modify an existing `City`
- `PostCity(city)` allows us to add a new `City`
- `DeleteCity(id)` allows us to delete an existing `City`

It definitely seems that we do have everything we need for our *front-end*. Before moving on to Angular, let's do the same for our `Countries`.

CountriesController

From Solution Explorer, right-click the `/Controllers/` folder and perform the same set of tasks we performed to add `CitiesController`—except for the name, which will obviously be `CountriesController`.

For the sake of simplicity, we won't waste additional pages by repeating the auto-generated code: we have a dedicated GitHub repository to look out for that, after all. However, we're going to get the same set of methods we mentioned previously to handle the countries.

That concludes our journey through Entity Framework. Now, we need to connect the dots and plant what we've sown using our favorite *front-end* framework.

Testing it out

Now that our controllers are ready, we can perform a quick test to see if they're working as expected.

Hit *F5* to launch our web application in debug mode, then copy the following URL into the browser's address bar: `https://localhost:44334/api/Cities/`

If we made everything properly, we should see something like this:

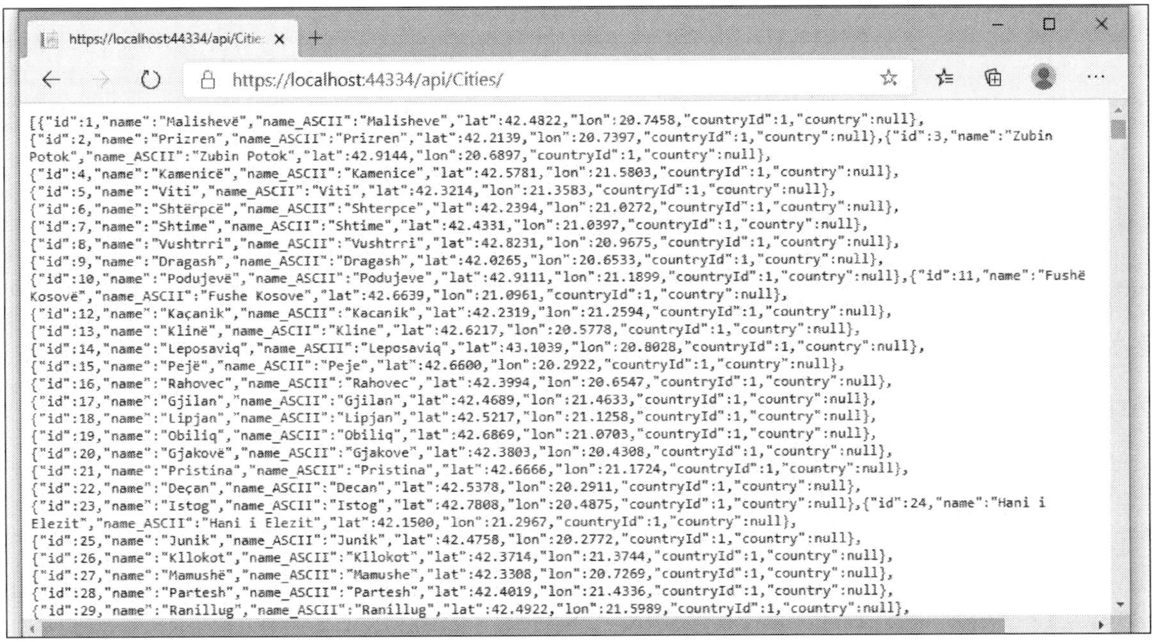

Figure 4.33: Testing CitiesController

Here come our cities!

While we're here, let's check the countries as well with the following URL: `https://localhost:44334/api/Countries/`

This is what we should receive from our browser:

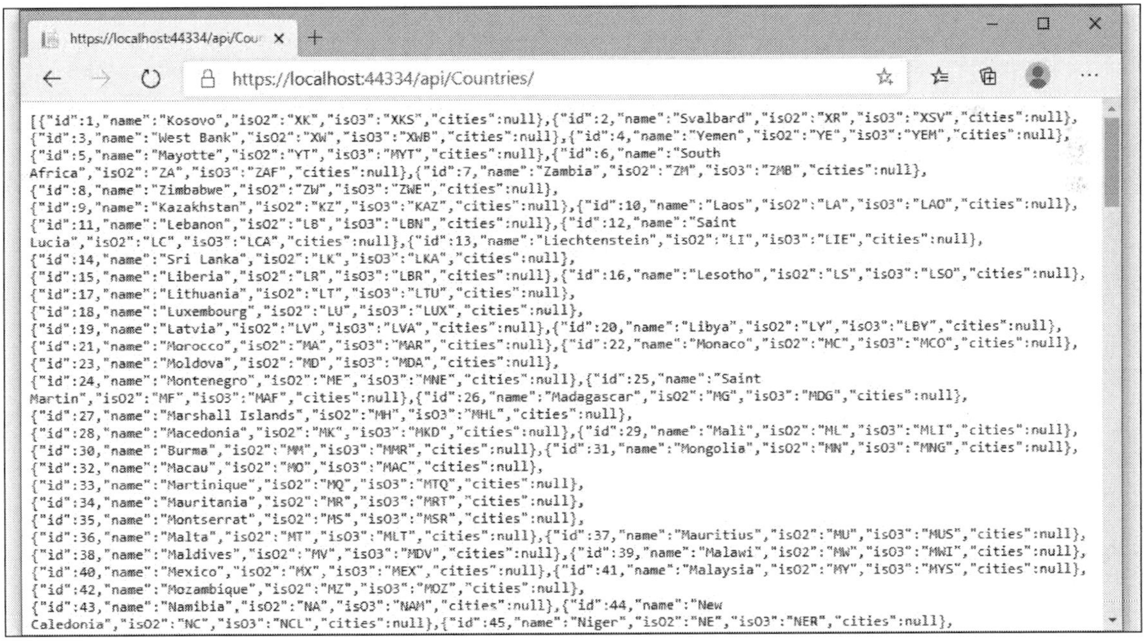

Figure 4.34: Testing CountriesController

Here they are.

Our job here is done: let's move on to the next chapter, where we'll see how to present this data to the *front-end*.

Summary

We started this chapter by enumerating a number of things that simply cannot be done without a proper data provider. To overcome these limitations, we decided to provide ourselves with a DBMS engine and a persistent database for reading and/or writing data. To avoid messing with what we did in the previous chapters, we created a brand-new web application project to deal with that, which we called `WorldCities`.

Then, we chose a suitable data source for our new project: a list of world cities and countries that we could download for free in a handy MS Excel file.

Right after that, we moved on to the data model: Entity Framework Core seemed an obvious choice to get what we wanted, so we added its relevant packages to our project. We briefly enumerated the available data modeling approaches and resorted to using Code-First due to its flexibility. Once done, we created our two entities, `City` and `Country`, both of which are based on the data source values we had to store within our database, along with a set of data annotations and relationships taking advantage of the renowned Entity Framework Core's convention-over-configuration approach. Then, we built our `ApplicationDbContext` class accordingly.

After we created our data model, we evaluated the various options for configuring and deploying our DBMS engine: we reviewed the DMBS local instances and cloud-based solutions such as MS Azure, and we explained how to implement both of them.

Last but not least, we created our .NET controller classes to deal with the data: `SeedController` to read the Excel file and seed our database, `CitiesController` to deal with cities, and `CountriesController` to handle countries.

After completing all of these tasks, we ran our application in debug mode to verify that everything was still working as intended. Now, we're ready to mess with the *front-end* part of our app. In the next chapter, we'll learn how to properly fetch this data from the server and bring it to the user in a fashionable way.

Angular, here we come!

Suggested topics

Web API, in-memory Web API, data source, data server, data model, data provider, ADO. NET, ORM, Entity Framework Core, Code-First, Database-First, Model-First, Entity class, Data Annotations, DbContext, CRUD operations, data migration, dependency injection, ORM mapping, JSON, ApiController.

References

- *Angular In-Memory Web API*: `https://github.com/angular/in-memory-web-api/`
- *Wikipedia: ISO 3166*: `https://en.wikipedia.org/wiki/ISO_3166`
- *Wikipedia: ISO 3166 alpha-2*: `https://en.wikipedia.org/wiki/ISO_3166-1_alpha-2`
- *Wikipedia: ISO 3166 alpha-3*: `https://en.wikipedia.org/wiki/ISO_3166-1_alpha-3`
- *ISO 3166 country codes*: `https://www.iso.org/iso-3166-country-codes.html`
- *SQL Server 2019 official page*: `https://www.microsoft.com/en-us/sql-server/sql-server-2019`
- *SQL Server 2019 – compare SQL Server versions*: `https://www.microsoft.com/en-us/sql-server/sql-server-2019-comparison`
- *SQL Server 2019 on Linux*: `https://docs.microsoft.com/en-US/sql/linux/sql-server-linux-overview`
- *Installing SQL Server on Windows*: `https://docs.microsoft.com/en-US/sql/database-engine/install-windows/installation-for-sql-server`
- *Installing SQL Server on Linux*: `https://docs.microsoft.com/en-US/sql/linux/sql-server-linux-setup`
- *Download SQL Server Management Studio (SSMS)*: `https://docs.microsoft.com/en-us/sql/ssms/download-sql-server-management-studio-ssms`
- *Create a SQL Server Database on Azure*: `https://azure.microsoft.com/en-us/resources/videos/create-sql-database-on-azure/`
- *Azure free account FAQ*: `https://azure.microsoft.com/en-in/free/free-account-faq/`
- *Azure SQL Server Managed Instance*: `https://azure.microsoft.com/en-us/services/sql-database/`
- *Use tags to organize your Azure resources*: `https://docs.microsoft.com/en-us/azure/azure-resource-manager/management/tag-resources`
- *Choose the right deployment option in Azure SQL*: `https://docs.microsoft.com/en-US/azure/sql-database/sql-database-paas-vs-sql-server-iaas`
- *Create an Azure SQL Database managed instance*: `https://docs.microsoft.com/en-us/azure/sql-database/sql-database-managed-instance-get-started`
- *Entity Framework Core: Loading Related Data*: `https://docs.microsoft.com/en-US/ef/core/querying/related-data`
- *Entity Framework Core: Modeling*: `https://docs.microsoft.com/en-us/ef/core/modeling/`
- *Entity Framework Core: Data Seeding*: `https://docs.microsoft.com/en-us/ef/core/modeling/data-seeding`
- *Entity Framework Core: DbContext*: `https://www.entityframeworktutorial.net/efcore/entity-framework-core-dbcontext.aspx`

- *EF Core .NET CLI reference*: `https://docs.microsoft.com/en-us/ef/core/miscellaneous/cli/dotnet`
- *EF Core PMC / PowerShell reference*: `https://docs.microsoft.com/en-us/ef/core/miscellaneous/cli/powershell`
- *#region (C# reference)*: `https://docs.microsoft.com/en-us/dotnet/csharp/language-reference/preprocessor-directives/preprocessor-region`
- *Are #regions an antipattern or code smell?*: `https://softwareengineering.stackexchange.com/questions/53086/are-regions-an-antipattern-or-code-smell`
- *PolyForm Noncommercial license*: `https://polyformproject.org/licenses/noncommercial/1.0.0/`
- *EPPlus library licensing change*: `https://www.epplussoftware.com/Home/LgplToPolyform`
- *DbExtensions.AsNoTracking Method*: `https://docs.microsoft.com/en-us/dotnet/api/system.data.entity.dbextensions.asnotracking`

5

Fetching and Displaying Data

In the previous chapter, we created a new `WorldCities` web application project and made a considerable effort to empower it with a DBMS-based data provider, built upon Entity Framework Core using the Code-First approach. Now that we have data persistence, we're ready to entrust our users with the ability to interact with our application; this means that we can implement some much-needed stuff, such as the following:

- **Fetching data**: Querying the data provider from the client side using HTTP requests and getting structured results back from the server side
- **Displaying data**: Populating typical client-side components such as tables, lists, and so on, ensuring a good user experience for the end user

In this chapter, we'll cover these two topics by adding a number of client-server interactions handled by standard HTTP request/response chains; it goes without saying that Angular will play a major role here, together with a couple of useful packages that will help us reach our goal.

Technical requirements

In this chapter, we're going to need all the technical requirements listed in the previous chapters, plus the following external libraries:

- `@angular/material` (Angular npm package)
- `System.Linq.Dynamic.Core` (.NET Core NuGet package)

As always, it's advisable to avoid installing them straight away; we're going to bring them in during this chapter to better contextualize their purpose within our project.

The code files for this chapter can be found at: `https://github.com/PacktPublishing/ASP.NET-Core-5-and-Angular/tree/main/Chapter_05`

Fetching data

As we already know from *Chapter 1, Getting Ready*, reading data from the database is mostly a matter of having the Angular *front-end* send HTTP requests to the ASP.NET *back-end* and fetching the corresponding HTTP responses accordingly; these data transfers will be mostly implemented using **JavaScript Object Notation (JSON)**, a lightweight data-interchange format that is natively supported by both frameworks.

In this section, we'll mostly talk about HTTP requests and responses, see how we can fetch data from the ASP.NET *back-end*, and lay out some raw UI examples using Angular components that will be further refined throughout the next sections.

Are we ready? Let's start!

Requests and responses

Let's start by taking a look at those HTTP requests and responses we'll be dealing with: hit *F5* to launch our `WorldCities` project in debug mode and type the following URL in the browser's address bar: `https://localhost:44334/api/Cities/`

If we did everything correctly, we should see a list of cities, each one with a unique `id`. From that list we can easily pick the `id` of each city and add it to our URL to retrieve that specific city only: for example, we can choose to use `9793`, which – in our specific scenario – corresponds to the city of New York.


```
{"id":9793,"name":"New York","name_ASCII":"New York","lat":40.6943,"lon":-73.9249,"countryId":235,"country":null}
```


Figure 5.1: Entry for New York

> **Important Note**: The IDs of the various cities and countries referenced throughout the book might likely differ from those present in the reader's own database, depending on various factors: the world cities file version/progress, the starting auto-incrementing `id` of the `[Cities]` database table we used to store the data source, and so on. Don't mind that: all the code samples should still work, regardless of any ID difference.

JSON conventions and defaults

As we can see, the JSON is basically a serialization of our `City` entity, with some built-in conventions such as the following:

- **camelCase instead of PascalCase**: We have `name` instead of `Name`, `countryId` instead of `CountryId`, and so on, meaning that all our PascalCase .NET class names and properties will be automatically converted into camelCase when they are serialized to JSON.

- **No indentation and no line feed/carriage return (LF/CR)**: Everything is stacked within a single line of text.

These conventions are the default options set by ASP.NET when dealing with JSON outputs. Most of them can be changed by adding some customization options to the MVC middleware. However, we don't need to do that as they are perfectly supported by Angular, which is what we're going to use to deal with those strings; we'll just have to ensure that the Angular interfaces that we'll create to mirror the entity classes have their names and properties set to camelCase.

> Anyone who wants to know why they chose camelCase instead of PascalCase as the default serialization option should check out the following GitHub thread: `https://github.com/aspnet/Mvc/issues/4283`

Anyway, for the sake of readability, let's add some indentation so that we'll be able to understand more of those outputs.

Open the `Startup.cs` file, locate the `ConfigureServices` method, and add the following code (new/updated lines highlighted):

```
public void ConfigureServices(IServiceCollection services)
{
    services.AddControllersWithViews()
        .AddJsonOptions(options => {
            // set this option to TRUE to indent the JSON output
            options.JsonSerializerOptions.WriteIndented = true;
            // set this option to NULL to use PascalCase instead of
            // camelCase (default)
            // options.JsonSerializerOptions.PropertyNamingPolicy =
            // null;
        });
    );
```

> As we can see, we also added the required configuration option to force PascalCase instead of camelCase; however, for the sake of these sample projects, we do prefer to enforce the camelCase convention on JSON and Angular, so we have chosen to comment that line.
>
> Those who want to uncomment it should be aware of the fact that they'll have to use camelCase for their Angular interfaces as well, changing our sample code accordingly.

Save the file, hit *F5*, and type the previous URL once more to see the following changes:

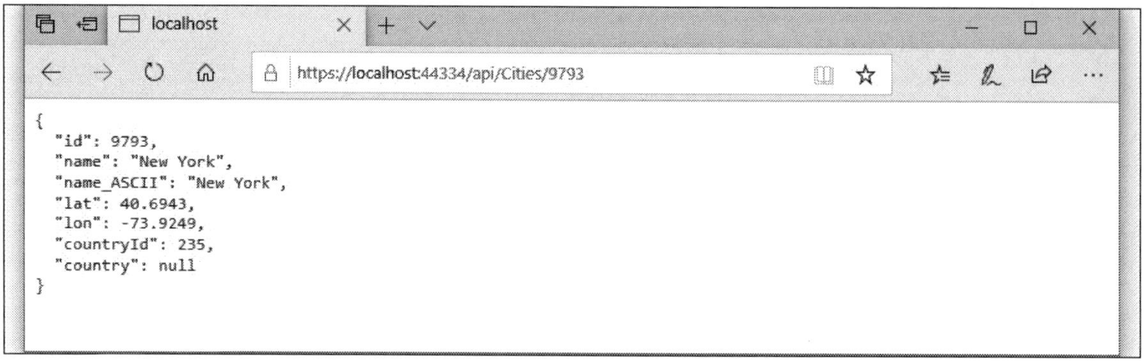
localhost
https://localhost:44334/api/Cities/9793
{
"id": 9793,
"name": "New York",
"name_ASCII": "New York",
"lat": 40.6943,
"lon": -73.9249,
"countryId": 235,
"country": null
}

Figure 5.2: New JSON file with camelCase and indentation changes

Here we go: now, the JSON is fully readable, with Angular still being able to properly access it.

A (very) long list

Let's now move to our Angular app and create a sample component to show a list of `Cities`. We already created a component in *Chapter 3*, *Front-End and Back-End Interactions*, so we know what to do.

From Solution Explorer, do the following:

1. Navigate to the `/ClientApp/src/app/` folder.
2. Create a new `/cities/` folder.
3. Within that folder, create the following new files:
    - `city.ts`
    - `cities.component.ts`
    - `cities.component.html`
    - `cities.component.css`

Once done, fill them with the following content.

city.ts

Open the `/ClientApp/src/app/cities/city.ts` file and add the following:

```
export interface City {
    id: number;
    name: string;
    lat: number;
    lon: number;
}
```

This small file contains our *city* interface, which we'll be using in our `CitiesComponent` class file. Since we're eventually going to use it in other components as well, it's better to create it within a separate file and decorate it with the `export` statement so that we'll be able to use it there as well when the time comes.

cities.component.ts

Open the `/ClientApp/src/app/cities/cities.component.ts` file and add the following:

```
import { Component, Inject, OnInit } from '@angular/core';
import { HttpClient } from '@angular/common/http';

import { City } from './city';

@Component({
  selector: 'app-cities',
  templateUrl: './cities.component.html',
  styleUrls: ['./cities.component.css']
})
export class CitiesComponent implements OnInit {
  public cities: City[];

  constructor(
    private http: HttpClient,
    @Inject('BASE_URL') private baseUrl: string) {
  }

  ngOnInit() {
    this.http.get<City[]>(this.baseUrl + 'api/Cities')
      .subscribe(result => {
        this.cities = result;
      }, error => console.error(error));
  }
}
```

As we can see, we added an `import` reference to the `City` interface we created a short while ago. We also used the `ngOnInit()` life cycle hook method to perform the HTTP request that will retrieve the cities, just like we did in *Chapter 3, Front-End and Back-End Interactions*, for our previous `HealthCheck` app.

cities.component.html

Open the `/ClientApp/src/app/cities/cities.component.html` file and add the following:

```
<h1>Cities</h1>

<p>Here's a list of cities: feel free to play with it.</p>

<p *ngIf="!cities"><em>Loading...</em></p>

<table class='table table-striped' aria-labelledby="tableLabel"
[hidden]="!cities">
  <thead>
    <tr>
      <th>ID</th>
      <th>Name</th>
      <th>Lat</th>
      <th>Lon</th>
    </tr>
  </thead>
  <tbody>
    <tr *ngFor="let city of cities">
      <td>{{ city.id }}</td>
      <td>{{ city.name }}</td>
      <td>{{ city.lat }}</td>
      <td>{{ city.lon }}</td>
    </tr>
  </tbody>
</table>
```

As we can see, the preceding HTML structure has nothing special: it's just a header, a paragraph, and a table with some standard loading logic to let the user know that we'll asynchronously load the data in a (hopefully) short while. However, there are at least two attributes that deserve a couple of words.

Bootstrap styling

If we take a look at the `<table>` HTML element, we can easily notice that we've applied a couple of CSS classes there: `table` and `table-striped`. These are two of the most used classes of the **Bootstrap** front-end framework when it comes to styling tables. In a nutshell, the former will apply some basic spacing and typography rules, while the latter will change the background color of the table's odd rows, thus reproducing a "striped" effect; both of them will greatly increase the table's readability.

> To read more about UI components and layout styling using Bootstrap, check out the official documentation at the following URL: `https://getbootstrap.com`

Now we could ask ourselves the following question: how can we use Bootstrap to begin with, since we haven't added a reference or stylesheet link to it anywhere in our project?

As a matter of fact, we never did; we inherited it from the ASP.NET and Angular template we started with. If we take a look at the `/ClientApp/angular.json` file, we can easily find a reference to it (row #28 or so):

```
[...]

"styles": [
  "node_modules/bootstrap/dist/css/bootstrap.min.css",
  "src/styles.css"
],

[...]
```

The reference points to the Bootstrap npm package, which is referenced in the `/ClientApp/package.json` file: now we know why we're able to use those CSS classes.

The [hidden] attribute

Shortly after the table's `class` definition, we can see that the `<table>` element features a strange `[hidden]` attribute. Why is it there, and why is it between square brackets?

As a matter of fact, the `hidden` attribute is an HTML5-valid content attribute that can be legitimately set on any HTML element. The role it's supposed to play is very similar to the CSS `display: none` setting: it indicates to the browser that the element and all of its descendants should not be visible or perceivable to any user. In other words, it's just another way to hide content from the user.

> For additional information regarding the `hidden` attribute, check out the following URL:
>
> **HTML Living Standard** (last updated on November 26, 2019): `https://html.spec.whatwg.org/multipage/interaction.html#the-hidden-attribute`

As for the square brackets, that's just the Angular syntax used to define a property binding, that is, an HTML property or attribute within the component template (our `.html` file) that gets its value from a variable, property, or expression defined within the component class (our `.ts` file). It's worth noting that such a binding flows in one direction: from the component class (the source) to the HTML element within the component template (the target).

As a direct consequence of what we have just said, every time the source value evaluates to `true`, the HTML property (or attribute) between square brackets will be set to *true* as well (and vice versa); this is a great way to deal with a lot of HTML attributes that work with Boolean values because we can dynamically set them through the whole component's life cycle. That's precisely what we do with the `<table>` element in the preceding code block: its `hidden` attribute will evaluate to `false` until the `cities` component variable is filled by the actual *cities* fetched from the server, which will only happen when the `HttpClient` module finishes its request/response task. Not bad, right?

Wait a minute: isn't that the same behavior of the `*ngIf` *structural directive* that we already know from *Chapter 3, Front-End and Back-End Interactions*? Why are we using this `[hidden]` attribute instead?

This is a very good question that gives us the chance to clarify the difference between these two similar - yet not identical - approaches:

- The `*ngIf` structural directive adds or removes the element from the **Document Object Model** (**DOM**) based on its corresponding condition or expression; this means that the element will be initialized and/or disposed of (together with all its children, events, and so on) every time its status changes.
- The `hidden` attribute, much like the `display: none` CSS setting, will only instruct the browser to show the element to or hide the element from the user; this means that the element will still be there, thus being fully available and reachable (for example, by JavaScript or other DOM-manipulating actions).

As we can see by looking at the preceding HTML code, we're using both of them: the `*ngIf` structural directive adds or removes the *loading* `<p>` element, while the `[hidden]` *attribute binding* shows or hides the main `<table>`. We have chosen to do this for a reason: the `<p>` element won't have children or events depending on it, while the `<table>` will soon become a complex object with a lot of features to initialize and preserve within the DOM.

cities.component.css

Here's the code for the `/ClientApp/src/app/cities/cities.component.css` file:

```
table {
  width: 100%;
}
```

That's it, at least for now: since we're using the bootstrap client framework, our component's CSS files will often be very small.

app.module.ts

Now that we've created the component, we need to add it to the `app.module.ts` file (new lines are highlighted):

```
import { BrowserModule } from '@angular/platform-browser';
import { NgModule } from '@angular/core';
```

```
import { FormsModule } from '@angular/forms';
import { HttpClientModule, HTTP_INTERCEPTORS } from '@angular/common/http';

import { AppRoutingModule } from './app-routing.module';

import { AppComponent } from './app.component';
import { NavMenuComponent } from './nav-menu/nav-menu.component';
import { HomeComponent } from './home/home.component';
import { CitiesComponent } from './cities/cities.component';

@NgModule({
  declarations: [
    AppComponent,
    NavMenuComponent,
    HomeComponent,
    CitiesComponent
  ],

[...]
```

Now that the component has its required reference here, we can deal with the routing part.

app-routing.module.ts

As we already know, this component can only be loaded – and can only be reached by Angular client-side routing – if we add it to the `app-routing.module.ts` file in the following way (new lines are highlighted):

```
import { NgModule } from '@angular/core';
import { Routes, RouterModule } from '@angular/router';
import { HomeComponent } from './home/home.component';
import { CitiesComponent } from './cities/cities.component';

const routes: Routes = [
  { path: '', component: HomeComponent, pathMatch: 'full' },
  { path: 'cities', component: CitiesComponent }
];

@NgModule({
  imports: [RouterModule.forRoot(routes)],
  exports: [RouterModule]
})
export class AppRoutingModule { }
```

Here we go.

nav-menu-component.html

Last but not least, we need to add a reference to the new component route within the app navigator component; otherwise, the user won't be able to see (and thus reach) it using the UI.

To do that, open the `nav-menu-component.html` file and add the following (highlighted) lines:

```
// ...existing code...

<ul class="navbar-nav flex-grow">
  <li
    class="nav-item"
    [routerLinkActive]="['link-active']"
    [routerLinkActiveOptions]="{ exact: true }"
  >
    <a class="nav-link text-dark" [routerLink]="['/']">Home</a>
  </li>
  <li class="nav-item" [routerLinkActive]="['link-active']">
    <a class="nav-link text-dark" [routerLink]="['/cities']"
      >Cities</a
    >
  </li>
</ul>

// ...existing code...
```

That's it. Now, we *could* hit *F5* to launch our app, click on the **Cities** link that will appear in the top-right part of the screen, and experience the following outcome:

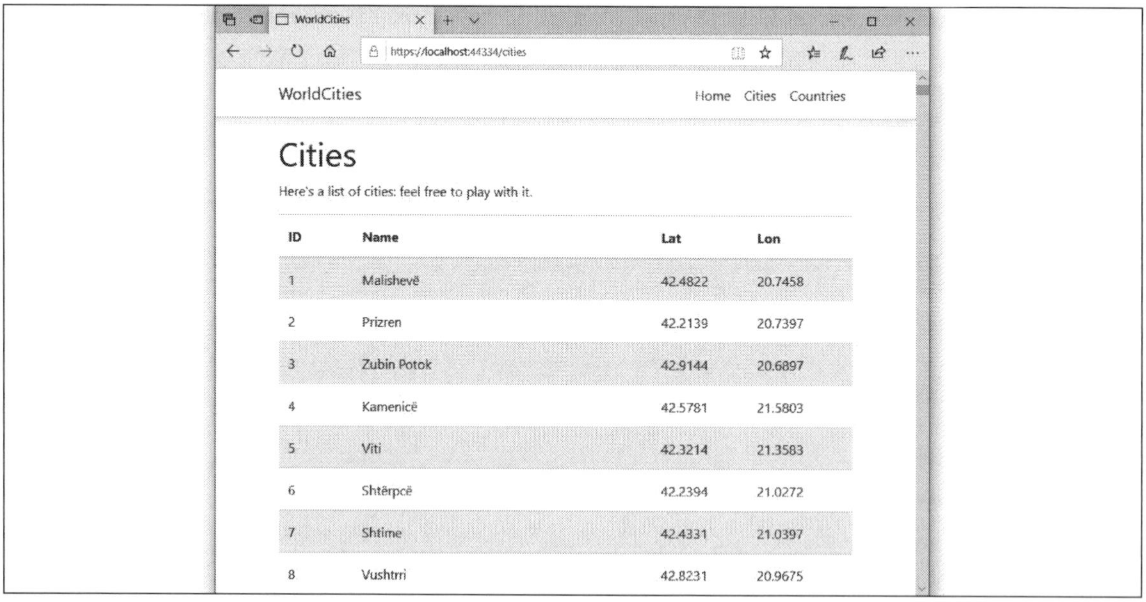

Figure 5.3: Cities table

As we can see by looking at the vertical scrollbar to the right, we would be overwhelmed by a huge HTML table consisting of 12,959 (or so) rows!

That's another huge performance stress for both ASP.NET and Angular - which should pass with flying colors on any average development machine since both frameworks can deal well with their respective tasks.

However, such a UI outcome is definitely a no-go in terms of user experience: we can't reasonably expect our end users to be happy if we force them to navigate through a 13k-row HTML table with a browser. They would go mad trying to find the city they're looking for!

To fix these major usability issues, we need to implement a few important features that are frequently used to deal with fat HTML tables: **paging**, **sorting**, and **filtering**.

Serving data with Angular Material

To implement a table with paging, sorting, and filtering features, we're going to use **Angular Material**, a UI component library that implements Material Design in Angular. As we most likely already know, Material Design is a UI design language that Google developed in 2014, which focuses on using grid-based layouts, responsive animations, transitions, padding, and depth effects such as lighting and shadows.

> Material Design was introduced by the Google designer Matías Duarte on June 25, 2014, at the 2014 Google I/O conference. To make UI designers familiarize themselves with its core concepts, he explained that "unlike real paper, our digital material can expand and reform intelligently. Material has physical surfaces and edges. Seams and shadows provide meaning about what you can touch."
>
> The main purpose of Material Design is to create a new UI language combining principles of good design with technical and scientific innovation in order to provide a consistent user experience across not only all Google platforms and applications but also any other web applications seeking to adopt such concepts. The language was revamped in 2018, providing more flexibility and advanced customization features based on themes.

As of 2020, Material Design is used on almost all Google web applications and tools - including Gmail, YouTube, Google Drive, Google Docs, Sheets, Slides, Google Maps, and all of the Google Play-branded applications, as well as most Android and Google OS UI elements. Such wide adoption also includes Angular, which has been provided with a dedicated npm package that can be added to any Angular-based project to implement Material Design in any Angular app; this package is called `@angular/material` and includes the native UI elements, the **Component Dev Kit** (**CDK**), a set of animations, and other useful stuff.

To install Angular Material, do the following:

1. Open Command Prompt.
2. Navigate to our project's `/ClientApp/` folder.
3. Type the following command:

```
> ng add @angular/material
```

Doing this will trigger the Angular Material command-line setup wizard, which will install the following npm packages:

- `@angular/material`
- `@angular/cdk` (prerequisite)

> **Important**: Be sure to install the same `@angular/material` version specified in the `package.json` of the GitHub project released with this book - `11.0.1` at the time of writing. Those who want to change or update the Angular version should pay special attention to updating the `@angular/material` package and/or manually fixing the potential breaking changes between the various versions.
>
> For additional information about Angular Material, check out the following URLs: `https://material.angular.io/`
>
> `https://github.com/angular/components`

During the installation process, the preceding command will ask us what pre-built theme we would like to install, as shown in the following screenshot:

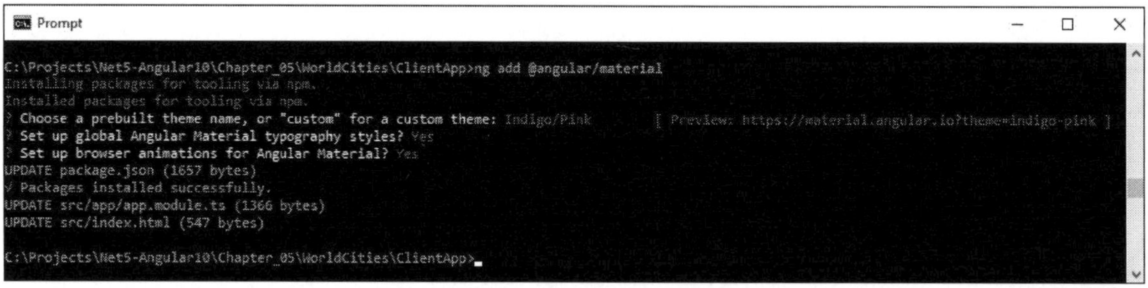

Figure 5.4: Angular Material installation

For the purpose of this chapter, we're going to pick `Indigo/Pink`, but we're free to choose any other theme we like. If we want to look at them before making our choice, we can visit the preview URIs listed in the preceding screenshot.

The setup wizard will also ask us if we would like to set up a couple of optional features:

- *Global Angular Material Typography* Styles (answer **YES** here): this option will add the `mat-typography` CSS class to the `<body>` element of our Angular app's `index.html` file, thus giving access to a lot of classes responsible for spacing, shadows, animations, and so on.

For additional info about this feature, check out the following URL:
`https://material.angular.io/guide/typography`

- *Browser animation for Angular Material* (answer **YES** here): this option will import the `BrowserAnimationsModule` into our application, thus enabling Angular's animation system.

For additional info about the `BrowserAnimationsModule` and Angular's animation system, check out the following URLs:

`https://angular.io/api/platform-browser/animations/BrowserAnimationsModule`

`https://angular.io/guide/animations`

Once done, the setup process will update the following files:

- `package.json`
- `/src/main.ts`
- `/src/app/app.module.ts`
- `angular.json`
- `src/index.html`
- `src/styles.css`

Now, we can proceed with the revamp of our **Cities** table.

MatTableModule

The Angular component we're going to use is `MatTableModule`, which provides a Material Design styled HTML table that can be used to display rows of data. Let's see how we can implement it in our existing Angular app.

From Solution Explorer, navigate to the `/ClientApp/src/app/` folder, create a new `angular-material.module.ts` file, and fill it with the following content:

```
import { NgModule } from '@angular/core';
import { MatTableModule } from '@angular/material/table';

@NgModule({
    imports: [
        MatTableModule
    ],
    exports: [
        MatTableModule
```

```
    ]
})

export class AngularMaterialModule { }
```

This is a brand new module that we're going to use for all the Angular Material modules we want to implement within our app; putting them here instead of using the `app.module.ts` file will keep that file smaller, which is great for project manageability.

Needless to say, for this *module container* to properly work, we need to add it within our existing `app.module.ts` file. Open it and add the following (highlighted) lines:

```
import { BrowserModule } from '@angular/platform-browser';
import { NgModule } from '@angular/core';
import { FormsModule } from '@angular/forms';
import { HttpClientModule, HTTP_INTERCEPTORS } from
 '@angular/common/http';

import { AppRoutingModule } from './app-routing.module';

import { AppComponent } from './app.component';
import { NavMenuComponent } from './nav-menu/nav-menu.component';
import { HomeComponent } from './home/home.component';
import { CitiesComponent } from './cities/cities.component';
import { BrowserAnimationsModule } from '@angular/platform-
 browser/animations';
import { AngularMaterialModule } from './angular-material.module';

@NgModule({
  declarations: [
    AppComponent,
    NavMenuComponent,
    HomeComponent,
    CitiesComponent
  ],
  imports: [
    BrowserModule.withServerTransition({ appId: 'ng-cli-universal' }),
    HttpClientModule,
    FormsModule,
    AppRoutingModule,
    BrowserAnimationsModule,
    AngularMaterialModule
  ],
  providers: [],
  bootstrap: [AppComponent]
})
export class AppModule { }
```

Here we go: now, everything we're going to put in the `angular-material.module.ts` file will also be referenced within our app.

Once we have done that, we can finally open our `/ClientApp/src/app/cities/cities.component.ts` file and add the following (highlighted) lines:

```
// ...existing code...

export class CitiesComponent implements OnInit {
  public displayedColumns: string[] = ['id', 'name', 'lat', 'lon'];
  public cities: City[];

  constructor(
    private http: HttpClient,
    @Inject('BASE_URL') private baseUrl: string) {
  }
}

// ...existing code...
```

Right after that, open the `/ClientApp/src/app/cities/cities.component.html` file and replace our previous table implementation with the new `MatTableModule` in the following way (updated code is highlighted):

```
<h1>Cities</h1>

<p>Here's a list of cities: feel free to play with it.</p>

<p *ngIf="!cities"><em>Loading...</em></p>

<table mat-table [dataSource]="cities"
  class="table-striped mat-elevation-z8"
  [hidden]="!cities">
  <!-- Id Column -->
  <ng-container matColumnDef="id">
    <th mat-header-cell *matHeaderCellDef>ID</th>
    <td mat-cell *matCellDef="let city">{{city.id}}</td>
  </ng-container>

  <!-- Name Column -->
  <ng-container matColumnDef="name">
    <th mat-header-cell *matHeaderCellDef>Name</th>
    <td mat-cell *matCellDef="let city">{{city.name}}</td>
  </ng-container>

  <!-- Lat Column -->
  <ng-container matColumnDef="lat">
```

```
    <th mat-header-cell *matHeaderCellDef>Latitude</th>
    <td mat-cell *matCellDef="let city">{{city.lat}}</td>
  </ng-container>

  <!-- Lon Column -->
  <ng-container matColumnDef="lon">
    <th mat-header-cell *matHeaderCellDef>Longitude</th>
    <td mat-cell *matCellDef="let city">{{city.lon}}</td>
  </ng-container>

  <tr mat-header-row *matHeaderRowDef="displayedColumns"></tr>
  <tr mat-row *matRowDef="let row; columns: displayedColumns;"></tr>
</table>
```

As we can see, `MatTableModule` kind of mimics the behavior of a standard HTML table, but with a template-based approach for each column; the template features a series of auxiliary structural directives (applied using the `*<directiveName>` syntax) that can be used to mark certain template sections and define their template section's actual role. As we can see, all these directives end with the `Def` postfix.

Here are the most relevant ones among those used in the preceding code:

- The `[hidden]` attribute binding is not a surprise as it was already present in the previous table for the exact same purpose: keeping the table hidden until the *cities* have been loaded.
- The `matColumnDef` directive identifies a given column with a unique key.
- The `matHeaderCellDef` directive defines how to display the header for each column.
- The `matCellDef` directive defines how to display the data cells for each column.
- The `matHeaderRowDef` directive, which can be found near the end of the preceding code, identifies a configuration element for the table header row and the display order of the header columns. As we can see, we had this directive expression pointing to a component variable called `displayedColumns`, which we defined in the `cities.component.ts` file early on; this variable hosts an array containing all the column keys we want to show, which need to be identical to the names specified via the various `matColumnDef` directives.

Let's hit *F5* and navigate to the **Cities** view to see what our brand new table looks like. This can be seen in the following screenshot:

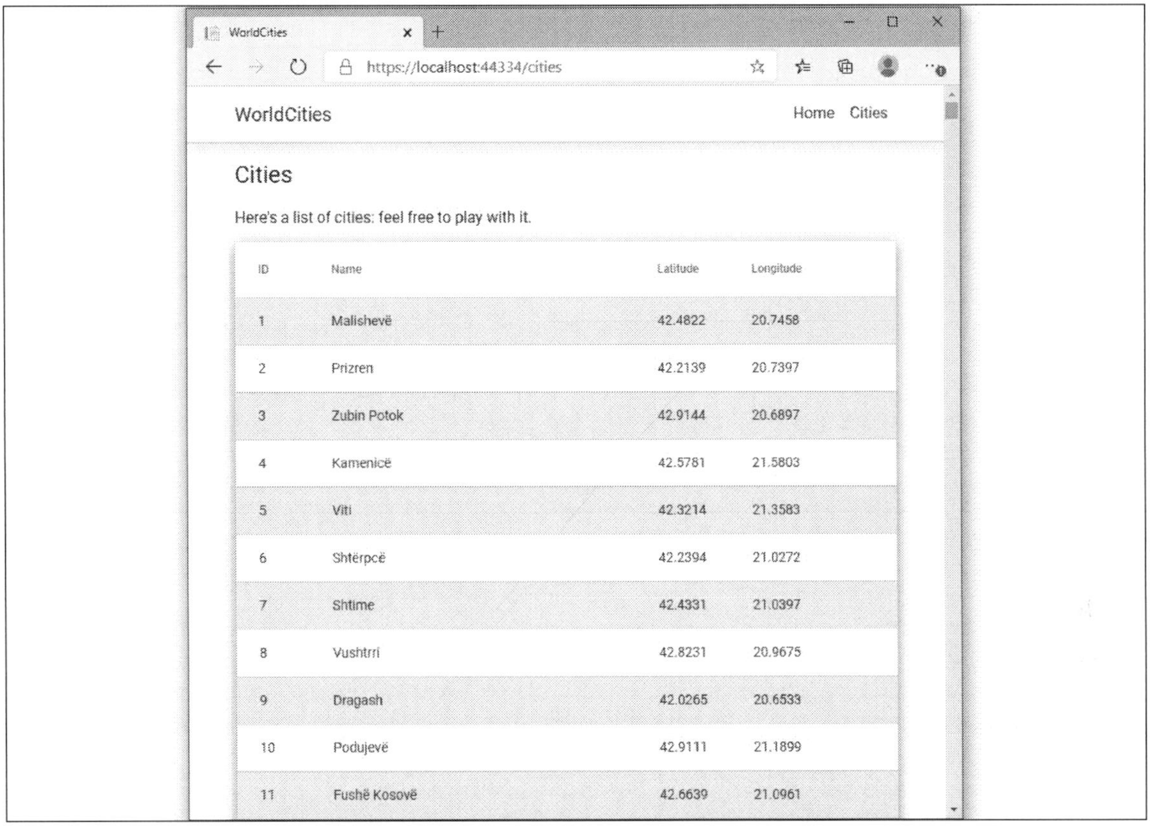

Figure 5.5: New Cities table implemented using MatTableModule

OK, Material Design is indeed there, but the table has the same UI/UX problems as before! For one, it's still very long; let's fix that by implementing the **paging** feature.

Adding pagination with MatPaginatorModule

Now that we are using Angular Material, implementing pagination is a rather easy task. The first thing we need to do is import the `MatPaginatorModule` service into the `angular-material.module.ts` file we created a short while ago.

Client-side paging

Here's how we can do that (new lines are highlighted):

```
import { NgModule } from '@angular/core';
import { MatTableModule } from '@angular/material/table';
import { MatPaginatorModule } from '@angular/material/paginator';

@NgModule({
    imports: [
        MatTableModule,
        MatPaginatorModule
    ],
    exports: [
        MatTableModule,
        MatPaginatorModule
    ]
})

export class AngularMaterialModule { }
```

Right after that, we need to open the `cities.component.ts` file and import the `MatPaginator`, `MatTableDataSource`, and `ViewChild` services:

```
import { Component, Inject, OnInit, ViewChild } from '@angular/core';
import { HttpClient } from '@angular/common/http';
import { MatTableDataSource } from '@angular/material/table';
import { MatPaginator } from '@angular/material/paginator';

import { City } from './city';

@Component({
  selector: 'app-cities',
  templateUrl: './cities.component.html',
  styleUrls: ['./cities.component.css']
})
export class CitiesComponent implements OnInit {
  public displayedColumns: string[] = ['id', 'name', 'lat', 'lon'];
```

```
  public cities: MatTableDataSource<City>;

  @ViewChild(MatPaginator) paginator: MatPaginator;

  constructor(
    private http: HttpClient,
    @Inject('BASE_URL') private baseUrl: string) {
  }

  ngOnInit() {
    this.http.get<City[]>(this.baseUrl + 'api/Cities')
      .subscribe(result => {
        this.cities = new MatTableDataSource<City>(result);
        this.cities.paginator = this.paginator;
      }, error => console.error(error));
  }
}
```

Once done, open the `cities.component.html` file and add the following pagination directive (highlighted) right after the `</table>` closing tag:

```
// ...existing code...

  <tr mat-header-row *matHeaderRowDef="displayedColumns"></tr>
  <tr mat-row *matRowDef="let row; columns: displayedColumns;"></tr>
</table>

<!-- Pagination directive -->
<mat-paginator [hidden]="!cities"
    [pageSize]="10"
    [pageSizeOptions]="[10, 20, 50]"
    showFirstLastButtons></mat-paginator>
```

As we can see, we used the `[hidden]` *attribute binding* again to keep the paginator hidden until the *cities* were loaded. The other properties that we can see on the `<mat-paginator>` element configure some of the `MatPaginatorModule` UI options, such as the default page size and an array of all the page size options that we want to make available to the users.

Now, we can hit *F5* and take a look at our efforts:

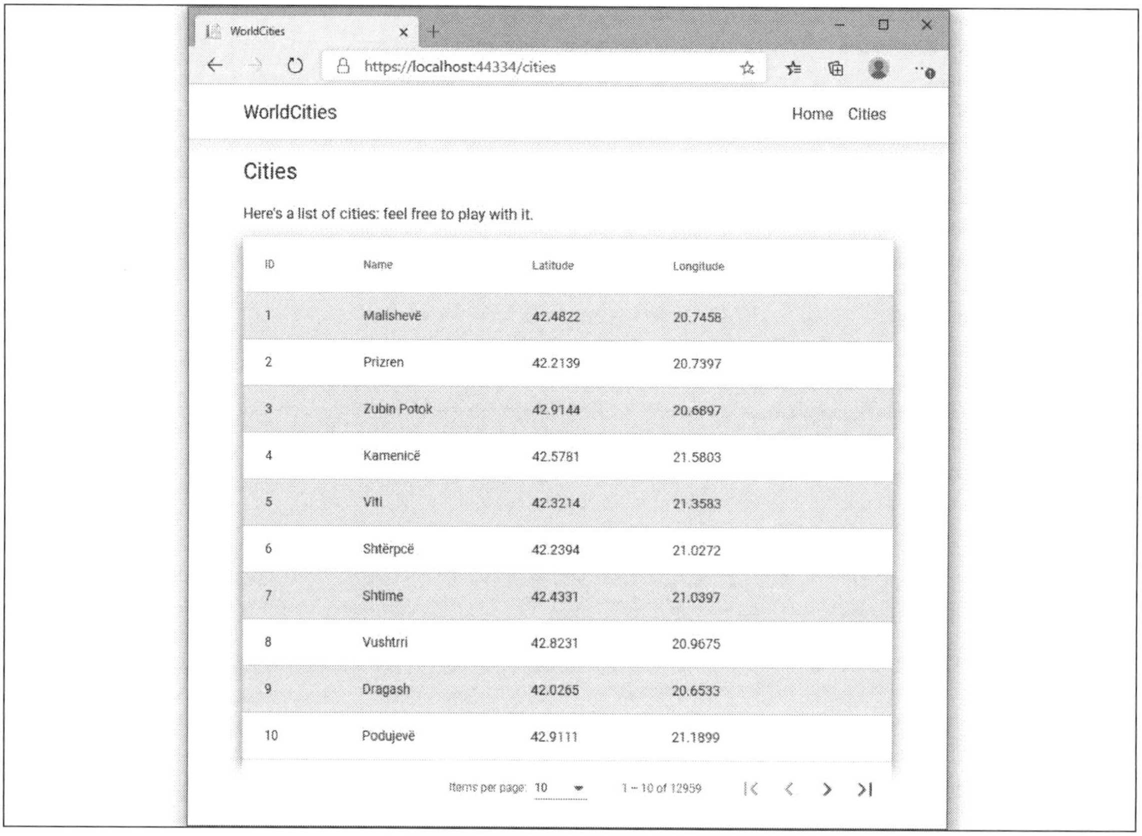

Figure 5.6: Cities table with pagination

Now, our table only shows the first 10 cities. It has also got a neat paginator at its bottom-right corner that can be used to navigate through the various pages using arrows. Our end user can even choose how many items per page to display using a neat drop-down list (10, 20, or 50 cities per page, as specified in the `[pageSizeOptions]` property). It definitely seems like we did it!

However, if we think about it, we can easily acknowledge that we're not quite there yet. Sure, now our users can browse the table nicely without having to scroll up and down for ages, but it doesn't take a genius to understand that all those rows are still there on the page: we never told the server to actually support a paginated request, so we still fetch all of the cities from our data provider (and through the ASP.NET API Controller) just like before: as a matter of fact, they're just not rendered by the *front-end*.

This basically means that we still have the same performance impact that we had before on the server side (huge SQL query result, massive JSON) and only a partial performance improvement on the client side: even if fewer HTML elements are now added to the DOM, there are still lots of HTML rows to show/hide on each paginator action, leading to a page change.

In order to mitigate the aforementioned issues, we need to move from client-side paging to server-side paging – which is precisely what we'll do in the next section.

Server-side paging

Implementing server-side paging is a bit more complex than its client-side counterpart. Here's what we need to do:

- Change our `CitiesController` ASP.NET class to make it support paged HTTP GET requests
- Create a new `ApiResult` .NET class that we can use to improve the JSON response of our ASP.NET Controllers
- Change our `cities.controller.ts` Angular component – and the current `MatPaginatorModule` configuration – to make it able to issue the new GET request and deal with the new JSON response

Let's do this!

CitiesController

The `GetCities` method of our `CitiesController` returns a JSON array of all the ~13,000 cities in our database by default; that's definitely a no-go in terms of server-side performance, so we need to change it. Ideally, we would like to only return a small number of `Cities`, which is something we can easily pull off by adding some (required) variables in the method signature, such as `pageIndex` and `pageSize`.

Here's how we could change that to enforce such behavior (updated lines highlighted):

```
// ...existing code...

[HttpGet]
public async Task<ActionResult<IEnumerable<City>>> GetCities(
    int pageIndex = 0,
    int pageSize = 10)
{
    return await _context.Cities
                .Skip(pageIndex * pageSize)
                .Take(pageSize)
                .ToListAsync();
}

// ...existing code...
```

That's it; we also specified some reasonable default values for those variables in order to avoid huge JSON responses *by default*.

Let's quickly test what we just did: hit *F5* and type the following URL in the browser's address bar: `https://localhost:44334/api/Cities/?pageIndex=0&pageSize=10`

Here's what we should get:

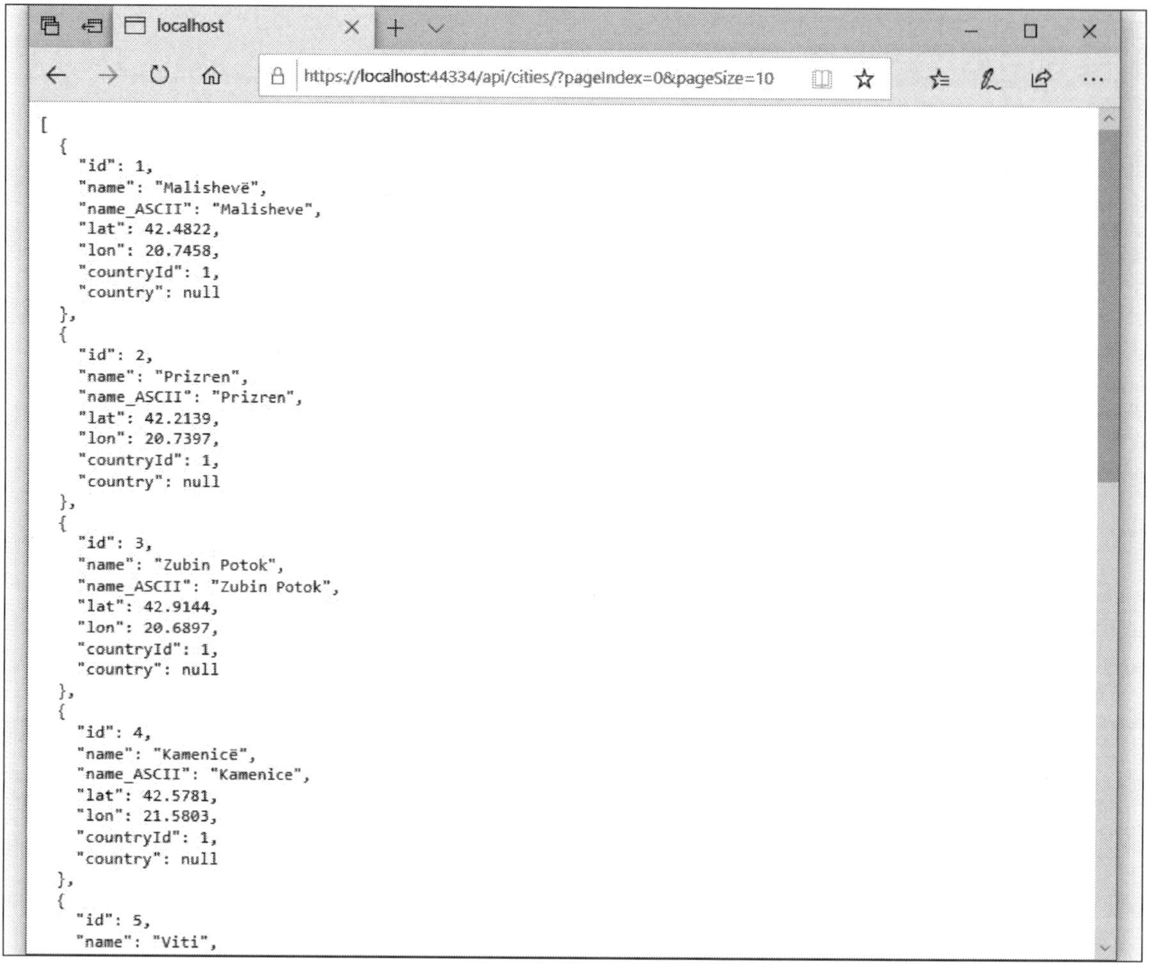

Figure 5.7: A snippet of the JSON array of 10 cities

It definitely seems that our plan is working!

However, there is a major issue we have to deal with: if we just return a JSON array of 10 cities, there will be no way for our Angular app to actually know how many cities are present in our database. Without that information, there is little chance that the paginator would reasonably work the way it did when we implemented the client-side pagination early on.

Long story short, we need to find a way to tell our Angular app some additional information, such as the following:

- The total number of pages (and/or records) available
- The current page
- The number of records on each page

Truth be told, the only required information is the first one as the Angular client would then be able to keep track of the other two; however, since we need to implement that one, we might as well return them all, thus making our *front-end* life a lot easier.

In order to do that, the best thing we can do is create a dedicated *response-type* class – which we're going to use a lot from now on.

ApiResult

From Solution Explorer, right-click the `Data` folder and add a new `ApiResult.cs` C# class file. Then, fill it up with the following content:

```
using Microsoft.EntityFrameworkCore;
using System;
using System.Collections.Generic;
using System.Linq;
using System.Threading.Tasks;

namespace WorldCities.Data
{
    public class ApiResult<T>
    {
        /// <summary>
        /// Private constructor called by the CreateAsync method.
        /// </summary>
        private ApiResult(
            List<T> data,
            int count,
            int pageIndex,
            int pageSize)
        {
            Data = data;
            PageIndex = pageIndex;
            PageSize = pageSize;
            TotalCount = count;
            TotalPages = (int)Math.Ceiling(count / (double)pageSize);
        }

        #region Methods
        /// <summary>
        /// Pages a IQueryable source.
        /// </summary>
        /// <param name="source">An IQueryable source of generic
        /// type</param>
        /// <param name="pageIndex">Zero-based current page index
```

```
/// (0 = first page)</param>
/// <param name="pageSize">The actual size of each
/// page</param>
/// <returns>
/// A object containing the paged result
/// and all the relevant paging navigation info.
/// </returns>
public static async Task<ApiResult<T>> CreateAsync(
    IQueryable<T> source,
    int pageIndex,
    int pageSize)
{
    var count = await source.CountAsync();
    source = source
        .Skip(pageIndex * pageSize)
        .Take(pageSize);

    var data = await source.ToListAsync();

    return new ApiResult<T>(
        data,
        count,
        pageIndex,
        pageSize);
}
#endregion

#region Properties
/// <summary>
/// The data result.
/// </summary>
public List<T> Data { get; private set; }

/// <summary>
/// Zero-based index of current page.
/// </summary>
public int PageIndex { get; private set; }

/// <summary>
/// Number of items contained in each page.
/// </summary>
public int PageSize { get; private set; }

/// <summary>
/// Total items count
```

```
        /// </summary>
        public int TotalCount { get; private set; }

        /// <summary>
        /// Total pages count
        /// </summary>
        public int TotalPages { get; private set; }

        /// <summary>
        /// TRUE if the current page has a previous page,
        /// FALSE otherwise.
        /// </summary>
        public bool HasPreviousPage
        {
            get
            {
                return (PageIndex > 0);
            }
        }

        /// <summary>
        /// TRUE if the current page has a next page, FALSE otherwise.
        /// </summary>
        public bool HasNextPage
        {
            get
            {
                return ((PageIndex +1) < TotalPages);
            }
        }
        #endregion
    }
}
```

This `ApiResult` class contains some really interesting stuff. Let's try to summarize the most relevant things:

- `Data`: A property of the `List<T>` type that will be used to contain the paged data (it will be translated to a JSON array)
- `PageIndex`: Returns the zero-based index of the current page (0 for the first page, 1 for the second, and so on)
- `PageSize`: Returns the total page size (`TotalCount / PageSize`)
- `TotalCount`: Returns the total `Item` count number
- `TotalPages`: Returns the total number of pages taking into account the total `Items` count (`TotalCount / PageSize`)

- `HasPreviousPage`: Returns `True` if the current page has a previous page, `False` otherwise
- `HasNextPage`: Returns `True` if the current page has a next page, `False` otherwise

Those properties are precisely what we were looking for; the underlying logic to calculate their values should be quite easy to understand by looking at the preceding code.

Other than that, the class basically revolves around the static method `CreateAsync<T>(IQueryable<T> source, int pageIndex, int pageSize)`, which can be used to paginate an Entity Framework `IQueryable` object.

> It's worth noting that the `ApiResult` class cannot be instantiated from the outside since its constructor has been marked as `private`; the only way to create it is by using the static `CreateAsync` factory method. There are good reasons to do that: since it is not possible to define an `async` constructor, we have resorted to using a static `async` method that returns a class instance; the constructor has been set to `private` to prevent developers from directly using it instead of the factory method, since it's the only reasonable way to instantiate this class.

Here's how we can make use of our brand new `ApiResult` class in the `GetCities` method of our `CitiesController`:

```
// ...existing code...

// GET: api/Cities
// GET: api/Cities/?pageIndex=0&pageSize=10
[HttpGet]
public async Task<ActionResult<ApiResult<City>>> GetCities(
        int pageIndex = 0,
        int pageSize = 10)
{
    return await ApiResult<City>.CreateAsync(
            _context.Cities,
            pageIndex,
            pageSize
            );
}

// ...existing code...
```

Here we go! Now, we should have our 10 cities and all the information we were looking for.

Let's hit *F5* and navigate to the same URL as before to see what's changed: `https://localhost:44334/api/Cities/?pageIndex=0&pageSize=10`.

Here's the updated JSON response:

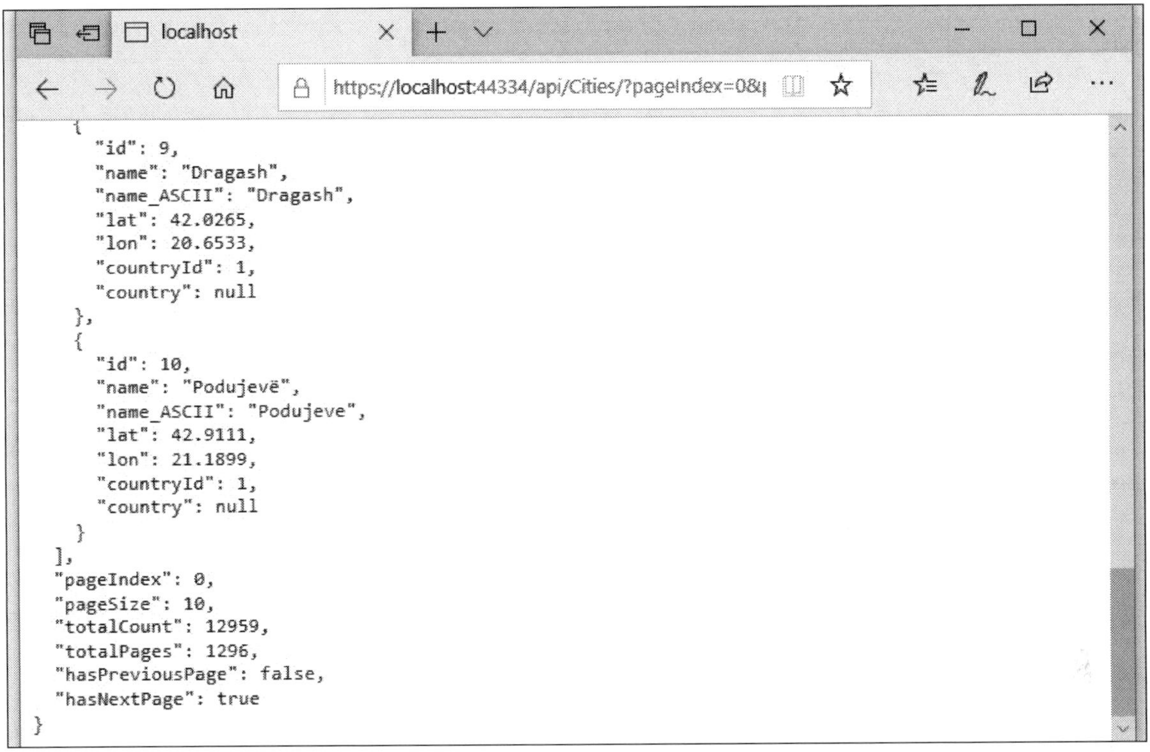

Figure 5.8: The updated JSON array containing extra page information

If we scroll down to the bottom of the page, we will see that our much-needed properties are all there.

The only downside of this implementation is that the URL we need to call to get such a result is rather ugly; before moving on to Angular, it could be useful to spend some time seeing if there's a way to make it sleeker.

Theoretically speaking, we could do better than what we did by implementing a dedicated route in the `CitiesController.cs` file in the following way (updated lines are highlighted, but *do not perform such a change on your code* – just have a look):

```
// ...existing code...

// GET: api/Cities
// GET: api/Cities/?pageIndex=0&pageSize=10
// GET: api/Cities/0/10
[HttpGet]
[Route("{pageIndex?}/{pageSize?}")]
public async Task<ActionResult<ApiResult<City>>> GetCities(
        int pageIndex = 0,
        int pageSize = 10)
{
```

```
        return await ApiResult<City>.CreateAsync(
                _context.Cities,
                pageIndex,
                pageSize
                );
    }

    // ...existing code...
```

By implementing that route, we could call the `GetCities` action method with this new URL: `https://localhost:44334/api/Cities/0/10`

This is arguably better than the following URL: `https://localhost:44334/api/Cities/?pageIndex=0&pageSize=10`

However, *let's not do that,* at least for now; relying on a given route would mean becoming unable to add additional parameters, which could be a huge loss in terms of customization options – as we'll see in a short while.

Let's now move to our Angular's `CitiesComponent` and update it to use this new, optimized way of fetching our cities from the server.

CitiesComponent

The only Angular files we need to change are the following:

- The `CitiesComponent` TypeScript file, which is where we put all the data-retrieval logic that we now need to update
- The `CitiesComponent` HTML file, to bind a specific event to our `MatPaginator` element

Let's do this.

Open the `cities.component.ts` file and perform the following changes (new/updated lines are highlighted):

```
import { Component, Inject, OnInit, ViewChild } from '@angular/core';
import { HttpClient, HttpParams } from '@angular/common/http';
import { MatTableDataSource } from '@angular/material/table';
import { MatPaginator, PageEvent } from '@angular/material/paginator';

import { City } from './city';

@Component({
  selector: 'app-cities',
  templateUrl: './cities.component.html',
  styleUrls: ['./cities.component.css']
```

```
})
export class CitiesComponent implements OnInit {
  public displayedColumns: string[] = ['id', 'name', 'lat', 'lon'];
  public cities: MatTableDataSource<City>;

  @ViewChild(MatPaginator) paginator: MatPaginator;

  constructor(
    private http: HttpClient,
    @Inject('BASE_URL') private baseUrl: string) {
  }

  ngOnInit() {
    var pageEvent = new PageEvent();
    pageEvent.pageIndex = 0;
    pageEvent.pageSize = 10;
    this.getData(pageEvent);
  }

  getData(event: PageEvent) {
    var url = this.baseUrl + 'api/Cities';
    var params = new HttpParams()
      .set("pageIndex", event.pageIndex.toString())
      .set("pageSize", event.pageSize.toString());
    this.http.get<any>(url, { params })
      .subscribe(result => {
        this.paginator.length = result.totalCount;
        this.paginator.pageIndex = result.pageIndex;
        this.paginator.pageSize = result.pageSize;
        this.cities = new MatTableDataSource<City>(result.data);
      }, error => console.error(error));
  }
}
```

Let's try to summarize what we did here:

- We used the `@ViewChild` decorator to set a static view query and store its result to the `paginator` variable; this allows us to access and manipulate the `MatPaginator` instance that we previously set up in our component's template from within the component class.
- We removed the `HttpClient` from the `ngOnInit()` life cycle hook method and placed the whole data-retrieval login in a separate `getData()` method. In order to do this, we had to define a couple of internal class variables to `host` the `HttpClient` and the `baseUrl` to persist them so that we'll be able to use them multiple times (that is, on multiple `getData()` calls).

- We changed the data-retrieval logic to match our new JSON response object.
- We modified our paginator configuration strategy to manually set the values we get from the server side instead of having it figuring them out automatically; doing that is required, otherwise it would just take into account (and *paginate*) the small portion of cities we retrieve upon each HTTP request instead of the full batch.

Among the various new stuff we've implemented with the preceding code, the @ViewChild decorator deserves a couple more words: in a nutshell, it can be used to get a reference of a DOM template element from within the Angular component, thus making it a very useful feature whenever we need to manipulate the element's properties.

As we can see from the preceding code, the @ViewChild decorator is defined using a *selector* parameter, which is required to access the DOM element: this *selector* can be a class name (if the class has either the @Component or @Directive decorator), a template reference variable, a provider defined in the child component tree, and so on. In our specific scenario, we've used the MatPaginator class name, since it does have the @Component decorator.

> While we're at it, it can be useful to know that the @ViewChild decorator also accepts a second parameter, which was required until Angular 8 and became optional since Angular 9: a static flag, which can be either true or false (from Angular 9, it defaults to false). If this flag is explicitly set to true, the @ViewChild is retrieved from the template before the Change Detection phase runs (that is, even before the ngOnInit() life cycle); conversely, the component/element retrieval task is resolved either after the Change Detection phase if the element is inside a nested view (for example, a view with a *ngIf conditional display directive), or before Change Detection if it isn't.
>
> Since we've used the [hidden] attribute binding in the template instead of the *ngIf directive, our MatPaginator won't run into initialization issues, even without having to set that flag to true.
>
> For additional information about the @ViewChild decorator, we suggest you take a look at the Angular docs: https://angular.io/api/core/ViewChild

As for the cities.component.html file, we just need to add a single line to the <mat-paginator> directive to bind the getData() event upon each paging event. Here's how to do that (the new line is highlighted):

```
// ...existing code

<!-- Pagination directive -->
<mat-paginator [hidden]="!cities"
    (page)="getData($event)"
    [pageSize]="10"
```

```
    [pageSizeOptions]="[10, 20, 50]"
    showFirstLastButtons></mat-paginator>
```

This simple binding plays a very important role: it ensures that the `getData()` event is called every time the user interacts with the `paginator` element to perform a page change, asking for the previous/next page, first/last page, changing the number of items to display, and so on. As we can easily understand, such a call is required for server-side pagination since we need to fetch the updated data from the server every time we have to display different rows.

Once done, let's try the new magic by hitting *F5* and then navigating to the **Cities** view. If we did everything properly, we should get the same UI that we could see before:

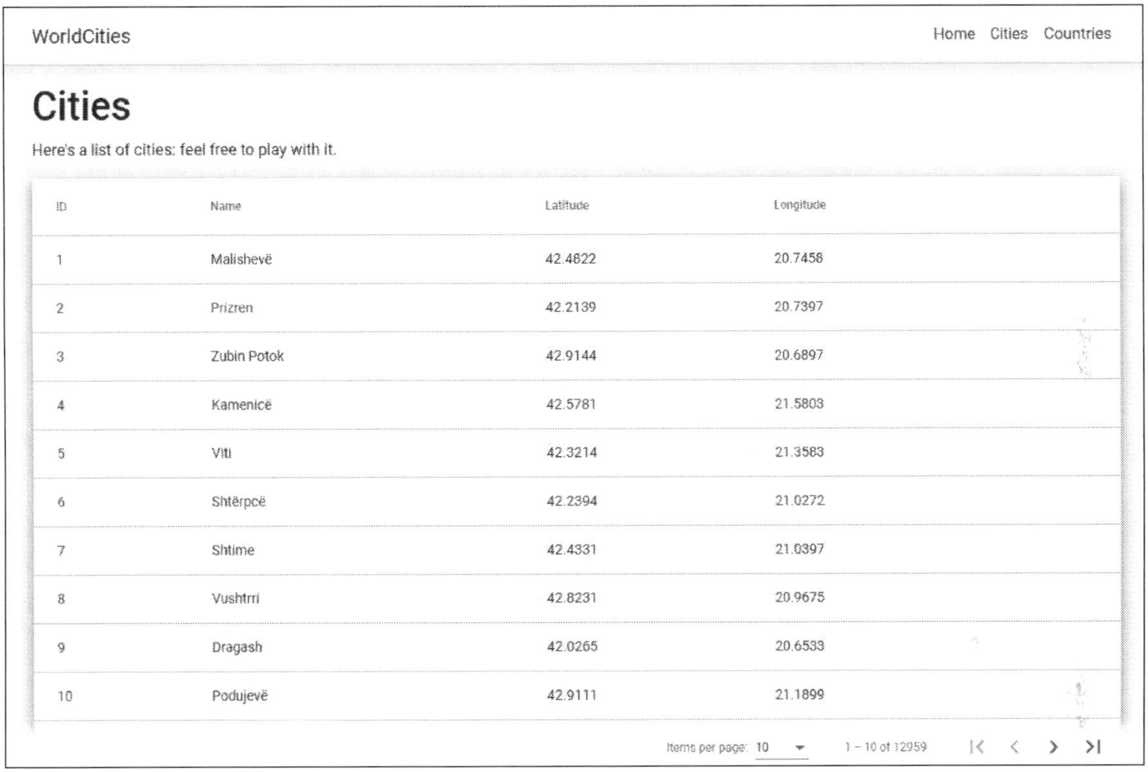

Figure 5.9: The same paginated Cities table with better performance

However, this time, we should experience better overall performance and faster response times. That's because we're not dealing with thousands of JSON items and HTML table rows under the hood; we're fetching only a few of them at a time (that is, those we get to see) using our improved server-side logic.

Since we're done with paging, we can finally deal with **sorting**.

Adding sorting with MatSortModule

In order to implement sorting, we're going to use `MatSortModule`, which can be implemented just like the `paginator` module.

This time, we won't make client-side sorting experiments as we did with paging early on; we're going for the server-side pattern right from the start.

> In general terms, whenever we deal with paging and sorting, we should always take the server-side implementation into account, since it will likely improve the overall performance of our apps while often preventing the need to handle that kind of stuff using additional client-side code.

Extending ApiResult

Let's start with the ASP.NET *back-end* part.

Do you remember the `ApiResult` class we created earlier? It's time to improve its source code to add sorting support.

From Solution Explorer, open the `/Data/ApiResult.cs` file and update its content accordingly (new/updated lines are highlighted):

```
using Microsoft.EntityFrameworkCore;
using System;
using System.Collections.Generic;
using System.Linq;
using System.Threading.Tasks;
using System.Linq.Dynamic.Core;
using System.Reflection;

namespace WorldCities.Data
{
    public class ApiResult<T>
    {
        /// <summary>
        /// Private constructor called by the CreateAsync method.
        /// </summary>
        private ApiResult(
            List<T> data,
            int count,
            int pageIndex,
            int pageSize,
            string sortColumn,
            string sortOrder)
        {
            Data = data;
```

```
            PageIndex = pageIndex;
            PageSize = pageSize;
            TotalCount = count;
            TotalPages = (int)Math.Ceiling(count / (double)pageSize);
            SortColumn = sortColumn;
            SortOrder = sortOrder;
        }

        #region Methods
        /// <summary>
        /// Pages and/or sorts a IQueryable source.
        /// </summary>
        /// <param name="source">An IQueryable source of generic
        /// type</param>
        /// <param name="pageIndex">Zero-based current page index
        /// (0 = first page)</param>
        /// <param name="pageSize">The actual size of each
        /// page</param>
        /// <param name="sortColumn">The sorting column name</param>
        /// <param name="sortOrder">The sorting order ("ASC" or
        /// "DESC")</param>
        /// <returns>
        /// A object containing the IQueryable paged/sorted result
        /// and all the relevant paging/sorting navigation info.
        /// </returns>
        public static async Task<ApiResult<T>> CreateAsync(
            IQueryable<T> source,
            int pageIndex,
            int pageSize,
            string sortColumn = null,
            string sortOrder = null)
        {
            var count = await source.CountAsync();

            if (!string.IsNullOrEmpty(sortColumn)
                && IsValidProperty(sortColumn))
            {
                sortOrder = !string.IsNullOrEmpty(sortOrder)
                    && sortOrder.ToUpper() == "ASC"
                    ? "ASC"
                    : "DESC";
                source = source.OrderBy(
                    string.Format(
                        "{0} {1}",
                        sortColumn,
                        sortOrder)
```

```
                );
            }

            source = source
                .Skip(pageIndex * pageSize)
                .Take(pageSize);

            var data = await source.ToListAsync();

            return new ApiResult<T>(
                data,
                count,
                pageIndex,
                pageSize,
                sortColumn,
                sortOrder);
        }
        #endregion

        #region Methods
        /// <summary>
        /// Checks if the given property name exists
        /// to protect against SQL injection attacks
        /// </summary>
        public static bool IsValidProperty(
            string propertyName,
            bool throwExceptionIfNotFound = true)
        {
            var prop = typeof(T).GetProperty(
                propertyName,
                BindingFlags.IgnoreCase |
                BindingFlags.Public |
                BindingFlags.Instance);
            if (prop == null && throwExceptionIfNotFound)
                throw new NotSupportedException(
                    string.Format(
                        "ERROR: Property '{0}' does not exist.",
                        propertyName)
                    );
            return prop != null;
        }
        #endregion

        #region Properties
        /// <summary>
        /// The data result.
```

```
/// </summary>
public List<T> Data { get; private set; }

/// <summary>
/// Zero-based index of current page.
/// </summary>
public int PageIndex { get; private set; }

/// <summary>
/// Number of items contained in each page.
/// </summary>
public int PageSize { get; private set; }

/// <summary>
/// Total items count
/// </summary>
public int TotalCount { get; private set; }

/// <summary>
/// Total pages count
/// </summary>
public int TotalPages { get; private set; }

/// <summary>
/// TRUE if the current page has a previous page,
/// FALSE otherwise.
/// </summary>
public bool HasPreviousPage
{
    get
    {
        return (PageIndex > 0);
    }
}

/// <summary>
/// TRUE if the current page has a next page, FALSE otherwise.
/// </summary>
public bool HasNextPage
{
    get
    {
        return ((PageIndex +1) < TotalPages);
    }
}
```

```
            /// <summary>
            /// Sorting Column name (or null if none set)
            /// </summary>
            public string SortColumn { get; set; }

            /// <summary>
            /// Sorting Order ("ASC", "DESC" or null if none set)
            /// </summary>
            public string SortOrder { get; set; }
            #endregion
        }
    }
```

What we did was add two new `sortColumn` and `sortOrder` attributes to the main class static method and implement them through the code; while we were there, we also took the chance to define two new properties with the same name (in uppercase) so that the sorting details will be part of the JSON response, just like the paging ones.

It's worth noting that since we're now assembling our **Language-Integrated Query** (**LINQ**)-to-SQL queries with literal data coming from the client, we also added a new `IsValidProperty()` method that will check that the `sortColumn` specified does actually exist as a typed property of the generic `<T>` entity we're dealing with; as the method comment clearly says, that's actually a security countermeasure against SQL injection attempts. This is a very important security issue that we'll be talking about in a short while.

> In the unlikely case that you've never heard of LINQ, don't worry: we'll get there soon.

If we try to build our project right after these changes, we'll most likely be greeted by some compiler errors, such as the following one:

```
Error CS0246: The type or namespace name System.Linq.Dynamic could not be found
(are you missing a using directive or an assembly reference?).
```

Don't worry, it's perfectly normal: we just need to add a new NuGet package to our project.

Installing System.Linq.Dynamic.Core

The `IQueryable<T>.OrderBy()` extension method that we used in the improved `ApiResult` source code to programmatically apply the column sorting is part of the `System.Linq.Dynamic.Core` namespace; thanks to this library, it's possible to write Dynamic LINQ queries (string-based) on an `IQueryable`, which is just like what we did in the preceding code.

Unfortunately, `System.Linq.Dynamic.Core` is not part of the ASP.NET stock binaries; therefore, in order to use these features, we need to add it via NuGet.

The fastest way to do that is to open Visual Studio's **Package Manager Console** and issue the following command:

```
> Install-Package System.Linq.Dynamic.Core
```

> **IMPORTANT**: Be sure to install `System.Linq.Dynamic.Core` and not `System.Linq.Dynamic`, which is its .NET Framework 4.0 counterpart; the latter won't work with our ASP.NET web application project.
>
> At the time of writing, the most recent version of the `System.Linq.Dynamic.Core` package is 1.2.6, which works absolutely fine for our purposes.
>
> For those who want to retrieve additional information regarding this great package, we suggest you take a look at the following resources:
>
> NuGet website: `https://www.nuget.org/packages/System.Linq.Dynamic.Core/`
>
> GitHub project: `https://github.com/StefH/System.Linq.Dynamic.Core`

What is LINQ?

Before moving forward, let's spend a couple of minutes talking about LINQ in the unlikely case you have never heard anything about it.

Also known as Language-Integrated Query, LINQ is the code name of a Microsoft .NET Framework set of technologies that adds data query capabilities to .NET languages such as C# and VB.NET. LINQ was first released in 2007 and was one of the major new features of .NET Framework 3.5.

The main purpose of LINQ is to make the developer able to express structured queries against data using a first-class language construct, without having to learn different query languages for each type of data source (collection types, SQL, XML, CSV, and so on). For each of these *major* data source types, there's a LINQ implementation that provides the same query experience for objects (*LINQ to Objects*), Entity Framework entities (*LINQ to Entities*), relational databases (*LINQ to SQL*), XML (*LINQ to XML*), and so on.

LINQ structured queries can be expressed using two alternative - yet also complementary - approaches:

- **Lambda expressions**, such as the following:

  ```
  var city = _context.Cities.Where(c => c.Name == "New York").First();
  ```

- **Query expressions**, such as the following:

  ```
  var city = (from c in _context.Cities where c.Name == "New York" select
  c).First();
  ```

Both yield the same result with the same performance, since query expressions are translated into their lambda expression equivalents before they're compiled.

> For additional information about LINQ, lambda expressions, and query expressions, check out the following links:
>
> LINQ: `https://docs.microsoft.com/en-us/dotnet/csharp/linq/`
>
> LINQ lambda expressions (C# Programming Guide): `https://docs.microsoft.com/en-us/dotnet/csharp/programming-guide/statements-expressions-operators/lambda-expressions`
>
> LINQ query expression basics: `https://docs.microsoft.com/en-us/dotnet/csharp/linq/query-expression-basics`

Linq.Dynamic.Core pros and cons

Now, since LINQ has been built in with .NET Framework since v3.5 and it's shipped with each subsequent ASP.NET version ever since, what does the `System.Linq.Dynamic.Core` package actually do and why are we using it?

As we can see from the two preceding examples, both lambda expressions and query expressions work with a strongly typed approach: whenever we *query* an object of any type using LINQ, the source type – together with all the properties we want our query to check for – must be known by the compiler. This means that we would be unable to use these techniques with generic objects (`object`) or types (`<T>`). That's where `Linq.Dynamic` comes to the rescue, allowing the developer to write lambda expressions and query expressions with literal strings and translate them into their strongly typed equivalents using **reflection**.

Here's the same query as before written using `System.Linq.Dynamic.Core`:

```
var city = _context.Cities.Where("Name = @1", "New York").First();
```

We can immediately see the difference – and also the tremendous advantage we can get by using such an approach: we will be able to build our queries dynamically, regardless of whether we're dealing with strongly typed objects or generic types, just like we did within the source code of `ApiResult` a short while ago.

However, such an approach will also have a major downside: our code will be less testable and way too error-prone, for at least two important reasons:

- We'll be just *a literal string away* from query errors that will almost always lead to major crashes
- The risk of unwanted queries (including SQL injection attacks) could increase exponentially, depending on how we build those queries and/or where we get our *dynamic* strings from

> Those who don't know what SQL injections are and/or why they are dangerous should definitely take a look at the following guide, written by Tim Sammut and Mike Schiffman from the Cisco Security Intelligence team:
>
> Understanding SQL Injections: `https://tools.cisco.com/security/center/resources/sql_injection`

The former issue is bad, but the latter is even worse: being open to SQL injection attacks could be devastating and therefore is something we should avoid at any cost - including getting rid of the `System.Linq.Dynamic.Core` package.

Preventing SQL injections

Luckily enough, we don't need to do that; although we're getting *two* potentially harmful variable strings coming from the client - `sortColumn` and `sortOrder` - we have already put in place effective countermeasures for both of them in the preceding source code of `ApiResult`.

Here's what we did for `sortOrder`:

```
//... existing code...

sortOrder = !string.IsNullOrEmpty(sortOrder)
    && sortOrder.ToUpper() == "ASC"
    ? "ASC"
    : "DESC";

//... existing code...
```

As we can see, we'll convert it into either `"ASC"` or `"DESC"` before using it anywhere, thus leaving no openings to SQL injections.

The `sortColumn` parameter is way more complex to handle because it can theoretically contain any possible column name mapped to any of our entities: `id`, `name`, `lat`, `lon`, `iso2`, `iso3`... if we were to check them all, we would need a very long conditional block! Not to mention the fact that it would also be very hard to maintain whenever we added new entities and/or properties to our project.

For that very reason, we chose a completely different - and arguably better - approach, which relies upon the following `IsValidProperty` method:

```
// ...existing code...

public static bool IsValidProperty(
    string propertyName,
    bool throwExceptionIfNotFound = true)
{
    var prop = typeof(T).GetProperty(
        propertyName,
        BindingFlags.IgnoreCase |
        BindingFlags.Public |
        BindingFlags.Instance);
    if (prop == null && throwExceptionIfNotFound)
        throw new NotSupportedException(
            string.Format(
                "ERROR: Property '{0}' does not exist.",
```

```
                propertyName)
            );
    return prop != null;
}

// ...existing code...
```

As we can see, this method checks that the given `propertyName` corresponds to an existing typed `Property` within our `<T>` generic entity class: if it does, it returns `True`; otherwise, it throws a `NotSupportedException` (or returns `False`, depending on how we call it). This is a great way to shield our code against SQL injection because there's absolutely no way that a harmful string would match one of our entity's properties.

> The property name check has been implemented through `System.Reflection`, a technique that's used to inspect and/or retrieve metadata on types at runtime. To work with reflection, we need to include the `System.Reflection` namespace in our class – which is precisely what we did at the beginning of the source code of our improved `ApiResult`.
>
> For additional information about `System.Reflection`, check out the following guide: `https://docs.microsoft.com/en-us/dotnet/csharp/programming-guide/concepts/reflection`

As we can see by looking back at the `ApiResult` source code, such a method is being called in the following way:

```
if (!string.IsNullOrEmpty(sortColumn)
    && IsValidProperty(sortColumn))
{
    /// if we are here, sortColumn is safe to use
}
```

Those curly brackets define our SQL injection safety zone: as long as we deal with `sortColumn` within them, we have nothing to worry about.

> Truth be told, even after implementing this defensive approach, there's still a minor threat we could be exposed to: if we have some reserved columns/properties that we don't want the client to interact with (system columns, for example), the preceding countermeasure won't block it from doing that; although being unable to acknowledge their existence or to read their data, an experienced user could still be able to "order" the table results by them – provided that the user knows their precise name somehow.
>
> If we want to prevent this remote – yet theoretically possible – leak, we can set these properties to `private` (since we told our `IsValidProperty` method to only check for `public` properties) and/or rethink the whole method logic so that it better suits our security needs.

Updating CitiesController

Now that we have improved our `ApiResult` class, we can implement it within our `CitiesController`.

Open the `/Controllers/CitiesController.cs` file and change its contents accordingly (updated lines are highlighted):

```
// ..existing code...

// GET: api/Cities
// GET: api/Cities/?pageIndex=0&pageSize=10
// GET: api/Cities/?pageIndex=0&pageSize=10&sortColumn=name&
//   sortOrder=asc
[HttpGet]
public async Task<ActionResult<ApiResult<City>>> GetCities(
        int pageIndex = 0,
        int pageSize = 10,
        string sortColumn = null,
        string sortOrder = null)
{
    return await ApiResult<City>.CreateAsync(
            _context.Cities,
            pageIndex,
            pageSize,
            sortColumn,
            sortOrder);
}

// ..existing code...
```

Thanks to these two new parameters, our `GetCities` method will be able to sort the cities the way we want.

We're done with the *back-end* part; let's move on to the *front-end*.

Updating the Angular app

As always, we need to change three files:

- The `angular-material.module.ts` file, where we need to add the new `@angular/material` module
- The `cities.component.ts` file, to implement the sorting business logic
- The `cities.component.html` file, to bind the new variables, methods, and references defined in the `.ts` file within the UI template

angular-material.module.ts

Open the `/ClientApp/src/app/angular-material.module.ts` file and change it in the following way (updated lines are highlighted):

```
import { NgModule } from '@angular/core';
import { MatTableModule } from '@angular/material/table';
import { MatPaginatorModule } from '@angular/material/paginator';
import { MatSortModule } from '@angular/material/sort';

@NgModule({
  imports: [
    MatTableModule,
    MatPaginatorModule,
    MatSortModule
  ],
  exports: [
    MatTableModule,
    MatPaginatorModule,
    MatSortModule
  ]
})

export class AngularMaterialModule { }
```

From now on, we'll be able to `import` the `MatSortModule`-related classes in any Angular component.

cities.component.ts

Once done, open the `cities.component.ts` file and make the following modifications (updated lines are highlighted):

```
import { Component, Inject, OnInit, ViewChild } from '@angular/core';
import { HttpClient, HttpParams } from '@angular/common/http';
import { MatTableDataSource } from '@angular/material/table';
import { MatPaginator, PageEvent } from '@angular/material/paginator';
import { MatSort } from '@angular/material/sort';

import { City } from './city';

@Component({
  selector: 'app-cities',
  templateUrl: './cities.component.html',
  styleUrls: ['./cities.component.css']
})
export class CitiesComponent implements OnInit {
```

```
  public displayedColumns: string[] = ['id', 'name', 'lat', 'lon'];
  public cities: MatTableDataSource<City>;

  defaultPageIndex: number = 0;
  defaultPageSize: number = 10;
  public defaultSortColumn: string = "name";
  public defaultSortOrder: string = "asc";

  @ViewChild(MatPaginator) paginator: MatPaginator;
  @ViewChild(MatSort) sort: MatSort;

  constructor(
    private http: HttpClient,
    @Inject('BASE_URL') private baseUrl: string) {
  }

  ngOnInit() {
    this.loadData();
  }

  loadData() {
    var pageEvent = new PageEvent();
    pageEvent.pageIndex = this.defaultPageIndex;
    pageEvent.pageSize = this.defaultPageSize;
    this.getData(pageEvent);
  }

  getData(event: PageEvent) {
    var url = this.baseUrl + 'api/Cities';
    var params = new HttpParams()
      .set("pageIndex", event.pageIndex.toString())
      .set("pageSize", event.pageSize.toString())
      .set("sortColumn", (this.sort)
        ? this.sort.active
        : this.defaultSortColumn)
      .set("sortOrder", (this.sort)
        ? this.sort.direction
        : this.defaultSortOrder);
      this.http.get<any>(url, { params })
        .subscribe(result => {
          console.log(result);
          this.paginator.length = result.totalCount;
          this.paginator.pageIndex = result.pageIndex;
          this.paginator.pageSize = result.pageSize;
          this.cities = new MatTableDataSource<City>(result.data);
        }, error => console.error(error));
    }
}
```

Here's a breakdown of the most relevant changes:

- We imported the `MatSort` reference from the `@angular/material` package.
- We added four new class variables to set the paging and sorting default values: `defaultPageIndex`, `defaultPageSize`, `defaultSortColumn`, and `defaultSortOrder`. Two of them have been defined as `public` because we need to use them from the HTML template via two-way data binding.
- We moved the initial `getData()` call from the class constructor to a new centralized `loadData()` function so that we can bind it to the table (as we'll see in a short while).
- We added the `sortColumn` and `sortOrder` HTTP GET parameters to our `HttpParams` object so that we can send the sorting information to the server side.

cities.component.html

Right after that, open the `cities.component.html` file and make the following modifications (updated lines are highlighted):

```
// ...existing code

<table mat-table [dataSource]="cities"
  class="table-striped mat-elevation-z8"
  [hidden]="!cities"
  matSort (matSortChange)="loadData()"
  matSortActive="{{defaultSortColumn}}"
  matSortDirection="{{defaultSortOrder}}">

  <!-- Id Column -->
  <ng-container matColumnDef="id">
    <th mat-header-cell *matHeaderCellDef mat-sort-header>ID</th>
    <td mat-cell *matCellDef="let city"> {{city.id}} </td>
  </ng-container>

  <!-- Name Column -->
  <ng-container matColumnDef="name">
    <th mat-header-cell *matHeaderCellDef mat-sort-header>Name</th>
    <td mat-cell *matCellDef="let city"> {{city.name}} </td>
  </ng-container>

  <!-- Lat Column -->
```

```
  <ng-container matColumnDef="lat">
    <th mat-header-cell *matHeaderCellDef mat-sort-header>Latitude
    </th>
    <td mat-cell *matCellDef="let city"> {{city.lat}} </td>
  </ng-container>

  <!-- Lon Column -->
  <ng-container matColumnDef="lon">
    <th mat-header-cell *matHeaderCellDef mat-sort-header>Longitude
    </th>
    <td mat-cell *matCellDef="let city"> {{city.lon}} </td>
  </ng-container>

  <tr mat-header-row *matHeaderRowDef="displayedColumns"></tr>
  <tr mat-row *matRowDef="let row; columns: displayedColumns;"></tr>
</table>

// ...existing code...
```

Here's what we did in a nutshell:

- We added the following attributes to the `<table mat-table>` element:
    - `matSort`: A reference to the `matSort` local variable we added to the `cities.component.ts` file early on
    - `(matSortChange)`: An event binding that will execute the `sortData()` method (also defined in the `.ts` file earlier) upon each sorting attempt by the user
    - `matSortActive` and `matSortDirection`: Two data bindings to the `defaultSortColumn` and `defaultSortOrder` variables that we defined in the `.ts` file early on
- We added the `mat-sort-header` attribute to each `<th mat-header-cell>` element (one for each table column).

> Now we can see why we didn't use the sleek URL we defined early on in our ASP.NET `CitiesController` and opted for the standard GET parameters instead: this approach allows us to programmatically add an indefinite number of HTTP GET parameters to our request thanks to the `HttpParams` class from the `@angular/common/http` package.

Let's quickly test it out by hitting *F5* and navigating to the **Cities** view. Here's what we should be able to see:

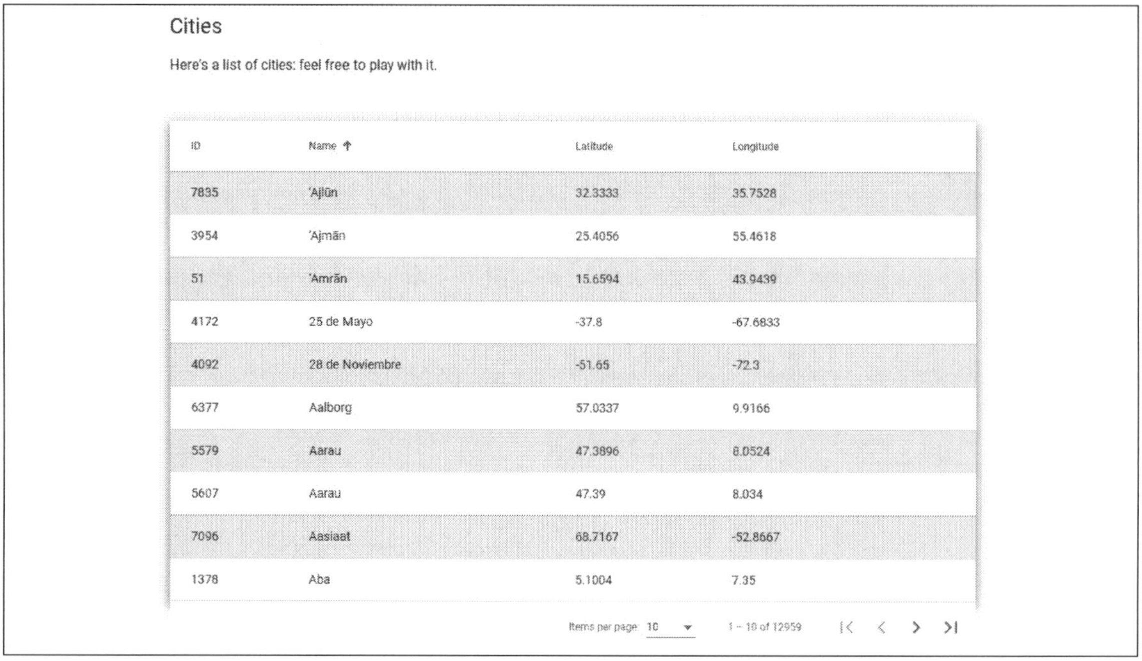

Cities
Here's a list of cities: feel free to play with it.
ID
Name
Latitude
Longitude
7835 'Ajlūn 32.3333 35.7528
3954 'Ajmān 25.4056 55.4618
51 'Amrān 15.6594 43.9439
4172 25 de Mayo -37.8 -67.6833
4092 28 de Noviembre -51.65 -72.3
6377 Aalborg 57.0337 9.9166
5579 Aarau 47.3896 8.0524
5607 Aarau 47.39 8.034
7096 Aasiaat 68.7167 -52.8667
1378 Aba 5.1004 7.35
Items per page: 10
1 – 10 of 12959

Figure 5.10: Cities table with pagination and sorting

The cities are now sorted alphabetically in ascending order. If we click on the various column headers, we can change their order as we please: the first click will sort the content in ascending order, while the second will do the opposite.

> It's worth noting how the paging and sorting features are able to coexist without issues; needless to say, whenever we try to change the table sorting, the paging will just roll back to the first page.

Now that the sorting has been implemented, there's only one missing feature left: **filtering**.

Adding filtering

If we think that we'll be able to get away with another component, this time, we're going to be disappointed: Angular Material does not provide a specific module to be used for filtering purposes. This means that we cannot rely on a standard approach to add filtering to our table; we have to figure out a reasonable approach by ourselves.

In general terms, the best thing to do whenever we need to code a feature by ourselves is start to visualize what we want it to look like: for example, we can imagine a **Search** input field lying on top of our table that would trigger our `CitiesComponent` to reload the cities data from the server – through its `getData()` method – whenever we type something in it. How does that sound?

Let's try to lay down an action plan:

1. As always, we'll need to extend our `ApiResult` class to programmatically handle the filtering task on the server side.
2. We'll also need to change the signature of the `GetCities()` action method of our .NET `CitiesController` so we can get the additional information from the client.
3. Right after that, we'll have to implement the filtering logic within our Angular `CitiesComponent`.
4. Eventually, we'll need to add the input textbox in the `CitiesComponent` HTML template file and bind an event to it to trigger the data retrieval process upon typing something.
5. Before moving further, we'll take the chance to talk about the performance impact of our filtering feature and how we can address it.

Now that we have made it, let's do our best to put this plan into action.

Extending ApiResult (again)

It seems like we need to perform another upgrade to our beloved `ApiResult` class to add filtering support to the already existing paging and sorting logic.

Truth be told, we're not forced to do everything within the `ApiResult` class: we could skip that part entirely and just add the following to our existing `CitiesController`:

```
// ...existing code...

[HttpGet]
public async Task<ActionResult<ApiResult<City>>> GetCities(
        int pageIndex = 0,
        int pageSize = 10,
        string sortColumn = null,
        string sortOrder = null,
        string filterColumn = null,
        string filterQuery = null)
{
    // first we perform the filtering...
    var cities = _context.Cities;
    if (!string.IsNullOrEmpty(filterColumn)
        && !string.IsNullOrEmpty(filterQuery))
    {
        cities= cities.Where(c => c.Name.Contains(filterQuery));
    }

    // ... and then we call the ApiResult
    return await ApiResult<City>.CreateAsync(
            cities,
            pageIndex,
```

```
                pageSize,
                sortColumn,
                sortOrder);
}


// ...existing code...
```

That's definitely a viable approach. As a matter of fact, if we weren't using the `System.Linq.Dynamic.Core` package library, this would most likely be the only possible approach; we would have no way to programmatically set a column filter using an external class that works with generic `IQueryable<T>` objects, because such a class would be unaware of the entity type and property names.

Luckily enough, we do have that package, so we can avoid performing the preceding changes (or roll them back, if we have already done that) and modify our `/Data/ApiResult.cs` class file in the following way instead:

```
using Microsoft.EntityFrameworkCore;
using System;
using System.Collections.Generic;
using System.Linq;
using System.Threading.Tasks;
using System.Linq.Dynamic.Core;
using System.Reflection;

namespace WorldCities.Data
{
    public class ApiResult<T>
    {
        /// <summary>
        /// Private constructor called by the CreateAsync method.
        /// </summary>
        private ApiResult(
            List<T> data,
            int count,
            int pageIndex,
            int pageSize,
            string sortColumn,
            string sortOrder,
            string filterColumn,
            string filterQuery)
        {
            Data = data;
            PageIndex = pageIndex;
            PageSize = pageSize;
            TotalCount = count;
```

```
        TotalPages = (int)Math.Ceiling(count / (double)pageSize);
        SortColumn = sortColumn;
        SortOrder = sortOrder;
        FilterColumn = filterColumn;
        FilterQuery = filterQuery;
    }

    #region Methods
    /// <summary>
    /// Pages, sorts and/or filters a IQueryable source.
    /// </summary>
    /// <param name="source">An IQueryable source of generic
    /// type</param>
    /// <param name="pageIndex">Zero-based current page index
    /// (0 = first page)</param>
    /// <param name="pageSize">The actual size of
    /// each page</param>
    /// <param name="sortColumn">The sorting column name</param>
    /// <param name="sortOrder">The sorting order ("ASC" or
    /// "DESC")</param>
    /// <param name="filterColumn">The filtering column
    ///  name</param>
    /// <param name="filterQuery">The filtering query (value to
    /// lookup)</param>
    /// <returns>
    /// A object containing the IQueryable paged/sorted/filtered
    /// result
    /// and all the relevant paging/sorting/filtering navigation
    /// info.
    /// </returns>
    public static async Task<ApiResult<T>> CreateAsync(
        IQueryable<T> source,
        int pageIndex,
        int pageSize,
        string sortColumn = null,
        string sortOrder = null,
        string filterColumn = null,
        string filterQuery = null)
    {
        if (!string.IsNullOrEmpty(filterColumn)
            && !string.IsNullOrEmpty(filterQuery)
            && IsValidProperty(filterColumn))
        {
            source = source.Where(
                string.Format("{0}.Contains(@0)",
                filterColumn),
```

```
                    filterQuery);
            }

            var count = await source.CountAsync();

            if (!string.IsNullOrEmpty(sortColumn)
                && IsValidProperty(sortColumn))
            {
                sortOrder = !string.IsNullOrEmpty(sortOrder)
                    && sortOrder.ToUpper() == "ASC"
                    ? "ASC"
                    : "DESC";
                source = source.OrderBy(
                    string.Format(
                        "{0} {1}",
                        sortColumn,
                        sortOrder)
                    );
            }

            source = source
                .Skip(pageIndex * pageSize)
                .Take(pageSize);

            var data = await source.ToListAsync();

            return new ApiResult<T>(
                data,
                count,
                pageIndex,
                pageSize,
                sortColumn,
                sortOrder,
                filterColumn,
                filterQuery);
        }

        /// <summary>
        /// Checks if the given property name exists
        /// to protect against SQL injection attacks
        /// </summary>
        public static bool IsValidProperty(
            string propertyName,
            bool throwExceptionIfNotFound = true)
        {
            var prop = typeof(T).GetProperty(
```

```
            propertyName,
            BindingFlags.IgnoreCase |
            BindingFlags.Public |
            BindingFlags.Static |
            BindingFlags.Instance);
        if (prop == null && throwExceptionIfNotFound)
            throw new NotSupportedException(
                string.Format(
                    "ERROR: Property '{0}' does not exist.",
                    propertyName)
                );
        return prop != null;
    }
    #endregion

    #region Properties
    /// <summary>
    /// IQueryable data result to return.
    /// </summary>
    public List<T> Data { get; private set; }

    /// <summary>
    /// Zero-based index of current page.
    /// </summary>
    public int PageIndex { get; private set; }

    /// <summary>
    /// Number of items contained in each page.
    /// </summary>
    public int PageSize { get; private set; }

    /// <summary>
    /// Total items count
    /// </summary>
    public int TotalCount { get; private set; }

    /// <summary>
    /// Total pages count
    /// </summary>
    public int TotalPages { get; private set; }

    /// <summary>
    /// TRUE if the current page has a previous page,
    /// FALSE otherwise.
    /// </summary>
    public bool HasPreviousPage
```

```
        {
            get
            {
                return (PageIndex > 0);
            }
        }

        /// <summary>
        /// TRUE if the current page has a next page, FALSE otherwise.
        /// </summary>
        public bool HasNextPage
        {
            get
            {
                return ((PageIndex +1) < TotalPages);
            }
        }

        /// <summary>
        /// Sorting Column name (or null if none set)
        /// </summary>
        public string SortColumn { get; set; }

        /// <summary>
        /// Sorting Order ("ASC", "DESC" or null if none set)
        /// </summary>
        public string SortOrder { get; set; }

        /// <summary>
        /// Filter Column name (or null if none set)
        /// </summary>
        public string FilterColumn { get; set; }

        /// <summary>
        /// Filter Query string
        /// (to be used within the given FilterColumn)
        /// </summary>
        public string FilterQuery { get; set; }
        #endregion
    }
}
```

And that's it. As we can see, we were able to programmatically implement the `IQueryable<T>.Where()` method – which actually performs the filtering task – thanks to another useful extension method provided by the `System.Linq.Dynamic.Core` package.

Needless to say, we took the chance to use our `IsValidProperty` method again to shield our code against possible SQL injection attempts: the filtering-related logic (and dynamic LINQ query) will only be executed if it returns `True`, that is, if the `filterColumn` parameter value matches with an existing entity's public property.

While we were there, we also added two additional properties (`FilterColumn` and `FilterQuery`), so that we'll have them on the JSON response object, and modified the constructor method signature accordingly.

CitiesController

Now, we can open our `/Controllers/CitiesController.cs` file and make the following changes:

```
[HttpGet]
public async Task<ActionResult<ApiResult<City>>> GetCities(
        int pageIndex = 0,
        int pageSize = 10,
        string sortColumn = null,
        string sortOrder = null,
        string filterColumn = null,
        string filterQuery = null)
{
    return await ApiResult<City>.CreateAsync(
            _context.Cities,
            pageIndex,
            pageSize,
            sortColumn,
            sortOrder,
            filterColumn,
            filterQuery);
}
```

The preceding code is very similar to the alternative implementation that we assumed in the previous section; as we mentioned earlier, both approaches are viable, depending on our tastes. However, since we're going to use this same implementation for the *countries* in a short while, making good use of `System.Linq.Dynamic.Core` and centralizing all the `IQueryable` logic is arguably a better approach since it keeps our source code as DRY as possible.

> **Don't Repeat Yourself** (**DRY**) is a widely achieved principle of software development. Whenever we violate it, we fall into a **WET** approach, which could mean **Write Everything Twice**, **We Enjoy Typing**, or **Waste Everyone's Time**, depending on what we like the most.

The .NET part is done; let's move on to Angular.

CitiesComponent

Open the `/ClientApp/src/app/cities/cities.component.ts` file and update its content in the following way (modified lines are highlighted):

```
import { Component, Inject, OnInit, ViewChild } from '@angular/core';
import { HttpClient, HttpParams } from '@angular/common/http';
import { MatTableDataSource } from '@angular/material/table';
import { MatPaginator, PageEvent } from '@angular/material/paginator';
import { MatSort } from '@angular/material/sort';

import { City } from './city';

@Component({
  selector: 'app-cities',
  templateUrl: './cities.component.html',
  styleUrls: ['./cities.component.css']
})
export class CitiesComponent implements OnInit {
  public displayedColumns: string[] = ['id', 'name', 'lat', 'lon'];
  public cities: MatTableDataSource<City>;

  defaultPageIndex: number = 0;
  defaultPageSize: number = 10;
  public defaultSortColumn: string = "name";
  public defaultSortOrder: string = "asc";

  defaultFilterColumn: string = "name";
  filterQuery:string = null;

  @ViewChild(MatPaginator) paginator: MatPaginator;
  @ViewChild(MatSort) sort: MatSort;

  constructor(
      private http: HttpClient,
      @Inject('BASE_URL') private baseUrl: string) {
  }

  ngOnInit() {
      this.loadData(null);
  }

  loadData(query: string = null) {
    var pageEvent = new PageEvent();
    pageEvent.pageIndex = this.defaultPageIndex;
    pageEvent.pageSize = this.defaultPageSize;
```

```
    if (query) {
        this.filterQuery = query;
    }
    this.getData(pageEvent);
  }

  getData(event: PageEvent) {
    var url = this.baseUrl + 'api/Cities';
    var params = new HttpParams()
      .set("pageIndex", event.pageIndex.toString())
      .set("pageSize", event.pageSize.toString())
      .set("sortColumn", (this.sort)
        ? this.sort.active
        : this.defaultSortColumn)
      .set("sortOrder", (this.sort)
        ? this.sort.direction
        : this.defaultSortOrder);

    if (this.filterQuery) {
        params = params
            .set("filterColumn", this.defaultFilterColumn)
            .set("filterQuery", this.filterQuery);
    }

    this.http.get<any>(url, { params })
      .subscribe(result => {
        this.paginator.length = result.totalCount;
        this.paginator.pageIndex = result.pageIndex;
        this.paginator.pageSize = result.pageSize;
        this.cities = new MatTableDataSource<City>(result.data);
    }, error => console.error(error));
  }
}
```

This time, the new code only consists of a few additional lines; we've just changed the signature of the `loadData()` method (with a `null` default value, so that we won't break anything) and conditionally added a couple of parameters to our HTTP request – that's it.

CitiesComponent template (HTML) file

Let's see what we need to add in the `/ClientApp/src/app/cities/cities.component.html` template file:

```
<h1>Cities</h1>

<p>Here's a list of cities: feel free to play with it.</p>

<p *ngIf="!cities"><em>Loading...</em></p>

<mat-form-field [hidden]="!cities">
    <input matInput (keyup)="loadData($event.target.value)"
        placeholder="Filter by name (or part of it)...">
</mat-form-field>

<table mat-table [dataSource]="cities"
  class="table-striped mat-elevation-z8"
  [hidden]="!cities"
  matSort (matSortChange)="loadData()"
  matSortActive="{{defaultSortColumn}}"
  matSortDirection="{{defaultSortOrder}}">

// ...existing code...
```

As we can see, we just added a `<mat-form-field>` element with the usual `[hidden]` attribute binding (to make it appear only after our cities have been loaded) and a `(keyup)` event binding that will trigger the `loadData()` method upon each keypress; this call will also contain the input value, which will be handled by our component class by the means we just implemented there.

CitiesComponent style (CSS) file

Before testing it out, we need to make a minor change to the `/ClientApp/src/app/cities/cities.component.css` file as well:

```
table {
  width: 100%;
}

.mat-form-field {
  font-size: 14px;
  width: 100%;
}
```

This is required to make our new `MatInputModule` span through the entire available space (it's limited to `180px` by default).

AngularMaterialModule

Wait a minute: did we just say `MatInputModule`? That's correct: as a matter of fact, it seems like we have actually used an Angular Material module in our filtering implementation after all – and for good reason, since it looks much better than a vanilla HTML input textbox!

However, since we did that, we need to reference it within our `AngularMaterialModule` container or we'll get a compiler error. To do that, open the `/ClientApp/src/app/angular-material.module.ts` file and add the following lines:

```
import { NgModule } from '@angular/core';
import { MatTableModule } from '@angular/material/table';
import { MatPaginatorModule } from '@angular/material/paginator';
import { MatSortModule } from '@angular/material/sort';
import { MatInputModule } from '@angular/material/input';

@NgModule({
  imports: [
    MatTableModule,
    MatPaginatorModule,
    MatSortModule,
    MatInputModule
  ],
  exports: [
    MatTableModule,
    MatPaginatorModule,
    MatSortModule,
    MatInputModule
  ]
})

export class AngularMaterialModule { }
```

That's it: now, we can hit *F5* and navigate to the **Cities** view to test the new filtering feature. If we did everything properly, we should be able to see something similar to the following screenshot:

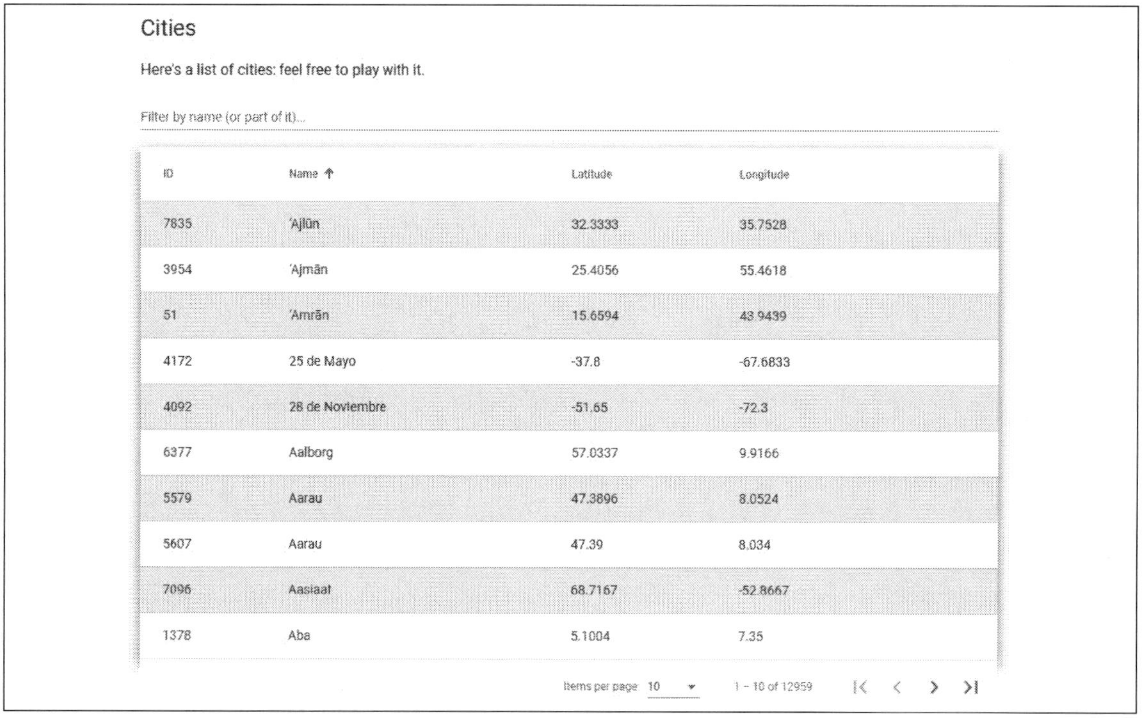

Figure 5.11: Cities table with pagination, sorting, and filtering

Looks pretty good, right?

If we try to type something into the filter textbox, we should see the table and the paginator update accordingly in real time. Look at what happens if we type `New York` in the filter textbox:

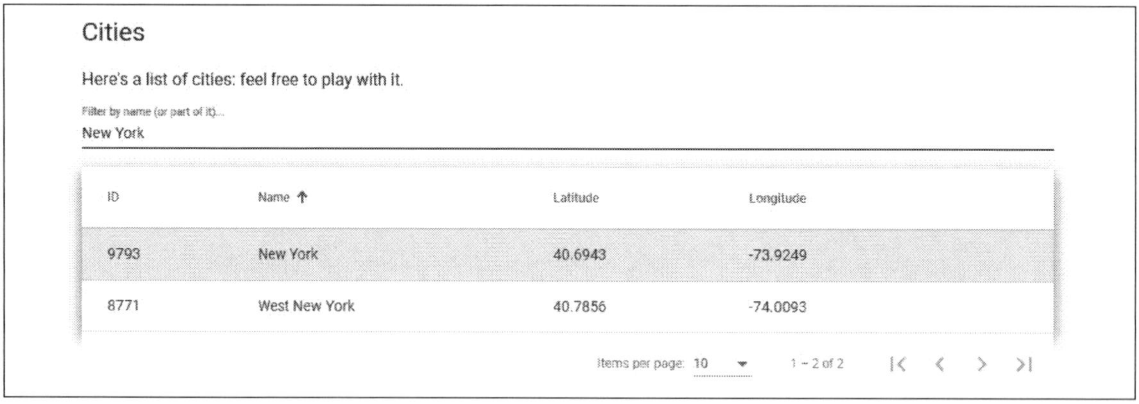

Figure 5.12: Cities table filtered for "New York"

That's definitely a good real-time filtering feature.

Performance considerations

Before moving further, it would be wise to spend a few minutes talking about the performance impact of the filter we've just implemented.

As we can see, the call to the `loadData` method is directly bound to the HTML input's *keyup* event, meaning that will fire upon each user's keystroke. This is great in terms of user experience, because our users will immediately get filtered data as they type; however, this real-time filter also has a serious downside in terms of performance impact: every time the filter text changes (that is, upon each keystroke), Angular fires an HTTP request to the back-end to retrieve the updated list of results. Such behavior is intrinsically resource-intensive and can easily become a huge performance issue, especially if we're dealing with large tables and/or non-indexed columns.

Are there ways to improve this approach without compromising the results obtained in terms of user experience? As a matter of fact, the answer is yes, but we won't do that now: we'll talk more about it in *Chapter 6, Forms and Data Validation*, when we introduce the concepts of *debouncing* and *throttling*.

Adding the countries to the loop

Before moving on, how about getting the countries up to speed? Yeah, it would mean redoing everything that we just did a second time; however, now that we know how to do this, we'll arguably be able to do it in a flash...... or maybe not.

Nonetheless, we should definitely spend a reasonable amount of time doing that now, because it would be a great way to plant everything we have learned so far in our muscle memory.

Let's do this now so that we can move on to trying something else. To avoid wasting pages, we'll just focus on the most relevant steps here, leaving everything else to what we just did with the cities - and to our GitHub repository, which hosts the full source code of what we need to do.

ASP.NET

Let's start with the ASP.NET part.

CountriesController

We should already have our `CountriesController` ready from *Chapter 4, Data Model with Entity Framework Core*, right? Open that file and replace the `GetCountries()` default action method with the following code:

```
// ...existing code...

[HttpGet]
public async Task<ActionResult<ApiResult<Country>>> GetCountries(
        int pageIndex = 0,
```

```
        int pageSize = 10,
        string sortColumn = null,
        string sortOrder = null,
        string filterColumn = null,
        string filterQuery = null)
{
    return await ApiResult<Country>.CreateAsync(
            _context.Countries,
            pageIndex,
            pageSize,
            sortColumn,
            sortOrder,
            filterColumn,
            filterQuery);
}

// ...existing code...
```

Luckily enough, our `ApiResult` class is type-agnostic; therefore, we can use it there with no issues. Also, since we have centralized all the hard work there, the .NET server-side part is already done.

An odd JSON naming issue

Before moving on, let's quickly test the component: hit *F5* and type the following URL into the browser's address bar: `https://localhost:44334/api/Countries/?pageIndex=0&pageSize=2`.

As soon as we hit *Enter*, we should be able to see the following interface:

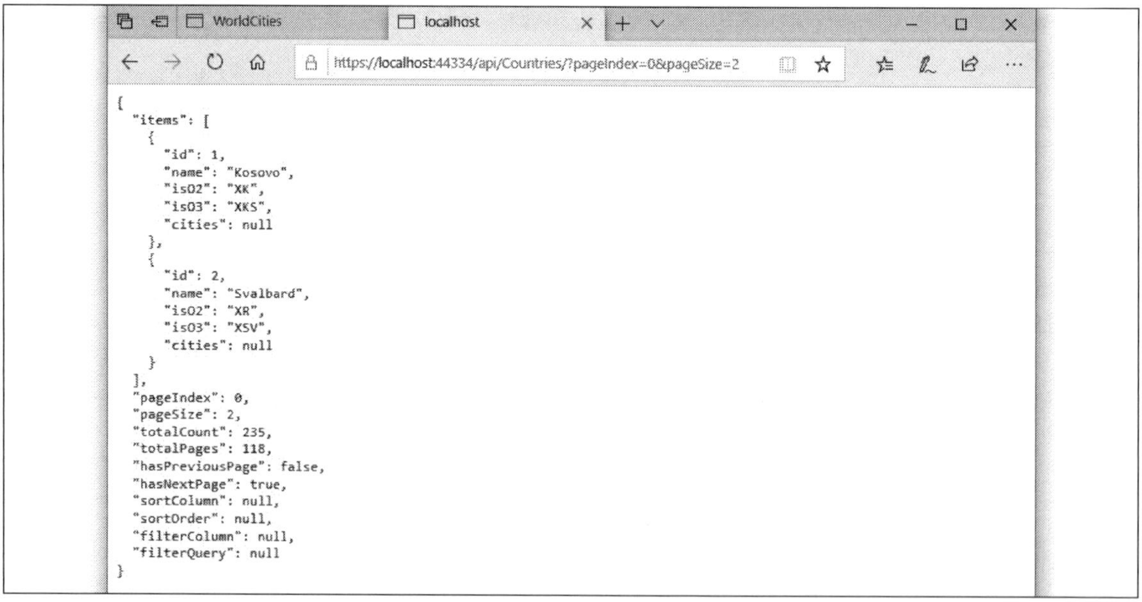

Figure 5.13: JSON array for the countries

It seems like it's all g... Hey, wait a minute: what's up with those `isO2` and `isO3` property names? They shouldn't be capitalized like that!

In order to understand what happened there, we need to take a step back and acknowledge something we might have underestimated so far: the camelCase conversion that the brand new `System.Text.Json` API (introduced with .NET Core 3) automatically does when serializing all our .NET classes to JSON. We already talked about this issue early on in this chapter, when we saw the .NET `CitiesController` JSON output for the first time, and we said that it wasn't a big deal since Angular is also camelCase-oriented - we would just have to define the various interfaces using camelCase as well.

Unfortunately, such automatic camelCase conversion might cause unwanted side effects when dealing with all-uppercase properties such as those two; whenever this happens, we need to adapt our source code to properly deal with that:

- The most obvious thing to do would be to just define them in our Angular interface in the exact same way, that is, using that exact casing; however, this would mean dealing with those `isO2` and `isO3` variable names throughout our whole Angular code, which is rather ugly and might also be quite misleading.
- If we don't want to adopt those hideous property names, there is an alternative - and arguably better - workaround we can use: we can decorate our offending properties with the `[JsonPropertyName]` data annotation, which allows us to force a JSON property name, regardless of the default casing convention (be it camelCase or PascalCase) specified within the `Startup` class.

The `[JsonPropertyName]` workaround seems the most reasonable fix we can apply to our specific scenario; let's just go with it and get rid of this problem for good!

Open the `/Data/Models/Country.cs` file and add the following lines to the existing code (new lines are highlighted):

```
// ...existing code...

/// <summary>
/// Country code (in ISO 3166-1 ALPHA-2 format)
/// </summary>
[JsonPropertyName("iso2")]
public string ISO2 { get; set; }

/// <summary>
/// Country code (in ISO 3166-1 ALPHA-3 format)
/// </summary>
[JsonPropertyName("iso3")]
public string ISO3 { get; set; }

// ...existing code...
```

Now, we can see whether those properties will respect this behavior by hitting *F5* and typing the same URL as before into the browser's address bar: `https://localhost:44334/api/Countries/?pageIndex=0&pageSize=2`:

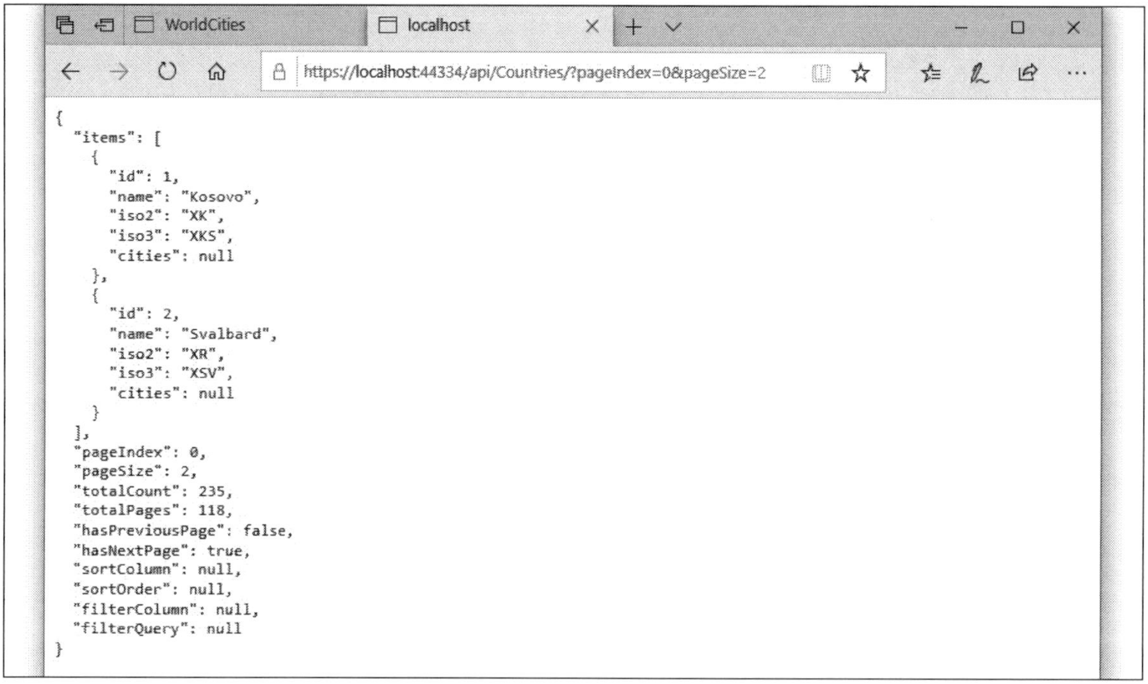

Figure 5.14: Amended JSON array for countries

It definitely seems like they do; thanks to this unexpected issue, we had the chance to add a powerful new weapon to our ASP.NET arsenal.

Now, we just need to create and configure the Angular component.

Angular

The Angular implementation will be less trivial than the ASP.NET one since we'll have to deal with multiple aspects:

- Adding the `CountriesComponent` TS, HTML, and CSS files and implementing the `Countries` table, as well as the paging, sorting, and filtering features as we did with the cities
- Configuring the `AppModule` to properly reference it and add the corresponding route
- Updating the `NavComponent` to add the navigation link

Let's do this! From Solution Explorer, do the following:

1. Navigate to the `/ClientApp/src/app/` folder.
2. Create a new `/countries/` folder.

3. Within that folder, create the following new files:
    - `country.ts`
    - `countries.component.ts`
    - `countries.component.html`
    - `countries.component.css`

Once done, fill them with the following content.

country.ts

Here's the source code for the `/ClientApp/src/app/countries/country.ts` interface file:

```
export interface Country {
    id: number;
    name: string;
    iso2: string;
    iso3: string;
}
```

Nothing new here – the code is very similar to what we did when we created the `city.ts` interface file.

countries.component.ts

Here's the source code for the `/ClientApp/src/app/countries/countries.component.ts` file:

```
import { Component, Inject, OnInit, ViewChild } from '@angular/core';
import { HttpClient, HttpParams } from '@angular/common/http';
import { MatTableDataSource } from '@angular/material/table';
import { MatPaginator, PageEvent } from '@angular/material/paginator';
import { MatSort } from '@angular/material/sort';

import { Country } from './country';

@Component({
  selector: 'app-countries',
  templateUrl: './countries.component.html',
  styleUrls: ['./countries.component.css']
})
export class CountriesComponent implements OnInit {
  public displayedColumns: string[] = ['id', 'name', 'iso2', 'iso3'];
  public countries: MatTableDataSource<Country>;

  defaultPageIndex: number = 0;
  defaultPageSize: number = 10;
```

```
public defaultSortColumn: string = "name";
public defaultSortOrder: string = "asc";

defaultFilterColumn: string = "name";
filterQuery: string = null;

@ViewChild(MatPaginator) paginator: MatPaginator;
@ViewChild(MatSort) sort: MatSort;

constructor(
private http: HttpClient,
@Inject('BASE_URL') private baseUrl: string) {
}

ngOnInit() {
this.loadData(null);
}

loadData(query: string = null) {
var pageEvent = new PageEvent();
pageEvent.pageIndex = this.defaultPageIndex;
pageEvent.pageSize = this.defaultPageSize;
if (query) {
this.filterQuery = query;
}
this.getData(pageEvent);
}

getData(event: PageEvent) {
var url = this.baseUrl + 'api/Countries';
var params = new HttpParams()
.set("pageIndex", event.pageIndex.toString())
.set("pageSize", event.pageSize.toString())
.set("sortColumn", (this.sort)
? this.sort.active
: this.defaultSortColumn)
.set("sortOrder", (this.sort)
? this.sort.direction
: this.defaultSortOrder);

if (this.filterQuery) {
params = params
.set("filterColumn", this.defaultFilterColumn)
.set("filterQuery", this.filterQuery);
}
```

```
this.http.get<any>(url, { params })
.subscribe(result => {
this.paginator.length = result.totalCount;
this.paginator.pageIndex = result.pageIndex;
this.paginator.pageSize = result.pageSize;
this.countries = new MatTableDataSource<Country>(result.data);
}, error => console.error(error));
}
}
```

Again, this is basically a mirror of the `cities.component.ts` file.

countries.component.html

Here's the source code for the `/ClientApp/src/app/countries/countries.component.html` file:

```
<h1>Countries</h1>

<p>Here's a list of countries: feel free to play with it.</p>

<p *ngIf="!countries"><em>Loading...</em></p>

<mat-form-field [hidden]="!countries">
  <input matInput (keyup)="loadData($event.target.value)"
      placeholder="Filter by name (or part of it)...">
</mat-form-field>

<table mat-table [dataSource]="countries"
  class="table-striped mat-elevation-z8"
  [hidden]="!countries"
  matSort (matSortChange)="loadData()"
  matSortActive="{{defaultSortColumn}}"
  matSortDirection="{{defaultSortOrder}}">

  <!-- Id Column -->
  <ng-container matColumnDef="id">
    <th mat-header-cell *matHeaderCellDef mat-sort-header>ID</th>
    <td mat-cell *matCellDef="let country"> {{country.id}} </td>
  </ng-container>

  <!-- Name Column -->
  <ng-container matColumnDef="name">
    <th mat-header-cell *matHeaderCellDef mat-sort-header>Name</th>
    <td mat-cell *matCellDef="let country"> {{country.name}} </td>
  </ng-container>
```

```
  <!-- Lat Column -->
  <ng-container matColumnDef="iso2">
    <th mat-header-cell *matHeaderCellDef mat-sort-header>ISO 2</th>
    <td mat-cell *matCellDef="let country"> {{country.iso2}} </td>
  </ng-container>

  <!-- Lon Column -->
  <ng-container matColumnDef="iso3">
    <th mat-header-cell *matHeaderCellDef mat-sort-header>ISO 3</th>
    <td mat-cell *matCellDef="let country"> {{country.iso3}} </td>
  </ng-container>

  <tr mat-header-row *matHeaderRowDef="displayedColumns"></tr>
  <tr mat-row *matRowDef="let row; columns: displayedColumns;"></tr>
</table>

<!-- Pagination directive -->
<mat-paginator [hidden]="!countries"
    (page)="getData($event)"
    [pageSize]="10"
    [pageSizeOptions]="[10, 20, 50]"
    showFirstLastButtons></mat-paginator>
```

The template, just as expected, is almost identical to the `cities.component.html` template file.

countries.component.css

Here's the source code for the `/ClientApp/src/app/countries/countries.component.css` file:

```
table {
  width: 100%;
}

.mat-form-field {
  font-size: 14px;
  width: 100%;
}
```

The preceding file is so similar to the `cities.components.css` file that we could even reference it instead of creating a new one; however, dealing with separate files is almost always a better choice, considering that we might need to apply different changes to the `Cities` and `Countries` tables later on.

AppModule

Now let's register our new component to the `AppModule` configuration file.

Open the `/ClientApp/src/app/app.module.ts` file and add the following highlighted lines:

```
import { BrowserModule } from '@angular/platform-browser';
import { NgModule } from '@angular/core';
import { FormsModule } from '@angular/forms';
import { HttpClientModule, HTTP_INTERCEPTORS } from '@angular/common/http';

import { AppRoutingModule } from './app-routing.module';

import { AppComponent } from './app.component';
import { NavMenuComponent } from './nav-menu/nav-menu.component';
import { HomeComponent } from './home/home.component';
import { CitiesComponent } from './cities/cities.component';
import { CountriesComponent } from './countries/countries.component';
import { BrowserAnimationsModule } from '@angular/platform-browser/animations';
import { AngularMaterialModule } from './angular-material.module';

@NgModule({
  declarations: [
    AppComponent,
    NavMenuComponent,
    HomeComponent,
    CitiesComponent,
    CountriesComponent
  ],

[...]
```

Once done, we can get to the routing part.

AppRoutingModule

The routing rule that we need to add is very similar to the one we added for the `CitiesComponent` a while ago:

```
import { NgModule } from '@angular/core';
import { Routes, RouterModule } from '@angular/router';
import { HomeComponent } from './home/home.component';
import { CitiesComponent } from './cities/cities.component';
```

```
import { CountriesComponent } from './countries/countries.component';

const routes: Routes = [
  { path: '', component: HomeComponent, pathMatch: 'full' },
  { path: 'cities', component: CitiesComponent },
  { path: 'countries', component: CountriesComponent }
];

@NgModule({
  imports: [RouterModule.forRoot(routes)],
  exports: [RouterModule]
})
export class AppRoutingModule { }
```

The new routing rule will make our new `CountriesComponent` get served by Angular when the client browser points to the `/countries` dedicated route. However, our users won't know that such a route exists if we don't add a visible link to it within our `NavComponent` menu; that's precisely why we're going to add it next.

NavComponent

Open the `/ClientApp/src/app/nav-menu/nav-menu.component.html` file and add the following highlighted lines to the existing code:

```
// ...existing code...

<ul class="navbar-nav flex-grow">
  <li
    class="nav-item"
    [routerLinkActive]="['link-active']"
    [routerLinkActiveOptions]="{ exact: true }"
  >
    <a class="nav-link text-dark" [routerLink]="['/']">Home</a>
  </li>
  <li class="nav-item" [routerLinkActive]="['link-active']">
    <a class="nav-link text-dark" [routerLink]="['/cities']"
      >Cities</a
    >
  </li>
  <li class="nav-item" [routerLinkActive]="['link-active']">
    <a class="nav-link text-dark" [routerLink]="['/countries']"
      >Countries</a
    >
  </li>
</ul>
```

```
// ...existing code...
```

... and that's it!

Our `CountriesComponent` is done, and – if we didn't make mistakes – it should work in about the same way as our beloved `CitiesComponent` that took so much time to finalize.

Testing CountriesComponent

It's time to see the results of our hard work: hit *F5*, navigate to the **Countries** view, and expect to see the following:

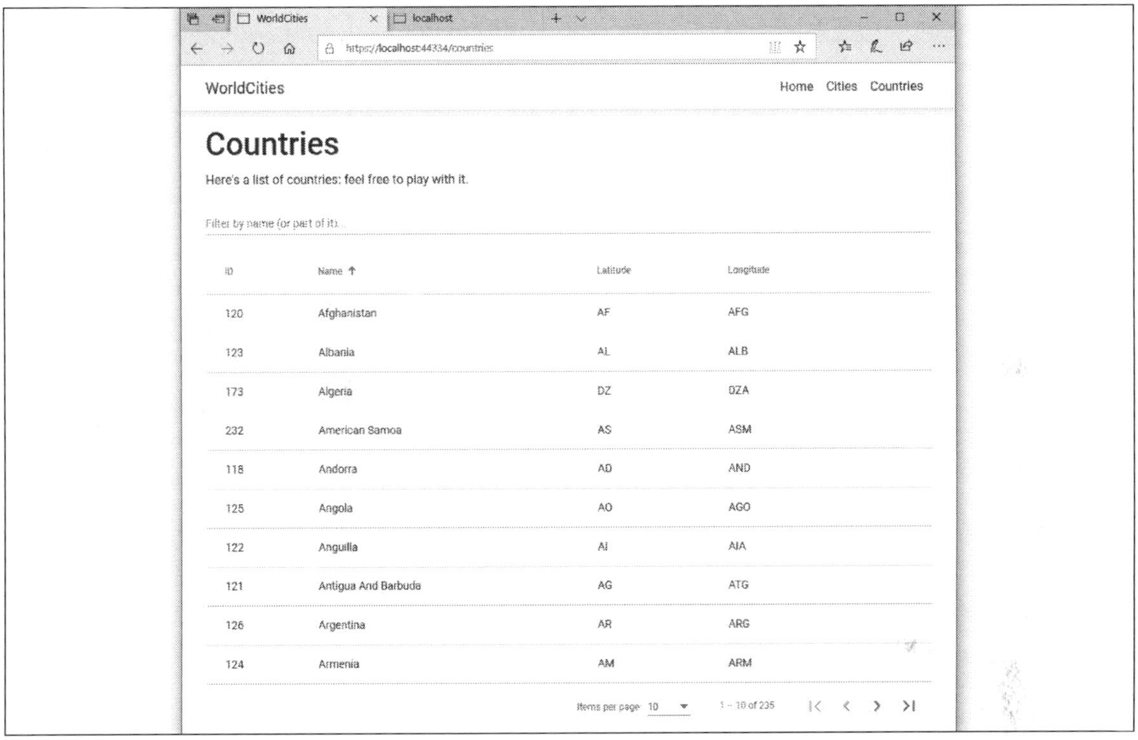

Figure 5.15: Countries table with pagination, sorting, and filtering

If we're able to get this same output on our first attempt, it definitely means that we have learned what to do; if we didn't, don't worry: we'll just have to check what we did wrong and fix it. Practice makes perfect.

IMPORTANT: don't be fooled by appearances; be sure to check that paging, sorting, and filtering are properly working before going further.

> The browser's console log can be a very useful tool for debugging server-side and client-side errors; most Angular errors come with well-documented exception text and a contextual link to the corresponding file and source code line, thus making it quite easy for the developer to understand what happens under the hood.

Summary

This chapter was all about reading data from the ASP.NET *back-end* and finding a way to properly show it to the browser with the Angular *front-end*.

We started by using our existing `CitiesController` to fetch a large number of cities with Angular components; although both frameworks are perfectly able to deal with massive data, we quickly understood that we need to improve the whole data request, response, and render flow process to grant our users a decent user experience.

For this very reason, we chose to adopt the `System.Linq.Dynamic.Core` .NET package to revamp our server-side business logic and the Angular Material npm package to greatly improve our client-side UI. By combining the powerful features of these two packages, we managed to pull off a bunch of interesting features: paging, sorting, and filtering. During our development journey, we also took the chance to identify, address, and mitigate some important security issues, such as a harmful SQL injection risk.

Right after finishing our work with `Cities`, we moved on to `Countries`, taking the chance to retrace our steps and cement what we just learned into our muscle memory.

After all our hard work, we can definitely say that we did a great job and fulfilled our goal: being able to read our data from the .NET *back-end* and gracefully present it through the *front-end* with Angular, thus making the end users fully able to see and interact with it.

We're now ready to add another layer of complexity to our application: give our users the chance to modify the existing data and/or add new data using HTML forms; these features are a must-have for most interactive web applications such as CMSes, forums, social networks, chat rooms, and the like. In the next chapter, we'll see how we can deal with such tasks using reactive forms, a pivotal Angular module that provides a model-driven approach to handling form inputs whose values change over time.

Suggested topics

JSON, RESTful conventions, HTTP verbs, HTTP status, life cycle hooks, client-side paging, server-side paging, sorting, filtering, dependency injection, SQL injection

ASP.NET

System.Linq, System.Linq.Dynamic.Core, IQueryable, Entity Framework Core

Angular

Components, Routing, Modules, AppModule, HttpClient, ngIf, hidden, Data Binding, Property Binding, Attribute Binding, ngFor, Directives, Structural Directives, interpolations, templates

References

- *Add sorting, filtering, and paging – ASP.NET MVC with EF Core*: `https://docs.microsoft.com/en-us/aspnet/core/data/ef-mvc/sort-filter-page`
- *Bootstrap Official Website*: `https://getbootstrap.com`
- *Angular Material official website*: `https://material.angular.io/`
- *Angular Material GitHub repository*: `https://github.com/angular/components`
- *Angular Material Typography*: `https://material.angular.io/guide/typography`
- *Angular BrowserAnimationsModule*: `https://angular.io/api/platform-browser/animations/BrowserAnimationsModule`
- *Angular Animation System*: `https://angular.io/guide/animations`
- *Angular Material: table overview*: `https://material.angular.io/components/table/overview`
- *Angular – ViewChild*: `https://angular.io/api/core/ViewChild`
- *System.Linq.Dynamic.Core project page on GitHub*: `https://github.com/StefH/System.Linq.Dynamic.Core`
- *LINQ Overview*: `https://docs.microsoft.com/en-us/dotnet/csharp/linq/`
- *LINQ (Language Integrated Query)*: `https://docs.microsoft.com/en-us/dotnet/csharp/programming-guide/concepts/linq/`
- *LINQ Lambda Expressions (C# Programming Guide)*: `https://docs.microsoft.com/en-us/dotnet/csharp/programming-guide/statements-expressions-operators/lambda-expressions`
- *LINQ Query expression basics*: `https://docs.microsoft.com/en-us/dotnet/csharp/linq/query-expression-basics`
- *Reflection (C#)*: `https://docs.microsoft.com/en-us/dotnet/csharp/programming-guide/concepts/reflection`
- *.NET Core and Entity Framework: set IQueryable<T> Column Names programmatically with Dynamic LINQ*: `https://www.ryadel.com/en/asp-net-core-set-column-name-programmatically-dynamic-linq-where-iqueryable/`
- *Understanding SQL Injections*: `https://tools.cisco.com/security/center/resources/sql_injection`

6
Forms and Data Validation

In this chapter, we'll mostly deal with forms, data input, and validation techniques. As we already know, HTML forms are one of the most important and delicate aspects of any business application. Nowadays, forms are used to fulfill almost any task involving user-submitted data, such as registering or logging in to a website, issuing a payment, reserving a hotel room, ordering a product, performing and retrieving search results, and more.

If we were asked to define a form from a developer's perspective, we would come out with the statement that *a form is a UI-based interface that allows authorized users to enter data that will be sent to a server for processing*. The moment we accept this definition, two additional considerations should come to mind:

- Each form should provide a data entry experience good enough to efficiently guide our users through the expected workflow; otherwise, they won't be able to use it properly.
- Each form, as long as it brings potentially insecure data to the server, could have a major security impact in terms of data integrity, data security, and system security, unless the developer possesses the required *know-how* to adopt and implement the appropriate countermeasures.

These two considerations provide a good summary of what we'll do in this chapter: we'll do our best to guide our users into submitting data in the most appropriate way, and we'll also learn how to check these input values properly to prevent, avoid, and/or minimize a wide spectrum of integrity and security threats. It's also important to understand that these two considerations are frequently intertwined with each other; hence, we'll often deal with them at the same time.

In this chapter, we'll cover the following topics:

- **Angular forms**, where we'll deal with **Template-Driven Forms** as well as **Reactive Forms**, all while understanding the pros and cons of both approaches and looking at which is the most suitable to use in various common scenarios.

- **Data validation**, where we'll learn how to double-check our users' input data in the *front-end* and also from the *back-end*, as well as the various techniques to give visual feedback when they send incorrect or invalid values.
- **Form builder**, where we'll implement another Reactive Form using some factory methods instead of manually instantiating the various form model elements.

At the end of each task, we'll also take some time to verify the result of our work using our web browser.

Technical requirements

In this chapter, we're going to need all the technical requirements that we mentioned in the previous chapters, with no additional resources, libraries, or packages.

The code files for this chapter can be found at: `https://github.com/PacktPublishing/ASP.NET-Core-5-and-Angular/tree/main/Chapter_06`

Exploring Angular forms

If we take a look at our current .NET Core with Angular projects, we will see how none of them allow our users to *interact* with the data:

- For the `HealthCheck` app, this is expected since there's simply no data to deal with: this is a monitor app that doesn't store anything and requires no input from the user.
- The `WorldCities` app, however, tells a whole different story: we do have a database that we use to return results to our users, who could – at least theoretically – be allowed to make changes.

It goes without saying that the `WorldCities` app would be our best candidate for implementing our forms. In the following sections, we'll do just that, starting with the Angular *front-end* and then moving to the .NET Core *back-end*.

Forms in Angular

Let's take a minute to briefly review our `WorldCities` app in the state we left it in at the end of *Chapter 5, Fetching and Displaying Data*. If we take a look at the `CitiesComponent` and `CountriesComponent` templates, we will see that we actually already have a data input element of some sort: we're clearly talking about <mat-form-field>, which is the *selector* of Angular Material's `MatInputModule`, which we added to the loop during *Chapter 5, Fetching and Displaying Data*, to let our users filter the `cities` and `countries` by their names.

Here's the relevant code snippet:

```
<mat-form-field [hidden]="!cities">
    <input matInput (keyup)="loadData($event.target.value)"
        placeholder="Filter by name (or part of it)...">
</mat-form-field>
```

This means that we are already accepting some kind of user action – consisting of a single input string – and reacting to it accordingly: such an action + reaction chain is the basis of an interaction between the user and the app, which is basically what the vast majority of forms are all about.

However, if we look at the generated HTML code, we can clearly see that we do not have any actual `<form>` element. We can test it by right-clicking that view's input element from our browser window and selecting **Inspect element**, as shown in the following screenshot:

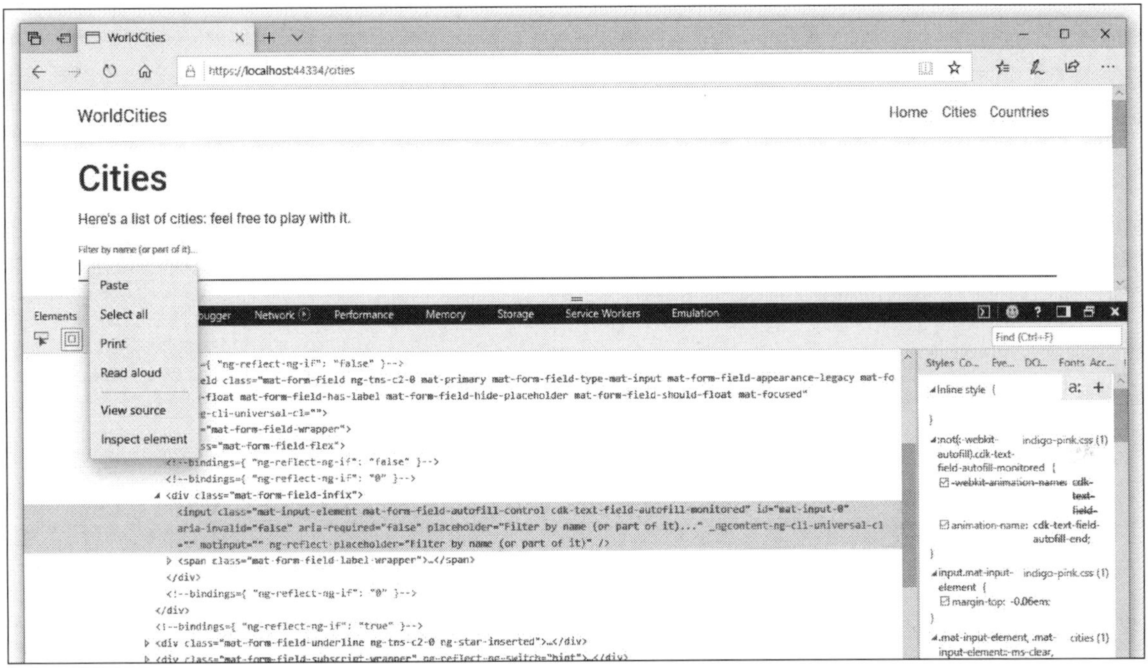

Figure 6.1: Inspecting the HTML of the input element

As we can see, there is no main form, only a single `input` field that perfectly handles the task we've assigned to it. The absence of the form is not missed because we're not submitting anything using FORM DATA: we're performing our data fetching using the Angular `HttpClient` module, which technically does this using an asynchronous **XMLHttpRequest** (**XHR**) through JavaScript – in one word, AJAX.

Such an approach does not require a `<form>` container element and is capable of handling the data encoding and transmission tasks using the following supported methods:

- `application/x-www-form-urlencoded`
- `multipart/form-data`
- `text/plain`

It only needs the actual input elements to get the required values from the user.

> For further details regarding the encoding method supported by the HTML `<form>` element, take a look at the following specifications:
>
> *URL Living Standard, – URL-encoded Form Data*: `https://url.spec.whatwg.org/#concept-urlencoded`
>
> *HTML Living Standard, section 4.10.21.7 – Multipart Form Data*: `https://html.spec.whatwg.org/multipage/form-control-infrastructure.html#multipart-form-data`
>
> *HTML Living Standard, section 4.10.21.8 – Plain Text Form Data*: `https://html.spec.whatwg.org/multipage/form-control-infrastructure.html#plain-text-form-data`

Although not required, a `form` element – or any HTML container for our input elements – might be very useful for a number of important tasks that don't fall into the data encoding and transmission subjects. Let's see what they are and why we may need them.

Reasons to use forms

Let's try to summarize the most blatant shortcomings of our current formless approach:

- We cannot keep track of the global form state since there's no way we can tell whether the input text is valid or not.
- We have no easy way to display an error message to the users to let them know what they have to do to make the form valid.
- We don't verify the input data in any way; we just collect and toss it to the server without thinking twice.

That's absolutely fine in our specific scenario since we're only dealing with a single text string and we don't care too much about its length, the input text, and so on. However, if we have to deal with multiple input elements and several value types, such limitations could seriously hinder our work – in terms of either data flow control, data validation, or user experience.

Sure, we could easily work around most of the aforementioned issues by implementing some custom methods within our form-based *components*; we could throw some errors such as `isValid()`, `isNumber()`, and so on here and there, and then hook them up to our template syntax and show/hide the validation messages with the help of structural directives such as `*ngIf`, `*ngFor`, and the like. However, it would definitely be a horrible way to address our problem; we didn't choose a feature-rich client-side framework such as Angular to work that way.

Luckily enough, we have no reason to do that since Angular provides us with a couple of alternative strategies to deal with these common form-related scenarios:

- **Template-Driven Forms**
- **Model-Driven Forms**, also known as **Reactive Forms**

Both of them are highly coupled with the framework and thus extremely viable; they both belong to the `@angular/forms` library and also share a common set of form control classes. However, they also have their own specific sets of features, along with their pros and cons, which could ultimately lead to us choosing one of them.

Let's try to quickly summarize these differences.

Template-Driven Forms

If you've come from AngularJS, there's a high chance that the Template-Driven approach will ring a bell or two. As the name implies, Template-Driven Forms host most of the logic in the template code; working with a Template-Driven Form means:

- Building the form in the `.html` template file
- Binding data to the various input fields using an `ngModel` instance
- Using a dedicated `ngForm` object related to the whole form and containing all the inputs, with each being accessible through their name

These things need to be done in order to perform the required validity checks.

To understand this, here's what a Template-Driven Form looks like:

```
<form novalidate autocomplete="off" #form="ngForm"
    (ngSubmit)="onSubmit(form)">

    <input type="text" name="name" value="" required
        placeholder="Insert the city name..."
        [(ngModel)]="city.Name" #title="ngModel"
        />

    <span *ngIf="(name.touched || name.dirty) &&
     name.errors?.required">
        Name is a required field: please enter a valid city name.
    </span>

    <button type="submit" name="btnSubmit"
      [disabled]="form.invalid">
      Submit
    </button>

</form>
```

As we can see, we can access any element, including the form itself, with some convenient aliases – the attributes with the `#` sign – and check for their current states to create our own validation workflow. These states are provided by the framework and will change in real time, depending on various things: `touched`, for example, becomes `True` when the control has been visited at least once; `dirty`, which is the opposite of `pristine`, means that the control value has changed, and so on. We used both `touched` and `dirty` in the preceding example because we want our validation message to only be shown if the user moves their focus to the `<input name="name">` and then goes away, leaving it blank by either deleting its value or not setting it.

These are Template-Driven Forms in a nutshell; now that we've had an overall look at them, let's try to summarize the pros and cons of this approach.

The pros

Here are the main advantages of Template-Driven Forms:

- **Template-Driven Forms are very easy to write**. We can recycle most of our HTML knowledge (assuming that we have any). On top of that, if we came from AngularJS, we already know how well we can make them work once we've mastered the technique.
- **They are rather easy to read and understand**, at least from an HTML point of view; we have a plain, understandable HTML structure containing all the input fields and validators, one after another. Each element will have a name, a two-way binding with the underlying `ngModel`, and (possibly) Template-Driven logic built upon aliases that have been hooked to other elements that we can also see, or to the form itself.

The cons

Here are their weaknesses:

- **Template-Driven Forms require a lot of HTML code**, which can be rather difficult to maintain and is generally more error-prone than pure TypeScript.
- For the same reason, **these forms cannot be unit tested**. We have no way to test their validators or to ensure that the logic we implemented will work, other than running an end-to-end test with our browser, which is hardly ideal for complex forms.
- **Their readability will quickly drop** as we add more and more validators and input tags. Keeping all their logic within the template might be fine for small forms, but it doesn't scale well when dealing with complex data items.

Ultimately, we can say that Template-Driven Forms might be the way to go when we need to build small forms with simple data validation rules, where we can benefit more from their simplicity. On top of that, they are quite similar to the typical HTML code we're already used to (assuming that we do have a plain HTML development background); we just need to learn how to decorate the standard `<form>` and `<input>` elements with aliases and throw in some validators handled by structural directives such as the ones we've already seen, and we'll be set in (almost) no time.

> For additional information on Template-Driven Forms, we highly recommend that you read the official Angular documentation at: `https://angular.io/guide/forms`

That being said, the lack of unit testing, the HTML code bloat that they will eventually produce, and the scaling difficulties will eventually lead us toward an alternative approach for any non-trivial form.

Model-Driven/Reactive Forms

The Model-Driven approach was specifically added in Angular 2+ to address the known limitations of Template-Driven Forms. The forms that are implemented with this alternative method are known as **Model-Driven Forms** or Reactive Forms, which are the exact same thing.

The main difference here is that (almost) nothing happens in the template, which acts as a mere reference to a more complex TypeScript object that gets defined, instantiated, and configured programmatically within the component class: the form **model**.

To understand the overall concept, let's try to rewrite the previous form in a Model-Driven/Reactive way (the relevant parts are highlighted). The outcome of doing this is as follows:

```
<form [formGroup]="form" (ngSubmit)="onSubmit()">

    <input formControlName="name" required />

    <span *ngIf="(form.get('name').touched || form.get('name').dirty)
        && form.get('name').errors?.required">
        Name is a required field: please enter a valid city name.
    </span>

    <button type="submit" name="btnSubmit"
        [disabled]="form.invalid">
        Submit
    </button>

</form>
```

As we can see, the amount of required code is much lower.

Here's the underlying form model that we will define in the component class file (the relevant parts are highlighted in the following code):

```
import { FormGroup, FormControl } from '@angular/forms';

class ModelFormComponent implements OnInit {
  form: FormGroup;

  ngOnInit() {
    this.form = new FormGroup({
        title: new FormControl()
    });
  }
}
```

Let's try to understand what's happening here:

- The `form` property is an instance of `FormGroup` and represents the form itself.
- `FormGroup`, as the name suggests, is a container of form controls sharing the same purpose. As we can see, the `form` itself acts as a `FormGroup`, which means that we can nest `FormGroup` objects inside other `FormGroup` objects (we didn't do that in our sample, though).
- Each data input element in the form template – in the preceding code, `name` – is represented by an instance of `FormControl`.
- Each `FormControl` instance encapsulates the related control's current state, such as `valid`, `invalid`, `touched`, and `dirty`, including its actual value.
- Each `FormGroup` instance encapsulates the state of each child control, meaning that it will only be valid if/when all its children are also valid.

Also, note that we have no way of accessing the `FormControls` directly like we were doing in Template-Driven Forms; we have to retrieve them using the `.get()` method of the main `FormGroup`, which is the form itself.

At first glance, the Model-Driven template doesn't seem too different from the Template-Driven one; we still have a `<form>` element, an `<input>` element hooked to a `<span>` validator, and a `submit` button; on top of that, checking the state of the input elements takes a bigger amount of source code since they have no aliases we can use. What's the real deal, then?

To help us visualize the difference, let's look at the following diagrams: here's a schema depicting how **Template-Driven Forms** work:

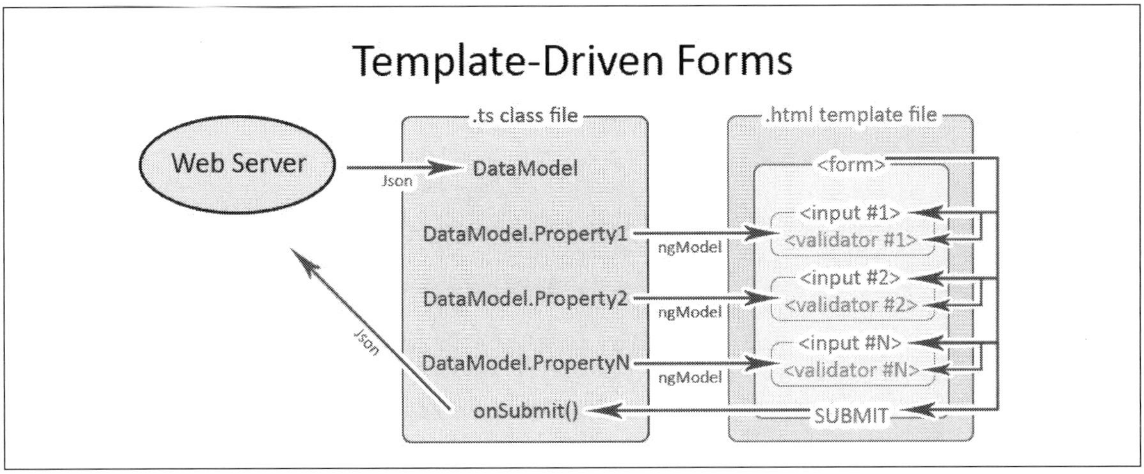

Figure 6.2: Template-Driven Forms schematic

By looking at the arrows, we can easily see that, in **Template-Driven Forms**, everything happens in the template; the HTML form elements are directly bound to the **DataModel** component represented by a property filled with an asynchronous HTML request to the **Web Server**, much like we did with our cities and country table. That **DataModel** will be updated as soon as the user changes something, that is, unless a validator prevents them from doing that. If we think about it, we can easily understand how there isn't a single part of the whole workflow that happens to be under our control; Angular handles everything by itself using the information in the data bindings defined within our template. This is what *Template-Driven* actually means: the template is calling the shots.

Now, let's take a look at the **Model-Driven Forms** (or Reactive Forms) approach:

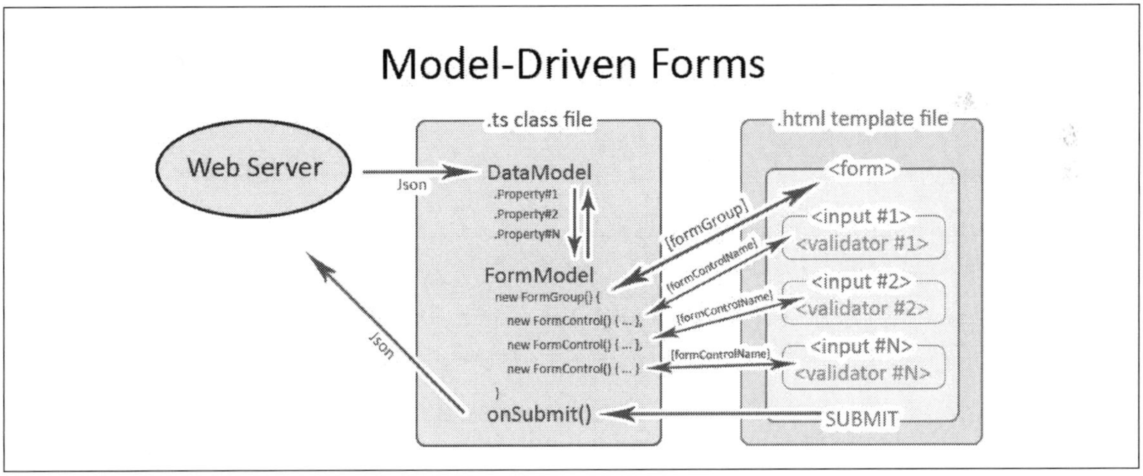

Figure 6.3: Model-Driven/Reactive Forms schematic

As we can see, the arrows depicting the **Model-Driven Forms** workflow tell a whole different story. They show how the data flows between the **DataModel** component – which we get from the **Web Server** – and a UI-oriented form model that retains the states and the values of the HTML form (and its children input elements) that are presented to the user. This means that we'll be able to get in-between the data and the form control objects and perform a number of tasks firsthand: push and pull data, detect and react to user changes, implement our own validation logic, perform unit tests, and so on.

Instead of being superseded by a template that's not under our control, we can track and influence the workflow programmatically, since the form model that calls the shots is also a `TypeScript` class; that's what Model-Driven Forms are about. This also explains why they are also called **Reactive Forms** – an explicit reference to the Reactive programming style that favors explicit data handling and change management throughout the workflow.

> For additional information on Model-Driven/Reactive Forms, we highly recommend reading the official Angular documentation at: `https://angular.io/guide/reactive-forms`

Enough with the theory; it's time to empower our components with some Reactive Forms.

Building our first Reactive Form

In this section, we'll create our first Reactive Form. More specifically, we're going to build a `CityEditComponent` that will give our users the chance to edit an existing *city* record.

To do that, we'll do the following:

- Add a reference to the `ReactiveFormsModule` to our `AppModule` class.
- Create the `CityEditComponent` TypeScript and template files.

Let's get started.

ReactiveFormsModule

The first thing we have to do to start working with Reactive Forms is add a reference to the `ReactiveFormsModule` in the `AppModule` class.

From Solution Explorer, open the `/ClientApp/src/app/app.module.ts` file and add the following code (the updated source code is highlighted):

```
import { BrowserModule } from '@angular/platform-browser';
import { NgModule } from '@angular/core';
import { FormsModule } from '@angular/forms';
import { HttpClientModule, HTTP_INTERCEPTORS } from '@angular/common/http';
```

```
import { AppRoutingModule } from './app-routing.module';

import { AppComponent } from './app.component';
import { NavMenuComponent } from './nav-menu/nav-menu.component';
import { HomeComponent } from './home/home.component';
import { CitiesComponent } from './cities/cities.component';
import { CountriesComponent } from './countries/countries.component';
import { BrowserAnimationsModule } from '@angular/platform-browser/animations';
import { AngularMaterialModule } from './angular-material.module';
import { ReactiveFormsModule } from '@angular/forms';

@NgModule({
  declarations: [
    AppComponent,
    NavMenuComponent,
    HomeComponent,
    CitiesComponent,
    CountriesComponent
  ],
  imports: [
    BrowserModule.withServerTransition({ appId: 'ng-cli-universal' }),
    HttpClientModule,
    FormsModule,
    AppRoutingModule,
    BrowserAnimationsModule,
    AngularMaterialModule,
    ReactiveFormsModule
  ],
  providers: [],
  bootstrap: [AppComponent]
})
export class AppModule { }
```

Now that we've added a reference to the `ReactiveFormsModule` in our app's `AppModule` file, we can implement the Angular component that will host the actual form.

CityEditComponent

Since our `CityEditComponent` is meant to allow our users to modify a city, we'll need to let it know which city it has to fetch from (and send to) the server. The best way to do that is by using a `GET` parameter, such as the city `id`.

Therefore, we're going to implement a standard **Master/Detail** UI pattern, much like the following one:

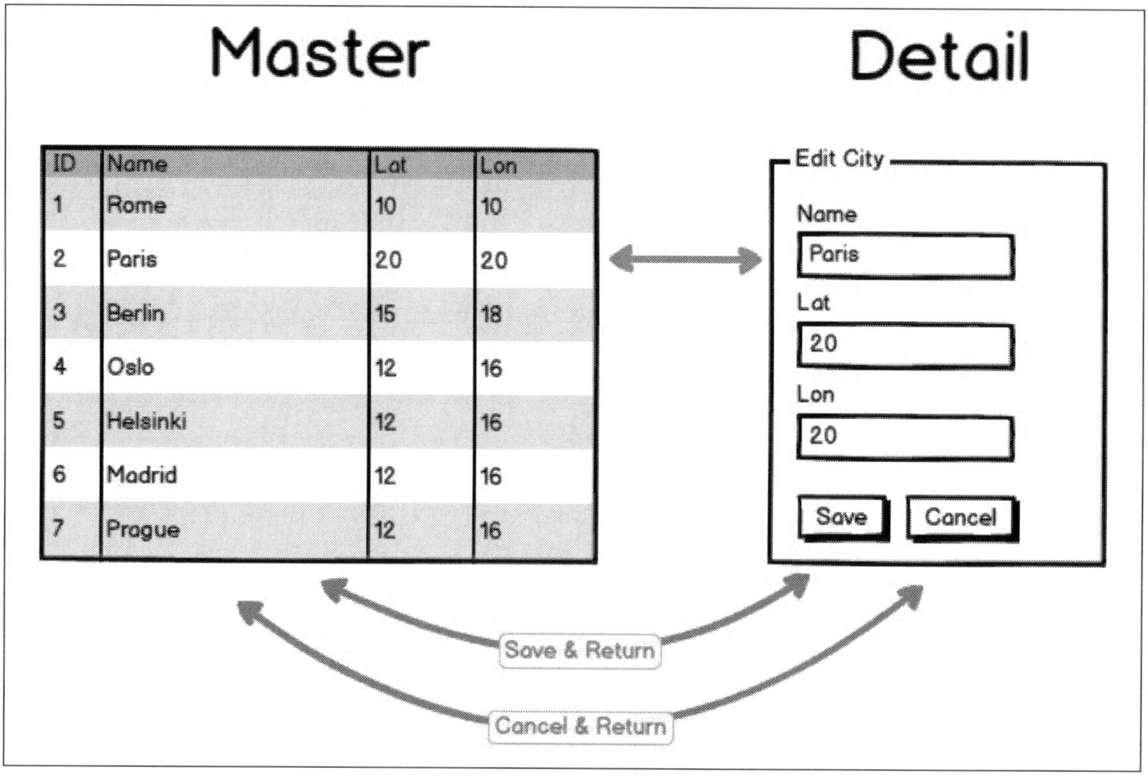

Figure 6.4: A Master/Detail UI pattern

This editing pattern, other than being the most used in the world when dealing with a list of items, is a perfect fit for our scenario. Sounds like a plan: let's do it!

From the Solution Explorer of our `WorldCities` project, do the following:

1. Navigate to the `/ClientApp/src/app/cities` folder.
2. Right-click the folder's name and select **Add | New Item** three times to create the following files:
    - `city-edit.component.ts`
    - `city-edit.component.html`
    - `city-edit.component.css`

We know what we're doing here due to what we learned about in *Chapter 3, Front-End and Back-End Interactions*: we're creating a new Angular component.

city-edit.component.ts

Once you're done, open the three new (and empty) files and fill them with the following, the source code for the `/ClientApp/src/app/cities/city-edit.component.ts` file:

```
import { Component, Inject, OnInit } from '@angular/core';
import { HttpClient } from '@angular/common/http';
import { ActivatedRoute, Router } from '@angular/router';
import { FormGroup, FormControl } from '@angular/forms';

import { City } from './City';

@Component({
  selector: 'app-city-edit',
  templateUrl: './city-edit.component.html',
  styleUrls: ['./city-edit.component.css']
})
export class CityEditComponent implements OnInit {

  // the view title
  title: string;

  // the form model
  form: FormGroup;

  // the city object to edit
  city: City;

  constructor(
    private activatedRoute: ActivatedRoute,
    private router: Router,
    private http: HttpClient,
    @Inject('BASE_URL') private baseUrl: string) {
  }

  ngOnInit() {
    this.form = new FormGroup({
      name: new FormControl(''),
      lat: new FormControl(''),
      lon: new FormControl('')
    });

    this.loadData();
  }

  loadData() {
```

```
    // retrieve the ID from the 'id' parameter
    var id = +this.activatedRoute.snapshot.paramMap.get('id');

    // fetch the city from the server
    var url = this.baseUrl + "api/Cities/" + id;
    this.http.get<City>(url).subscribe(result => {
      this.city = result;
      this.title = "Edit - " + this.city.name;

      // update the form with the city value
      this.form.patchValue(this.city);
    }, error => console.error(error));
  }

  onSubmit() {

    var city = this.city;

    city.name = this.form.get("name").value;
    city.lat = +this.form.get("lat").value;
    city.lon = +this.form.get("lon").value;

    var url = this.baseUrl + "api/Cities/" + this.city.id;
    this.http
      .put<City>(url, city)
        .subscribe(result => {

          console.log("City " + city.id + " has been updated.");

          // go back to cities view
          this.router.navigate(['/cities']);
        }, error => console.error(error));
    }
}
```

This is a fair amount of source code: luckily enough, there are a lot of comments that should help us understand the purpose of each relevant step.

Let's try to summarize what we did here:

- We added some `import` references to the modules we're about to use within this class: among them, we can see a couple of new kids on the block: `@angular/router` and `@angular/form`. The former is required to define some internal routing patterns, while the latter contains the `FormGroup` and `FormControl` classes that we need in order to build our form.

- Right below the class definition, we created a `FormGroup` instance within a `form` variable: that's our form model.
- The `form` variable instance contains three `FormControl` objects that will store the *city* values we want to allow our users to change: `name`, `lat`, and `lon`. We don't want to make them change the `Id` or the `CountryId` - at least, not for now.
- Right below the `form` variable, we defined a `city` variable that will host the actual city when we retrieve it from the database.
- The city retrieval task is handled by the `loadData()` method, which is rather similar to the one we implemented in the `cities.component.ts` file: a standard data-fetching task handled by an `HttpClient` module that's injected (as usual) through the `constructor()`. The most relevant difference here is that the method, right after the HTTP request/response cycle, proactively loads the retrieved city data within the form model (by using the form's `patchValue()` method) instead of relying on the Angular data-binding feature: that's hardly a surprise since we're using the Model-Driven/Reactive approach and not the Template-Driven one.
- The `onSubmit()` method is where the update magic takes place: `HttpClient` plays a major role here as well by issuing a PUT request to the server sending the `city` variable properly. Once the *Observable* subscription has been processed, we use the `router` instance to redirect the user back to the `CitiesComponent` (the *Master* view).

> Before moving further, it could be wise to spend a couple of words talking about the `patchValue()` method that we used in the preceding code.
>
> The `@angular/forms` package gives us two ways to update a Reactive Form's model: the `setValue()` method, which sets a new value for each individual control, and the `patchValue()` method, which will replace any properties that have been defined in the object that have changed in the form model.
>
> The main difference between them is that `setValue()` performs a strict check of the source object and will throw errors if it doesn't fully adhere to the model structure (including all nested `FormControl` elements), while `patchValue()` will silently fail on those errors.
>
> Therefore, we can say that the former method might be a better choice for complex forms and/or whenever we need to catch nesting errors, while the latter is the way to go when things are simple enough - like in our current samples.

The `@angular/router` package deserves a special mention because it's the first time we have seen it in a component TypeScript file, and we've only used it twice before:

- In the `app.module.ts` file, to define our client-side routing rules
- In the `nav.component.html` file, to implement the aforementioned routing rules and make them appear as navigation links within the web application's main menu

This time, we had to `import` it because we needed a way to retrieve the *City* `id` parameter from the URL. To do this, we used the `ActivatedRoute` interface, which allows us to retrieve information about the currently active route, as well as the GET parameter we were looking for.

city-edit.component.html

Here's the content for the `/ClientApp/src/app/cities/city-edit.component.html` template file:

```
<div class="city-edit">
    <h1>{{title}}</h1>

    <p *ngIf="!city"><em>Loading...</em></p>

    <div class="form" [formGroup]="form" (ngSubmit)="onSubmit()">

        <div class="form-group">
            <label for="name">City name:</label>
            <br />
            <input type="text" id="name"
                   formControlName="name" required
                   placeholder="City name..."
                   class="form-control" />
        </div>

        <div class="form-group">
            <label for="lat">City latitude:</label>
            <br />
            <input type="text" id="lat"
                   formControlName="lat" required
                   placeholder="Latitude..."
                   class="form-control" />
        </div>

        <div class="form-group">
            <label for="lon">City longitude:</label>
            <br />
            <input type="text" id="lon"
                   formControlName="lon" required
                   placeholder="Latitude..."
                   class="form-control" />
        </div>

        <div class="form-group commands">
            <button type="submit"
```

```
                    (click)="onSubmit()"
                    class="btn btn-success">
                Save
            </button>
            <button type="submit"
                    [routerLink]="['/cities']"
                    class="btn">
                Cancel
            </button>
        </div>
    </div>
</div>
```

Wait a minute: where's our `<form>` HTML element? Didn't we say that we were working with form-based approaches because they are way better than placing a bunch of separate `<input>` fields here and there?

As a matter of fact, we **do** have a form: we just used a `<div>` rather than the classic `<form>` element. As you may have guessed at this point, forms in Angular don't necessarily have to be created using the `<form>` HTML element, since we won't be using its distinctive features. For that very reason, we are free to define them using `<div>`, `<p>`, or any HTML block-level element that could reasonably contain `<input>` fields.

city-edit.component.css

Last but not least, here's our `/ClientApp/src/app/cities/city-edit.component.css` content:

```
/* empty */
```

Yeah, that's it: we don't need a specific style at the moment, so we'll just leave it empty for now: we'll pimp it later on.

Adding the navigation link

Now that our `CityEditComponent` is ready, we need to enforce our master/detail pattern by adding a navigation link that will allow our users to navigate from our city listing (master) to the city edit form (detail).

To do that, we need to perform two tasks:

- Create a new route within the `app.module.ts` file.
- Implement the preceding route in the template code of `CitiesComponent`.

Let's do this!

app.module.ts

Open the `/ClientApp/src/app/app.module.ts` file and add a reference for the new component:

```
import { BrowserModule } from '@angular/platform-browser';
import { NgModule } from '@angular/core';
import { FormsModule } from '@angular/forms';
import { HttpClientModule, HTTP_INTERCEPTORS } from '@angular/common/http';

import { AppRoutingModule } from './app-routing.module';

import { AppComponent } from './app.component';
import { NavMenuComponent } from './nav-menu/nav-menu.component';
import { HomeComponent } from './home/home.component';
import { CitiesComponent } from './cities/cities.component';
import { CityEditComponent } from './cities/city-edit.component';
import { CountriesComponent } from './countries/countries.component';
import { BrowserAnimationsModule } from '@angular/platform-browser/animations';
import { AngularMaterialModule } from './angular-material.module';
import { ReactiveFormsModule } from '@angular/forms';

@NgModule({
  declarations: [
    AppComponent,
    NavMenuComponent,
    HomeComponent,
    CitiesComponent,
    CityEditComponent,
    CountriesComponent
  ],
  imports: [
    BrowserModule.withServerTransition({ appId: 'ng-cli-universal' }),
    HttpClientModule,
    FormsModule,
    AppRoutingModule,
    BrowserAnimationsModule,
    AngularMaterialModule,
    ReactiveFormsModule
  ],
  providers: [],
  bootstrap: [AppComponent]
})
export class AppModule { }
```

That's it: now we can deal with the routing part.

app-routing.module.ts

Right after that, add a new route to the `app-routing.module.ts` file with the following source code (new lines are highlighted):

```
import { NgModule } from '@angular/core';
import { Routes, RouterModule } from '@angular/router';
import { HomeComponent } from './home/home.component';
import { CitiesComponent } from './cities/cities.component';
import { CityEditComponent } from './cities/city-edit.component';
import { CountriesComponent } from './countries/countries.component';

const routes: Routes = [
  { path: '', component: HomeComponent, pathMatch: 'full' },
  { path: 'cities', component: CitiesComponent },
  { path: 'city/:id', component: CityEditComponent },
  { path: 'countries', component: CountriesComponent },
];

@NgModule({
  imports: [RouterModule.forRoot(routes)],
  exports: [RouterModule]
})
export class AppRoutingModule { }
```

As we can see, we imported the `CityEditComponent`, added it to the `@NgModule` declarations list, and – last but not least – defined a new `city/:id` corresponding to the route. The syntax we used will route any URL composed by `city` and a parameter that will be registered with the `id` name.

cities.component.html

Now that we have the navigation route, we need to implement it within the *Master* view so that the *Detail* view can be reached.

Open the `/ClientApp/src/app/cities/cities.component.html` file and change the HTML template code for the city's `Name` column in the following way:

```
<!-- ...existing code... -->

<!-- Name Column -->
<ng-container matColumnDef="name">
  <th mat-header-cell *matHeaderCellDef mat-sort-header>Name</th>
  <td mat-cell *matCellDef="let city">
    <a [routerLink]="['/city', city.id]">{{city.name}}</a>
  </td>
</ng-container>
```

```
<!-- ...existing code... -->
```

Once you're done, test it out by hitting *F5* and navigating to the **Cities** view. As shown in the following screenshot, the city names are now clickable links:

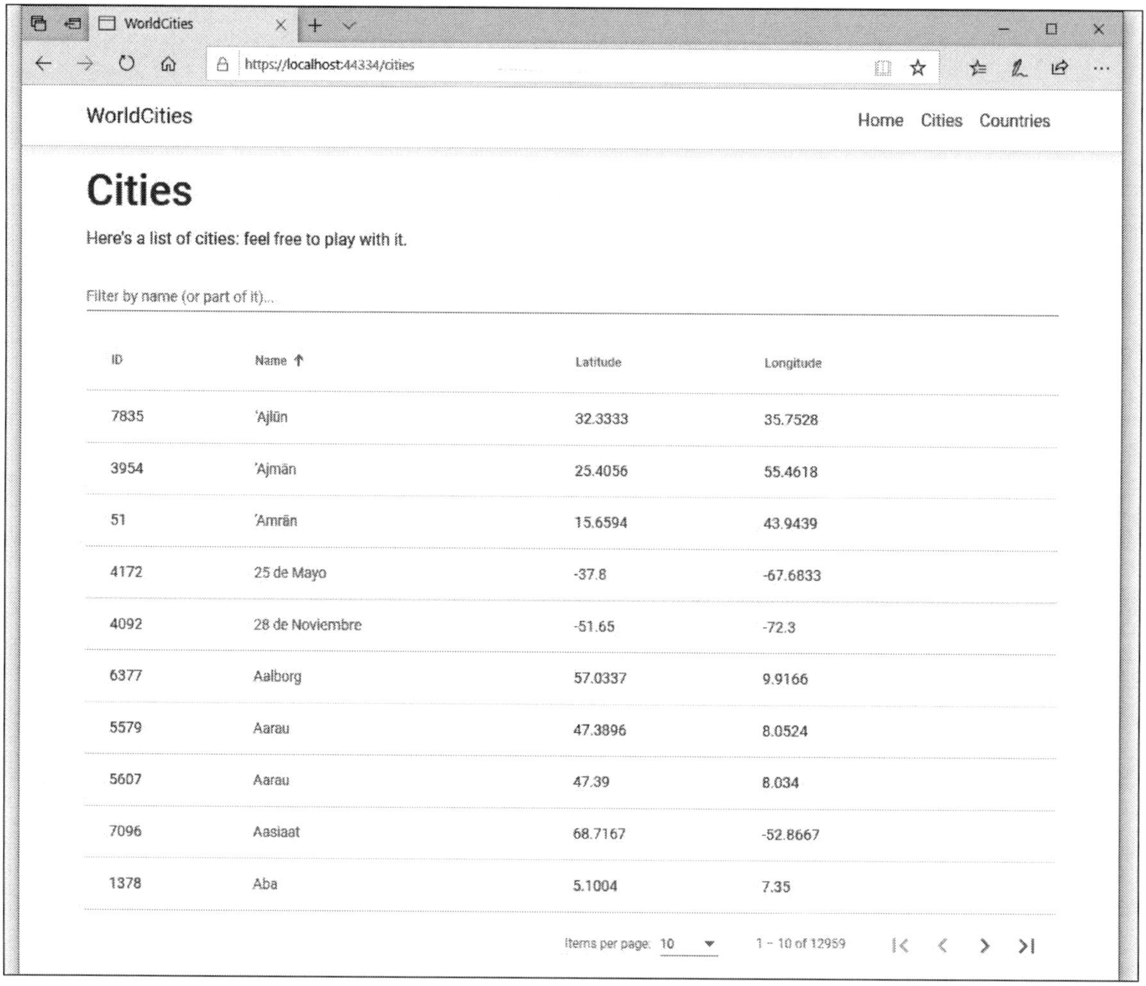

Figure 6.5: Cities table with clickable links

From there, filter the table for `Paris` and click on the first result to access the `CityEditComponent`, which we'll finally be able to see (as shown in the following screenshot):

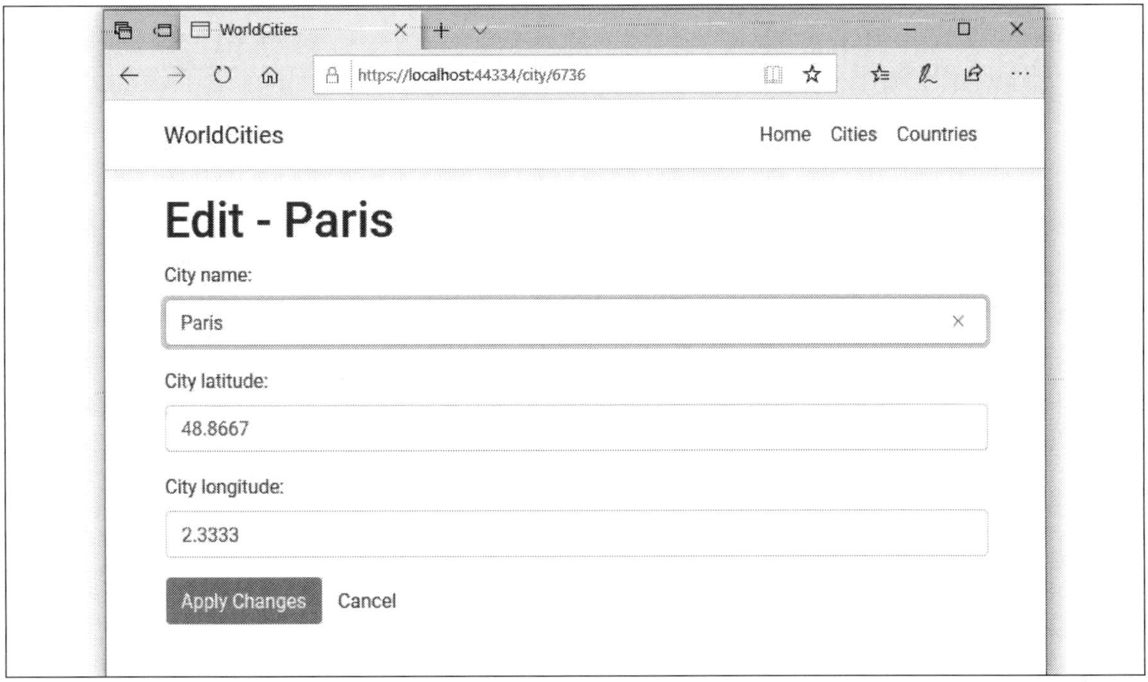

Figure 6.6: The CityEditComponent

As we can see, everything is much as we would expect it to be. We have three textboxes, as well as a **Save** button and a **Cancel** button, both of which are ready to perform the task they have been assigned. The **Save** button will send the modified text to the server for the update and then redirect the user to the *Master* view, while the **Cancel** button will redirect the user without performing any changes.

That's definitely a good start! However, we're far from done: we still have to add validators, implement error handling, and write a couple of unit tests for the client side and the server side. Let's get started.

Adding a new city

Before going any further, let's spend a couple more minutes adding a very useful feature to our `CityEditComponent`: the chance to add a brand-new `City`. This is a rather classic requirement of a *Detail* view with editing capabilities, which can be handled with the same component – as long as we perform some small modifications to enable it to handle a new feature (adding a new city) as well as the existing one (editing an existing city) in a seamless way.

To do that, we'll have to perform the following steps:

1. **Extend the functionalities of CityEditComponent** to make it able to add new cities, as well as edit existing ones.
2. **Add a new Add City button** to our component's template file and bind it to a new client-side route.
3. Implement the required functionalities to **select a country** for the newly added city, which will also be useful in edit mode (it will allow users to change the country for existing cities).

Let's get to work!

Extending the CityEditComponent

Open the `/ClientApp/src/app/cities/city-edit.component.ts` file and add the following code (the new/updated lines are highlighted):

```
import { Component, Inject, OnInit } from '@angular/core';
import { HttpClient } from '@angular/common/http';
import { ActivatedRoute, Router } from '@angular/router';
import { FormGroup, FormControl } from '@angular/forms';

import { City } from './City';

@Component({
  selector: 'app-city-edit',
  templateUrl: './city-edit.component.html',
  styleUrls: ['./city-edit.component.css']
})
export class CityEditComponent implements OnInit {

  // the view title
  title: string;

  // the form model
  form: FormGroup;

  // the city object to edit or create
  city: City;

  // the city object id, as fetched from the active route:
  // It's NULL when we're adding a new city,
  // and not NULL when we're editing an existing one.
  id?: number;

  constructor(
```

```
    private activatedRoute: ActivatedRoute,
    private router: Router,
    private http: HttpClient,
    @Inject('BASE_URL') private baseUrl: string) {
    }

  ngOnInit() {
    this.form = new FormGroup({
      name: new FormControl(''),
      lat: new FormControl(''),
      lon: new FormControl('')
    });

    this.loadData();
  }


  loadData() {

    // retrieve the ID from the 'id'
    this.id = +this.activatedRoute.snapshot.paramMap.get('id');
    if (this.id) {
      // EDIT MODE

      // fetch the city from the server
      var url = this.baseUrl + "api/Cities/" + this.id;
      this.http.get<City>(url).subscribe(result => {
        this.city = result;
        this.title = "Edit - " + this.city.name;

        // update the form with the city value
        this.form.patchValue(this.city);
      }, error => console.error(error));
    }
    else {
      // ADD NEW MODE

      this.title = "Create a new City";
    }
  }

  onSubmit() {

    var city = (this.id) ? this.city : <City>{};

    city.name = this.form.get("name").value;
```

```
    city.lat = +this.form.get("lat").value;
    city.lon = +this.form.get("lon").value;

    if (this.id) {
      // EDIT mode

      var url = this.baseUrl + "api/Cities/" + this.city.id;
      this.http
        .put<City>(url, city)
        .subscribe(result => {

          console.log("City " + city.id + " has been updated.");

          // go back to cities view
          this.router.navigate(['/cities']);
        }, error => console.error(error));
    }
    else {
      // ADD NEW mode
      var url = this.baseUrl + "api/Cities";
      this.http
        .post<City>(url, city)
        .subscribe(result => {

          console.log("City " + result.id + " has been created.");

          // go back to cities view
          this.router.navigate(['/cities']);
        }, error => console.error(error));
    }
  }
}
```

Thanks to these modifications, our code will now be able to distinguish between the two different user actions (adding a new city or editing an existing one) and properly deal with both of them.

The HTML template file may also perform a minor update to notify the user of the new feature.

Open the `/ClientApp/src/app/cities/cities-edit.component.html` file and modify it in the following way (the new/updated lines are highlighted).

Add the following highlighted code near the beginning of the file:

```
<!-- ... existing code ... -->

<p *ngIf="this.id && !city"><em>Loading...</em></p>

<!-- ... existing code ... -->
```

With such an improvement, we'll ensure that the `"Loading..."` message won't appear when we're adding a new city since the `city` variable will be empty.

Also, add the following highlighted code toward the end of the file:

```
<!-- ... existing code ... -->
<div class="form-group commands">
    <button *ngIf="id" type="submit"
            (click)="onSubmit()"
            class="btn btn-success">
        Save
    </button>
    <button *ngIf="!id" type="submit"
            (click)="onSubmit()"
            class="btn btn-success">
        Create
    </button>
    <button type="submit"
            [routerLink]="['/cities']"
            class="btn">
        Cancel
    </button>
</div>

<!-- ... existing code ... -->
```

This minor yet useful addition will let us know if the form is working as expected: whenever we add a new city, we will see a more appropriate **Create** button instead of the **Save** one, which will still be visible in edit mode.

Now, we need to do two things:

1. Find a nice way to let our users know that they can add new cities as well as modify the existing ones.
2. Make them able to access this new feature.

A simple **Add a new City** button will fix both these issues at once: let's add it to our `CitiesComponent`.

Adding the "Add a new City" button

Open the `/ClientApp/src/app/cities/cities.component.html` file and add the following code:

```
<!-- ... existing code ... -->

<h1>Cities</h1>

<p>Here's a list of cities: feel free to play with it.</p>

<p *ngIf="!cities"><em>Loading...</em></p>

<div class="commands text-right" *ngIf="cities">
  <button type="submit"
          [routerLink]="['/city']"
          class="btn btn-success">
      Add a new City
  </button>
</div>

<!-- ... existing code ... -->
```

Here we go. There's nothing new here; we've added the usual *route*-based button within a container and a `*ngIf` *structural directive* to make it appear after the *Cities* array becomes available.

Adding a new route

Now, we need to define the new route that we referenced for the **Add a new City** button.

To do that, open the `/ClientApp/src/app/app-routing.module.ts` file and update the code, as follows:

```
// ...existing code...

RouterModule.forRoot([
  { path: '', component: HomeComponent, pathMatch: 'full' },
  { path: 'cities', component: CitiesComponent },
  { path: 'city/:id', component: CityEditComponent },
  { path: 'city', component: CityEditComponent },
  { path: 'countries', component: CountriesComponent },
]),

// ...existing code...
```

As we can see, the (new) route to add a new city and the (existing) route to edit an existing city are very similar since they both redirect the user to the same component; the only difference is that the latter doesn't have the `id` parameter, which is the technique we used to make our component aware of which task it has been called for. If the `id` is present, the user is editing an existing city; otherwise, they're adding a new one.

We are doing well... but we're not quite there yet. If we were to test what we've done so far by hitting *F5* and trying to add a new city, our `HttpClient` module would be greeted by an `HTTP 500 - Internal Server Error` from the server, similar to the one shown in the following screenshot:

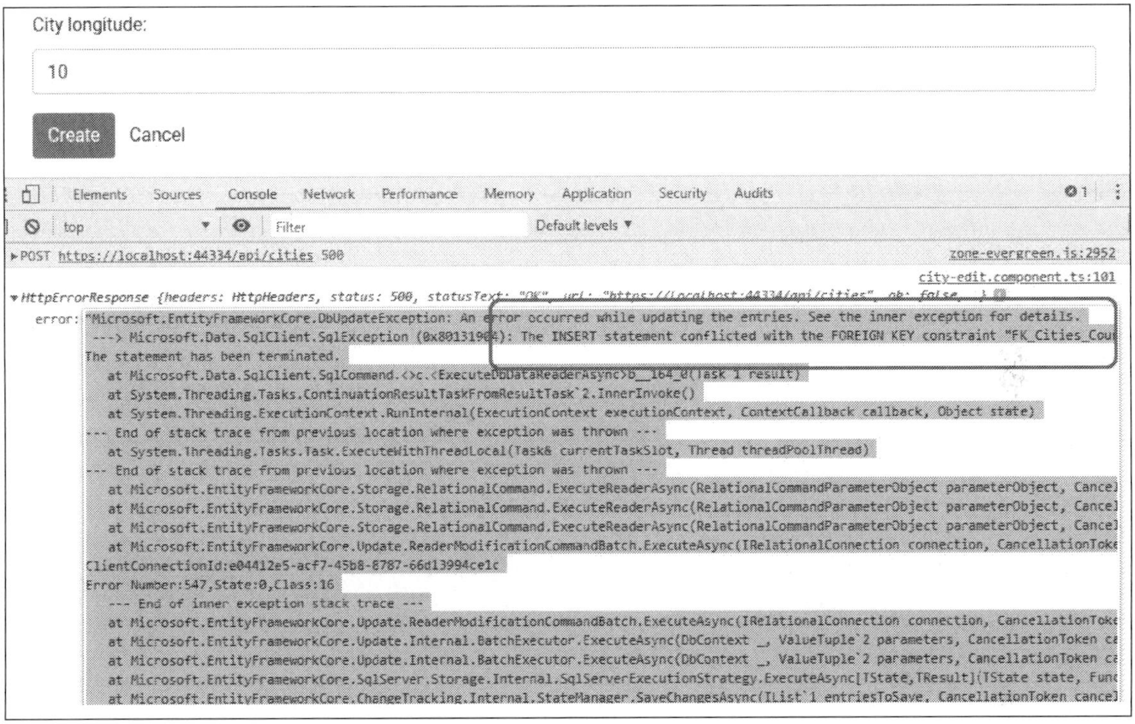

Figure 6.7: HTTP 500 error after trying to add a new city

Here's the full error text (with the relevant parts highlighted):

```
---> Microsoft.Data.SqlClient.SqlException (0x80131904): The INSERT statement
conflicted with the FOREIGN KEY constraint "FK_Cities_Countries_CountryId". The
conflict occurred in database "WorldCities", table "dbo.Countries", column 'Id'.
 The statement has been terminated.
```

It definitely seems like we forgot the `CountryId` property of the `City` entity: we did that on purpose when we had to define the Angular city interface because we didn't need it at that time. We didn't suffer from its absence when we implemented the city edit mode because that property was *silently* fetched from the server and then stored within our Angular local variable, which we were sending back to the server while the HTTP `PUT` request was performing the update. However, now that we do want to create a new city from scratch, such a missing property will eventually take its toll.

To fix this, we need to add the `countryId` property to the `/ClientApp/src/app/cities/city.ts` file in the following way (the new lines are highlighted):

```
export interface City {
    id: number;
    name: string;
    lat: number;
    lon: number;
    countryId: number;
}
```

However, this won't be enough: we also need to give our users the chance to assign a specific `Country` to the new city; otherwise, the `countryId` property will never see an actual value – unless we define it programmatically with a fixed value, which would be a rather ugly workaround (to say the least).

Let's fix this in a decent way by adding a list of countries to `CityEditComponent` so that the user will be able to select one before hitting the **Create** button. Such a new feature will be very useful – even when the component runs in edit mode – since it will allow our users to change the country for existing cities.

HTML select

The easiest way to allow our users to pick a country from a list of countries would be to use a `<select>` element and populate it by fetching our data from the .NET *back-end* via the CountriesController's `GetCountries()` method. Let's do that now.

Open the `/ClientApp/src/app/cities/city-edit.component.ts` file and add the following code (the new lines are highlighted):

```
import { Component, Inject, OnInit } from '@angular/core';
import { HttpClient, HttpParams } from '@angular/common/http';
import { ActivatedRoute, Router } from '@angular/router';
import { FormGroup, FormControl } from '@angular/forms';

import { City } from './City';
import { Country } from './../countries/Country';

@Component({
  selector: 'app-city-edit',
  templateUrl: './city-edit.component.html',
  styleUrls: ['./city-edit.component.css']
})
export class CityEditComponent implements OnInit {

  // the view title
  title: string;
```

```
// the form model
form: FormGroup;

// the city object to edit or create
city: City;

// the city object id, as fetched from the active route:
// It's NULL when we're adding a new city,
// and not NULL when we're editing an existing one.
id?: number;

// the countries array for the select
countries: Country[];

constructor(
  private activatedRoute: ActivatedRoute,
  private router: Router,
  private http: HttpClient,
  @Inject('BASE_URL') private baseUrl: string) {
}

ngOnInit() {
  this.form = new FormGroup({
    name: new FormControl(''),
    lat: new FormControl(''),
    lon: new FormControl(''),
    countryId: new FormControl('')
  });

  this.loadData();
}

loadData() {

  // load countries
  this.loadCountries();

  // retrieve the ID from the 'id'
  this.id = +this.activatedRoute.snapshot.paramMap.get('id');
  if (this.id) {
    // EDIT MODE

    // fetch the city from the server
    var url = this.baseUrl + "api/Cities/" + this.id;
    this.http.get<City>(url).subscribe(result => {
```

```
      this.city = result;
      this.title = "Edit - " + this.city.name;

      // update the form with the city value
      this.form.patchValue(this.city);
    }, error => console.error(error));
  }
  else {
    // ADD NEW MODE

    this.title = "Create a new City";
  }
}

loadCountries() {
  // fetch all the countries from the server
  var url = this.baseUrl + "api/Countries";
  var params = new HttpParams()
    .set("pageIndex", "0")
    .set("pageSize", "9999")
    .set("sortColumn", "name");

  this.http.get<any>(url, { params }).subscribe(result => {
    this.countries = result.data;
  }, error => console.error(error));
}

onSubmit() {

  var city = (this.id) ? this.city : <City>{};

  city.name = this.form.get("name").value;
  city.lat = +this.form.get("lat").value;
  city.lon = +this.form.get("lon").value;
  city.countryId = +this.form.get("countryId").value;

  if (this.id) {
    // EDIT mode

    var url = this.baseUrl + "api/Cities/" + this.city.id;
    this.http
      .put<City>(url, city)
      .subscribe(result => {

        console.log("City " + city.id + " has been updated.");
```

```
            // go back to cities view
            this.router.navigate(['/cities']);
          }, error => console.error(error));
      }
      else {
        // ADD NEW mode
        var url = this.baseUrl + "api/Cities";
        this.http
          .post<City>(url, city)
          .subscribe(result => {

            console.log("City " + result.id + " has been created.");

            // go back to cities view
            this.router.navigate(['/cities']);
          }, error => console.error(error));
      }
    }
}
```

What did we do here?

- We added the `HttpParams` module to the `import` list of `@angular/common/http`.
- We added a reference to our `Country` interface since we need to handle countries as well.
- We added a `countries` variable to store our countries.
- We added a `countryId` form control (with a required validator, since it's a required value) to our form.
- We added a `loadCountries()` method to fetch the countries from the server.
- We added a call to the `loadCountries()` method from the `loadData()` method so that we'll asynchronously fetch the countries while we do the rest of the `loadData()` stuff (such as loading the city and/or setting up the form).
- We updated the city's `countryId` so that it matches the one that's selected in the form in the `onSubmit()` method; this means that it will be sent to the server for the insert or update task.

> It's worth noting how, in the `loadCountries()` method, we had to set up some GET parameters for the `/api/Countries` URL to comply with the strict default values that we set in *Chapter 5, Fetching and Displaying Data*: we don't need paging here since we need to fetch the entire countries list to populate our select list. More specifically, we set a `pageSize` of `9999` to ensure that we get all our countries, as well as an appropriate `sortColumn` to have them ordered by their name.

Now, we can use our brand-new `countries` variable on our HTML template.

Open the `/ClientApp/src/app/cities/city-edit.component.html` file and add the following code (the new lines are highlighted):

```
<!-- ...existing code... -->

<div class="form-group">
    <label for="lon">City longitude:</label>
    <br />
    <input type="text" id="lon"
            formControlName="lon" required
            placeholder="Latitude..."
            class="form-control" />
</div>

<div class="form-group" *ngIf="countries">
    <label for="countryId">Country:</label>
    <br />
    <select id="countryId" class="form-control"
      formControlName="countryId">
      <option value="">--- Select a country ---</option>
      <option *ngFor="let country of countries" [value]="country.id">
        {{country.name}}
      </option>
    </select>
</div>

<!-- ...existing code... -->
```

If we press *F5* to test our code and navigate to the **Add a new City** or **Edit City** view, we'll see the following output:

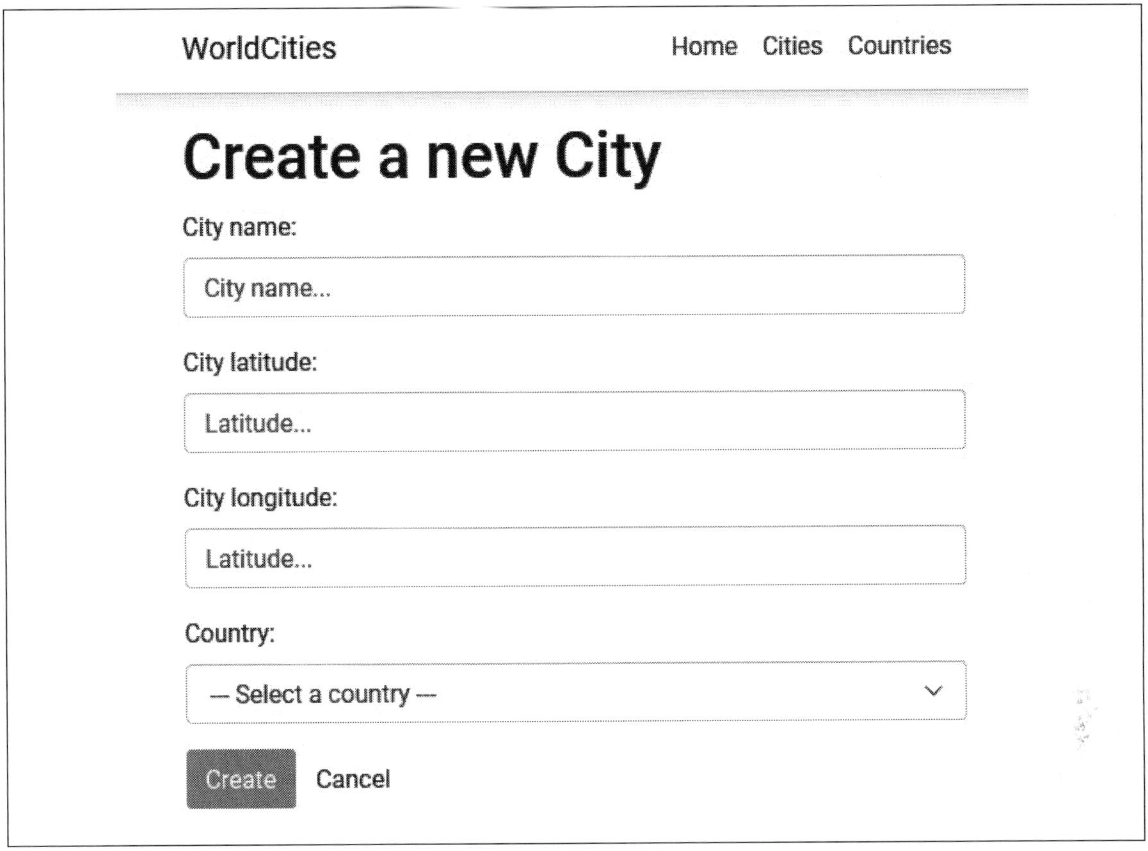

Figure 6.8: The CityEditComponent with a Country dropdown list

Now, by clicking the **--- Select a country ---** dropdown list, our users will be able to pick a country from the ones that are available. That's not bad, right?

However, we can do even better: we can improve the user experience of our view by replacing our standard HTML `select` with a more powerful component from the **Angular Material** package library: `MatSelectModule`.

Angular Material select (MatSelectModule)

Since we've never used `MatSelectModule` before, we need to add it to the `/ClientApp/src/app/angular-material.module.ts` file, just like we did for `MatPaginatorModule`, `MatSortModule`, and `MatInputModule` back in *Chapter 5, Fetching and Displaying Data.*

Here's how to do that (the new lines are highlighted):

```
import { NgModule } from '@angular/core';
import { MatTableModule } from '@angular/material/table';
import { MatPaginatorModule } from '@angular/material/paginator';
import { MatSortModule } from '@angular/material/sort';
import { MatInputModule } from '@angular/material/input';
import { MatSelectModule } from '@angular/material/select';

@NgModule({
  imports: [
    MatTableModule,
    MatPaginatorModule,
    MatSortModule,
    MatInputModule,
    MatSelectModule
  ],
  exports: [
    MatTableModule,
    MatPaginatorModule,
    MatSortModule,
    MatInputModule,
    MatSelectModule
  ]
})

export class AngularMaterialModule { }
```

Right after that, we can replace the `<select>` HTML element we added to the `/ClientApp/src/app/cities/city-edit.component.html` file a short while ago in the following way (the updated lines are highlighted):

```
<!-- ...existing code... -->

<div class="form-group">
    <label for="countryId">Country:</label>
    <br />
    <mat-form-field *ngIf="countries">
      <mat-label>Select a Country...</mat-label>
      <mat-select id="countryId" formControlName="countryId">
        <mat-option *ngFor="let country of countries"
```

```
            [value]="country.id">
            {{country.name}}
          </mat-option>
        </mat-select>
      </mat-form-field>
</div>

<!-- ...existing code... -->
```

And that's it! We can see the updated result by hitting *F5* (see the following screenshot for the output):

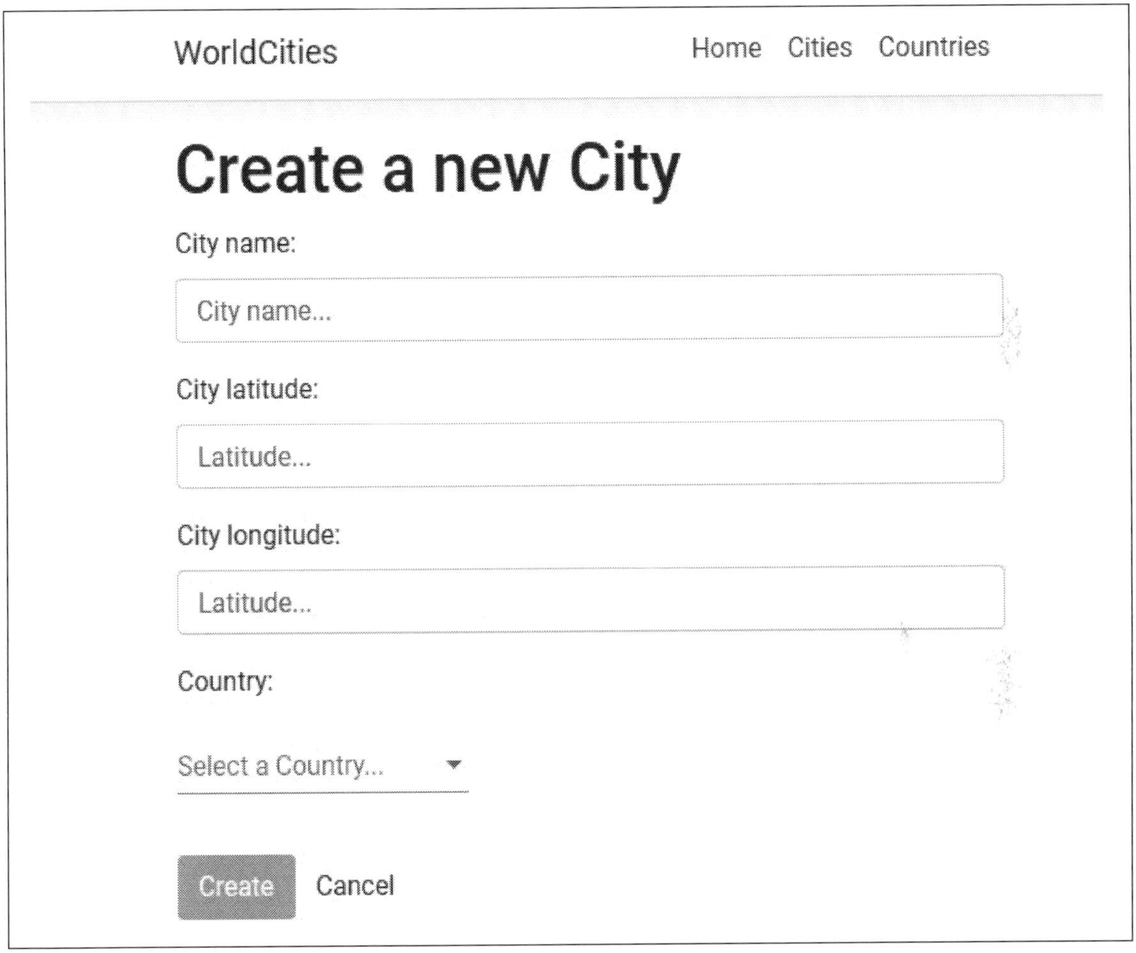

Figure 6.9: The CityEditComponent using MatSelectModule for the Country dropdown

The `MatSelectModule` is definitely prettier than the stock `<select>` HTML element, all while retaining the same features: we don't even need to change the underlying component class file since it uses the same binding interface.

Now, we can add our brand-new city to our database. Let's do this using the following data:

- **Name**: `New Tokyo`
- **Latitude**: `35.685`
- **Longitude**: `139.7514`
- **Country**: `Japan`

Fill in our `Create a new City` form with these values and click the **Create** button. If everything went well, we should be brought back to the **Cities** view, where we'll be able to find our `New Tokyo` city using the filter (see the following screenshot):

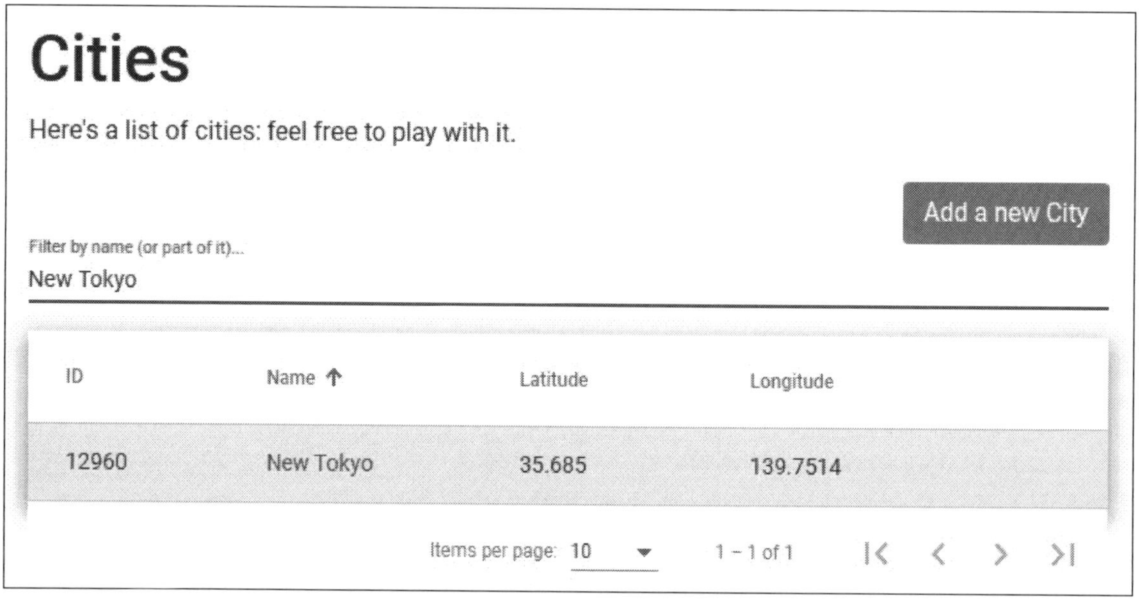

Figure 6.10: Cities list after filtering for New Tokyo

Here we go: we successfully added our first city!

Now that our Reactive Form is working properly and we have decent know-how about how it works, we're ready to spend some time tweaking it by adding something that could be very useful in a production scenario: some error-handling capabilities. We'll obtain these by adding some data validators.

Understanding data validation

Adding data validation to a form is hardly an option: it's a required feature to check the user input in terms of accuracy and completeness to improve the overall data quality by validating the data we want – or need – to collect. It's also very useful in terms of user experience because the error-handling capabilities it comes with will make our users able to understand why the form doesn't work and what they can do to fix the issues preventing them from submitting their data.

To understand such a concept, let's take our current `CityEditComponent` Reactive Form: it works fine if our users fill out all the required fields; however, there's no way for them to understand what the required values actually are, or what happens if they forget to fill all of them out... except for a console error message, which is what our source code currently does whenever our PUT and POST requests end up with a *back-end* error of any sort.

In this section, we'll learn how we can validate user input from the *front-end* UI and display useful validation messages using our current Reactive Form. While we're there, we'll also take the chance to create an `Edit Country/Add new Country` form and learn something new in the process.

Template-driven validation

For the sake of simplicity, we've chosen to not mess around with Template-Driven Forms and bring our focus to Model-Driven/Reactive Forms instead. However, it might be wise to spend a couple of minutes understanding how we can add validation to a Template-Driven Form as well.

The good news about this is that we can use the same standard validation attributes that we would normally use to validate a native HTML form: the Angular framework uses directives to match them with validator functions internally and in a fully transparent way. More specifically, every time the value of a form control changes, Angular will run these functions and generate either a list of validation errors, thus resulting in an invalid status, or null, meaning that the form is valid.

The form's state - as well as each form control's state - can be checked/inspected by exporting `ngModel` to a local template variable. Here's an example that can help clarify this:

```
<input id="name" name="name" class="form-control" required minlength="4"
    [(ngModel)]="city.name" #name="ngModel">

<div *ngIf="name.invalid && (name.dirty || name.touched)" class="alert alert-
danger">
    <div *ngIf="name.errors?.required">Name is required.</div>
    <div *ngIf="name.errors?.minlength">Name must be at least 4
      characters long.</div>
</div>
```

The *data validation directives* are highlighted in bold. As we can see, the preceding form will raise an error - and show a `<div>` element with an alert style to the user - whenever the city's `name` is not present or its character count is smaller than 4, since this is the minimum allowed length for the name input.

It's worth noting that we're checking two properties that might sound rather odd: `name.dirty` and `name.touched`. Here's a brief explanation of what they mean and why it's wise to check for their status:

- The `dirty` property starts as being `false` and becomes `true` whenever the user changes its starting values.
- The `touched` property starts as being `false` and becomes `true` whenever the user blurs the form control element, that is, clicks (or taps, or "tabs") away from it after having it in focus.

Now that we know how these properties work, we should be able to understand why we are checking them: we want our data validator error to only be seen if/when the user goes away from the control, leaving it with an invalid value - or no value at all.

> That's it for Template-Driven validation, at least for the purposes of this book. Those who need additional information should check out the following guide at: `https://angular.io/guide/forms#template-driven-forms`

The Safe Navigation Operator

Before moving on, it could be useful to spend a couple of minutes explaining the meaning of the ? question mark that we've been using whenever we need to check for the presence of form errors, such as in the following example, which has been taken from the preceding code:

```
name.errors?.required
```

This question mark is TypeScript's Safe Navigation Operator, also known as the **Elvis Operator**, and is very useful for protecting against null and undefined values in property paths. When the Safe Navigation Operator is present, TypeScript stops evaluating the expression when it hits the first `null` value. In the preceding code, if `name.errors` is `null`, the whole expression would return false without checking the `required` property, thus avoiding the following null-reference exception:

TypeError: Cannot read property 'required' of null.

As a matter of fact, the Safe Navigation Operator makes us able to navigate an object path - even when we are not aware of whether such a path exists or not - by returning either the value of the object path (if it exists) or null. Such behavior is perfect if we wish to check for the conditional presence of errors in Angular forms, where a `null` return value has the same meaning as *false* (that is, no errors). For this very reason, we're going to use it a lot from now on.

> It's worth noting that the *Safe Navigation Operator* has been part of the Angular HTML template language since Angular 2 and was only recently added to TypeScript. This much-needed addition occurred in November 2019, with the release of TypeScript v3.7:
>
> `https://www.typescriptlang.org/docs/handbook/release-notes/typescript-3-7.html`
>
> For more information about the *Safe Navigation Operator*, check out the following URL: `https://angular.io/guide/template-expression-operators#safe-navigation-operator`

Model-driven validation

When dealing with Reactive Forms, the whole validation approach is rather different. In a nutshell, we could say that most of this job has to be done within the component class: instead of adding validators using HTML attributes in the template, we'll have to add validator functions directly to the form control model in the component class so that Angular will be able to call them whenever the value of the control changes.

Since we'll mostly be dealing with functions, we'll also get the option to make them sync or async, thus getting the chance to add synchronous and/or asynchronous validators:

- **Sync validators** immediately return either a set of validation errors or `null`. They can be set up using the second argument when we instantiate the `FormControl` they need to check (the first one being the default value).
- **Async validators** return a *Promise* or *Observable* that's been configured to emit a set of validation errors or `null`. They can be set up using the third argument when we instantiate the `FormControl` they need to check.

> It's important to know that `async` validators will only be executed/checked after the `sync` validators, and only if all of them successfully pass. Such an architectural choice has been made for performance reasons.

In the upcoming sections, we'll create both of them and add them to our form.

Our first validators

Enough with the theory: let's add our first set of validators in our `CityEditComponent` form.

Open the `/ClientApp/src/app/cities/city-edit.component.ts` file and add the following code:

```
import { Component, Inject, OnInit } from '@angular/core';
import { HttpClient, HttpParams } from '@angular/common/http';
import { ActivatedRoute, Router } from '@angular/router';
import { FormGroup, FormControl, Validators } from '@angular/forms';

import { City } from './City';
import { Country } from './../countries/Country';

@Component({
  selector: 'app-city-edit',
  templateUrl: './city-edit.component.html',
  styleUrls: ['./city-edit.component.css']
})
export class CityEditComponent implements OnInit {

  // the view title
  title: string;

  // the form model
  form: FormGroup;

  // the city object to edit or create
  city: City;

  // the city object id, as fetched from the active route:
  // It's NULL when we're adding a new city,
  // and not NULL when we're editing an existing one.
  id?: number;

  // the countries array for the select
  countries: Country[];

  constructor(
    private activatedRoute: ActivatedRoute,
    private router: Router,
    private http: HttpClient,
    @Inject('BASE_URL') private baseUrl: string) {
  }

  ngOnInit() {
    this.form = new FormGroup({
      name: new FormControl('', Validators.required),
      lat: new FormControl('', Validators.required),
```

```
        lon: new FormControl('', Validators.required),
        countryId: new FormControl('', Validators.required)
      });

      this.loadData();
    }

  // ...existing code...
```

As we can see, we added the following:

- An `import` reference to the `Validators` class from the `@angular/forms` package.
- A `Validators.required` to each of our `FormControl` elements. As the name suggests, such a validator expects a non-null value for these fields; otherwise, it will return an `invalid` status.

> `Validators.required` is a built-in sync validator among those available from the `Validators` class. Other built-in validators provided by this class include `min`, `max`, `requiredTrue`, `email`, `minLength`, `maxLength`, `pattern`, `nullValidator`, `compose`, and `composeAsync`.
>
> For more information regarding Angular's built-in validators, take a look at the following URL: `https://angular.io/api/forms/Validators`

Once you're done, open the `/ClientApp/src/app/cities/city-edit.component.html` file and add the following code:

```
<div class="city-edit">
    <h1>{{title}}</h1>

    <p *ngIf="this.id && !city"><em>Loading...</em></p>

    <div class="form" [formGroup]="form" (ngSubmit)="onSubmit()">

        <div class="form-group">
            <label for="name">City name:</label>
            <br />
            <input type="text" id="name"
                formControlName="name" required
                placeholder="City name..."
                class="form-control"
                />

            <div *ngIf="form.get('name').invalid &&
                (form.get('name').dirty || form.get('name').touched)"
                class="invalid-feedback">
```

```
                <div *ngIf="form.get('name').errors?.required">
                  Name is required.
                </div>
            </div>
        </div>

        <div class="form-group">
            <label for="lat">City latitude:</label>
            <br />
            <input type="text" id="lat"
                   formControlName="lat" required
                   placeholder="Latitude..."
                   class="form-control" />

            <div *ngIf="form.get('lat').invalid &&
                 (form.get('lat').dirty || form.get('lat').touched)"
                 class="invalid-feedback">
                <div *ngIf="form.get('lat').errors?.required">
                  Latitude is required.
                </div>
            </div>
        </div>


        <div class="form-group">
            <label for="lon">City longitude:</label>
            <br />
            <input type="text" id="lon"
                   formControlName="lon" required
                   placeholder="Latitude..."
                   class="form-control" />

            <div *ngIf="form.get('lon').invalid &&
                 (form.get('lon').dirty || form.get('lon').touched)"
                 class="invalid-feedback">
                <div *ngIf="form.get('lon').errors?.required">
                  Longitude is required.
                </div>
            </div>
        </div>

        <div class="form-group">
            <label for="countryId">Country:</label>
            <br />
            <mat-form-field *ngIf="countries">
              <mat-label>Select a Country...</mat-label>
```

```
            <mat-select id="countryId" formControlName="countryId">
              <mat-option *ngFor="let country of countries"
                [value]="country.id">
                {{country.name}}
              </mat-option>
            </mat-select>
          </mat-form-field>

          <div *ngIf="form.get('countryId').invalid &&
                (form.get('countryId').dirty ||
                  form.get('countryId').touched)"
                class="invalid-feedback">
              <div *ngIf="form.get('countryId').errors?.required">
                Please select a Country.
              </div>
          </div>
        </div>

        <div class="form-group commands">
          <button *ngIf="id" type="submit"
                  (click)="onSubmit()"
                  [disabled]="form.invalid"
                  class="btn btn-success">
              Save
          </button>
          <button *ngIf="!id" type="submit"
                  (click)="onSubmit()"
                  [disabled]="form.invalid"
                  class="btn btn-success">
              Create
          </button>
          <button type="button"
                  [routerLink]="['/cities']"
                  class="btn">
              Cancel
          </button>
        </div>
    </div>
</div>
```

Here, we added four `<div>` elements (one for each input) to check the input value and conditionally return an error. As we can see, these validators are all working in the same way:

- The first `<div>` (the parent) checks if the `FormControl` is valid or not. It only appears if it's invalid and either dirty or touched, so that it won't be shown until the user has had the chance to set it.

- The second `<div>` (the child) checks for the required validator.

We used this approach because we could have multiple validators for each `FormControl`. Therefore, it can be useful to have a separate child element for each of them and a single *parent* element that encompasses them all (`invalid` is set to `true` whenever any of the configured validators doesn't pass).

While we were there, we added a `[disabled]` property bound to the `Create` and `Save` buttons to conditionally disable them whenever the form has an invalid state. This is a great way to prevent the user from submitting wrong or invalid values.

Right after that, open the `/ClientApp/src/app/cities/city-edit.component.css` file and add the following code:

```
input.ng-valid {
  border-left: 5px solid green;
}

input.ng-invalid.ng-dirty,
input.ng-invalid.ng-touched {
  border-left: 5px solid red;
}

input.ng-valid ~ .valid-feedback,
input.ng-invalid ~ .invalid-feedback {
  display: block;
}
```

These simple yet powerful styles leverage existing Angular and Bootstrap CSS classes so that they decorate our input fields whenever they have a valid or invalid status.

Let's quickly check everything we've done so far: hit *F5*, navigate to the **Cities** view, click on the **Add a new City** button, and play with the form while trying to trigger the validators.

Here's what happens when we cycle through the various input values without typing anything:

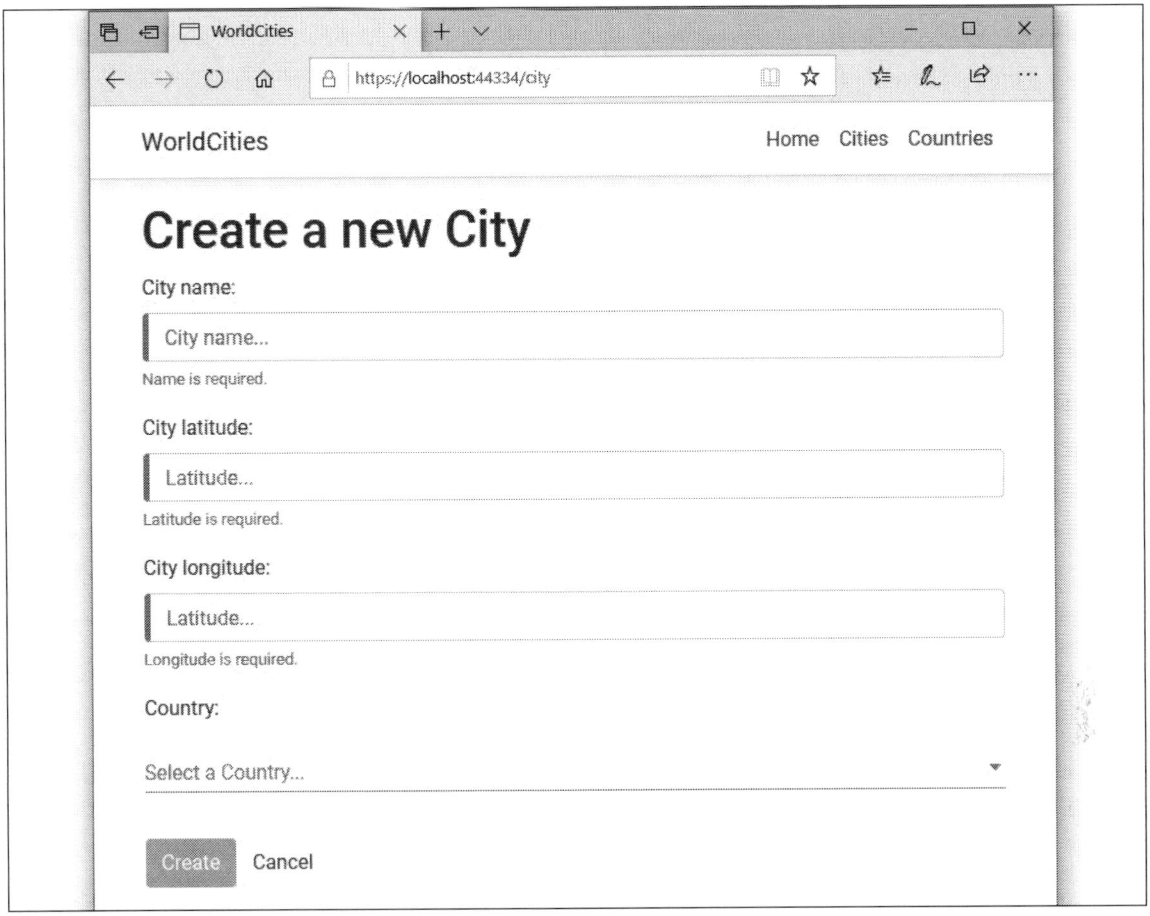

Figure 6.11: Testing the CityEditComponent form validators

Not bad, right? The input errors couldn't be more visible, and the **Create** button will stay disabled until they are all fixed, thus preventing accidental submits. All of these colored warnings should help our users understand what they're doing wrong and fix these issues.

Before ending our data validation journey, there's still one topic we need to cover: server-side validation, which can often be the only reasonable way to prevent some complex errors.

Server-side validation

Server-side validation is the process of checking for errors (and handling them accordingly) on the server side, that is, after the data has been sent to the *back-end*. This is a whole different approach to **client-side validation**, where the data is checked by the *front-end*, that is, before the data is sent to the server.

Handling errors on the *client side* has a lot of advantages in terms of speed and performance because the user immediately knows whether the input data is valid or not without having to query the server. However, *server-side* validation is a required feature of any decent web application because it prevents a lot of potentially harmful scenarios, such as the following:

- **Implementation errors** of the *client-side validation* process, which can fail to block badly-formatted data
- **Client-side hacks** performed by experienced users, browser extensions, or plugins that might want to allow the user to send unsupported input values to the *back-end*
- **Request forgery**, that is, false HTTP requests containing incorrect or malicious data

All of these techniques are based upon circumventing the *client-side validators*, which is always possible because we have no way to prevent our users (or hackers) from skipping, altering, or eliminating them; conversely, *server-side validators* cannot be avoided because they will be performed by the same *back-end* that will process the input data.

Therefore, in a nutshell, we could reasonably say that *client-side validation* is an optional and convenient feature, while *server-side validation* is a requirement for any decent web application that cares about the quality of the input data.

> To avoid confusion, it is important to understand that server-side validation, although being implemented on the back-end, also requires a front-end implementation, such as calling the back-end and then showing the validation results to the user. The main difference between client-side validation and server-side validation is that the former only exists on the client-side and never calls the back-end, while the latter relies upon a front-end and back-end coordinated effort, thus being more complex to implement and test.

Moreover, there are some scenarios where server-side validation is the only possible way to check for certain conditions or requirements that cannot be verified by *client-side* validation alone. To explain this concept, let's look at a quick example.

Launch our `WorldCities` app in *debug* mode by hitting *F5*, go to our **Cities** view, and type `paris` into the filter textbox.

You should see the following output:

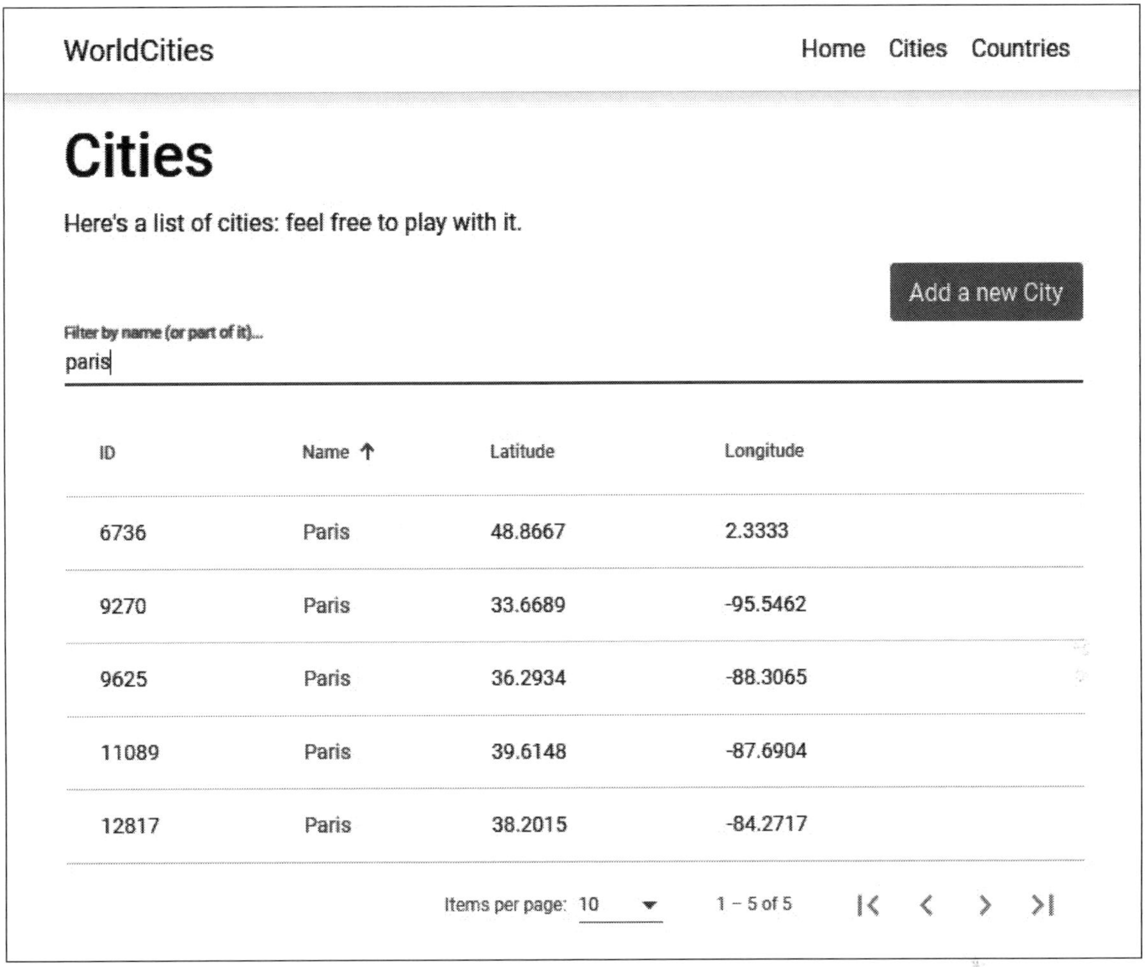

Figure 6.12: Cities list after filtering for "paris"

The preceding screenshot tells us the following things:

- There are at least *five* cities called `Paris` all over the world (!)
- Multiple cities can have the same identical name

That's not surprising: when we created our database using Entity Framework with *code-first*, we didn't make the `name` field *unique* since we knew that there was a high chance of *homonymous* cities. Luckily enough, this isn't an issue since we can still distinguish between them by looking at the `lat`, `lon`, and `country` values.

> For example, if we check the first three on *Google Maps*, we will see that the first one is in *France*, the second is in *Texas* (US), and the third is in *Tennessee* (US). Same name, different cities.

Now, what about adding a *validator* that could check if the city we are trying to add has the same `name`, `lat`, and `lon` values as a city already present in our database? Such a feature would block our users from inserting the same identical city multiple times, thus avoiding real duplicates, without blocking the *homonyms* that have different coordinates.

Unfortunately, there's no way to do that on the *client-side* only. To fulfill this task, we would need to create an Angular *custom validator* that could *asynchronously* check these values against the *server* and then return an *OK* (*valid*) or *KO* (*invalid*) result: in other words, a *server-side validation* task.

Let's try to do that now.

DupeCityValidator

In this section, we'll create a custom validator that will perform an asynchronous call to our .NET Core *back-end* to ensure that the city we're trying to add doesn't have the same `name`, `lat`, `lon`, and `country` as an existing one.

city-edit.component.ts

The first thing we have to do is create the validator itself and bind it to our Reactive Form. To do that, open the `/ClientApp/src/app/cities/city-edit.component.ts` file and change its contents accordingly (the new/updated lines are highlighted):

```
import { Component, Inject } from '@angular/core';
import { HttpClient, HttpParams } from '@angular/common/http';
import { ActivatedRoute, Router } from '@angular/router';
import { FormGroup, FormControl, Validators, AbstractControl, AsyncValidatorFn }
from '@angular/forms';
import { Observable } from 'rxjs';
import { map } from 'rxjs/operators';

import { City } from './City';
import { Country } from './../countries/Country';

// ...existing code...

  ngOnInit() {
    this.form = new FormGroup({
      name: new FormControl('', Validators.required),
      lat: new FormControl('', Validators.required),
      lon: new FormControl('', Validators.required),
```

```
      countryId: new FormControl('', Validators.required)
    }, null, this.isDupeCity());

    this.loadData();
  }

// ...existing code...

  isDupeCity(): AsyncValidatorFn {
    return (control: AbstractControl): Observable<{ [key: string]: any } | null>
=> {

      var city = <City>{};
      city.id = (this.id) ? this.id : 0;
      city.name = this.form.get("name").value;
      city.lat = +this.form.get("lat").value;
      city.lon = +this.form.get("lon").value;
      city.countryId = +this.form.get("countryId").value;

      var url = this.baseUrl + "api/Cities/IsDupeCity";
      return this.http.post<boolean>(url, city).pipe(map(result => {

        return (result ? { isDupeCity: true } : null);
      }));
    }
  }
}
```

As we can see, we've made some important changes in the preceding code:

- We added some `import` references (`AbstractControl`, `AsyncValidatorFn`, `Observable`, and `map`) that we used to implement our new async custom validator. If you don't get what we need them for, don't worry: we'll be talking about this topic later on.
- We created a new `isDupeCity()` method, which contains the whole implementation of our async custom validator.
- We configured the new validator to be used by the main `FormGroup` (the one related to the whole form).

As for our custom validator, it seems way more complex than it actually is. Let's try to summarize what it does:

- The first thing worth mentioning is that the function is defined as an `AsyncValidatorFn` that returns an `Observable`: this means that we're not returning a value but a *subscriber function instance* that will eventually return a value – which will be either a *key/value* object or `null`. Such a value will only be *emitted* when the *Observable* is executed.

- The *inner function* creates a temporary `city` object, fills it with the real-time form data, calls an `IsDupeCity` *back-end* URL that we don't know yet (but we will soon enough), and eventually returns either `true` or `null`, depending on the result. It's worth noting that we're not *subscribing* to the `HttpClient` this time, as we often did in the past: we're manipulating it using the `pipe` and `map` *ReactJS* (*RxJS*) operators, which we'll be talking about in a short while.

> For more information regarding custom async validators, read the following guide: `https://angular.io/guide/form-validation#implementing-a-custom-async-validator`

Since our custom validator relies on an HTTP request being sent to our .NET Core *back-end*, we need to implement that method as well.

CitiesController

Open the `/Controllers/CitiesController.cs` file and add the following method at the bottom of the file:

```
// ...existing code...

private bool CityExists(int id)
{
    return _context.Cities.Any(e => e.Id == id);
}

[HttpPost]
[Route("IsDupeCity")]
public bool IsDupeCity(City city)
{
    return _context.Cities.Any(
        e => e.Name == city.Name
        && e.Lat == city.Lat
        && e.Lon == city.Lon
        && e.CountryId == city.CountryId
        && e.Id != city.Id
    );
}

// ...existing code...
```

The .NET method is very straightforward: it checks the data model for a `City` that has the same `Name`, `Lat`, `Lon`, and `CountryId` as the one provided by the *front-end* (as well as a different **Id**) and returns `true` or `false` as the result. The `Id` check has been added to conditionally disable the *dupe check* when the user is editing an existing city.

If that's the case, using the *same* `Name`, `Lat`, `Lon`, and `CountryId` would be allowed since we're basically overwriting the same city and not creating a new one. When the user adds a new city, that `Id` value will always be set to *zero*, preventing the *dupe check* from being disabled.

city-edit.component.html

Now that the *back-end* code is ready, we need to create a suitable error message from the UI. Open the `/ClientApp/src/app/cities/city-edit.component.html` file and update its content in the following way (the new lines are highlighted):

```
<div class="city-edit">
    <h1>{{title}}</h1>

    <p *ngIf="this.id && !city"><em>Loading...</em></p>

    <div class="form" [formGroup]="form" (ngSubmit)="onSubmit()">

        <div *ngIf="form.invalid && form.errors &&
            form.errors?.isDupeCity"
            class="alert alert-danger">
              <strong>ERROR</strong>:
              A city with the same <i>name</i>, <i>lat</i>,
              <i>lon</i> and <i>country</i> already exists.
        </div>

<!-- ...existing code... -->
```

As shown in the preceding code, the alert `<div>` we added will only be shown if all of the following three conditions are met:

- The form is invalid
- There are errors that are strictly related to the form itself
- The `isDupeCity` error is returning `true`

It's very important to check all of them, otherwise we risk showing such an alert even when it doesn't have to be shown.

Testing it out

Now that the component HTML template has been set up, we can test the result of our hard work. Press *F5*, navigate to the **Cities** view, click the **Add a new City** button, and insert the following values:

- **Name**: `New Tokyo`
- **Latitude**: `35.685`
- **Longitude**: `139.7514`
- **Country**: `Japan`

If you did everything properly, you should be greeted by the following error message:

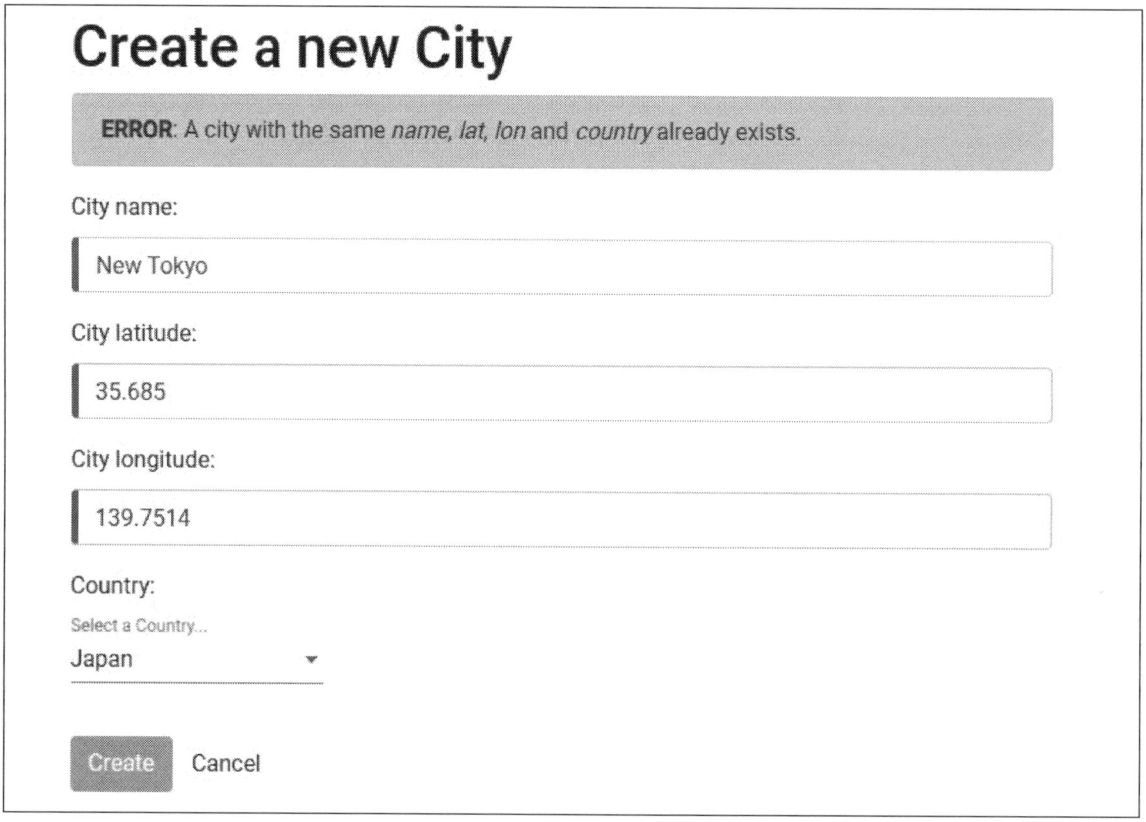

Figure 6.13: Testing the duplicate city validator

That's great! Our custom *async* validator is working fine and triggers both the *front-end* and the *back-end* validation logic.

Observables and RxJS operators

The *async* logic that's used to perform the call makes extensive use of the *Observable/RxJS* pattern: this time, though, instead of relying on the `subscribe()` method we've already used a number of times, we opted for a `pipe` + `map` approach. These are two very important *RxJS* operators that allow us to perform our data manipulation tasks while retaining the *Observable* status of the returned value, while subscriptions will *execute* the *Observable* and return actual data instead.

This concept might be quite difficult to understand. Let's try to put it in other words:

- We should use the `subscribe()` method when we want to execute the *Observable* and get its actual result; for example, a JSON structured response. Such a method returns a *Subscription* that can be canceled but **can't be subscribed to** anymore.

- We should use the `map()` operator when we want to transform/manipulate the data events of the *Observable* without executing it so that it can be passed to other *async* actors that will also manipulate (and eventually execute) it. Such a method returns an *Observable* that **can be subscribed to**.

As for the `pipe()`, it's just an *RxJS* operator that composes/chains other operators (such as `map`, `filter`, and so on).

The most important difference between *Observable* methods and *RxJS* operators is that the latter always return *Observables*, while the former return a different (and mostly final) object type. Does this ring a bell?

If we think about what we learned back in *Chapter 5, Fetching and Displaying Data*, when dealing with .NET *Entity Framework*, it should definitely sound familiar. Remember when we were playing around with the `IQueryable<T>` interface? The various `Where`, `OrderBy`, and `CountAsync` IQueryable methods that we used when we built our `ApiResult` class are quite similar to what we can do in Angular by chaining multiple `map` functions with the `pipe` operator. Conversely, the `subscribe()` method strictly resembles the various `ToListAsync()`/`ToArrayAsync()` methods that we used in .NET to execute the `IQueryable` and retrieve its result in a usable object.

Performance issues

Before moving on, let's try to answer the following question: *when will this validator be checked?* In other words, can we reasonably expect performance issues, considering the fact it performs a *server-side* API call upon each check?

If we recall what we said earlier, the *asynchronous* validators will only be checked when all the *synchronous* validators return `true`. Since `isDupeCity` is *async*, it won't be called until all the `Validators.required` that we previously set up in all the `FormControl` elements return `true`. That's a piece of great news indeed, since there would be no sense in checking for an existing city with `name`, `lat`, `lon`, and/or `countryId` being null or empty.

Based on what we have just said, we can reasonably expect the `isDupeCity` validator to be called once or twice for each form submission, which is perfectly fine in terms of performance impact. Everything is fine, then. Let's move on.

Introducing the FormBuilder

Now that our `CityEditComponent` has been set up, we might be tempted to reuse the same techniques to create a `CountryEditComponent` and get the job done, just like we did in *Chapter 5, Fetching and Displaying Data*, with our `CitiesComponent` and `CountryComponent` files. However, we won't be doing this. Instead, we'll take the chance to introduce a new tool to our shed that can be very useful when dealing with multiple forms: the `FormBuilder` service.

In the following chapters, we'll do the following:

- Create our `CountryEditComponent` with all the required TypeScript, HTML, and CSS files.
- Learn how to use the `FormBuilder` service to generate form controls in a better way.
- Add a new set of `Validators` (including a brand-new `isDupeCountry` custom validator) to the new form implementation.
- Test our new `FormBuilder`-based implementation to check that everything works.

By the end of this section, we'll have a fully-functional `CountryEditComponent` that will work in the same way that `CityEditComponent` does, except it will be based on a slightly different approach.

Creating the CountryEditComponent

Let's start by laying down the files we need. From the Solution Explorer of our `WorldCities` project, do the following:

1. Navigate to the `/ClientApp/src/app/countries` folder.
2. Right-click the folder's name and select **Add | New Item** three times to create the following files:
    - `country-edit.component.ts`
    - `country-edit.component.html`
    - `country-edit.component.css`

Once you're done, fill them with the following content.

country-edit.component.ts

Open the `/ClientApp/src/app/countries/country-edit.component.ts` file and fill it with the following code. Watch out for the highlighted parts, which are rather different from the previous `CityEditComponent`; other minor differences, such as `country` instead of `city`, are not highlighted, since they're more than expected:

```
import { Component, Inject, OnInit } from '@angular/core';
import { HttpClient, HttpParams } from '@angular/common/http';
import { ActivatedRoute, Router } from '@angular/router';
import { FormGroup, FormBuilder, Validators, AbstractControl, AsyncValidatorFn }
from '@angular/forms';
import { map } from 'rxjs/operators';
import { Observable } from 'rxjs';

import { Country } from './../countries/Country';

@Component({
```

```
    selector: 'app-country-edit',
    templateUrl: './country-edit.component.html',
    styleUrls: ['./country-edit.component.css']
})
export class CountryEditComponent implements OnInit {

  // the view title
  title: string;

  // the form model
  form: FormGroup;

  // the city object to edit or create
  country: Country;

  // the city object id, as fetched from the active route:
  // It's NULL when we're adding a new country,
  // and not NULL when we're editing an existing one.
  id?: number;

  constructor(
    private fb: FormBuilder,
    private activatedRoute: ActivatedRoute,
    private router: Router,
    private http: HttpClient,
    @Inject('BASE_URL') private baseUrl: string) {
      this.loadData();
  }

  ngOnInit() {
    this.form = this.fb.group({
      name: ['',
        Validators.required,
        this.isDupeField("name")
      ],
      iso2: ['',
        [
          Validators.required,
          Validators.pattern(/^[a-zA-Z]{2}$/)
        ],
        this.isDupeField("iso2")
      ],
      iso3: ['',
        [
          Validators.required,
          Validators.pattern(/^[a-zA-Z]{3}$/)
```

```
          ],
          this.isDupeField("iso3")
        ]
      });

      this.loadData();
    }

    loadData() {

      // retrieve the ID from the 'id'
      this.id = +this.activatedRoute.snapshot.paramMap.get('id');
      if (this.id) {
        // EDIT MODE

        // fetch the country from the server
        var url = this.baseUrl + "api/Countries/" + this.id;
        this.http.get<Country>(url).subscribe(result => {
            this.country = result;
            this.title = "Edit - " + this.country.name;

            // update the form with the country value
            this.form.patchValue(this.country);
        }, error => console.error(error));
      }
      else {
        // ADD NEW MODE

        this.title = "Create a new Country";
      }
    }

    onSubmit() {

      var country = (this.id) ? this.country : <Country>{};

      country.name = this.form.get("name").value;
      country.iso2 = this.form.get("iso2").value;
      country.iso3 = this.form.get("iso3").value;

      if (this.id) {
        // EDIT mode

        var url = this.baseUrl + "api/Countries/" + this.country.id;
        this.http
          .put<Country>(url, country)
```

```
        .subscribe(result => {

          console.log("Country " + country.id + " has been updated.");

          // go back to cities view
          this.router.navigate(['/countries']);
        }, error => console.error(error));
    }
    else {
      // ADD NEW mode
      var url = this.baseUrl + "api/Countries";
      this.http
        .post<Country>(url, country)
        .subscribe(result => {

          console.log("Country " + result.id + " has been created.");

          // go back to cities view
          this.router.navigate(['/countries']);
        }, error => console.error(error));
    }
  }

  isDupeField(fieldName: string): AsyncValidatorFn {
    return (control: AbstractControl): Observable<{ [key: string]: any
      } | null> => {

      var params = new HttpParams()
        .set("countryId", (this.id) ? this.id.toString() : "0")
        .set("fieldName", fieldName)
        .set("fieldValue", control.value);
      var url = this.baseUrl + "api/Countries/IsDupeField";
      return this.http.post<boolean>(url, null, { params })
        .pipe(map(result => {
          return (result ? { isDupeField: true } : null);
      }));
    }
  }
}
```

As we can see, the component's source code is quite similar to `CityEditComponent`, except for some limited yet important differences that we're going to summarize here:

- The `FormBuilder` service has been added to the `@angular/forms` import list, replacing the `FormControl` reference that we don't need anymore. As a matter of fact, we're still creating form controls, but we'll do that via the `FormBuilder` instead of manually instantiating them, which means we don't need to *explicitly reference* them.

- The `form` variable is now instantiated using a different approach that strongly relies upon the new `FormBuilder` service.
- The various `FormControl` elements that get instantiated within the `form` feature are some *validators* that we have never seen before.

The `FormBuilder` service gives us three *factory methods* so that we can create our form structure: `control()`, `group()`, and `array()`. Each generates an instance of the corresponding `FormControl`, `FormGroup`, and `FormArray` class. In our example, we're creating a single containing group with three controls, each with its own set of *validators*.

As for the *validators*, we can see two new entries:

- `Validators.pattern`: A built-in *validator* that requires the control's *value* to match a given regular expression (*regex*) pattern. Since our `ISO2` and `ISO3` country fields are defined using a strict format, we're going to use them to ensure that the user will input correct values.
- `isDupeField`: This is a custom async validator that we implemented here for the first time. It's similar to the `isDupeCity` validator we created for our `CityEditComponent` but with some key differences that we're going to summarize in the next section.

> Those who don't know much about regular expressions (or regex for short) and want to use the `Validators.pattern` to its full extent should definitely visit the following website, which contains a good number of resources regarding regex and a great online builder and tester with full JavaScript and PHP/PCRE regex support: `https://regexr.com/`

The isDupeField validator

As we can see by looking at the preceding component's source code, the `isDupeField` custom validator is not assigned to the main `FormGroup` like `isDupeCity` is; instead, it's set three times: one for each `FormControl` it needs to check. The reason for this is simple: compared to `isDupeCity`, which was meant to check for duplicate cities using a four-field dupe key, `isDupeField` needs to **individually check** each field it's assigned to. We need to do that because we don't want more than one country having the same `name`, **or** the same `iso2`, **or** the same `iso3`.

This also explains why we need to specify a `fieldname` and a corresponding `fieldValue` instead of passing a `Country` interface: the `isDupeField` *server-side* API will have to perform a different check for each `fieldName` we're going to pass, instead of relying on a single general-purpose check like the `isDupeCity` API does.

As for the `countryId` parameter, it's required to prevent the *dupe-check* from raising a validation error when editing an existing *country*. In the `isDupeCity` validator, it was passed as a property of the `city` class. Now, we need to explicitly add it to the `POST` parameters.

The IsDupeField server-side API

Now, we need to implement our custom validator's *back-end* API.

Open the `/Controllers/CountriesController.cs` file and add the following method at the bottom of the file:

```
// ...existing code...

private bool CountryExists(int id)
{
    return _context.Countries.Any(e => e.Id == id);
}

[HttpPost]
[Route("IsDupeField")]
public bool IsDupeField(
    int countryId,
    string fieldName,
    string fieldValue)
{
    switch (fieldName)
    {
        case "name":
            return _context.Countries.Any(
                c => c.Name == fieldValue && c.Id != countryId);
        case "iso2":
            return _context.Countries.Any(
                c => c.ISO2 == fieldValue && c.Id != countryId);
        case "iso3":
            return _context.Countries.Any(
                c => c.ISO3 == fieldValue && c.Id != countryId);
        default:
            return false;
    }
}
```

Although the code resembles the `IsDupeCity` *server-side* API, we're switching the `fieldName` parameter and performing a different *dupe-check* depending on its value; such logic is implemented with a standard `switch/case` conditional block with *strongly-typed* LINQ lambda expressions for each field we can reasonably expect. Again, we're also checking that the `countryId` is different so that our users can *edit* an existing country.

If the `fieldName` that's received from the client differs from the three supported values, our API will respond with `false`.

An alternative approach using Linq.Dynamic

Before moving on, we may want to ask ourselves why we've implemented the `IsDupeField` API using *strongly-typed* LAMBDA expressions inside a `switch...case` block, instead of relying on the `System.Linq.Dynamic.Core` library.

As a matter of fact, we did that for the sake of simplicity, since the *dynamic* approach would require us having to write additional code to protect our method from *SQL injection* attacks. However, since we already implemented such a task in the `IsValidProperty()` method of our `ApiResult` class, maybe we can use it and shrink the preceding code down: after all, we've made it *public* and *static* so that we can use it anywhere.

Here's an alternative implementation using the aforementioned tools (the old code is commented, while the new code is highlighted):

```
using System.Linq.Dynamic.Core;

// ...existing code...

[HttpPost]
[Route("IsDupeField")]
public bool IsDupeField(
    int countryId,
    string fieldName,
    string fieldValue)
{
    // Default approach (using strongly-typed LAMBA expressions)
    //switch (fieldName)
    //{
    // case "name":
    // return _context.Countries.Any(c => c.Name == fieldValue);
    // case "iso2":
    // return _context.Countries.Any(c => c.ISO2 == fieldValue);
    // case "iso3":
    // return _context.Countries.Any(c => c.ISO3 == fieldValue);
    // default:
    // return false;
    //}

    // Alternative approach (using System.Linq.Dynamic.Core)
    return (ApiResult<Country>.IsValidProperty(fieldName, true))
        ? _context.Countries.Any(
            string.Format("{0} == @0 && Id != @1", fieldName),
            fieldValue,
            countryId)
        : false;
}
```

Not bad, right?

The *alternative dynamic* approach definitely looks more DRY and versatile than the *default* one, all while retaining the same security level against *SQL injection* attacks. The only downside may be due to the additional overhead brought by the `System.Linq.Dynamics.Core` library, which will likely have some minor performance impact. Although this shouldn't be an issue in most scenarios, whenever we want our APIs to respond to HTTP requests as quickly as possible, we should arguably favor the default approach.

country-edit.component.html

It's time to implement the template of our `CountryEditComponent`.

Open the `/ClientApp/src/app/countries/country-edit.component.html` file and fill it with the following code. Once again, pay attention to the highlighted parts, which are rather different from the template of `CityEditComponent`; other minor differences, such as `country` instead of `city`, are not highlighted since they're more than expected:

```
<div class="country-edit">
    <h1>{{title}}</h1>

    <p *ngIf="this.id && !country"><em>Loading...</em></p>

    <div class="form" [formGroup]="form" (ngSubmit)="onSubmit()">

        <div class="form-group">
            <label for="name">Country name:</label>
            <br />
            <input type="text" id="name"
                formControlName="name" required
                placeholder="Country name..."
                class="form-control"
                />

            <div *ngIf="form.get('name').invalid &&
                 (form.get('name').dirty || form.get('name').touched)"
                 class="invalid-feedback">
                <div *ngIf="form.get('name').errors?.required">
                  Name is required.
                </div>
                <div *ngIf="form.get('name').errors?.isDupeField">
                  Name already exists: please choose another.
                </div>
            </div>
        </div>

        <div class="form-group">
```

```
      <label for="iso2">ISO 3166-1 ALPHA-2 Country Code (2
        letters)</label>
      <br />
      <input type="text" id="iso2"
            formControlName="iso2" required
            placeholder="2 letters country code..."
            class="form-control" />

      <div *ngIf="form.get('iso2').invalid &&
           (form.get('iso2').dirty || form.get('iso2').touched)"
           class="invalid-feedback">
          <div *ngIf="form.get('iso2').errors?.required">
            ISO 3166-1 ALPHA-2 country code is required.
          </div>
          <div *ngIf="form.get('iso2').errors?.pattern">
            ISO 3166-1 ALPHA-2 country code requires 2 letters.
          </div>
          <div *ngIf="form.get('iso2').errors?.isDupeField">
            This ISO 3166-1 ALPHA-2 country code already exists:
             please choose another.
          </div>
      </div>
  </div>

        <div class="form-group">
      <label for="iso3">ISO 3166-1 ALPHA-3 Country Code (3
        letters)</label>
      <br />
      <input type="text" id="iso3"
            formControlName="iso3" required
            placeholder="3 letters country code..."
            class="form-control" />

      <div *ngIf="form.get('iso3').invalid &&
           (form.get('iso3').dirty || form.get('iso3').touched)"
           class="invalid-feedback">
          <div *ngIf="form.get('iso3').errors?.required">
            ISO 3166-1 ALPHA-3 country code is required.
          </div>
          <div *ngIf="form.get('iso3').errors?.pattern">
            ISO 3166-1 ALPHA-3 country code requires 3 letters.
          </div>
          <div *ngIf="form.get('iso3').errors?.isDupeField">
            This ISO 3166-1 ALPHA-3 country code already exists:
             please choose another.
          </div>
```

```
            </div>
        </div>

        <div class="form-group commands">
            <button *ngIf="id" type="submit"
                    (click)="onSubmit()"
                    [disabled]="form.invalid"
                    class="btn btn-success">
                Save
            </button>
            <button *ngIf="!id" type="submit"
                    (click)="onSubmit()"
                    [disabled]="form.invalid"
                    class="btn btn-success">
                Create
            </button>
            <button type="button"
                    [routerLink]="['/countries']"
                    class="btn">
                Cancel
            </button>
        </div>
    </div>
</div>
```

As we can see, the most relevant differences are all related to the HTML code that's required to show the new *pattern* and `isDupeField` validators. Now, we have as many as *three* different validators for our fields, which is pretty awesome: our users won't be given a chance to input wrong values!

country-edit.component.css

Last but not least, let's apply the UI styling.

Open the `/ClientApp/src/app/countries/country-edit.component.css` file and fill it with the following code:

```
input.ng-valid {
  border-left: 5px solid green;
}

input.ng-invalid.ng-dirty,
input.ng-invalid.ng-touched {
  border-left: 5px solid red;
}
input.ng-valid ~ .valid-feedback,
input.ng-invalid ~ .invalid-feedback {
```

```
    display: block;
  }
```

No surprises here; the preceding stylesheet code is identical to the one we used for `CityEditComponent`.

Our component is finally done! Now, we need to reference it in the `AppModule` file and implement the *navigation routes* in the `CountriesComponent`.

AppModule

Open the `/ClientApp/src/app/app.module.ts` file and add the following code (the new lines are highlighted):

```
import { BrowserModule } from '@angular/platform-browser';
import { NgModule } from '@angular/core';
import { FormsModule } from '@angular/forms';
import { HttpClientModule, HTTP_INTERCEPTORS } from '@angular/common/http';

import { AppRoutingModule } from './app-routing.module';

import { AppComponent } from './app.component';
import { NavMenuComponent } from './nav-menu/nav-menu.component';
import { HomeComponent } from './home/home.component';
import { CitiesComponent } from './cities/cities.component';
import { CityEditComponent } from './cities/city-edit.component';
import { CountriesComponent } from './countries/countries.component';
import { CountryEditComponent } from './countries/country-edit.component';
import { BrowserAnimationsModule } from '@angular/platform-browser/animations';
import { AngularMaterialModule } from './angular-material.module';
import { ReactiveFormsModule } from '@angular/forms';

@NgModule({
  declarations: [
    AppComponent,
    NavMenuComponent,
    HomeComponent,
    CitiesComponent,
    CityEditComponent,
    CountriesComponent,
    CountryEditComponent
  ],
  imports: [
    BrowserModule.withServerTransition({ appId: 'ng-cli-universal' }),
    HttpClientModule,
    FormsModule,
    AppRoutingModule,
```

```
    BrowserAnimationsModule,
    AngularMaterialModule,
    ReactiveFormsModule
  ],
  providers: [],
  bootstrap: [AppComponent]
})
export class AppModule { }
```

Once done, we can add the required routes for `CountryEditComponent`.

AppRoutingModule

By now, we should know what to do. Open the `app-routing.module.ts` file and add the following routing rules (new lines are highlighted):

```
import { NgModule } from '@angular/core';
import { Routes, RouterModule } from '@angular/router';
import { HomeComponent } from './home/home.component';
import { CitiesComponent } from './cities/cities.component';
import { CityEditComponent } from './cities/city-edit.component';
import { CountriesComponent } from './countries/countries.component';
import { CountryEditComponent } from './countries/country-edit.component';

const routes: Routes = [
  { path: '', component: HomeComponent, pathMatch: 'full' },
  { path: 'cities', component: CitiesComponent },
  { path: 'city/:id', component: CityEditComponent },
  { path: 'city', component: CityEditComponent },
  { path: 'countries', component: CountriesComponent },
  { path: 'country/:id', component: CountryEditComponent },
  { path: 'country', component: CountryEditComponent }
];

@NgModule({
  imports: [RouterModule.forRoot(routes)],
  exports: [RouterModule]
})
export class AppRoutingModule { }
```

Now that we've laid down the two routes so that we can `edit` and `add` countries, we just need to implement them in the `CountriesComponent` template file.

countries.component.html

Open the /ClientApp/src/app/countries/countries.component.html file and add the following code (the new lines are highlighted):

```
<h1>Countries</h1>

<p>Here's a list of countries: feel free to play with it.</p>

<p *ngIf="!countries"><em>Loading...</em></p>

<div class="commands text-right" *ngIf="countries">
  <button type="submit"
          [routerLink]="['/country']"
          class="btn btn-success">
      Add a new Country
  </button>
</div>

<mat-form-field [hidden]="!countries">
  <input matInput (keyup)="loadData($event.target.value)"
      placeholder="Filter by name (or part of it)...">
</mat-form-field>

<table mat-table [dataSource]="countries"
  class="table-striped mat-elevation-z8"
  [hidden]="!countries"
  matSort (matSortChange)="loadData()"
  matSortActive="{{defaultSortColumn}}"
  matSortDirection="{{defaultSortOrder}}">

  <!-- Id Column -->
  <ng-container matColumnDef="id">
    <th mat-header-cell *matHeaderCellDef mat-sort-header>ID</th>
    <td mat-cell *matCellDef="let country"> {{country.id}} </td>
  </ng-container>

  <!-- Name Column -->
  <ng-container matColumnDef="name">
    <th mat-header-cell *matHeaderCellDef mat-sort-header>Name</th>
    <td mat-cell *matCellDef="let country">
      <a [routerLink]="['/country', country.id]">{{country.name}}</a>
    </td>
  </ng-container>

<!-- ...existing code... -->
```

... And that's it! Now, we're ready to test everything out.

Testing the CountryEditComponent

Now, it's time to press *F5* and admire the result of our hard work.

Once the app has been launched in *debug* mode, navigate to the **Countries** view to see the **Add a new Country** button and the edit links on the various country names, as shown in the following screenshot:

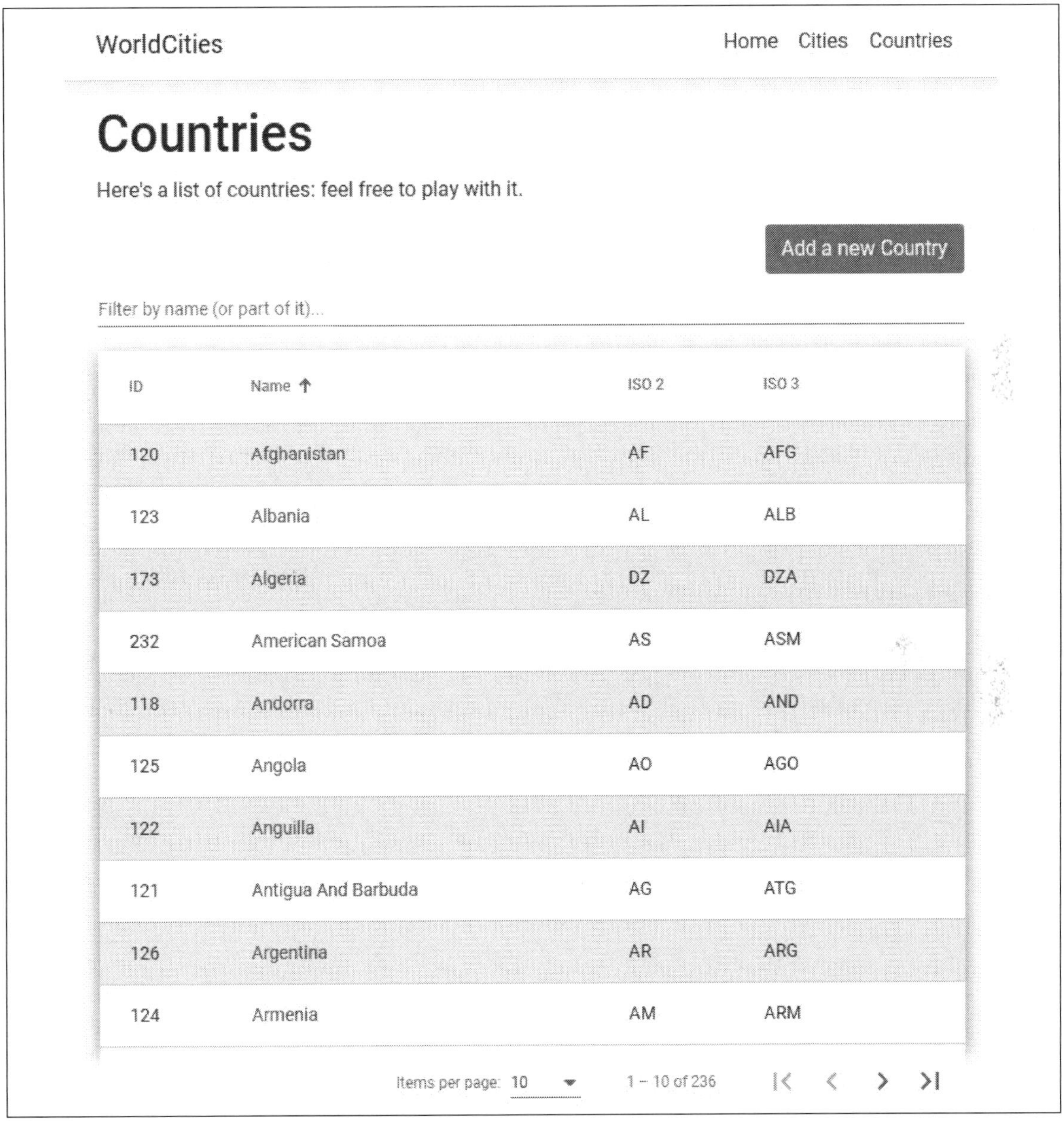

Figure 6.14: Countries list with the Add a new Country button and edit links

Now, let's search for `Denmark` using our filter and click on the name to enter the `CountryEditComponent` in *edit mode*. If everything works fine, the `name`, `iso2`, and `iso3` fields should all be green, meaning that our `isDupeField` custom validator(s) are not raising errors:

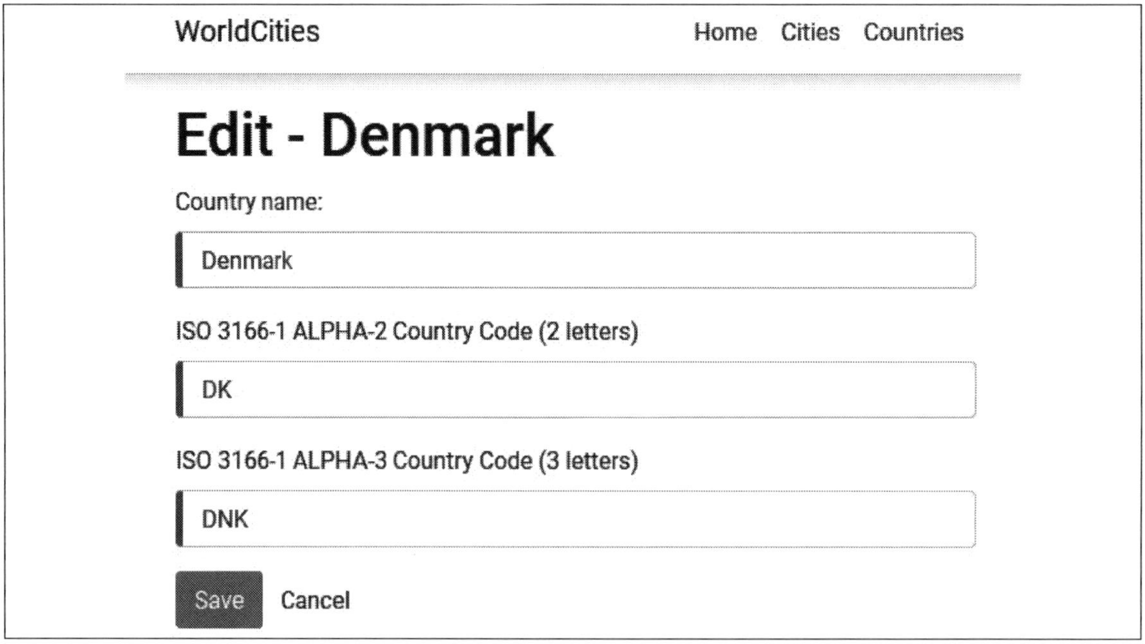

Figure 6.15: CountryEditComponent for Denmark

Now, let's try to change the **Country name** to `Japan` and the **ISO 3166-1 ALPHA-2 Country Code** to `IT` and see what happens:

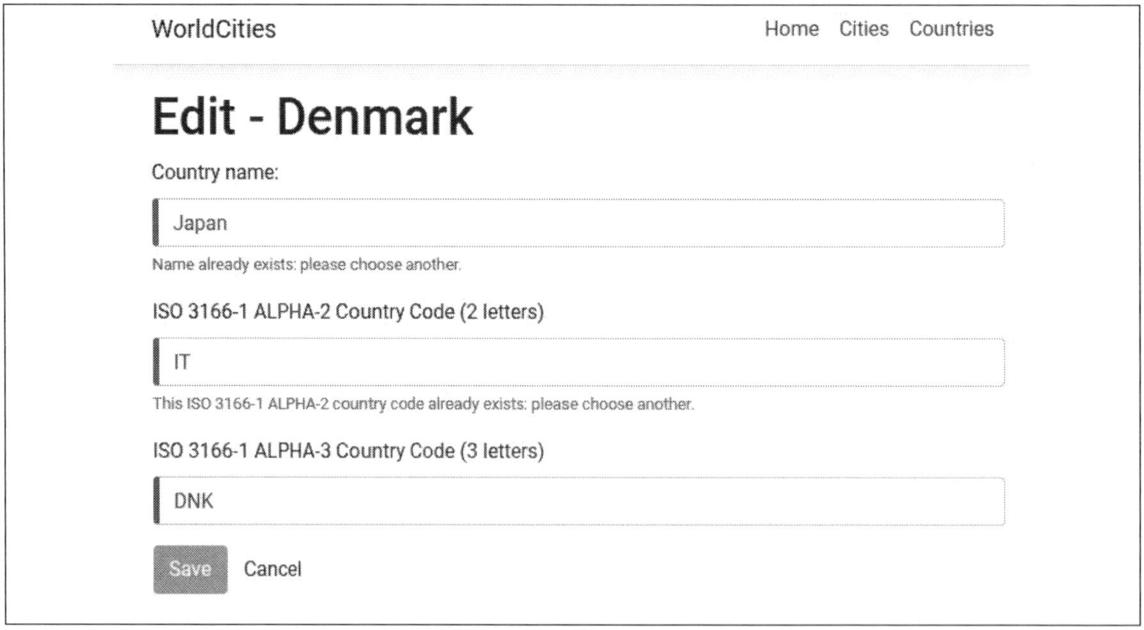

Figure 6.16: Duplicate error messages when trying to edit Denmark

This is a great result: this means that our custom validators are doing their job, positively raising some dupe errors since these values have been reserved for other existing countries (`Japan` and `Italy`, respectively).

Now, let's hit the **Cancel** button and go back to the **Countries** view. From there, click the **Add a new Country** button and try to insert a country with the following values:

- **Country name**: `New Japan`
- **ISO 3166-1 ALPHA-2 Country Code**: `JP`
- **ISO 3166-1 ALPHA-3 Country Code**: `NJ2`

If everything is working fine, we should raise two more validation errors, as shown in the following screenshot:

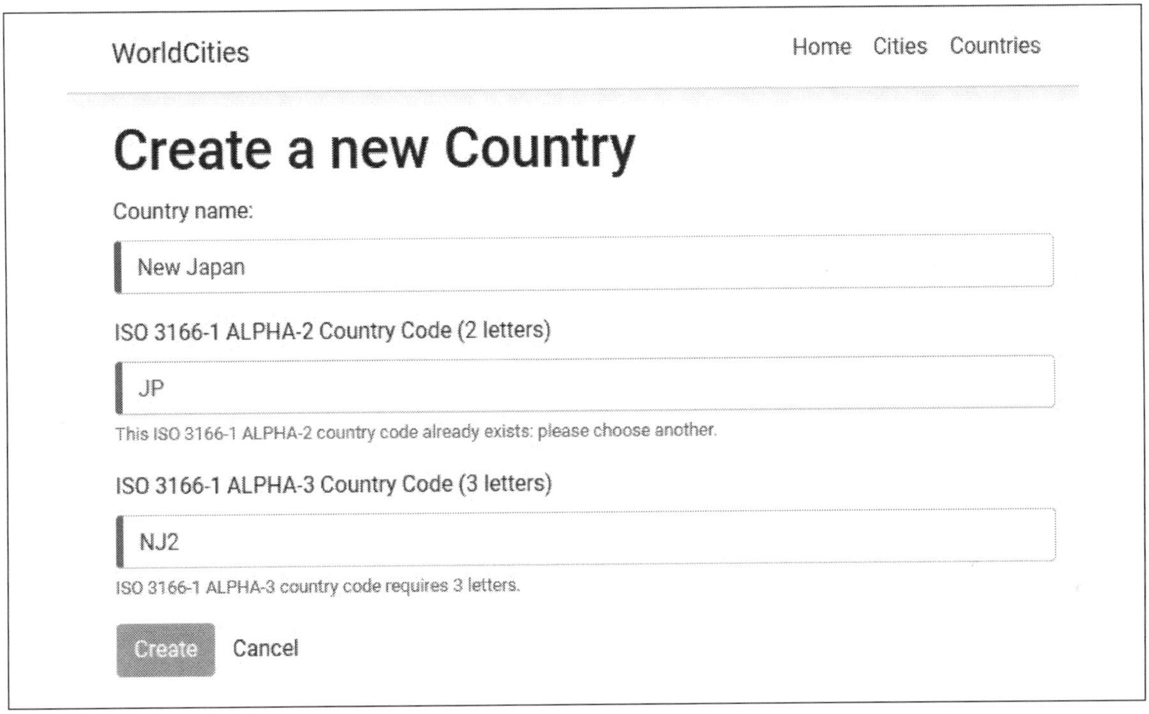

Figure 6.17: Duplicate errors while trying to add a new Country

The former error is raised by our `isDupeField` custom validator and is due to the fact that the ALPHA-2 country code already belongs to an existing country (`Japan`); the latter one is raised by the built-in `Validators.pattern`, which we configured with a *regular expression*, `/^[a-zA-Z]{3}$/`, that doesn't allow digits.

Let's fix these errors by typing in the following values:

- **Country name**: `New Japan`
- **ISO 3166-1 ALPHA-2 Country Code**: `NJ`
- **ISO 3166-1 ALPHA-3 Country Code**: `NJP`

Once you're done, click **Create** to create the new country. If everything is working as expected, the view should redirect us to the main **Countries** view.

From there, we can type `New Japan` into our text filter to ensure that our brand-new country is actually there:

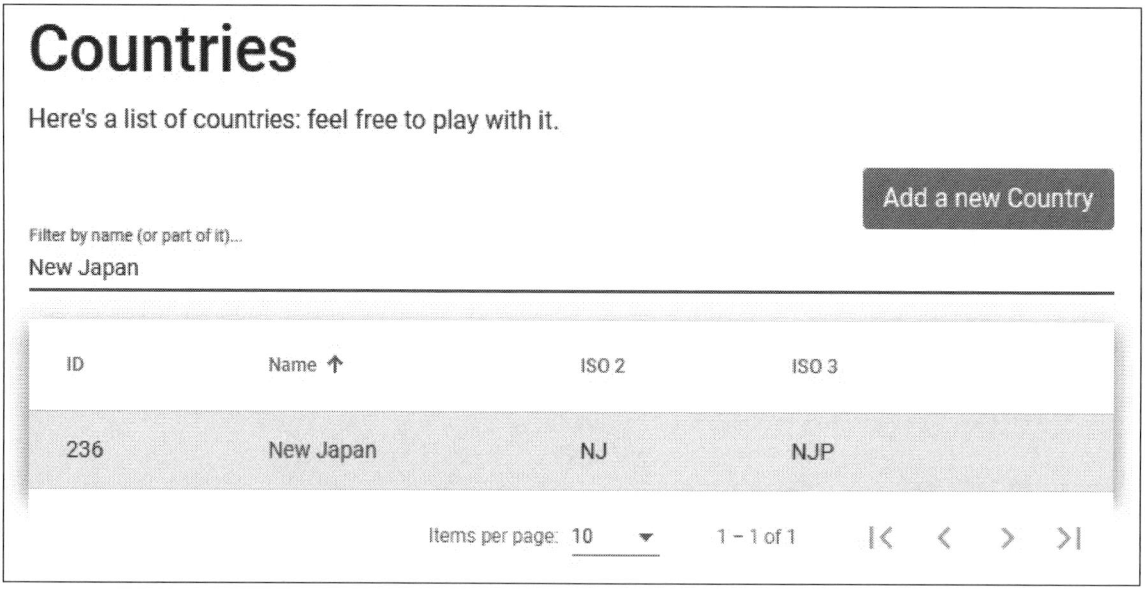

Figure 6.18: Countries list after filtering for New Japan

... Here it is! This means that we're finally done with `CountryEditComponent` and ready to move on to new, exciting tasks.

Improving the filter behavior

The real-time filter that we've implemented in our Cities and Countries listing views works well and should be very helpful for our users: however, every time the filter text changes (that is, upon each keystroke), Angular fires an HTTP request to the back-end to retrieve the updated list of results. Such behavior is intrinsically resource-intensive and can easily become a huge performance issue, especially if we're dealing with large tables and/or non-indexed columns.

Are there ways to improve this approach without compromising the results obtained in terms of user experience? As a matter of fact, the answer is yes, as long as we're willing to implement a couple of widely used techniques specifically meant to improve the performance of code that gets executed repeatedly within a short period of time.

Throttling and debouncing

If we think about it, our everyday life is full of situations where we are forced to do something while our attention is captured by something else: social networks like Twitter and instant messaging apps such as WhatsApp are a perfect example of that, since they literally flood us with notifications regardless of what we're doing.

What do we usually do in these cases? Let's consider the following alternatives:

- **Respond to all notifications in real time**, which would be great for the requesting party but would compromise what we're doing.
- **Take no immediate action** and check our messages only once every, let's say, five minutes.
- **Take no immediate action** and check our messages only when no new notifications have come in for the last five minutes.

The first approach is what our app is currently doing; the second is called *throttling*, while the third is called *debouncing*. Let's try to better understand what these terms actually mean.

Definitions

In software development, **throttling** is used to define a behavior that enforces a maximum number of times a function can be called over time. To put it in other words, it's a way to say, "*let's execute this function at most once every N milliseconds*". No matter how many times the user fires the event, that function will be executed only once in a given time interval.

The term **debouncing** is used to define a technique that prevents a function from being called until a certain amount of time has passed without it being called: in other words, it's a way to say, "*let's execute this function only if N milliseconds have passed without it being called*". The concept has some similarities with the throttling technique, with an important difference: no matter how many times the user fires the event, the attached function will be executed only after the specified time once the user stops firing the event.

In a nutshell, we can say that the main difference between throttling and debouncing is that throttling executes the function at a regular interval, while debouncing executes the function only after a cooling period.

Why would we want to throttle or debounce our code?

Let's cut it short: in information technology, throttling and debouncing are mostly useful for two main reasons: optimization and performance. They are widely used in JavaScript because they can be very helpful to efficiently handle some resource-intensive DOM-related tasks, such as scrolling and resizing HTML components, as well as retrieving data from the server.

In our given scenario, we can think of them as two ways to optimize event handling, thus lifting some work from our server (controller and database): more specifically, we want to find a way to reduce the HTTP requests that Angular currently makes to our server upon each keystroke.

Shall we do that using throttling or debouncing?

If we think about how the filter function works in terms of user experience, we can easily determine the correct answer. Since we're talking about a textbox that can be used to filter the listing results to those that contain one or more characters typed by the user, we can reasonably conclude that we could defer the HTTP request until the user stops typing, as long as we process it right after it does. Such behavior won't hinder the user experience granted by the current filter while preventing a good number of unnecessary HTTP calls.

In other words, we need to *debounce* our calls to the back-end: let's see how we can do that.

Debouncing calls to the back-end

An easy approach to debouncing with Angular is given by *RxJS*, the Reactive Extensions for JavaScript library that allows us to use *Observables*, which we introduced in *Chapter 3, Front-End and Back-End Interactions*.

Since we're using an *Observable* to perform the HTTP call, we're halfway done: we just need to make use of the handy `debounceTime` RxJS operator, which will emit a value from the source *Observable* only after a particular time span has passed without another source emission. While we are there, we can also take the chance to add the `distinctUntilChanged` operator as well, which emits a value only if it's different from the last one inserted by the user: this will prevent any HTTP call identical to the previous one, which could happen – for example – if the user writes a sentence, then adds a letter and immediately deletes it.

Updating the CitiesComponent

To implement such logic, open the `/ClientApp/src/app/cities/cities.component.ts` file and perform the following changes:

```
// [...]

import { MatSort } from '@angular/material/sort';

import { Subject } from 'rxjs';
import { debounceTime, distinctUntilChanged } from 'rxjs/operators';

import { City } from './city';

// [...]

  @ViewChild(MatPaginator) paginator: MatPaginator;
```

```
  @ViewChild(MatSort) sort: MatSort;

  filterTextChanged: Subject<string> = new Subject<string>();

// [...]

  ngOnInit() {
    this.loadData(null);
  }

  // debounce filter text changes
  onFilterTextChanged(filterText: string) {
    if (this.filterTextChanged.observers.length === 0) {
      this.filterTextChanged
        .pipe(debounceTime(1000), distinctUntilChanged())
        .subscribe(query => {
          this.loadData(query);
        });
    }
    this.filterTextChanged.next(filterText);
  }

  loadData(query: string = null) {
    var pageEvent = new PageEvent();
    pageEvent.pageIndex = this.defaultPageIndex;
    pageEvent.pageSize = this.defaultPageSize;
    if (query) {
      this.filterQuery = query;
    }
    this.getData(pageEvent);
  }

// [...]
```

As we can see, we haven't touched the `loadData` method at all, so that we won't mess up anything that we've done up to now; we added a new `onFilterTextChanged` method instead, which will be called by the filter's input and will transparently handle the debouncing task.

If we take a closer look at the `onFilterTextChanged` method, we can see that it works with a new `filterTextChanged` variable that we've also added to our component class: this variable hosts a *Subject*, a special type of *Observable* that allows values to be multi-casted to many *Observers*.

In a nutshell, here's what this new method does every time it gets called by the filter's input method:

- Checks the `filterTextChanged` *Subject* to see if there are *Observers* listening; if there are no *Observers* yet, pipes the `debounceTime` and `distinctUntilChanged` operators and adds a new subscription for the `loadData` method.
- Feeds a new value to the *Subject*, which will be multi-casted to the *Observers* registered to listen to it.

> For space reasons, we won't say any more about *Subjects* here, but the topic can be further studied by taking a look at the following page from the RxJS official guide: `https://rxjs-dev.firebaseapp.com/guide/subject#`

Although we've already explained what these operators do, let's quickly recap their role again:

- `debounceTime` will emit the value after 1,000 milliseconds of no source input coming from the user.
- `distinctUntilChanged` will emit the value only if it's different than the last inserted one.

Now that we've implemented the debouncing logic in the Angular class, we just need to update the component's template file to make the filter's input call the new `onFilterTextChanged` method instead of `loadData`.

Open the `/ClientApp/src/app/cities/cities.component.html` file and apply the following changes:

```
<mat-form-field [hidden]="!cities">
    <input matInput
        (keyup)="onFilterTextChanged($event.target.value)"
        placeholder="Filter by name (or part of it)...">
</mat-form-field>
```

That's it.

Updating the CountriesComponent

Before going further, let's update the `CountriesComponent` in the exact same way. This can be done by opening the following files:

- `/ClientApp/src/app/countries/countries.component.ts`
- `/ClientApp/src/app/countries/countries.component.html`

and applying the same changes that we did on the `CitiesComponent` files.

> For space reasons, we won't demonstrate how to perform these changes here; however, the updated `CountriesComponent` source code can be found in the GitHub repository.

Delaying these HTTP requests in these two components will shut out most unnecessary HTTP requests coming from our Angular app, thus preventing our database from being called over and over rapidly.

What about throttling?

As a matter of fact, our WorldCities Angular app doesn't have tasks or features that could benefit from throttling. However, it's worth noting that such a technique can be implemented using the same approach that we've used for debouncing, replacing the `debounceTime` RxJS operator with `throttleTime`.

> For additional info regarding these RxJS operators, refer to the following pages from the RxJS official guide:
>
> `https://rxjs-dev.firebaseapp.com/api/operators/debounceTime`
>
> `https://rxjs-dev.firebaseapp.com/api/operators/throttleTime`

Summary

This chapter was entirely dedicated to Angular forms. We started by clarifying what a form actually is and enumerated the features it needs to have in order to fulfill its duties, grouping them into two main requirements: providing a good user experience and properly handling the submitted data.

Then, we turned our focus to the Angular framework and to the two form design models it offers: the *Template-Driven* approach, mostly inherited from AngularJS, and the *Model-Driven* or *Reactive* alternative. We took some valuable time to analyze the pros and cons provided by both of them, and then we performed a detailed comparison of the underlying logic and workflow. At the end of the day, we chose to embrace the *Reactive* way of doing things, as it gives the developer more control and enforces a more consistent separation of duties between the *Data Model* and the *Form Model*.

Right after that, we went from theory to practice by creating a `CityEditComponent` and used it to implement a fully-featured *Reactive Form*; we also added the *client-side* and *server-side* data validation logic by making good use of the *Angular template syntax* in conjunction with the classes and directives granted by Angular's `ReactiveFormsModule`. Once done, we did the same with `CountryEditComponent`, where we took the chance to try and use a `FormBuilder` instead of the `FormGroup`/`FormControl` instances we used previously.

Once done, we performed a surface test with our browser to check all the *built-in* and *custom* validators, ensuring that they worked properly on the *front-end* as well as on their *back-end* APIs.

Last but not least, we spent some valuable time analyzing some performance issues of our filter feature and found a way to mitigate them by implementing a debouncing technique: this allowed us to learn how to use some very useful features from the RxJS library: `Subject`, `debounceTime`, and `distinctUntilChanged`.

In the next chapter, we're going to refine what we've done so far by refactoring some rough aspects of our Angular components in a better way. By doing so, we'll learn how to post-process the data, add decent error handling, implement some retry logic to deal with connection issues, debug our form using the Visual Studio *client-side* debugger, and - most importantly - perform some *unit tests*.

Suggested topics

Template-Driven Forms, Model-Driven Forms, Reactive Forms, JSON, RFC 7578, RFC 1341, URL Living Standard, HTML Living Standard, data validation, Angular validators, custom validators, asynchronous validators, regular expressions (regex), Angular pipes, FormBuilder, RxJS, Observables, Safe Navigation Operator (Elvis Operator), RxJS operators, Subject, debounceTime, throttleTime.

References

- *The application/www-form-urlencoded format draft-hoehrmann-urlencoded-01*: `https://tools.ietf.org/html/draft-hoehrmann-urlencoded-01`
- *RFC 7578 - Returning Values from Forms: multipart/form-data*: `https://tools.ietf.org/html/rfc7578`
- *RFC 1341, section 7.2 - The Multipart Content-Type*: `https://www.w3.org/Protocols/rfc1341/7_2_Multipart.html`
- *URL Living Standard - URL-encoded Form Data*: `https://url.spec.whatwg.org/#concept-urlencoded`
- *HTML Living Standard, section 4.10.21.7 - Multipart form data*: `https://html.spec.whatwg.org/multipage/form-control-infrastructure.html#multipart-form-data`
- *HTML Living Standard, section 4.10.21.8 - Plain Text Form Data*: `https://html.spec.whatwg.org/multipage/form-control-infrastructure.html#plain-text-form-data`
- *Angular: Template-driven forms*: `https://angular.io/guide/forms#template-driven-forms`
- *Angular: Reactive forms*: `https://angular.io/guide/reactive-forms`
- *Angular: Form validation*: `https://angular.io/guide/form-validation`
- *Angular: Validators*: `https://angular.io/api/forms/Validators`

- *Angular: Custom Async Validators*: `https://angular.io/guide/form-validation#implementing-a-custom-async-validator`
- *RegExr: Learn, Build, and Test RegEx*: `https://regexr.com/`
- *TypeScript 3.7 Release Notes*: `https://www.typescriptlang.org/docs/handbook/release-notes/typescript-3-7.html`
- *Angular Template expression operators*: `https://angular.io/guide/template-expression-operators#safe-navigation-operator`
- *RxJS Subject*: `https://rxjs-dev.firebaseapp.com/guide/subject#`
- *RxJS debounceTime operator*: `https://rxjs-dev.firebaseapp.com/api/operators/debounceTime`
- *RxJS throttleTime operator*: `https://rxjs-dev.firebaseapp.com/api/operators/throttleTime`

7
Code Tweaks and Data Services

Our `WorldCities` web application is now a full-fledged project providing a number of interesting features: we can **retrieve a list** of all the *cities* and *countries* available in our DBMS and browse them through paged tables that we can *order* and *filter*; thanks to our *master/detail* UI pattern, we can also access a detailed view of each *city* and *country*, where we can **read** and/or **edit** the most relevant fields for both of them; and last, but not least, we can **create** new *cities* and *countries* thanks to the "add new" capabilities of the aforementioned *Detail* view.

Now, before going further, it could be wise to spend some time consolidating what we've learned so far and improve the basic patterns we have followed. After all, refining our *front-end* and *back-end* and the overall logic they're currently relying upon will definitely make them more *versatile* and *fail-proof* for what is yet to come.

This chapter is entirely dedicated to those tasks. Here's what we're going to do through the various sections that we're about to face:

- **Optimizations and tweaks**, where we'll implement some high-level source code and UI refinements.
- **Bug fixes and improvements**, where we'll leverage the preceding tweaks to enhance our app's consistency and add some new features.
- **Data services**, where we'll learn how to migrate from our current simplified implementation – where we used the raw `HttpClient` service directly inside the components – to a more versatile approach that would allow us to add features such as post-processing, error handling, retry logic, and more.

All these changes will be worth their time because they'll strengthen our app's source code and prepare it for the *debugging* and *testing* phase that will appear in the next chapter.

All right, then...let's get to work.

Technical requirements

In this chapter, we're going to need all the previous technical requirements that were listed in all the previous chapters, with no additional resources, libraries, or packages.

The code files for this chapter can be found at: `https://github.com/PacktPublishing/ASP.NET-5-and-Angular/tree/master/Chapter_07/`

Optimizations and tweaks

In computer programming, the term **code bloat** is commonly used to describe an unnecessarily long, slow, or wasteful amount of source code. Such code is hardly desirable because it inevitably makes our app more vulnerable to human errors, regression bugs, logical inconsistencies, wasted resources, and so on. It also makes *debugging* and *testing* a lot more difficult and stressful; for all of the previously mentioned reasons, we should try to prevent that from happening as much as we can.

The most effective way to counter *code bloat* is to adopt and adhere to the **Don't Repeat Yourself (DRY)** principle, which is something that any developer should try to follow whenever they can. As already stated in *Chapter 5, Fetching and Displaying Data*, DRY is a widely achieved principle of software development: whenever we violate it, we fall into a *WET* approach, which could mean *Write Everything Twice*, *We Enjoy Typing*, or *Waste Everyone's Time*, depending on what we like the most.

In this section, we'll try to address some rather *WET* parts of our current code and see how we can make them more *DRY*: doing that will greatly help our *debugging* and testing *sessions* later on.

Template improvements

If we take another look at our `CityEditComponent` and `CountryEditComponent` template files, we can definitely see a certain amount of code bloat. The `form.get()` method is called no less than *10* times per form, and poses a serious threat to our template's readability. And we're talking about very small and easy forms. What would happen when dealing with big ones? Is there a way to address that?

As a matter of fact, there is: whenever we feel like we're writing too much code or repeating a complex task too many times, we can create one or more helper methods within our component class in order to centralize the underlying logic. These helper methods will act as *shortcuts* that we can call instead of repeating the whole validation logic. Let's try to add them to our *form*-related Angular Components.

Form validation shortcuts

Let's see how to do that in the `CityEditComponent` class.

Open the `/ClientApp/src/app/cities/city-edit.component.ts` file and add the following methods:

```
// retrieve a FormControl
getControl(name: string) {
    return this.form.get(name);
}

// returns TRUE if the FormControl is valid
isValid(name: string) {
    var e = this.getControl(name);
    return e && e.valid;
}

// returns TRUE if the FormControl has been changed
isChanged(name: string) {
    var e = this.getControl(name);
    return e && (e.dirty || e.touched);
}

// returns TRUE if the FormControl is raising an error,
// i.e. an invalid state after user changes
hasError(name: string) {
    var e = this.getControl(name);
    return e && (e.dirty || e.touched) && e.invalid;
}
```

The comments are self-explanatory, so there's nothing more to say. These helper methods grant us the chance to shrink our previous validation code, as follows:

```
<!-- ...existing code... --->

<div *ngIf="hasError('name')"
      class="invalid-feedback">
    <div *ngIf="form.get('name').errors?.required">
      Name is required.
    </div>
</div>

<!-- ...existing code... --->

<div *ngIf="hasError('lat')"
      class="invalid-feedback">
    <div *ngIf="form.get('lat').errors?.required">
      Latitude is required.
    </div>
</div>

<!-- ...existing code... --->
```

... and so on. Much better, right?

Let's do the same for all the form controls for `CityEditComponent`, and then switch to `CountryEditComponent` and do the same there as well...

... Or not.

Wait a minute: didn't we just say we would adhere to the *DRY* pattern as much as we can? How can we reasonably expect to do that if we're about to *copy and paste* the same identical methods throughout different classes? What if we had 10 form-based components to patch instead of just 2? That doesn't sound anything but *WET*. Now that we've found a good way to shrink our template code, we also need to find a decent way to implement those form-related methods without spawning clones everywhere.

Luckily enough, TypeScript provides a great way to handle these kinds of scenarios: **class inheritance**. Let's see how we can use such features to our advantage.

Class inheritance

Object-oriented programming (**OOP**) is usually defined by two core concepts: *polymorphism* and *inheritance*. Although both concepts are related, they are not the same. Here's what they mean in a nutshell:

- **Polymorphism** allows us to assign multiple interfaces on the same *entity* (such as a *variable*, *function*, *object*, or *type*), and/or to assign the same interface on different *entities*: in other words, it allows *entities* to have more than one form.
- **Inheritance** allows us to *extend* an object or class by *deriving* it from another object (*prototype-based inheritance*) or class (*class-based inheritance*), while retaining a similar implementation; the extended class is commonly called a **subclass** or **child class**, while the inherited class takes the name of *superclass* or *base class*.

Let's now focus on **inheritance**: in TypeScript, as in most class-based, object-oriented languages, a type created through *inheritance* (a *child* class) acquires all the properties and behaviors of the parent type, except constructors, destructors, overloaded operators, and *private* members of the *base class*.

If we think about it, it's just what we need in our scenario: if we create a base class and implement all our form-related methods there, we'll just need to *extend* our current component class without having to write it more than once.

Let's see how we can pull this off.

Implementing a BaseFormComponent

From Solution Explorer, right-click on the `/ClientApp/src/app/` folder and create a new `base.form.component.ts` file. Open it, and fill it with the following content:

```
import { Component } from '@angular/core';
import { FormGroup } from '@angular/forms';
```

```
@Component({
  template: ''
})
export abstract class BaseFormComponent {

  // the form model
  form: FormGroup;

  constructor() { }

  // retrieve a FormControl
  getControl(name: string) {
    return this.form.get(name);
  }

  // returns TRUE if the FormControl is valid
  isValid(name: string) {
    var e = this.getControl(name);
    return e && e.valid;
  }

  // returns TRUE if the FormControl has been changed
  isChanged(name: string) {
    var e = this.getControl(name);
    return e && (e.dirty || e.touched);
  }

  // returns TRUE if the FormControl is raising an error,
  // i.e. an invalid state after user changes
  hasError(name: string) {
    var e = this.getControl(name);
    return e && (e.dirty || e.touched) && e.invalid;
  }
}
```

> From now on, we'll take it for granted that we've got the logic behind our code samples; consequently, we're going to present them in a more succinct way to avoid wasting more pages by saying the obvious: please bear with it! After all, whenever we need to see the full file, we can always find it on the book's online source code repository on **GitHub**.

Now, we do have a `BaseFormComponent` *superclass* that we can use to *extend* our subclasses; as we can see, there's nothing much there, only the form-related methods and the `form` variable itself, because it's used (and therefore is required) by those methods. Also, we've purposely added the `abstract` modifier since we don't plan to ever instantiate this class; we only want other classes to derive from it.

> The fact that we'll never instantiate this abstract base class relieves us from having to import and declare it in the `/ClientApp/src/app/app.module.ts` file, like we did for all "standard" classes. Furthermore, declaring it `abstract` explicitly prevents us from being able to do that (adding an abstract class to the `declarations` array of `AppModule` would raise a TS2322 error).

Right after that, we can update our current `CityEditComponent` TypeScript file in order to extend its class accordingly.

Extending CityEditComponent

Open the `/ClientApp/src/app/cities/city-edit.component.ts` file, then add the `BaseFormComponent` *superclass* at the end of the `import` list at the beginning of the file:

```
import { Component, Inject, OnInit } from '@angular/core';
import { HttpClient, HttpParams } from '@angular/common/http';
import { ActivatedRoute, Router } from '@angular/router';
import { FormGroup, FormControl, Validators, AbstractControl,
 AsyncValidatorFn } from '@angular/forms';
import { Observable } from 'rxjs';
import { map } from 'rxjs/operators';

import { City } from './city';
import { Country } from '../countries/country';

import { BaseFormComponent } from '../base.form.component';

// ...existing code...
```

Now, we need to implement the class inheritance using the `extends` modifier that is right after the class declaration:

```
// ...existing code...

export class CityEditComponent
    extends BaseFormComponent implements OnInit {

// ...existing code...
```

That's it: `CityEditComponent` has now officially become a *child class* of the `BaseFormComponent` *superclass*.

Last but not least, we need to invoke the *superclass* constructor by calling `super()` inside the *child class* constructor's implementation:

```
// ...existing code...

constructor(
    private activatedRoute: ActivatedRoute,
    private router: Router,
    private http: HttpClient,
    @Inject('BASE_URL') private baseUrl: string) {
    super();
}

// ...existing code...
```

And that's it: now we can freely remove all the form-related methods that we added early on – `getControl`, `isValid`, `isChanged`, and `hasError` – to the `CityEditComponent` class file, as our *child class* will now transparently *inherit* them from its *superclass*.

> As for the `form` variable, it's worth noting that we're actually **overriding** it in the child class source code: in TypeScript, this can be done without any fancy modifier. We just need to redefine it; since we have already got it, we don't need to do anything.

Let's now test what we did by hitting *F5* and navigating through `CityEditComponent` in both the *edit* and *add new* modes. If we did everything correctly, we should see no issues: everything should work just like it was, with a fairly smaller amount of source code.

> Don't forget to test our validators, since the form-related methods that we have implemented mostly impact them: if the form validators are still working and show their errors when triggered, this means that the child class is able to inherit and use its base class methods, thereby proving that our brand-new superclass/subclass implementation is working fine.

Extending CountryEditComponent

As soon as we're sure that everything is working fine, we can extend the `CountryEditComponent` class and make it become a *child class* of `BaseFormComponent` as well. Let's quickly do this, so that we can move on.

We're not going to show the source code changes here because the required steps are almost identical to what we've just seen; if we've got any doubts, we can refer to this chapter's source code on the GitHub repository.

Now that we've optimized our components' code, let's see what we can do to improve our app's user experience.

Bug fixes and improvements

Let's be honest: although we made a decent job of building up our *master/detail* UI pattern, and we assembled both views using the most relevant *city* and *country* fields, our app is still lacking something that our users might want to see. More specifically, the following detail is missing:

- **Our City Detail view doesn't validate the lat and lon input values properly**: for example, we are allowed to type letters instead of numbers, which utterly crashes the form.
- **Our Countries view doesn't show the number of cities** that each *country* actually contains.
- **Our Cities view doesn't show the country name** for each listed city.

Let's do our best to fix all of these issues for good.

Validating lat and lon

Let's start with the only real *bug*: a form that can be broken from the *front-end* is something that we should always avoid, even if those input types are implicitly checked in the *back-end* by our ASP.NET Core API.

Luckily enough, we already know how to fix those kinds of errors: we need to add some *pattern-based validators* to the `lat` and `lon` *FormControls* for `CityEditComponent`, just like we did with the `iso2` and `iso3` controls in the `CountryEditComponent` files. As we already know, we'll need to update two files:

- The `CityEditComponent` *class* file, in order to implement the validators and define a *validation pattern* based upon a *regex*
- The `CityEditComponent` *template* file, in order to implement the validators' error messages and their show/hide logic

Let's do this!

city-edit.component.ts

Open the `/ClientApp/src/app/cities/city-edit.component.ts` file and update its content accordingly (new/updated lines are highlighted):

```
// ...existing code...

  ngOnInit() {
    this.form = new FormGroup({
      name: new FormControl('', Validators.required),
      lat: new FormControl('', [
```

```
        Validators.required,
        Validators.pattern(/^[-]?[0-9]+(\.[0-9]{1,4})?$/)
      ]),
      lon: new FormControl('', [
        Validators.required,
        Validators.pattern(/^[-]?[0-9]+(\.[0-9]{1,4})?$/)
      ]),
      countryId: new FormControl('', Validators.required)
    }, null, this.isDupeCity());

    this.loadData();
  }

// ...existing code...
```

Here we go. As we already know from *Chapter 6, Forms and Data Validation*, this form's implementation is still based on the manually instantiated `FormGroup` and `FormControl` objects instead of using `FormBuilder`; however, there's no reason to change it now, since we were still able to implement `Validators.pattern` without any issues.

Let's spend a couple minutes explaining the *regular expression* that we've used there:

- `^` defines the start of the *user input* string that we need to check.
- `[-]?` allows the presence of an *optional* minus sign, which is required when dealing with negative coordinates.
- `[0-9]+` asks for *one or more* numbers between 0 and 9.
- `(\.[0-9]{1,4})?` defines an *optional group* (thanks to `?` at the end), which, if present, needs to respect the following rules:
    - `\.`: requires the input to start with *a single dot* (the decimal sign). The dot is escaped because it's a reserved *regex* character, which, when unescaped, means *any character*.
    - `[0-9]{1,4}` asks for *one to four* numbers between 0 and 9 (since we do want *between 1 and 4 decimal values* after the dot).
- `$` defines the end of the *user input* string.

> We could've used `\d` (any digit) as an alternative to `[0-9]`, which is a slightly more succinct syntax; however, we have chosen to stick with `[0-9]` for better readability. Feel free to replace it with `\d` at any time.

Now that the validators have been set in place, we need to add the error messages to the `CityEditComponent` template file.

city-edit.component.html

Open the `/ClientApp/src/app/cities/city-edit.component.html` file and update its content accordingly (new/updated lines are highlighted):

```
<!-- ...existing code -->

        <div *ngIf="form.get('lat').errors?.required">
          Latitude is required.
        </div>
        <div *ngIf="form.get('lat').errors?.pattern">
          Latitude requires a positive or negative number with 0-4
           decimal values.
        </div>

<!-- ...existing code -->

        <div *ngIf="form.get('lon').errors?.required">
          Longitude is required.
        </div>
        <div *ngIf="form.get('lon').errors?.pattern">
          Longitude requires a positive or negative number with 0-4
           decimal values.
        </div>

<!-- ...existing code -->
```

Here we go.

Let's quickly test it:

1. Hit *F5* to start the app in *debug* mode.
2. Navigate through the **Cities** view.
3. Filter the list to find **Madrid**.
4. Type some invalid characters in the **City latitude** and **City longitude** input fields.

If the validators have been implemented properly, we should see our error messages appear in all their glory and the **Save** button disabled, just like in the following screenshot:

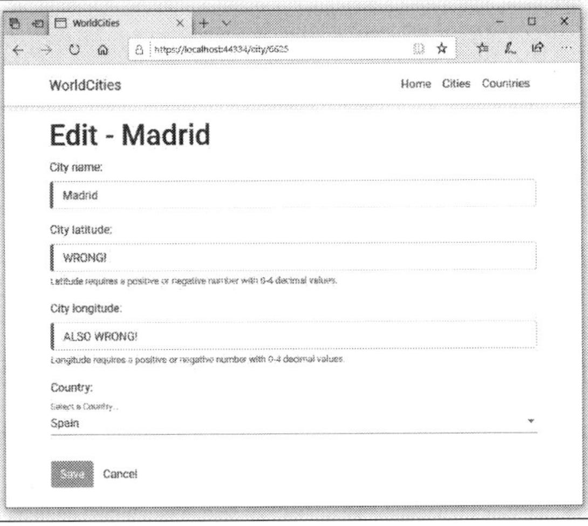

Figure 7.1: Error messages when inputting invalid latitude and longitude

That's it. Now that we have fixed our first UI bug, let's move on to the next task.

Adding the number of cities

What we need to do now is find a way to show an additional column in the **Countries** view that will allow users to instantly see the *number of cities* for each listed *country*. In order to do that, we definitely need to improve our *back-end* web API, because we know that there's currently no way to retrieve such info from the server.

Well, technically speaking, there is a way: we could use the CitiesController's `GetCities()` method with a huge `pageSize` parameter (99,999 or so) and a suitable filter to retrieve the whole set of cities for each given country, then count that collection and output the number.

However, doing this would indeed have a *huge* performance impact: not only would we have to retrieve all the cities for all the listed *countries*, but we would have to do that by issuing a separate HTTP request for each table row. That's definitely not what we want if we are aiming to fulfill our task in a smart and efficient way.

Here's what we're going to do instead:

- Find a smart and efficient way to count the number of cities for each listed country from the *back-end*.
- Add a `TotCities` property to our `Country` Angular *interface* to store that same number on the *client*.

Let's do this.

CountriesController

Let's start with the *back-end* part. Finding a smart and efficient way to count the number of cities for each country might be harder than it seems.

If we want to retrieve this value in a single shot, that is, without making additional API requests with Angular, there's no doubt that we need to improve our current CountriesController's `GetCountries()` method, which is what we're currently using to fetch the *countries* data.

Let's open our `/Controllers/CountriesController.cs` file and see how ASP.NET Core and **Entity Framework Core** (**EF Core**) can help us to perform what we want.

Here's the `GetCountries()` method that we need to update:

```
public async Task<ActionResult<ApiResult<Country>>> GetCountries(
        int pageIndex = 0,
        int pageSize = 10,
        string sortColumn = null,
        string sortOrder = null,
        string filterColumn = null,
        string filterQuery = null)
{
    return await ApiResult<Country>.CreateAsync(
            _context.Countries,
            pageIndex,
            pageSize,
            sortColumn,
            sortOrder,
            filterColumn,
            filterQuery);
}
```

As we can see, there's no trace of `Cities`. Although we know that our `Country` entity contains a `Cities` property that is meant to store a list of *cities*, we also remember (from *Chapter 4, Data Model with Entity Framework Core*) that this property is set to `null`, since we've never told EF Core to load the entity's related data.

What if we do it now? We could be tempted to solve our issue by activating the *Eager Loading* ORM pattern (as discussed in *Chapter 4, Data Model with Entity Framework Core*) and filling our `Cities` property with actual values with which to feed our Angular client. Here's how we could do that:

```
return await ApiResult<Country>.CreateAsync(
            _context.Countries
                .Include(c => c.Cities),
            pageIndex,
            pageSize,
            sortColumn,
            sortOrder,
            filterColumn,
            filterQuery);
```

However, it doesn't take a genius to understand that such a workaround is hardly smart and efficient: a *country* entity might have lots of cities, sometimes *hundreds* of them. Do we really think it would be acceptable for our *back-end* to retrieve them all from the DBMS? Are we really going to flood our Angular *front-end* with those huge JSON arrays?

That's definitely a no-go: we can do better than that. Especially considering that, after all, we don't need to retrieve each country's entire cities data to fulfill our goal: we just need to know their *number*.

Here's how we can do that:

```
[HttpGet]
public async Task<ActionResult<ApiResult<CountryDTO>>> GetCountries(
int pageIndex = 0,
int pageSize = 10,
string sortColumn = null,
string sortOrder = null,
string filterColumn = null,
string filterQuery = null)
{
    return await ApiResult<CountryDTO>.CreateAsync(
            _context.Countries
                .Select(c => new CountryDTO()
                {
                    Id = c.Id,
                    Name = c.Name,
                    ISO2 = c.ISO2,
                    ISO3 = c.ISO3,
                    TotCities = c.Cities.Count
                }),
```

```
                pageIndex,
                pageSize,
                sortColumn,
                sortOrder,
                filterColumn,
                filterQuery);
}
```

As we can see, we went for a totally different approach: the `Include()` method is out of the way; now, instead of eagerly loading the cities, we're using the `Select()` method to *project* our resulting *countries* into a brand-new `CountryDTO` object that contains the exact same properties of its source, plus a new `TotCities` variable: that way, we never get the cities, we only fetch their number.

> It's also worth noting that, since we switched out our `Country` entity class for a new `CountryDTO` class, we had to change the `ApiResult` generic type (from `ApiResult<Country>` to `ApiResult<CountryDTO>`) in the method's return type.

Although this method is a bit more complex to pull off, it's definitely a *smart and efficient* way to deal with our task; the only downside is that we need to create the `CountryDTO` class, which doesn't exist yet.

Creating the CountryDTO class

From Solution Explorer, right-click on the `/Data/` folder, then add a new `CountryDTO.cs` file, open it, and fill it with the following content:

```
using System.Text.Json.Serialization;

namespace WorldCities.Data
{
    public class CountryDTO
    {
        public CountryDTO() { }

        #region Properties
        public int Id { get; set; }

        public string Name { get; set; }

        [JsonPropertyName("iso2")]
        public string ISO2 { get; set; }

        [JsonPropertyName("iso3")]
        public string ISO3 { get; set; }
```

```
        public int TotCities { get; set; }
        #endregion
    }
}
```

As we can see, the `CountryDTO` class contains most of the properties that are already provided by the `Country` entity class, without the `Cities` property – which we know we won't need here – and a single, additional `TotCities` property: it's a **Data Transfer Object** (**DTO**) *class* that serves only the purpose of feeding the client with (only) the data that we need to send.

> As the name implies, a DTO is an object that carries data between processes. It's a widely used concept when developing web services and micro-services, where each HTTP call is an expensive operation that should always be cut to the bare minimum amount of required data.
>
> The difference between DTOs and business objects and/or data access objects (such as DataSets, DataTables, DataRows, IQueryables, Entities, and so on) is that a DTO should only store, serialize, and deserialize its own data.

It's worth noting that we had to use the `[JsonPropertyName]` attributes here as well, since this class will be converted to JSON and the `ISO2` and `ISO3` properties won't be converted in the way that we expect (as we've already seen in *Chapter 5, Fetching and Displaying Data*).

Angular front-end updates

It is time to switch to Angular and update the *front-end* accordingly, with the new changes applied to the *back-end*.

Follow these steps:

1. Open the `/ClientApp/src/app/countries/country.ts` file to add the `TotCities` property to the `Country` interface in the following way:

```
export interface Country {
    id: number;
    name: string;
    iso2: string;
    iso3: string;
    totCities: number;
}
```

2. Right after that, open the `/ClientApp/src/app/countries/countries.component.ts` file and update the `displayedColumns` inner variable in the following way:

```
// ...existing code...

public displayedColumns: string[] = ['id', 'name', 'iso2',
```

```
  'iso3', 'totCities'];

// ...existing code...
```

3. Once done, open the `/ClientApp/src/app/countries/countries.component.html` file and add the `TotCities` column to *Angular Material*'s `MatTable` template in the following way (updated lines are highlighted):

```
<!-- ...existing code... -->

<!-- Lon Column -->
<ng-container matColumnDef="iso3">
  <th mat-header-cell *matHeaderCellDef mat-sort-header>
    ISO 3
  </th>
  <td mat-cell *matCellDef="let country"> {{country.iso3}} </td>
</ng-container>

<!-- TotCities Column -->
<ng-container matColumnDef="totCities">
  <th mat-header-cell *matHeaderCellDef mat-sort-header>
    Tot. Cities
  </th>
  <td mat-cell *matCellDef="let country"> {{country.totCities}} </td>
</ng-container>

<tr mat-header-row *matHeaderRowDef="displayedColumns"></tr>
<tr mat-row *matRowDef="let row; columns: displayedColumns;"></tr>

<!-- ...existing code... -->
```

4. Now, we can finally hit *F5* and see the results of our hard work. If we did everything correctly, we should be able to see the new **Tot. Cities** column, as shown in the following screenshot:

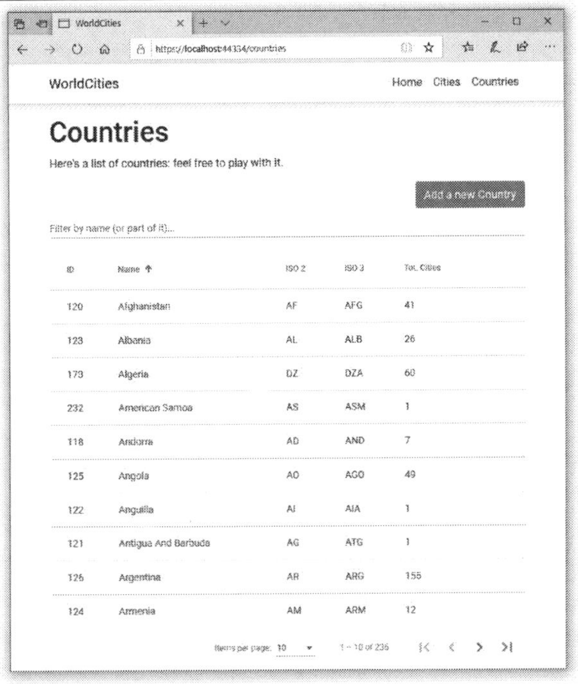

Figure 7.2: Countries table with the total cities column

Not bad at all: on top of that, the new column will also be *sortable*, meaning that we can order our countries by the number of listed cities in *ascending* or *descending* order, using one or two clicks. Thanks to this new feature, we can learn that the United States is the country that has the most listed cities (4,864), while New Japan, the imaginary country that we created back in *Chapter 6, Forms and Data Validation*, still has *zero*.

While we're here, let's quickly fix this by going to the **Cities** view, using it to edit **New Tokyo**, and changing its *country* in the following way:

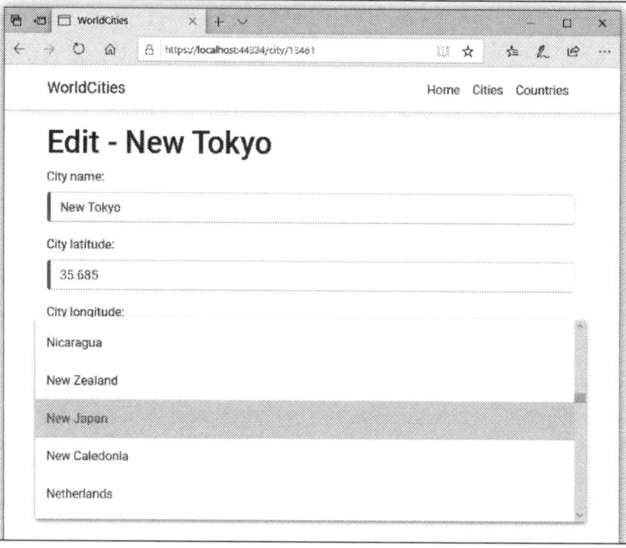

Figure 7.3: Changing the country New Tokyo belongs to

If we set the New Tokyo's *country* to **New Japan**, hit the **Save** button to apply the changes, and then go back to the **Countries** view, we should see that **New Japan** now has a single city (as shown in the following screenshot):

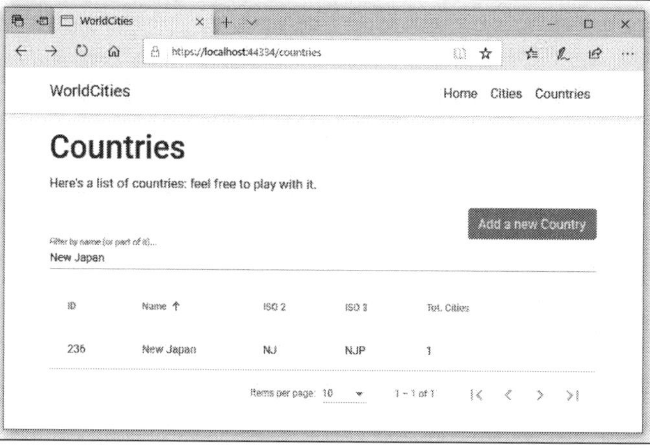

Figure 7.4: Filtering the Countries list for New Japan

Now that we've successfully shown the number of cities for each *country* in our **Countries** views – and bound **New Japan** together with **New Tokyo** in the process – we're ready to move on to the third improvement.

However, before doing that, it could be useful to spend some time thinking about that *DTO class* that we had to create to fulfill our latest task.

DTO classes – should we really use them?

Now that we've seen how similar the `Country` *entity class* and the `CountryDTO` *class* actually are, we should be asking ourselves whether we could do something better than that. For example, we could inherit the `Country` entity class in the `CountryDTO` class, thus avoiding the repetition of four properties; or we could entirely avoid the `CountryDTO` class, and just add the `TotCities` property to the `Country` entity instead.

Well, the answer is **yes**: we could've definitely used those workarounds, thereby avoiding the need to create additional properties (or classes) and keeping the code undeniably more *DRY*. Why didn't we do that?

The answer is rather simple: because both of the previous workarounds come with some relevant design and *security* flaws. Let's do our best to address them and understand why they should be avoided whenever we can.

Separation of concerns

As a general rule of thumb, *entity classes* shouldn't be burdened with properties that only exist to fulfill our *client-side* needs: whenever we need to create them, it's wise to create an intermediate class, and then separate the *entity* from the output object that we send to the client through the web APIs.

> If we've worked with the ASP.NET MVC Framework, we can relate this separation of concerns with the one that distinguishes the **Model** from the **ViewModel** in the **Model-View-ViewModel** (**MVVM**) presentation pattern. The scenario is basically the same: both are simple classes with attributes, but they do have different audiences – the controller and the view. In our scenario, the view is nothing less than our Angular client.

Now, it goes without saying that putting a `TotCities` property within an *Entity* class would break that *separation of concerns*. There's no `TotCities` column in our `Countries` database table; that property would only be there to send some additional data to the *front-end.*

On top of that, there would be no relations between the `TotCities` property and the already existing `Cities` property: if we do activate the EF Core *Eager Loading* pattern and fill the `Cities` property, the `TotCities` property will still be set to zero (and vice versa); such misleading behavior would be a bad design choice and could even result in implementation errors for those who reasonably expect our *Entity classes* to be a C# version of our data source.

Security considerations

Keeping entity classes separate from the *client-side* API output classes is often a good choice, even for security purposes: now that we're dealing with *cities* and *countries*, we don't really suffer from it, but what if we were to handle a *users* table with personal and/or login data? If we think about it, there are a lot of possible scenarios where it wouldn't be wise to just pull all the fields from the database and send them to the client in JSON format. The default methods created by ASP.NET Core Web API Controllers when we add them from the Visual Studio interface – which is what we did in *Chapter 4, Data Model with Entity Framework Core* – don't care about that, which is perfectly fine for code samples and even simple API-based projects. However, when things become more complex, it's recommended to feed the client with limited data and in a controlled way.

That said, the most effective way to do that in .NET is to create and serve thinner, and more secure, *DTO classes* instead of the main *Entities*: this is precisely what we have done with the `CountryDTO` class in the preceding sections.

DTO classes versus anonymous types

The only acceptable alternative to the aforementioned *DTO classes* would be using the `Select()` method to *project* the main Entity classes to *anonymous types*, and serve them, instead.

Here's another version of the previous CountriesController's `GetCountries()` method using an *anonymous type* instead of the `CountryDTO` *class* (relevant changes are highlighted in the following code):

```
[HttpGet]
public async Task<ActionResult<ApiResult<dynamic>>> GetCountries(
    int pageIndex = 0,
    int pageSize = 10,
    string sortColumn = null,
    string sortOrder = null,
    string filterColumn = null,
    string filterQuery = null)
{
    return await ApiResult<dynamic>.CreateAsync(
            _context.Countries
                .Select(c => new
                {
                    id = c.Id,
                    name = c.Name,
                    iso2 = c.ISO2,
                    iso3 = c.ISO3,
                    totCities = c.Cities.Count
                }),
            pageIndex,
            pageSize,
            sortColumn,
            sortOrder,
            filterColumn,
            filterQuery);
}
```

As expected, we had to change our `ApiResult` generic type to `dynamic` in the code, and also in the method's *return value*; other than that, the preceding method seems to be fine and it will definitely work just like the previous one.

What should we use then? *DTO classes* or *anonymous types*?

Truth be told, both methods are perfectly fine. *Anonymous types* can often be a great alternative, especially when we need to quickly define JSON return types; however, there are some specific scenarios (such as *unit testing*, as we're going to see later on) where we would prefer to deal with *named types* instead. The choice, as always, depends on the situation. In our current scenario, we'll stick to the `CountryDTO` class, but we're going to use *anonymous types* as well in the near future.

> For additional info on the anonymous types in C#, read the following document: `https://docs.microsoft.com/en-us/dotnet/csharp/programming-guide/classes-and-structs/anonymous-types`

Securing entities

If we don't want to use *DTO classes*, and *anonymous types* aren't our cup of tea, there's a third viable alternative that we might want to consider: securing our *entities* to prevent them from either giving incorrect instructions (such as creating wrong columns) to EF Core, or sending too much data through our RESTful APIs: if we manage to do that, we could just continue to use them and keep our web API code DRY.

We can achieve such a result by decorating our entities' properties with some specific *Data Annotation attributes*, such as the following:

- `[NotMapped]`: Prevents EF Core from creating a *database column* for that property
- `[JsonIgnore]`: Prevents a property from being serialized or deserialized
- `[JsonPropertyName("name")]`: Allows us to override the property name upon the JSON class serialization and deserialization, overriding the property name and any naming policy that is specified by the `JsonNamingPolicy` settings within the `Startup.cs` file

The first attribute requires the `Microsoft.EntityFrameworkCore` namespace, while the others are part of the `System.Text.Json.Serialization` namespace.

We've already used the `[JsonPropertyName]` *attribute* back in *Chapter 5, Fetching and Displaying Data*, where we had to specify a JSON property name for the `ISO2` and `ISO3` properties of the `Country` *entity*. Let's now implement the other two as well.

[NotMapped] and [JsonIgnore] attributes

Open the `/Data/Models/Country.cs` file and update the existing code at the end of the file as follows (new/updated lines are highlighted):

```
#region Client-side properties
/// <summary>
/// The number of cities related to this country.
/// </summary>
[NotMapped]
public int TotCities
{
    get
    {
        return (Cities != null)
            ? Cities.Count
            : _TotCities;
    }
    set { _TotCities = value; }
}

private int _TotCities = 0;
#endregion

#region Navigation Properties
/// <summary>
/// A list containing all the cities related to this country.
/// </summary>
[JsonIgnore]
public virtual List<City> Cities { get; set; }
#endregion
```

Here's what we've done, in a nutshell:

- We have implemented the `TotCities` property in the *Entity* code and decorated it with the `[NotMapped]` attribute, so that EF Core won't create its corresponding database column upon any *migration* and/or *update* task.
- While we were there, we took the chance to write some additional logic to *link* this property to the `Cities` property value (only when it's not `null`): that way, our *Entity* won't give misleading info, such as having 20+ cities in the `Cities` list property and a `TotCities` value of zero at the same time.
- Last but not least, we added the `[JsonIgnore]` attribute to the `Cities` properties, thus preventing such info from being sent to the client (regardless of its value, even when `null`).

> The [NotMapped] attribute, which we've never used before, helps mitigate the fact that we're using an entity to store the properties that are required by the front-end, and are therefore completely unrelated to the data model. In a nutshell, such an attribute will tell EF Core that we do not want to create a database column for that property in the database.
>
> Since we've created our database using EF Core's code-first approach (see *Chapter 4, Data Model with Entity Framework Core*), and we're using migrations to keep the database structure updated, we need to use that attribute each and every time we want to create an extra property on our entity classes. Whenever we forget to do that, we will definitely end up with unwanted database fields.

Using [JsonIgnore] to prevent the server from sending away the Cities property might seem like overkill: why would we even want to skip such a value, since it's currently null?

As a matter of fact, we've taken this decision as a precaution. Since we're using *entities* directly, instead of relying upon *DTO classes* or *anonymous types*, we want to implement a restrictive approach with our data. Whenever we don't need it, it's wise to apply [JsonIgnore] to be sure we won't be disclosing anything more than we need to; we could call it a *Data Protection by Default* approach, which will hopefully help us to keep our web API under control and prevent it from sharing too much. After all, we can always remove that attribute whenever we need to.

It goes without saying that, if we want to adopt the *Secured Entities* alternative approach, we won't need the CountryDTO.cs class anymore; therefore, we could *revert* the /Controllers/CountriesController.cs file's GetCountries() method, which we changed a short while ago, and put the Country reference back where it was:

```
return await ApiResult<Country>.CreateAsync(
        _context.Countries
            .Select(c => new Country()
            {
                Id = c.Id,
                Name = c.Name,
                ISO2 = c.ISO2,
                ISO3 = c.ISO3,
                TotCities = c.Cities.Count
            }),
        pageIndex,
        pageSize,
        sortColumn,
        sortOrder,
        filterColumn,
        filterQuery);
```

However, before doing all that, we should spend a couple minutes carefully evaluating the downsides of this alternative *Securing Entities* approach.

The downsides of Swiss Army Knives

The *Securing Entities* approach that we've just discussed might sound like a valid DTO alternative: it gives us the chance to write less code by "shrinking" all the logic within the Entity class, which will become a "jack of all trades." Is it really as good as it looks?

Unfortunately, the answer is no. Although such an alternative method will work, it exposes our code base to several downsides that we should want to avoid.

Here's a list of reasons that should lead us to avoid this method:

- Entity classes are meant to be object wrappers for database tables and views; directly using them to "configure" the JSON data output for our client-side app will break the **Single Responsibility Principle** (**SRP**), which states that every module, class, or function in a computer program should have responsibility over a single part of that program's functionality.
- Entities can likely contain a lot of data that the user and/or the client-side app should never be able to see, such as password hashes, personal data, and so on. Hiding these properties with `[JsonIgnore]` attributes will continuously force the developer to over-complicate their source code, which will eventually lead to a confusing code base.
- Entity classes will likely evolve over the course of time. For example, in the database table, they are meant to "wrap" changes; all developers working on the project will have to be aware of the fact that all new properties will be served by the API response, unless it's properly "secured": a single missing `[JsonIgnore]` attribute could cause a dangerous leak.

All in all, such an approach will eventually expose our database data to potential leaks due to an increased chance of developer mistakes, with the only real advantage of having fewer (useful) classes to deal with. Is it worth it? We don't think so: we don't need a few *Swiss Army Knives*, but several well-made and readable classes that can deal with their required tasks in the best (and most efficient) possible way.

> A **Swiss Army Knife**, sometimes also known as a **Kitchen Sink**, is a name that most developers give to excessively complex class interfaces explicitly designed to meet all possible needs; such an approach often overcomplicates things instead of simplifying them, thus ending up in a futile attempt that negates most of their premises. For this very reason, it is almost always considered a bad practice.

Final thoughts

All three alternative implementations of the `GetCountries()` method that have been discussed in this section – `CountryDTO`, `dynamic`, and `Country` – are available in the `/Controllers/CountriesController.cs` file in the GitHub source code for *Chapter 7*. The first is what we'll be using for this book's samples, while the other two have been commented out and put there for reference only. Readers are encouraged to switch them at will in order to find the most suitable approach for their programming style. That said, we strongly suggest taking our advice into consideration in order to make the most responsible choice.

That's it. Now we can finally move on to our third and final task.

Adding the country name

Now, we need to find a way to add a `Country` column to the **Cities** view, so that our users will be able to see the *country* name for each listed city. Considering what we just did with the *countries*, this should be a rather straightforward task.

CitiesController

As always, let's start with the web API. Follow these steps:

1. Open the `/Controllers/CitiesController.cs` file and change the `GetCities()` method in the following way:

```
// ...existing code...

[HttpGet]
public async Task<ActionResult<ApiResult<CityDTO>>> GetCities(
        int pageIndex = 0,
        int pageSize = 10,
        string sortColumn = null,
        string sortOrder = null,
        string filterColumn = null,
        string filterQuery = null)
{
    return await ApiResult<CityDTO>.CreateAsync(
            _context.Cities
                .Select(c => new CityDTO()
                {
                    Id = c.Id,
                    Name = c.Name,
                    Lat = c.Lat,
                    Lon = c.Lon,
                    CountryId = c.Country.Id,
                    CountryName = c.Country.Name
                }),
            pageIndex,
            pageSize,
            sortColumn,
            sortOrder,
            filterColumn,
            filterQuery);
}

// ...existing code...
```

As we can see, we're sticking to the DTO-based pattern, meaning that we'll have to create an additional `CountryDTO` class.

2. Use the Visual Studio Solution Explorer to add a new `/Data/CityDTO.cs` file and fill it with the following content:

```
namespace WorldCities.Data
{
    public class CityDTO
    {
        public CityDTO() { }

        public int Id { get; set; }

        public string Name { get; set; }

        public string Name_ASCII { get; set; }

        public decimal Lat { get; set; }

        public decimal Lon { get; set; }

        public int CountryId { get; set; }

        public string CountryName { get; set; }
    }
}
```

That's it. Our web API is ready, so let's move to Angular.

> As we've seen when working with the CountriesController's `GetCountries()` method early on, we could have implemented the web API by using anonymous types, or with a secured `City` entity, thus avoiding having to write the `CityDTO` class.

Angular front-end updates

Let's start with the `/ClientApp/src/app/cities/city.ts` interface, where we need to add the `countryName` property. Open that file and update its content in the following way:

```
interface City {
    id: number;
```

```
    name: string;
    lat: number;
    lon: number;
    countryId: number;
  countryName: string;
}
```

Once done, open the `/ClientApi/src/app/cities/cities.component.ts` class, where we need to add the `countryName` column definition:

```
// ...existing code...

public displayedColumns: string[] = ['id', 'name', 'lat', 'lon', 'countryName'];

// ...existing code...
```

Then, open the `/ClientApi/src/app/cities/cities.component.html` class and add a new `<ng-container>` accordingly:

```
<!-- ...existing code... -->

<!-- Lon Column -->
<ng-container matColumnDef="lon">
  <th mat-header-cell *matHeaderCellDef mat-sort-header>Longitude</th>
  <td mat-cell *matCellDef="let city"> {{city.lon}} </td>
</ng-container>

<!-- CountryName Column -->
<ng-container matColumnDef="countryName">
  <th mat-header-cell *matHeaderCellDef mat-sort-header>Country</th>
  <td mat-cell *matCellDef="let city">
    <a [routerLink]="['/country',
      city.countryId]">{{city.countryName}}</a>
  </td>
</ng-container>

<!-- ...existing code... -->
```

As we can see, we wrapped `countryName` within `routerLink`, pointing to the *Edit Country* view, so that our users will be able to use it as a navigation element.

Let's test what we did. Hit *F5* to launch the app in *debug* mode, then go to the **Cities** view. If we did everything properly, we should be welcomed by the following result:

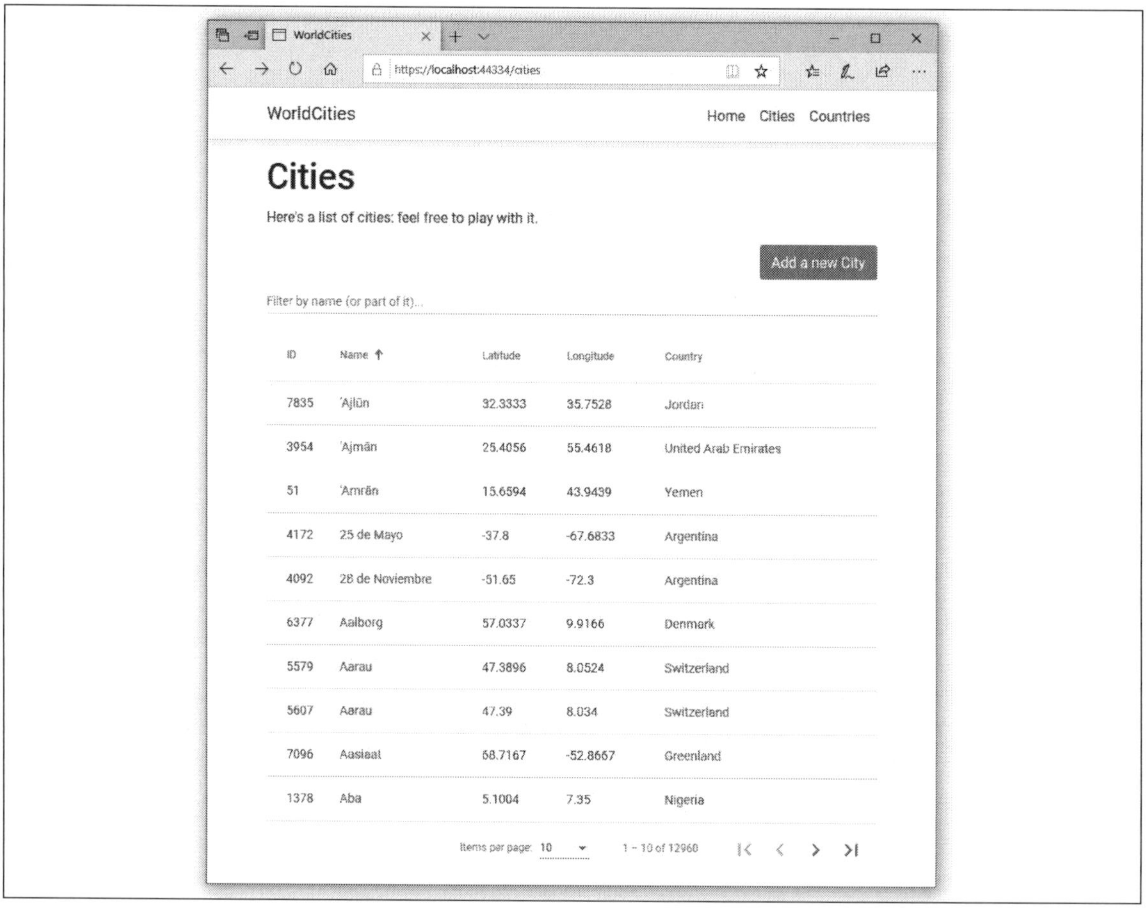

Figure 7.5: Cities list with an added Country column

Not bad, right?

From there, if we click on a *country* name, let's say, Jordan, we should be brought to the *Edit Country* view:

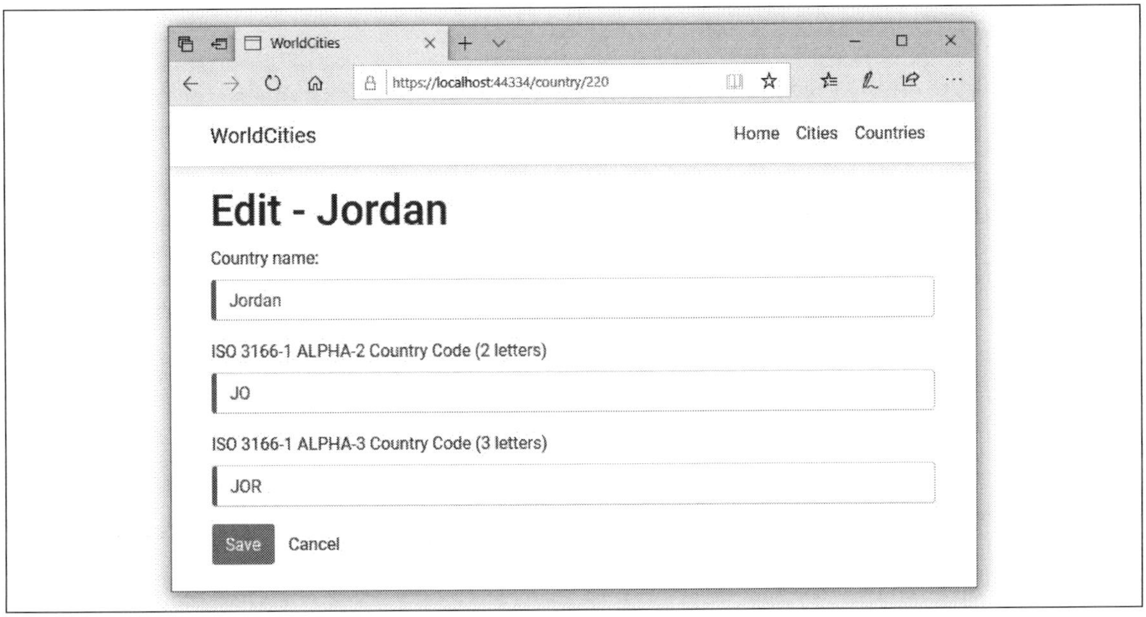

Figure 7.6: View when editing Jordan

That's awesome!

This brings us to the end of the *minor* code improvements and UI tweaks. In the next section, we'll face a more demanding task, which will require a *code refactoring* of all the Angular Components that we've created so far.

> In software development, code refactoring is the process of restructuring existing source code without changing its external behavior. There could be multiple reasons to perform refactoring activities, such as improving the code's readability, extensibility, or performance, making it more secure, reducing its complexity, and so on.
>
> For additional information regarding the code refactoring high-level concept, check out the following URL: `https://docs.microsoft.com/en-us/visualstudio/ide/refactoring-in-visual-studio`

Data services

The two web applications that we have created so far – `HealthCheck` in *Chapters 1* to *3*, and `WorldCities` in *Chapters 4* to *7* – both feature *front-end* to *back-end* communication over the HTTP(S) protocol, and in order to establish such communication, we made good use of the `HttpClient` class, a built-in Angular HTTP API client shipped with the `@angular/common/http` package that rests on the `XMLHttpRequest` interface.

Angular's `HttpClient` class has a lot of benefits, including testability features, *request* and *response* typed objects, *request* and *response* interception, *Observable* APIs, and streamlined error handling. It can even be used without a *data server* thanks to the *in-memory web API package*, which emulates CRUD operations over a RESTful API: we briefly talked about that at the beginning of *Chapter 4*, *Data Model with Entity Framework Core*, when we were asking ourselves if we really needed a *data server* or not (the answer was no, therefore we didn't use it).

For all of the previously mentioned reasons, making good use of the `HttpClient` class is arguably the most logical choice for anyone who wants to develop a *front-end* web app using the Angular framework; that said, there are multiple ways to implement it, depending on how much we want to take advantage of its valuable features.

In this section, after a brief look at other available alternatives, we'll see how to refactor our app in order to replace our current `HttpClient` implementation with a more versatile approach, based upon a dedicated *HTTP Data Service*.

XMLHttpRequest versus Fetch (versus HttpClient)

As we said a moment ago, Angular's `HttpClient` class is based on **XMLHttpRequest** (**XHR**), an API consisting of an object that is provided by the browser through its JavaScript engine, which can be used to transfer data between a web browser and a web server in an *asynchronous* way, and without having to reload the whole page. This technique, which recently celebrated its 20-year anniversary, was basically the only available alternative until 2017, when the **Fetch API** eventually came out.

The Fetch API is another interface for fetching resources that aims to be a modern alternative to the `XMLHttpRequest` API, providing a more powerful and flexible feature set; in the next section, we'll quickly review both of them and discuss their pros and cons.

XMLHttpRequest

The concept behind this made its first appearance back in 1999, when Microsoft released the first version of **Outlook Web Access** (**OWA**) for MS Exchange Server 2000.

Here's an excerpt of a very old post written by Alex Hopmann, one of the developers who gave birth to it:

"XMLHTTP actually began its life out of the Exchange 2000 team. I had joined Microsoft in November 1996 and moved to Redmond in the spring of 1997, working initially on some Internet Standards stuff as related to the future of Outlook. I was specifically doing some work on meta-data for web sites including an early proposal called "Web Collections". During this time period Thomas Reardon one day dragged me down the hall to introduce me to this guy named Jean Paoli that had just joined the company. Jean was working on this new thing called XML that some people suspected would be very big someday (for some unclear reason at the time)."

– Alex Hopmann, The Story of XMLHTTP.

> The quote comes from a post on his blog, which unfortunately doesn't seem to be online anymore: `http://www.alexhopmann.com/xmlhttp.htm`
>
> However, there's an archived copy here: `http://archive.is/7i5l`

Alex was right: a few months later, his team released an interface called `IXMLHTTPRequest`, which was implemented in the second version of the **Microsoft XML Core Services** (**MSXML**) library. That version was then shipped with Internet Explorer 5.0 in March 1999, which arguably was the first browser that was able to access that interface (through ActiveX).

Soon after that, the Mozilla project developed an interface called `nsIXMLHttpRequest`, and implemented it into their Gecko layout engine; this was very similar to the Microsoft interface, but it also came with a wrapper that allowed it to be used through JavaScript, thanks to an object that was returned by the browser. The object, which was made accessible on Gecko v0.6 on December 6, 2000, was called `XMLHttpRequest`.

In the following years, the `XMLHttpRequest` object became a de facto standard in all major browsers, being implemented in *Safari 1.2* (February 2004), *Opera 8.0* (April 2005), *iCab 3.0b352* (September 2005), and *Internet Explorer 7* (October 2006). These early adoptions allowed Google engineers to develop and release *Gmail* (2004) and *Google Maps* (2005), two pioneering web applications, which were entirely based upon the `XMLHttpRequest` API. A single look at these apps was enough to understand that web development had entered a new era.

The only thing missing for this exciting technology was a name, which was found on February 18, 2005, when *Jesse James Garrett* wrote an iconic article called *AJAX: A New Approach to Web Applications*.

This was the first known **appearance of the term AJAX**, the acronym for **Asynchronous JavaScript + XML**, a set of web development techniques that can be used to create asynchronous web applications from the *client side*, where the `XMLHttpRequest` object played a pivotal role.

On April 5, 2006, the **World Wide Web Consortium** (**W3C**) released the first draft specification for the `XMLHttpRequest` object, in an attempt to create an official web standard.

> The latest draft of the `XMLHttpRequest` object was published on October 6, 2016, and is available at the following URL: `https://www.w3.org/TR/2016/NOTE-XMLHttpRequest-20161006/`

The W3C draft paved the way to the wide adoption of AJAX development. However, the first implementations were rather difficult for most web developers, due to some relevant differences among the various browsers' implementation of the involved APIs. Luckily enough, things became a lot easier thanks to the many cross-browser JavaScript libraries – such as *jQuery*, *Axios*, and *MooTools* – that were smart enough to add it to their available set of tools. This allowed developers to use the underlying `XMLHttpRequest` object functionality indirectly, through a standardized set of high-level methods.

Over time, the XHR data format quickly switched from XML to *JSON*, *HTML*, and *plain text*, which were more suited to work with the DOM page, without changing the overall approach. Also, when the **Reactive Extensions for JavaScript** (**RxJS**) library came out, the `XMLHttpRequest` object could be easily put behind `Observable`, thus gaining a lot of advantages (such as being able to mix and match it with other observables, *subscribe/unsubscribe*, *pipe/map*, and so on).

This is the main idea behind Angular's `HttpClient` class, which can be described as *the Angular way to deal with XMLHttpRequest*: a very convenient wrapper that allows developers to effectively use it through the `Observable` pattern.

Fetch

During its early years, using the raw `XMLHttpRequest` object was rather difficult for most web developers, and could easily lead to a large amount of JavaScript source code that was often difficult to read and understand; these issues were eventually solved by the *superstructures* that were brought by libraries such as *jQuery* and the like, but at the cost of some inevitable code (and resource) overheads.

The Fetch API was released to address such issues in a cleaner way, using a *built-in, promise-based* approach, which could be used to perform the same *asynchronous* server requests in an easy way, without requiring third-party libraries.

Here's an example of an HTTP request using *XHR*:

```
var oReq = new XMLHttpRequest();
oReq.onload = function() {
  // success
  var jsonData = JSON.parse(this.responseText);
};
oReq.onerror = function() {
  // error
  console.error(err);
};
```

```
oReq.open('get', './api/myCmd', true);
oReq.send();
```

And here's the same request performed using `fetch`:

```
fetch('./api/myCmd')
  .then((response) => {
    response.json().then((jsonData) => {
       // success
    });
  })
  .catch((err) => {
    // error
    console.error(err);
  });
```

As we can see, the fetch-based code is definitely more readable. Its generic interfaces provide better consistency, the native JSON capabilities make the code more DRY, and the *Promises* it returns permit easier *chaining* and *async/await* tasks without having to define callbacks.

Long story short, it doesn't take a genius to see that if we compare the raw XHR implementation with the brand-new `fetch()` API, the latter clearly wins.

HttpClient

However, thanks to Angular's `HttpClient` class, using raw XHR is out of the question; what we'll use is the built-in abstraction that is provided by the client, which allows us to write the previous code in the following way:

```
this.http.get('./api/myCmd')
  .subscribe(jsonData => {
    // success
  },
  error => {
    // error
    console.error(error));
  };
```

As we can see, the *Observable*-based code of `HttpClient` in the previous code provides similar benefits to the *fetch*-based code that we've seen before: we get a consistent interface, native JSON capabilities, *chaining*, and *async/await* tasks.

On top of that, *Observables* can also be converted into *Promises*, meaning that we could even do the following:

```
this.http.get('./api/myCmd')
  .toPromise()
  .then((response) => {
```

```
    response.json().then((jsonData) => {
      // success
    });
  })
  .catch((err) => {
    // error
    console.error(err);
  });
```

> At the same time, it's true that Promises can also be converted to Observables using the RxJS library.

All in all, both the *JavaScript-native* Fetch API and the *Angular-native* `HttpClient` class are perfectly viable and either of them can be effectively used in an Angular app.

Here are the major advantages of using **Fetch**:

- It's the *newest* industry standard that can be used to handle HTTP *requests* and *responses*.
- It's *JavaScript-native*; therefore, it can be used not only on *Angular*, but also on any other JavaScript-based *front-end* framework (such as *React*, *Vue*, and so on).
- It simplifies working with *service workers*, as the *Request* and *Response* objects are the same as the ones we are using in our normal code.
- It's built around the *norm* that HTTP requests have *single return values*, thus returning a *Promise* instead of a stream-like type, like the *Observer* is (this can be an advantage in most scenarios, but it can also become a disadvantage).

And here are the most relevant advantages of using `HttpClient`:

- It's *Angular-native*, and therefore widely supported and constantly updated by the framework (and will most likely be in the future as well).
- It allows easy mixing and matching of multiple *Observables*.
- Its abstraction level allows us to easily implement some *HTTP magic* (such as defining *auto-retry* attempts in case of request failures).
- *Observers* are arguably more versatile and feature-rich than *Promises*, which can be useful in some complex scenarios, such as performing *sequencing calls*, being able to cancel HTTP *requests* after they have been sent, and so on.
- It can be *injected*, and therefore used to write *unit tests* for various scenarios.

For all of these reasons, after careful consideration, we genuinely think that adopting `HttpClient` in Angular might be a better choice, and therefore we'll be sticking to it for the rest of the book. That said, since the Fetch API is almost as viable in most scenarios, readers can definitely try both approaches and see which one is the most fitting for any given task.

For the sake of simplicity, we're not going any further with these topics. Those who wants to know more about XMLHttpRequest, Fetch API, Observables, and Promises, are encouraged to check out the following URIs:

XMLHttpRequest Living Standard (September 24, 2019): https://xhr.spec.whatwg.org/

Fetch API - Concepts and usage: https://developer.mozilla.org/en-US/docs/Web/API/Fetch_API

RxJS - Observable: https://angular.io/guide/observables

MDN - Promise: https://developer.mozilla.org/en-US/docs/Web/JavaScript/Reference/Global_Objects/Promise

Building a data service

Since we've chosen to stick with the Angular's HttpClient class that we've already used everywhere, this means we're good, right?

Well, as a matter of fact, no. Although using HttpClient is definitely a good choice, we have implemented it using an oversimplified approach. If we look at our Angular source code, we can see how the actual HTTP calls are placed inside the *components*, which could be acceptable for small-scale sample apps, but it's definitely not the best way of doing it in real-life scenarios. What if we want to handle the HTTP errors in a more complex way (for example, sending them all to a remote server for statistical purposes)? What if we need to *cache* and/or *post-process* the data that we fetch through the *back-end* API? Not to mention the fact that we would definitely implement a retry logic in order to deal with potential connectivity issues, which is a typical requirement of any *Progressive Web App*.

Shall we implement all of the previous stuff within each *component's* set of methods? That's definitely not an option if we want to stick to the DRY pattern; maybe we could define a *superclass*, provide it with HTTP capabilities, and adapt our *subclasses'* source code to perform everything by calling the *super* methods with a bunch of highly customized parameters. Such a workaround could work for small tasks, but it could easily become a mess once things become more complex.

As a general rule, we should try our best to prevent our *TypeScript* classes - be they *standard*, *super*, or *sub* - from being cluttered with huge amounts of data access code. As soon as we fall into that pit, our component will become much more difficult to understand, and we will have a hard time whenever we want to upgrade, standardize, and/or test them. In order to avoid such an outcome, it's highly advisable to separate the *Data Access Layer* from the *Data Presentation Logic*, which can be done by encapsulating the former in a separate service, and then *injecting* that service into the component itself.

This is precisely what we're about to do.

Creating the BaseService

Since we're dealing with multiple component classes that handle different tasks depending on their *context* (that is, the data source that they need to access), it's highly advisable to create multiple services, one for each *context*.

More specifically, we'll need the following:

- `CityService`, to deal with the *city-related* Angular Components and ASP.NET Core web APIs
- `CountryService`, to deal with the *country-related* Angular Components and ASP.NET Core web APIs

Also, assuming that they will most likely have some relevant things in common, it might be useful to provide them both with a *superclass* that will act as a *common interface*. Let's do it.

> Using an abstract superclass as a common interface might seem a bit counter-intuitive: why don't we just create an interface, then? We already have two of them, for cities (`/cities/city.ts`) and countries (`/countries/country.ts`).
>
> As a matter of fact, we did that for a good reason: *Angular does not allow us to provide interfaces as providers*, because interfaces aren't compiled in the JavaScript output of TypeScript. Therefore, in order to create an interface for a service to an interface, the most effective way to do that is to use an abstract class.

From Solution Explorer, browse to the `/ClientApp/src/app/` folder, *right-click* to create a new `base.service.ts` file, and fill its contents with the following code:

```
import { HttpClient } from '@angular/common/http';

export abstract class BaseService {
  constructor(
    protected http: HttpClient,
    protected baseUrl: string
  ) {
  }
}
```

The preceding source code (minus the `abstract` and `protected` highlighted modifiers) is also the *core* of a typical HTTP data service: we're going to use it as a *base class* with which to `extend` our service classes; more precisely, we'll have a single *superclass* (`BaseService`) containing a *common interface* for the two different *subclasses* (`CityService` and `CountryService`) that will be injected in our *components*.

As for the two highlighted modifiers, let's try to shed some light on them:

- `abstract`: We've already used this modifier in the `BaseFormComponent` class early on. While we're here, let's talk a bit more about it. In TypeScript, an abstract class is a class that may have some unimplemented methods: these methods are called **abstract methods**. Abstract classes can't be created as instances, but other classes can extend the abstract class, and therefore reuse its constructor and members.
- `protected`: The `HttpClient` class will be required by all the service *subclasses*. Therefore, it's the first member that we're going to make available to them (and also the only one, at least for now). In order to do that, we need to use an *access modifier* that allows the subclasses to use it. In our sample, we've used *protected*, but we could have used *public* as well.

Before going any further, it might be useful to briefly recap how many *access modifiers* are supported by TypeScript and how they actually work. If we already know them from C# or other object-oriented programming languages, it'll be a familiar story for the most part.

TypeScript access modifiers

Access modifiers are a TypeScript concept that allow developers to declare methods and properties as *public*, *private*, *protected*, and *read-only*. If no modifier is provided, then the method or property is assumed to be *public*, meaning that it can be accessed internally and externally without issues. Conversely, if it is marked as *private*, that method or property will only be accessible within the class, *not including its subclasses* (if any). *Protected* implies that the method or property is accessible only internally *within the class and all its subclasses*, that is, any class that extends it, but not externally. Finally, *read-only* will cause the TypeScript compiler to throw an error if the value of the property is changed after its initial assignment in the class constructor.

However, it's important to keep in mind that *these access modifiers will be enforced only at compile time*. The TypeScript transpiler will warn us about all inappropriate uses, but it won't be able to stop inappropriate usage at runtime.

Adding the common interface methods

Let's now expand our `BaseService` *common interface* with some high-level methods that correspond to what we'll need to do in our subclasses. Since the *components* we're refactoring are already there, the best way to define these *common interface methods* is by reviewing their source code and acting accordingly.

Here's a good start:

```
import { HttpClient } from '@angular/common/http';
import { Observable } from 'rxjs';

export abstract class BaseService {
  constructor(
    protected http: HttpClient,
    protected baseUrl: string
  ) {
```

```
  }

  abstract getData<ApiResult>(
    pageIndex: number,
    pageSize: number,
    sortColumn: string,
    sortOrder: string,
    filterColumn: string,
    filterQuery: string): Observable<ApiResult>;

    abstract get<T>(id: number): Observable<T>;
    abstract put<T>(item: T): Observable<T>;
    abstract post<T>(item: T): Observable<T>;
}

export interface ApiResult<T> {
  data: T[];
  pageIndex: number;
  pageSize: number;
  totalCount: number;
  totalPages: number;
  sortColumn: string;
  sortOrder: string;
  filterColumn: string;
  filterQuery: string;
}
```

Let's briefly review each one of the preceding abstract methods:

- `getData<ApiResult>()`: This is meant to replace our current implementation for the `getData()` methods in our `CitiesComponent` and `CountriesComponent` TypeScript files to retrieve, respectively, the *cities* and *countries* lists. As we can see, we took the chance to specify a new *strongly typed* interface – `ApiResult` – which will be populated with the structured JSON output that we already receive from the `GetCities` and `GetCountries` ASP.NET Core web APIs.
- `get<T>()`: This will replace our current implementation for the `loadData()` methods of our `CityEditComponent` and `CountryEditComponent` TypeScript files.
- `put<T>()` and `post<T>()`: These will replace our current implementations for the `submit()` methods of our `CityEditComponent` and `CountryEditComponent` TypeScript files.

Since we're using a good number of generic-type variables, it may be useful to briefly recap what they are and how they can help us to define our common interfaces.

Type variables and generic types – <T> and <any>

It's worth noting that for the *get*, *put*, and *post* methods, we didn't use a *strongly typed* interface, but we went for a *type variable* instead; we were kind of forced to do that because these methods will return either a `City` or a `Country` interface, depending on the *derived* class that will implement them.

Taking that into account, we will choose to use `<T>`, instead of `<any>`, so that we won't lose the information about what that type was when the function returns. The `<T>` generic type allows us to defer the specification of the returned variable type until the class or method is declared and instantiated by the client code, meaning that *we'll be able to capture the type of the given argument whenever we implement the method in the derived class* (that is, when we know what is being returned).

> The type `<T>` variable is a great way to deal with unknown types in an interface, to the point that we've also used it in the preceding `ApiResult` Angular interface, just like we did in the `/Data/ApiResult.cs` C# file in the .NET back-end.

These concepts are nothing new, since we've already used them in our *back-end* code: it's just great that we can also use them on the Angular *front-end*, thanks to the TypeScript programming language.

Why return Observables and not JSON?

Before moving on, it could be wise to briefly explain why we've chosen to return `Observable` types instead of the actual *JSON-based interfaces* that we already have, such as `City`, `Country`, and `ApiResult`. Wouldn't it be a more practical choice?

As a matter of fact, it's the exact opposite: our *interface* types have extremely limited options if we compare them to the feature-rich `Observable` collections that we've talked about a number of times since *Chapter 3, Front-End and Back-End Interactions*. Why would we want to limit ourselves – and the components that will call these methods? Even if we wanted (or needed) to actually execute the HTTP call and retrieve the data from within them, we could always recreate `Observable`, and return it after such a task. We'll talk about this more in the next chapters.

Creating the CityService

Let's now create our first derived service, that is, our first BaseService's *derived* class (or *subclass*).

From Solution Explorer, browse to the `/ClientApp/src/app/cities/` folder, *right-click* to create a new `city.service.ts` file, and fill it with the following code:

```
import { Injectable, Inject } from '@angular/core';
import { HttpClient, HttpParams } from '@angular/common/http';
import { BaseService, ApiResult } from '../base.service';
import { Observable } from 'rxjs';

import { City } from './city';

@Injectable({
  providedIn: 'root',
})
export class CityService
  extends BaseService {
  constructor(
    http: HttpClient,
    @Inject('BASE_URL') baseUrl: string) {
      super(http, baseUrl);
  }

  getData<ApiResult>(
    pageIndex: number,
    pageSize: number,
    sortColumn: string,
    sortOrder: string,
    filterColumn: string,
    filterQuery: string
    ): Observable<ApiResult> {
    var url = this.baseUrl + 'api/Cities';
    var params = new HttpParams()
      .set("pageIndex", pageIndex.toString())
      .set("pageSize", pageSize.toString())
      .set("sortColumn", sortColumn)
      .set("sortOrder", sortOrder);

      if (filterQuery) {
        params = params
          .set("filterColumn", filterColumn)
          .set("filterQuery", filterQuery);
      }

      return this.http.get<ApiResult>(url, { params });
  }

  get<City>(id): Observable<City> {
```

```
    var url = this.baseUrl + "api/Cities/" + id;
    return this.http.get<City>(url);
  }

  put<City>(item): Observable<City> {
    var url = this.baseUrl + "api/Cities/" + item.id;
    return this.http.put<City>(url, item);
  }

  post<City>(item): Observable<City> {
    var url = this.baseUrl + "api/Cities";
    return this.http.post<City>(url, item);
  }
}
```

The most relevant aspect of the preceding source code is the `providedIn` property in the service's `@Injectable()` decorator, which we've set to `root`. This will tell Angular to provide this injectable in the application root, thus making it a *singleton* service, by all means.

> A singleton service is a service for which only one instance exists in an app. In other words, Angular will create only one instance of that service, which will be shared with all the components that will use it (through dependency injection) in our application. Although Angular services are not required to be singleton, such a technique provides an efficient use of memory and good performance, thereby making it the most frequently used implementation approach.
>
> For additional info about singleton services, check out the following URL: `https://angular.io/guide/singleton-services`

Other than that, there's nothing new in the preceding code: we just copied (and slightly adapted) the implementation that already exists in our `CitiesComponent` and `CityEditComponent` TypeScript files. The main difference is that we're now using `HttpClient` here, meaning that we can remove it from the component classes and abstract its usage with `CityService` instead.

Implementing the CityService

Let's now refactor our Angular Components to use our brand-new `CityService` instead of the raw `HttpClient`. As we'll be able to see in a short while, the new singleton services pattern that we used (and talked about) earlier will make things slightly easier than before.

AppModule

In Angular versions prior to 6.0, the only way to make a *singleton* service available throughout the app would have been to reference it within the `AppModule` file in the following way:

```
// ...existing code...

import { CityService } from './cities/city.service';

// ...existing code...

  providers: [ CityService ],

// ...existing code...
```

As we can see, we should have added the `import` statement for the new service at the beginning of the `AppModule` file, and also registered the service itself in the existing (albeit still empty) `providers: []` section.

Luckily enough, since we've used the `providedIn: root` approach that was introduced with Angular 6.0, the previous technique is no longer required – although it is still supported as a viable alternative.

> As a matter of fact, the `providedIn: root` approach is preferable, because it makes our service tree-shakable. **Tree shaking** is a method of optimizing the JavaScript-compiled code bundles by eliminating any code from the final file that isn't actually being used.
>
> For additional info about tree shaking in JavaScript, take a look at the following URL: `https://developer.mozilla.org/en-US/docs/Glossary/Tree_shaking`

Long story short, thanks to the new approach, we no longer have to update the `AppModule` file: we just need to refactor the components that will use the service.

CitiesComponent

From Solution Explorer, open the `/ClientApp/src/app/cities/cities.component.ts` file and update its content accordingly:

```
import { Component, Inject, OnInit, ViewChild } from '@angular/core';
// import { HttpClient, HttpParams } from '@angular/common/http';
import { MatTableDataSource } from '@angular/material/table';
import { MatPaginator, PageEvent } from '@angular/material/paginator';
import { MatSort } from '@angular/material/sort';

import { Subject } from 'rxjs';
import { debounceTime, distinctUntilChanged } from 'rxjs/operators';

import { City } from './city';
import { CityService } from './city.service';
import { ApiResult } from '../base.service';
```

```
@Component({
  selector: 'app-cities',
  templateUrl: './cities.component.html',
  styleUrls: ['./cities.component.css']
})

// ...existing code...

  constructor(
    private cityService: CityService) {
  }

// ...existing code...

getData(event: PageEvent) {

  var sortColumn = (this.sort)
    ? this.sort.active
    : this.defaultSortColumn;

  var sortOrder = (this.sort)
    ? this.sort.direction
    : this.defaultSortOrder;

  var filterColumn = (this.filterQuery)
    ? this.defaultFilterColumn
    : null;

  var filterQuery = (this.filterQuery)
    ? this.filterQuery
    : null;

  this.cityService.getData<ApiResult<City>>(
    event.pageIndex,
    event.pageSize,
    sortColumn,
    sortOrder,
    filterColumn,
    filterQuery)
      .subscribe(result => {
        this.paginator.length = result.totalCount;
        this.paginator.pageIndex = result.pageIndex;
        this.paginator.pageSize = result.pageSize;
        this.cities = new MatTableDataSource<City>(result.data);
```

```
        }, error => console.error(error));
    }
}
```

As we can see, we just had to perform some minor updates:

- In the `import` section, we added some references to our new files.
- In the constructor, we switched the existing `http` variable of the `HttpClient` type with a brand-new `cityService` variable of the `CityService` type. We could also have retained the old variable name and just changed the type, but we preferred to change that as well, to avoid confusion.
- Since we're no longer dealing with the `HttpClient` directly, we don't need `BASE_URL` to be injected into this component class. Therefore, we removed the DI entry from the constructor's parameters.
- Last but not least, we changed the `getData()` method's existing implementation—based upon the `HttpClient`—for a new one that relies upon the new `CityService`.

It's worth noting that we have commented out all the `import` references from the `@angular/common/http` package, simply because we no longer need them now that we're not directly using that stuff in this class.

CityEditComponent

Implementing `CityService` in `CityEditComponent` is going to be just as easy as it was for `CitiesComponents`.

From Solution Explorer, open the `/ClientApp/src/app/cities/city-edit.component.ts` file and update its content accordingly:

```
import { Component, Inject, OnInit } from '@angular/core';
import { HttpClient, HttpParams } from '@angular/common/http';
import { ActivatedRoute, Router } from '@angular/router';
import { FormGroup, FormControl, Validators, AbstractControl, AsyncValidatorFn }
from '@angular/forms';
import { Observable } from 'rxjs';
import { map } from 'rxjs/operators';
import { BaseFormComponent } from '../base.form.component';

import { City } from './city';
import { Country } from '../countries/country';
import { CityService } from './city.service';
import { ApiResult } from '../base.service';

// ...existing code...

  constructor(
    private activatedRoute: ActivatedRoute,
```

```
    private router: Router,
    private http: HttpClient,
    private cityService: CityService,
    @Inject('BASE_URL') private baseUrl: string) {
      super();
  }

// ...existing code...

  onSubmit() {

    var city = (this.id) ? this.city : <City>{};

    city.name = this.form.get("name").value;
    city.lat = +this.form.get("lat").value;
    city.lon = +this.form.get("lon").value;
    city.countryId = +this.form.get("countryId").value;

    if (this.id) {
      // EDIT mode
      this.cityService
        .put<City>(city)
        .subscribe(result => {

          console.log("City " + city.id + " has been updated.");

          // go back to cities view
          this.router.navigate(['/cities']);
        }, error => console.error(error));
    }
    else {
      // ADD NEW mode
      this.cityService
        .post<City>(city)
        .subscribe(result => {

          console.log("City " + result.id + " has been created.");

          // go back to cities view
          this.router.navigate(['/cities']);
        }, error => console.error(error));
    }
  }

// ...existing code...
```

As we can see, this time we weren't able to get rid of the `@angular/common/http` package reference, because we still need `HttpClient` to perform some specific tasks – `loadCountries()` and `isDupeCity()` – that we can't handle with our current service. In order to fix these issues, it definitely seems like we need to implement two more methods in `CityService`.

Let's do this!

Implementing loadCountries and IsDupeCity in CityService

From Solution Explorer, open the `/ClientApp/src/app/cities/city.service.ts` file and add the following methods at the end of the file, just before the last curly bracket:

```
// ...existing code...

getCountries<ApiResult>(
  pageIndex: number,
  pageSize: number,
  sortColumn: string,
  sortOrder: string,
  filterColumn: string,
  filterQuery: string
): Observable<ApiResult> {
  var url = this.baseUrl + 'api/Countries';
  var params = new HttpParams()
    .set("pageIndex", pageIndex.toString())
    .set("pageSize", pageSize.toString())
    .set("sortColumn", sortColumn)
    .set("sortOrder", sortOrder);

  if (filterQuery) {
    params = params
      .set("filterColumn", filterColumn)
      .set("filterQuery", filterQuery);
  }

  return this.http.get<ApiResult>(url, { params });
}

isDupeCity(item): Observable<boolean> {
  var url = this.baseUrl + "api/Cities/IsDupeCity";
  return this.http.post<boolean>(url, item);
}
```

With this new service method, we can patch our `CityEditComponent` class file in the following way:

```
import { Component, Inject, OnInit } from '@angular/core';
```

```
// import { HttpClient, HttpParams } from '@angular/common/http';

// ...existing code...

  constructor(
    private activatedRoute: ActivatedRoute,
    private router: Router,
    private cityService: CityService) {
    super();
  }

// ...existing code...

  loadData() {

    // load countries
    this.loadCountries();

    // retrieve the ID from the 'id'
    this.id = +this.activatedRoute.snapshot.paramMap.get('id');
    if (this.id) {
      // EDIT MODE

      // fetch the city from the server
      this.cityService.get<City>(this.id).subscribe(result => {
        this.city = result;
        this.title = "Edit - " + this.city.name;

        // update the form with the city value
        this.form.patchValue(this.city);
      }, error => console.error(error));
    }
    else {
      // ADD NEW MODE

      this.title = "Create a new City";
    }
  }

  loadCountries() {
    // fetch all the countries from the server
    this.cityService.getCountries<ApiResult<Country>>(
      0,
      9999,
      "name",
      null,
```

```
        null,
        null,
        ).subscribe(result => {
          this.countries = result.data;
        }, error => console.error(error));
    }

  // ...existing code...

    isDupeCity(): AsyncValidatorFn {
      return (control: AbstractControl): Observable<{ [key: string]:
       any } | null> => {

        var city = <City>{};
        city.id = (this.id) ? this.id : 0;
        city.name = this.form.get("name").value;
        city.lat = +this.form.get("lat").value;
        city.lon = +this.form.get("lon").value;
        city.countryId = +this.form.get("countryId").value;

        return this.cityService.isDupeCity(city)
          .pipe(map(result => {
            return (result ? { isDupeCity: true } : null);
          }));
      }
    }
  }
```

And that's it! Now, we are able to remove the `@angular/common/http` references, the `HttpClient` usage, and the `BASE_URL` injected parameter from our `CityEditComponent` code.

In the next section, we'll do the same with the *country-related* components.

> Before going further, it would be wise to check what we have done so far by hitting *F5* and ensuring that everything is still working as before. If we did everything correctly, we should see no differences: our new `CityService` should be able to transparently perform all the tasks that were previously handled by `HttpClient`. That's expected, since we're still using it under the hood!

Creating the CountryService

It's now time to create `CountryService`, which will be our second – and last – BaseService's *derived* class (or *subclass*).

From Solution Explorer, browse to the `/ClientApp/src/app/countries/` folder, *right-click* to create a new `country.service.ts` file, and fill it with the following code:

```
import { Injectable, Inject } from '@angular/core';
import { HttpClient, HttpParams } from '@angular/common/http';
import { BaseService, ApiResult } from '../base.service';
import { Observable } from 'rxjs';

import { Country } from './country';

@Injectable({
  providedIn: 'root',
})
export class CountryService
  extends BaseService {
  constructor(
    http: HttpClient,
    @Inject('BASE_URL') baseUrl: string) {
    super(http, baseUrl);
  }

  getData<ApiResult>(
    pageIndex: number,
    pageSize: number,
    sortColumn: string,
    sortOrder: string,
    filterColumn: string,
    filterQuery: string
  ): Observable<ApiResult> {
    var url = this.baseUrl + 'api/Countries';
    var params = new HttpParams()
      .set("pageIndex", pageIndex.toString())
      .set("pageSize", pageSize.toString())
      .set("sortColumn", sortColumn)
      .set("sortOrder", sortOrder);

    if (filterQuery) {
      params = params
      .set("filterColumn", filterColumn)
      .set("filterQuery", filterQuery);
    }

      return this.http.get<ApiResult>(url, { params });
  }

  get<Country>(id): Observable<Country> {
```

```
    var url = this.baseUrl + "api/Countries/" + id;
    return this.http.get<Country>(url);
  }

  put<Country>(item): Observable<Country> {
    var url = this.baseUrl + "api/Countries/" + item.id;
    return this.http.put<Country>(url, item);
  }

  post<Country>(item): Observable<Country> {
    var url = this.baseUrl + "api/Countries";
    return this.http.post<Country>(url, item);
  }

  isDupeField(countryId, fieldName, fieldValue): Observable<boolean> {
    var params = new HttpParams()
      .set("countryId", countryId)
      .set("fieldName", fieldName)
      .set("fieldValue", fieldValue);
    var url = this.baseUrl + "api/Countries/IsDupeField";
    return this.http.post<boolean>(url, null, { params });
  }
}
```

As we can see, this time we went ahead of time and took the chance to directly add the `isDupeField()` method, since we're definitely going to need it to refactor the validator of our `CountryEditComponent` in a short while.

As always, now that we have created the service, we need to implement it within our app. Luckily enough, as we already explained earlier on, we don't have to reference it in our `AppModule` file; we just need to properly implement it in our country-related components.

CountriesComponent

From Solution Explorer, open the `/ClientApp/src/app/countries/countries.component.ts` file and update its content accordingly:

```
import { Component, Inject, OnInit, ViewChild } from '@angular/core';
// import { HttpClient, HttpParams } from '@angular/common/http';
import { MatTableDataSource } from '@angular/material/table';
import { MatPaginator, PageEvent } from '@angular/material/paginator';
import { MatSort } from '@angular/material/sort';

import { Subject } from 'rxjs';
import { debounceTime, distinctUntilChanged } from 'rxjs/operators';

import { Country } from './country';
import { CountryService } from './country.service';
```

```
import { ApiResult } from '../base.service';

@Component({
  selector: 'app-countries',
  templateUrl: './countries.component.html',
  styleUrls: ['./countries.component.css']
})
export class CountriesComponent implements OnInit {
  public displayedColumns: string[] = ['id', 'name', 'iso2', 'iso3',
'totCities'];
  public countries: MatTableDataSource<Country>;

  defaultPageIndex: number = 0;
  defaultPageSize: number = 10;
  public defaultSortColumn: string = "name";
  public defaultSortOrder: string = "asc";

  defaultFilterColumn: string = "name";
  filterQuery: string = null;

  @ViewChild(MatPaginator) paginator: MatPaginator;
  @ViewChild(MatSort) sort: MatSort;

  constructor(
    private countryService: CountryService) {
  }

  // ...existing code...

  getData(event: PageEvent) {

    var sortColumn = (this.sort)
      ? this.sort.active
      : this.defaultSortColumn;

    var sortOrder = (this.sort)
      ? this.sort.direction
      : this.defaultSortOrder;

    var filterColumn = (this.filterQuery)
      ? this.defaultFilterColumn
      : null;

    var filterQuery = (this.filterQuery)
      ? this.filterQuery
      : null;

    this.countryService.getData<ApiResult<Country>>(
```

```
      event.pageIndex,
      event.pageSize,
      sortColumn,
      sortOrder,
      filterColumn,
      filterQuery)
      .subscribe(result => {
        this.paginator.length = result.totalCount;
        this.paginator.pageIndex = result.pageIndex;
        this.paginator.pageSize = result.pageSize;
        this.countries = new MatTableDataSource<Country>(result.data);
      }, error => console.error(error));
  }
}
```

Nothing new here; we just repeated what we did with `CitiesComponent` a short while ago.

CountryEditComponent

From Solution Explorer, open the `/ClientApp/src/app/countries/country-edit.component.ts` file and change its content in the following way:

```
import { Component, Inject, OnInit } from '@angular/core';
// import { HttpClient, HttpParams } from '@angular/common/http';
import { ActivatedRoute, Router } from '@angular/router';
import { FormGroup, FormBuilder, Validators, AbstractControl, AsyncValidatorFn }
from '@angular/forms';
import { map } from 'rxjs/operators';
import { Observable } from 'rxjs';
import { BaseFormComponent } from '../base.form.component';

import { Country } from '../countries/country';
import { CountryService } from './country.service';

@Component({
  selector: 'app-country-edit',
  templateUrl: './country-edit.component.html',
  styleUrls: ['./country-edit.component.css']
})
export class CountryEditComponent
  extends BaseFormComponent implements OnInit {

  // the view title
  title: string;

  // the form model
  form: FormGroup;
```

```
// the city object to edit or create
country: Country;

// the city object id, as fetched from the active route:
// It's NULL when we're adding a new country,
// and not NULL when we're editing an existing one.
id?: number;

constructor(
  private fb: FormBuilder,
  private activatedRoute: ActivatedRoute,
  private router: Router,
  private countryService: CountryService) {
  super();
}

ngOnInit() {
  this.form = this.fb.group({
    name: ['',
      Validators.required,
      this.isDupeField("name")
    ],
    iso2: ['',
      [
        Validators.required,
        Validators.pattern(/^[a-zA-Z]{2}$/)
      ],
      this.isDupeField("iso2")
    ],
    iso3: ['',
      [
        Validators.required,
        Validators.pattern(/^[a-zA-Z]{3}$/)
      ],
      this.isDupeField("iso3")
    ]
  });

  this.loadData();
}

loadData() {

  // retrieve the ID from the 'id'
  this.id = +this.activatedRoute.snapshot.paramMap.get('id');
```

```
    if (this.id) {
      // EDIT MODE

      // fetch the country from the server
      this.countryService.get<Country>(this.id)
        .subscribe(result => {
          this.country = result;
          this.title = "Edit - " + this.country.name;

          // update the form with the country value
          this.form.patchValue(this.country);
        }, error => console.error(error));
    }
    else {
      // ADD NEW MODE

      this.title = "Create a new Country";
    }
  }

  onSubmit() {

    var country = (this.id) ? this.country : <Country>{};

    country.name = this.form.get("name").value;
    country.iso2 = this.form.get("iso2").value;
    country.iso3 = this.form.get("iso3").value;

    if (this.id) {
      // EDIT mode
      this.countryService
        .put<Country>(country)
        .subscribe(result => {

          console.log("Country " + country.id + " has been updated.");

          // go back to cities view
          this.router.navigate(['/countries']);
        }, error => console.error(error));
    }
    else {
      // ADD NEW mode
      this.countryService
        .post<Country>(country)
```

```
        .subscribe(result => {
          console.log("Country " + result.id + " has been created.");

          // go back to cities view
          this.router.navigate(['/countries']);
        }, error => console.error(error));
    }
  }

  isDupeField(fieldName: string): AsyncValidatorFn {
    return (control: AbstractControl): Observable<{ [key: string]:
      any } | null> => {

      var countryId = (this.id) ? this.id.toString() : "0";

      return this.countryService.isDupeField(
        countryId,
        fieldName,
        control.value)
        .pipe(map(result => {
          return (result ? { isDupeField: true } : null);
      }));
    }
  }
}
```

As we can see, the code changes that we applied here are very similar to what we did in `CityEditComponent`. Since we took the chance to preventively add the `isDupeField()` method in our `CountryService` class, this time we were able to get rid of the `@angular/common/http` package in a single shot.

That's it, at least for now. In the next chapter, we'll make good use of these new services. However, before going further, you are strongly advised to perform some debug runs (by hitting *F5*) in order to ensure that everything is still working.

Summary

In this chapter, we have spent some valuable time consolidating the existing source code of our WorldCities Angular app. We successfully implemented some optimizations and tweaks by making good use of the TypeScript class inheritance features, and we learned how to create base classes (*superclasses*) and derived classes (*subclasses*), thus making our source code more maintainable and DRY. At the same time, we took the chance to perform some bug fixing and add a couple of new features to our app's UI.

Right after that, we refined the data fetching capabilities of our Angular app by switching from a direct usage of the Angular's `HttpClient` class in our components to a more versatile *service-based* approach. Eventually, we created `CityService` and `CountryService` – both extending a `BaseService` abstract class – to deal with all the HTTP requests, thus paving the way for post-processing, error handling, retry logic, and more interesting stuff that will be introduced in the upcoming chapter.

Suggested topics

Object-oriented programming, polymorphism, inheritance, AJAX, XMLHttpRequest, Fetch API, Angular HttpClient, Angular services, RxJS, Observables, Promises, tree shaking, singleton services, TypeScript access modifiers, TypeScript generic types, base classes and derived classes, superclasses and subclasses, access modifiers.

References

- *Jesse James Garrett – AJAX: A New Approach to Web Applications*: `https://web.archive.org/web/20061107032631/http://www.adaptivepath.com/publications/essays/archives/000385.php`
- *The XMLHttpRequest Object – W3C First Working Draft (April 5, 2006)*: `https://www.w3.org/TR/2006/WD-XMLHttpRequest-20060405/`
- *Alex Hopmann talks about XMLHttpRequest (currently offline)*: `http://www.alexhopmann.com/xmlhttp.htm`
- *Alex Hopmann talks about XMLHttpRequest (archived copy)*: `http://archive.is/7i5l`
- *XMLHttpRequest Level 1 – W3C Latest Draft (October 6, 2016)*: `https://www.w3.org/TR/2016/NOTE-XMLHttpRequest-20161006/`
- *XMLHttpRequest Living Standard (September 24, 2019)*: `https://xhr.spec.whatwg.org/`
- *Fetch API – Concepts and usage*: `https://developer.mozilla.org/en-US/docs/Web/API/Fetch_API`
- *RxJS – Observable*: `https://angular.io/guide/observables`
- *MDN – Promise*: `https://developer.mozilla.org/en-US/docs/Web/JavaScript/Reference/Global_Objects/Promise`
- *Angular – Singleton services*: `https://angular.io/guide/singleton-services`
- *Tree shaking in JavaScript*: `https://developer.mozilla.org/en-US/docs/Glossary/Tree_shaking`
- *TypeScript: Access Modifiers*: `http://www.typescriptlang.org/docs/handbook/classes.html#public-private-and-protected-modifiers`
- *TypeScript: Generic Types*: `https://www.typescriptlang.org/docs/handbook/generics.html`

- *Anonymous Types in C#*: `https://docs.microsoft.com/en-us/dotnet/csharp/programming-guide/classes-and-structs/anonymous-types`
- *Create Data Transfer Objects (DTOs)*: `https://docs.microsoft.com/en-us/aspnet/web-api/overview/data/using-web-api-with-entity-framework/part-5`
- *Pros and Cons of Data Transfer Objects*: `https://docs.microsoft.com/en-us/archive/msdn-magazine/2009/brownfield/pros-and-cons-of-data-transfer-objects`
- *Microsoft.EntityFrameworkCore Namespace*: `https://docs.microsoft.com/en-us/dotnet/api/microsoft.entityframeworkcore`
- *System.Text.Json.Serialization Namespace*: `https://docs.microsoft.com/en-us/dotnet/api/system.text.json.serialization`
- *Refactoring code*: `https://docs.microsoft.com/en-us/visualstudio/ide/refactoring-in-visual-studio`

8

Back-End and Front-End Debugging

One of the most relevant features of all *programming* languages (such as C#) and most *scripting* languages (such as JavaScript) is the debugging capabilities they offer to developers.

> *"If debugging is the process of removing software bugs, then programming must be the process of putting them in."*
>
> – *E. W. Dijkstra*

The term debugging universally refers to the process of finding and resolving the issues and/or problems, commonly called **bugs**, that prevent a program or an application from working as expected. In a nutshell, we can say that the debugging process allows the developer to better understand how the source code is being executed under the hood and why it produces the result that it does.

Debugging is a very important skill for any developer, arguably as much as programming itself; it's a skill that all developers have to learn with theory, practice, and experience, just like coding.

The best way to fulfill these tasks is by making use of a debugger—a tool that allows running the target program under controlled conditions. This enables the developer to track its operations in real time, halting them using breakpoints, executing them step by step, viewing the values of the underlying type, and so on. Advanced debugger features also allow the developer to access the memory contents, CPU registers, storage device activities, and so on, viewing or altering their values to reproduce specific conditions that might be causing the addressed issues.

Luckily enough, **Visual Studio** provides a set of debuggers that can be used to track any .NET application. Although most of its features have been designed to debug the managed code portion of our app (for example, our C# files), some of them—when configured properly—can be very useful to track the client-side code as well. Throughout this chapter, we'll learn how to use them, as well as the various debugging tools built into some web browsers such as Chrome, Firefox, and Edge to constantly monitor and keep under control the whole HTTP workflow of our *WorldCities* app.

For practical reasons, the debugging process has been split into two separate sections:

- The back-end, where the debug tasks are mostly being handled using the Visual Studio and .NET Core tools
- The front-end, where both Visual Studio and the web browser play a major role

The last section of the chapter is dedicated to back-end logging using the .NET logging API and a third-party logging provider (Serilog).

By the end of this chapter, we'll have learned how to properly debug our web application's Web API, as well as our Angular components, using the various debugging and logging tools provided by Visual Studio and ASP.NET Core to their full extent.

Technical requirements

In this chapter, we're going to need all the technical requirements listed in the previous chapters, plus the following external libraries:

- The `Serilog.AspNetCore` NuGet package
- The `Serilog.Settings.Configuration` NuGet package
- The `Serilog.Sinks.MSSqlServer` NuGet package

The code files for this chapter can be found here: `https://github.com/PacktPublishing/ASP.NET-5-and-Angular/tree/master/Chapter_08/`

Back-end debugging

In this section, we'll learn how to make use of the debug features offered by the Visual Studio environment to take a look at the server-side life cycle of our web application and understand how we can properly troubleshoot some potential flaws.

However, before doing that, let's spend a couple of minutes seeing how it works for the various operating systems available.

Windows or Linux?

For the sake of simplicity, we'll take for granted that we're using the Visual Studio Community, Professional, or Enterprise edition for Windows operating systems. However, since .NET Core and .NET 5 have been designed to be cross-platform, there are at least two options for those who want to debug in other environments, such as Linux or macOS:

- Using Visual Studio Code, a lightweight and open source alternative to Visual Studio available for Windows, Linux, and macOS with full debug support
- Using Visual Studio, thanks to the Docker container tools available since Visual Studio 2017 and built into Visual Studio 2019 since version 16.3

> Visual Studio Code can be downloaded for free (under the MIT license) from the following URL: `https://code.visualstudio.com/download`
>
> Visual Studio Docker container tools require Docker for Windows, which can be installed from the following URL: `https://docs.docker.com/docker-for-windows/install/`
>
> The container tools usage information is available here: `https://docs.microsoft.com/en-us/aspnet/core/host-and-deploy/docker/visual-studio-tools-for-docker`
>
> For additional information about the .NET Core debugging features under Linux and macOS, check out the following URL: `https://github.com/Microsoft/MIEngine/wiki/Offroad-Debugging-of-.NET-Core-on-Linux---OSX-from-Visual-Studio`

In this book, for the sake of simplicity, we'll stick to the Windows environment, thus making use of the Visual Studio set of debuggers available for Windows.

The basics

We'll take for granted that everyone who is reading this book already knows all the basic debugging features offered by Visual Studio, such as the following:

- Debug versus Release build configuration modes
- Breakpoints and how to set and use them
- Stepping in and out of a program
- The *Watch*, *Call Stack*, *Locals*, and *Immediate* windows

> For those who don't know (or remember) them well enough, here's a great tutorial that can be useful if you want a quick recap: `https://docs.microsoft.com/en-US/dotnet/core/tutorials/debugging-with-visual-studio?tabs=csharp`

In the following section, we'll briefly introduce some advanced debug options that can be useful in our specific scenarios.

Conditional breakpoints

The conditional breakpoint is a useful debugging feature that is often unknown to (or underutilized by) most developers; it acts just like a normal breakpoint, but it only triggers when certain conditions are met.

To set a conditional breakpoint, just click on the *Settings* contextual icon (the one with a cogwheel) that appears when we create a standard breakpoint, as shown in the following screenshot:

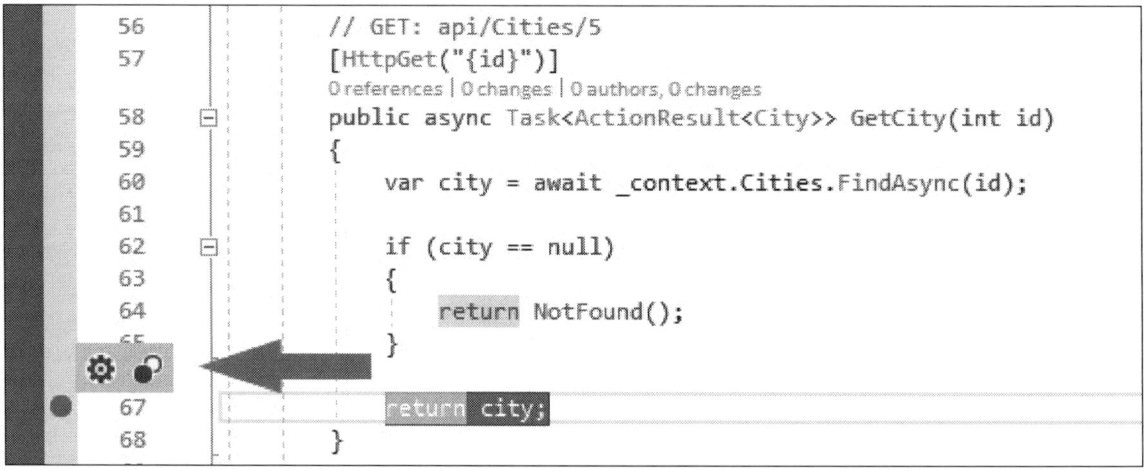

Figure 8.1: Creating a conditional breakpoint

As soon as we do that, a panel will appear at the bottom of the window showing a number of possible conditional settings that we can configure for that breakpoint:

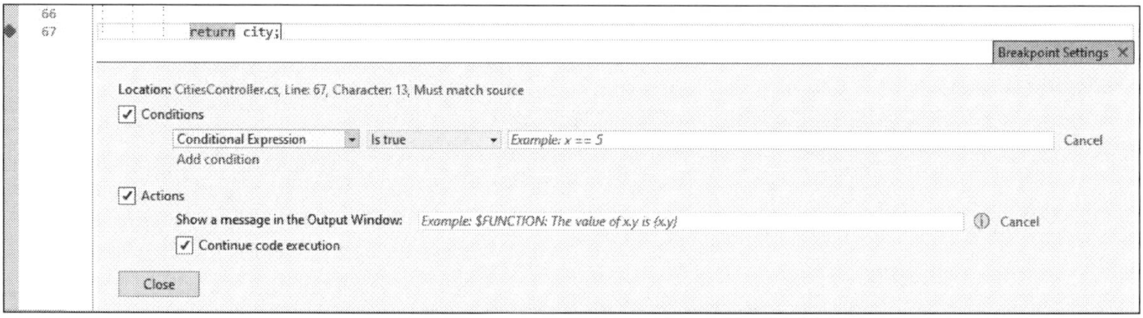

Figure 8.2: Conditional breakpoint settings panel

As we can see, there are a number of possible settings available (**Conditions**, **Actions**, and so on). Let's see how we can use them.

Conditions

If we check the **Conditions** checkbox, we'll be able to define the code condition that will trigger the breakpoint.

To better explain how it works, let's perform a quick debugging test:

1. From **Solution Explorer**, open the `/Controllers/CitiesController.cs` file.
2. Set a breakpoint on the last line of the `GetCity()` method (the one that returns the city to the client once it has been found—see the following screenshot for details).
3. Click the **Settings** icon to access the **Breakpoint Settings** panel.
4. Activate the **Conditions** checkbox.
5. Select **Conditional Expression** and **Is true** in the two drop-down lists.
6. Type the following condition into the textbox to the right: `city.Name == "Moscow"`.

Once done, our **Breakpoint Settings** panel should look like the following screenshot:

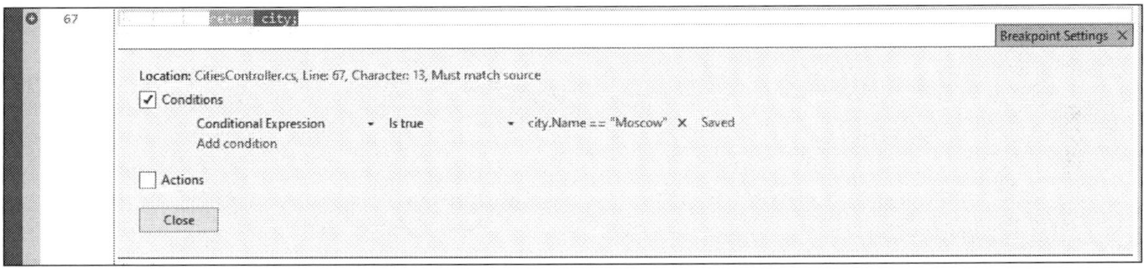

Figure 8.3: Activating the Conditions checkbox

As we can see, our condition has been created; the interface lets us add other conditions, as well as perform certain **Actions** by activating the checkbox below it.

Actions

The **Actions** feature can be used to show a custom message in the **Output** window (such as, **Hey, we're currently editing Moscow from Angular!**) and/or choose whether the code execution should continue or not. If no **Action** is specified, the breakpoint will behave normally, without emitting messages and halting the code execution.

While we're here, let's take the chance to test the **Actions** feature as well. Activate the checkbox, then type the message in the previous paragraph into the rightmost textbox.

Once done, our **Breakpoint Settings** panel should look like the following screenshot:

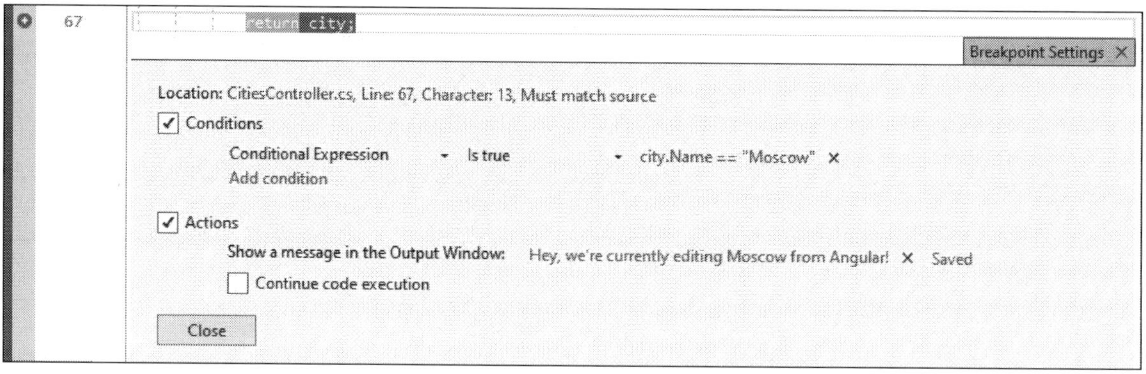

Figure 8.4: Activating the Actions checkbox

We've just created our first conditional breakpoint; let's quickly test it to see how it works.

Testing the conditional breakpoint

To test what happens when the breakpoint is hit, run the `WorldCities` app in debug mode (by hitting *F5*), navigate to the **Cities** view, filter the table to locate the city of **Moscow**, and click on its name to enter edit mode.

If everything has been done properly, our conditional breakpoint should trigger and behave in the following way:

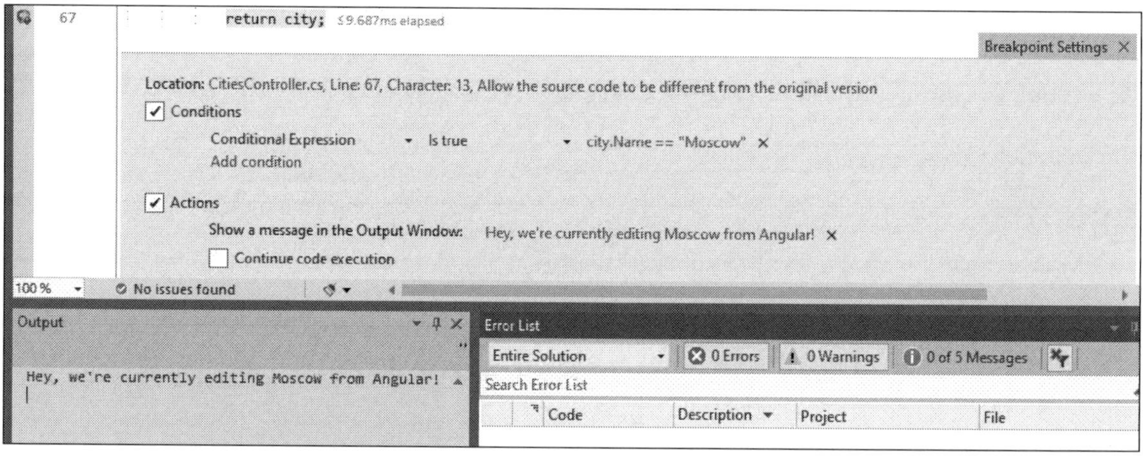

Figure 8.5: Outcome after triggering the conditional breakpoint

As we can see, the **Output** window has been populated with our custom message as well. If we now repeat the same test with any other city with a different name (for example, Rome, Prague, or New York), that same breakpoint won't trigger at all; nothing will happen.

> It's worth mentioning that there are two cities called Moscow in our WorldCities database: the Russian capital city and a city in Idaho, USA. It goes without saying that our conditional breakpoint will trigger on both of them because it only checks for the `Name` property. If we wanted to limit its scope to the Russian city only, we should refine the conditional expression to also match the `CityId`, the `CountryId`, or any other suitable property.

All good so far; let's move on.

The Output window

In the previous section, we talked about the Visual Studio **Output** window, which we used to write a custom message whenever our conditional breakpoint was being hit.

If you have some experience with the Visual Studio debugger, you'll know about the utmost importance of this window for understanding what happens behind the curtains. The **Output** window shows the status messages for various features in the IDE, meaning that most .NET middlewares, libraries, and packages write their relevant information there, just like we did with our conditional breakpoint.

> To open the **Output** window, either choose **View** | **Output** from the main menu bar or press *Ctrl* + *Alt* + *O*.

If we take a look at what happened in the **Output** window during the test we have just performed, we can see a lot of interesting stuff:

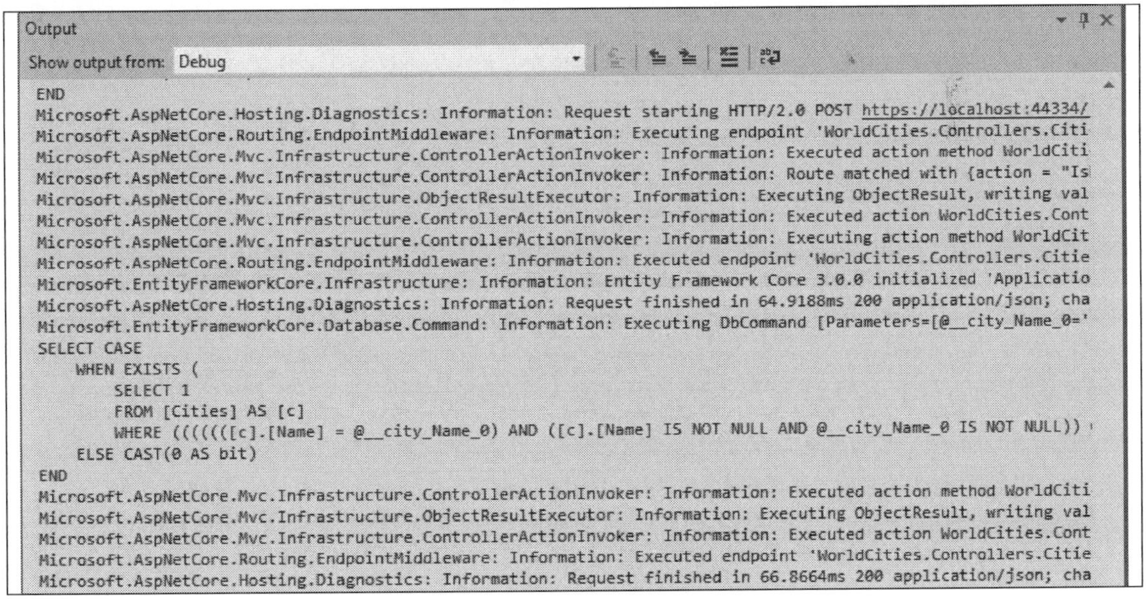
Output
Show output from: Debug
END
Microsoft.AspNetCore.Hosting.Diagnostics: Information: Request starting HTTP/2.0 POST https://localhost:44334/
Microsoft.AspNetCore.Routing.EndpointMiddleware: Information: Executing endpoint 'WorldCities.Controllers.Citi
Microsoft.AspNetCore.Mvc.Infrastructure.ControllerActionInvoker: Information: Executed action method WorldCiti
Microsoft.AspNetCore.Mvc.Infrastructure.ControllerActionInvoker: Information: Route matched with {action = "Is
Microsoft.AspNetCore.Mvc.Infrastructure.ObjectResultExecutor: Information: Executing ObjectResult, writing val
Microsoft.AspNetCore.Mvc.Infrastructure.ControllerActionInvoker: Information: Executed action WorldCities.Cont
Microsoft.AspNetCore.Mvc.Infrastructure.ControllerActionInvoker: Information: Executing action method WorldCit
Microsoft.AspNetCore.Routing.EndpointMiddleware: Information: Executed endpoint 'WorldCities.Controllers.Citie
Microsoft.EntityFrameworkCore.Infrastructure: Information: Entity Framework Core 3.0.0 initialized 'Applicatio
Microsoft.AspNetCore.Hosting.Diagnostics: Information: Request finished in 64.9188ms 200 application/json; cha
Microsoft.EntityFrameworkCore.Database.Command: Information: Executing DbCommand [Parameters=[@__city_Name_0='
SELECT CASE
WHEN EXISTS (
SELECT 1
FROM [Cities] AS [c]
WHERE (((((([c].[Name] = @__city_Name_0) AND ([c].[Name] IS NOT NULL AND @__city_Name_0 IS NOT NULL))
ELSE CAST(0 AS bit)
END
Microsoft.AspNetCore.Mvc.Infrastructure.ControllerActionInvoker: Information: Executed action method WorldCiti
Microsoft.AspNetCore.Mvc.Infrastructure.ObjectResultExecutor: Information: Executing ObjectResult, writing val
Microsoft.AspNetCore.Mvc.Infrastructure.ControllerActionInvoker: Information: Executed action WorldCities.Cont
Microsoft.AspNetCore.Routing.EndpointMiddleware: Information: Executed endpoint 'WorldCities.Controllers.Citie
Microsoft.AspNetCore.Hosting.Diagnostics: Information: Request finished in 66.8664ms 200 application/json; cha

Figure 8.6: The Visual Studio Output window

As we can see, there are pieces of information coming out from a number of different sources, including the following:

- `Microsoft.AspNetCore.Hosting.Diagnostics`: The .NET Core middleware dedicated to exception handling, exception display pages, and diagnostics information. It handles developer exception page middleware, exception handler middleware, runtime information middleware, status code page middleware, and welcome page middleware. In a nutshell, it's the king of the **Output** window when debugging web applications.
- `Microsoft.AspNetCore.Mvc.Infrastructure`: The namespace that handles (and tracks) the controller's actions and responds to the .NET Core MVC middleware.
- `Microsoft.AspNetCore.Routing`: The .NET Core middleware that handles static and dynamic routing, such as all our web application's URI endpoints.
- `Microsoft.EntityFrameworkCore`: The .NET Core middleware that handles the connections to the data source; for example, our SQL server, which we extensively talked about in *Chapter 4, Data Model with Entity Framework Core*.

All this information is basically a sequential log of everything that happens during our web application's execution. We can learn a lot from the .NET Core life cycle just by performing a user-driven action and reading it.

Configuring the Output window

Needless to say, the Visual Studio interface allows us to filter the output and/or choose the level of detail of the captured information.

To configure what to show and what to hide, select **Tools | Options** from the main menu, then navigate to **Debugging | Output Window** from the tree menu item to the right. From that panel, we can select (or deselect) a number of output messages: **Exception Messages**, **Module Load Messages/Module Unload Messages**, **Process Exit Messages**, **Step Filtering Messages**, and so on:

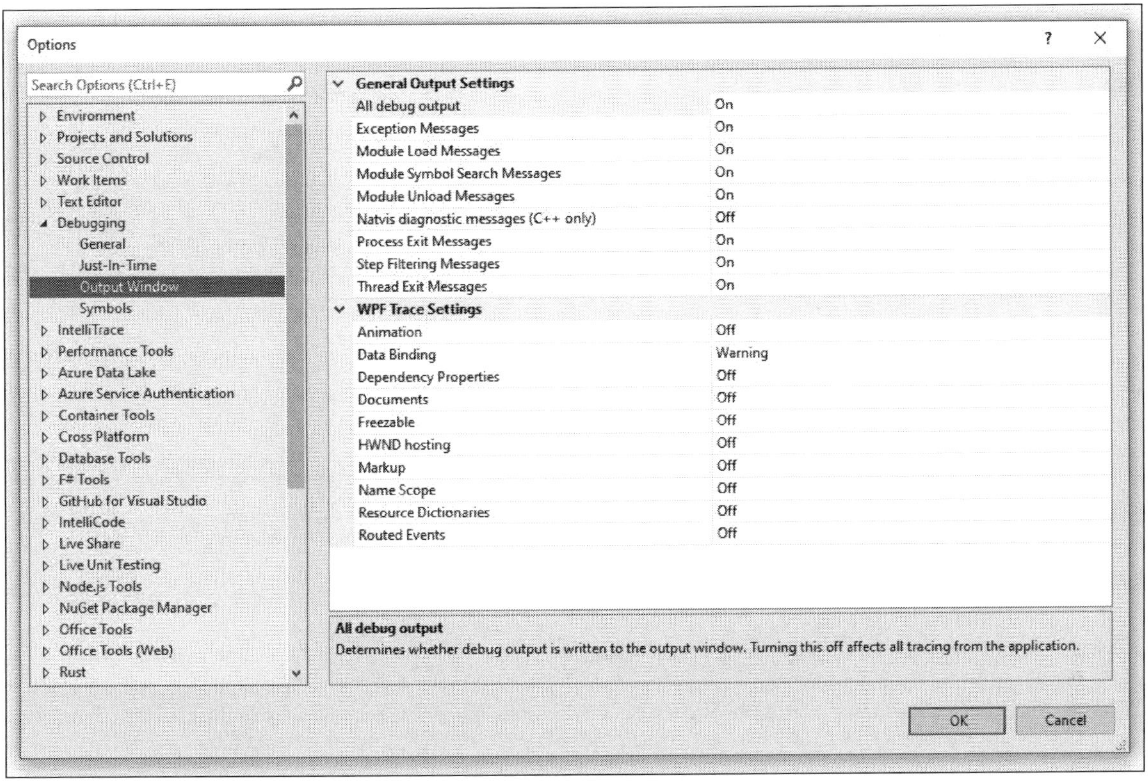

Figure 8.7: Output window configuration

Now that we've got the gist of the back-end debugging output, let's move our focus to one of the middlewares that arguably requires special attention: **Entity Framework** (**EF**) **Core**.

Debugging EF Core

If we take a look at the **Output** window right after one of our web application's runs in debug mode, we should be able to see a bunch of SQL queries written in plain text. These are the queries used by the underlying **LINQ to SQL provider**, which is in charge of translating all our lambda expressions, query expressions, IQueryable objects, and expression trees into valid T-SQL queries.

Here's the output information line emitted by the `Microsoft.EntityFrameworkCore` middleware containing the SQL query used to retrieve the city of Moscow (the actual SQL query is highlighted):

```
Microsoft.EntityFrameworkCore.Database.Command: Information: Executing DbCommand
[Parameters=[@__p_0='?' (DbType = Int32), @__p_1='?' (DbType = Int32)],
CommandType='Text', CommandTimeout='30']
SELECT [c].[Id], [c].[Name], [c].[Lat], [c].[Lon], [c0].[Id] AS [CountryId],
[c0].[Name] AS [CountryName]
FROM [Cities] AS [c]
INNER JOIN [Countries] AS [c0] ON [c].[CountryId] = [c0].[Id]
WHERE CHARINDEX(N'moscow', [c].[Name]) > 0
ORDER BY [c].[Name]
OFFSET @__p_0 ROWS FETCH NEXT @__p_1 ROWS ONLY
```

Not bad, right? These SQL queries in clear text might be very useful to determine whether the LINQ to SQL provider does a good job or not when converting our lambda or LINQ query expressions in terms of performance.

The GetCountries() SQL query

Let's try to use this same technique to retrieve the SQL query that corresponds to the CountriesController's `GetCountries()` method implementation, which we refined during *Chapter 7, Code Tweaks and Data Services*, to include the cities count.

Here's the source code snippet:

```
return await ApiResult<CountryDTO>.CreateAsync(
        _context.Countries
            .Select(c => new CountryDTO()
            {
                Id = c.Id,
                Name = c.Name,
                ISO2 = c.ISO2,
                ISO3 = c.ISO3,
                TotCities = c.Cities.Count
            }),
        pageIndex,
        pageSize,
        sortColumn,
        sortOrder,
        filterColumn,
        filterQuery);
```

To see how it was converted into T-SQL, do the following:

1. Hit *F5* to run the web app in debug mode.
2. Navigate to the **Countries** view.
3. Take a look at the resulting **Output** window (searching for `TotCities` will help there).

Here's the SQL query that we should find there:

```
SELECT [c0].[Id], [c0].[Name], [c0].[ISO2], [c0].[ISO3], (
    SELECT COUNT(*)
    FROM [Cities] AS [c]
    WHERE [c0].[Id] = [c].[CountryId]) AS [TotCities]
FROM [Countries] AS [c0]
ORDER BY [c0].[Name]
OFFSET @__p_0 ROWS FETCH NEXT @__p_1 ROWS ONLY
```

That's not bad; the LINQ to SQL provider converted it using a subquery, which is a good choice in terms of performance. The `OFFSET` part of the SQL query, together with the `DBCommand` parameters mentioned in the preceding code snippet, handles the pagination and ensures that we're only getting the rows we've been asking for.

However, the Visual Studio **Output** window is not the only way to take a look at those SQL queries—we can provide ourselves with an even better alternative by implementing a simple, yet effective, extension method, as we're going to see in the following sections.

Getting the SQL code programmatically

The **Output** window is good enough for most scenarios, but what if we want to retrieve the SQL code from an `IQueryable<T>` programmatically? Such an option might be very useful to debug (or conditionally debug) some parts of our app, especially if we want to automatically save these SQL queries outside the **Output** window (for example, a log file or a log aggregator service).

In order to achieve such a result, we need to create a dedicated helper function that will be able to do that using `System.Reflection`. Let's quickly do that and test out how it works.

From the Solution Explorer, right-click the `/Data/` folder, create a new `IQueryableExtensions.cs` file, and fill its content with the following source code:

```
using Microsoft.Data.SqlClient;
using Microsoft.EntityFrameworkCore.Query;
using Microsoft.EntityFrameworkCore.Query.Internal;
using Microsoft.EntityFrameworkCore.Query.SqlExpressions;
using System;
using System.Collections;
using System.Collections.Generic;
using System.Linq;
using System.Reflection;
```

```
namespace WorldCities.Data
{
    public static class IQueryableExtension
    {
        public static (string, IEnumerable<SqlParameter>)  ToParametrizedSql
(this IQueryable query)
        {
            string relationalCommandCacheText = "_relationalCommandCache";
            string selectExpressionText = "_selectExpression";
            string querySqlGeneratorFactoryText = "_querySqlGeneratorFactory";
            string relationalQueryContextText = "_relationalQueryContext";

            string cannotGetText = "Cannot get";

            var enumerator = query.Provider.Execute<IEnumerable>(query.
Expression).GetEnumerator();
            var relationalCommandCache = enumerator.Private(relationalCommandCac
heText) as RelationalCommandCache;
            var queryContext = enumerator.Private<RelationalQueryContext>(relat
ionalQueryContextText) ?? throw new InvalidOperationException($"{cannotGetText}
{relationalQueryContextText}");
            var parameterValues = queryContext.ParameterValues;

            string sql;
            IList<SqlParameter> parameters;
            if (relationalCommandCache != null)
            {
#pragma warning disable EF1001 // Internal EF Core API usage.
                var command = relationalCommandCache.GetRelationalCommand(parame
terValues);
#pragma warning restore EF1001 // Internal EF Core API usage.
                var parameterNames = new HashSet<string>(command.Parameters.
Select(p => p.InvariantName));
                sql = command.CommandText;
                parameters = parameterValues.Where(pv => parameterNames.
Contains(pv.Key)).Select(pv => new SqlParameter("@" + pv.Key, pv.Value)).
ToList();
            }
            else
            {
                SelectExpression selectExpression = enumerator.Private<SelectExp
ression>(selectExpressionText) ?? throw new InvalidOperationException($"{cannotG
etText} {selectExpressionText}");
                IQuerySqlGeneratorFactory factory = enumerator.Private<IQuerySql
GeneratorFactory>(querySqlGeneratorFactoryText) ?? throw new InvalidOperationExc
eption($"{cannotGetText} {querySqlGeneratorFactoryText}");
```

```
                var sqlGenerator = factory.Create();
                var command = sqlGenerator.GetCommand(selectExpression);
                sql = command.CommandText;
                parameters = parameterValues.Select(pv => new SqlParameter("@" +
pv.Key, pv.Value)).ToList();
            }

            return (sql, parameters);
        }

        private static readonly BindingFlags bindingFlags = BindingFlags.
Instance | BindingFlags.NonPublic;
        private static object Private(this object obj, string privateField) =>
obj?.GetType().GetField(privateField, bindingFlags)?.GetValue(obj);
        private static T Private<T>(this object obj, string privateField) => (T)
obj?.GetType().GetField(privateField, bindingFlags)?.GetValue(obj);
    }
}
```

As we can see, we took the chance to create the helper class as an `IQueryable<T>` extension method. This allows us to extend the functionality of the `IQueryable<T>` type without creating a new derived type, modifying the original type, or creating a static function that will explicitly require it as a reference parameter.

> For those who have never heard of them, C# extension methods are static methods that can be called as if they were instance methods on the extended type. For further information, take a look at the following URL from the Microsoft C# programming guide: `https://docs.microsoft.com/en-us/dotnet/csharp/programming-guide/classes-and-structs/extension-methods`

Now that we've created the `IQueryableExtension` static class, we can use the `ToParametrizedSql()` extension method in any other class, as long as it includes a reference to the `WorldCities.Data` namespace.

Let's see how we can implement the previous extension in our `ApiResult.cs` class, which is the place where most of our `IQueryable<T>` objects get executed.

Implementing the ToParametrizedSql() method

From Solution Explorer, select the `/Data/ApiResult.cs` file, open it for editing, and add the following lines to the existing `CreateAsync` method implementation (the new lines are highlighted):

```
// ...existing code...
```

```
public static async Task<ApiResult<T>> CreateAsync(
    IQueryable<T> source,
    int pageIndex,
    int pageSize,
    string sortColumn = null,
    string sortOrder = null,
    string filterColumn = null,
    string filterQuery = null)
{
    if (!string.IsNullOrEmpty(filterColumn)
        && !string.IsNullOrEmpty(filterQuery)
        && IsValidProperty(filterColumn))
    {
        source = source.Where(
            string.Format("{0}.Contains(@0)",
            filterColumn),
            filterQuery);
    }

    var count = await source.CountAsync();

    if (!string.IsNullOrEmpty(sortColumn)
        && IsValidProperty(sortColumn))
    {
        sortOrder = !string.IsNullOrEmpty(sortOrder)
            && sortOrder.ToUpper() == "ASC"
            ? "ASC"
            : "DESC";
        source = source.OrderBy(
            string.Format(
                "{0} {1}",
                sortColumn,
                sortOrder)
            );
    }

    source = source
        .Skip(pageIndex * pageSize)
        .Take(pageSize);

    // retrieve the SQL query (for debug purposes)
    var sql = source.ToParametrizedSql();

    var data = await source.ToListAsync();

    return new ApiResult<T>(
```

```
        data,
        count,
        pageIndex,
        pageSize,
        sortColumn,
        sortOrder,
        filterColumn,
        filterQuery);
}

// ...existing code...
```

As we can see, we added a single variable to store the results of our new extension method. Let's quickly test it out to see how it works.

> It's worth noting that, since the `ApiResult.cs` class is part of the `WorldCities.Data` namespace, we didn't have to add the `using` reference at the top.

Put a breakpoint on the line of the `ApiResult.cs` class, immediately below the new lines we added earlier on (as shown in the following screenshot). Once done, hit *F5* to run the web application in debug mode, then navigate to the **Countries** view.

The breakpoint should hit, as shown in the following screenshot:

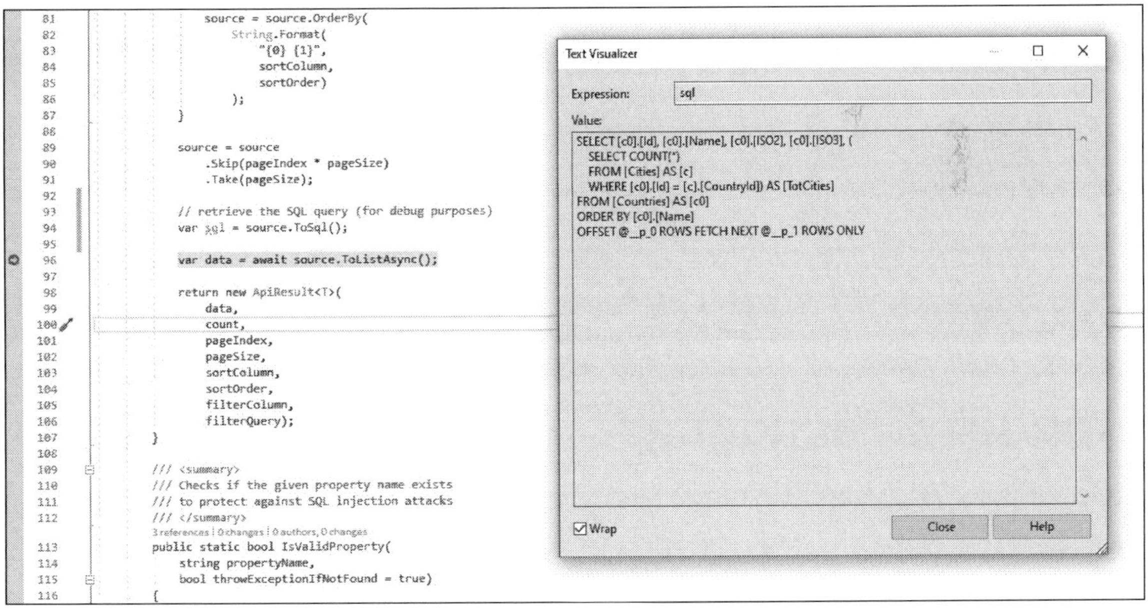

Figure 8.8: Seeing the SQL query when the breakpoint is triggered

If we move our mouse cursor over the `sql` variable and click the magnifier lens icon, we'll be able to see the SQL query in the **Text Visualizer** window. Now, we know how to quickly view the SQL queries produced by EF Core from our `IQueryable<T>` objects.

Using the #if preprocessor

If we are worried about the performance hit of the `ToParametrizedSql()` method task, we can definitely tweak the previous code using the `#if` preprocessor in the following way:

```
// retrieve the SQL query (for debug purposes)
#if DEBUG
{
    var sql = source.ToParametrizedSql();
    // do something with the sql string
}
#endif
```

As we can see, we have wrapped the `ToParametrizedSql()` method call in an `#if` *preprocessor directive* block: when the C# compiler encounters these directives, it will compile the code between them only if the specified symbol is defined. More specifically, the `DEBUG` symbol that we used in the previous code will prevent that wrapped code from being compiled unless the web application is being run in debug mode, thus avoiding any performance loss in release/production builds.

> For additional information regarding the C# preprocessor directives, take a look at the following URLs:
>
> C# preprocessor directives: `https://docs.microsoft.com/en-us/dotnet/csharp/language-reference/preprocessor-directives/`
>
> `#if` preprocessor directives: `https://docs.microsoft.com/en-us/dotnet/csharp/language-reference/preprocessor-directives/preprocessor-if`

There is still a lot to say about the back-end debugging features offered by Visual Studio and .NET Core; however, for reasons of space, it's better to stop here for the time being and move on to the front-end.

Front-end debugging

In this section, we'll briefly review the various front-end debugging options we have available (Visual Studio or the browser's developer tools). Right after that, we'll take a look at some Angular features that we can leverage to increase our awareness of the various tasks performed by our client-side application under the hood and debug them.

Visual Studio JavaScript debugging

Front-end debugging works just like back-end debugging, thanks to the **JavaScript debugging** feature of Visual Studio. The JavaScript debugger is not enabled by default, but the Visual Studio IDE will automatically ask whether to activate it or not the first time we put a breakpoint on a JavaScript (or TypeScript) file and run our app in debug mode.

As of the time of writing, client-side debugging support is only provided for Chrome and Microsoft Edge. On top of that, since we're using TypeScript and not JavaScript directly, the use of source maps is required if we want to set and hit breakpoints in the TypeScript file (our Angular component class file) and not in the JavaScript-transpiled file.

Luckily enough, the Angular template we're using (see *Chapter 1*, *Getting Ready*, and *Chapter 2*, *Looking Around*) already provides source map support, as we can see by taking a look at the `sourceMap` parameter value in the `/ClientApp/tsconfig.json` file:

```
[...]

"sourceMap": true

[...]
```

This means that we can do the following:

1. Open the `/ClientApp/src/app/countries/countries.component.ts` file.
2. Place a breakpoint inside the subscription to the `Observable` returned by the `countryService` (see the following screenshot for details).
3. Hit *F5* to launch the web application in debug mode.

If we did everything correctly, the Visual Studio IDE should ask us whether we want to enable JavaScript debugging, as shown in the following screenshot:

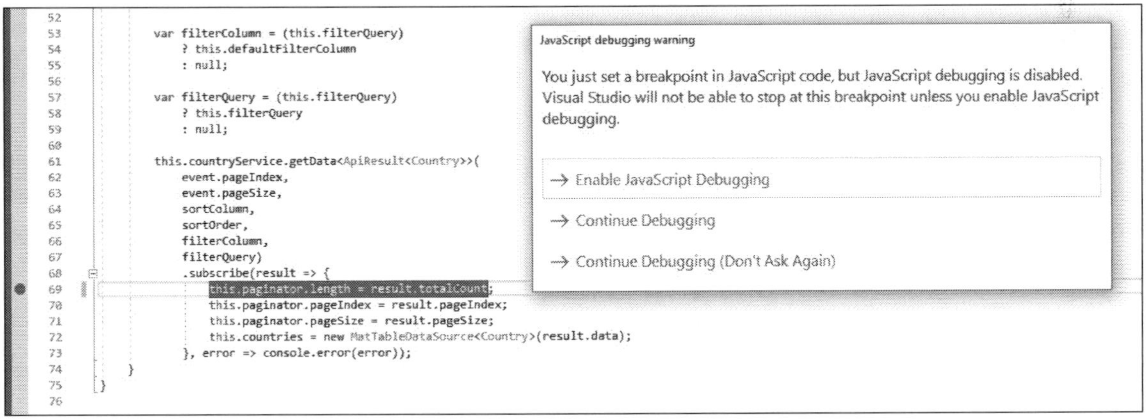

Figure 8.9: JavaScript debugging warning popup

Once enabled, the runtime environment will stop the program execution as soon as we navigate to the **Countries** view. Needless to say, we'll be able to inspect the various members of the Angular component class:

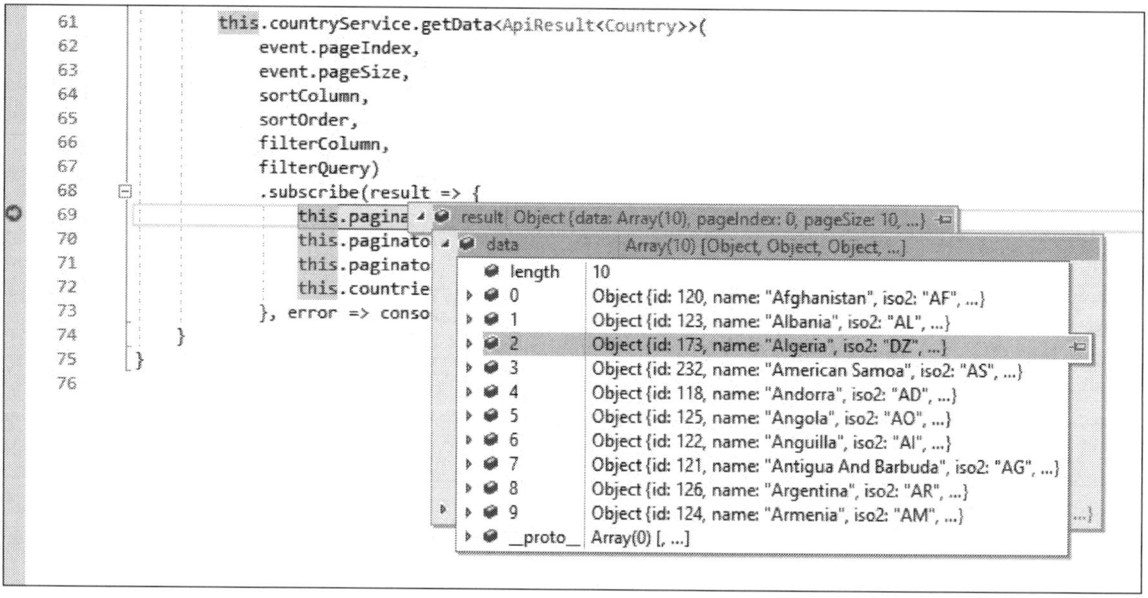

Figure 8.10: Inspecting the Angular Component class

That's pretty cool, right? We can even define conditional breakpoints and use the *Watch*, *Call Stack*, *Locals*, and *Immediate* windows without significant flaws.

> For additional information about debugging a TypeScript or JavaScript app in Visual Studio, take a look at the following URL: `https://docs.microsoft.com/en-US/visualstudio/javascript/debug-nodejs`

In the next section, we're going to introduce another important front-end debugging resource: JavaScript source maps.

JavaScript source maps

For those who don't know what source maps actually are, let's try to briefly summarize the concept.

Technically speaking, a source map is a file that maps the code within a compressed, combined, minified, and/or transpiled file back to its original position in a source file. Thanks to these mappings, we can debug our applications even after our assets have been optimized.

> **Minification**, also known as **minimisation** or **minimization**, is the process of removing all unnecessary characters from the source code of interpreted programming languages or markup languages without changing its functionality: white spaces, new line/carriage returns, comments, and everything that is not required for the code to be executed. Minification is good for a production environment because it will reduce the size of the source code, thus making its transmission more efficient in terms of bandwidth.

As we saw a moment ago, source maps are extensively used by the Visual Studio JavaScript debugger to enable us to set breakpoints within the TypeScript source code, and they are also supported by the Google Chrome, Mozilla Firefox, and Microsoft Edge developer tools, thus allowing these browsers' built-in debuggers to display the unminified and uncombined source to the developer, even when dealing with compressed and minified files.

> For additional information about JavaScript source maps, check out the following URLs:
>
> *Introduction to JavaScript Source Maps*, Ryan Seddon: `https://www.html5rocks.com/en/tutorials/developertools/sourcemaps/`
>
> *An Introduction to Source Maps*, Matt West: `https://blog.teamtreehouse.com/introduction-source-maps`

However, given our specific scenario, the debugging capabilities of the aforementioned browsers might not be ideal; in the next section, we'll do our best to explain why.

Browser developer tools

As we can easily guess, the Visual Studio JavaScript debugging feature is not the only way we can debug a client-side script. However, since we're dealing with a TypeScript application, it's arguably the best available option due to the fact that it allows the debugging of the `.ts` files through the autogenerated source maps.

Although the browser's built-in debugging tools can definitely use the source maps to make us deal with the unminified and uncombined files, they cannot do anything to revert these transpiled files back into their former TypeScript classes—because they have never seen them to begin with.

For that very reason, if we try to activate, for example, the Chrome developer tools to debug our `CountriesComponent` Angular class, we'll experience something like this:

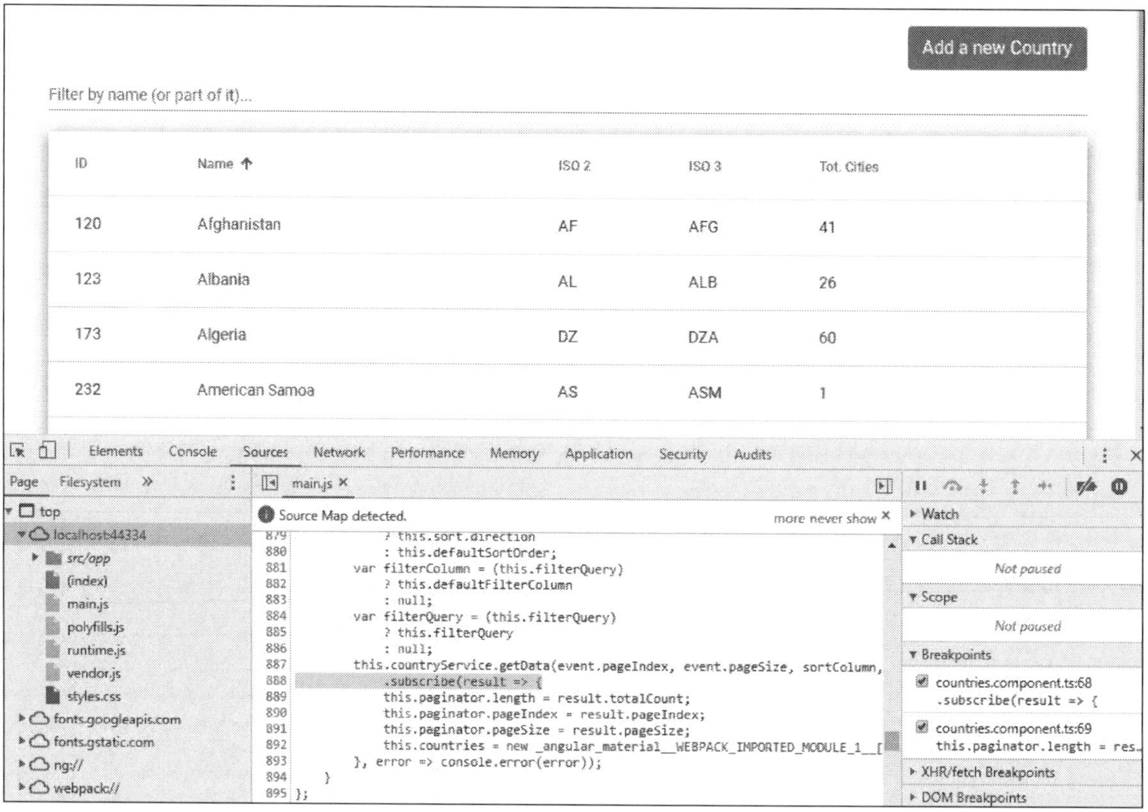

Figure 8.11: Chrome developer tools

As we can see, the TypeScript file is not there. The browser is dealing with a huge `main.js` transpiled file, which basically contains all the Angular components. In that file, the aforementioned line of the `CountriesComponent` class (line 69 or so) corresponds to line 888 (see the previous screenshot; the actual line number might vary).

However, as soon as we click on that line to set a breakpoint there, the corresponding TypeScript file will also become accessible, just like in Visual Studio:

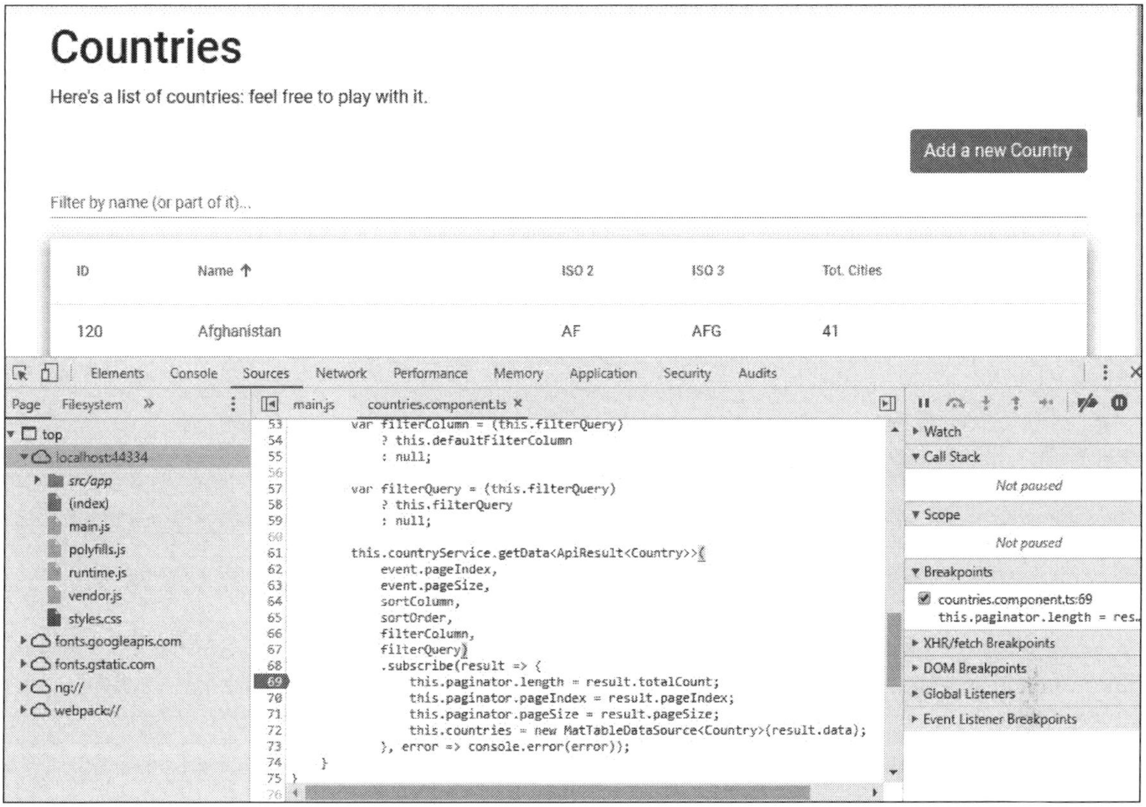

Figure 8.12: Seeing the countries.components.ts file after setting a breakpoint

How is such a thing possible? Didn't we just say that the browser doesn't know anything about the TypeScript class?

As a matter of fact, it doesn't; however, since we're running the app in a development environment, our .NET Core application is using `AngularCliMiddleware` to serve our Angular app, thus forwarding all the HTTP requests there.

We've already seen this setting in the `Startup.cs` file:

```
// [...]

app.UseSpa(spa =>
{
    // To learn more about options for serving an Angular SPA from
    // ASP.NET Core,
    // see https://go.microsoft.com/fwlink/?linkid=864501

    spa.Options.SourcePath = "ClientApp";

    if (env.IsDevelopment())
    {
        spa.UseAngularCliServer(npmScript: "start");
    }
});

// [...]
```

The `UseAngularCliServer()` method will internally invoke `AngularCliMiddleware`, which will do the following:

1. Start an npm instance (using a dynamic port)
2. Use that dynamic port to perform an `ng serve` (serve the Angular app)
3. Create a transparent proxy to forward all the HTTP requests to the Angular dev server

Thanks to all this, the browser, although receiving only the `main.js` JavaScript transpiled file, will still be able to follow the source map to reach the underlying TypeScript files.

However, even if we set the breakpoint on the TypeScript page, as soon as we make it trigger, we'll be brought back to the `main.js` file, as shown in the following screenshot:

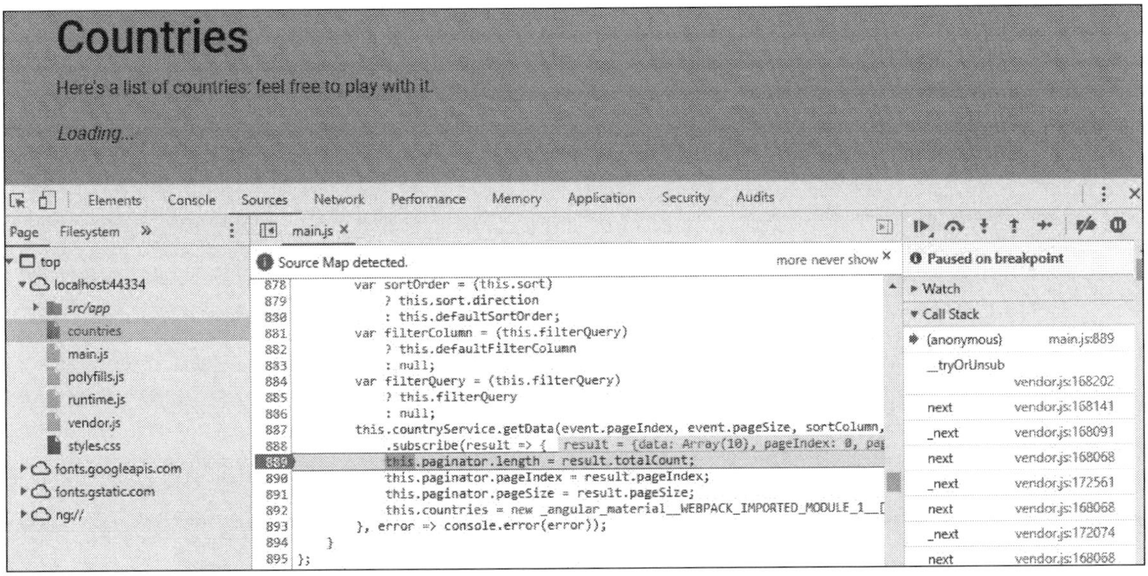

Figure 8.13: View of main.js after triggering a breakpoint set on the TypeScript page

This behavior is hardly a surprise; the browser's built-in debugger can retrieve the TypeScript classes from the proxy using the source maps, yet it's clearly unable to directly handle/debug them.

For that very reason, at least in our specific scenario, the Visual Studio front-end debugging features (using the built-in JavaScript debugger) are arguably the most effective way to debug our Angular application nowadays.

Angular form debugging

In this section, we're going to spend some of our valuable time understanding some key concepts related to form debugging.

As we mentioned in *Chapter 6, Forms and Data Validation*, one of the advantages granted by the model-driven approach is the fact that it allows us to have granular control over our form elements. How can we use these features to our advantage and translate them into writing more robust code?

In the following sections, we'll try to address this question by showing some useful techniques that can be used to gain more control over our forms.

A look at the Form Model

We talked a lot about the Form Model in *Chapter 6, Forms and Data Validation*, yet we've never seen it up close. It would greatly help to have it on screen while developing the form templates, especially if it can be updated in real time as we play with the form inputs and controls.

Here's a convenient HTML snippet containing the template syntax required to let it happen:

```
<!-- Form debug info panel -->
<div class="card bg-light mb-3">
  <div class="card-header">Form Debug Info</div>
  <div class="card-body">
    <div class="card-text">
      <div><strong>Form value:</strong></div>
      <div class="help-block">
        {{ form.value | json }}
      </div>
      <div class="mt-2"><strong>Form status:</strong></div>
      <div class="help-block">
        {{ form.status | json }}
      </div>
    </div>
  </div>
</div>
```

We can put this snippet on any of our form-based components, for example, `CityEditComponent`, to obtain the following result:

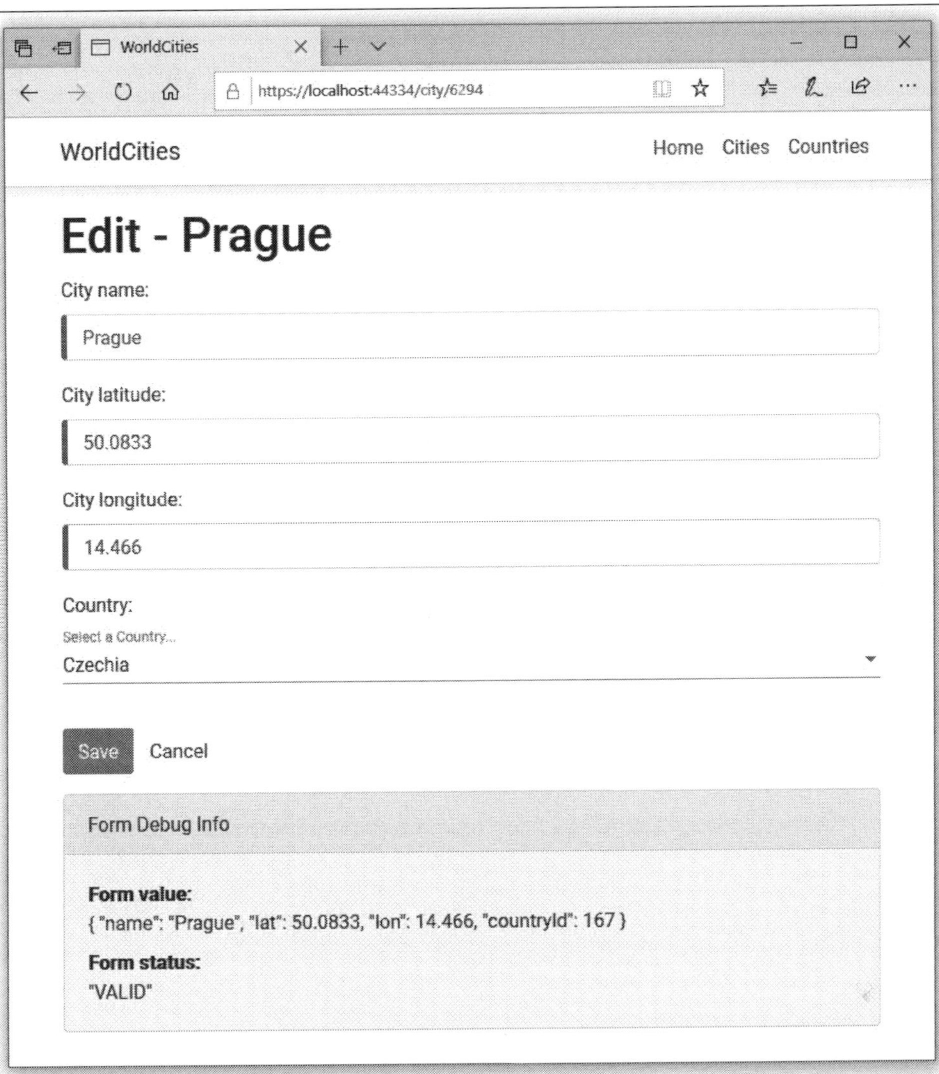

Figure 8.14: The Form Debug Info window while editing Prague

Pretty useful, right? If we play with the form a bit, we can see how the values contained in the **Form Debug Info** panel will change as we change the input controls; something like that will definitely come in handy when dealing with complex forms.

The pipe operator

By looking at the highlighted lines of the preceding source code, we can see how we used the pipe operator (|), which is another useful tool coming from the Angular template syntax.

To quickly summarize what it does, we can say the following: the `pipe` operator allows the use of some transformation functions that can be used to perform various tasks such as format strings, join array elements into a string, uppercase/lowercase a text, and sort a list.

Here are the pipes that come built-in with Angular:

- `DatePipe`
- `UpperCasePipe`
- `LowerCasePipe`
- `CurrencyPipe`
- `PercentPipe`
- `JsonPipe`

These are all available for use in any template. Needless to say, we used the last pipe in the preceding script to transform the `form.value` and `form.status` objects into readable JSON strings.

> It's worth noting that we can also chain multiple pipes and define custom pipes; however, we don't need to do that for the time being, and talking about such a topic would take us far away from the scope of this chapter. Those who want to know more about pipes should take a look at the official Angular documentation at: `https://angular.io/guide/pipes`

Reacting to changes

One of the reasons we chose the Reactive approach was to be able to react to the changes issued by the user. We can do that by subscribing to the `valueChanges` property exposed by the `FormGroup` and `FormControl` classes, which returns an *RxJS Observable* that emits the latest values.

We've been using observables since *Chapter 3, Front-End and Back-End Interactions*, when we subscribed to the `get()` method of `HttpClient` to handle the `HTTP` response received by the web server for the first time. We used them again in *Chapter 6, Forms and Data Validation*, when we had to implement support for the `put()` and `post()` methods as well.

Last but not least, we extensively talked about them in *Chapter 7, Code Tweaks and Data Services*, when we explained their pros and cons against Promises, learned about some of their most relevant features, and integrated them in to our `CityService` and `CountryService`. As a matter of fact, we'll likely keep using them wherever and whenever we need to fetch the JSON data that feeds our Data Model interfaces and Form Model objects.

In the following section, we're going to use them to demonstrate how we can perform some arbitrary operations whenever the user changes something within a form. More precisely, we'll try to observe the observable by implementing a custom activity log.

The activity log

Once again, `CityEditComponent` will be our lab rat.

Open the `/ClientApp/src/app/cities/city-edit.component.ts` class file and update its code with the following highlighted lines:

```
// ...existing code...

  // Activity Log (for debugging purposes)
  activityLog: string = '';

  constructor(
    private activatedRoute: ActivatedRoute,
    private router: Router,
    private cityService: CityService,
    @Inject('BASE_URL') private baseUrl: string) {
      super();
    }

  ngOnInit() {
    this.form = new FormGroup({
      name: new FormControl('', Validators.required),
      lat: new FormControl('', [
        Validators.required,
        Validators.pattern(/^[-]?[0-9]+(\.[0-9]{1,4})?$/)
      ]),
      lon: new FormControl('', [
        Validators.required,
        Validators.pattern(/^[-]?[0-9]+(\.[0-9]{1,4})?$/)
      ]),
      countryId: new FormControl('', Validators.required)
    }, null, this.isDupeCity());

    // react to form changes
    this.form.valueChanges
      .subscribe(() => {
        if (!this.form.dirty) {
          this.log("Form Model has been loaded.");
        }
        else {
          this.log("Form was updated by the user.");
        }
      });
```

```
        this.loadData();
    }

    log(str: string) {
        this.activityLog += "["
            + new Date().toLocaleString()
            + "] " + str + "<br />";
    }

    // ...existing code
```

In the preceding code, we provided our Form Model with a simple, yet effective, logging feature that will register any change activity performed by the framework and/or by the user.

As we can see, all the logic has been put within the constructor because this is where the component class gets initialized, along with the observable we need to monitor. The log() function is just a shortcut to append a basic timestamp to the log activity string and add it to the activityLog local variable in a centralized way.

In order to enjoy our new logging feature to the fullest, we have to find a way to put the activityLog on screen.

To do that, open the /ClientApp/src/app/cities/city-edit.component.html template file and append the following HTML code snippet at the end of the file, right below the previous **Form Debug Info** panel:

```
<!-- Form activity log panel -->
<div class="card bg-light mb-3">
  <div class="card-header">Form Activity Log</div>
  <div class="card-body">
    <div class="card-text">
      <div class="help-block">
        <span *ngIf="activityLog"
            [innerHTML]="activityLog"></span>
      </div>
    </div>
  </div>
</div>
```

That's it; now, the activity log will be shown in real time, meaning in a truly reactive way.

> It's worth noting that we didn't use the double curly braces of interpolation here—we went straight for the [innerHTML] directive instead. The reason for that is very simple. The interpolation strips the HTML tags from the source string; hence, we would've lost the <br /> tag that we used in the log() function to separate all log lines with a line feed. If not for that, we would have used the {{ activityLog }} syntax instead.

Testing the activity log

All we need to do now is test our new activity log.

To do so, run the project in debug mode, go straight to `CityEditComponent` by editing an already-existing city (for example, **Prague**), play with the form fields, and see what happens in the **Form Activity Log** panel:

Figure 8.15: Testing the activity log

The first log line should trigger automatically as soon as the `HttpClient` retrieves the city JSON from the back-end Web API and the Form Model gets updated. Then, the form will log any updates performed by the user; all we can do is change the various input fields, yet that's more than enough for our humble reactivity test to complete successfully.

Extending the activity log

Reacting to the Form Model changes is not the only thing we can do; we can extend our subscriptions to observe any form control as well. Let's perform a further upgrade on our current activity log implementation to demonstrate that.

Open the `/ClientApp/src/app/cities/city-edit.component.ts` class file and update the code in the `constructor` method with the following highlighted lines:

```
// ...existing code...

// react to form changes
this.form.valueChanges
  .subscribe(val => {
    if (!this.form.dirty) {
      this.log("Form Model has been loaded.");
    }
    else {
      this.log("Form was updated by the user.");
    }
  });

// react to changes in the form.name control
this.form.get("name")!.valueChanges
  .subscribe(() => {
    if (!this.form.dirty) {
      this.log("Name has been loaded with initial values.");
    }
    else {
      this.log("Name was updated by the user.");
    }
  });

// ...existing code...
```

The preceding code will add further log lines within the **Form Activity Log**, all related to the changes occurring in the `name` form control, which contains the city name, as follows:

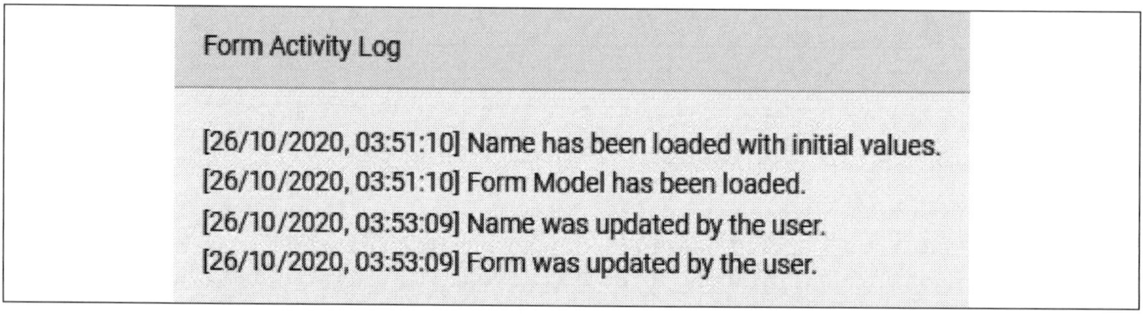

Figure 8.16: Inspecting the Form Activity Log for changes in the name form control

What we just did here is more than enough to demonstrate the wonders of the `valueChanges` observable property; let's move on to the next topic.

> We can definitely keep the **Form Debug Info** and **Form Activity Log** panels in the `CityEditComponent` template for further reference, yet there's no need to copy/paste it within the other form-based components' templates or anywhere else: after all, this logging info will be unnecessary for the average user and shouldn't be visible in the application user interface, for demonstration purposes.

Client-side debugging

Another great advantage of observables is that we can use them to debug a good part of the whole Reactive workflow by placing breakpoints within our subscription source code. To quickly demonstrate this, just add a Visual Studio breakpoint to our latest subscription, as follows:

```
// react to changes in the form.name control
this.form.get("name")!.valueChanges
    .subscribe(val => {
        if (!this.form.dirty) {
            this.log("Name has been loaded with initial values.");
        }
        else {
            this.log("Name was updated by the user.");
        }
    });
```

Figure 8.17: Adding a Visual Studio breakpoint

Once done, run the project in debug mode and navigate to `CityEditComponent`; the breakpoint will be hit as soon as the Form Model is loaded, since the `name` control will be updated as well, and also every time we make a change to that control. Whenever this happens, we'll be able to use all the Visual Studio JavaScript debugging tools and features that are available on client-side debugging, such as *Watch*, *Locals*, *Autos*, *Immediate*, *Call Stack*, and more.

> For additional information about client-side debugging with Google Chrome, we strongly suggest reading the following post on the official MSDN blog: `https://blogs.msdn.microsoft.com/webdev/2016/11/21/client-side-debugging-of-asp-net-projects-in-google-chrome/`

Unsubscribing the Observables

Observables are a great way to monitor our client-side app's behavior: once we subscribe to them, we can be sure that our event handlers will be called every time a new value is emitted.

However, with great power comes great responsibility: if we subscribe to *observables* and don't unsubscribe from them, they will never `complete` and therefore will live on indefinitely, even when the component that originated them is destroyed, thus ending up with a memory leak until the whole Angular app is removed from memory—such as when we navigate away to a different site.

In order to avoid such behavior, we need to learn how to properly deal with them: in a word, **unsubscribe**. Let's briefly introduce some ways to do that using imperative, declarative, and automatic approaches.

The unsubscribe() method

The first approach we should consider is to collect all the subscriptions that we can declare within our `CityEditComponent` class in a single `Subscription` instance in the following way:

```
import { Subscription } from 'rxjs';

// ... existing code...

private subscriptions: Subscription = new Subscription();
```

And then use it to store all our existing subscriptions:

```
// ...existing code...

// react to form changes
this.subscriptions.add(this.form.valueChanges
  .subscribe(val => {
    if (!this.form.dirty) {
      this.log("Form Model has been loaded.");
    }
    else {
      this.log("Form was updated by the user.");
    }
  }));

// react to changes in the form.name control
this.subscriptions.add(this.form.get("name")!.valueChanges
  .subscribe(() => {
    if (!this.form.dirty) {
      this.log("Name has been loaded with initial values.");
    }
    else {
      this.log("Name was updated by the user.");
    }
  }));

// ...existing code...
```

If we do that, we can then unsubscribe all the "collected" subscriptions in the ngOnDestroy lifecycle hook, which gets called when the component is destroyed:

```
ngOnDestroy() {
    this.subscriptions.unsubscribe();
}
```

That's it: in the preceding code, we make good use of a neat built-in mechanism provided by the Subscription class that does most of the unsubscribe job for us; we just have to "wrap up" all the subscriptions that we want to get rid of and implement the ngOnDestroy method above.

The takeUntil() operator

If we prefer to use a declarative approach, we can use another fancy mechanism provided by the RxJS library: the takeUntil operator.

Here's how we can implement it in the CityEditComponent class, replacing the previous unsubscribe() approach:

```
// ...existing code...

import { Subject } from 'rxjs';
import { takeUntil } from 'rxjs/operators';

// ...existing code...

private destroySubject: Subject<boolean> = new Subject<boolean>();

// ...existing code...

// react to form changes
this.form.valueChanges
  .pipe(takeUntil(this.destroySubject))
  .subscribe(val => {
    if (!this.form.dirty) {
      this.log("Form Model has been loaded.");
    }
    else {
      this.log("Form was updated by the user.");
    }
  });

// react to changes in the form.name control
this.form.get("name")!.valueChanges
 .pipe(takeUntil(this.destroySubject))
  .subscribe(() => {
    if (!this.form.dirty) {
```

```
      this.log("Name has been loaded with initial values.");
    }
    else {
      this.log("Name was updated by the user.");
    }
  });

// ...existing code...

ngOnDestroy() {
    // emit a value with the takeUntil notifier
    this.destroySubject.next(true);
    // unsubscribe from the notifier itself
    this.destroySubject.unsubscribe();
}
```

In a nutshell, here's what we've done:

- We've added a `destroySubject` internal variable of type `Subject`, a special type of Observable which we introduced in *Chapter 7, Code Tweaks and Data Services*, that allows values to be multi-casted to many observers.
- We've piped the `takeUntil()` operator to all our observable chains; the operator will register `destroySubject` as a notifier, meaning that it will emit the values emitted by the source observable until `destroySubject` emits a value.
- We've implemented the `ngOnDestroy` life cycle hook where our notifier emits a value (thus stopping all the subscriptions) and then unsubscribes itself.

As we can see, this method allows us to declare our observable chain beforehand with everything that it needs to accommodate for the whole life cycle from start to end: a viable alternative to the `unsubscribe()` method......as long as we don't forget to implement the `ngOnDestroy` interface! To help us remember it, we could acquire the (good) habit of explicitly declaring the `OnDestroy` interface in all our component classes:

```
import { Component, Inject, OnInit, OnDestroy } from '@angular/core';

// ... existing code...

export class CityEditComponent
  extends BaseFormComponent implements OnInit, OnDestroy {
```

For the time being, let's do this in our `CityEditComponent` and move on.

In order to give a proper source code reference to the reader, we've implemented the `takeUntil()` method—as well as the `OnDestroy` explicit declaration—in `CityEditComponent`: the code can be found in the book's GitHub repository for this chapter.

Other viable alternatives

There are many other ways of unsubscribing from observables, most of them being even more efficient and concise for some specific scenarios.

For example, if we only need a single result to be emitted, we can use the `first()` or `take(1)` operators: these operators can be "piped" before the subscription just like the `takeUntil()` operator and will automatically complete after receiving the first result, without having to create a `destroySubject` notifier; if we want to unsubscribe from the source stream once the emitted value no longer matches a certain condition, we can use the `takeWhile()` operator.

A great advantage of all these RxJS operators is that they will automatically unsubscribe, without having to perform it manually (and risking forgetting about it).

Furthermore, whenever we use a subscription to feed data to our templates, we can use the Angular `async pipe`, which subscribes and unsubscribes automatically when the component is destroyed. This basically means that, in our `CityEditComponent` TypeScript class file, instead of doing this:

```
// ...

// the countries array for the select
countries: Country[];

// ...

loadCountries() {
  // fetch all the countries from the server
  this.cityService.getCountries<ApiResult<Country>>(
    0,
    9999,
    "name",
    null,
    null,
    null,
  ).subscribe(result => {
    this.countries = result.data;
  }, error => console.error(error));
}
```

We could do this:

```
// ...

// the countries observable for the select (using async pipe)
countries: Observable<ApiResult<Country>>;

// ...
```

```
loadCountries() {
  // fetch all the countries from the server
  this.countries = this.cityService
    .getCountries<ApiResult<Country>>(
      0,
      9999,
      "name",
      null,
      null,
      null,
    );
}
```

And then handle the updated `countries` variable (which is now an *observable*) by modifying the `city-edit.component.html` template file in the following way:

```
<!-- ... -->

<mat-form-field *ngIf="countries | async as result">
  <mat-label>Select a Country...</mat-label>
  <mat-select id="countryId" formControlName="countryId">
    <mat-option *ngFor="let country of result.data" [value]="country.id">
      {{country.name}}
    </mat-option>
  </mat-select>
</mat-form-field>

<!-- ... -->
```

Now the async pipe will automatically subscribe to the observable, return the latest value, and then unsubscribe from it, thus avoiding memory leaks.

Let's quickly implement this valuable sample in our `CityEditComponent` (TypeScript and HTML files) and move on; as always, those who encounter issues while trying to do that can find the full source code reference in the GitHub repository.

> Unfortunately, for obvious reasons of space, we won't have the chance to talk much more about these techniques within this book; however, the reader can learn how to use them by taking a look at the following posts:
>
> **No need to unsubscribe - RxJS operators will help you out**, by *Wojciech Trawiński*: `https://medium.com/javascript-everyday/no-need-to-unsubscribe-rxjs-operators-will-help-you-out-f8b8ce7bf26a`
>
> **Async Pipe all the Things!**, by *Joaquin Cid*: `https://medium.com/@joaqcid/async-pipe-all-the-things-2607a7bc6732`

Should we always unsubscribe?

As a matter of fact, no; however, in order to determine when we should unsubscribe, we need to understand where our "enemy" actually hides.

In a nutshell, the memory leaks that we would like to avoid occur when we destroy and recreate our components without cleaning up existing subscriptions: if those components are re-created, which will likely happen if the user keeps browsing around the app, they will spawn more and more subscriptions, and so on, thus producing the leak.

This brief analysis should be more than enough to help you understand when we should use the unsubscribe method(s) explained previously: as a general rule, we should do it for the observables that get subscribed in components that are meant to be instantiated and destroyed multiple times, such as the components hosting the views.

Conversely, any component that gets instantiated only once during the application startup won't have the chance to generate multiple "endless subscriptions" and therefore doesn't require any "unsubscription" logic. `AppComponent`, as well as most of the services, are good examples: they are meant to live for the whole duration of the application lifetime and won't produce any memory leak while the app is running.

> For additional info regarding this topic, we strongly suggest reading the following articles by Tomas Trajan and Maciej Treder:
>
> `https://medium.com/angular-in-depth/the-best-way-to-unsubscribe-rxjs-observable-in-the-angular-applications-d8f9aa42f6a0`
>
> `https://www.twilio.com/blog/prevent-memory-leaks-angular-observable-ngondestroy`

Now that we've dealt with unsubscribing and we know how to properly debug our back-end code, let's switch to a slightly different topic.

Application logging

As all developers most likely know, the term logging—when used in any IT context, from programming languages to computer science—is mostly used to define the process of recording application actions and state to a *secondary* channel. To better understand this definition, we need to grasp the difference between a *primary* and *secondary* channel.

All applications are meant to communicate with their users through a dedicated interface, which is often called the **user interface**, or UI:

- **Desktop applications**, for example, use the **Graphical User Interface** (**GUI**) provided by the Windows (or other operating systems) libraries
- **Console applications** rely upon the operating system terminal
- **Web applications** display their data through the web browser

... and so on. In all the preceding examples, the *user interface* is the main output mechanism used by the software to communicate with their users, thus being the application's *primary* channel.

At the same time, it's often very useful for an application to keep track of the various actions it performs while it works: state changes, access to internal resources, event handlers that trigger in response to user interactions, and so on. We made something like that in Angular early on in this chapter, when we implemented the activity log.

Now, that level of info is often neglectable for the average user, as long as the application works as expected; not to mention the fact that such low-level details could easily disclose some internal mechanics and/or behaviors of our web application that shouldn't be made available to the public for obvious security reasons.

At the same time, these logs might become extremely useful for developers and system administrators whenever the app hangs or behaves in an unexpected way, because they could greatly help them to understand what is going wrong and how to fix it. Truth be told, any experienced developer knows that logging is a must-have feature for any application, as it is necessary for detecting, investigating, and debugging issues.

Which brings us to the main question: if the *primary* channel is not an option, where should we put such info? The answer lies in the definition of logging that we have stated a short while ago: in a *secondary* channel that only developers, system administrators, and other interested (and authorized) parties will be able to access.

If we think of a client-side framework such as Angular, the best *secondary* channel we have available is the browser's console log, which can be accessed using the `console.log` and/or `debug.log` JavaScript commands; ideally, that's the place where we should move all our activity log's output, thus keeping the user interface—the *primary* channel—as clear as possible.

Doing this would be simple, and we should just change a couple of things:

- Remove the **Form Activity Log** panel (up to the root `<div>` element)
- Remove the `this.activityLog` variable (in the `city-edit.component.ts` file)
- Modify the `CityEditComponent`'s `log` method in the following way:

```
log(str: string) {
  console.log("["
    + new Date().toLocaleString()
    + "] " + str);
}
```

That's it for the client side.

> The "on-screen" implementation will be kept in the book's GitHub source code for reference purposes; however, the reader is strongly encouraged to rely upon `console.log` for most real-case scenarios.

What about server-side logging? We've previously seen that we have the **Output** window, but that's only available when we're running our app from Visual Studio, right?

Or not?

Introducing ASP.NET Core logging

.NET 5 natively supports a logging API that can be used to collect, display, and/or store logs using a default interface (`ILogger`) that has been implemented by a variety of built-in and third-party logging providers.

In a typical ASP.NET Core web application, the built-in logging providers are automatically added to our web application by the `Program.cs` file's `CreateDefaultBuilder` helper method, which we saw back in *Chapter 2, Looking Around*. More precisely, the following providers are enabled:

- **Console**, which logs output to the console
- **Debug**, which writes log output by using the `System.Diagnostics.Debug` class
- **Event Source**, which writes to a cross-platform event source with the name `Microsoft-Extensions-Logging`
- **EventLog**, which sends log output to the Windows event log (Windows operating system only)

As a matter of fact, the content that we see within Visual Studio's **Output** window entirely comes from the **Debug** built-in provider.

DBMS structured logging with Serilog

As we can see, there are no native logging providers that can be used to have these logs stored within a DBMS, which would certainly be very useful as it would allow us to review our logs using a *structured* approach. As a matter of fact, structured logging would definitely be a great way to produce readable, filterable, indexed, and exportable logs.

Luckily enough, we can achieve this using one of the many third-party logging providers that implement the `ILogger` interface available on NuGet: its name is **Serilog** and it's pretty awesome.

In the following sections, we'll see how we can implement it within our WorldCities app to save its logs in a dedicated SQL Server database in a structured way.

Installing the NuGet packages

The first thing we must do is add the following NuGet packages to our project:

- `Serilog.AspNetCore`
- `Serilog.Settings.Configuration`
- `Serilog.Sinks.MSSqlServer`

As always, these packages can be installed using Visual Studio's GUI (Manage NuGet Packages) or the Package Manager Console interface in the following way:

```
PM> Install-Package Serilog.AspNetCore
PM> Install-Package Serilog.Settings.Configuration
PM> Install-Package Serilog.Sinks.MSSqlServer
```

`Serilog.Sinks.MSSqlServer` is required in our scenario since we're using an MS SQL Server; however, there are many other connectors ("sinks") available for MySQL, MariaDB, PostgreSQL, and even NoSQL databases, such as RavenDB and MongoDB.

Configuring Serilog

Once the required NuGet packages have been installed, we can configure Serilog using our web application's configuration files. More precisely, we're going to update the `Program.cs` file, where the `IHostBuilder` is created with its set of built-in logging providers.

From **Solution Explorer**, open the `Program.cs` file and add the following `using` statements at the beginning of the file, just below the existing ones:

```
using System.IO;
using Serilog;
using Serilog.Sinks.MSSqlServer;
using Serilog.Events;
```

Once done, scroll down and modify the `Main()` method in the following way (new/updated lines highlighted):

```
[...]

public static void Main(string[] args)
{
    var configuration = new ConfigurationBuilder()
        .SetBasePath(Directory.GetCurrentDirectory())
        .AddJsonFile("appsettings.json",
            optional: false,
            reloadOnChange: true)
        .AddJsonFile(string.Format("appsettings.{0}.json",
            Environment.GetEnvironmentVariable("ASPNETCORE_ENVIRONMENT")
                ?? "Production"),
            optional: true,
            reloadOnChange: true)
        .AddUserSecrets<Startup>(optional: true, reloadOnChange: true)
        .Build();
```

```
    Log.Logger = new LoggerConfiguration()
        .WriteTo.MSSqlServer(
            connectionString:
                configuration.GetConnectionString("DefaultConnection"),
            restrictedToMinimumLevel: LogEventLevel.Information,
            sinkOptions: new MSSqlServerSinkOptions {
                TableName = "LogEvents",
                AutoCreateSqlTable = true
            })
        .WriteTo.Console()
        .CreateLogger();

    CreateHostBuilder(args).UseSerilog().Build().Run();
}

[...]
```

As we can see, we've performed three different tasks here:

1. We created a new `IConfiguration` object so that we can use it to read the `appsettings.json` and `secrets.json` file content and use the settings we've defined there. It's worth noting that we've also added the specific file for the currently running environment (using the `Environment.GetEnvironmentVariable` method) and the `secrets.json` file (using the `AddUserSecrets` method).
2. We instantiated the `Serilog` `ILogger` interface using an appropriate `LoggerConfiguration` that reads the connection string from the `IConfiguration` object and writes the logs to the *LogEvents* table, creating the table if it doesn't exist. Notice that we're using the same connection string that we used to instantiate our `ApplicationDbContext` in *Chapter 4, Data Model with Entity Framework Core*, which means that the *LogEvents* table will be created within the **WorldCities** database. While we were there, we also used the `restrictedToMinimumLevel` configuration setting to cut out the less relevant info (such as the `LogEventLevel.Verbose` system messages) from our logs. Last but not least, we chained a `WriteTo.Console()` command before creating the logger to ensure that the console logging that we can read from within Visual Studio will still be written together with the DBMS one.
3. We added **Serilog** as a logging provider for our app's `IHost` using the `UseSerilog()` extension method.

> All the **Serilog** configuration settings that we've added from within the code could've been defined in the `appsettings.json` file using a `"Serilog"` key. For additional info on how to do that and regarding the settings syntax, read the MSSqlServer sink official docs on GitHub: `https://github.com/serilog/serilog-sinks-mssqlserver`

Before we can test our implementation, let's spend a minute adding another useful logging feature to our application: the `SerilogRequestLogging` middleware.

Logging HTTP requests

Another great feature of Serilog is that we can use it to log the incoming HTTP requests. Once implemented, this feature will produce the following log message:

```
HTTP GET /cities responded 200 in 1348.6188 ms
```

In order to do that, we need to open our `Startup.cs` file and add the following middleware at the end of the `Configure` method:

```
public void Configure(IApplicationBuilder app, IWebHostEnvironment env)
{
    // ... existing code...

    // Use the Serilog request logging middleware to log HTTP requests.
    app.UseSerilogRequestLogging();
}
```

That's it.

Now that everything is set, we just have to perform a quick test to confirm that our new Serilog-based logging provider actually works.

Accessing the logs

Since we've told **Serilog** to auto-create the *LogEvents* table if it doesn't exist yet, we just have to launch our project in debug mode by hitting *F5* and see what happens to the database.

As soon as the web app is fully loaded, open SQL Server Management Studio and access the **WorldCities** database following the instructions given in *Chapter 4, Data Model with Entity Framework Core*.

If we did everything as expected, we should be able to see the new *LogEvents* table and a bunch of initialization logs, just as shown in the following screenshot:

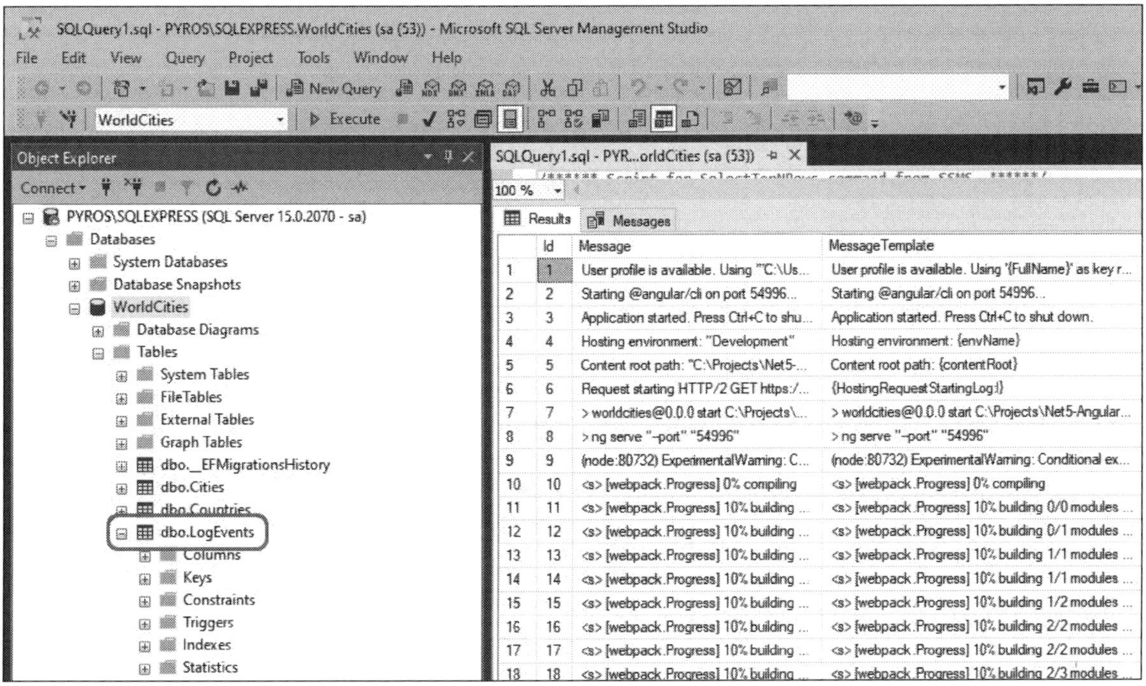

Figure 8.18: Viewing our new LogEvents table

Now we can conveniently access our log in a structured way using SQL queries.

Furthermore, we can use this new feature to log whatever we want using the convenient `Serilog.Log` static entry point provided by the library.

Here's how we can do that from a controller:

```
public class SampleController : Controller
{
    public SampleController()
    {
        Serilog.Log.Information("SampleController initialized.");
    }
}
```

And here's how to call it within a view:

```
@ Serilog.Log.Information("SampleView shown to the user");
```

If we don't like the `Serilog.Log` static entry point, we can still use the standard `ILogger` interface using *dependency injection* and achieve the same result, since it will also use the new Serilog outputs/sinks.

Here's how to implement the `ILogger` interface in a controller:

```
using  Microsoft.Extensions.Logging;

[...]

public class SampleController : Controller
{
    public ILogger<SampleController> Logger { get; set; }

    public SampleController(ILogger<SampleController> logger)
    {
        Logger = logger;
        Logger.LogInformation("SampleController initialized.");
    }
}
```

And here's the same approach within a view:

```
@using Microsoft.Extensions.Logging
@inject ILogger<_Views_Dress_Edit> logger

@logger.LogInformation("SampleView shown to the user");
```

The `Serilog.Log` static entry point is great and provides a lot of additional features; that said, the standard `ILogger` interface is often the most advisable approach because it will make it easier to connect our app with other MS-based telemetry and monitoring tools (such as Application Insights on MS Azure).

> It's important to understand that we've only scratched the surface of **Serilog** here, just to demonstrate how easy it is to set it up to write logs to a DBMS of our choice; for example, we could've used a different database within the same SQL Server instance—or even a different DBMS engine; we could've modified the default *EventLog* table name and/or column names, as well as adding additional columns; and so on.
>
> Those who want to know more about Serilog and all the available settings can check out the following URL: `https://serilog.net/`

Summary

Throughout this chapter, we talked about a number of debugging features and techniques that can be very useful during development. Let's try to quickly summarize what we've learned so far.

We started our journey with the Visual Studio server-side debugging features. These are a set of runtime debugging features that can be used to prevent most compiler errors on our Web API and allow us to track the whole back-end application life cycle: from the middleware initialization, through to the whole HTTP request/response pipeline, down to the controllers, entities, and `IQueryable` objects.

Right after that, we moved to the Visual Studio client-side debugging feature. This is a neat JavaScript debugger that, thanks to the source maps created by the TypeScript transpiler, allows us to directly debug our TypeScript classes and access variables, subscriptions, and initializers in a truly efficient way.

Furthermore, we designed and implemented a real-time activity log. This is a quick and effective way to exploit the Reactive features of the various observables exposed by the Angular modules to keep track of what happens to our components; not to mention the fact that the Visual Studio TypeScript transpiler (and IntelliSense) will hopefully shield us from most syntax, semantic, and logical programming errors, freeing us from the pests of script-based programming, at least for the most part.

Last but not least, we saw how to implement a handy third-party library (*Serilog*) to store our application logs in the database, so that we'll be able to access them in a structured way.

However, what if we want to test our forms against some specific use cases? Is there a way we can mock our back-end ASP.NET Core controllers' behaviors, as well as those of our front-end Angular components, and perform unit tests?

The answer is yes. As a matter of fact, our two frameworks of choice provide various open source testing tools to perform unit tests. In the next chapter, we'll learn how to use them to improve the quality of our code and prevent bugs during refactoring, regression, and new implementation processes.

Suggested topics

Visual Studio Code, debugger, server-side debugging, client-side debugging, extension methods, C# preprocessor directives, JavaScript source maps, Angular pipes, Observable, Subject, unsubscribe, RxJS operators, async pipe, ILogger, Serilog.

References

- *Visual Studio Code*: https://code.visualstudio.com/
- *Visual Studio Container Tools with ASP.NET Core*: https://docs.microsoft.com/en-us/aspnet/core/host-and-deploy/docker/visual-studio-tools-for-docker
- *Offroad Debugging of .NET Core on Linux OSX from Visual Studio*: https://github.com/Microsoft/MIEngine/wiki/Offroad-Debugging-of-.NET-Core-on-Linux---OSX-from-Visual-Studio
- *Debug an application using Visual Studio*: https://docs.microsoft.com/en-US/dotnet/core/tutorials/debugging-with-visual-studio?tabs=csharp
- *Extension Methods*: https://docs.microsoft.com/en-us/dotnet/csharp/programming-guide/classes-and-structs/extension-methods
- *Microsoft.EntityFrameworkCore Namespace*: https://docs.microsoft.com/en-us/dotnet/api/microsoft.entityframeworkcore
- *C# Preprocessor Directives*: https://docs.microsoft.com/en-us/dotnet/csharp/language-reference/preprocessor-directives/
- *The #IF preprocessor directive in C#*: https://docs.microsoft.com/en-us/dotnet/csharp/language-reference/preprocessor-directives/preprocessor-if
- *Debug a JavaScript or TypeScript app in Visual Studio*: https://docs.microsoft.com/en-US/visualstudio/javascript/debug-nodejs
- *Introduction to JavaScript Source Maps*: https://www.html5rocks.com/en/tutorials/developertools/sourcemaps/
- *An Introduction to Source Maps*: https://blog.teamtreehouse.com/introduction-source-maps
- *Angular Pipes*: https://angular.io/guide/pipes
- *No need to unsubscribe – RxJS operators will help you out*: https://medium.com/javascript-everyday/no-need-to-unsubscribe-rxjs-operators-will-help-you-out-f8b8ce7bf26a
- *Async Pipe all the Things!*: https://medium.com/@joaqcid/async-pipe-all-the-things-2607a7bc6732
- *Client-side debugging of ASP.NET projects in Google Chrome*: https://blogs.msdn.microsoft.com/webdev/2016/11/21/client-side-debugging-of-asp-net-projects-in-google-chrome/
- *Angular Debugging*: https://blog.angular-university.io/angular-debugging/
- *The best way to unsubscribe RxJS observables in Angular*: https://medium.com/angular-in-depth/the-best-way-to-unsubscribe-rxjs-observable-in-the-angular-applications-d8f9aa42f6a0
- *Preventing Memory Leaks in Angular Observables with ngOnDestroy*: https://www.twilio.com/blog/prevent-memory-leaks-angular-observable-ngondestroy
- *Serilog*: https://serilog.net
- *Serilog MSSqlServer sink*: https://github.com/serilog/serilog-sinks-mssqlserver

9

ASP.NET Core and Angular Unit Testing

Unit testing is the name given to a method of software testing that helps to determine whether the isolated modules of a program (units) are working correctly. After the various units have been verified, they can be merged together and tested as a whole (integration testing and system testing) and/or released in production.

Given this definition, it's pretty easy to understand the importance of properly defining and isolating the various units. These are the smallest testable parts of our software, featuring a few inputs and a single output. In **Object-Oriented Programming** (**OOP**), where the program's source code is split into classes, a unit is often a method of a super, abstract, or derived class, yet it can also be a static function of a helper class.

Although they've become a *de facto* standard for high-quality projects, unit tests are often underestimated by most developers and project managers who are eager to speed up the whole development process and therefore reduce its overall cost. Such an approach may not be acceptable for small-scale projects with low profit margins, since creating unit tests undeniably requires some additional work. However, it's very important to understand their huge benefits for medium-to-big projects and enterprise solutions, especially if they require the coordinated effort of a large number of developers.

This chapter is entirely dedicated to unit tests. More precisely, we'll learn how to define, implement, and perform the following:

- **Back-end unit tests in ASP.NET Core**, using the **xUnit.net** testing tool.
- **Front-end unit tests in Angular**, using the **Jasmine** testing framework and the **Karma** test runner that we briefly saw in *Chapter 2, Looking Around*.

We'll also get the opportunity to briefly introduce some widely used testing practices that can help us to get the most out of our tests, such as **Test-Driven Development** (**TDD**) and **Behavior-Driven Development** (**BDD**). By the end of this chapter, we'll have learned how to properly design and implement *back-end* and *front-end* unit tests following these practices.

For the sake of simplicity, we're going to perform our unit test in our existing `WorldCities` Angular app. However, to do this, we're going to add some new packages to our project.

Technical requirements

In this chapter, we're going to need all of the technical requirements listed in previous chapters, with the following additional packages:

- `Microsoft.NET.Test.Sdk`
- `xunit`
- `xunit.runner.visualstudio`
- `Moq`
- `Microsoft.EntityFrameworkCore.InMemory`

As always, it's advisable to avoid installing them straight away. We're going to bring them in during this chapter to better contextualize their purpose within our project.

The code files for this chapter can be found here: `https://github.com/PacktPublishing/ASP.NET-5-and-Angular/tree/master/Chapter_09/`

ASP.NET Core unit tests

In this section, we'll learn how to build an ASP.NET Core unit test project using xUnit.net, a free, open-source, community-focused unit testing tool for .NET created by Brad Wilson, who also developed NUnit v2. We've chosen this tool because it's arguably one of the most powerful and easy-to-use unit testing tools available today. It's part of the .NET Foundation, hence operating under their code of conduct, and is licensed under the Apache License, version 2.

Before moving on, we'll also take the opportunity to talk about TDD and BDD in the following sections. These are two widely used testing approaches that have a number of similarities and differences that are worth exploring.

Creating the WorldCities.Test project

The first thing to do is to add a second project to our `WorldCities` solution.

The best way to handle this is to have the `WorldCities.sln` solution file in a dedicated solution folder:

```
/Projects/WorldCities/WorldCities.sln
```

And the `WorldCities.csproj` file, as well as all the other project files and folders, in a subfolder:

```
/Projects/WorldCities/WorldCities/WorldCities.csproj
/Projects/WorldCities/WorldCities/ClientApp
/Projects/WorldCities/WorldCities/Controllers
/Projects/WorldCities/WorldCities/wwwroot
/Projects/WorldCities/WorldCities/[...other files & folders...]
```

If we created the solution by putting the `.sln` file and the `.csproj` files in the same folder, we can easily migrate to that folder structure using Windows 10's **File Explorer** app in the following way:

1. Create the `/WorldCities/` subfolder inside our current project's root folder
2. Move everything there, except for the `.sln` file
3. Open the project's solution
4. From Solution Explorer, remove the (missing) `WorldCities` project from the solution's projects
5. From Solution Explorer, right-click on the solution node, select **Add Existing Project**, and re-add the "moved" `WorldCities` project

Once we have the solution file in a root folder and the csproj file (as well as the other project files) in a subfolder, we can add a new test project to our solution with the following steps:

1. Open a command-line terminal
2. Navigate to the `WorldCities` solution's root folder (be careful: the *solution* root folder, not the project one!)
3. Type the following command and hit *Enter*:

```
> dotnet new xunit -o WorldCities.Tests
```

The .NET CLI should create a new project for us and process some post-creation actions. Once done, a text message will inform us that the `restore` task has been completed (**Restore succeeded**). If we have done everything correctly, a new `WorldCities.Test` project should be present at the same folder level as the existing `WorldCities` project.

Immediately after this, we can add our new `WorldCities.Tests` project to our main solution in the following way:

1. From Solution Explorer, right-click on the root solution's node and select **Add Existing Project**
2. Navigate inside the `/WorldCities.Tests/` folder and select the `WorldCities.Tests.proj` file

The new `WorldCities.Tests` project will be loaded in the existing solution, right below the existing `WorldCities` project, as shown in the following screenshot:

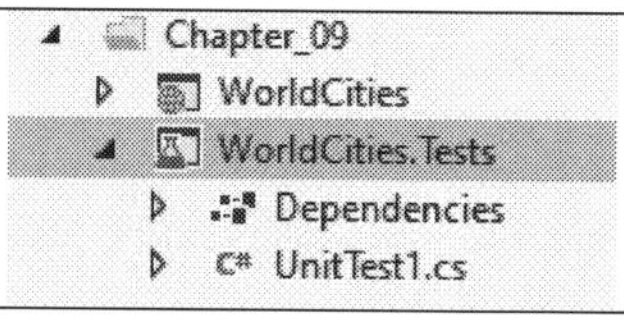

Figure 9.1: The new WorldCities.Tests project

> Alternatively, we could add the new project to the solution file directly from the CLI with the following command: `dotnet sln add WorldCities.Tests`

Let's delete the existing `UnitTest1.cs` file, since we won't need it. We'll create our own unit testing classes in a short while.

The new `WorldCities.Test` project should already have the following NuGet package references:

- **Microsoft.NET.Test.Sdk** (version 16.8.3 or later)
- **xunit** (version 2.4.1 or later)
- **xunit.runner.visualstudio** (version 2.4.3 or later)

> The preceding packages' version numbers are the latest at the time of writing and the ones that we're going to use in this book.

However, we also require two more NuGet packages: `Moq` and `Microsoft.EntityFrameworkCore.InMemory`. Let's see how to add them in the following sections.

Moq

`Moq` is arguably the most popular and friendly mocking framework for .NET. To better understand why we need it, we need to introduce the concept of mocking.

Mocking is a convenient feature that we can use in unit testing whenever the unit that we want to test has external dependencies that cannot be easily created within the testing project. The main purpose of a mocking framework is to create replacement objects that simulate the behavior of the real ones. `Moq` is a minimalistic framework that will do just that.

To install it, do the following:

1. From Solution Explorer, right-click on the `WorldCities.Test` project and choose **Manage NuGet Packages**

2. Search for the `Moq` keyword
3. Find and install the `Moq` NuGet package

Alternatively, just type the following command in Visual Studio's Package Manager Console (setting `WorldCities.Tests` as the default project):

```
> Install-Package Moq
```

> At the time of writing, we're using `Moq 4.15.2`, this being the latest stable version. To be sure that you are using this version as well, just add `-version 4.15.2` to the preceding command.
>
> The latest **Moq** NuGet package, as well as all of the previous versions, are available here: `https://www.nuget.org/packages/moq/`

That's it! We now need to install another NuGet package.

Microsoft.EntityFramework.InMemory

`Microsoft.EntityFrameworkCore.InMemory` is an in-memory database provider for Entity Framework Core that can be used for testing purposes. This is basically the same concept as the Angular in-memory Web API that we talked about in *Chapter 4, Data Model with Entity Framework Core*. In a nutshell, we can think of it as a convenient database mock.

To install it, do the following:

1. From Solution Explorer, right-click on the `WorldCities.Test` project and choose **Manage NuGet Packages**
2. Search for the `Microsoft.EntityFrameworkCore.InMemory` keyword
3. Find and install the `Microsoft.EntityFrameworkCore.InMemory` NuGet package

Alternatively, just type the following command in Visual Studio's Package Manager Console:

```
> Install-Package Microsoft.EntityFrameworkCore.InMemory
```

> At the time of writing, we're using `Microsoft.EntityFrameworkCore.InMemory 5.0.0`, this being the latest stable version. To be sure that you are using this version as well, just add `-version 5.0.0` to the preceding command.
>
> The latest `Microsoft.EntityFrameworkCore.InMemory` NuGet package, as well as all of the previous versions, are available here: `https://www.nuget.org/packages/Microsoft.EntityFrameworkCore.InMemory/`

With this, we're all set.

Adding the WorldCities dependency reference

The next thing we need to do is to add a reference to the main project in our new `WorldCities.Test` project's dependencies so that we'll be able to import the required classes and types.

To do that, right-click on the **Dependencies** node of the new project to add a new `Project Reference` to the `WorldCities` project, as shown in the following screenshot, and press **OK**:

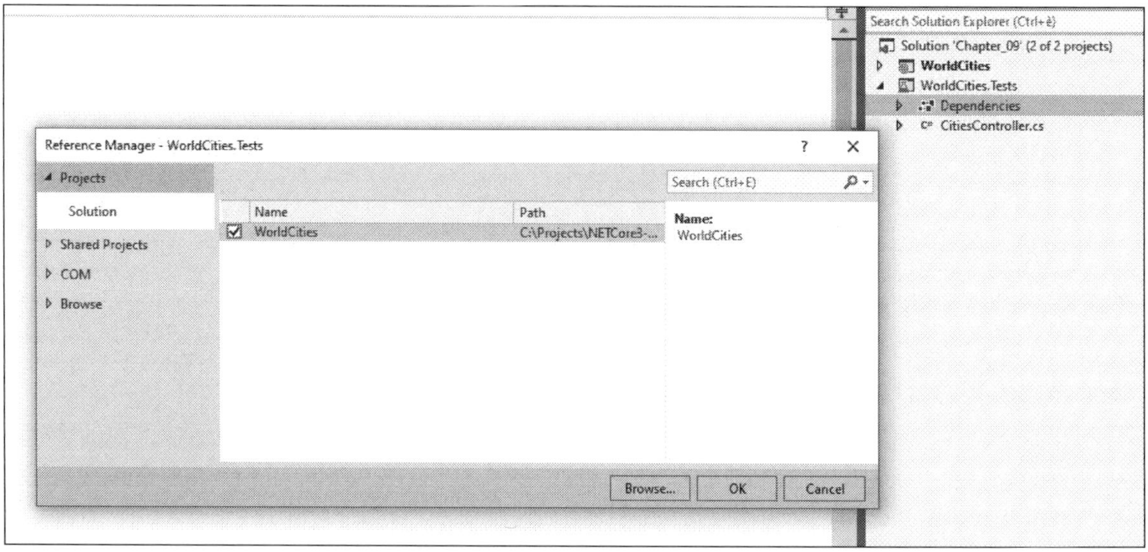

Figure 9.2: Adding a new Project Reference

By doing this, our test project will be able to access (and hence test) the whole `WorldCities` code.

We're now ready to learn how `xUnit` actually works. As always, the best way to do this is to create our first unit test.

Our first test

In Standard Testing Development practice, which we're going to call STD from now on, unit tests are often used to ensure that our existing code is working properly. Once ready, those units will be protected against regression bugs and breaking changes.

Since our *back-end* code is a Web API, the first thing we can cover with our unit tests should be the individual controllers' methods. However, instantiating our controllers outside our web application's life cycle is not that simple, since they do have at least two important dependencies: `HttpContext` and `ApplicationDbContext`. Is there a way to instantiate them too in our `WorldCities.Test` project?

Thanks to `Microsoft.EntityFrameworkCore.InMemory`, this can be a rather easy task... as soon as we understand how to use it.

From Solution Explorer, open the `WorldCities.Test` project. Create a new `CitiesController_Test.cs` file in the project's root and fill it with the following content:

```
using Microsoft.EntityFrameworkCore;
using WorldCities.Controllers;
using WorldCities.Data;
using WorldCities.Data.Models;
using Xunit;

namespace WorldCities.Tests
{
    public class CitiesController_Tests
    {
        /// <summary>
        /// Test the GetCity() method
        /// </summary>
        [Fact]
        public async void GetCity()
        {
            #region Arrange
            // todo: define the required assets
            #endregion

            #region Act
            // todo: invoke the test
            #endregion

            #region Assert
            // todo: verify that conditions are met.
            #endregion
        }
    }
}
```

As we can see by looking at the highlighted regions, we have split the unit test into three code blocks, or phases:

- **Arrange**: Defines the assets required to run the test
- **Act**: Invokes the testing subject's behavior
- **Assert**: Verifies that the expected conditions are met by evaluating the behavior's return value or measuring it against some user-defined rules

Such an approach is known as the **Arrange**, **Act**, **Assert** pattern. This is a typical way to describe the various phases of software testing in TDD. However, there are also alternative names used to describe these same test phases; for example, BDD frameworks usually refer to them as *Given*, *When*, and *Then*.

> TDD and BDD are two development practices that enforce a different coding approach when compared to **Standard Testing Development** (**STD**). We'll talk more about these soon enough.

Regardless of the names, the important thing here is to understand the following key concepts:

- Separating the three phases increases the readability of the test
- Executing the three phases in the proper order makes the test easier to understand

Let's now take a look at how we have implemented the three phases.

Arrange

The `Arrange` phase is the place where we define the assets required to run the test. In our scenario, since we're going to test the functionality of the `GetCity()` method of `CitiesController`, we need to provide our controller with a suitable `ApplicationDbContext`.

However, since we're not testing `ApplicationDbContext` itself, instantiating the real thing wouldn't be advisable, at least for now. We don't want our test to fail just because the database is unavailable, or the database connection is incorrect, because these are different units and therefore should be checked by different unit tests. Moreover, we definitely can't allow our unit tests to operate against our actual data source: what if we want to test an update or a delete task?

The best thing we can do to test our Web API controllers is to find a way to provide them with a replacement object that can behave just like our real `ApplicationDbContext`; in other words, a mock. This is where the `Microsoft.EntityFrameworkCore.InMemory` NuGet package that we installed earlier on might come in handy.

Here's how we can use it to properly implement the `Arrange` phase:

```
// ...existing code...

#region Arrange
var options = new DbContextOptionsBuilder<ApplicationDbContext>()
    .UseInMemoryDatabase(databaseName: "WorldCities")
    .Options;
using (var context = new ApplicationDbContext(options))
{
    context.Add(new City() {
        Id = 1,
        CountryId = 1,
        Lat = 1,
        Lon = 1,
```

```
        Name = "TestCity1"
    });
    context.SaveChanges();
}
City city_existing = null;
City city_notExisting = null;
#endregion

// ...existing code...
```

As we can see, we've used the `UseInMemoryDatabase` extension method provided by the `Microsoft.EntityFrameworkCore.InMemory` package to create a suitable `DbContextOptionsBuilder`. Once we have it, we can use it to instantiate an `ApplicationDbContext` session with an in-memory database instead of the SQL server used by the `WorldCities` project.

Once created, that `context` can be populated by creating new cities, which is what we did in the preceding code, creating `TestCity1` with some random data. This will allow our `GetCity()` method of `CitiesController` to actually retrieve something, provided that we pass a city `Id`.

Other than that, we have defined two `City` objects that will contain the two specimens for this test.

Act

The `Act` phase is where the test takes place. It often consists of a single instruction that corresponds to the behavior of the unit that we want to check.

Here's the `Act` phase implementation:

```
// ...existing code...

#region Act
using (var context = new ApplicationDbContext(options))
{
    var controller = new CitiesController(context);
    city_existing = (await controller.GetCity(1)).Value;
    city_notExisting = (await controller.GetCity(2)).Value;
}
#endregion

// ...existing code...
```

As we can see, the entire implementation is enclosed by a `using` directive, which ensures that our in-memory `ApplicationDbContext` instance will be properly disposed of as soon as the phase ends.

The remainder of the code is quite self-explanatory. We have created a `CitiesController` instance using the in-memory context and we execute the `GetCity()` method two times:

- The first occasion is to retrieve an existing city (using the same `Id` that we used to populate our in-memory database with)
- The second occasion is to retrieve a non-existing city (using a different `Id`)

The two return values are then stored in the `city_existing` and `city_notExisting` variables. Ideally, the first one should contain `TestCity1`, which we created in the `Arrange` phase, while the latter should be `null`.

Assert

The purpose of the `Assert` phase is to verify that the conditions that we expect are properly met by the values retrieved by the `Act` phase. To do this, we'll make use of the `Assert` class provided by **xUnit**, which contains various static methods that can be used to verify that these conditions are met.

Here's the `Assert` phase implementation:

```
#region Assert
Assert.NotNull(city_existing);
Assert.Null(city_notExisting);
#endregion
```

As we can see, we're just checking the values of the two variables that contain the return values of the two `GetCity()` method calls of `CitiesController` made in the `Act` phase. We reasonably expect `city_existing` not to be `null`, while `city_notExisting` should definitely be `null`.

Our test is now ready, so let's see how we can execute it.

Executing the test

Each unit test can be executed in two ways:

- **From the command line**, using the .NET CLI
- **From the Visual Studio GUI**, using Visual Studio's built-in test runner (Test Explorer)

Let's quickly try both of these approaches.

Using the CLI

To execute our test unit(s) by using the .NET CLI, perform the following steps:

1. Open Command Prompt
2. Navigate to the `WorldCities.Tests` project root folder

3. Execute the following command:

```
> dotnet test
```

If we have done everything correctly, we should see something like this:

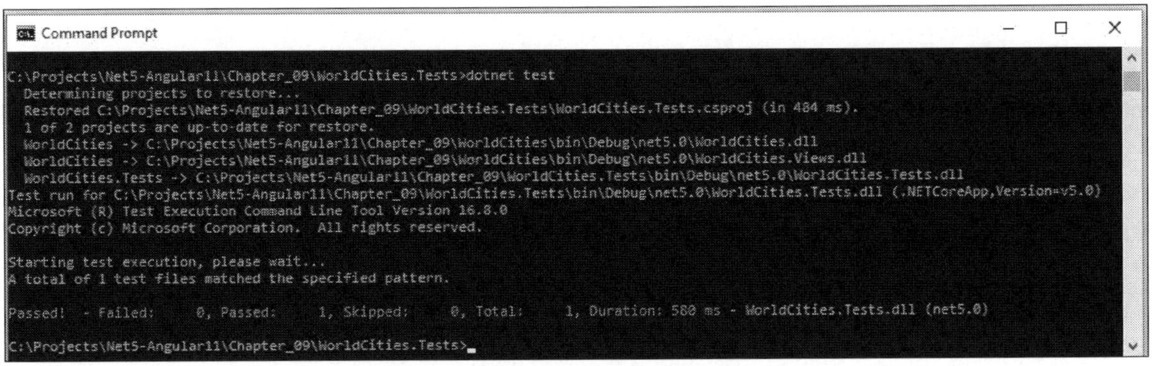

Command Prompt
C:\Projects\Net5-Angular11\Chapter_09\WorldCities.Tests>dotnet test
Determining projects to restore...
Restored C:\Projects\Net5-Angular11\Chapter_09\WorldCities.Tests\WorldCities.Tests.csproj (in 484 ms).
1 of 2 projects are up-to-date for restore.
WorldCities -> C:\Projects\Net5-Angular11\Chapter_09\WorldCities\bin\Debug\net5.0\WorldCities.dll
WorldCities -> C:\Projects\Net5-Angular11\Chapter_09\WorldCities\bin\Debug\net5.0\WorldCities.Views.dll
WorldCities.Tests -> C:\Projects\Net5-Angular11\Chapter_09\WorldCities.Tests\bin\Debug\net5.0\WorldCities.Tests.dll
Test run for C:\Projects\Net5-Angular11\Chapter_09\WorldCities.Tests\bin\Debug\net5.0\WorldCities.Tests.dll (.NETCoreApp,Version=v5.0)
Microsoft (R) Test Execution Command Line Tool Version 16.8.0
Copyright (c) Microsoft Corporation. All rights reserved.
Starting test execution, please wait...
A total of 1 test files matched the specified pattern.
Passed! - Failed: 0, Passed: 1, Skipped: 0, Total: 1, Duration: 580 ms - WorldCities.Tests.dll (net5.0)
C:\Projects\Net5-Angular11\Chapter_09\WorldCities.Tests>

Figure 9.3: Command Prompt output after executing the test

That's it. Our test is working and it passes, meaning that the `GetCity()` method of `CitiesController` is behaving as expected.

Using the Visual Studio Test Explorer

Being able to run our tests from the command line can be a great feature if we want to automate these kinds of tasks. However, in most cases, we'll instead want to be able to run these tests directly from within the Visual Studio GUI.

Luckily enough, this is definitely possible thanks to the Test Explorer window, which can be activated by pressing *Ctrl* + *E*, *T*, or from **Menu** | **View**, as shown in the following screenshot:

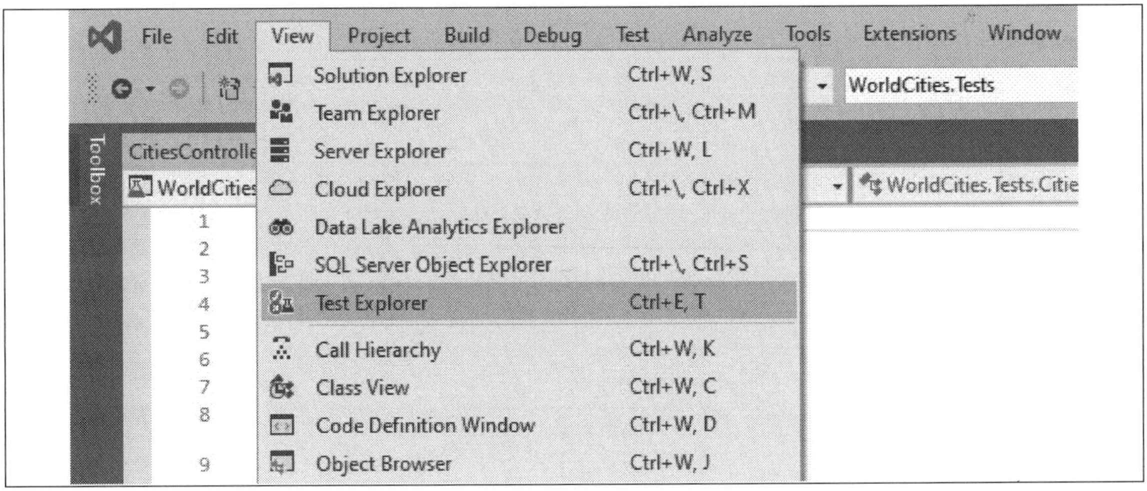

Figure 9.4: Navigating to Test Explorer in Visual Studio

Once activated, the **Test Explorer** window should be accessible in the rightmost part of the Visual Studio GUI, just below the **Solution Explorer** window. From there, we can either run all tests or just the current test by pressing the first two green *play* icons placed in the top-left part of the panel, called **Run All** and **Run**, respectively (refer to the following screenshot):

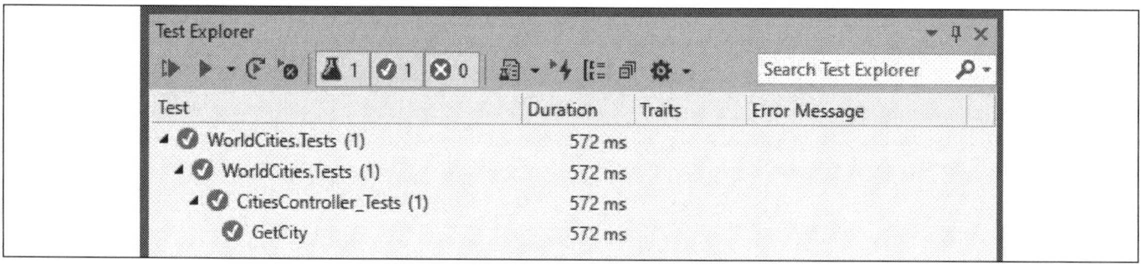

Figure 9.5: The Test Explorer window

Since we only have a single test, for now, either command will do the same thing: run our unit test and show the results using either a green check (success) or a red cross (failure).

> As we can see in the preceding screenshot, those green and/or red icons will be used to determine the combined results of the testing class, the namespace, and the whole assembly.

Before moving further, we should spend another couple of minutes learning how to debug these unit tests.

Debugging tests

If we click on the *arrow handle* next to the second *Run* icon in the top-left part of the **Test Explorer** window, we can see that there are a number of other possible commands we can give to our tests, including **Debug**, **Debug All Tests**, and **Debug Last Run** (refer to the following screenshot):

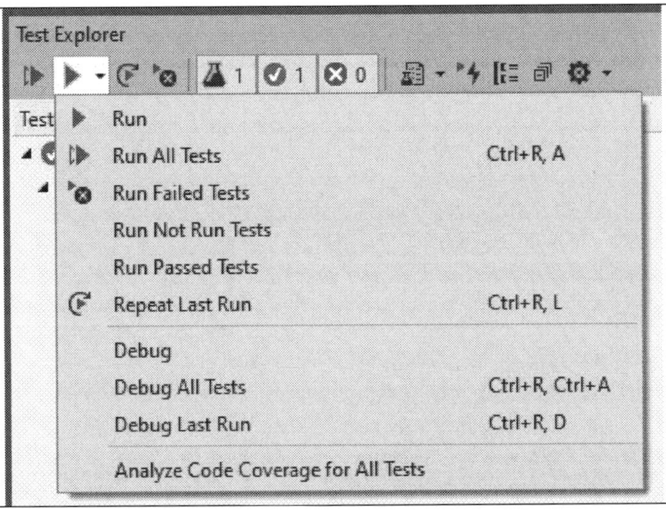

Figure 9.6: Viewing the test run and debug options

Alternatively, we can use the **Debug Tests** command that is shown when we right-click on the `WorldCities.Tests` project node from the **Solution Explorer** window:

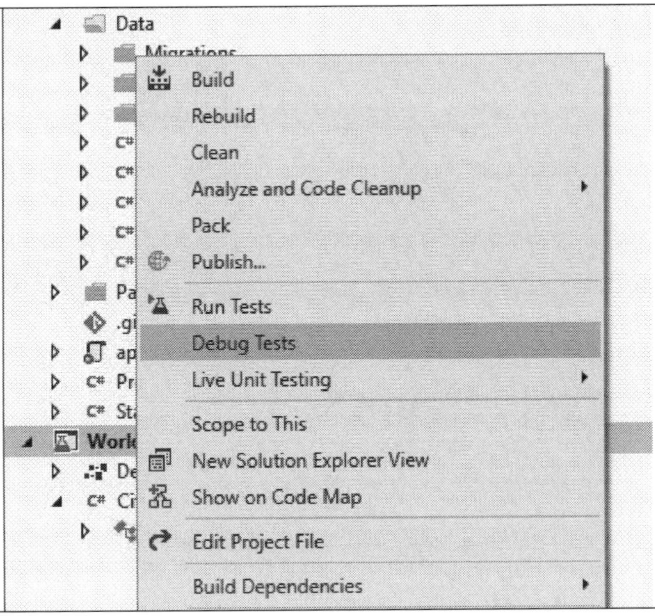

Figure 9.7: Viewing the Debug Tests option

Both commands will execute our test in debug mode, meaning that we can set breakpoints (or conditional breakpoints) and evaluate the results.

To quickly test it, set a breakpoint on the first line of the `Assert` region, then execute the preceding **Debug Tests** command, and wait for the hit:

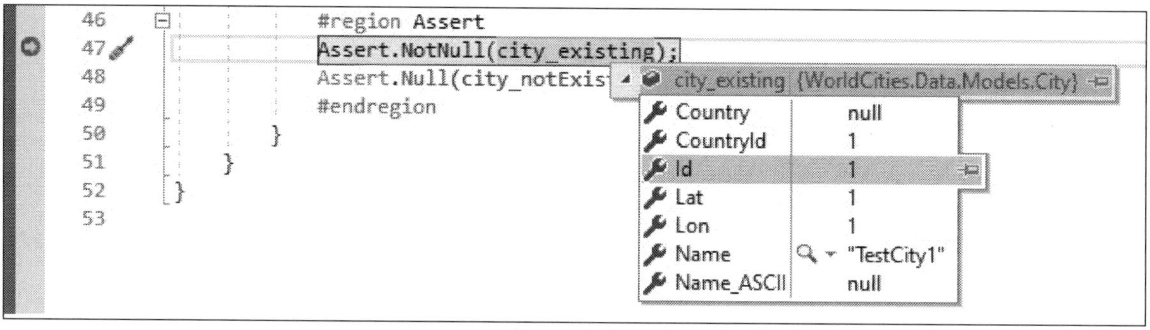

Figure 9.8: Hitting the breakpoint

There we go. Now, we know how to debug our unit tests. This can be very useful during the adoption phase when we still don't know how to properly use them and/or we're still learning the various xUnit.net commands.

> Those readers who want to know more about `xUnit.net` for ASP.NET Core and the unique unit test classes and methods provided by this package are strongly encouraged to check out the following URL: `https://xunit.net/docs/getting-started/netcore/cmdline`

Before switching to the *front-end*, it might be worthwhile spending a couple of minutes familiarizing ourselves with the concepts of TDD and BDD, since this is something that could greatly help us to create useful and relevant tests.

Test-driven development

TDD is more of a programming practice than a testing approach, and it can be a very good practice, at least for certain scenarios.

In a nutshell, a software developer that adopts the TDD methodology will convert all of the software requirements into specific test cases, and then write the new code, or improve the existing code, so that the tests will pass.

Let's try to visualize the actual life cycle of these programming practices with the help of a small diagram:

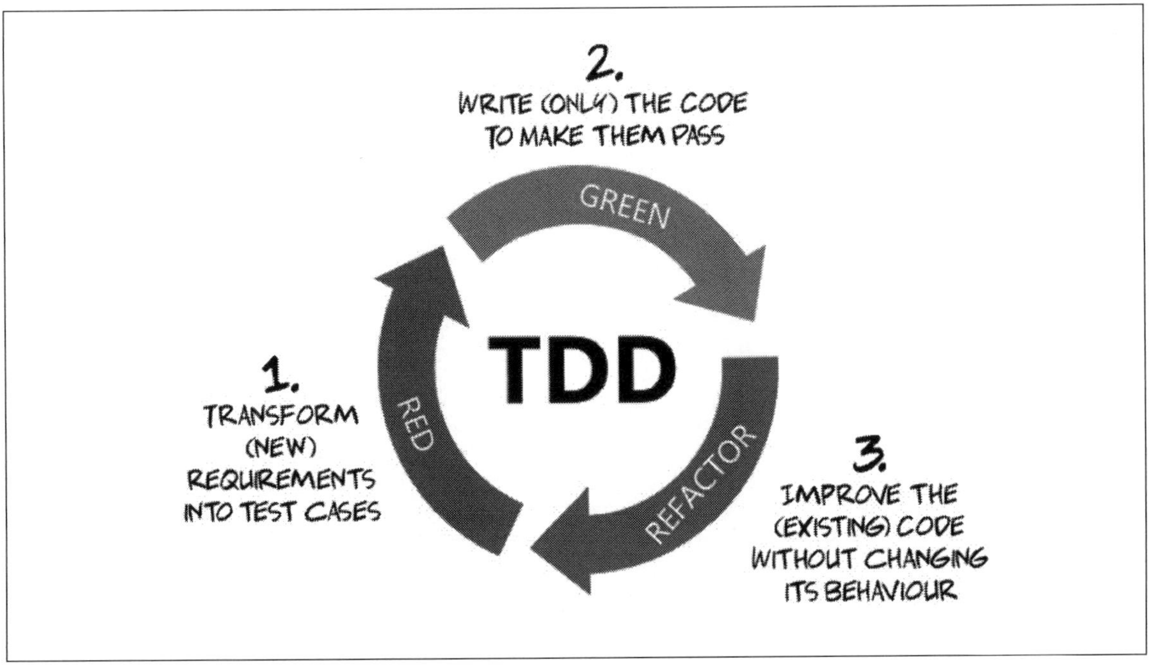

Figure 9.9: Test-driven development life cycle

As we can see, TDD is mostly a way of designing the code that requires developers to **start writing test cases that express what they intend the code to do before writing any actual code (RED)**. Once done, it asks them to **only write the code required to make the test cases pass (GREEN)**. Eventually, **when all of the test cases pass, the existing code can be improved (REFACTOR)**, until more test cases appear. This short development cycle is conventionally called **RED-GREEN-REFACTOR** and is the backbone of the TDD practice. It's worth noting that **RED** is always the initial step of any cycle since the tests will always fail at the start because the code that could allow them to pass is yet to be written.

Such a practice is very different from the STD practice, where we first generate the code and then (maybe) the tests. In other words, our source code can be (and therefore usually gets) written before (or even without) test cases. The main difference between the two approaches is that, in TDD, tests are the requirement conditions that we need to fulfill, while in STD, as we have already said a short while ago, they are mostly the proof that our existing code is working.

In the next chapter, when dealing with authentication and authorization, we'll try to create a couple of *back-end* unit tests using the TDD approach; after all, since the TDD practice requires the creation of test cases only when we have to implement additional requirements, the best way to use it is when we have some new features to add.

Behavior-driven development

BDD is an agile software development process that shares the same test-first approach as TDD but **emphasizes results from the end-user's perspective instead of focusing on implementation**.

To better understand the key differences between TDD and BDD, we can ask ourselves the following question:

What are we testing for?

That's a great question to ask when we're about to write some unit tests.

If we want to test the actual implementation of our methods/units, TDD might be the proper way to go. However, if we aim to figure out the end-user behavior of our application under specific circumstances, TDD might give us false positives, especially if the system evolves (as Agile-driven projects often do). More specifically, we could encounter a scenario where one or more units are passing their tests despite failing to deliver the expected end-user outcome.

In more general terms, we can say the following:

- TDD is meant to **enforce developers' control over the source code they write**
- BDD aims to **satisfy both the developer** *and* **the end-user** (or customer)

Therefore, we can easily see how BDD supersedes TDD instead of replacing it.

Let's try to wrap up these concepts in a diagram:

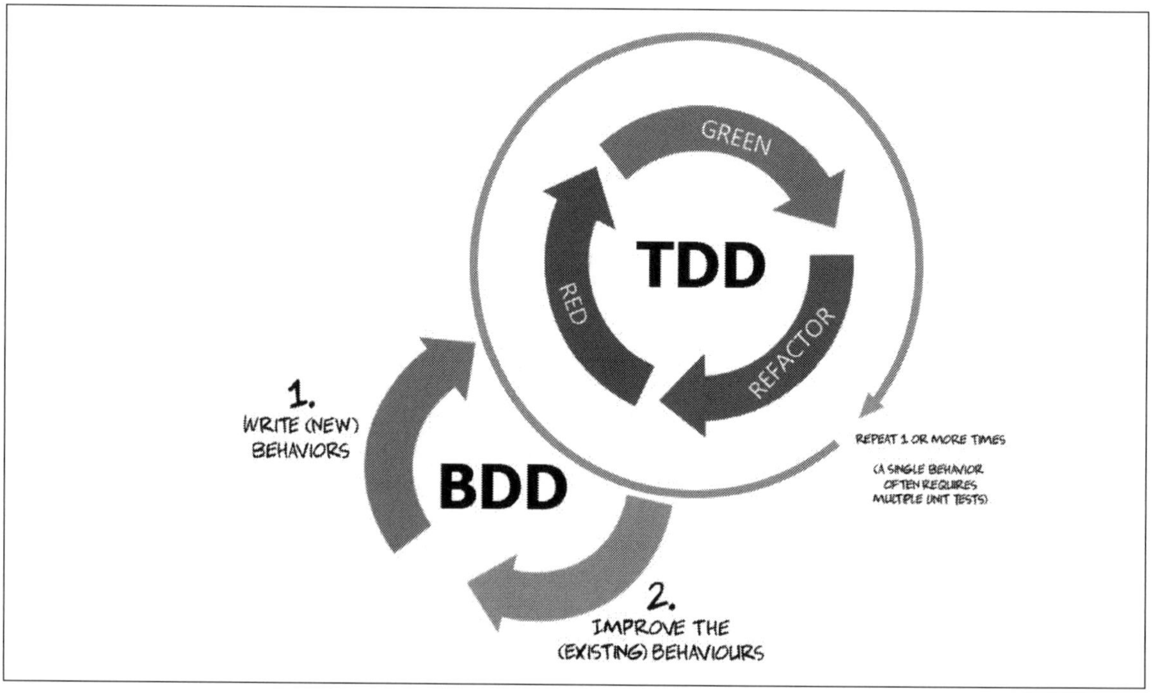

Figure 9.10: Behavior-driven development life cycle

As we can see, BDD acts just like an extension to TDD. Instead of writing the test cases, we start by writing a behavior. As soon as we do that, we will develop the required code for our application to be able to perform it (arguably using TDD), and then we move on to define additional behaviors or refactor the existing ones.

Since these behaviors are aimed at the end-user, they must also be written using understandable terms. For that very reason, the BDD tests are usually defined using a semi-formal format that is borrowed from Agile's user stories, with a strong narrative and explicit contextualization. These user stories are generally meant to comply with the following structure:

- **Title**: An explicit title, such as *Editing an Existing City*
- **Narrative**: A descriptive section that uses the *Role/Feature/Benefit* pattern from Agile user stories, such as: *As a user, I want to edit an existing City, so that I can change its values*
- **Acceptance criteria**: A description of the three test phases, using the *Given/When/Then* model, which is basically a more understandable version of the *Arrange/Act/Assert* cycle used in TDD, such as: **Given** *a world cities database containing one or more cities;* **When** *the user selects a City;* **Then** *the app must retrieve it from the DB and display it on the front-end*

As we can see, we just tried to describe the unit test we created a while ago using a typical BDD approach. Although it mostly works, it's evident that a single behavior might require multiple *back-end* and *front-end* unit tests. This lets us understand another distinctive feature of the BDD practice. Emphasizing the utmost importance of the *front-end* testing phase is the best way to test user behavior rather than an implementation spec.

All in all, BDD can be a great way to extend a standard TDD approach to design our tests in a way that their results can address a wider audience—provided we're able to properly design the required *front-end* and *back-end* tests.

In the next section, we're going to learn how we can do that.

Angular unit tests

Everything we have said in the previous sections of this chapter regarding the ASP.NET Core testing purposes, meanings, and approaches is also valid for Angular.

Luckily enough, this time, we won't need to install anything since the ASP.NET Core and Angular Visual Studio template that we've used to create our `WorldCities` project already contains everything we need to write app tests for our Angular application.

More specifically, we can already count on the following packages, which we briefly introduced in *Chapter 2, Looking Around*:

- **Jasmine**: A JavaScript testing framework that fully supports the BDD approach that we talked about earlier
- **Karma**: A tool that lets us spawn browsers and run our Jasmine tests inside them (and show their results) from the command line

- **Protractor**: An end-to-end test framework that runs tests against Angular applications from within a real browser, interacting with it as if it were a real user

> For additional information regarding Jasmine and Karma, check out the following guides:
>
> **Karma**: `https://karma-runner.github.io/`
>
> **Jasmine**: `https://jasmine.github.io/`
>
> **Protractor**: `https://www.protractortest.org/`
>
> **Angular unit test**: `https://angular.io/guide/testing`

In the following sections, we're going to do the following:

- **Review the testing configuration files** still present in our `WorldCities` Angular app
- **Introduce the TestBed interface**, one of the most important concepts of Angular testing
- **Explore Jasmine and Karma** to understand how they actually work
- **Create some .spec.ts files** to test our existing components
- **Set up and configure some tests** for our Angular app

Let's get started!

General concepts

In contrast to what we did in ASP.NET Core, where we created our unit tests in separate `WorldCities.Tests` projects, all our *front-end* tests will be written in the same project that hosts our Angular app.

As a matter of fact, we've already seen one of these tests in *Chapter 2, Looking Around*, when we explored the Angular folders for the first time. The test was written in the `counter.component.spec.ts` file, which we then deleted at the end of that chapter because we no longer required `CounterComponent`.

Luckily enough, we didn't delete the following files from the `/ClientApp/src/app/` folder:

- `karma.conf.js`: The application-specific Karma configuration file, containing information about the reporters, the browser to use, the TCP port, and so on
- `test.ts`: The Angular entry point for the project's unit test; this is where Angular initializes the testing environment, configures the `.spec.ts` extensions to identify the test files, and loads the required modules from the `@angular/core/testing` and `@angular/platform-browser-dynamic/testing` packages

That's a good thing because now we just need to write tests for our new components. However, before doing that, it would be wise to spend a bit longer explaining how Angular testing actually works.

Introducing the TestBed interface

The **TestBed** interface is one of the most important concepts of the Angular testing approach. In a nutshell, TestBed is a dynamically constructed Angular test module that emulates the behavior of an Angular `@NgModule`.

The TestBed concept was first introduced with Angular 2 as a convenient way to test a component with a real DOM behind it. The TestBed interface significantly assists in this regard thanks to its support for injecting services (either real or mock) into our components, as well as automatically binding components and templates.

To better understand how TestBed actually works and how we can use it, let's take a look at the TestBed implementation provided within the `counter.component.spec.ts` file that we deleted back in *Chapter 2*, *Looking Around*:

```
TestBed.configureTestingModule({
  declarations: [ CounterComponent ]
})
  .compileComponents();
```

In the preceding code, we can see how TestBed reproduces the behavior of a minimalistic `AppModule` file—the bootstrap `@NgModule` of an Angular app—with the sole purpose of compiling the components that we need to test. It uses the Angular module system (which we talked about in *Chapter 3*, *Front-End and Back-End Interactions*) to declare and compile `CounterComponent` so that we can use its source code in our tests.

Testing with Jasmine

Jasmine tests are usually constructed using the following three main APIs:

- `describe()`: A wrapping context used to create a group of tests (also called a *test suite*)
- `it()`: The declaration of a single test
- `expect()`: The expected result of a test

These APIs will be available within our `*.spec.ts` files in the form of static methods thanks to the built-in Angular integration with the Jasmine testing framework.

Keeping this in mind, let's create our first testing class file for our Angular app.

Our first Angular test suite

Let's now try to create our own test suite, and a corresponding TestBed, for one of our existing Angular components. We'll use `CitiesComponent` since we know it very well.

> Unfortunately, the Angular CLI doesn't (yet) provide a way to automatically generate `spec.ts` files for existing component classes. However, there are a number of third-party libraries that generate specs based on Angular CLI spec presets.
>
> The most popular (and widely used) package that does that is called `ngx-spec` and is available on GitHub at the following URL: `https://github.com/smnbbrv/ngx-spec`
>
> However, we're not going to use it in our specific scenario; we'll create and implement our `spec.ts` files manually so that we can better understand how they work.

From **Solution Explorer**, create a new `/ClientApp/src/app/cities/cities.component.spec.ts` file and open it. Since we're going to write a fair amount of source code, it would be wise to separate it into multiple blocks.

The import section

Let's start by defining the required `import` statements:

```
import { async, ComponentFixture, TestBed } from
 '@angular/core/testing';
import { BrowserAnimationsModule } from
 '@angular/platform-browser/animations';
import { AngularMaterialModule } from '../angular-material.module';
import { RouterTestingModule } from '@angular/router/testing';
import { of } from 'rxjs';

import { CitiesComponent } from './cities.component';
import { City } from './city';
import { CityService } from './city.service';
import { ApiResult } from '../base.service';

// ...to be continued...
```

As we can see, we added a bunch of modules that we already used in our `AppModule` and `CitiesComponent` classes. This is certainly anticipated since our TestBed will need to reproduce a suitable `@NgModule` for our tests to run.

The describe and beforeEach sections

Now that we have got all of our required references, let's see how we can use the `describe()` API to lay out our testing suite:

```
// ...existing code...

describe('CitiesComponent', () => {
  let fixture: ComponentFixture<CitiesComponent>;
  let component: CitiesComponent;

  // async beforeEach(): TestBed initialization
  beforeEach(async(() => {

    // todo: initialize the required providers

    TestBed.configureTestingModule({
      declarations: [CitiesComponent],
      imports: [
        BrowserAnimationsModule,
        AngularMaterialModule,
        RouterTestingModule
      ],
      providers: [

        // todo: reference the required providers

      ]
    })
      .compileComponents();
  }));

  // synchronous beforeEach(): fixtures and components setup
  beforeEach(() => {
    fixture = TestBed.createComponent(CitiesComponent);
    component = fixture.componentInstance;

    // todo: configure fixture/component/children/etc.

  });

  // todo: implement some tests

});
```

As we can see by looking at the preceding code, everything happens within a single `describe()` wrapping context, which represents our `CitiesComponent` test suite. All of the tests related to our `CitiesComponent` class will be implemented inside this suite.

The first thing we have done in the test suite is to define two important variables that will be used extensively in our tests:

- `fixture`: This property hosts a fixed state of `CitiesComponent` for running tests; we can use this fixture to interact with the instantiated component and its child elements
- `component`: This property will contain the `CitiesComponent` instance created from the preceding fixture

Immediately after this, we defined two consecutive `beforeEach()` method calls. To better distinguish them, we have provided them with a different name using the inline comments:

- `async beforeEach()`, where TestBed is created and initialized
- `synchronous beforeEach()`, where fixtures and components are instantiated and configured

Inside `async beforeEach()`, we have defined a TestBed by declaring our `CitiesComponent` and importing its two required modules—`BrowserAnimationModule` and `AngularMaterialModule`. As we can see from the *todo* comments we've left, we'll also need to define and configure our `providers` (such as `CityService`), otherwise, `CitiesComponent` won't be able to inject them; we'll do that in a short while.

Inside `synchronous beforeEach()`, we have instantiated our `fixture` and `component` variables. Since we'll likely have to properly set them up and/or configure some of our component's child elements, we've left another *todo* comment there as well.

At the end of the file, there's another *todo* comment. This is where we'll get to implement our tests using the `it()` and `expect()` APIs provided by the Jasmine framework.

Adding a mock CityService

Now, we're going to replace our first and second *todos* by implementing a *mock* `CityService` so that we can reference it within our TestBed.

> As we already know from back-end testing using ASP.NET Core and xUnit, a mock is a replacement object that simulates the behavior of the real one.

Just like ASP.NET Core and xUnit, Jasmine provides multiple ways to set up mock objects. In the following sections, we'll briefly review some of the most frequently used approaches.

Fake service class

We can create a fake `CityService`, which just returns whatever we want for our test. Once done, we can `import` it in the `.spec.ts` class and add it to TestBed's `providers` list so that it will be called by our component just like the real one.

Extending and overriding

Instead of creating a whole double class, we can just extend the real service and then override the methods we need in order to perform our tests. Once done, we can set up an instance of the extended class in our TestBed using `@NgModule's useValue` feature.

Interface instance

Instead of creating a new double or extended class, we can just instantiate the interface of our service, implementing just the method that we need for our tests. Once done, we can set up that instance in our TestBed using `@NgModule's useValue` feature.

Spy

This approach relies upon a Jasmine-specific feature called *spy*, which lets us take an existing class, function, or object and mock it so that we can control its return values. Since the real method won't be executed, a spy method will work just like an override, without having to create an extended class.

We can use such a feature to create a real instance of our service, spy the method that we want to override, and then set up that specific instance in our TestBed using `@NgModule's useValue` feature. Alternatively, we can use the `jasmine.createSpyObj()` static function to create a mock object with multiple spy methods that we can then configure in various ways.

Implementing the mock CityService

Which route should we take? Unfortunately, there's no one best answer for all scenarios, since the best approach often depends on the complexity of the features we want to test and/or how we want to structure our test suite.

Theoretically speaking, creating a whole **fake service class** is arguably the safest and most versatile choice since we can fully customize our mock service return values. However, it can also be time-consuming and often unnecessary, when we're dealing with simple services and/or small-scale tests. Conversely, the **extend and override**, **interface**, and **spy** approaches are often a great way to address the basic requirements of most tests, yet they might give unexpected results in complex testing scenarios, unless we pay close attention to overriding/spying all of the required methods.

Everything considered, since our `CityService` is quite small and features a simple implementation with a small number of methods, we're going to use the spy approach, which seems to be the most apt for our given scenario.

Let's go back to the `/ClientApp/src/cities/cities.components.spec.ts` file. Once there, the following line of code needs to be replaced:

```
// todo: initialize the required providers
```

The preceding line of code has to be replaced with the following code:

```
// Create a mock cityService object with a mock 'getData' method
const cityService = jasmine.createSpyObj<CityService>('CityService',
['getData']);

// Configure the 'getData' spy method
cityService.getData.and.returnValue(
  // return an Observable with some test data
  of<ApiResult<City>>(<ApiResult<City>>{
    data: [
      <City>{
        name: 'TestCity1',
        id: 1, lat: 1, lon: 1,
        countryId: 1, countryName: 'TestCountry1'
      },
      <City>{
        name: 'TestCity2',
        id: 2, lat: 1, lon: 1,
        countryId: 1, countryName: 'TestCountry1'
      },
      <City>{
        name: 'TestCity3',
        id: 3, lat: 1, lon: 1,
        countryId: 1, countryName: 'TestCountry1'
      }
    ],
    totalCount: 3,
    pageIndex: 0,
    pageSize: 10
  }));
```

That's it. Now, we can add our new mock `CityService` to the TestBed configuration, replacing the second *todo*:

```
// todo: reference the required providers
```

This is replaced with the highlighted lines of the following code:

```
// ...existing code...

TestBed.configureTestingModule({
```

```
  declarations: [CitiesComponent],
  imports: [
    BrowserAnimationsModule,
    AngularMaterialModule,
    RouterTestingModule
  ],
  providers: [
    {
      provide: CityService,
      useValue: cityService
    }
  ]
})
  .compileComponents();

// ...existing code...
```

That mock `CityService` will now be injected into `CitiesComponent`, thereby making us able to control the data returned for each test.

Alternative implementation using the interface approach

Here's how we could have implemented the mock `CityService` using the interface approach:

```
// Create a mock cityService object with a mock 'getData' method
const cityService = <CityService>{
  get: () => { return null; },
  put: () => { return null; },
  post: () => { return null; },
  getCountries: () => { return null; },
  isDupeCity: () => { return null; },
  http: null,
  baseUrl: null,
  getData: () => {
    // return an Observable with some test data
    return of<ApiResult<City>>(<ApiResult<City>>{
      data: [
        <City>{
          name: 'TestCity1',
          id: 1, lat: 1, lon: 1,
          countryId: 1, countryName: 'TestCountry1'
        },
        <City>{
          name: 'TestCity2',
          id: 2, lat: 1, lon: 1,
          countryId: 1, countryName: 'TestCountry1'
        },
```

```
        <City>{
          name: 'TestCity3',
          id: 3, lat: 1, lon: 1,
          countryId: 1, countryName: 'TestCountry1'
        }
      ],
      totalCount: 3,
      pageIndex: 0,
      pageSize: 10
    });
  }
};
```

As we can see, the code is rather similar, but implementing the interface requires additional code if we want to maintain the `<CityService>` type assertion. That's why we've used the **spy** approach instead.

Configuring the fixture and the component

It's now time to remove the third *todo* in our `/ClientApp/src/cities/cities.components.spec.ts` class:

```
// todo: configure fixture/component/children/etc.
```

This needs to be replaced with the following highlighted lines:

```
// ...existing code...

// synchronous beforeEach(): fixtures and components setup
beforeEach(() => {
  fixture = TestBed.createComponent(CitiesComponent);
  component = fixture.componentInstance;

  component.paginator = jasmine.createSpyObj(
    "MatPaginator", ["length", "pageIndex", "pageSize"]
  );

  fixture.detectChanges();
});

// ...existing code...
```

The preceding code will perform the following steps directly before each test:

- Create a mock `MatPaginator` object instance
- Trigger a change detection run on our component

> As we might easily surmise, change detection isn't done automatically there, so we have to manually trigger it by calling the `detectChanges` method on our **fixture**. This will make our `ngOnInit()` method fire and populate the table with the cities. Since we're testing the component behavior, that's definitely something to do before running our tests.

Creating the title test

We're finally ready to create our first test.

The last remaining *todo* line in our `/ClientApp/src/cities/cities.components.spec.ts` class needs to be replaced:

```
// todo: implement some tests
```

The preceding line of code needs to be replaced as follows:

```
it('should display a "Cities" title', async(() => {
  let title = fixture.nativeElement
    .querySelector('h1');
  expect(title.textContent).toEqual('Cities');
}));
```

As we can see, we're finally using the `it()` and `expect()` Jasmine methods. The former declares the meaning of our test, while the latter evaluates the component's behavior against the expected one and determines the test result.

In this first test, we want to check that the component displays a `Cities` title to the user. Since we know that our component's template holds the title inside an `<H1>` HTML element, we can check it by performing a DOM query against `fixture.nativeElement`, the root component element that contains all of the rendered HTML content.

Once we get the `title` element, we check its `textContent` property to see whether it's what we expect (`Cities`). This is what will make the test pass or fail.

Creating the cities tests

Before running our test suite, let's add another test.

Open the `/ClientApp/src/cities/cities.components.spec.ts` file again and add the following lines right below the previous test:

```
// ...existing code...

it('should contain a table with a list of one or more cities', async(() => {
  let table = fixture.nativeElement
    .querySelector('table.mat-table');
  let tableRows = table
```

```
      .querySelectorAll('tr.mat-row');
    expect(tableRows.length).toBeGreaterThan(0);
  }));

  // ...existing code...
```

This time, we're checking the table that contains the list of cities. More precisely, we're counting the table body rows to ensure that the resulting number is greater than zero, meaning that the table has been filled with at least one city. To perform such a count, we're using the CSS classes that Angular Material assigns to its `MatTable` component by default.

To better understand this, take a look at the following screenshot:

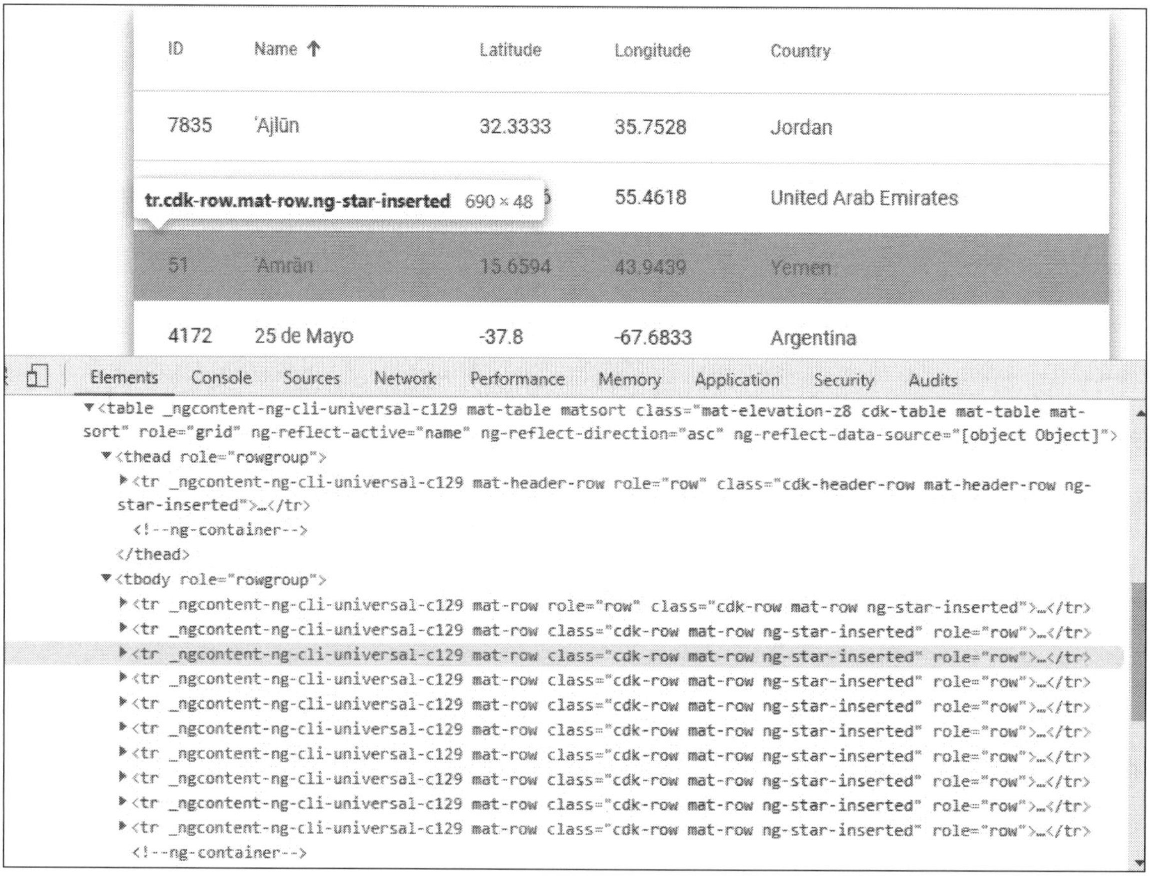

Figure 9.11: Inspecting rows of our Cities list

As we can see, the `mat-row` CSS class is only applied to the table body rows, while the table header rows have the `mat-header-row` class. Therefore, if the test passes, it definitely means that the component created at least one row within the table.

> **IMPORTANT**: It goes without saying that relying upon CSS classes applied by a third-party package to define our tests is not a good practice. We're doing this just to demonstrate what we can do with our current implementation. A safer approach for such DOM-based tests would arguably require defining custom CSS classes and checking for their presence instead.

Running the test suite

It's now time to run our test suite and see what we've got.

To do this, perform the following steps:

1. Open Command Prompt
2. Navigate to the `/ClientApp/` folder of the `WorldCities` app
3. Execute the following command:

```
> ng test
```

This will launch the Karma test runner, which will open a dedicated browser to run the tests in. If we have done everything correctly, we should be able to see the following results:

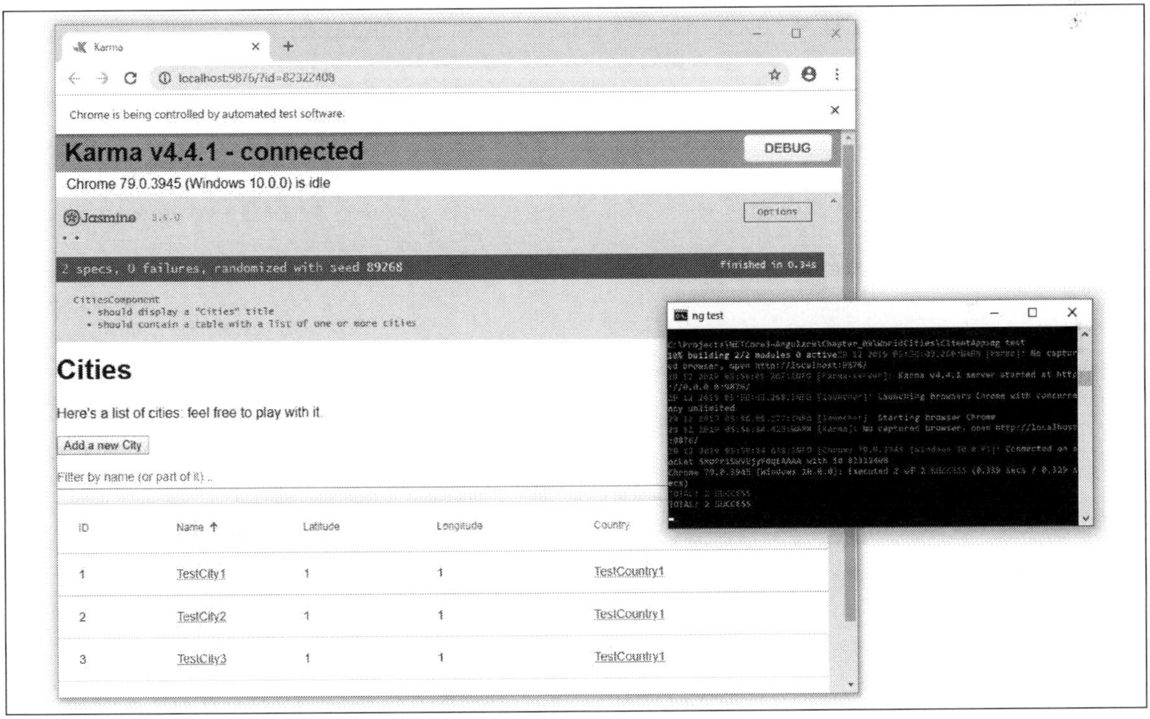

Figure 9.12: Results of our test

That's it; both tests passed. To be 100% certain that we did everything properly, let's now try to make them fail.

Open the `/ClientApp/src/cities/cities.components.spec.ts` file again and modify the test's source code in the following way (the updated lines are highlighted):

```
it('should display a "Cities" title', async(() => {
  let title = fixture.nativeElement
    .querySelector('h1');
  expect(title.textContent).toEqual('Cities!!!');
}));

it('should contain a table with a list of one or more cities', async(() => {
  let table = fixture.nativeElement
    .querySelector('table.mat-table');
  let tableRows = table
    .querySelectorAll('tr.mat-row');
  expect(tableRows.length).toBeGreaterThan(3);
}));
```

Now, our first test will expect an incorrect title value, and the second is looking for more than three rows, which won't be the case since our mock `CityService` has been configured to serve three of them.

As soon as we save the file, the Karma test runner should automatically reload the testing page and show the updated results (refer to the following screenshot):

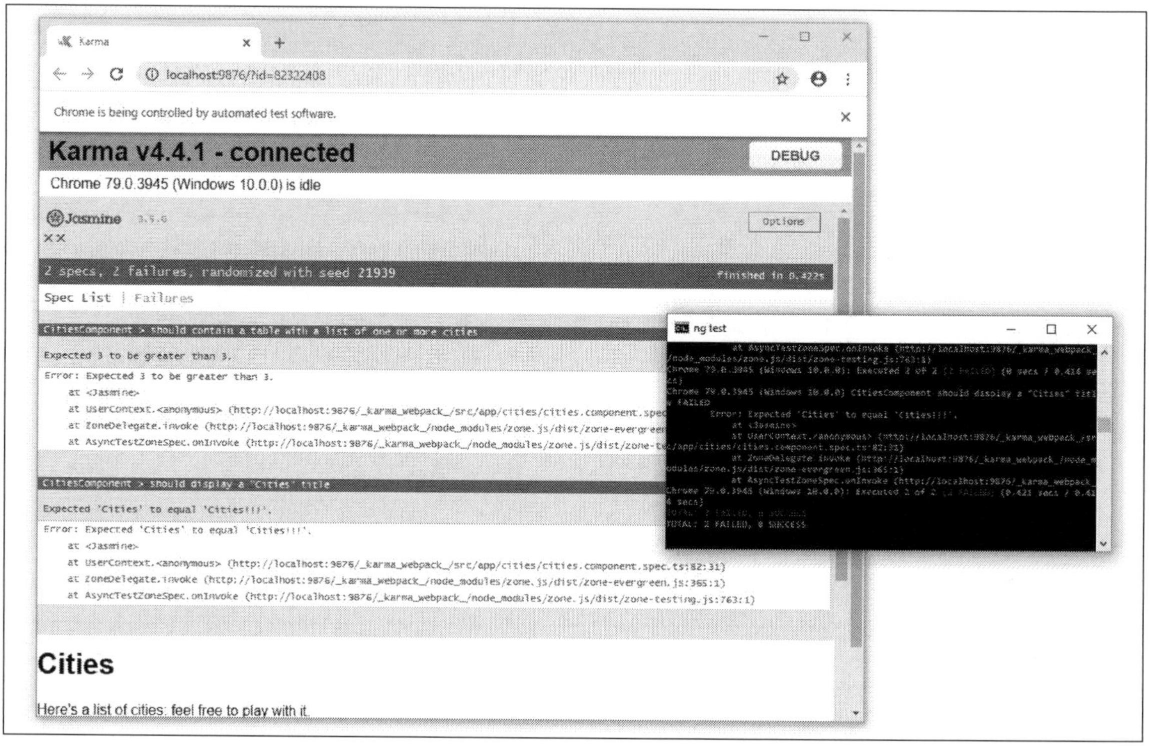

Figure 9.13: Results showing the test has failed

There we go. Now, we are experiencing two failures, just as expected. The Jasmine framework is also telling us what's wrong so that we can address the issues promptly.

Let's do this. Open the `/ClientApp/src/cities/cities.components.spec.ts` file and revert the test's source code back to how it was before:

```
it('should display a "Cities" title', async(() => {
  let title = fixture.nativeElement
    .querySelector('h1');
  expect(title.textContent).toEqual('Cities');
}));

it('should contain a table with a list of one or more cities', async(() => {
  let table = fixture.nativeElement
    .querySelector('table.mat-table');
  let tableRows = table
    .querySelectorAll('tr.mat-row');
  expect(tableRows.length).toBeGreaterThan(0);
}));
```

That's it. Now that we have *tested* our test suite, we can close the test runner by pressing *Ctrl + C* on the `ng test` Terminal window and then choosing *Y* (and hitting *Enter*) to terminate the batch job.

With this, we've concluded our learning journey through *front-end* testing.

Summary

This chapter was entirely dedicated to the concepts of testing and unit testing. After a brief introduction, where we explained the meaning of these concepts and the various testing practices available, we spent some valuable time learning how to implement them properly.

We started focusing on *back-end* testing with the help of the xUnit.net testing tool. Such an approach required us to create a new test project, where we implemented our first *back-end* unit tests. While working at it, we learned the importance of some test-related concepts, such as mocking, which we used to emulate the behavior of our `ApplicationDbContext` class to provide some in-memory data instead of using our SQL Server data source.

The *back-end* testing approach greatly helped us to understand the meaning of TDD and its similarities and differences vis-à-vis the BDD approach, which is a distinctive *front-end* testing practice.

Such a comparison guided us to Angular, where we used the **Jasmine** testing framework and the **Karma** test runner to develop some *front-end* tests. Here, we got the opportunity to learn some good testing practices as well as other important concepts strictly related to the Jasmine framework, such as TestBed, test suites, and spies. Eventually, we successfully saw our tests in action in our `WorldCities` app.

In the next chapter, we'll try to design some more tests when dealing with the authorization and authentication topics. The concepts that we learned here will definitely be very useful when having to implement the registration and login workflows.

Suggested topics

Unit Testing, xUnit, Moq, TDD, BDD, Mock, Stub, Fixture, Jasmine, Karma, Protractor, Spy, test suite, TestBed.

References

- *Getting Started with xUnit.net*: `https://xunit.net/docs/getting-started/netcore/cmdline`
- *Unit testing in .NET*: `https://docs.microsoft.com/en-US/dotnet/core/testing/`
- *Unit test controller logic in ASP.NET Core*: `https://docs.microsoft.com/en-us/aspnet/core/mvc/controllers/testing`
- *The using statement (C#)*: `https://docs.microsoft.com/en-US/dotnet/csharp/language-reference/keywords/using-statement`
- *xUnit.net – Using ASP.NET Core with the .NET SDK command line*: `https://xunit.net/docs/getting-started/netcore/cmdline`
- *Angular – Testing*: `https://angular.io/guide/testing`
- *Protractor: End-to-end testing for Angular*: `https://www.protractortest.org/`
- *Jasmine: Behavior-Driven JavaScript*: `https://jasmine.github.io/`
- *Karma: Spectacular Test Runner for JavaScript*: `https://karma-runner.github.io/latest/index.html`
- *Angular Testing: ComponentFixture*: `https://angular.io/api/core/testing/ComponentFixture`
- *Angular References: ngAfterViewInit*: `https://ngrefs.com/latest/core/ng-after-view-init`

10
Authentication and Authorization

Generally speaking, the term *authentication* refers to any process of verification that someone, be it a human being or an automated system, is who (or what) they claim to be. This is also true within the context of the **World Wide Web (WWW)**, where that same word is mostly used to denote any technique used by a website or service to collect a set of login information from a user agent, typically a web browser, and authenticate them using a membership and/or identity service.

Authentication should never be confused with *authorization*, as this is a different process and is in charge of a very different task. To give a quick definition, we can say that the purpose of authorization is to confirm that the requesting user is allowed to have access to the action they want to perform. In other words, while authentication is about who they are, authorization is about what they're allowed to do.

To better understand the difference between these two apparently similar concepts, we can think of two real-world scenarios:

- A free, yet registered, account trying to gain access to a paid or premium-only service or feature. This is a common example of authenticated, yet not authorized access; we know who they are, yet they're not allowed to go there.
- An anonymous user trying to gain access to a publicly available page or file; this is an example of non-authenticated, yet authorized, access; we don't know who they are, yet they can access public resources just like everyone else.

Authentication and authorization will be the main topics of this chapter, which we'll try to address from both theoretical and practical points of view. More precisely, we're going to do the following:

- **Discuss some typical scenarios** where authentication and authorization could either be required or not.
- **Introduce ASP.NET Core Identity**, a modern membership system that allows developers to add login functionality to their applications, as well as `IdentityServer`, middleware designed to add **OpenID Connect** and OAuth 2.0 endpoints to any ASP.NET Core application.

- **Implement ASP.NET Core Identity and IdentityServer** to add login and registration functionalities to our existing `WorldCities` app.
- **Explore the Angular authorization API** provided by the .NET Core and Angular Visual Studio project template, which implements the **oidc-client** npm package to interact with the URI endpoints provided by the ASP.NET Core Identity system, as well as some key Angular features, such as **route guards** and **HTTP interceptors**, to handle the whole authorization flow.
- **Integrate the aforementioned back-end and front-end APIs** into our `WorldCities` project in order to give our users a satisfying authentication and authentication experience.
- **Implement an email sending service**, so that our app will be able to properly authenticate registered users using a typical email confirmation flow.

Let's do our best!

Technical requirements

In this chapter, we're going to need all the technical requirements listed in the previous chapters, with the following additional packages:

- `Microsoft.AspNetCore.Identity.EntityFrameworkCore`
- `Microsoft.AspNetCore.ApiAuthorization.IdentityServer`
- `Microsoft.AspNetCore.Identity.UI`
- `SendGrid`
- `MailKit`

As always, it's advisable to avoid installing them straight away; we're going to bring them in during the chapter to better contextualize their purposes within our project.

The code files for this chapter can be found at: `https://github.com/PacktPublishing/ASP.NET-5-and-Angular/tree/master/Chapter_10/`

To auth, or not to auth

As a matter of fact, implementing authentication and/or authorization logic isn't mandatory for most web-based applications or services; there are a number of websites that still don't do that, mostly because they serve content that can be accessed by anyone at any time. This used to be pretty common among most corporate, marketing, and informative websites until some years ago; that was before their owners learned how important it is to build a network of registered users and how much these "loyal" contacts are worth nowadays.

We don't need to be experienced developers to acknowledge how much the WWW has changed in the last few years; each and every website, regardless of its purpose, has an increasing and more or less legitimate interest in tracking its users nowadays, giving them the chance to customize their navigation experience, interact with their social networks, collect email addresses, and so on. None of the preceding can be done without an authentication mechanism of some sort.

There are billions of websites and services that require authentication to work properly, as most of their content and/or intents depend upon the actions of registered users: forums, blogs, shopping carts, subscription-based services, and even collaborative tools such as wikis.

Long story short, the answer is yes, as long as we want to have users performing **Create, Read, Update, and Delete** (**CRUD**) operations within our client app, there is no doubt that we should implement some kind of authentication and authorization procedure. If we're aiming for a production-ready **Single-Page Application** (**SPA**) featuring some user interactions of any kind, we definitely want to know who our users are in terms of names and email addresses. It is the only way to determine who will be able to view, add, update, or delete our records, not to mention perform administrative-level tasks, keep track of our users, and so on.

Authentication

Since the origin of the WWW, the vast majority of authentication techniques rely upon **HTTP/HTTPS implementation standards**, and all of them work more or less in the following way:

1. A non-authenticated user agent asks for content that cannot be accessed without some kind of permission.
2. The web application returns an authentication request, usually in the form of an HTML page containing an empty web form to complete.
3. The user agent fills in the web form with their credentials, usually a username and a password, and then sends it back with a `POST` command, which is most likely issued by a click on a **Submit** button.
4. The web application receives the `POST` data and calls the aforementioned server-side implementation, which will try to authenticate the user with the given input and return an appropriate result.
5. If the result is successful, the web application will authenticate the user and store the relevant data somewhere, depending on the chosen authentication method: sessions/cookies, tokens, signatures, and so on (we'll talk about these later on). Conversely, the result will be presented to the user as a readable outcome inside an error page, possibly asking them to try again, contact an administrator, or something else.

This is still the most common approach nowadays. Almost all websites we can think of are using it, albeit with a number of big or small differences regarding security layers, state management, **JSON Web Tokens** (**JWTs**) or other RESTful tokens, basic or digest access, single sign-on properties, and more.

Third-party authentication

Being forced to have a potentially different username and password for each website visit can be frustrating, as well as requiring users to develop custom password storage techniques that might lead to security risks. In order to overcome this issue, a large number of IT developers started to look around for an alternative way to authenticate users that could replace the standard authentication technique based on usernames and passwords with an authentication protocol based on trusted third-party providers.

The rise and fall of OpenID

Among the first successful attempts to implement a third-party authentication mechanism was the first release of **OpenID**, an open and decentralized authentication protocol promoted by the non-profit OpenID Foundation. Available since 2005, it was quickly and enthusiastically adopted by some big players such as Google and Stack Overflow, who originally based their authentication providers on it.

Here's how it works in a few words:

- Whenever our application receives an OpenID authentication request, it opens a transparent connection interface through the requesting user and a trusted third-party authentication provider (for example, the **Google identity provider**); the interface can be a popup, an AJAX-populated modal window, or an API call, depending on the implementation.
- The user sends their username and password to the aforementioned third-party provider, who performs the authentication accordingly and communicates the result to our application by redirecting the user to where they came from, along with a security token that can be used to retrieve the authentication result.
- Our application consumes the token to check the authentication result, authenticating the user in the event of success or sending an error response in the event of failure.

Despite the great enthusiasm between 2005 and 2009, with a good number of relevant companies publicly declaring their support for OpenID and even joining the foundation—including PayPal and Facebook—the original protocol didn't live up to its great expectations: legal controversies, security issues, and, most importantly, the massive popularity surge of the social networks with their improper—yet working—**OAuth-based** social logins in the 2009-2012 period basically killed it.

> Those who don't know what OAuth is, have some patience; we'll get there soon enough.

OpenID Connect

In a desperate attempt to keep their flag flying after the takeover of the **OAuth/OAuth 2** social logins, the OpenID Foundation released the third generation of the OpenID technology in February 2014; this was called **OpenID Connect (OIDC)**.

Despite the name, the new installment has little to nothing to do with its ancestor; it's merely an authentication layer built upon the OAuth 2 authorization protocol. In other words, it's little more than a standardized interface to help developers use OAuth 2 as an authentication framework in a less improper way, which is kind of funny, considering that OAuth 2 played a major role in taking out OpenID 2.0 in the first place.

The choice of giving up on OpenID in favor of OIDC was highly criticized in 2014; however, after all these years, we can definitely say that OIDC can still provide a useful, standardized way to obtain user identities. It allows developers to request and receive information about authenticated users and sessions using a convenient, RESTful-based JSON interface; it features an extensible specification that also supports some promising optional features such as encryption of identity data, auto-discovery of OpenID providers, and even session management. In short, it's still useful enough to be used instead of relying on pure OAuth 2.

> For additional information about OpenID, we strongly suggest reading the following specifications from the OpenID Foundation official website:
>
> **OpenID Connect**:
> `http://openid.net/specs/openid-connect-core-1_0.html`
>
> **OpenID 2.0 to OIDC migration guide**:
> `http://openid.net/specs/openid-connect-migration-1_0.html`

Authorization

In most standard implementations, including those featured by ASP.NET, the authorization phase kicks in right after authentication, and it's mostly based on permissions or roles; any authenticated user might have their own set of permissions and/or belong to one or more roles and thus be granted access to a specific set of resources. These *role-based* checks are usually set by the developer in a declarative fashion within the application source code and/or configuration files.

Authorization, as we said, shouldn't be confused with authentication, despite the fact that it can be easily exploited to perform an implicit authentication as well, especially when it's delegated to a third-party actor.

Third-party authorization

The best-known third-party authorization protocol nowadays is the 2.0 release of OAuth, also known as OAuth 2, which supersedes the former release (OAuth 1, or simply OAuth) originally developed by Blaine Cook and Chris Messina in 2006.

We have already talked a lot about it for good reason: OAuth 2 has quickly become the industry-standard protocol for authorization and is currently used by a gigantic number of community-based websites and social networks, including Google, Facebook, and Twitter. It basically works like this:

- Whenever an existing user requests a set of permissions to our application via OAuth, we open a transparent connection interface between them and a third-party authorization provider that is trusted by our application (for example, Facebook)
- The provider acknowledges the user and, if they have the proper rights, responds by entrusting them with a temporary, specific access key
- The user presents the access key to our application and will be granted access

We can clearly see how easy it is to exploit this authorization logic for authentication purposes as well; after all, if Facebook says I can do something, shouldn't it also imply that I am who I claim to be? Isn't that enough?

The short answer is no. It might be the case for Facebook because their OAuth 2 implementation implies that subscribers receiving the authorization must have authenticated themselves to Facebook first; however, this assurance is not written anywhere. Considering how many websites are using it for authentication purposes, we can assume that Facebook won't likely change their actual behavior, yet we have no guarantees of this.

Theoretically speaking, these websites can split their authorization system from their authentication protocol at any time, thus leading our application's authentication logic to an unrecoverable state of inconsistency. More generally, we can say that presuming something from something else is almost always a bad practice, unless that assumption lies upon very solid, well-documented, and (most importantly) highly guaranteed grounds.

Proprietary versus third-party

Theoretically speaking, it's possible to entirely delegate the authentication and/or authorization tasks to existing external, third-party providers such as those we mentioned before; there are a lot of web and mobile applications that proudly follow this route nowadays. There are a number of undeniable advantages to using such an approach, including the following:

- **No user-specific database tables/data models**, just some provider-based identifiers to use here and there as reference keys.
- **Immediate registration**, since there's no need to fill in a registration form and wait for a confirmation email—no username, no password. This will be appreciated by most users and will probably increase our conversion rates as well.
- **Few or no privacy issues**, as there's no personal or sensitive data on the application server.
- **No need to handle usernames and passwords** and implement automatic recovery processes.

- **Fewer security-related issues** such as form-based hacking attempts or brute-force login attempts.

Of course, there are also some downsides:

- **There won't be an actual user base**, so it will be difficult to get an overview of active users, get their email address, analyze statistics, and so on.
- **The login phase might be resource-intensive**, since it will always require an external, back-and-forth secure connection with a third-party server.
- **All users will need to have (or open) an account with the chosen third-party provider(s)** in order to log in.
- **All users will need to trust our application** because the third-party provider will ask them to authorize it to access their data.
- **We will have to register our application with the provider** in order to be able to perform a number of required or optional tasks, such as receiving our public and secret keys, authorizing one or more URI initiators, and choosing the information we want to collect.

Taking all these pros and cons into account, we can say that relying on third-party providers might be a great time-saving choice for small-scale apps, including ours; however, building our own account management system seems to be the only way to overcome the aforementioned governance and control-based flaws undeniably brought by that approach.

In this book, we'll explore both of these routes, in an attempt to get the most—if not the best—of both worlds. In this chapter, we'll create an **internal membership provider** that will handle authentication and provide its very own set of authorization rules; in the following chapter, we'll further leverage that same implementation to demonstrate how we can give our users the chance to log in using a sample third-party auth provider (Facebook) and use its SDK and API to fetch the data that we need to create our corresponding internal users, thanks to the built-in features provided by the ASP.NET Core Identity package.

Proprietary auth with .NET Core

The authentication patterns made available by ASP.NET Core are basically the same as those supported by the previous versions of ASP.NET:

- **No authentication**, if we don't feel like implementing anything or if we want to use (or develop) a self-made auth interface without relying upon the ASP.NET Core Identity system
- **Individual user accounts**, when we set up an internal database to store user data using the standard ASP.NET Core Identity interface
- **Azure Active Directory** (AD), which implies using a token-based set of API calls handled by the **Azure AD Authentication Library** (ADAL)
- **Windows authentication**, which is only viable for local-scope applications within Windows domains or AD trees

However, the implementation patterns introduced by the ASP.NET Core team over the past few years are constantly evolving in order to match the latest security practices available.

All the aforementioned approaches—excluding the first one—are handled by the **ASP.NET Core Identity system**, a membership system that allows us to add authentication and authorization functionalities to our application.

> For additional info about the ASP.NET Core Identity APIs, check out the following URL:
>
> `https://docs.microsoft.com/en-us/aspnet/core/security/authentication/identity`

Starting with .NET Core 3.0, ASP.NET Core Identity has been integrated with a new API authorization mechanism to handle authentication in SPAs; this new feature is based on `IdentityServer`, a piece of open-source OIDC and OAuth 2.0 middleware that has been part of the .NET Foundation since .NET Core 3.0.

> Further information about `IdentityServer` can be retrieved from the official documentation website, which is available at the following URLs:
>
> `https://identityserver.io/`
> `http://docs.identityserver.io/en/latest/`

With ASP.NET Core Identity, we can easily implement a login mechanism that will allow our users to create an account and log in with a username and a password. On top of that, we can also give them the chance to use an external login provider—as long as it's supported by the framework; as of the time of writing, the list of available providers includes Facebook, Google, Microsoft account, Twitter, and more.

In this section, we're going to do the following:

- **Introduce the ASP.NET Core Identity model**, the framework provided by ASP.NET Core to manage and store user accounts
- **Set up an ASP.NET Core Identity implementation** by installing the required NuGet packages to our existing `WorldCities` app
- **Extend ApplicationDbContext** using the Individual User Accounts authentication type
- **Configure the Identity service** in our application's `Startup` class
- **Update the existing SeedController** by adding a method to create our default users with the .NET Identity API providers

Right after that, we'll also say a couple of words about the ASP.NET Core **Task Asynchronous Programming** (**TAP**) model.

The ASP.NET Core Identity model

ASP.NET Core provides a unified framework to manage and store user accounts that can be easily used in any .NET Core application (even non-web ones); this framework is called **ASP.NET Core Identity** and provides a set of APIs that allows developers to handle the following tasks:

- Design, set up, and implement user registration and login functionalities
- Manage users, passwords, profile data, roles, claims, tokens, email confirmation, and so on
- Support external (third-party) login providers such as Facebook, Google, Microsoft account, Twitter, and more

The ASP.NET Core Identity source code is open-source and available on GitHub at: `https://github.com/aspnet/AspNetCore/tree/master/src/Identity`

It goes without saying that ASP.NET Core Identity requires a persistent data source to store (and retrieve) the identity data (usernames, passwords, and profile data), such as a SQL Server database; for that very reason, it features built-in integration mechanisms with Entity Framework Core.

This means that, in order to implement our very own identity system, we'll basically extend what we did in *Chapter 4, Data Model with Entity Framework Core*; more specifically, we'll update our existing `ApplicationDbContext` to support the additional entity classes required to handle users, roles, and so on.

Entity types

The ASP.NET Core Identity platform strongly relies upon the following entity types, each one of them representing a specific set of records:

- `User`: The users of our application
- `Role`: The roles that we can assign to each user
- `UserClaim`: The claims that a user possesses
- `UserToken`: The authentication token that a user might use to perform auth-based tasks (such as logging in)
- `UserLogin`: The login account associated with each user
- `RoleClaim`: The claims that are granted to all users within a given role
- `UserRole`: The lookup table to store the relationship between users and their assigned roles

These entity types are related to each other in the following ways:

- Each `User` can have many `UserClaim`, `UserLogin`, and `UserToken` entities (*one-to-many*)
- Each `Role` can have many associated `RoleClaim` entities (*one-to-many*)
- Each `User` can have many associated `Role` entities, and each `Role` can be associated with many `User` entities (*many-to-many*)

The many-to-many relationship requires a join table in the database, which is represented by the `UserRole` entity.

Luckily enough, we won't have to manually implement all these entities from scratch, because ASP.NET Core Identity provides some default **Common Language Runtime** (**CLR**) types for each one of them:

- `IdentityUser`
- `IdentityRole`
- `IdentityUserClaim`
- `IdentityUserToken`
- `IdentityUserLogin`
- `IdentityRoleClaim`
- `IdentityUserRole`

These types can be used as *base classes* for our own implementation, whenever we need to explicitly define an identity-related entity model; moreover, most of them don't have to be implemented in most common authentication scenarios, since their functionalities can be handled at a higher level thanks to the ASP.NET Core Identity sets of APIs, which can be accessed from the following classes:

- `RoleManager<TRole>`: Provides the APIs for managing roles
- `SignInManager<TUser>`: Provides the APIs for signing users in and out (login and logout)
- `UserManager<TUser>`: Provides the APIs for managing users

Once the ASP.NET Core Identity service has been properly configured and set up, these providers can be injected into our .NET controllers using **Dependency Injection** (**DI**), just like we did with `ApplicationDbContext`; in the following section, we'll see how we can do that.

Setting up ASP.NET Core Identity

In *Chapter 1*, *Getting Ready*, and *Chapter 3*, *Front-End and Back-End Interactions*, when we created our `HealthCheck` and `WorldCities` .NET Core projects, we always made the choice to go with an empty project featuring no authentication. That was because we didn't want Visual Studio to install **ASP.NET Core Identity** within our application's startup files right from the start. However, now that we're using it, we need to manually perform the required setup steps.

Adding the NuGet packages

Enough with the theory, let's put the plan into action.

From Solution Explorer, right-click on the `WorldCities` tree node, then select **Manage NuGet Packages**. Look for the following two packages and install them:

- `Microsoft.AspNetCore.Identity.EntityFrameworkCore`
- `Microsoft.AspNetCore.ApiAuthorization.IdentityServer`

Alternatively, open `Package Manager Console` and install them with the following commands:

```
> Install-Package Microsoft.AspNetCore.Identity.EntityFrameworkCore
> Install-Package Microsoft.AspNetCore.ApiAuthorization.IdentityServer
```

At the time of writing, the latest version for both of them is **5.0.0**; as always, we are free to install a newer version, as long as we know how to adapt our code accordingly to fix potential compatibility issues.

Creating ApplicationUser

Now that we have installed the required identity libraries, we need to create a new `ApplicationUser` entity class with all the features required by the ASP.NET Core Identity service to use it for auth purposes. Luckily enough, the package comes with a built-in `IdentityUser` base class that can be used to extend our own implementation, thus granting it all that we need.

From Solution Explorer, navigate to the `/Data/Models/` folder, then create a new `ApplicationUser.cs` class and fill its content with the following code:

```
using Microsoft.AspNetCore.Identity;
using System;
using System.Collections.Generic;
using System.Linq;
using System.Threading.Tasks;

namespace WorldCities.Data.Models
{
    public class ApplicationUser : IdentityUser
    {
    }
}
```

As we can see, we don't need to implement anything there, at least not for the time being; we'll just extend the `IdentityUser` base class, which already contains everything we need for now.

Extending ApplicationDbContext

In order to support the .NET Core authentication mechanism, our existing `ApplicationDbContext` needs to be extended from a different database abstraction base class that supports ASP.NET Core Identity and `IdentityServer`.

Open the `/Data/ApplicationDbContext.cs` file and update its contents accordingly (updated lines are highlighted):

```
using IdentityServer4.EntityFramework.Options;
using Microsoft.AspNetCore.ApiAuthorization.IdentityServer;
using Microsoft.EntityFrameworkCore;
using Microsoft.Extensions.Options;
using WorldCities.Data.Models;

namespace WorldCities.Data
{
    public class ApplicationDbContext
        : ApiAuthorizationDbContext<ApplicationUser>
    {
        public ApplicationDbContext(
            DbContextOptions options,
            IOptions<OperationalStoreOptions> operationalStoreOptions)
            : base(options, operationalStoreOptions)
        {
        }

        public DbSet<City> Cities { get; set; }
        public DbSet<Country> Countries { get; set; }
    }
}
```

As we can see from the preceding code, we replaced the current `DbContext` base class with the new `ApiAuthorizationDbContext` base class; the new class strongly relies on the `IdentityServer` middleware, which also required a change in the constructor signature to accept some options that are required for properly configuring the operational context.

> For additional information about the .NET authentication and authorization system for SPAs, the ASP.NET Core Identity API, and the .NET Core `IdentityServer`, check out the following URL:
>
> `https://docs.microsoft.com/en-us/aspnet/core/security/authentication/identity-api-authorization`

Adjusting our unit tests

As soon as we save the new `ApplicationDbContext` file, our existing `CitiesController_Tests.cs` class in the `WorldCities.Tests` project will likely throw a compiler error, as shown in the following screenshot:

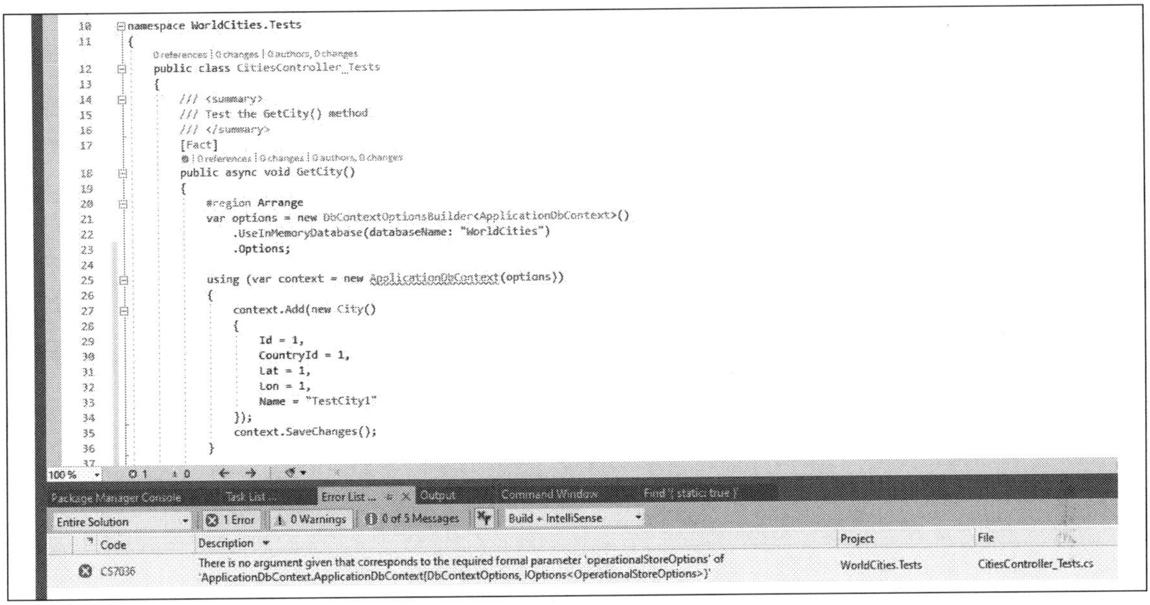

Figure 10.1: Compiler error after changing ApplicationDbContext.cs

The reason for that is well explained in the **Error List** panel: the constructor signature of `ApplicationDbContext` changed, requiring an additional parameter that we don't pass here.

> It's worth noting that this issue doesn't affect our main application's controllers since `ApplicationDbContext` is injected through DI there.

To quickly fix that, update the `CitiesController_Tests.cs` existing source code in the following way (new and updated lines are highlighted):

```
using IdentityServer4.EntityFramework.Options;

// ...existing code...

var storeOptions = Options.Create(new OperationalStoreOptions());

using (var context = new ApplicationDbContext(options, storeOptions))

// ...existing code...
```

Now the error should disappear (and the test should still pass).

Configuring the ASP.NET Core Identity middleware

Now that we're done with all the prerequisites, we can open the `Startup.cs` file and add the following highlighted lines in the `ConfigureServices` method to set up the middleware required by the ASP.NET Core Identity system:

```
// ...existing code...

// This method gets called by the runtime. Use this method to add
// services to the container.
public void ConfigureServices(IServiceCollection services)
{
    services.AddControllersWithViews()
      .AddJsonOptions(options => {
        // set this option to TRUE to indent the JSON output
        options.JsonSerializerOptions.WriteIndented = true;
        // set this option to NULL to use PascalCase instead of
        // CamelCase (default)
        // options.JsonSerializerOptions.PropertyNamingPolicy = null;
     });


    // In production, the Angular files will be served from
    // this directory
    services.AddSpaStaticFiles(configuration =>
    {
        configuration.RootPath = "ClientApp/dist";
    });

    // Add ApplicationDbContext.
    services.AddDbContext<ApplicationDbContext>(options =>
        options.UseSqlServer(
            Configuration.GetConnectionString("DefaultConnection")
            )
    );

    // Add ASP.NET Core Identity support
    services.AddDefaultIdentity<ApplicationUser>(options =>
```

```
        {
            options.SignIn.RequireConfirmedAccount = true;
            options.Password.RequireDigit = true;
            options.Password.RequireLowercase = true;
            options.Password.RequireUppercase = true;
            options.Password.RequireNonAlphanumeric = true;
            options.Password.RequiredLength = 8;
        })
        .AddRoles<IdentityRole>()
        .AddEntityFrameworkStores<ApplicationDbContext>();

    services.AddIdentityServer()
        .AddApiAuthorization<ApplicationUser, ApplicationDbContext>();

    services.AddAuthentication()
        .AddIdentityServerJwt();
}

// ...existing code...
```

And then, in the `Configure` method, add the following highlighted lines:

```
// ...existing code...

app.UseRouting();

app.UseAuthentication();
app.UseIdentityServer();
app.UseAuthorization();

app.UseEndpoints(endpoints =>

// ...existing code...
```

The preceding code strictly resembles the default .NET Core Identity implementation for SPA projects. If we created a new **ASP.NET Core web application** using the Visual Studio wizard, by selecting the **Individual User Accounts** authentication method (see the following screenshot), we would end up with the same code, with some minor differences:

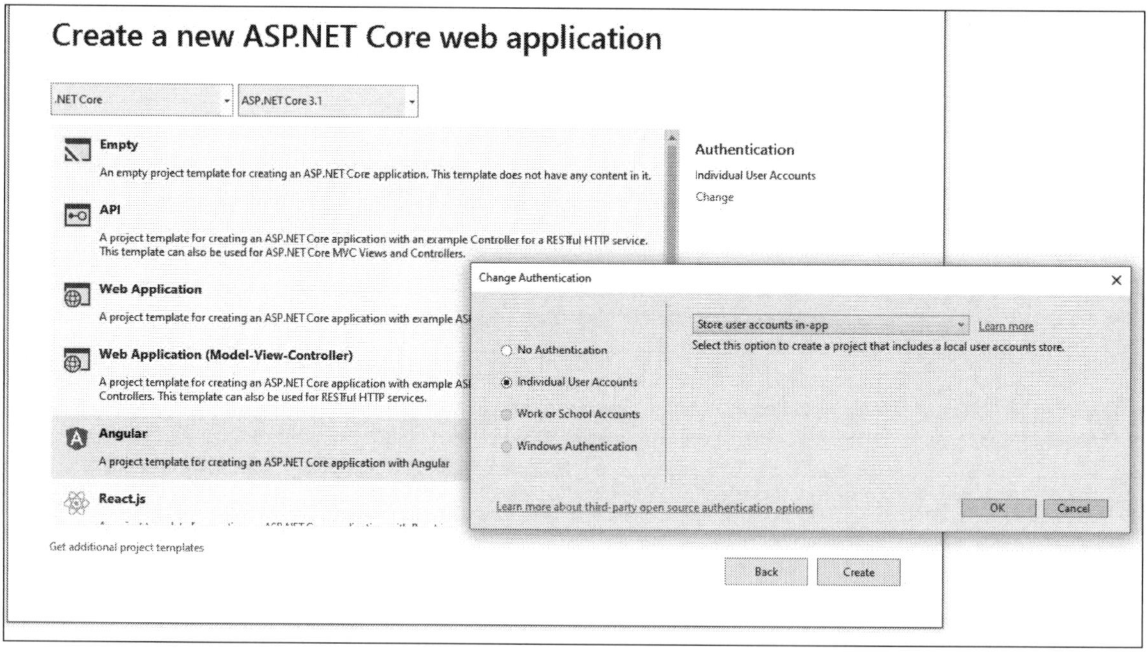

Figure 10.2: Creating a new ASP.NET Core web app using the Visual Studio wizard

In the opposite way to the default implementation, in our code, we took the chance to override some of the default password policy settings to demonstrate how we can configure the Identity service to better suit our needs.

Let's take another look at the preceding code, emphasizing the changes (highlighted lines):

```
options.SignIn.RequireConfirmedAccount = true;
options.Password.RequireLowercase = true;
options.Password.RequireUppercase = true;
options.Password.RequireDigit = true;
options.Password.RequireNonAlphanumeric = true;
options.Password.RequiredLength = 8;
```

As we can see, we didn't change the `RequireConfirmedAccount` default settings, which require a confirmed user account (verified through email) to sign in. What we did instead was explicitly set our password strength requirements so that all our users' passwords would need to have the following:

- At least one lowercase letter
- At least one uppercase letter
- At least one digit character
- At least one non-alphanumeric character
- A minimum length of eight characters

That will grant our app a decent level of authentication security, should we ever want to make it publicly accessible on the web. Needless to say, we can change these settings depending on our specific needs; a development sample could probably live with more relaxed settings, as long as we don't make it available to the public.

It's worth noting that the preceding code will require a reference to the new identity-related packages that we installed a moment ago:

```
// ...existing code...

using Microsoft.AspNetCore.Authentication;
using Microsoft.AspNetCore.Identity;

// ...existing code...
```

Furthermore, we'll also need to reference the namespace that we used for our data models, since we're now referencing the `ApplicationUser` class:

```
// ...existing code...

using WorldCities.Data.Models;

// ...existing code...
```

Now that we have properly configured our `Setup` class, we need to do the same with `IdentityServer`.

Configuring IdentityServer

In order to properly set up the `IdentityServer` middleware, we need to add the following lines to our existing `appSettings.json` configuration file (new lines are highlighted):

```
{
  "Logging": {
      "LogLevel": {
      "Default": "Information",
      "Microsoft": "Warning",
      "Microsoft.Hosting.Lifetime": "Information"
      }
    },
  "IdentityServer": {
    "Clients": {
      "WorldCities": {
        "Profile": "IdentityServerSPA"
      }
    }
  },
"AllowedHosts": "*"
}
```

As we can see, we added a single client for `IdentityServer`, which will be our Angular app. The `"IdentityServerSPA"` profile indicates the application type and it's used internally to generate the server defaults for that type—in our scenario, an SPA is hosted alongside `IdentityServer` as a single unit.

Here are the defaults that `IdentityServer` will load for our application type:

- `redirect_uri` defaults to `/authentication/login-callback`
- `post_logout_redirect_uri` defaults to `/authentication/logout-callback`
- The set of scopes includes `openID`, `Profile`, and every scope defined for the APIs in the app
- The set of allowed OIDC response types is `id_token token` or each of them individually (`id_token`, `token`)
- The allowed response mode is *fragment*

Other available profiles include the following:

- **SPA**: An SPA that is not hosted with `IdentityServer`
- **IdentityServerJwt**: An API that is hosted alongside `IdentityServer`
- **API**: An API that is not hosted with `IdentityServer`

Before going further, we need to perform another `IdentityServer`-related update to our `appSettings.Development.json` file.

Updating the appSettings.Development.json file

As we know from *Chapter 2*, *Looking Around*, the `appSettings.Development.json` file is used to specify additional configuration key/value pairs (and/or override the existing ones) for the *development* environment. This is precisely what we need to do now since `IdentityServer` requires some development-specific settings that shouldn't be put in production.

Open the `appSettings.Development.json` file and add the following content (new lines are highlighted):

```
{
  "Logging": {
    "LogLevel": {
      "Default": "Debug",
      "System": "Information",
      "Microsoft": "Information"
    },
    "IdentityServer": {
      "Key": {
        "Type": "Development"
      }
    }
  }
}
```

The "Key" element that we added in the preceding code describes the key that will be used to sign tokens; for the time being, since we're still in development, that key type will work just fine. However, when we want to deploy our app to production, we'll need to provision and deploy a real key alongside our app. When we come to that, we'll have to add a "Key" element to our appSettings.json production file and configure it accordingly; we'll talk more about this in *Chapter 12, Windows, Linux, and Azure Deployment*.

Until then, it's better to avoid adding it in the production settings to prevent our web app from running in an insecure mode.

> For additional information about IdentityServer and its configuration parameters, check out the following URL:
>
> https://docs.microsoft.com/en-us/aspnet/core/security/authentication/identity-api-authorization

Now we're ready to create our users.

Revising SeedController

The best way to create a new user from scratch would be from SeedController, which implements the *seeding mechanism* that we set up in *Chapter 4, Data Model with Entity Framework Core*; however, in order to interact with the .NET Core Identity APIs required to do that, we need to inject them using DI, just like we already did with ApplicationDbContext.

Adding RoleManager and UserManager through DI

From Solution Explorer, open the /Controllers/SeedController.cs file of the WorldCities project and update its content accordingly with the following code (new/updated lines are highlighted):

```
using Microsoft.AspNetCore.Identity;

// ...existing code...

public class SeedController : ControllerBase
{
    private readonly ApplicationDbContext _context;
    private readonly RoleManager<IdentityRole> _roleManager;
    private readonly UserManager<ApplicationUser> _userManager;
    private readonly IWebHostEnvironment _env;

    public SeedController(
        ApplicationDbContext context,
        RoleManager<IdentityRole> roleManager,
        UserManager<ApplicationUser> userManager,
        IWebHostEnvironment env)
```

```
    {
        _context = context;
        _roleManager = roleManager;
        _userManager = userManager;
        _env = env;
    }

// ...existing code...
```

As we can see, we added the `RoleManager<TRole>` and `UserManager<TUser>` providers that we talked about early on; we did that using DI, just like we did with `ApplicationDbContext` and `IWebHostEnvironment` back in *Chapter 4, Data Model with Entity Framework Core*. We'll see how we can use these new providers to create our users and roles soon enough.

Now, let's define the following method at the end of the `/Controllers/SeedController.cs` file, right below the existing `Import()` method:

```
// ...existing code...

[HttpGet]
public async Task<ActionResult> CreateDefaultUsers()
{
    throw new NotImplementedException();
}

// ...existing code...
```

> In a typical `ApiController`, adding another action method with the `[HttpGet]` attribute would create an ambiguous route that will conflict with the original method accepting HTTP GET requests (the `Import()` method): this code will not run when you hit the endpoint. However, since our `SeedController` has been configured to take the action names into account thanks to the `[Route("api/[controller]/[action]")]` routing rule that we placed above the class constructor back in *Chapter 4, Data Model with Entity Framework Core*, we're entitled to add this method without creating a conflict.

In the opposite way to what we usually do, we're not going to implement this method straight away; we'll take this chance to embrace the **Test-Driven Development** (**TDD**) approach, which means that we'll start with creating a (failing) unit test.

Defining the CreateDefaultUser() unit test

From Solution Explorer, create a new `/SeedController_Tests.cs` file in the `WorldCities.Tests` project; once done, fill its content with the following code:

```
using IdentityServer4.EntityFramework.Options;
using Microsoft.AspNetCore.Hosting;
using Microsoft.AspNetCore.Identity;
```

```
using Microsoft.AspNetCore.Identity.EntityFrameworkCore;
using Microsoft.EntityFrameworkCore;
using Microsoft.Extensions.Logging;
using Microsoft.Extensions.Options;
using Moq;
using System;
using WorldCities.Controllers;
using WorldCities.Data;
using WorldCities.Data.Models;
using Xunit;

namespace WorldCities.Tests
{
    public class SeedController_Tests
    {
        /// <summary>
        /// Test the CreateDefaultUsers() method
        /// </summary>
        [Fact]
        public async void CreateDefaultUsers()
        {
            #region Arrange
            // create the option instances required by the
            // ApplicationDbContext
            var options = new
             DbContextOptionsBuilder<ApplicationDbContext>()
                .UseInMemoryDatabase(databaseName: "WorldCities")
                .Options;
            var storeOptions = Options.Create(new
             OperationalStoreOptions());

            // create a IWebHost environment mock instance
            var mockEnv = new Mock<IWebHostEnvironment>().Object;

            // define the variables for the users we want to test
            ApplicationUser user_Admin = null;
            ApplicationUser user_User = null;
            ApplicationUser user_NotExisting = null;
            #endregion

            #region Act

            // create a ApplicationDbContext instance using the
            // in-memory DB
            using (var context = new ApplicationDbContext(options,
             storeOptions))
```

```
{
    // create a RoleManager instance
    var roleStore = new RoleStore<IdentityRole>(context);
    var roleManager = new RoleManager<IdentityRole>(
        roleStore,
        new IRoleValidator< IdentityRole >[0],
        new UpperInvariantLookupNormalizer(),
        new Mock<IdentityErrorDescriber>().Object,
        new Mock<ILogger<RoleManager<IdentityRole>>>(
        ).Object);

    // create a UserManager instance
    var userStore = new
     UserStore<ApplicationUser>(context);
    var userManager = new UserManager<ApplicationUser>(
        userStore,
        new Mock<IOptions<IdentityOptions>>().Object,
        new Mock<IPasswordHasher< ApplicationUser>>().Object,
        new IUserValidator< ApplicationUser>[0],
        new IPasswordValidator<ApplicationUser>[0],
        new UpperInvariantLookupNormalizer(),
        new Mock<IdentityErrorDescriber>().Object,
        new Mock<IServiceProvider>().Object,
        new Mock<ILogger<UserManager<ApplicationUser>>>(
        ).Object);

    // create a SeedController instance
    var controller = new SeedController(
        context,
        roleManager,
        userManager,
        mockEnv
        );

    // execute the SeedController's CreateDefaultUsers()
    // method to create the default users (and roles)
    await controller.CreateDefaultUsers();

    // retrieve the users
    user_Admin = await userManager.FindByEmailAsync(
     "admin@email.com");
    user_User = await userManager.FindByEmailAsync(
     "user@email.com");
    user_NotExisting = await userManager.FindByEmailAsync(
     "notexisting@email.com");
}
```

```
            #endregion

            #region Assert
            Assert.NotNull(user_Admin);
            Assert.NotNull(user_User);
            Assert.Null(user_NotExisting);
            #endregion
        }
    }
}
```

As we can see, we are creating *real instances* (not *mocks*) of the `RoleManager` and `UserManager` providers, since we'll need them to actually perform some read/write operations to the *in-memory* database that we have defined in the options of `ApplicationDbContext`; this basically means that these providers will perform their job for real, but everything will be done on the in-memory database instead of the SQL Server data source. That's an ideal scenario for our tests.

At the same time, we still made good use of the `Moq` package library to create a number of *mocks* to emulate a number of parameters required to instantiate `RoleManager` and `UserManager`. Luckily enough, most of them are internal objects that won't be needed to perform our current tests; for those that are required, we had to create a real instance.

> For example, for both providers, we were forced to create a real instance of `UpperInvariantLookupNormalizer`—which implements the `ILookupNormalizer` interface—because it's being used internally by `RoleManager` (to look up existing roles) as well as `UserManager` (to look up existing usernames); if we had mocked it instead, we would've hit some nasty runtime errors while trying to make these tests pass.

While we are here, it could be useful to move the `RoleManager` and `UserManager` generation logic to a separate helper class, so that we'll be able to use it in other tests without having to repeat it every time.

From Solution Explorer, create a new `IdentityHelper.cs` file in the `WorldCities.Tests` project. Once done, fill its content with the following code:

```
using Microsoft.AspNetCore.Identity;
using Microsoft.Extensions.Logging;
using Microsoft.Extensions.Options;
using Moq;
using System;
using System.Collections.Generic;
using System.Text;

namespace WorldCities.Tests
{
```

```
    public static class IdentityHelper
    {
        public static RoleManager<TIdentityRole>
         GetRoleManager<TIdentityRole>(
            IRoleStore<TIdentityRole> roleStore) where TIdentityRole :
             IdentityRole
        {
            return new RoleManager<TIdentityRole>(
                    roleStore,
                    new IRoleValidator<TIdentityRole>[0],
                    new UpperInvariantLookupNormalizer(),
                    new Mock<IdentityErrorDescriber>().Object,
                    new Mock<ILogger<RoleManager<TIdentityRole>>>(
                    ).Object);
        }

        public static UserManager<TIDentityUser>
         GetUserManager<TIDentityUser>(
            IUserStore<TIDentityUser> userStore) where TIDentityUser :
             IdentityUser
        {
            return new UserManager<TIDentityUser>(
                    userStore,
                    new Mock<IOptions<IdentityOptions>>().Object,
                    new Mock<IPasswordHasher<TIDentityUser>>().Object,
                    new IUserValidator<TIDentityUser>[0],
                    new IPasswordValidator<TIDentityUser>[0],
                    new UpperInvariantLookupNormalizer(),
                    new Mock<IdentityErrorDescriber>().Object,
                    new Mock<IServiceProvider>().Object,
                    new Mock<ILogger<UserManager<TIDentityUser>>>(
                    ).Object);
        }
    }
}
```

As we can see, we created two methods—`GetRoleManager` and `GetUserManager`—which we can use to create these providers for other tests.

Now we can call these two methods from `SeedController` by updating its code in the following way (updated lines are highlighted):

```
// ...existing code...

// create a RoleManager instance
var roleManager = IdentityHelper.GetRoleManager(
    new RoleStore<IdentityRole>(context));
```

```
// create a UserManager instance
var userManager = IdentityHelper.GetUserManager(
    new UserStore<ApplicationUser>(context));

// ...existing code...
```

With this, our unit test is ready; we just need to execute it to see it fail.

To do that, right-click the `WorldCities.Test` node from Solution Explorer and select **Run Tests**.

> Alternatively, just switch to the **Test Explorer** window and use the topmost buttons to run the tests from there.

If we did everything correctly, we should be able to see our `CreateDefaultUsers()` test failing, just like in the following screenshot:

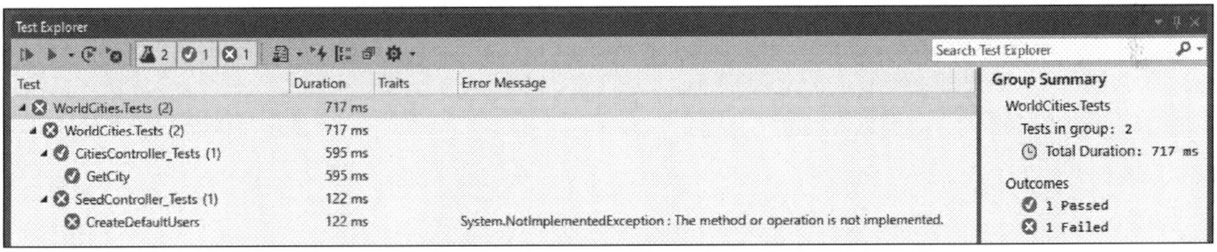

Figure 10.3: Failure of our CreateDefaultUsers() test

That's it; all we have to do now is to implement the `CreateDefaultUsers()` method of `SeedController` to make the preceding test pass.

Implementing the CreateDefaultUsers() method

Add the following method at the end of the `/Controllers/SeedController.cs` file, right below the existing `Import()` method:

```
// ...existing code...

[HttpGet]
public async Task<ActionResult> CreateDefaultUsers()
{
    // setup the default role names
    string role_RegisteredUser = "RegisteredUser";
    string role_Administrator = "Administrator";

    // create the default roles (if they don't exist yet)
```

```
if (await _roleManager.FindByNameAsync(role_RegisteredUser) ==
 null)
    await _roleManager.CreateAsync(new
     IdentityRole(role_RegisteredUser));

if (await _roleManager.FindByNameAsync(role_Administrator) ==
 null)
    await _roleManager.CreateAsync(new
     IdentityRole(role_Administrator));

// create a list to track the newly added users
var addedUserList = new List<ApplicationUser>();

// check if the admin user already exists
var email_Admin = "admin@email.com";
if (await _userManager.FindByNameAsync(email_Admin) == null)
{
    // create a new admin ApplicationUser account
    var user_Admin = new ApplicationUser()
    {
        SecurityStamp = Guid.NewGuid().ToString(),
        UserName = email_Admin,
        Email = email_Admin,
    };

    // insert the admin user into the DB
    await _userManager.CreateAsync(user_Admin, "MySecr3t$");

    // assign the "RegisteredUser" and "Administrator" roles
    await _userManager.AddToRoleAsync(user_Admin,
     role_RegisteredUser);
    await _userManager.AddToRoleAsync(user_Admin,
     role_Administrator);

    // confirm the e-mail and remove lockout
    user_Admin.EmailConfirmed = true;
    user_Admin.LockoutEnabled = false;

    // add the admin user to the added users list
    addedUserList.Add(user_Admin);
}

// check if the standard user already exists
var email_User = "user@email.com";
if (await _userManager.FindByNameAsync(email_User) == null)
{
```

```
            // create a new standard ApplicationUser account
            var user_User = new ApplicationUser()
            {
                SecurityStamp = Guid.NewGuid().ToString(),
                UserName = email_User,
                Email = email_User
            };

            // insert the standard user into the DB
            await _userManager.CreateAsync(user_User, "MySecr3t$");

            // assign the "RegisteredUser" role
            await _userManager.AddToRoleAsync(user_User,
             role_RegisteredUser);

            // confirm the e-mail and remove lockout
            user_User.EmailConfirmed = true;
            user_User.LockoutEnabled = false;

            // add the standard user to the added users list
            addedUserList.Add(user_User);
        }

        // if we added at least one user, persist the changes into the DB
        if (addedUserList.Count > 0)
            await _context.SaveChangesAsync();

        return new JsonResult(new
        {
            Count = addedUserList.Count,
            Users = addedUserList
        });
    }

// ...existing code...
```

The code is quite self-explanatory, and it has a lot of comments explaining the various steps; however, here's a convenient summary of what we just did:

- We started by defining some default role names (`RegisteredUsers` for the standard registered users, `Administrator` for the administrative-level ones).
- We created a logic to check whether these roles already exist. If they don't exist, we create them. As expected, both tasks have been performed using `RoleManager`.
- We defined a user list local variable to track the newly added users, so that we can output it to the user in the JSON object we'll return at the end of the action method.

- We created a logic to check whether a user with the `admin@email.com` username already exists; if it doesn't, we create it and assign it both the `RegisteredUser` and `Administrator` roles, since it will be a standard user *and also* the administrative account of our app.
- We created a logic to check whether a user with the `user@email.com` username already exists; if it doesn't, we create it and assign it the `RegisteredUser` role.
- At the end of the action method, we configured the JSON object that we'll return to the caller; this object contains a count of the added users and a list containing them, which will be serialized into a JSON object that will show their entity values.

> The `Administrator` and `RegisteredUser` roles we just implemented here will be the core of our authorization mechanism; all of our users will be assigned to at least one of them. Note how we assigned both of them to the **Admin** user to make them able to do everything a standard user can do, plus more: all the other users only have the latter role, so they'll be unable to perform any administrative-level tasks—as long as they're not provided with the `Administrator` role.

Before moving on, it's worth noting that we're using the user's email address for both the `Email` and `UserName` fields. We did that on purpose, because those two fields in the ASP.NET Core Identity system are used interchangeably by default; whenever we add a user using the default APIs, the `Email` provided is saved in the `UserName` field as well, even if they are two separate fields in the `AspNetUsers` database table. Although this behavior can be changed, we're going to stick to the default settings so that we'll be able to use the default settings without changing them throughout the whole ASP.NET Identity system.

Rerunning the unit test

Now that we have implemented the test, we can rerun the `CreateDefaultUsers()` test and see whether it passes. As usual, we can do that by right-clicking the `WorldCities.Test` root node from Solution Explorer and selecting **Run Tests**, or from within the **Test Explorer** panel.

If we did everything correctly, we should see something like this:

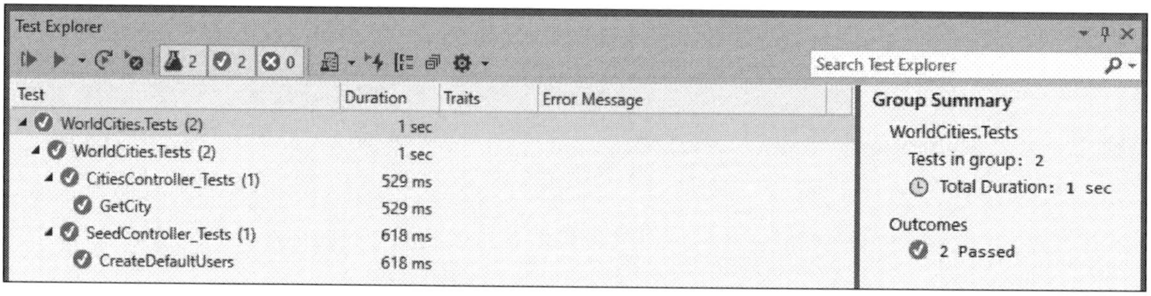

Figure 10.4: CreateDefaultUsers() test passed

That's it; now we're finally done updating our project's classes.

A word on async tasks, awaits, and deadlocks

As we can see by looking at the preceding `CreateDefaultUsers()` method, all the ASP.NET Core Identity system API's relevant methods are *asynchronous*, meaning that they return an *async task* rather than a given return value. For that very reason, since we need to execute these various tasks one after another, we had to prepend all of them with the `await` keyword.

Here's an example of `await` usage taken from the preceding code:

```
await _userManager.AddToRoleAsync(user_Admin, role_RegisteredUser);
```

The `await` keyword, as the name implies, awaits the completion of the async task before going forward. It's worth noting that such an expression does not block the thread on which it is executing; instead, it causes the compiler to sign up the rest of the `async` method as a continuation of the awaited task, thus returning the thread control to the caller. Eventually, when the task completes, it invokes its continuation, thus resuming the execution of the `async` method where it left off.

> That's the reason why the `await` keyword can only be used within `async` methods; as a matter of fact, the preceding logic requires the caller to be `async` as well, otherwise, it wouldn't work.

Alternatively, we could have used the `Wait()` method, in the following way:

```
_userManager.AddToRoleAsync(user_Admin, role_RegisteredUser).Wait();
```

However, we didn't do that—for good reason. In the opposite way to the `await` keyword, which tells the compiler to *asynchronously wait* for the async task to complete, the parameterless `Wait()` method will *block the calling thread* until the async task has completed execution; therefore, the calling thread will unconditionally wait until the task completes.

To better explain how such techniques impact our .NET Core application, we should spend a little time better understanding the concept of async tasks, as they are a pivotal part of the ASP.NET Core TAP model.

One of the first things we should learn when working with sync methods invoking async tasks in ASP.NET is that when the top-level method awaits a task, its current execution context gets blocked until the task completes. This won't be a problem unless that context allows only one thread to run at a time, which is precisely the case of `AspNetSynchronizationContext`. If we combine these two things, we can easily see that *blocking* an `async` method (that is, a method returning an async task) will expose our application to a high risk of *deadlock*.

A *deadlock*, from a software development perspective, is a dreadful situation that occurs whenever a process or thread enters a waiting state indefinitely, usually because the resource it's waiting for is held by another waiting process. In any legacy ASP.NET web application, we would face a deadlock every time we're blocking a task, simply because that task, in order to complete, will require the same execution context as the invoking method, which is kept blocked by that method until the task completes!

Luckily enough, we're not using legacy ASP.NET here; we're using ASP.NET Core, where the legacy ASP.NET pattern based upon the `SynchronizationContext` has been replaced by a *contextless* approach layered upon a versatile, deadlock-resilient thread pool.

This basically means that *blocking the calling thread* using the `Wait()` method isn't that problematic anymore; therefore, if we switched our `await` keywords with it, our method would still run and complete just fine. However, by doing so, we would basically use synchronous code to perform asynchronous operations, which is generally considered a bad practice; moreover, we would lose all the benefits brought by asynchronous programming, such as performance and scalability.

For all those reasons, the `await` approach is definitely the way to go there.

> For additional information regarding threads, async task awaits, and asynchronous programming in ASP.NET, we highly recommend checking out the outstanding articles written by Stephen Cleary on the topic, which will greatly help in understanding some of the most tricky and complex scenarios that we could face when developing with these technologies. Some of them were written a while ago, yet they never really age:
>
> `https://blog.stephencleary.com/2012/02/async-and-await.html`
>
> `https://blogs.msdn.microsoft.com/pfxteam/2012/04/12/asyncawait-faq/`
>
> `http://blog.stephencleary.com/2012/07/dont-block-on-async-code.html`
>
> `https://msdn.microsoft.com/en-us/magazine/jj991977.aspx`
>
> `https://blog.stephencleary.com/2017/03/aspnetcore-synchronization-context.html`
>
> Also, we strongly suggest checking out this excellent article about asynchronous programming with async and await at:
>
> `https://docs.microsoft.com/en-us/dotnet/csharp/programming-guide/concepts/async/index`

Updating the database

It's time to create a new migration and reflect the code changes to the database by taking advantage of the Code-First approach we chose in *Chapter 4, Data Model with Entity Framework Core*.

Here's a list of what we're going to do in this section:

- **Add the identity migration** using the `dotnet-ef` command, just like we did in *Chapter 4, Data Model with Entity Framework Core*.

- **Apply the migration to the database**, updating it without altering the existing data or performing a drop and recreate.
- **Seed the data** using the `CreateDefaultUsers()` method of `SeedController` that we implemented earlier on.

Let's get to work.

Adding identity migration

The first thing we need to do is to add a new migration to our data model to reflect the changes that we have implemented by extending the `ApplicationDbContext` class.

To do that, open a command line or PowerShell prompt and go to our `WorldCities` project's root folder, then write the following:

```
dotnet ef migrations add "Identity" -o "Data/Migrations"
```

A new migration should then be added to the project, as shown in the following screenshot:

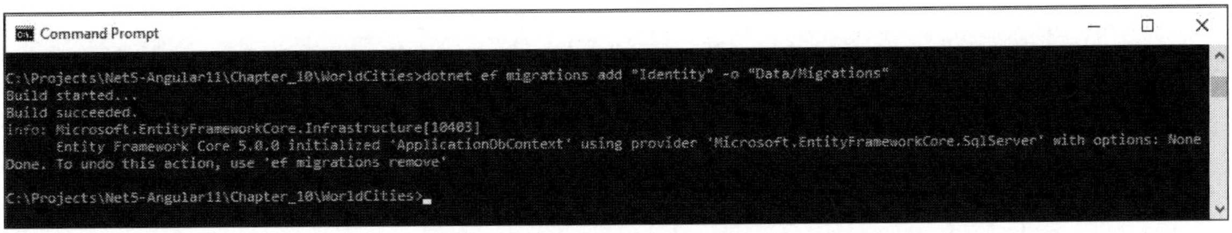
Command Prompt
C:\Projects\Net5-Angular11\Chapter_10\WorldCities>dotnet ef migrations add "Identity" -o "Data/Migrations"
Build started...
Build succeeded.
info: Microsoft.EntityFrameworkCore.Infrastructure[10403]
Entity Framework Core 5.0.0 initialized 'ApplicationDbContext' using provider 'Microsoft.EntityFrameworkCore.SqlServer' with options: None
Done. To undo this action, use 'ef migrations remove'
C:\Projects\Net5-Angular11\Chapter_10\WorldCities>

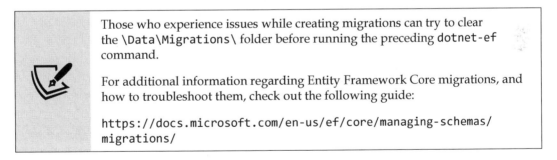

Figure 10.5: Adding a new migration

The new migration files will be autogenerated in the `\Data\Migrations\` folder.

> Those who experience issues while creating migrations can try to clear the `\Data\Migrations\` folder before running the preceding `dotnet-ef` command.
>
> For additional information regarding Entity Framework Core migrations, and how to troubleshoot them, check out the following guide:
>
> `https://docs.microsoft.com/en-us/ef/core/managing-schemas/migrations/`

Applying the migration

The next thing to do is to apply the new migration to our database. We can choose between two options:

- **Updating the existing data model schema** while keeping all its data as it is
- **Dropping and recreating the database** from scratch

As a matter of fact, the whole purpose of the EF Core migration feature is to provide a way to incrementally update the database schema while preserving existing data in the database; for that very reason, we're going to follow the former path.

> Before applying migrations, it's always advisable to perform a full database backup; this advice is particularly important when dealing with production environments. For small databases such as the one currently used by our `WorldCities` web app, it would take a few seconds.
>
> For additional information about how to perform a full backup of a SQL Server database, read the following guide:
>
> `https://docs.microsoft.com/en-us/sql/relational-databases/backup-restore/create-a-full-database-backup-sql-server`

Updating the existing data model

To apply the migration to the existing database schema without losing the existing data, run the following command from our `WorldCities` project's root folder:

```
dotnet ef database update
```

The `dotnet ef` tool will then apply the necessary updates to our SQL database schema and output the relevant information—as well as the actual SQL queries—in the console buffer, as shown in the following screenshot:

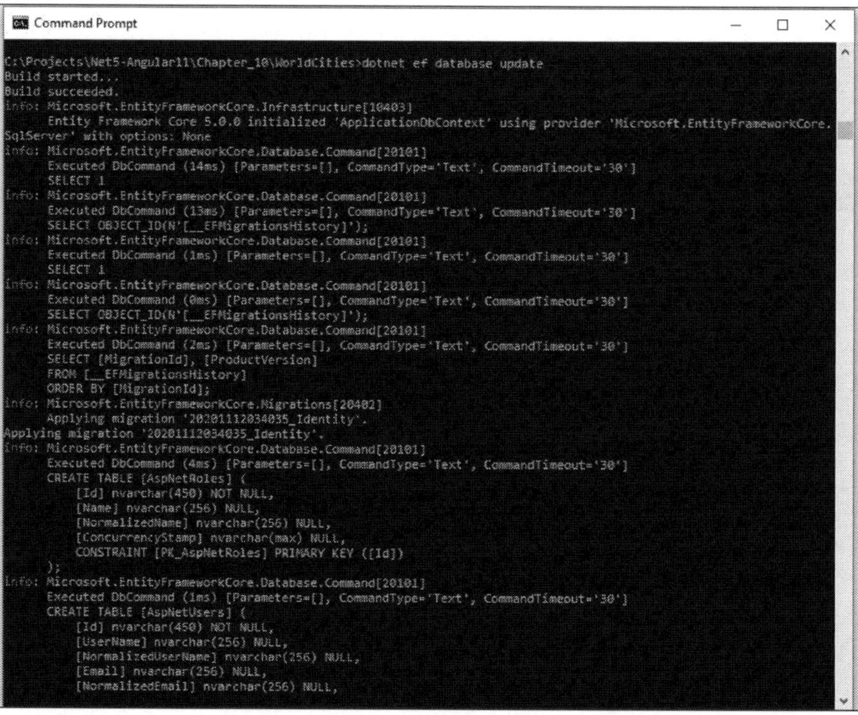

Figure 10.6: Applying the migration to the existing database schema

Once the task has been completed, we should connect to our database using the **SQL Server Management Studio** tool that we installed back in *Chapter 4, Data Model with Entity Framework Core*—and check for the presence of the new identity-related tables.

If everything went well, we should be able to see the new identity tables together with our existing `Cities` and `Countries` tables:

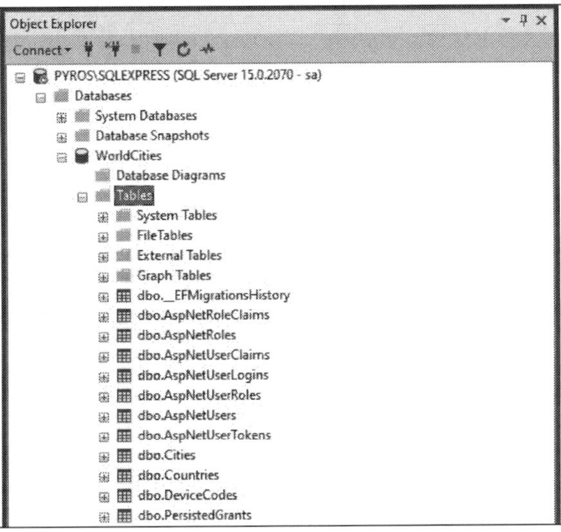

Figure 10.7: Viewing the new identity tables in Object Explorer

As we can easily guess, these tables are still empty; to populate them, we'll have to run the `CreateDefaultUsers()` method of `SeedController`, which is something that we're going to do in a short while.

Dropping and recreating the data model from scratch

For completeness, let's spend a little time looking at how to recreate our data model and **database schema** (**DB schema**) from scratch. Needless to say, if we opt for that route, we will lose all our existing data. However, we could always reload everything using the `Import()` method of `SeedController`, hence it wouldn't be a great loss; as a matter of fact, we would only lose what we did during our CRUD-based tests in *Chapter 4, Data Model with Entity Framework Core*.

Although performing a database drop and recreate is not the suggested approach—especially considering that we've adopted the *migration* pattern precisely to avoid such a scenario—it can be a decent workaround whenever we lose control of our migrations, provided that we entirely back up the data before doing that and, most importantly, know how to restore everything afterward.

> Although it might seem a horrible way to fix things, that's definitely not the case; we're still in the development phase, hence we can definitely allow a full database refresh.

Should we choose to take this route, here are the **dotnet-ef** console commands to use:

```
> dotnet ef database drop
> dotnet ef database update
```

The `drop` command should ask for a Y/N confirmation before proceeding; when it does, hit the *Y* key and let it happen. When the drop and update tasks are both done, we can run our project in debug mode and pay a visit to the `Import()` method of `SeedController`; once done, we should have an updated database with ASP.NET Core Identity support.

Seeding the data

Regardless of the option we chose to update the database, we now have to repopulate it.

Hit *F5* to run the project in debug mode, then manually input the following URL in the browser's address bar: `https://localhost:44334/api/Seed/CreateDefaultUsers`

And let the `CreateDefaultUsers()` method of `SeedController` work its magic.

Once done, we should be able to see the following JSON response:

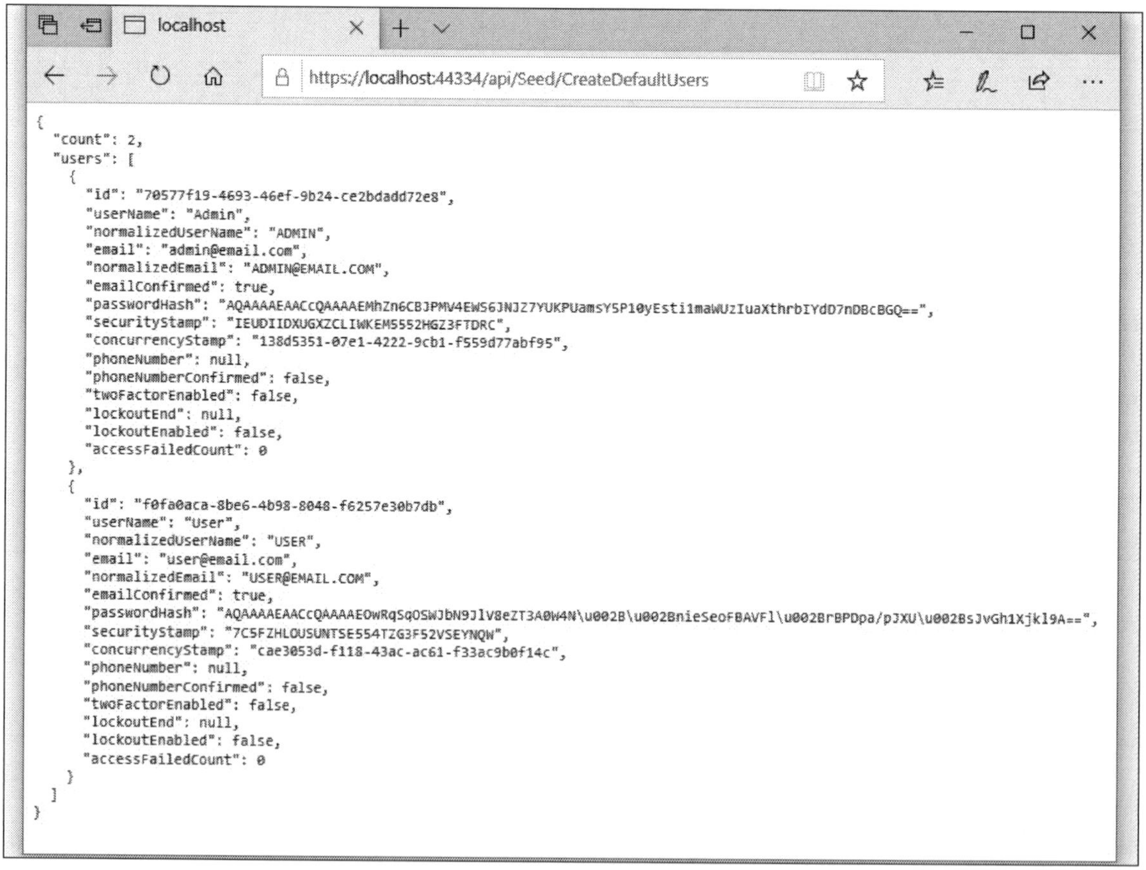

Figure 10.8: The CreateDefaultUsers() JSON response

This output already tells us that our first two users have been created and stored in our data model. However, we can also confirm that by connecting to our database using the SQL Server Management Studio tool and taking a look at the `dbo.AspNetUsers` table (see the following screenshot):

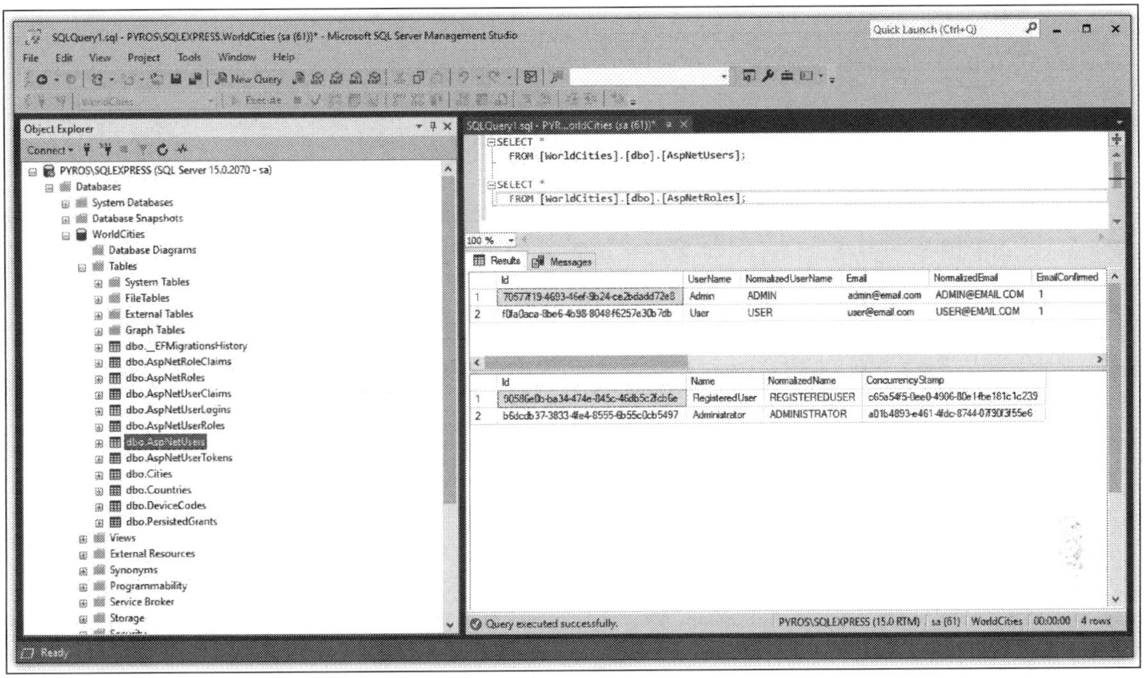

Figure 10.9: Querying dbo.AspNetUsers

As we can see, we used the following T-SQL queries to check for the existing users and roles:

```
SELECT *
  FROM [WorldCities].[dbo].[AspNetUsers];

SELECT *
  FROM [WorldCities].[dbo].[AspNetRoles];
```

Bingo! Our ASP.NET Core Identity system implementation is up, running, and fully integrated with our data model; now we just need to implement it within our controllers and hook it up with our Angular client app.

Authentication methods

Now that we have updated our database to support the ASP.NET Core Identity authentication workflow and patterns, we should spend some valuable time choosing which authentication method to adopt; more precisely, since we've already implemented the .NET Core `IdentityServer`, to properly understand whether the default authentication method that it provides for SPAs—JWTs—is safe enough to use or whether we should change it to a more secure mechanism.

As we most certainly know, the HTTP protocol is *stateless*, meaning that whatever we do during a request/response cycle will be lost before the subsequent request, including the authentication result. The only way we have to overcome this is to store that result somewhere, along with all its relevant data, such as user ID, login date/time, and last request time.

Sessions

Since a few years ago, the most common and traditional method to do this was to store that data on the server using either a memory-based, disk-based, or external session manager. Each session can be retrieved using a unique ID that the client receives with the authentication response, usually inside a session cookie, which will be transmitted to the server on each subsequent request.

Here's a brief diagram showing the **Session-Based Authentication Flow**:

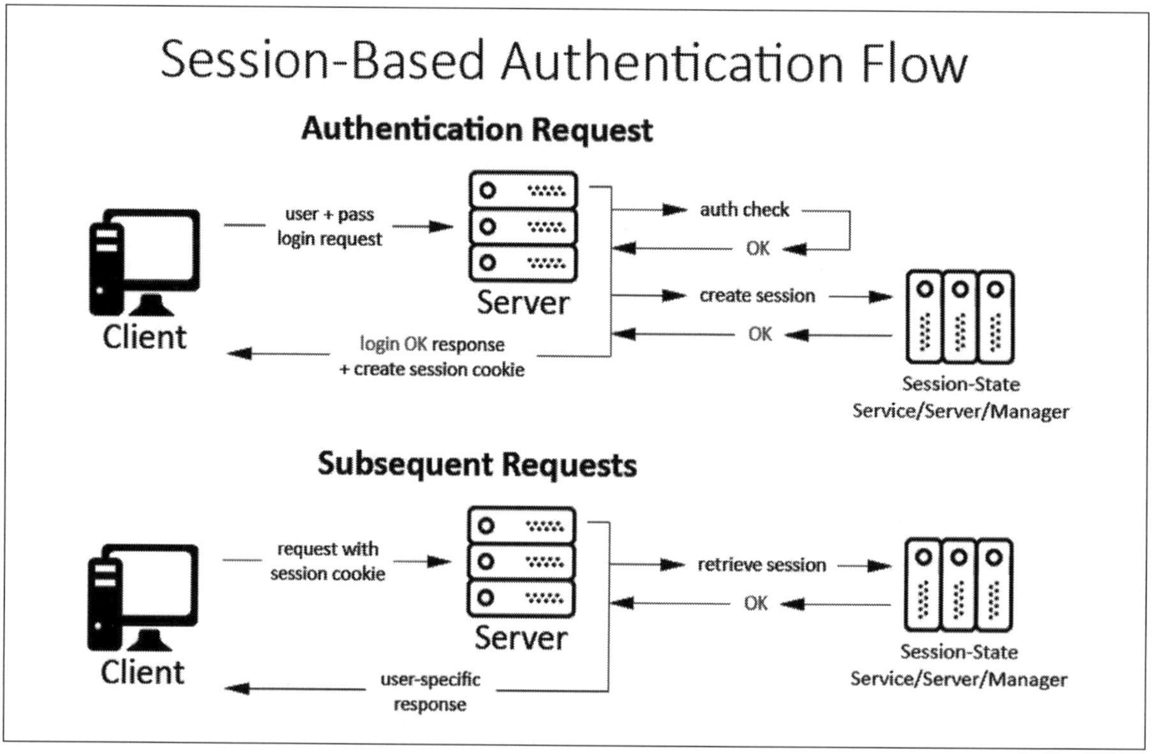

Figure 10.10: Session-based authentication flow

This is still a very common technique used by most web applications. There's nothing wrong with adopting this approach, as long as we are okay with its widely acknowledged downsides, such as the following:

- **Memory issues**: Whenever there are many authenticated users, the web server will consume more and more memory. Even if we use a file-based or external session provider, there will nonetheless be an intensive I/O, TCP, or socket overhead.

- **Scalability issues**: Replicating a session provider in a scalable architecture (*IIS web farm*, *load-balanced cluster*, and the like) might not be an easy task and will often lead to bottlenecks or wasted resources.
- **Cross-domain issues**: Session cookies behave just like standard cookies, so they cannot be easily shared between different origins/domains. These kinds of problems can often be solved with some workarounds, yet they will often lead to insecure scenarios to make things work.
- **Security issues**: There is a wide range of detailed literature on security-related issues involving sessions and session cookies: for instance, **Cross-Site Request Forgery** (**CSRF**) attacks, and a number of other threats that won't be covered here for the sake of simplicity. Most of them can be mitigated by some countermeasures, yet they can be difficult to handle for junior or novice developers.

As these issues have arisen over the years, there's no doubt that most analysts and developers have put a lot of effort into figuring out different approaches, as well as mitigating them.

> Regarding the mitigation part, a pivotal improvement was achieved in 2016 with the *SameSite cookies* draft, which suggested an HTTP security policy that was then improved by the *Cookies HTTP State Management Mechanism* (April 2019) and the *Incrementally Better Cookies* (May 2019) drafts:
>
> `https://tools.ietf.org/html/draft-west-first-party-cookies-07`
>
> `https://tools.ietf.org/html/draft-west-cookie-incrementalism-00`
>
> `https://tools.ietf.org/html/draft-west-first-party-cookies-07`
>
> Now that most browsers have adopted the **SameSite** cookie specification, cookie-based authentication is a lot safer than before.

Tokens

Token-based authentication has been increasingly adopted by **Single-Page Applications** (**SPAs**) and mobile apps in the last few years for a number of undeniably good reasons that we'll try to briefly summarize here.

The most important difference between session-based authentication and token-based authentication is that the latter is *stateless*, meaning that we won't be storing any user-specific information on the server memory, database, session provider, or other data containers of any sort.

This single aspect solves most of the downsides that we pointed out earlier for session-based authentication. We won't have sessions, so there won't be an increasing overhead; we won't need a session provider, so scaling will be much easier. Also, for browsers supporting `LocalStorage`, we won't even be using cookies, so we won't get blocked by *cross-origin* restrictive policies and, hopefully, we'll get around most security issues.

Here's a typical **Token-Based Authentication Flow**:

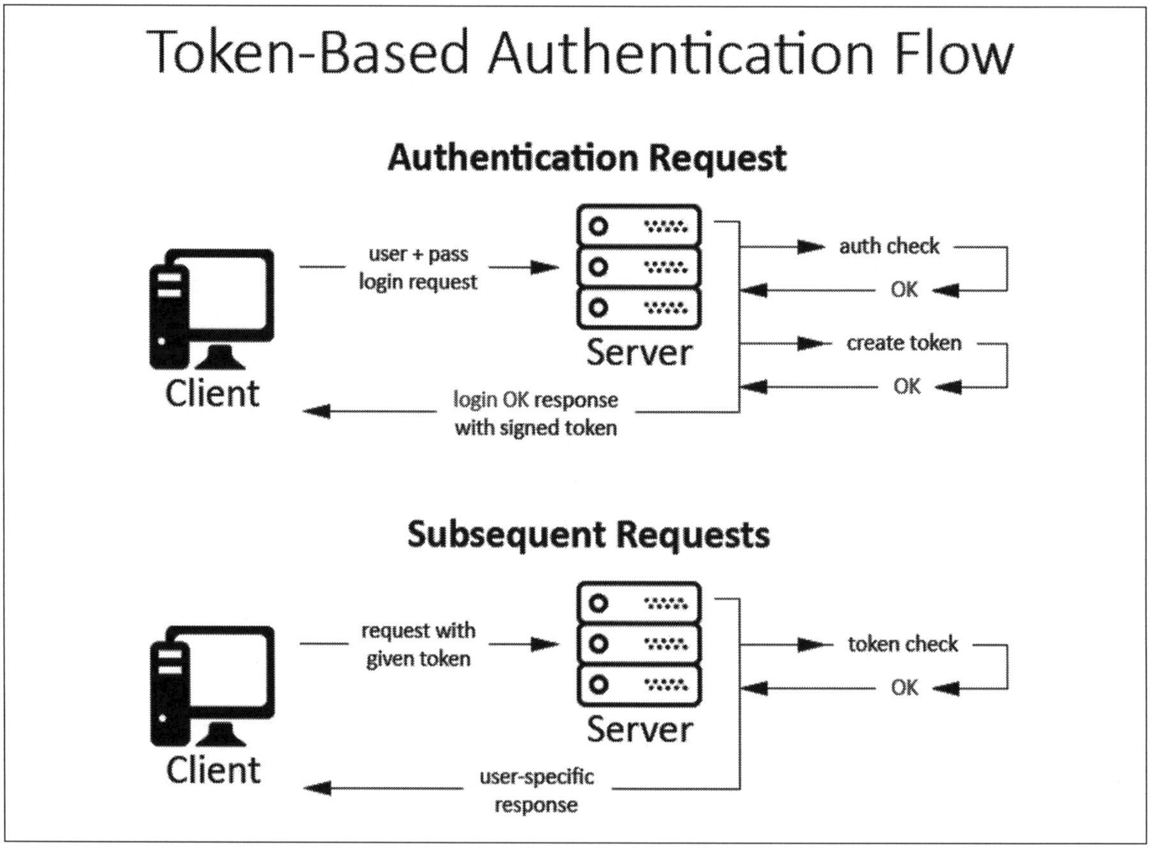

Figure 10.11: Token-based authentication flow

In terms of client-server interaction, these steps don't seem much different from the session-based authentication flow diagram; apparently, the only difference is that we'll be issuing and checking tokens instead of creating and retrieving sessions. The real deal is happening (or not happening) at the server side. We can immediately see that the token-based auth flow does not rely on a stateful session-state server, service, or manager. This will easily translate into a considerable boost in terms of performance and scalability.

Signatures

This is a method used by most modern API-based cloud-computing and storage services, including **Amazon Web Services** (**AWS**). In contrast to session-based and token-based approaches, which rely on a transport layer that can theoretically be accessed by or exposed to a third-party attacker, signature-based authentication performs a hash of the whole request using a previously shared private key. This ensures that no intruder or man-in-the-middle can ever act as the requesting user, as they won't be able to sign the request.

Two-factor

This is the standard authentication method used by most banking and financial accounts, being arguably the most secure one.

The implementation may vary, but it always relies on the following base workflow:

- The user performs a standard login with a username and password.
- The server identifies the user and prompts them with an additional, user-specific request that can only be satisfied by something obtained or obtainable through a different channel: an OTP password sent by SMS, a unique authentication card with a number of answer codes, a dynamic PIN generated by a proprietary device or a mobile app, and so on.
- If the user gives the correct answer, they are authenticated using a standard session-based or token-based method.

Two-Factor Authentication (**2FA**) has been supported by ASP.NET Core since its 1.0 release, which implemented it using SMS verification (SMS 2FA); however, starting with ASP.NET Core 2, the SMS 2FA approach was deprecated in favor of a **Time-Based One-Time Password** (**TOTP**) **algorithm**, which became the industry-recommended approach to implement 2FA in web applications.

> For additional information about SMS 2FA, check out the following URL:
>
> `https://docs.microsoft.com/en-us/aspnet/core/security/authentication/2fa`
>
> For additional information about TOTP 2FA, take a look at the following URL:
>
> `https://docs.microsoft.com/en-us/aspnet/core/security/authentication/identity-enable-qrcodes`

Conclusions

After reviewing all these authentication methods, we can definitely say that the token-based authentication approach provided by `IdentityServer` seems to be a great choice for our specific scenario.

Our current implementation is based on **JSON Web Tokens** (**JWTs**), a JSON-based open standard explicitly designed for native web applications, available in multiple languages, such as .NET, Python, Java, PHP, Ruby, JavaScript/Node.js, and Perl. We've chosen it because it's becoming a de facto standard for token authentication, as it's natively supported by most technologies.

> For additional information about JSON web tokens, check out the following URL:
>
> `https://jwt.io/`

Implementing authentication in Angular

In order to handle JWT-based token authentication, we need to set up our ASP.NET *back-end* and our Angular *front-end* to handle all the required tasks.

In the previous sections, we spent a good amount of time configuring the .NET Core Identity services as well as `IdentityServer`, meaning that we're halfway done; as a matter of fact, we're almost done with the *server-side* tasks. At the same time, we did nothing at the *front-end* level: the two users that we created in the previous section—`admin@email.com` and `user@email.com`—have no way to log in, and there isn't a registration form for creating new users.

Now, here's some (very) good news: the Visual Studio Angular template that we used to set up our apps comes with built-in support for the auth API that we've just added to our *back-end,* and the best part of it is that it actually works very well!

However, we've also got some bad news: since we chose *not* to add any authentication method to our projects when we created them, all the Angular modules, components, services, interceptors, and tests that would have handled this task *have been excluded* from our Angular app. As a consequence of that initial choice, when we started to explore our pre-made Angular app back in *Chapter 2, Looking Around,* we only had the `counter` and `fetch-data` components to play with.

As a matter of fact, we've chosen to exclude the authorization components for a reason: since we used that template as a sample application to learn more about the Angular structure, we didn't want to complicate our life early on by bringing in all the authentication and authorization stuff.

Luckily, all those missing classes can be easily retrieved and implemented in our current `WorldCities` project... which is precisely what we're going to do in this section.

More specifically, here's a list of our upcoming tasks:

- **Creating a brand-new .NET Core and Angular project**, which we'll use as a *code repository* to copy the auth-related Angular classes from; the new project name will be `AuthSample`
- **Exploring the Angular authorization APIs** to understand how they work
- **Testing the login and registration forms** provided by the aforementioned APIs from the `AuthSample` project

By the end of the section, we should be able to register new users, as well as log in with existing users, using the *front-end* authorization APIs shipped with the `AuthSample` app.

Creating the AuthSample project

The first thing we're going to do is create a new .NET Core and Angular web application project. As a matter of fact, it's the third time we're doing this: we created the `HealthCheck` project in *Chapter 1, Getting Ready,* and then the `WorldCities` project in *Chapter 3, Front-End and Back-End Interactions*; therefore, we already know most of what we have to do.

The name of our third project will be `AuthSample`; however, the required tasks to create it will be slightly different from (and definitely easier than) the last time we did this:

1. Create a new project with the `dotnet new angular -o AuthSample -au Individual` command.
2. Edit the `/ClientApp/package.json` file to update the existing npm package versions to the same version we're currently using in the existing `HealthCheck` and `WorldCities` Angular apps (see *Chapter 2, Looking Around,* for details on how to do this).
3. Remove the `@nguniversal/module-map-ngfactory-loader` and `ModuleMapLoaderModule` references from the `/ClientApp/package.json` and `/ClientApp/src/app/app.server.module.ts` files.

> Remember to execute the `npm update` and `npm install` commands to ensure that the npm packages will be updated.

That's it. As we can see, this time we added the `-au` switch (a shortcut for `--auth`), which will include all the auth-related classes that we purposely missed when creating the `HealthCheck` and `WorldCities` projects. Moreover, we didn't have to delete or update anything other than the npm package versions: the built-in Angular components, as well as the *back-end* classes and libraries, are more than enough to explore the auth-related code we've been missing until now.

Troubleshooting the AuthSample project

After updating the npm packages, the first thing we should do is launch the project in debug mode and ensure that the home page is properly working (see the following screenshot):

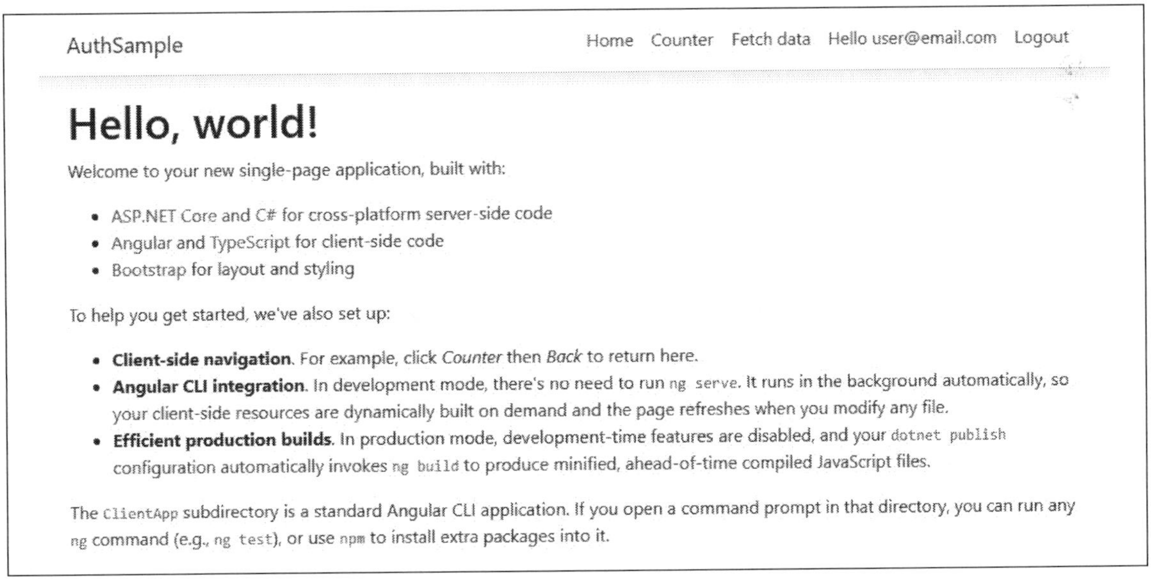

AuthSample
Home Counter Fetch data Hello user@email.com Logout
Hello, world!
Welcome to your new single-page application, built with:
ASP.NET Core and C# for cross-platform server-side code
Angular and TypeScript for client-side code
Bootstrap for layout and styling
To help you get started, we've also set up:
Client-side navigation. For example, click Counter then Back to return here.
Angular CLI integration. In development mode, there's no need to run ng serve. It runs in the background automatically, so your client-side resources are dynamically built on demand and the page refreshes when you modify any file.
Efficient production builds. In production mode, development-time features are disabled, and your dotnet publish configuration automatically invokes ng build to produce minified, ahead-of-time compiled JavaScript files.
The ClientApp subdirectory is a standard Angular CLI application. If you open a command prompt in that directory, you can run any ng command (e.g., ng test), or use npm to install extra packages into it.

Figure 10.12: AuthSample home page

If we run into package conflicts, JavaScript errors, or other npm-related issues, we can try to execute the following npm commands from the `/ClientApp/` folder to update them all and verify the package cache:

```
> npm install
> npm cache verify
```

This is shown in the following screenshot:

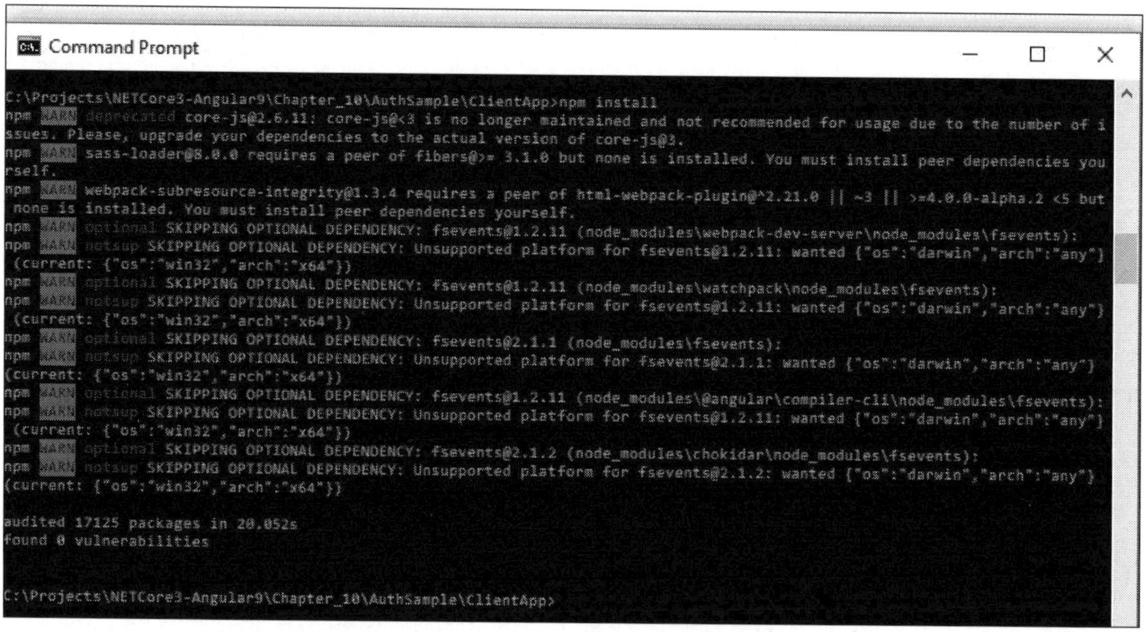

Figure 10.13: Updating npm packages and verifying package cache

Although Visual Studio should automatically update the npm packages as soon as we update the `package.json` file on disk, sometimes the auto-update process fails to work properly; when this happens, manual execution of the preceding npm commands from the command line is a convenient way to fix these kinds of issues.

If we experience some *back-end* runtime errors, it could be wise to briefly review the .NET code against what we did in the previous chapters—and also in this chapter—to fix any issue related to the template's source code, third-party references, NuGet package versions, and so on. As always, the GitHub repository provided by this book will greatly help us to troubleshoot our own code; be sure to check it out!

Exploring the Angular authorization APIs

In this section, we're going to take an extensive look at the authorization APIs provided by the .NET Core and Angular Visual Studio project template: a set of functionalities that rely upon the **oidc-client** library to allow an Angular app to interact with the URI endpoints provided by the ASP.NET Core Identity system.

> The **oidc-client** library is an open-source solution that provides OIDC and OAuth 2 protocol support for client-side, browser-based JavaScript client applications, including user session support and access token management. Its npm package reference is already present in the `package.json` file of our `WorldCities` app, therefore we won't have to manually add it.
>
> For additional info about the **oidc-client** library, check out the following URL: `https://github.com/IdentityModel/oidc-client-js`

As we'll be able to see, these APIs make use of some important Angular features—such as route guards and HTTP interceptors—to handle the authorization flow through the HTTP request/response cycle.

Let's start with a quick overview of the Angular app shipped with our new `AuthSample` project. If we observe the various files and folders within the `/ClientApp/` directory, we can immediately see that we're dealing with the same sample app that we already explored back in *Chapter 2, Looking Around*, before trimming it down to better suit our needs.

However, there's an additional folder that wasn't there at the time: we're talking about the `/ClientApp/src/app/api-authorization/` folder, which basically contains everything we missed back then—the Angular *front-end* implementation of the .NET Core Identity APIs and `IdentityServer` hook points.

Inside that folder there are a number of interesting files and subfolders, as shown in the following screenshot:

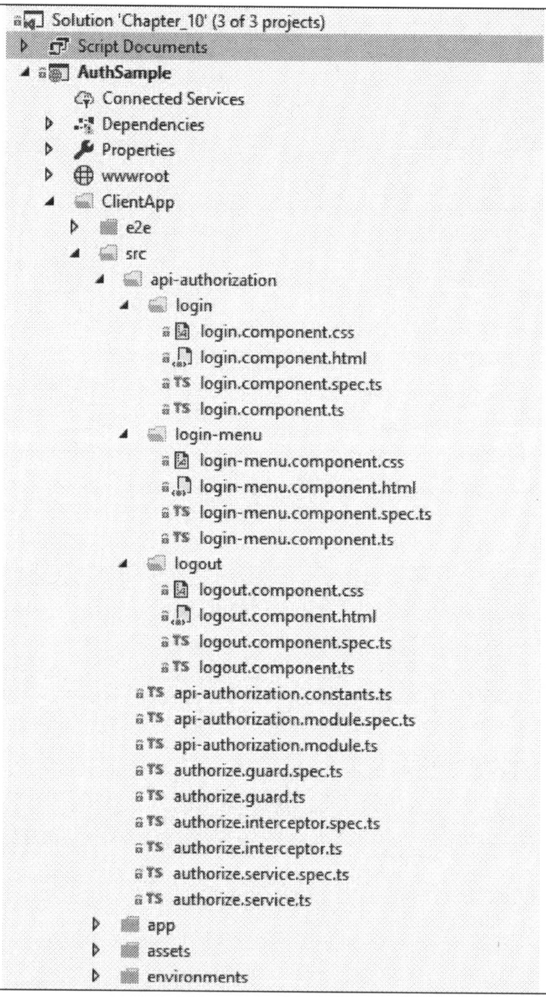

Figure 10.14: Exploring the api-authorization folder

Thanks to the knowledge we gained about the Angular architecture, we can easily understand the main role of each one of them:

- The first three subfolders—`/login/`, `/login-menu/`, and `/logout/`—contain three *components*, each one with their TypeScript class, HTML template, CSS file, and test suite.
- The `api-authorization.constants.ts` file contains a bunch of common *interfaces* and *constants* that are referenced and used by the other classes.
- The `api-authorization.module.ts` file is an `NgModule`, that is, a container for the authorization API's common feature set, just like the `AngularMaterialModule` that we created in our `WorldCities` app back in *Chapter 5, Fetching and Displaying Data*. If we open it, we can see that it contains some auth-specific routing rules.

- The `authorize.guard.ts` file introduces the concept of **route guards**, which is something that we've yet to learn; we'll talk more about this in a short while.
- The `authorize.interceptor.ts` file implements an **HTTP interceptor** class—another mechanism that we don't know yet; again, we'll talk more about this soon enough.
- The `authorize.service.ts` file contains the *data service* that will handle all the HTTP requests and responses; we know their role and how they work from *Chapter 7, Code Tweaks and Data Services*, where we implemented `CityService` and `CountryService` for our `WorldCities` app.

We've yet to mention the various `.spec.ts` files; as we learned in *Chapter 9, ASP.NET Core and Angular Unit Testing*, we know that they are the corresponding *test units* for the class files they share their names with.

Route Guards

As we learned in *Chapter 2, Looking Around*, the Angular router is the service that allows our users to navigate through the various *views* of our app; each view updates the *front-end* and (possibly) calls the *back-end* to retrieve content.

If we think about it, we can see how the Angular router is the *front-end* counterpart of the ASP.NET Core routing interface, which is responsible for mapping request URIs to *back-end* endpoints and dispatching incoming requests to those endpoints. Since both of these modules share the same behavior, they also have similar requirements that we have to take care of when we implement an authentication and authorization mechanism in our app.

Throughout the previous chapters, we've defined a lot of routes on the *back-end* as well as on the *front-end* to grant our users access to the various ASP.NET Core action methods and Angular views that we've implemented. If we think about it, we can see how all of these routes share a common feature: *anyone can access them*. To put it in other words, *any user is free to go anywhere within our web app*: they can edit cities and countries, they can interact with our `SeedController` to execute its database-seeding tasks, and so on.

It goes without saying that such behavior, although being acceptable in development, is highly undesirable in any production scenario; when the app goes live, we would definitely want to protect some of these routes by restricting them to authorized users only—in other words, to *guard* them.

Route guards are a mechanism to properly enforce such a requirement; they can be added to our route configuration to return values that can control the router's behavior in the following way:

- If a route guard returns `true`, the navigation process continues
- If it returns `false`, the navigation process stops
- If it returns a `UrlTree`, the navigation process is canceled and replaced by a new navigation to the given `UrlTree`

Available guards

The following route guards are currently available in Angular:

- `CanActivate`: Mediates navigation to a given *route*
- `CanActivateChild`: Mediates navigation to a given *child route*
- `CanDeactivate`: Mediates navigation away from the current *route*
- `Resolve`: Performs some arbitrary operations (such as custom data retrieval tasks) before activating the *route*
- `CanLoad`: Mediates navigation to a given asynchronous *module*

Each one of them is available through a *superclass* that acts as a *common interface*: whenever we want to create our own guard, we'll just have to extend the corresponding superclass and implement the relevant method(s).

Any route can be configured with multiple guards: `CanDeactivate` and `CanActivateChild` guards will be checked first, from the deepest child route to the top; right after that, the router will check `CanActivate` guards from the top down to the deepest child route. Once done, `CanLoad` routes will be checked for asynchronous modules. If any of these guards returns `false`, the navigation will be stopped and all pending guards will be canceled.

Let's now take a look at the `/ClientApp/src/api-authorization/authorize.guard.ts` file to see which route guards have been implemented by the *front-end* authorization API shipped with the `AuthSample` Angular app (relevant lines are highlighted):

```
import { Injectable } from '@angular/core';
import { CanActivate, ActivatedRouteSnapshot, RouterStateSnapshot,
 Router } from '@angular/router';
import { Observable } from 'rxjs';
import { AuthorizeService } from './authorize.service';
import { tap } from 'rxjs/operators';
import { ApplicationPaths, QueryParameterNames } from
 './api-authorization.constants';

@Injectable({
  providedIn: 'root'
})
export class AuthorizeGuard implements CanActivate {
  constructor(private authorize: AuthorizeService, private router:
   Router) {
  }
  canActivate(
```

```
    _next: ActivatedRouteSnapshot,
    state: RouterStateSnapshot): Observable<boolean> |
     Promise<boolean> | boolean {
      return this.authorize.isAuthenticated()
        .pipe(tap(isAuthenticated =>
         this.handleAuthorization(isAuthenticated, state)));
  }
  private handleAuthorization(isAuthenticated: boolean, state:
   RouterStateSnapshot) {
    if (!isAuthenticated) {
      this.router.navigate(ApplicationPaths.LoginPathComponents, {
        queryParams: {
          [QueryParameterNames.ReturnUrl]: state.url
        }
      });
    }
  }
}
```

As we can see, we're dealing with a guard that extends the `CanActivate` interface. As we can reasonably expect from an authorization API, that guard is checking the `isAuthenticated()` method of `AuthorizeService` (which is *injected* in the constructor through DI) and conditionally allows or blocks the navigation based on it; no wonder its name is `AuthorizeGuard`.

Once they have been created, guards can be bound to the various routes from within the route configuration itself, which provides a property for each guard type; if we take a look inside the `/ClientApp/src/app/app.module.ts` file of the `AuthSample` app, where the main routes are configured, we can easily identify the *guarded* route:

```
// ...

RouterModule.forRoot([
  { path: '', component: HomeComponent, pathMatch: 'full' },
  { path: 'counter', component: CounterComponent },
  { path: 'fetch-data', component: FetchDataComponent, canActivate:
    [AuthorizeGuard] },
])

// ...
```

This means that the `fetch-data` view, which brings the user to the `FetchDataComponent`, can only be activated by authenticated users; let's quickly give it a try to see if it works as expected.

Press *F5* to run the `AuthSample` app in debug mode, then try to navigate to the fetch data view by clicking the corresponding link to the top-right menu. Since we're not an authenticated user, we should be redirected to the **Log in** view, as shown in the following screenshot:

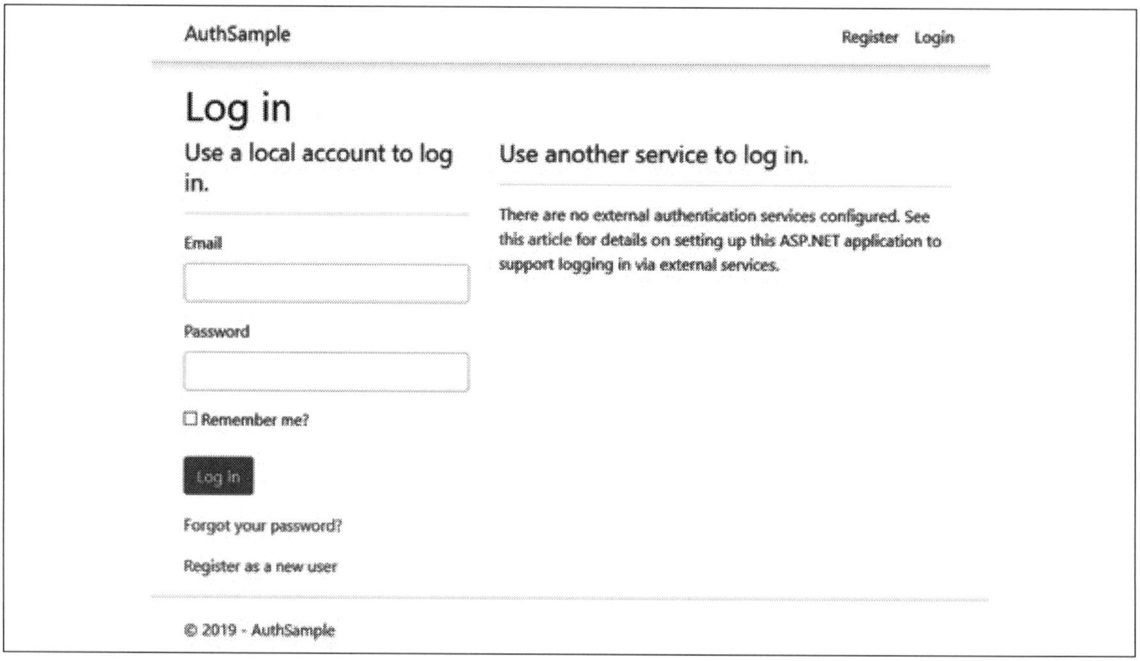

Figure 10.15: The Log in view

It seems that the route guard is working: if we now manually edit the `/ClientApp/src/app/app.module.ts` file, remove the `canActivate` property from the `fetch-data` route, and try again, we'll see that we'll be able to access that view without issues:

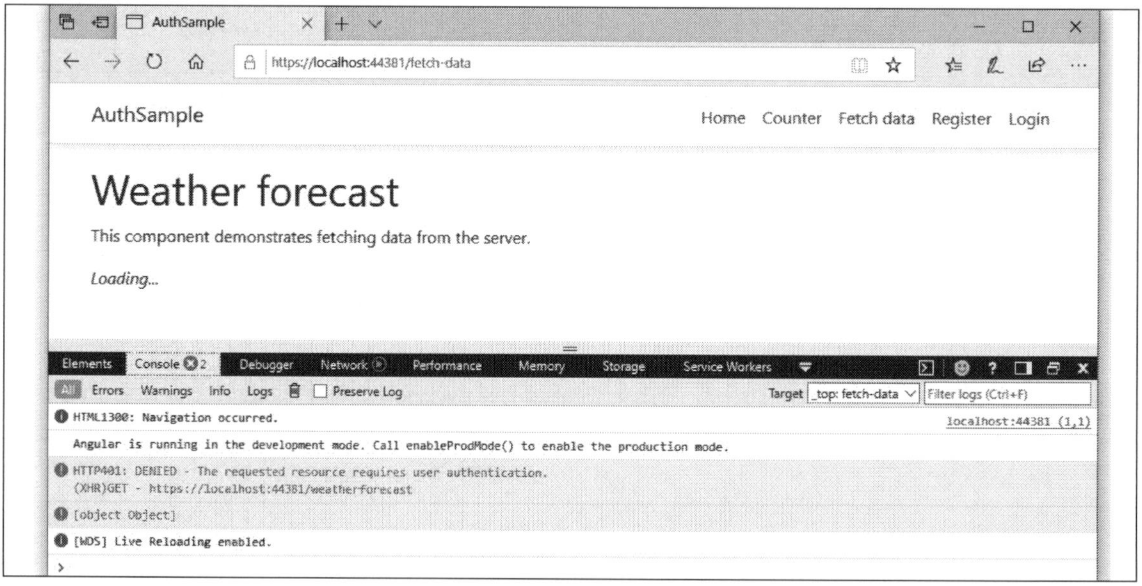

Figure 10.16: Trying to fetch the weather forecast data

... or maybe not.

As we can see from the **Console** log, even if the *front-end* allowed us to pass, the HTTP request issued to the *back-end* seems to have hit a 401 Unauthorized Error. What happened? The answer is really simple: by manually removing the route guard, we were able to *hack* our way through the Angular *front-end* routing system, but the .NET Core *back-end* routing also features similar protection against unauthorized access that can't be avoided from the client side.

This protection can easily be seen by opening the `/Controllers/WeatherForecastController.cs` file and looking at the existing class attributes (relevant line highlighted):

```
// ...

[Authorize]
[ApiController]
[Route("[controller]")]
public class WeatherForecastController : ControllerBase

// ...
```

In ASP.NET Core controllers, route authorization is controlled through the `AuthorizeAttribute` attribute. More specifically, the controller or action method that the `[Authorize]` attribute is applied to requires the authorization level specified by its parameters; if no parameters are given, applying the `AuthorizeAttribute` attribute to a controller or action will limit the access to *authenticated* users only.

Now we know why we are unable to fetch that data from the *back-end*; if we remove (or comment out) that attribute, we will finally be able to, as shown in the following screenshot:

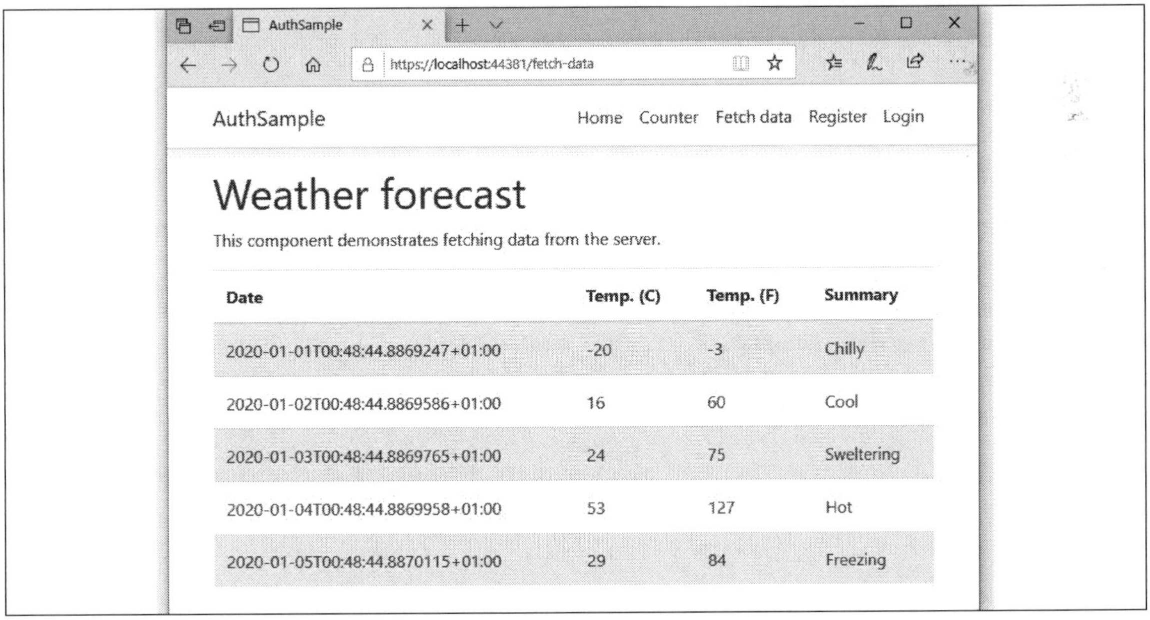

Figure 10.17: Successfully fetching the weather forecast data

Before proceeding, let's put the *front-end* route guard and the *back-end* `AuthorizeAttribute` back in their place; we need them to be there to properly test our navigation after performing an actual login and obtaining the authorization to access those resources.

However, before doing that, we have to finish our exploration journey; in the next section, we'll introduce another important Angular concept that we haven't talked about yet.

> For further information about route guards and their role in the Angular routing workflow, check out the following URLs:
>
> `https://angular.io/guide/router#preventing-unauthorized-access`
>
> `https://docs.microsoft.com/en-us/aspnet/core/fundamentals/routing`

HttpInterceptor

The Angular `HttpInterceptor` interface provides a standardized mechanism to intercept and/or transform outgoing HTTP requests or incoming HTTP responses; *interceptors* are quite similar to the ASP.NET *middleware* that we introduced in *Chapter 2*, *Looking Around*, and then played with in *Chapter 3*, *Front-End and Back-End Interactions*, except that they work at the *front-end* level.

Interceptors are a major feature of Angular since they can be used for a number of different tasks: they can inspect and/or log our app's HTTP traffic, modify the requests, cache the responses, and so on; they are a convenient way to centralize all these tasks so that we don't have to implement them explicitly on our *data services* and/or within the various `HttpClient`-based method calls. Moreover, they can also be chained, meaning that we can have multiple interceptors working together in a forward-and-backward chain of request/response handlers.

The `AuthorizeInterceptor` class shipped with the Angular authentication APIs we are exploring features a lot of inline comments that greatly help us to understand how it actually works.

To take a look at its source code, open the `/ClientApp/src/api-authorization/authorize.interceptor.ts` file (relevant lines are highlighted):

```
import { Injectable } from '@angular/core';
import { HttpInterceptor, HttpRequest, HttpHandler, HttpEvent }
 from '@angular/common/http';
import { Observable } from 'rxjs';
import { AuthorizeService } from './authorize.service';
import { mergeMap } from 'rxjs/operators';

@Injectable({
  providedIn: 'root'
})
export class AuthorizeInterceptor implements HttpInterceptor {
  constructor(private authorize: AuthorizeService) { }
```

```
  intercept(req: HttpRequest<any>, next: HttpHandler):
   Observable<HttpEvent<any>> {
    return this.authorize.getAccessToken()
      .pipe(mergeMap(token => this.processRequestWithToken(token, req,
       next)));
  }

  // Checks if there is an access_token available in the authorize
  // service and adds it to the request in case it's targeted at
  // the same origin as the single page application.
  private processRequestWithToken(token: string, req:
   HttpRequest<any>,
   next: HttpHandler) {
    if (!!token && this.isSameOriginUrl(req)) {
      req = req.clone({
        setHeaders: {
          Authorization: `Bearer ${token}`
        }
      });
    }

    return next.handle(req);
  }

  private isSameOriginUrl(req: any) {
    // It's an absolute url with the same origin.
    if (req.url.startsWith(`${window.location.origin}/`)) {
      return true;
    }

    // It's a protocol relative url with the same origin.
    // For example: //www.example.com/api/Products
    if (req.url.startsWith(`//${window.location.host}/`)) {
      return true;
    }

    // It's a relative url like /api/Products
    if (/^\/[^\/].*/.test(req.url)) {
      return true;
    }

    // It's an absolute or protocol relative url that
    // doesn't have the same origin.
    return false;
  }
}
```

As we can see, `AuthorizeInterceptor` implements the `HttpInterceptor` interface by defining an `intercept` method. That method's job is to intercept *all* the outgoing HTTP requests and conditionally add the JWT Bearer token to their HTTP headers; this condition is determined by the `isSameOriginUrl()` internal method, which will return `true` only if the request is addressed to an URL with the same *origin* as the Angular app.

Just like any other Angular class, the `AuthorizeInterceptor` needs to be properly configured within an `NgModule` in order to work; since it needs to inspect *any* HTTP request—including those not part of the authorization API—it has been configured in the `AppModule`, the root-level `NgModule`, of the `AuthSample` app.

To see the actual implementation, open the `/ClientApp/src/app/app.module.ts` file and look at the `providers` section:

```
// ...

providers: [
  { provide: HTTP_INTERCEPTORS, useClass: AuthorizeInterceptor,
    multi: true }
],

// ...
```

The `multi: true` property that we can see in the preceding code is a required setting, because `HTTP_INTERCEPTORS` is a multi-provider token that is expecting to *inject* an array of multiple values, rather than a single one.

> For additional information about HTTP interceptors, take a look at the following URLs:
>
> `https://angular.io/api/common/http/HttpInterceptor`
>
> `https://angular.io/api/common/http/HTTP_INTERCEPTORS`

The authorization components

Let's now take a look at the various Angular components included in the `/api-authorization/` folder.

LoginMenuComponent

The role of `LoginMenuComponent`, located in the `/ClientApp/src/api-authorization/login-menu/` folder, is to be included within `NavMenuComponent` (which we already know well) to add the `Login` and `Logout` actions to the existing navigation options.

We can check it out by opening the `/ClientApp/src/app/nav-menu/nav-menu.component.html` file and checking for the presence of the following line:

```
<app-login-menu></app-login-menu>
```

This is the root element of `LoginMenuComponent`; therefore, `LoginMenuComponent` is implemented as a *child component* of `NavMenuComponent`. However, if we look at its TypeScript file source code, we can see that it has some unique features strictly related to its tasks (relevant lines are highlighted):

```
import { Component, OnInit } from '@angular/core';
import { AuthorizeService } from '../authorize.service';
import { Observable } from 'rxjs';
import { map, tap } from 'rxjs/operators';

@Component({
  selector: 'app-login-menu',
  templateUrl: './login-menu.component.html',
  styleUrls: ['./login-menu.component.css']
})
export class LoginMenuComponent implements OnInit {
  public isAuthenticated: Observable<boolean>;
  public userName: Observable<string>;

  constructor(private authorizeService: AuthorizeService) { }

  ngOnInit() {
    this.isAuthenticated = this.authorizeService.isAuthenticated();
    this.userName = this.authorizeService.getUser().pipe(map(u => u &&
      u.name));
  }
}
```

As we can see, the component uses `authorizeService` (injected in the constructor through DI) to retrieve the following information about the visiting user:

- Whether that user is authenticated or not
- That user's username

The two values are stored in the `isAuthenticated` and `userName` local variables, which are then used by the template file to determine the component's behavior.

To better understand that, let's take a look at the `/ClientApp/src/api-authentication/login-menu/login-menu.component.html` template file (relevant lines highlighted):

```
<ul class="navbar-nav" *ngIf="isAuthenticated | async">
    <li class="nav-item">
        <a class="nav-link text-dark"
         [routerLink]='["/authentication/profile"]'
         title="Manage">Hello {{ userName | async }}</a>
    </li>
    <li class="nav-item">
        <a class="nav-link text-dark"
```

```
            [routerLink]='["/authentication/logout"]'
            [state]='{ local: true }' title="Logout">Logout</a>
    </li>
</ul>
<ul class="navbar-nav" *ngIf="!(isAuthenticated | async)">
  <li class="nav-item">
        <a class="nav-link text-dark"
         [routerLink]='["/authentication/register"]'>Register</a>
    </li>
    <li class="nav-item">
        <a class="nav-link text-dark"
         [routerLink]='["/authentication/login"]'>Login</a>
    </li>
</ul>
```

We can immediately see how the presentation layer is determined by two `ngIf` *structural directives* in the following way:

- If the user is *authenticated*, it will show the `Hello <username>` welcome message and the `Logout` link
- If the user is *not authenticated*, it will show the `Register` and `Login` links

That's a widely used approach to implement a login/logout menu; as we can see, all the links are pointing to the Razor pages provided by ASP.NET Core Identity UI that will transparently handle each task.

LoginComponent

`LoginComponent` performs various tasks required to properly handle the user's login process; consequently, any Angular component and/or ASP.NET Core controller that wants to restrict its access to authenticated users should perform an HTTP redirect to this component's route. As we can see by looking at the source code of the component's defining method, if the incoming request provides a `returnUrl` query parameter, the component will redirect the user back to it after performing the login:

```
//...

private async login(returnUrl: string): Promise<void> {
  const state: INavigationState = { returnUrl };
  const result = await this.authorizeService.signIn(state);
  this.message.next(undefined);
  switch (result.status) {
    case AuthenticationResultStatus.Redirect:
      break;
    case AuthenticationResultStatus.Success:
      await this.navigateToReturnUrl(returnUrl);
      break;
    case AuthenticationResultStatus.Fail:
```

```
        await this.router.navigate(
         ApplicationPaths.LoginFailedPathComponents, {
          queryParams: { [QueryParameterNames.Message]: result.message }
        });
        break;
      default:
        throw new Error(`Invalid status result ${(result as
         any).status}.`);
    }
  }

  // ...
```

The `LoginComponent` TypeScript source code is rather long, but it's very understandable as long as we keep in mind its main job: passing the user's authentication information to the ASP.NET Core `IdentityServer` using the default endpoint URIs and returning the results back to the client; it basically acts like a *front-end* to the *back-end* authentication proxy.

If we take a look at its template file, this role will become even more evident:

```
<p>{{ message | async }}</p>
```

That's it. As a matter of fact, this component has a very tiny template, simply because it will mostly redirect the user to some *back-end* pages that loosely mimic the visual style of our Angular components (!).

To quickly confirm that, hit *F5* to run the `AuthSample` project in debug mode and visit the **Log in** view, then look carefully at the UI elements highlighted in the following screenshot:

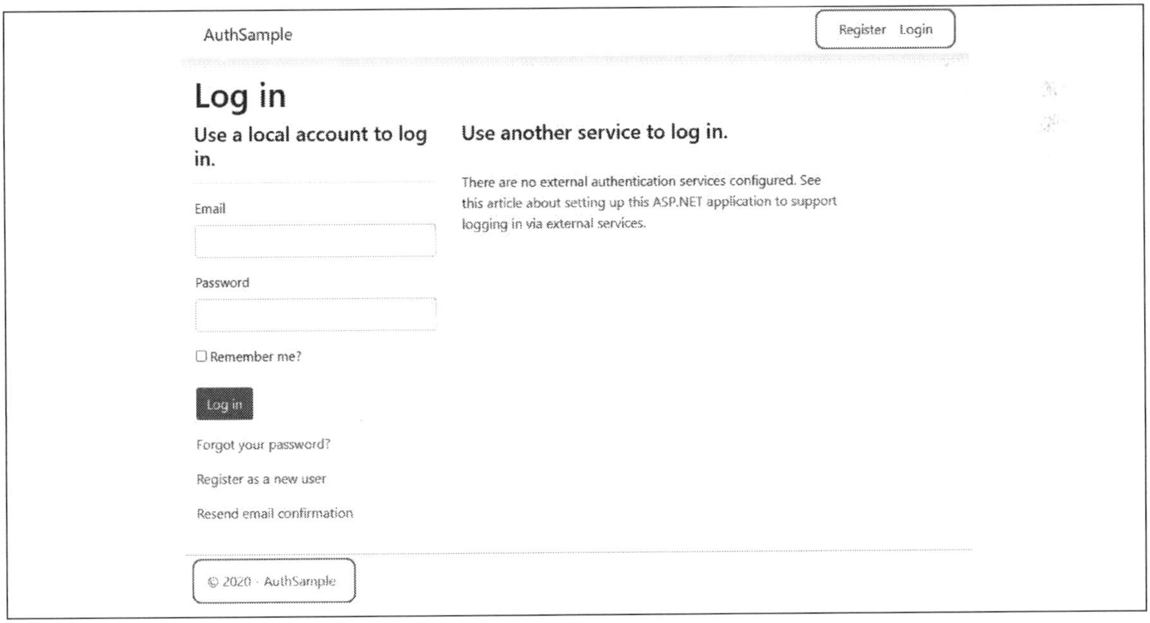

Figure 10.18: Inspecting UI elements on the Log in view

The two elements that we highlighted using the red squares don't match with the rest of our Angular app's GUI: the top-right menu is missing the **Counter** and **Fetch data** options, and the footer doesn't even exist; both of them have been generated from the *back-end*, just like the rest of the **Log in** view's HTML content.

As a matter of fact, the authentication API implementation shipped with the ASP.NET Core and Angular template is designed to work in the following way: both the login and registration forms are handled by the *back-end*, with `LoginComponent` playing a hybrid role—half a request handler, half a UI proxy.

> It's worth noting that these built-in Login and Registration pages provided by the ASP.NET Core back-end can be fully customized in their UI and/or behavior to make them compatible with the Angular app's look and feel: see the *Installing the ASP.NET Core Identity UI package* and *Customizing the default Identity UI* sections within this chapter for further details on how to do this.

This technique might seem a *hack*—and it actually is, at least to a certain extent, but it's a very smart one, since it *transparently* (well, not so much) works around a lot of the security, performance, and compatibility issues of most login mechanisms featuring a *pure front-end* implementation, while saving developers a lot of time.

> In one of my previous books (*ASP.NET Core 2 and Angular 5*), I chose to purposely avoid the ASP.NET Core `IdentityServer` and manually implement the registration and login workflows from the front-end: however, the .NET Core mixed approach has greatly improved in the last 2 years and now offers a great alternative to the standard, Angular-based implementation, thanks to a solid and highly configurable interface.
>
> Those who prefer to use the former method can take a look at the GitHub repository of the *ASP.NET Core 2 and Angular 5* book, (`Chapter_08` onward), which is still mostly compatible with the latest Angular versions:
>
> `https://github.com/PacktPublishing/ASP.NET-Core-2-and-Angular-5/`

If we don't like the *redirect to back-end* approach, the *built-in* authorization API features an alternative implementation that replaces the full-page HTTP redirects with popups.

To activate it, open the `/ClientApp/src/api-authorization/authorize.service.ts` file and change the `popUpDisabled` internal variable value from `true` to `false`, as shown in the following code:

```
// ...

export class AuthorizeService {
  // By default pop ups are disabled because they don't work properly
  // on Edge. If you want to enable pop up authentication simply set
```

```
    // this flag to false.

    private popUpDisabled = false;
    private userManager: UserManager;
    private userSubject: BehaviorSubject<IUser | null> = new
     BehaviorSubject(null);

  // ...
```

If we prefer to implement the auth feature through popups, we can change the preceding Boolean value to `false` and then test the outcome by launching our `AuthSample` project in debug mode.

Here's what the pop-up login page will look like:

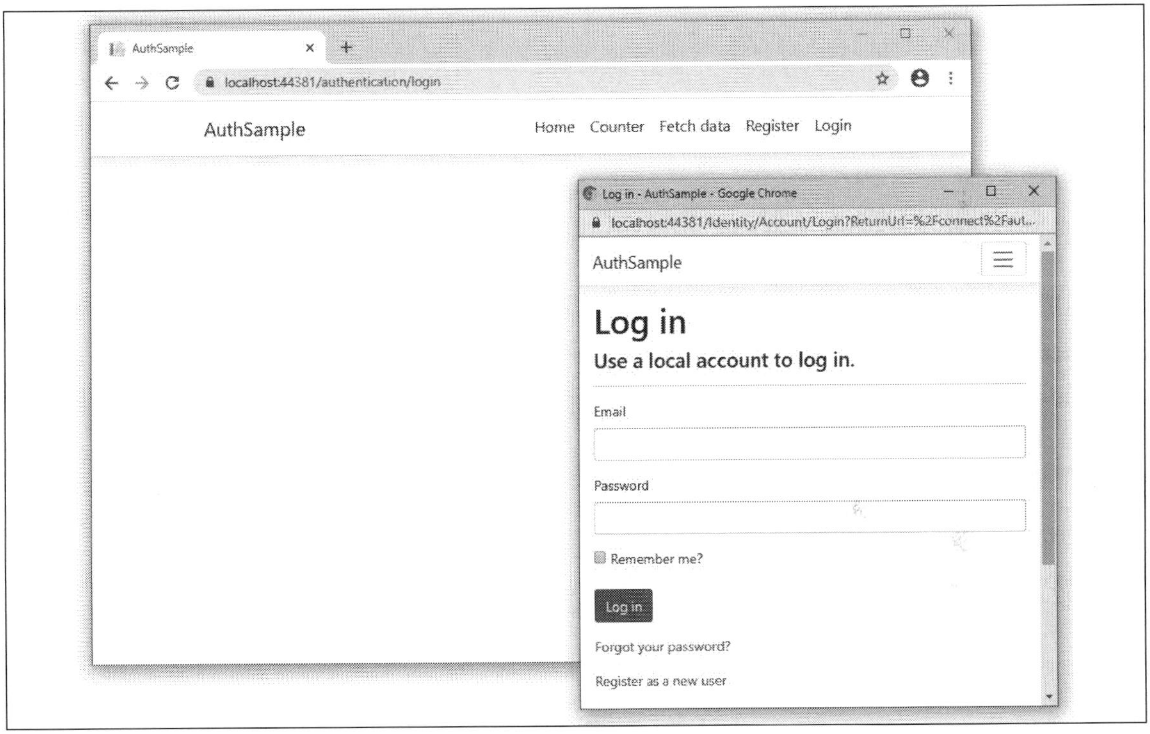

Figure 10.19: Pop-up login page

However, as the inline comments say, popups don't work properly on Microsoft Edge (and even the other browsers don't like them); for this reason, the *back-end*-generated pages are arguably a better choice—especially if we can customize them, as we'll see later on.

LogoutComponent

`LogoutComponent` is the counterpart of `LoginComponent`, as it handles the task of disconnecting our users and bringing them back to the home page.

There's not much to say there, because it works in a similar way to its sibling, redirecting the user to the ASP.NET Core Identity system endpoint URIs and then bringing the user's client back to the Angular app using the `returnUrl` parameter. The main difference is that there are no *back-end* pages this time, since the logout workflow doesn't require a user interface.

Testing registration and login

Now we're ready to test the registration and login workflow of the `AuthSample` Angular app; let's start with the registration phase, since we don't have any registered users here yet.

Hit *F5* to run the project in debug mode, then navigate to the **Register** view: insert a valid email and a password that matches the required password strength settings, and hit the **Register** button.

As soon as we do that, we should see the following message:

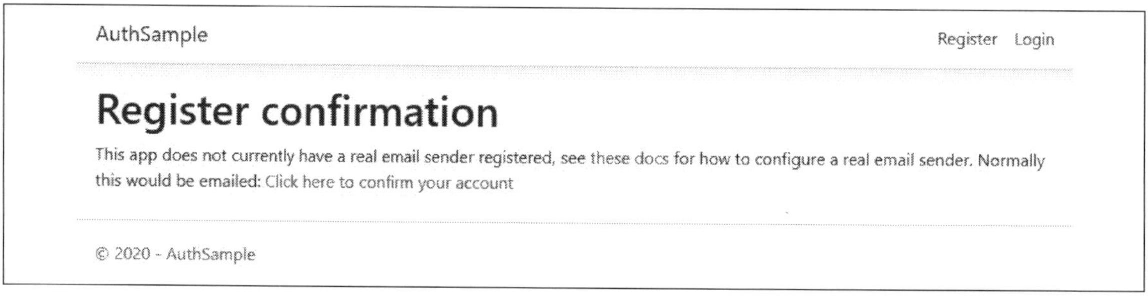

Figure 10.20: Register confirmation message

Click the confirmation link to create the account, then wait for a full-page reload.

> Actually, all these redirects and reloads performed by this implementation definitely break the SPA pattern that we talked about in *Chapter 1, Getting Ready*.
>
> However, when we compared the pros and cons of the Native Web Application, SPA, and Progressive Web Application approaches, we told ourselves that we would have definitely adopted some strategic HTTP round trips and/or other redirect techniques whenever we could use a microservice to lift off some workload from our app; that's precisely what we are doing right now.

When we're taken back to the **Log in** view, we can finally enter the credentials chosen a moment ago and perform the login.

Once done, we should be welcomed by the following screen:

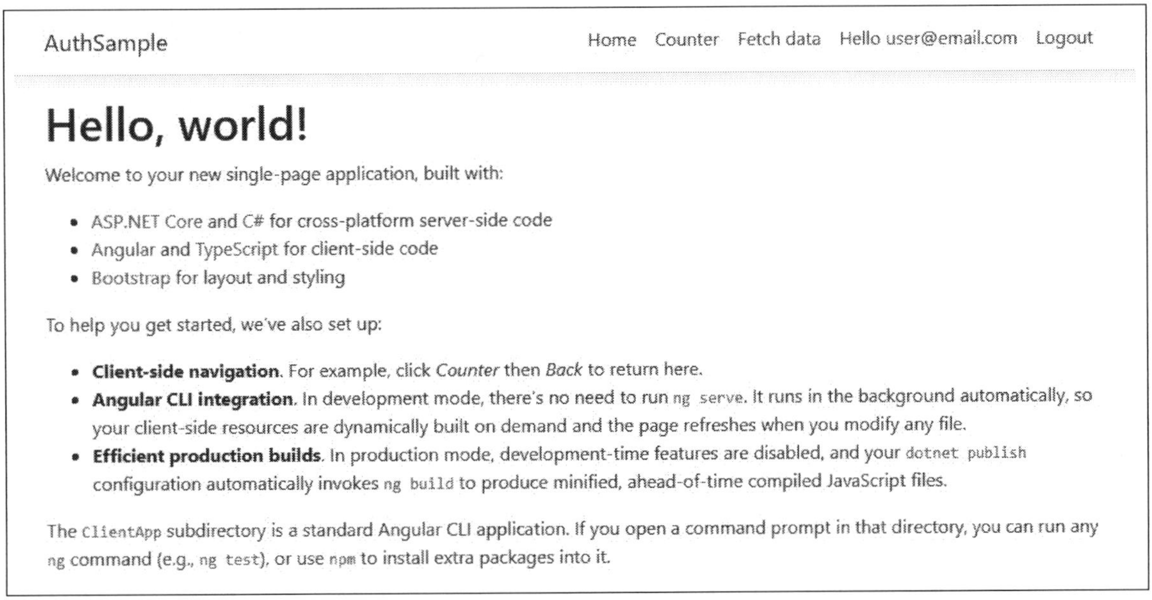
AuthSample
Home Counter Fetch data Hello user@email.com Logout
Hello, world!
Welcome to your new single-page application, built with:
ASP.NET Core and C# for cross-platform server-side code
Angular and TypeScript for client-side code
Bootstrap for layout and styling
To help you get started, we've also set up:
Client-side navigation. For example, click Counter then Back to return here.
Angular CLI integration. In development mode, there's no need to run ng serve. It runs in the background automatically, so your client-side resources are dynamically built on demand and the page refreshes when you modify any file.
Efficient production builds. In production mode, development-time features are disabled, and your dotnet publish configuration automatically invokes ng build to produce minified, ahead-of-time compiled JavaScript files.
The ClientApp subdirectory is a standard Angular CLI application. If you open a command prompt in that directory, you can run any ng command (e.g., ng test), or use npm to install extra packages into it.

Figure 10.21: Welcome screen after login

Here we go; we can see that we've logged in because the UI behavior of `LoginMenuComponent` has changed, meaning that its `isAuthenticated` internal variable now evaluates to `true`.

With this, we're done with our `AuthSample` app: now that we've understood how the *front-end* authorization API shipped with the .NET Core and Angular Visual Studio template actually works, we're going to bring it to our `WorldCities` app.

Implementing the auth API in the WorldCities app

In this section, we're going to implement the authorization API provided with the `AuthSample` app to our `WorldCities` app. Here's what we're going to do in detail:

- **Import the front-end authorization APIs** from the `AuthSample` app to the `WorldCities` app and integrate them into our existing Angular code
- **Adjust the existing back-end source code** to properly implement the authentication features
- **Test the login and registration forms** from the `WorldCities` project

By the end of the section, we should be able to log in with our existing users, as well as create new users, from the `WorldCities` app.

Importing the front-end authorization APIs

The first thing we need to do in order to import the *front-end* authorization APIs to our `WorldCities` Angular app is to copy the whole `/ClientApp/src/api-authorization/` folder from the `AuthSample` app. There are no drawbacks to doing this, so we can just do it with the Visual Studio Solution Explorer using the copy and paste GUI commands (or *Ctrl* + *C*/ *Ctrl* + *V*, if you prefer to use keyboard shortcuts).

Once done, we need to integrate the new *front-end* capabilities with the existing code.

api-authorization.constants

The first file we have to modify is the `/ClientApp/src/api-authorization/api-authorization.constants.ts` file, which contains a literal reference to the app name on the first line of its contents:

```
export const ApplicationName = 'AuthSample';

// ...
```

Change `'AuthSample'` to `'WorldCities'`, leaving the rest of the file as it is.

AppModule

Right after that, we need to update the `/ClientApp/src/app/app.module.ts` file, where we need to add the required references to the authorization API's classes:

```
// ...

import { HttpClientModule, HTTP_INTERCEPTORS } from '@angular/common/http';

// ...

import { ApiAuthorizationModule } from 'src/api-authorization/api-authorization.
module';
import { AuthorizeInterceptor } from 'src/api-authorization/authorize.
interceptor';

// ...

  imports: [
    BrowserModule.withServerTransition({ appId: 'ng-cli-universal' }),
    HttpClientModule,
    FormsModule,
    ApiAuthorizationModule,
    AppRoutingModule,
    BrowserAnimationsModule,
```

```
    AngularMaterialModule,
    ReactiveFormsModule
    ],
  providers: [
    {
      provide: HTTP_INTERCEPTORS,
      useClass: AuthorizeInterceptor,
      multi: true
    }
  ],
  bootstrap: [AppComponent]
})
export class AppModule { }
```

That's it.

AppRoutingModule

Now we need to protect our edit components using `AuthorizeGuard`, so that they will become accessible only to *registered* users. To do that, open the `/ClientApp/src/app/app-routing.module.ts` file and add the guard in the following way (new lines are highlighted):

```
import { NgModule } from '@angular/core';
import { Routes, RouterModule } from '@angular/router';
import { HomeComponent } from './home/home.component';
import { CitiesComponent } from './cities/cities.component';
import { CityEditComponent } from './cities/city-edit.component';
import { CountriesComponent } from './countries/countries.component';
import { CountryEditComponent } from './countries/country-edit.component';

import { AuthorizeGuard } from 'src/api-authorization/authorize.guard';

const routes: Routes = [
  {
    path: '',
    component: HomeComponent,
    pathMatch: 'full'
  },
  {
    path: 'cities',
    component: CitiesComponent
  },
  {
    path: 'city/:id',
    component: CityEditComponent,
    canActivate: [AuthorizeGuard]
```

```
  },
  {
    path: 'city',
    component: CityEditComponent,
    canActivate: [AuthorizeGuard]
  },
  {
    path: 'countries',
    component: CountriesComponent
  },
  {
    path: 'country/:id',
    component: CountryEditComponent,
    canActivate: [AuthorizeGuard]
  },
  {
    path: 'country',
    component: CountryEditComponent,
    canActivate: [AuthorizeGuard]
  }
];

@NgModule({
  imports: [RouterModule.forRoot(routes, {
    initialNavigation: 'enabled'
})],
  exports: [RouterModule]
})
export class AppRoutingModule { }
```

As we can see, other than adding the reference to the guard file, we've added `AuthorizeGuard` to all the routes pointing to components that perform writing activities to our database; this way we'll ensure that only registered and authorized users will be able to do that.

NavMenuComponent

Now we need to integrate `LoginMenuComponent` into our existing `NavMenuComponent`, just like in the `AuthSample` app.

Open the `/ClientApp/src/app/nav-menu/nav-menu.component.html` template file and add a reference to the menu within its content accordingly:

```
<header>
  <nav class="navbar navbar-expand-sm navbar-toggleable-sm
    navbar-light bg-white border-bottom box-shadow mb-3"
  >
    <div class="container">
```

```
      <a class="navbar-brand" [routerLink]="['/']">WorldCities</a>
      <button
        class="navbar-toggler"
        type="button"
        data-toggle="collapse"
        data-target=".navbar-collapse"
        aria-label="Toggle navigation"
        [attr.aria-expanded]="isExpanded"
        (click)="toggle()"
      >
        <span class="navbar-toggler-icon"></span>
      </button>
      <div
        class="navbar-collapse collapse d-sm-inline-flex
         flex-sm-row-reverse"
        [ngClass]="{ show: isExpanded }"
      >
        <app-login-menu></app-login-menu>
        <ul class="navbar-nav flex-grow">
          <li
            class="nav-item"
            [routerLinkActive]="['link-active']"
            [routerLinkActiveOptions]="{ exact: true }"
          >
            <a class="nav-link text-dark"
            [routerLink]="['/']">Home</a>

<!-- ...existing code... --->
```

Now we can switch to the *back-end* code.

Adjusting the back-end code

Let's start by importing `OidcConfigurationController`. The `AuthSample` project comes with a dedicated ASP.NET Core API controller to provide the URI endpoint that will serve the OIDC configuration parameters that the client needs to use.

Copy the `AuthSample` project's `/Controllers/OidcConfigurationController.cs` file to the `WorldCities` project's `/Controllers/` folder, then open the copied file and change its namespace accordingly:

```
// ...

namespace AuthSample.Controllers

// ...
```

Change `AuthSample.Controllers` to `WorldCities.Controllers` and go ahead.

Installing the ASP.NET Core Identity UI package

Remember when we talked about the login and registration pages generated from the *back-end* a short while ago? These are provided by the `Microsoft.AspNetCore.Identity.UI` package, which contains the default **Razor Pages** built-in UI for the .NET Core Identity framework. Since it's not installed by default, we need to manually add it to our `WorldCities` project using NuGet.

From Solution Explorer, right-click on the `WorldCities` tree node, then select **Manage NuGet Packages**, look for the following package, and install it:

```
Microsoft.AspNetCore.Identity.UI
```

Alternatively, open Package Manager Console and install it with the following command:

```
> Install-Package Microsoft.AspNetCore.Identity.UI
```

At the time of writing, this package's latest available version is **5.0.0**; as always, we are free to install a newer version, as long as we know how to adapt our code accordingly to fix potential compatibility issues.

Customizing the default Identity UI

The `AuthSample` project that we generated early on allows us to customize the top-level menu HTML snippet, which can be found within the `/Pages/Shared/_LoginPartial.cshtml` partial view: this can be useful to keep that menu "in sync" with the overall look and feel of our Angular app.

> When copying that file, don't forget to change `'@using AuthSample.Models;'` to `'@using WorldCities.Data.Models;'` near the top.

If changing the top-level menu isn't enough, we can extend such a technique to any other *login* and *registration* view and/or partial view provided by the `Microsoft.AspNetCore.Identity.UI` package using the *identity scaffolder* tool, which can be used to selectively add the files contained in the Identity **Razor Class Library** (**RCL**) to our project; once generated, those files will be available within a dedicated `/Areas/Identity/` folder, where we'll be able to change their appearance and/or behavior to better suit our needs.

> Generated (and modified) code will automatically take precedence over the default code in the Identity RCL.

To gain full control of the UI and not use the default RCL, see the following guides:

- `https://docs.microsoft.com/en-us/aspnet/core/security/authentication/scaffold-identity`
- `https://docs.microsoft.com/en-us/aspnet/core/security/authentication/scaffold-identity#full`
- `https://docs.microsoft.com/en-us/aspnet/core/razor-pages/ui-class`

> We'll use the scaffolding tool later in this chapter; for now, for the sake of simplicity, we'll just use the built-in *login* and *registration* pages.

Mapping Razor Pages to EndpointMiddleware

Now that we're (internally) using some Razor Pages, we need to map them to the *back-end* routing system; otherwise, our ASP.NET Core app won't forward the HTTP requests to them.

To do that, open the `WorldCities` project's `Startup.cs` file and add the following highlighted line in the `EndpointMiddleware` configuration block:

```
// ...

app.UseEndpoints(endpoints =>
{
    endpoints.MapControllerRoute(
        name: "default",
        pattern: "{controller}/{action=Index}/{id?}");

    endpoints.MapRazorPages();
});

// ...
```

That's it; now we're finally ready to log in.

Securing the back-end action methods

Before testing our authentication and authorization implementation, we should spend two more minutes to protect our *back-end* routes just like we did with the *front-end* ones. As we already know, we can do that using `AuthorizeAttribute`, which can restrict access to controllers and/or action methods to the registered users only.

To effectively shield our ASP.NET Core Web API against unauthorized access attempts, it can be wise to use it on the PUT, POST, and DELETE methods of all our controllers in the following way:

1. Open the /Controllers/CitiesController.cs file and add the [Authorize] attribute to the PutCity, PostCity, and DeleteCity methods:

```
using Microsoft.AspNetCore.Authorization;

// ...

[Authorize]
 [HttpPut("{id}")]
public async Task<IActionResult> PutCity(int id, City city)

// ...

[Authorize]
 [HttpPost]
public async Task<ActionResult<City>> PostCity(City city)

[Authorize]
[HttpDelete("{id}")]
public async Task<ActionResult<City>> DeleteCity(int id)

// ...
```

2. Open the /Controllers/CountriesController.cs file and add the [Authorize] attribute to the PutCountry, PostCountry, and DeleteCountry methods:

```
using Microsoft.AspNetCore.Authorization;

// ...

[Authorize]
 [HttpPut("{id}")]
public async Task<IActionResult> PutCountry(int id, Country country)

// ...
```

```
[Authorize]
 [HttpPost]
public async Task<ActionResult<Country>> PostCountry(Country country)

// ...

[Authorize]
 [HttpDelete("{id}")]
public async Task<ActionResult<Country>> DeleteCountry(int id)

// ...
```

> Don't forget to add a reference to the `using Microsoft.AspNetCore.Authorization` namespace at the top of both files.

Now all these action methods are protected against unauthorized access, as they will accept only requests coming from registered and logged-in users; those who don't have it will receive a 401 Unauthorized HTTP error response.

Testing login and registration

In this section, we're going to repeat the login and registration phases we already did for the `AuthSample` app a short while ago. However, this time, we'll do the login first, since we already have some existing users thanks to the `CreateDefaultUsers()` method of `SeedController`.

Launch the `WorldCities` app in debug mode by hitting *F5*. Once done, navigate to the login screen and insert the email and password of one of our existing users.

> If we didn't change them at the time, the sample values that we used in `SeedController` should be the following: email: `user@email.com` and password: `MySecr3t$`.

If we did everything correctly, we should see a screen like the one shown in the following screenshot:

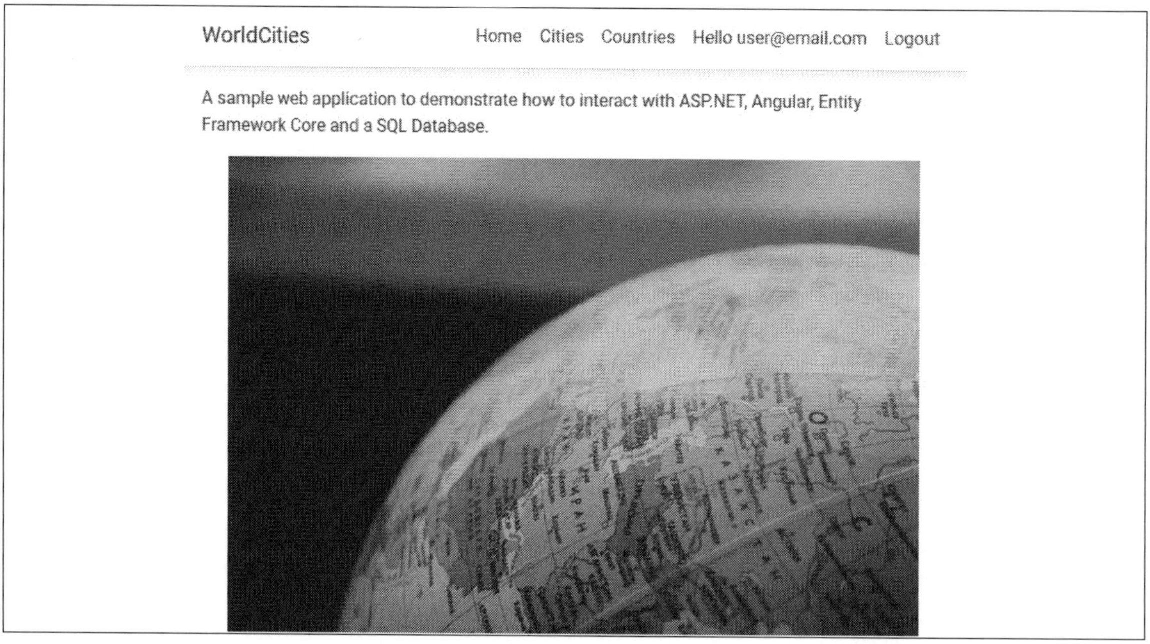

Figure 10.22: WorldCities home page

Right after that, we can perform the logout and try the registration workflow to register a new user, such as `newuser@ryadel.com`; if our login path worked so well, there's no reason why this action shouldn't succeed as well:

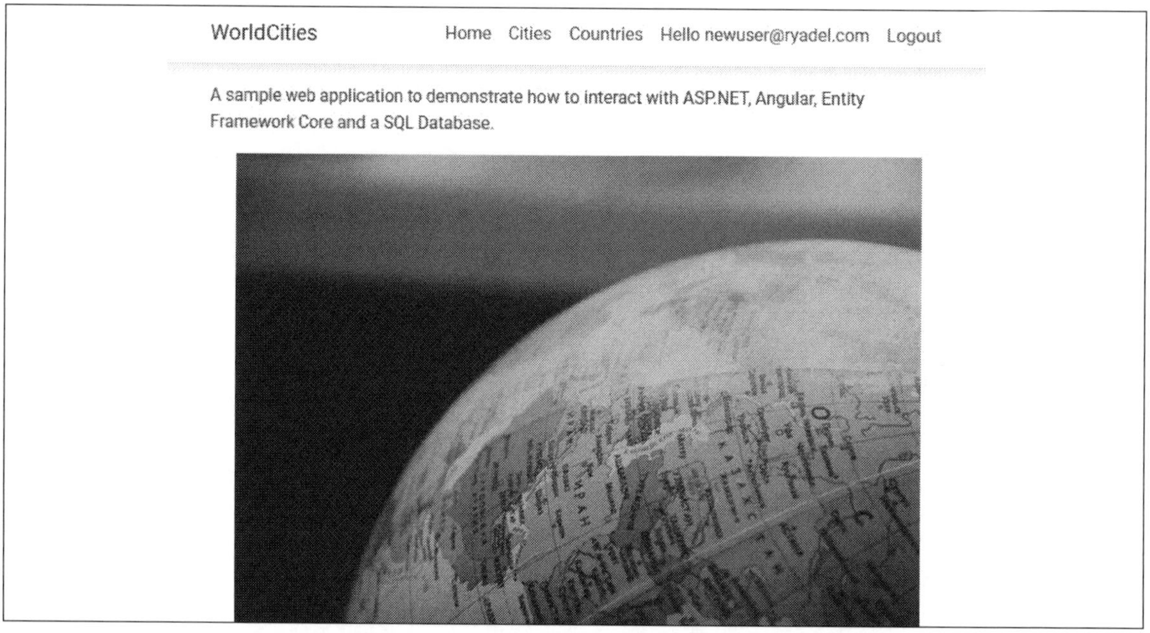

Figure 10.23: WorldCities home page after login with a newly created user

We did it! Now our `WorldCities` app contains fully featured authorization and authentication APIs.

As a matter of fact, we're still missing some key features, such as the following:

- The **email verification** step right after the registration phase, which would require an email sending service of some sort
- The **password change** and **password recovery** features, also requiring the aforementioned email service
- Some **third-party authentication providers** such as Facebook, Twitter, and so on (that is, **social login**)

In the next section, we'll see how we can take care of the first two features by implementing a custom email sender based upon the ASP.NET Core built-in `IEmailSender` interface, which will be used to connect to a dedicated external service or an SMTP server.

> For reasons of space, we won't be talking about how to enrich our existing authentication mechanism by adding a "social login" feature using third-party authentication providers. Those who are interested in doing so can take a look at this great guide with a lot of ready-to-use code samples to connect with external OAuth providers such as Facebook, Twitter, Google, and Microsoft:
>
> `https://docs.microsoft.com/en-us/aspnet/core/security/authentication/social/`

Adding an email sending service

The `IEmailSender` interface is a set of ASP.NET Core built-in APIs that fully supports the ASP.NET Core Identity default UI infrastructure: such an interface can be implemented by creating a custom IEmailSender-derived class that can be used within any web application to asynchronously send email messages in a structured, transparent, and consistent way.

> For additional info about the `IEmailSender` interface, check out the official documentation at the following URL:
>
> `https://docs.microsoft.com/en-us/dotnet/api/microsoft.aspnetcore.identity.ui.services.iemailsender`

In this section, we'll explain how we can implement such an interface in order to allow any ASP.NET Core web application to send email messages.

More precisely, we'll see how to achieve this result using two alternative methods:

- **A transactional email API** provided by a third-party service such as *SendGrid*, *Autopilot*, and the like
- **An external SMTP server** of any sort, just like the one we use to send our personal email messages

Are we ready? Let's start!

Transactional email API using SendGrid

Let's see how we can implement the `IEmailSender` interface to send email services using one of the many third-party marketing automation platforms that offer transactional email services. If we look for them using a search engine, we can easily find a lot of alternatives, such as:

- **SendGrid**
- **Autopilot**
- **Mailjet**
- **Sendinblue**
- **Mailgun**
- **Amazon SES**

... and many more.

For obvious reasons of space, we'll just pick one of them, which also happens to have a good .NET Core API and, most importantly, a free plan: *Twilio SendGrid*.

> For those who don't know what we're talking about, Twilio SendGrid (*SendGrid* from now on) is an all-in-one SaaS-based platform that offers transactional services such as email, SMS, chat (and more) through a versatile set of APIs that can be invoked and consumed from external websites or web services; its feature set makes it rather similar to the other alternatives, at least when it comes to email sending capabilities.
>
> For additional info about the SendGrid full feature set, check out its *Knowledge Center* at the following URL:
>
> `https://sendgrid.com/docs/`

Create a SendGrid account

The first thing we need to do is to create an account on SendGrid. Doing this is extremely easy; we just have to fill in the required fields, as shown in the following screenshot:

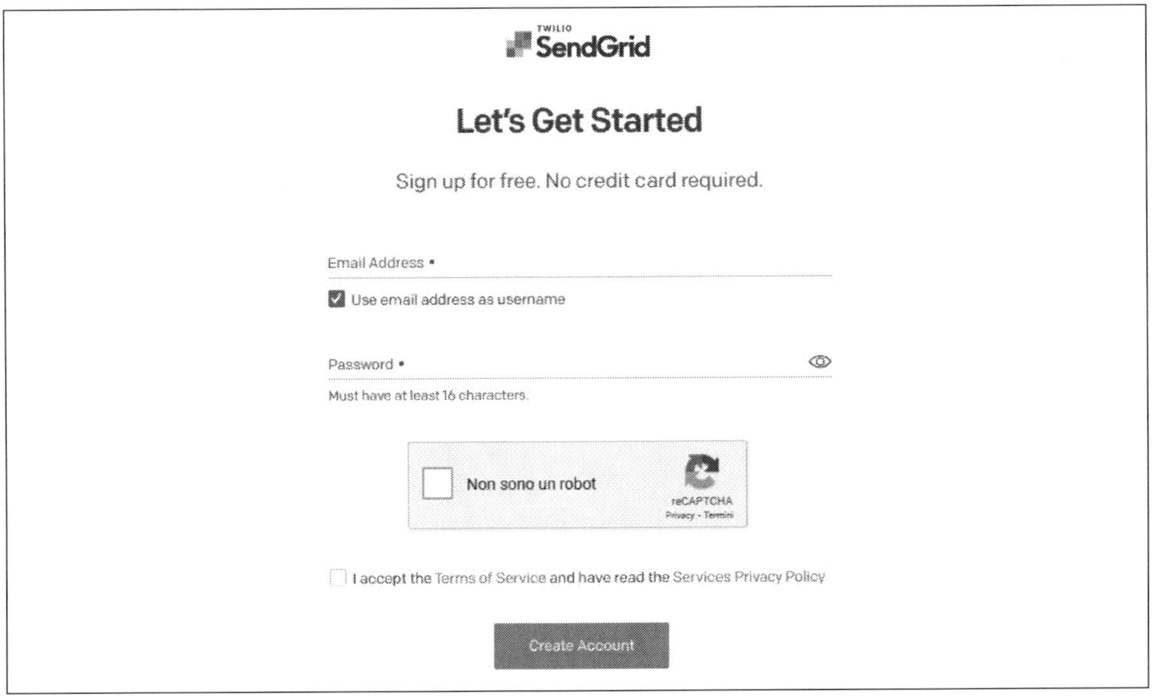

Figure 10.24: SendGrid account creation

Once done, we need to select one of the various pricing plans available: the best thing we can do, at least for the purpose of this book's samples, is to select the **Free** plan, which allows us to send up to 100 email messages per day; that's more than enough for testing out our implementation:

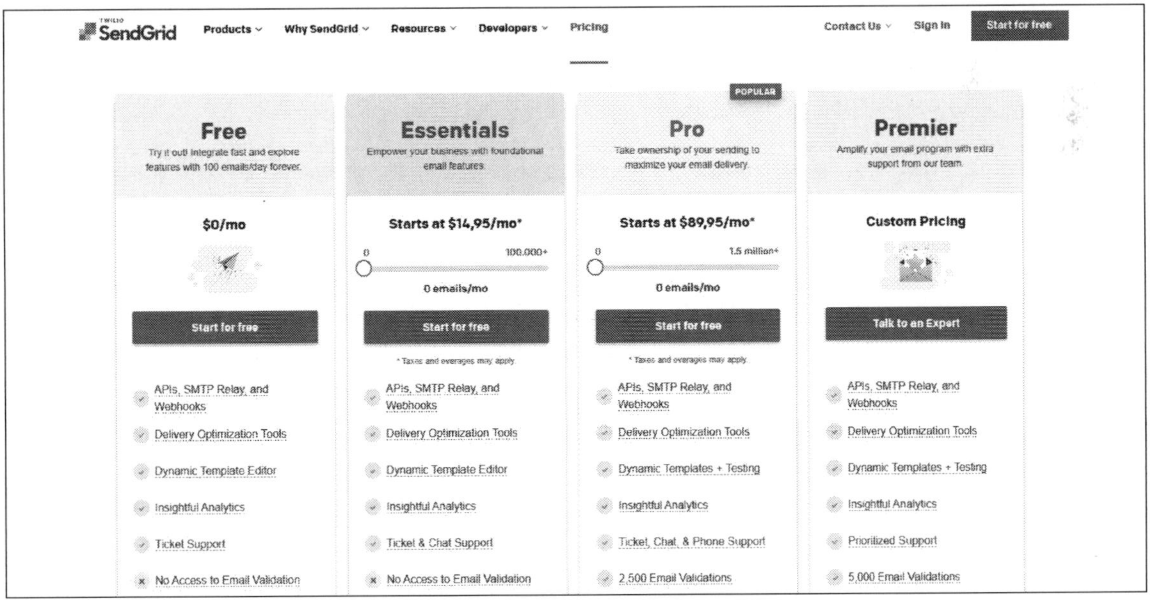

Figure 10.25: SendGrid plan selection

In order to complete the registration phase, we'll need to confirm our given email address: once done, we can proceed with the next step.

Get the Web API key

Right after completing the registration phase and performing the login, we'll be brought to SendGrid's main dashboard panel, which allows us to monitor our recent activities, as well as managing our campaigns, templates, settings, and more:

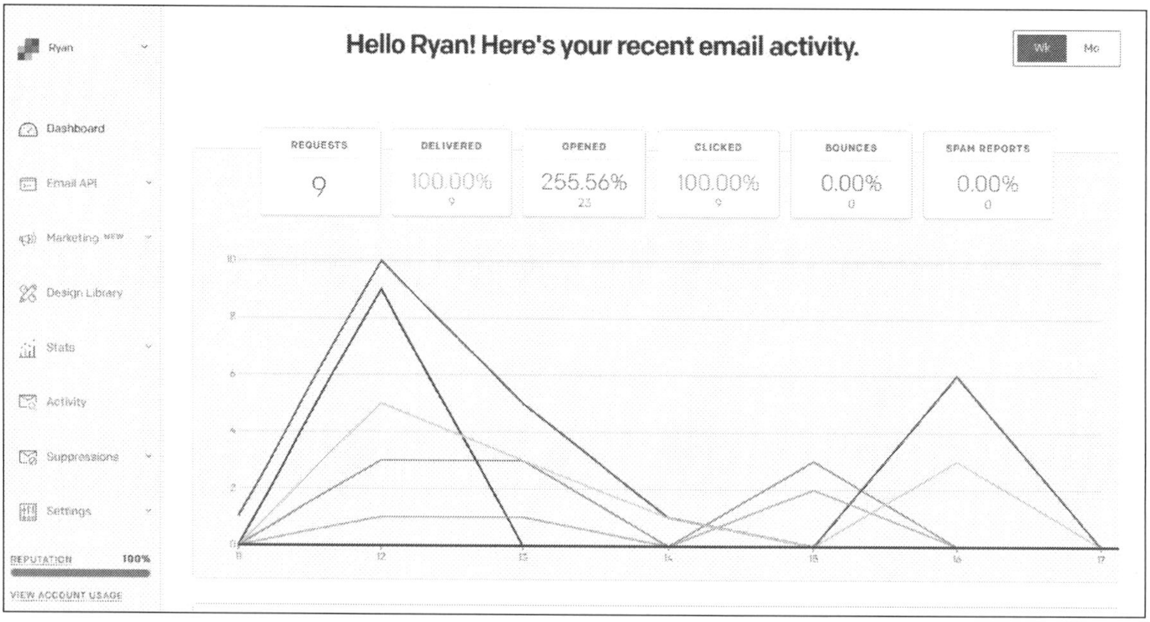

Figure 10.26: SendGrid main dashboard

Once there, select the **Email API** option from the left-side menu to access the **Integration guide** section, which is what we're going to use SendGrid for.

From the **Integration guide** section, we'll be prompted to choose between two available options:

- **Web API**, for direct app integration using the SendGrid official packages for the various supported languages (PHP, Ruby, Java, C#, and more).
- **SMTP Relay**, which can be used to retrieve the SendGrid SMTP data and implement it using a third-party email sender interface such as MailKit:

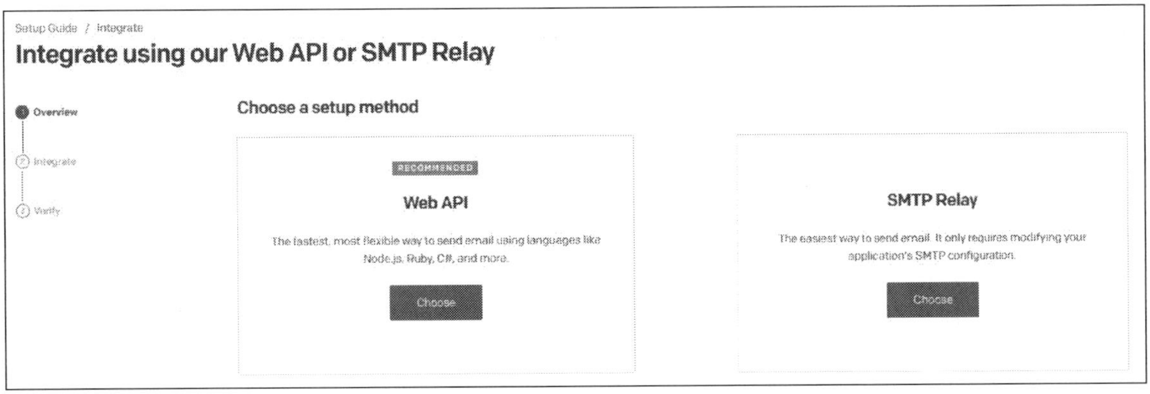

Figure 10.27: Choosing between Web API and SMTP Relay

Let's take the first choice for now, leaving the latter for the next section.

After selecting the Web API option, we'll access SendGrid's Web API setup guide: from there we can retrieve the *Web API key*, read all the required info, and even get a working code sample to get the stuff done:

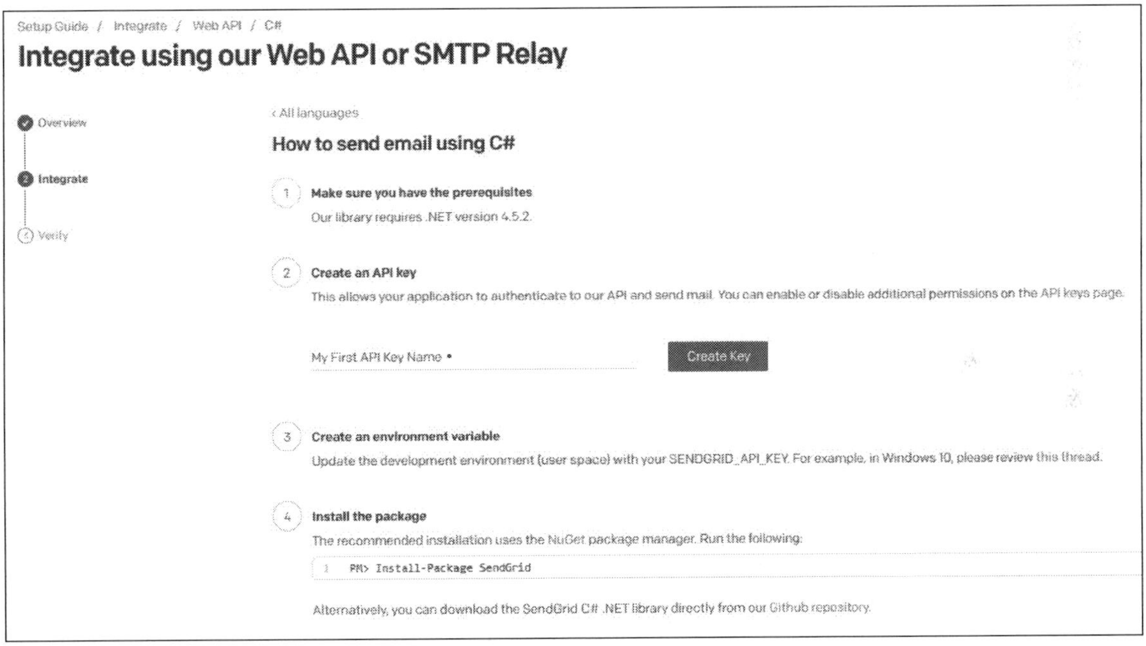

Figure 10.28: Web API setup guide

Here's a list of what we need to do here:

- **Create a new API key** and store it within our Visual Studio `secrets.json` file (as seen in *Chapter 4, Data Model with Entity Framework Core*)
- **Install the SendGrid ASP.NET Core NuGet package**
- **Verify the integration using the sample code** provided by the SendGrid page, modifying it to get the API key from the chosen *environment variable*, *user secret*, or plain text
- **Create our own implementation code** by adding the C# classes required by the `IEmailSender` interface, using the sample code as reference

Creating the API key is quite a straightforward process that can be dealt with from the website's interface.

Install the SendGrid NuGet package

To install the SendGrid NuGet package, open the Visual Studio Package Manager Console and type the following command:

```
PM> Install-Package Sendgrid -version 9.21.2
```

The specified version is the latest at the time of writing; feel free to remove the `-version` switch if you want to use the package's latest version.

Verify the integration

Here's what the SendGrid guide's sample code looks like: the single line of code where we need to put the API key value has been marked:

```
// using SendGrid's C# Library
// https://github.com/sendgrid/sendgrid-csharp
using SendGrid;
using SendGrid.Helpers.Mail;
using System;
using System.Threading.Tasks;

namespace Example
{
    internal class Example
    {
        private static void Main()
        {
            Execute().Wait();
        }
```

```
        static async Task Execute()
        {
            var apiKey = Environment.GetEnvironmentVariable("NAME_OF_THE_
ENVIRONMENT_VARIABLE_FOR_YOUR_SENDGRID_KEY");
            var client = new SendGridClient(apiKey);
            var from = new EmailAddress("test@example.com", "Example User");
            var subject = "Sending with SendGrid is Fun";
            var to = new EmailAddress("test@example.com", "Example User");
            var plainTextContent = "and easy to do anywhere, even with C#";
            var htmlContent = "<strong>and easy to do anywhere, even with C#</
strong>";
            var msg = MailHelper.CreateSingleEmail(from, to, subject,
plainTextContent, htmlContent);
            var response = await client.SendEmailAsync(msg);
        }
    }
}
```

> The preceding sample code has been published for reference purposes only; it's strongly advised to use the version found in the official SendGrid Web API C# integration guide.

In order to test the SendGrid integration, we need to implement the preceding code (more precisely, the `Execute` method) within our web application's `Program.cs` file, and then launch it from the existing `Main` method.

If we want to try that, since we don't plan to store the API key within an environment variable, we just need to replace the first line of the `Execute` method in the following way:

```
var apiKey = "PUT-YOUR-API-KEY-HERE";
```

in order to use our newly generated API key.

> If we don't want to alter our existing web app source code, we could skip this part and create a brand-new ASP.NET web application (or console application) project and test the SendGrid integration there instead... or we could just skip the test for now and just test our final implementation.

Here's the updated `Program.cs` file content (new lines are highlighted):

```
using Microsoft.AspNetCore.Hosting;
using Microsoft.Extensions.Hosting;
using SendGrid;
using SendGrid.Helpers.Mail;
using System.Threading.Tasks;
```

```
namespace WorldCities
{
    public class Program
    {
        public static void Main(string[] args)
        {
            // SendGrid implementation test
            Execute().Wait();

            CreateHostBuilder(args).Build().Run();
        }

        public static IHostBuilder CreateHostBuilder(string[] args) =>
            Host.CreateDefaultBuilder(args)
                .ConfigureWebHostDefaults(webBuilder =>
                {
                    webBuilder.UseStartup<Startup>();
                });


        /// <summary>
        /// SendGrid implementation test
        /// </summary>
        static async Task Execute()
        {
            var apiKey = "PUT-YOUR-API-KEY-HERE";
            var client = new SendGridClient(apiKey);
            var from = new EmailAddress("test@example.com", "Example User");
            var subject = "Sending with SendGrid is Fun";
            var to = new EmailAddress("test@example.com", "Example User");
            var plainTextContent = "and easy to do anywhere, even with C#";
            var htmlContent = "<strong>and easy to do anywhere, even with C#</
strong>";
            var msg = MailHelper.CreateSingleEmail(from, to, subject,
plainTextContent, htmlContent);
            var response = await client.SendEmailAsync(msg);
        }
    }
}
```

As we can see, we've just added the `Execute` method that we took from the SendGrid implementation sample and called it from the `Main` method of our `Program` class, right before running our web application.

> You will find the preceding sample in the GitHub project for *Chapter 10*, with the `Execute().Wait()` call commented out for performance reasons; feel free to uncomment it to have the test running.

We can check the verification process from the SendGrid page; as soon as we successfully do that, we can proceed with our own implementation.

Implement the IEmailSender interface

The first thing to do is to add the SendGrid API key to our project. Although the SendGrid sample code suggests the use of an environment variable, we strongly advise you to not do that and implement the API key using the Visual Studio *User Secrets* approach that we've already seen in *Chapter 4, Data Model with Entity Framework Core*.

To do that, open the Visual Studio `secrets.json` file and store it in the following way (new lines are highlighted):

```
{
  "ConnectionStrings": {
    "DefaultConnection": "Server=localhost\\SQLEXPRESS;Database=WorldCities;User
Id=WorldCities;Password=MyVeryOwn$721;Integrated Security=False;MultipleActiveRe
sultSets=True"
  },
  "ExternalProviders": {
    "SendGrid": {
      "ApiKey": "PUT-YOUR-API-KEY-HERE"
    }
  }
}
```

From now on, we'll be able to access our SendGrid API key in the following way:

```
Configuration["ExternalProviders:SendGrid:ApiKey"]
```

Now we can finally switch to the source code part.

In order to implement the `IEmailSender` interface, we need to create two classes:

- **A custom class derived from the EmailSender base class**: This is the class that will contain the main email sending logic.
- **An options class** that will contain the mail sender settings, which will be used as an initialization parameter of the main class.

Let's do this.

SendGridEmailSenderOptions

Let's start with the options class: from Solution Explorer, create a new `/Services/` folder in the root project's node, then add a new `SendGridEmailSenderOptions.cs` class file and fill it with the following content:

```
namespace WorldCities.Services
{
    public class SendGridEmailSenderOptions
    {
        public string ApiKey { get; set; }

        public string Sender_Email { get; set; }

        public string Sender_Name { get; set; }
    }
}
```

As we can see, this class will be used to store the API key that we created a short while ago and a couple of other settings.

SendGridEmailSender

Right after that, right-click on the `/Services/` folder again and add a new `SendGridEmailSender.cs` class file, filling it with the following content:

```
using Microsoft.AspNetCore.Identity.UI.Services;
using Microsoft.Extensions.Options;
using SendGrid;
using SendGrid.Helpers.Mail;
using System.Threading.Tasks;

namespace WorldCities.Services
{
    public class SendGridEmailSender : IEmailSender
    {
        public SendGridEmailSender(
            IOptions<SendGridEmailSenderOptions> options
            )
        {
            this.Options = options.Value;
        }

        public SendGridEmailSenderOptions Options { get; set; }

        public async Task SendEmailAsync(
            string email,
```

```
            string subject,
            string message)
        {
            await Execute(Options.ApiKey, subject, message, email);
        }

        private async Task<Response> Execute(
            string apiKey,
            string subject,
            string message,
            string email)
        {
            var client = new SendGridClient(apiKey);
            var msg = new SendGridMessage()
            {
                From = new EmailAddress(Options.Sender_Email, Options.
Sender_Name),
                Subject = subject,
                PlainTextContent = message,
                HtmlContent = message
            };
            msg.AddTo(new EmailAddress(email));

            // Disable tracking settings
            msg.SetClickTracking(false, false);
            msg.SetOpenTracking(false);
            msg.SetGoogleAnalytics(false);
            msg.SetSubscriptionTracking(false);

            return await client.SendEmailAsync(msg);
        }
    }
}
```

As we can see, we've altered the sample code provided by the SendGrid website to create a custom class that extends the `IEmailSender` interface. The action takes place within the interface's `Execute` method, where the email message is built, then configured using the `SendGridEmailSenderOptions` object that we've added early on, and eventually sent using the `SendEmailAsync` method provided by the SendGrid client.

> For additional info regarding the options that we used to disable tracking settings in the preceding code, check out the following URL:
>
> `https://sendgrid.com/docs/ui/account-and-settings/tracking/`

Startup class

Now that we do have our classes, we just need to configure them in a dedicated transient service that we can define in our application's `Startup` class.

Open the `Startup.cs` file and add the following code at the end of the existing `ConfigureServices` method:

```
// IEmailSender implementation using SendGrid
services.AddTransient<IEmailSender, SendGridEmailSender>();
services.Configure<SendGridEmailSenderOptions>(options =>
{
    options.ApiKey = Configuration["ExternalProviders:SendGrid:ApiKey"];
    options.Sender_Email = "test@example.com";
    options.Sender_Name = "WorldCities";
});
```

For the preceding code to work without compiler errors, we'll also need to add our new services namespace at the beginning of the file:

```
using WorldCities.Services;
```

As we can see by looking at the preceding code, we are still using the `test@example.com` testing email address taken from the SendGrid sample code. It goes without saying that, before being able to actually send email messages, we'll have to replace it with a real email address.

Create a new sender

This can be done with SendGrid's **Create new sender** feature (in the **Marketing** > **Sender** section), which allows us to add one or more new sender addresses and use them within the API. Once added, each sender must be verified, as explained in the notes that we can read in the SendGrid's **Add a Sender** modal window:

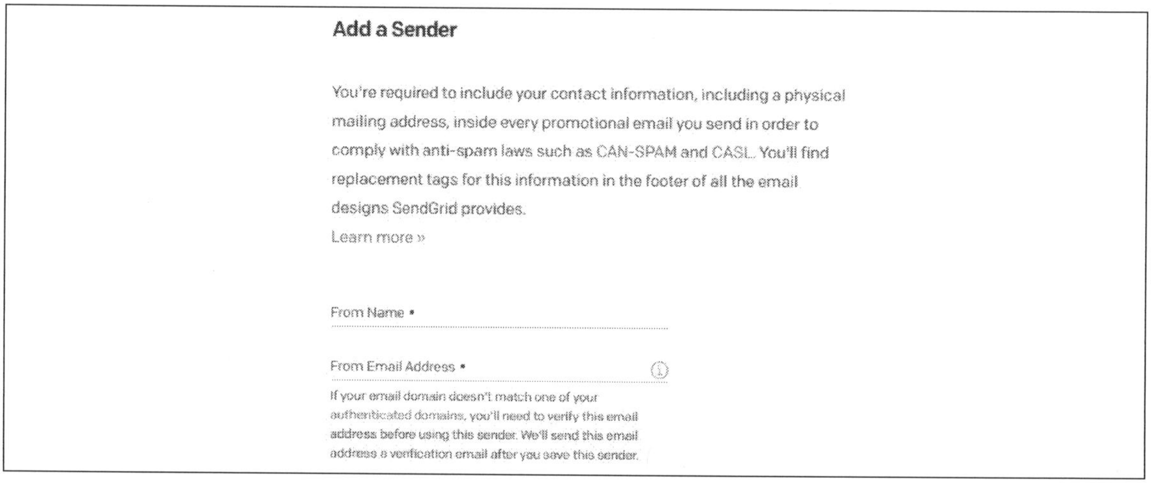

Figure 10.29: SendGrid's Add a Sender modal window

As we can see, SendGrid currently supports two verification methods:

- **Registering the email address domain** under the authenticated domains section
- **Answering a verification email** that will be sent to the email address registered as the sender

Both methods would be viable enough for most scenarios. In our case, for the sake of simplicity, we suggest validating a single email address, adding it to the startup `ConfigureServices` method (thus replacing `test@example.com` in the preceding code), and go ahead.

Since we have to do that, we can take the chance to move the `Sender_Email` and `Sender_Name` property values to the `secrets.json` file instead:

```
"SendGrid": {
  "ApiKey": "PUT-YOUR-API-KEY-HERE",
  "Sender_Email": "your.verified@email.com",
  "Sender_Name": "WorldCities "
},
```

And modify the `Startup.cs` code accordingly:

```
// IEmailSender implementation using SendGrid
services.AddTransient<IEmailSender, SendGridEmailSender>();
services.Configure<SendGridEmailSenderOptions>(options =>
{
    options.ApiKey = Configuration["ExternalProviders:SendGrid:ApiKey"];
    options.Sender_Email = Configuration["ExternalProviders:SendGrid:Sender_
Email"];
    options.Sender_Name = Configuration["ExternalProviders:SendGrid:Sender_
Name"];
});
```

This concludes our SendGrid implementation. Let's now see how we can use what we just did to send all the identity-related email messages, thus replacing the existing "no-send" behavior.

Scaffold the Identity pages

The best way to test our new `IEmailSender` implementation is to use the identity scaffolding tool that we've briefly introduced a while ago. This will allow us to view, modify, and debug all the account-related pages (login, registration, email confirmation, and so on).

From Solution Explorer, right-click the web application's root node and select **Add** > **New Scaffolded Item**. From the modal window that appears, select the **Identity** group and the **Identity** element within it, as shown in the following screenshot:

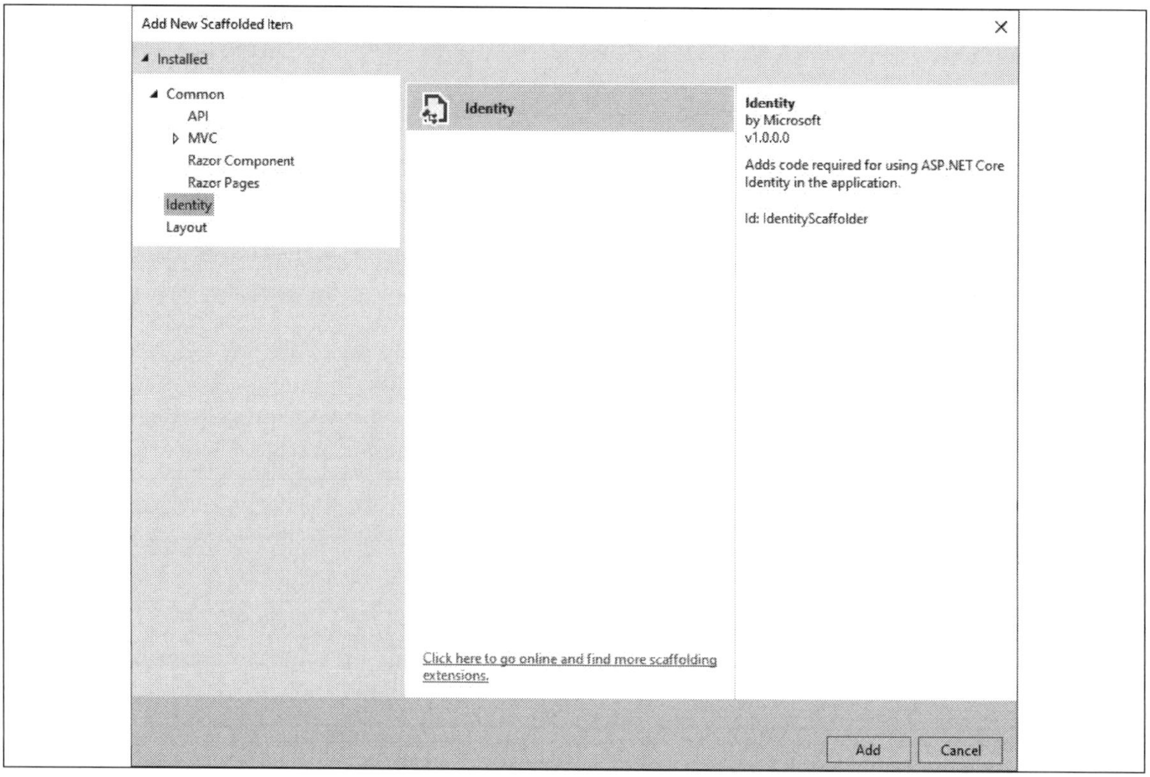

Figure 10.30: Add New Scaffolded Item modal window

Click on the **Add** button to access the next page of this mini-wizard; from there, we'll be asked to specify an existing layout page, select which files to override, and select our existing data context class.

Since we don't have an existing layout page or existing identity pages, we can leave the layout page textbox empty and select the **Override all files** checkbox. As for **Data context class**, select our `ApplicationDbContext` to ensure that the identity framework will perform its data accesses within that context:

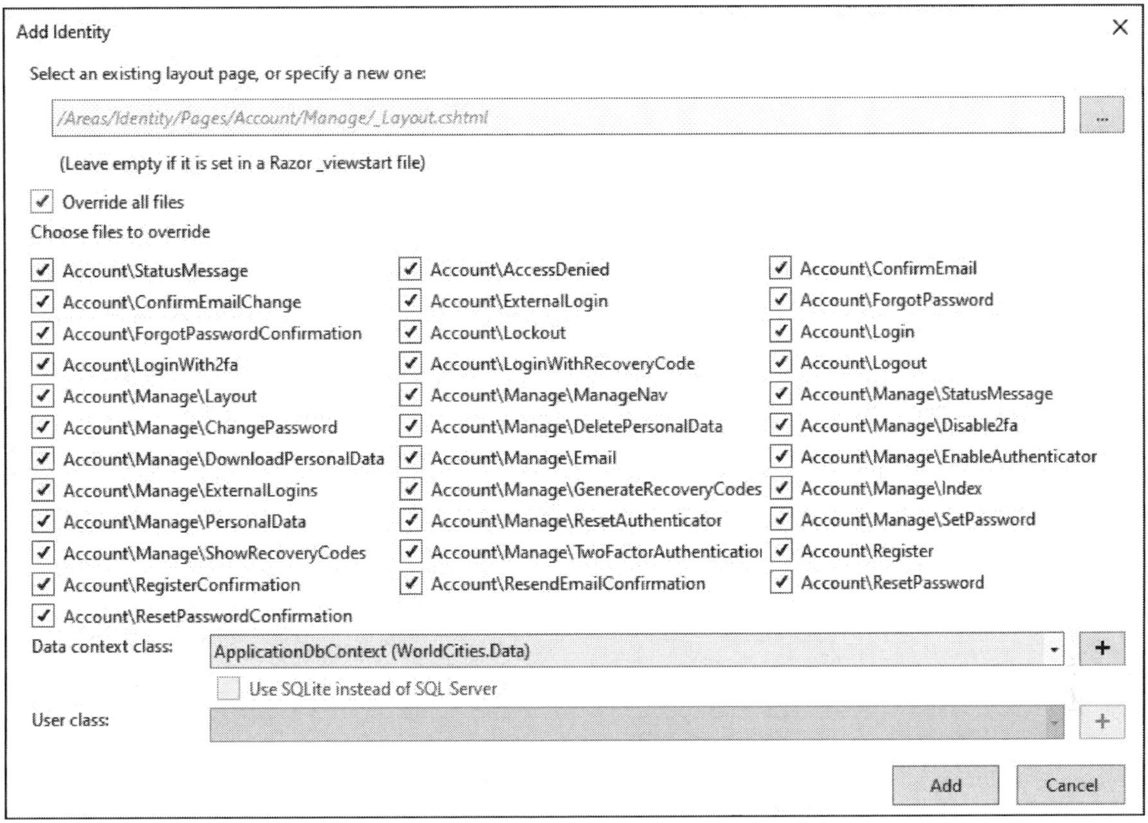

Figure 10.31: Add Identity window

After clicking the **Add** button, the scaffolding process will start; the whole code generation task will likely take some seconds:

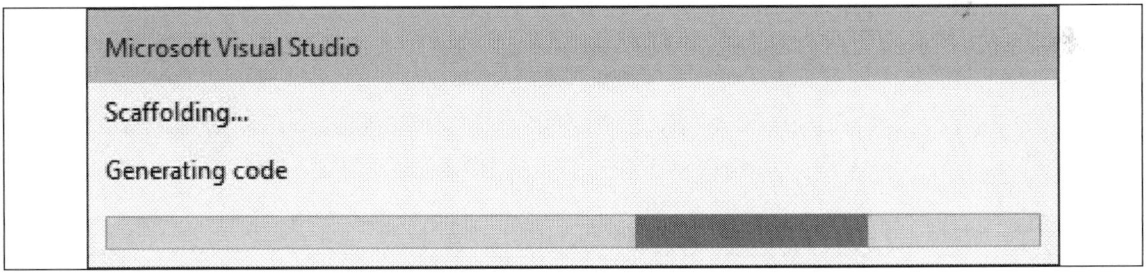

Figure 10.32: Scaffolding in progress

Eventually, a new `/Areas/` folder will be added to our project, containing all the Razor pages included in the **Identity Razor Class Library (RCL)**:

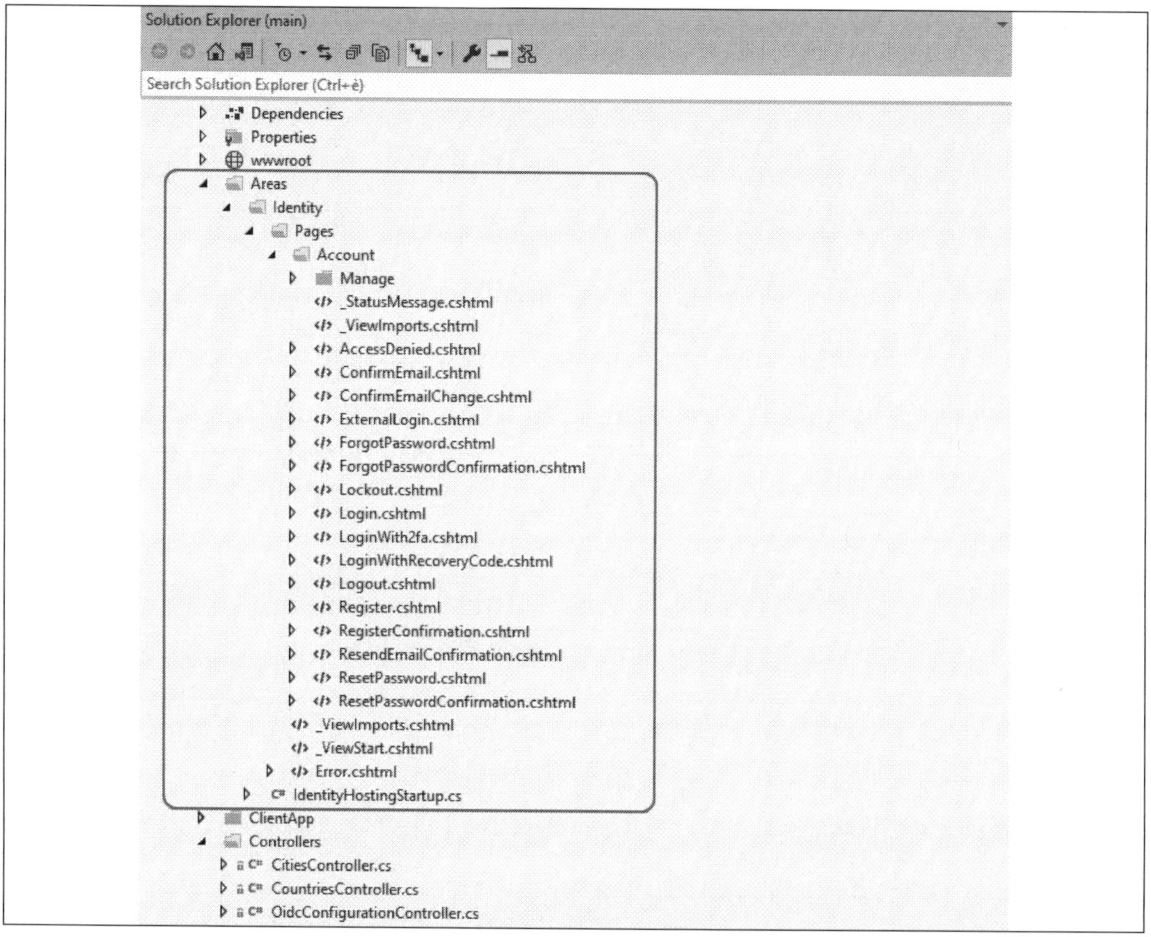

Figure 10.33: Examining the new Areas folder

These new Razor pages will allow us to edit the built-in HTML content that we saw a while ago when we first tested the login and registration views.

Disable link-based account verification

With the default templates, as we saw earlier on, when users submit their registration page by specifying the email address and password, they are redirected to the `RegisterConfirmation` page, where they can select a link to have the account confirmed. Such "automatic" account verification behavior is meant for testing purposes only and should definitely be disabled in a production app, possibly replacing it with an email-based verification process; this is precisely what we're going to do now.

From Solution Explorer, open the following page:

```
/Areas/Identity/Pages/Account/RegisterConfirmation.cshtml.cs
```

Locate the `OnGetAsync` method and set the `DisplayConfirmAccountLink` property to `false` in the following way (the single updated line is highlighted):

```
public async Task<IActionResult> OnGetAsync(string email, string returnUrl =
null)
{
    if (email == null)
    {
        return RedirectToPage("/Index");
    }

    var user = await _userManager.FindByEmailAsync(email);
    if (user == null)
    {
        return NotFound($"Unable to load user with email '{email}'.");
    }

    Email = email;
    // Once you add a real email sender, you should remove this code that lets
you confirm the account
    DisplayConfirmAccountLink = false;
    if (DisplayConfirmAccountLink)
    {
        var userId = await _userManager.GetUserIdAsync(user);
        var code = await _userManager.GenerateEmailConfirmationTokenAsync(user);
        code = WebEncoders.Base64UrlEncode(Encoding.UTF8.GetBytes(code));
        EmailConfirmationUrl = Url.Page(
            "/Account/ConfirmEmail",
            pageHandler: null,
            values: new { area = "Identity", userId = userId, code = code,
returnUrl = returnUrl },
            protocol: Request.Scheme);
    }

    return Page();
}
```

The preceding change will disable the link-based account verification process, thus leaving the email-based alternative the only possible way to confirm the user registration.

Test the email-based account verification

Now we just need to test the new email-based behavior. To do that, open the following file:

```
/Areas/Identity/Pages/Account/Register.cshtml.cs
```

And place a breakpoint to the `await _emailSender.SendEmailAsync` call (it should be around line 92 or so), just like shown in the following screenshot:

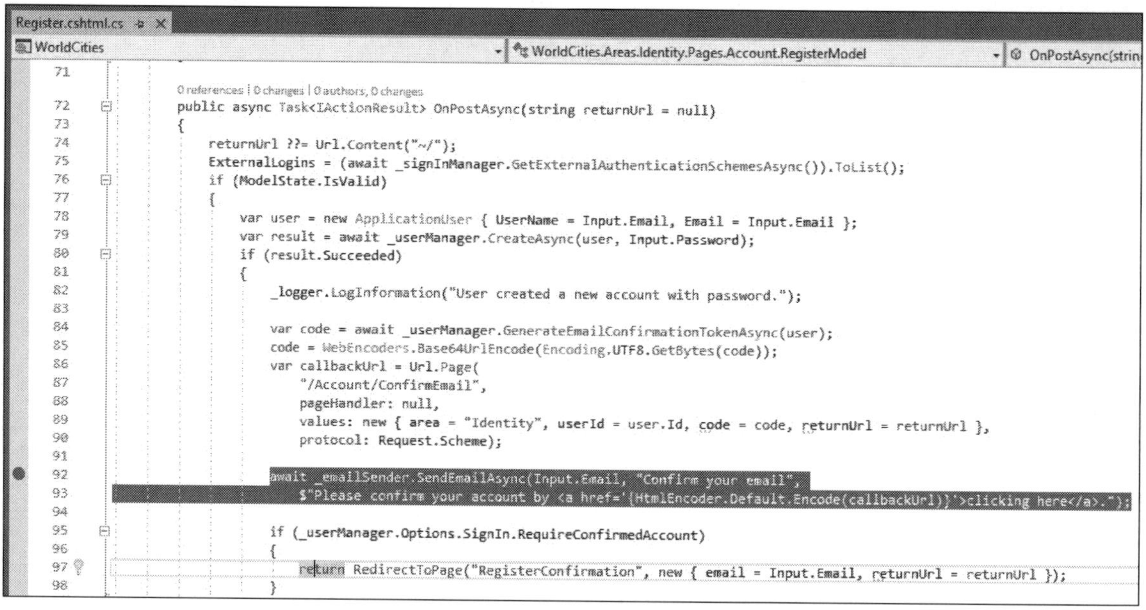
Register.cshtml.cs
WorldCities
WorldCities.Areas.Identity.Pages.Account.RegisterModel
OnPostAsync(strin
0 references | 0 changes | 0 authors, 0 changes
public async Task<IActionResult> OnPostAsync(string returnUrl = null)
{
returnUrl ??= Url.Content("~/");
ExternalLogins = (await _signInManager.GetExternalAuthenticationSchemesAsync()).ToList();
if (ModelState.IsValid)
{
var user = new ApplicationUser { UserName = Input.Email, Email = Input.Email };
var result = await _userManager.CreateAsync(user, Input.Password);
if (result.Succeeded)
{
_logger.LogInformation("User created a new account with password.");
var code = await _userManager.GenerateEmailConfirmationTokenAsync(user);
code = WebEncoders.Base64UrlEncode(Encoding.UTF8.GetBytes(code));
var callbackUrl = Url.Page(
"/Account/ConfirmEmail",
pageHandler: null,
values: new { area = "Identity", userId = user.Id, code = code, returnUrl = returnUrl },
protocol: Request.Scheme);
await _emailSender.SendEmailAsync(Input.Email, "Confirm your email",
$"Please confirm your account by <a href='{HtmlEncoder.Default.Encode(callbackUrl)}'>clicking here</a>.");
if (_userManager.Options.SignIn.RequireConfirmedAccount)
{
return RedirectToPage("RegisterConfirmation", new { email = Input.Email, returnUrl = returnUrl });
}

Figure 10.34: Adding a breakpoint to the await _emailSender.SendEmailAsync call

Once done, hit *F5* to run the app in debug mode. Click the **Register** menu item, fill out another registration form, and hit the **Register** button to send it, just like we already did in our previous test.

If we did everything correctly, the breakpoint should trigger:

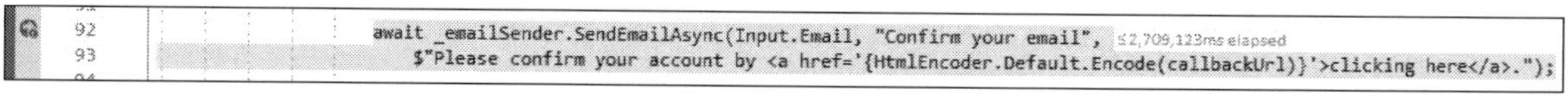
await _emailSender.SendEmailAsync(Input.Email, "Confirm your email", ≤2,709,123ms elapsed
$"Please confirm your account by <a href='{HtmlEncoder.Default.Encode(callbackUrl)}'>clicking here</a>.");

Figure 10.35: Triggering the breakpoint

This is one of the (many) parts of the auto-generated code that makes use of the `IEmailSender` interface to send the identity-related email messages.

Now, since we've implemented our very own `SendGridEmailSender` interface and configured it in the startup `ConfigureServices` method, we should reasonably expect that it will be used to fulfill such a task.

Let's see if that's the case. Open the `/Services/SendGridEmailSender.cs` file and place another breakpoint in the first line of the `Execute` method, then resume the app's execution by hitting *Continue* to release the previous breakpoint. The new breakpoint should trigger as well, demonstrating that our `IEmailSender` implementation successfully kicked in:

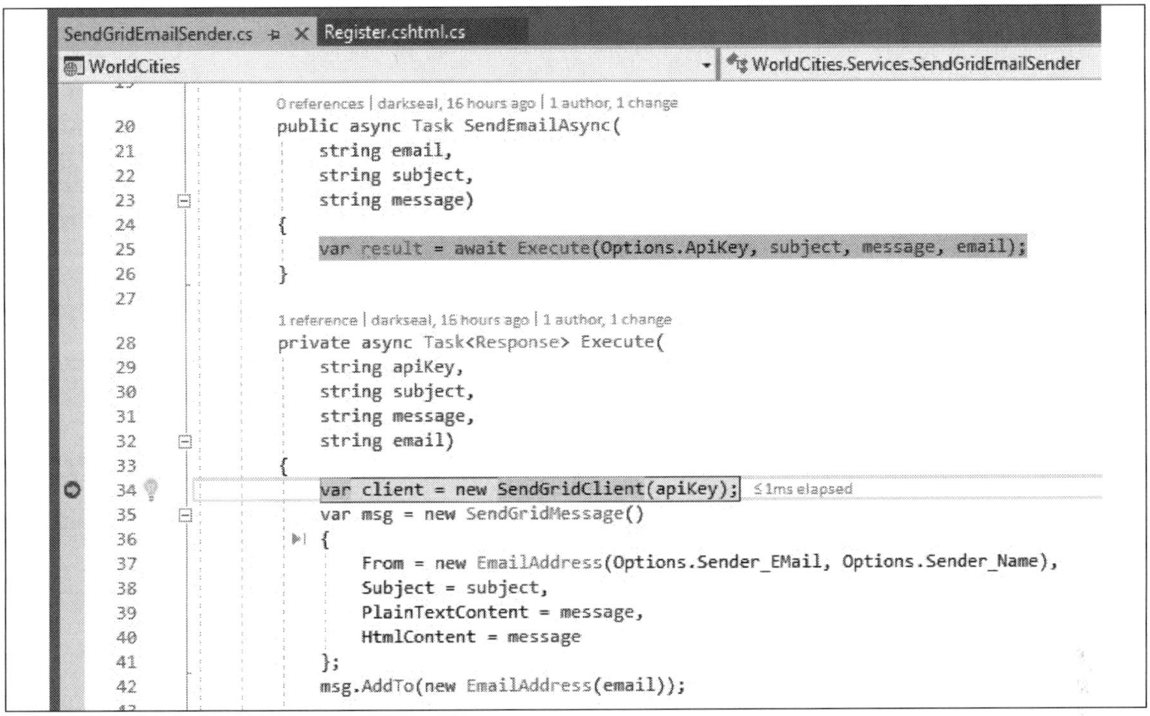

Figure 10.36: Triggering the second breakpoint

If we resume the app execution, and the SendGrid integration is working as expected, we should receive an email message containing the link to verify our email address, meaning that our web application now handles the verification task in a proper way.

The new behavior should be also confirmed by the **Register confirmation** view's revised look, which now shouldn't show the registration link anymore (as shown in the following screenshot):

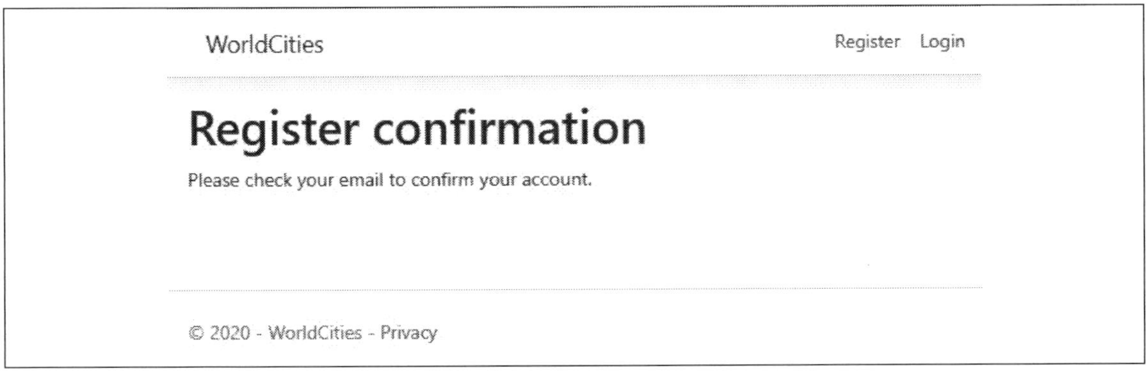

Figure 10.37: Register confirmation revised view

Our SendGrid-based `IEmailSender` implementation is done. It goes without saying that such an approach is not limited to the identity-related pages. From now on, we'll be able to send email messages from any of our controllers, as long as we provide it with an `IEmailSender` interface using *Dependency Injection*:

```
public class MyController : Controller
{
    private readonly IEmailSender _emailSender;

    public MyController(
        IEmailSender emailSender)
    {
        _emailSender = emailSender;
    }
}
```

And then call the `SendEmailAsync` method in the following way:

```
await _emailSender.SendEmailAsync("target0@email.com", "subject", "text");
```

In the next section, we'll see how to pull off a different approach that will allow us to use any SMTP server, including SendGrid's **SMTP Relay** method, which we talked about earlier on.

External SMTP server using MailKit

In this section, we'll see how to implement the `IEmailSender` interface to seamlessly send email messages through the SMTP server of our choice. To do that, we'll make use of **MailKit**, an open-source, cross-platform .NET mail-client library based on MimeKit that allows us to connect to the SMTP server and send email messages.

> For further details about it, check out the MailKit product page on NuGet at the following URL:
>
> `https://www.nuget.org/packages/MailKit`

Are we ready? Let's start!

Install the MailKit NuGet package

The first thing we need to do is to install the MailKit NuGet package, which can be done from the Package Manager Console in the following way:

```
PM> Install-Package MailKit -version 2.10.1
```

The specified version is the latest at the time of writing; feel free to remove the `-version` switch if you want to use the package's latest version.

Set up the SMTP settings

The best place to store our SMTP server's settings is—again—our `secrets.json` file. Open it and add the following highlighted keys to the existing JSON:

```
[...]

"ExternalProviders": {
  "SendGrid": {
    "ApiKey": "SG.XAM-t2eJTfe5Wo1qQpYc2Q.CiYD4nvaQBcx8B--
y91XaguyPN1bgbPBnH2WNSi6KuU",
    "Sender_Email": "WorldCities",
    "Sender_Name": "noreply@worldcities.com"
  },
  "MailKit": {
    "SMTP": {
      "Address": "my-smtp.server.com",
      "Port": "465",
      "Account": "my-smtp-username",
      "Password": "my-smtp-password",
      "Sender_Email": "noreply@worldcities.com",
      "Sender_Name": "WorldCities"
    }
  }
}

[...]
```

Be sure to replace the SMTP sample settings in the preceding code (address, port, and so on) with valid ones. If we don't have an SMTP server available, we can use the one provided by SendGrid when choosing the **SMTP Relay** method, which we talked about earlier on.

Implement the IEmailSender interface

Right after doing this, we need to create the two classes required to implement the `IEmailSender` interface: the *option class* and the *custom class*, just like we did a short while ago when dealing with the SendGrid implementation.

Let's quickly get done with that, since we already know what to do.

MailKitEmailSenderOptions

Again, let's start with the options class: from Solution Explorer, create a new `/Services/` folder in the root project's node, then add a new `MailKitEmailSenderOptions.cs` class file and fill it with the following content:

```
using MailKit.Security;
```

```
namespace WorldCities.Services
{
    public class MailKitEmailSenderOptions
    {
        public MailKitEmailSenderOptions()
        {
            Host_SecureSocketOptions = SecureSocketOptions.Auto;
        }

        public string Host_Address { get; set; }

        public int Host_Port { get; set; }

        public string Host_Username { get; set; }

        public string Host_Password { get; set; }

        public SecureSocketOptions Host_SecureSocketOptions { get; set; }

        public string Sender_EMail { get; set; }

        public string Sender_Name { get; set; }
    }
}
```

As we can see, this time there is no `ApiKey` property, simply because MailKit does not have a public API to deal with; however, in its place we had to add a bunch of additional properties related to the external SMTP server that we are going to use to send our e-mail messages.

MailKitEmailSender

MailKit's `IEmailSender` implementation will be quite similar to SendGrid's one, with some relevant differences in the main `Execute` method.

Right-click on the `/Services/` folder again and add a new `MailKitEmailSender.cs` class file, filling it with the following content:

```
using MailKit.Net.Smtp;
using Microsoft.AspNetCore.Identity.UI.Services;
using Microsoft.Extensions.Options;
using MimeKit;
using MimeKit.Text;
using System.Threading.Tasks;

namespace WorldCities.Services
{
    public class MailKitEmailSender : IEmailSender
```

```
{
    public MailKitEmailSender(
        IOptions<MailKitEmailSenderOptions> options
        )
    {
        this.Options = options.Value;
    }

    public MailKitEmailSenderOptions Options { get; set; }

    public Task SendEmailAsync(
        string email,
        string subject,
        string message)
    {
        return Execute(email, subject, message);
    }

    public Task Execute(
        string email,
        string subject,
        string message)
    {
        // create message
        var msg = new MimeMessage();
        msg.Sender = MailboxAddress.Parse(Options.Sender_EMail);
        if (!string.IsNullOrEmpty(Options.Sender_Name))
            msg.Sender.Name = Options.Sender_Name;
        msg.From.Add(msg.Sender);
        msg.To.Add(MailboxAddress.Parse(email));
        msg.Subject = subject;
        msg.Body = new TextPart(TextFormat.Html) { Text = message };

        // send email
        using (var smtp = new SmtpClient())
        {
            smtp.Connect(
                Options.Host_Address,
                Options.Host_Port,
                Options.Host_SecureSocketOptions);
            smtp.Authenticate(
                Options.Host_Username,
                Options.Host_Password);
            smtp.Send(msg);
            smtp.Disconnect(true);
        }
```

```
            return Task.FromResult(true);
        }
    }
}
```

Again, the `Execute` method is where the email message is built and configured using the `MailKitEmailSenderOptions` object, and then sent using the method provided by the client provided by the third-party package – an instance of the `MailKit.Net.Smtp.SmtpClient` class.

Startup class

Now we just have to implement the MailKit service within our `Startup.cs` class, which can be done by adding the following lines at the end of the `ConfigureService` method:

```
// IEmailSender implementation using MailKit
services.AddTransient<IEmailSender, MailKitEmailSender>();
services.Configure<MailKitEmailSenderOptions>(options =>
{
    options.Host_Address = Configuration["ExternalProviders:MailKit:SMTP:
Address"];
    options.Host_Port = Convert.ToInt32(Configuration["ExternalProviders:MailKit
:SMTP:Port"]);
    options.Host_Username = Configuration["ExternalProviders:MailKit:SMTP:
Account"];
    options.Host_Password = Configuration["ExternalProviders:MailKit:SMTP:
Password"];
    options.Sender_EMail = Configuration["ExternalProviders:MailKit:SMTP:
Sender_Email"];
    options.Sender_Name = Configuration["ExternalProviders:MailKit:SMTP:
Sender_Name"];
});
```

Important: Be sure to comment out the SendGrid service if you have added it before.

That's it: the MailKit implementation will work just like the SendGrid one, with the only difference being that it will internally relay the e-mail messages using the SMTP server instead of the transactional API service.

Summary

At the start of this chapter, we introduced the concepts of authentication and authorization, acknowledging the fact that most applications, including ours, do require a mechanism to properly handle authenticated and non-authenticated clients as well as authorized and unauthorized requests.

We took some time to properly understand the similarities and differences between authentication and authorization as well as the pros and cons of handling these tasks using our own internal provider or delegating them to third-party providers such as Google, Facebook, and Twitter. We also found out that, luckily enough, the ASP.NET Core Identity services, together with the `IdentityServer` API support, provide a convenient set of features that allow us to achieve the best of both worlds.

To be able to use it, we added the required packages to our project and did what was needed to properly configure them, such as performing some updates in our `Startup` and `ApplicationDbContext` classes and creating a new `ApplicationUser` entity; right after implementing all the required changes, we added a new Entity Framework Core migration to update our database accordingly.

We briefly enumerated the various web-based authentication methods available nowadays: sessions, tokens, signatures, and two-factor strategies of various sorts. After careful consideration, we chose to stick with the token-based approach using JWT that `IdentityServer` provides by default for the SPA clients, it being a solid and well-known standard for any *front-end* framework.

Since the default ASP.NET Core and Angular project template provided by Visual Studio features a built-in ASP.NET Core Identity system and `IdentityServer` support for Angular, we created a brand-new project—which we called `AuthSample`—to test it out. We spent some time reviewing its main features, such as route guards, HTTP interceptors, HTTP round trips to the *back-end*, and so on; while doing that, we took the time to implement the required *front-end* and *back-end* authorization rules to protect some of our application views, routes, and APIs from unauthorized access. Eventually, we imported those APIs into our `WorldCities` Angular app, changing our existing *front-end* and *back-end* code accordingly.

In the last part of the chapter, we took care of an important missing feature of our sample identity-based implementation: the email sending capabilities of our app. We saw how we can implement a custom email sender based upon the ASP.NET Core built-in `IEmailSender` interface using two different approaches: a third-party, API-driven transactional email service and an external SMTP server.

We're ready to switch to the next topic, **progressive web apps**, which will keep us busy throughout the next chapter.

Suggested topics

Authentication, authorization, HTTP protocol, Secure Socket Layer, session state management, indirection, single sign-on, Azure AD Authentication Library (ADAL), ASP.NET Core Identity, IdentityServer, OpenID, Open ID Connect (OIDC), OAuth, OAuth 2, Two-Factor Authentication (2FA), SMS 2FA, Time-Based One-Time Password Algorithm (TOTP), TOTP 2FA, IdentityUser, stateless, Cross-Site Scripting (XSS), Cross-Site Request Forgery (CSRF), Angular HttpClient, Route Guard, Http Interceptor, LocalStorage, Web Storage API, server-side prerendering, Angular Universal, browser types, generic types, JWTs, Claims, AuthorizeAttribute, SendGrid, MailKit, IEmailSender.

References

- *Introduction to Identity on ASP.NET Core*: `https://docs.microsoft.com/en-us/aspnet/core/security/authentication/identity`
- *Authentication and authorization for SPAs*: `https://docs.microsoft.com/en-us/aspnet/core/security/authentication/identity-api-authorization`
- *IdentityServer official documentation*: `http://docs.identityserver.io/en/latest/` *RoleManager<TRole> Class*: `https://docs.microsoft.com/en-us/dotnet/api/microsoft.aspnetcore.identity.rolemanager-1`
- *Identity model customization in ASP.NET Core*: `https://docs.microsoft.com/en-US/aspnet/core/security/authentication/customize-identity-model`
- *Overview of ASP.NET Core Security*: `https://docs.microsoft.com/en-us/aspnet/core/security/`
- *Async and Await*: `https://blog.stephencleary.com/2012/02/async-and-await.html`
- *Async/Await FAQ*: `https://blogs.msdn.microsoft.com/pfxteam/2012/04/12/asyncawait-faq/`
- *Don't Block on Async Code*: `http://blog.stephencleary.com/2012/07/dont-block-on-async-code.html`
- *Async/Await – Best Practices in Asynchronous Programming*: `https://msdn.microsoft.com/en-us/magazine/jj991977.aspx`
- *ASP.NET Core SynchronizationContext*: `https://blog.stephencleary.com/2017/03/aspnetcore-synchronization-context.html`
- *Asynchronous programming with async and await*: `https://docs.microsoft.com/en-us/dotnet/csharp/programming-guide/concepts/async/index`
- *EF Core Migrations*: `https://docs.microsoft.com/en-us/ef/core/managing-schemas/migrations/`
- *SQL Server: Create a Full Database Backup*: `https://docs.microsoft.com/en-us/sql/relational-databases/backup-restore/create-a-full-database-backup-sql-server`
- *Two-factor authentication with SMS in ASP.NET Core*: `https://docs.microsoft.com/en-us/aspnet/core/security/authentication/2fa`

- *Enable QR code generation for TOTP authenticator apps in ASP.NET Core*: `https://docs.microsoft.com/en-us/aspnet/core/security/authentication/identity-enable-qrcodes`
- *Angular: Router Guards*: `https://angular.io/guide/router#preventing-unauthorized-access`
- *Routing in ASP.NET Core*: `https://docs.microsoft.com/en-us/aspnet/core/fundamentals/routing`
- *Introduction to authorization in ASP.NET Core*: `https://docs.microsoft.com/en-us/aspnet/core/security/authorization/introduction`
- *Simple authorization in ASP.NET Core*: `https://docs.microsoft.com/en-us/aspnet/core/security/authorization/simple`
- *Authorize with a specific scheme in ASP.NET Core*: `https://docs.microsoft.com/en-us/aspnet/core/security/authorization/limitingidentitybyscheme`
- *Scaffold Identity in ASP.NET Core projects*: `https://docs.microsoft.com/en-us/aspnet/core/security/authentication/scaffold-identity`
- *ASP.NET Core Identity: Create full identity UI source*: `https://docs.microsoft.com/en-us/aspnet/core/security/authentication/scaffold-identity#full`
- *Create reusable UI using the Razor class library project in ASP.NET Core*: `https://docs.microsoft.com/en-us/aspnet/core/razor-pages/ui-class`
- *Angular: HttpInterceptor*: `https://angular.io/api/common/http/HttpInterceptor`
- *Role-based authorization in ASP.NET Core*: `https://docs.microsoft.com/en-us/aspnet/core/security/authorization/roles`
- *Account confirmation and password recovery in ASP.NET Core*: `https://docs.microsoft.com/en-us/aspnet/core/security/authentication/accconfirm`
- *IEmailSender interface*: `https://docs.microsoft.com/en-us/dotnet/api/microsoft.aspnetcore.identity.ui.services.iemailsender`
- *SendGrid Tracking Settings*: `https://sendgrid.com/docs/ui/account-and-settings/tracking/`
- *MailKit*: `https://www.nuget.org/packages/MailKit`

11

Progressive Web Apps

In this chapter, we'll focus on a topic that we just briefly mentioned back in *Chapter 1, Getting Ready*, when we first talked about the different development patterns for web applications available nowadays: **Progressive Web Apps** (**PWAs**).

As a matter of fact, both our `HealthCheck` and `WorldCities` apps currently stick to the **Single-Page Application** (**SPA**) model, at least for the most part; in the following sections, we'll see how we can turn them into PWAs by implementing several well-established capabilities required by such a development approach.

As we learned in *Chapter 1, Getting Ready*, a PWA is a web application that uses a modern web browser's capabilities to deliver an app-like experience to users. To achieve this, the PWA needs to meet some technical requirements, including (yet not limited to) a *Web App Manifest file* and a service worker to allow it to work in *offline mode* and behave just like a mobile app.

More precisely, here's what we're going to do:

- **Identify the technical requirements** required by a PWA by following its known specifications.
- **Implement those requirements** on our existing `HealthCheck` and `WorldCities` apps to turn them into PWAs. More precisely, we'll do that using two different approaches: manually performing all of the required steps for the `HealthCheck` app, and then using the *PWA automatic setup* offered by the Angular CLI for the `WorldCities` app.
- **Test the new PWA capabilities** of both of these apps.

By the end of this chapter, we'll have learned how to successfully convert an existing SPA into a PWA.

Technical requirements

In this chapter, we're going to need all previous technical requirements listed in *Chapters 1-10*, with the following additional packages:

- `@angular/service-worker` (npm package)
- `ng-connection-service` (npm package)
- `Microsoft.AspNetCore.Cors` (NuGet package)
- `WebEssentials.AspNetCore.ServiceWorker` (NuGet package, *optional*)
- `http-server` (npm package, *optional*)

As always, it's advisable to avoid installing them straight away; we're going to bring them in during this chapter to better contextualize their purpose within our project.

The code files for this chapter can be found at: `https://github.com/PacktPublishing/ASP.NET-5-and-Angular/tree/master/Chapter_11/`

PWA – distinctive features

Let's start by summarizing the main distinctive characteristics of a PWA:

- **Progressive**: A PWA should work for every user, regardless of the platform and/or browser used.
- **Responsive**: They must adapt well to any form factor: desktop, mobile, tablet, and so on.
- **Connectivity-independent**: They must be able to work offline—at least to some extent, such as informing the user that some features might not work in *offline mode*—or on low-quality networks.
- **App-like**: They need to provide the same navigation and interaction mechanics of mobile apps. This includes tap support, gesture-based scrolling, and so on.
- **Safe**: They must provide HTTPS support for better security, such as preventing snooping and ensuring that their content has not been tampered with.
- **Discoverable**: They have to be identifiable as *web applications* thanks to a W3C manifest file and a service worker registration scope so that search engines will be able to find, identify, and categorize them.
- **Re-engageable**: They should make re-engagement easy through features such as *push notifications.*
- **Installable**: They should allow users to install and keep them on their desktop and/or mobile home screen, just like any standard mobile app, yet without the hassle of having to download and install them from an app store.
- **Linkable**: They should be easily shared through a URL, without requiring complex installation.

> The preceding characteristics can be inferred from the following articles written by the Google developers and engineers who spent their efforts on introducing the PWA concept and defining its core specs:
>
> `https://developers.google.com/web/progressive-web-apps`
>
> `https://developers.google.com/web/fundamentals`
>
> `https://infrequently.org/2015/06/progressive-apps-escaping-tabs-without-losing-our-soul/`

These high-level requirements can be translated into a specific technical task that we have to implement. The best way to do that is by starting with the technical baseline criteria described by Alex Russell, the Google Chrome engineer that who coined the term PWA together with the designer Frances Berriman back in 2015:

- **Originate from a secure origin**: In other words, there's full HTTPS support with no mixed content (*green padlock* display)
- **Load while offline**, even if it's just an *offline* information page: This clearly implies that we need to implement a service worker
- **Reference a Web App Manifest** with at least the four key properties: `name`, `short_name`, `stat_url`, and `display` (with either a *standalone* or *fullscreen* value)
- **A 144 × 144 icon** in PNG format: Other sizes are supported, but the 144 x 144 one is the minimum requirement
- **Use vector graphics**, as they can scale indefinitely and require smaller file sizes

Each one of these technical requirements can be translated into a specific technical task that we have to implement. In the following sections, we're going to implement them all.

Secure origin

Implementing the **secure origin** feature basically means serving our app through an HTTPS certificate. Such a requirement is rather easy to fulfill nowadays: TLS certificates are quite cheap thanks to the many resellers available. A PositiveSSL certificate issued by Comodo Inc. can be purchased online for $10/year or so and is immediately available for download.

If we don't want to spend money, there's also a free alternative provided by **Let's Encrypt**: a free, automated, Open Certificate Authority that can be used to obtain a TLS certificate without costs. However, the method they use to release the certificate requires shell access (also known as **SSH access**) to the deployment web host.

> For additional information about **Let's Encrypt** and how to obtain an HTTPS certificate for free, check out the official site: `https://letsencrypt.org/`

For the sake of simplicity, we'll not cover the HTTPS certificate release and installation part; we'll take for granted that the reader will be able to properly install it, thanks to the many how-to guides available from the various resellers' websites (including **Let's Encrypt**).

Offline loading and Web App Manifest

Connection independency is one of the most important capabilities of PWAs; to properly implement it, we need to introduce—and implement—a concept that we've just barely mentioned until now: service workers. What are they, and how can they help our app to work while offline?

The best way to figure out what a service worker is would be to think of it as a *script that runs inside the web browser* and handles a specific task for the application that registered it: such tasks can include *caching support* and *push notifications*.

When properly implemented and registered, service workers will enhance the **user experience** (**UX**) provided by standard websites by delivering a UX similar to what can be achieved by native mobile apps; technically, their role is to intercept any ongoing HTTP request made by the user and—whenever it's directed to the web application they are registered for—check for the web application's availability and act accordingly. To put it in other words, we could say that they act as an HTTP proxy with fallback capabilities when the application is unable to handle the request.

Such a *fallback* can be configured by the developer to behave in many ways, such as the following:

- **Caching service** (also known as **offline mode**): The service worker will deliver a cached response by querying an internal (local) cache previously built from the app (when it was online)
- **Offline warning**: Whenever no cached content is available (or if we didn't implement a caching mechanism), the service worker can serve an *offline status* informative text, warning the user that the app is unable to work

> Those who are familiar with forward cache services might prefer to imagine service workers as reverse proxies (or CDN edges) installed in the end user's web browser instead.

The *caching service* feature is great for web applications that provide static content, such as HTML5-based gaming apps and Angular apps that don't require any *back-end* interaction. Unfortunately, it's not ideal for our two apps: both `HealthCheck` and `WorldCities` strongly rely upon the *back-end* web API provided by ASP.NET. Conversely, these apps can definitely benefit from an *offline mode*, so that their users will be informed that an internet connection is required—instead of getting a *connection error*, a `404 - Not Found` message, or any other message.

Service workers versus HttpInterceptors

If we remember the various Angular features that we introduced in *Chapter 10, Authentication and Authorization*, we can see how the aforementioned behavior reminds us of the role performed by `HttpInterceptors`.

However, since *interceptors* are part of the Angular app script bundle, they always cease to work whenever the user closes the browser tab that contains the web app. Furthermore, interceptors are only able to intercept calls made with Angular's `HttpClient`: they won't be able to handle browser requests issued to load scripts, stylesheets, images, and so on.

Conversely, service workers need to be preserved after the user closes the tab so that they can intercept the browser requests *before* connecting to the app.

Also, there's another important difference: `HttpInterceptors` can only intercept calls made with `HttpClient` and not browser requests like loading a <script> stylesheet, <img>, and so on.

Enough with the theory, let's now see how we can implement an *offline mode*, *Web App Manifest*, and *PNG icons* in our existing apps.

Introducing @angular/service-worker

Starting with version 5.0.0, Angular provides a fully featured service worker implementation that can be easily integrated into any app without needing to code against low-level APIs; such an implementation is handled by the `@angular/service-worker` npm package and relies upon a manifest file that is loaded from the server that describes the resources to cache and will be used as an index by the service worker, which behaves in the following way:

- **When the app is online**, each indexed resource will be checked to detect changes; if the source has changed, the service worker will update or rebuild the cache
- **When the app is offline**, the cached version will be served instead

The aforementioned manifest file is generated from a CLI-generated configuration file called `ngsw-config.json`, which we'll have to create and set up accordingly.

> It's worth mentioning that web browsers will always ignore service workers if the website that tries to register them is served over an unsecured (non-HTTPS) connection. The reason for that is quite simple to understand: since service workers' defining role is to proxy their source web application and potentially serve alternative content, malicious parties could be interested in tampering with them; therefore, allowing their registration to secure websites only will provide an additional security layer to the whole mechanism.

Here's an example of a manifest file similar to the one we need (and that we'll add in a short while):

```
{
  "name": "My Sample App",
  "short_name": " MySampleApp ",
  "start_url": ".",
  "display": "standalone",
  "background_color": "#fff",
  "description": "A simply readable Hacker News app.",
  "icons": [{
    "src": "images/touch/homescreen48.png",
    "sizes": "48x48",
    "type": "image/png"
  }, {
    "src": "images/touch/homescreen72.png",
    "sizes": "72x72",
    "type": "image/png"
  }, {

... multiple icon definitions ...

  }],
  "related_applications": [{
    "platform": "play",
    "url": "https://play.google.com/store/apps/details?id=my.sample.app "
  }]
}
```

The ASP.NET Core PWA middleware alternative

It's worth noting that `@angular/service-worker` isn't the only available approach we could adopt to implement the service worker and *Web App Manifest* file's PWA capabilities. As a matter of fact, ASP.NET Core provides its own way to deal with these requirements with a set of middleware that can be easily installed and integrated into our project's HTTP stack.

Among the various solutions provided, the most interesting one—at least in our opinion—is the `WebEssentials.AspNetCore.ServiceWorker` NuGet package developed by Mads Kristensen, a prolific author of Visual Studio extensions and ASP.NET Core libraries; the package provides fully featured ASP.NET Core PWA middleware that comes with full *Web App Manifest* support and pre-built service workers and is a valid *back-end* and *front-end* alternative to the pure *front-end* solution provided by the `@angular/service-worker` npm package.

> To get additional information about the `WebEssentials.AspNetCore.ServiceWorker` NuGet package, check out the following URLs:
>
> `https://github.com/madskristensen/WebEssentials.AspNetCore.ServiceWorker`
>
> `https://www.nuget.org/packages/WebEssentials.AspNetCore.ServiceWorker/`

All in all, it seems that we have two convenient ways to fulfill our PWA-related tasks: which one should we choose?

Ideally, we would've loved to implement both of them; however, for reasons of space, we'll just use the `@angular/service-worker` npm package, leaving the ASP.NET Core PWA middleware alternative for another time.

> Choosing the Angular service worker will also give us some advantages: since it's specifically designed for Angular, it will definitely help us to fix some common issues.

In the following section, we'll learn how to implement the `@angular/service-worker` package in our existing Angular apps following two very different—yet equally rewarding—approaches.

Implementing the PWA requirements

To perform the required implementation steps that we've focused on in the previous section, we have two choices:

- **Perform a manual update** of our app's source code
- **Use the automatic installation feature** provided by the Angular CLI

To learn the most from the experience, both of these paths should be taken at least once. Luckily enough, we have two existing Angular apps to experiment with. Therefore, we'll take the manual route for our `HealthCheck` app first, then we'll experience the automatic CLI setup for the `WorldCities` app.

Manual installation

In this section, we'll see how to manually implement the required technical steps we're still missing to make our `HealthCheck` app fully compliant with the PWA requirements.

Let's briefly recap them:

- Add the `@angular/service-worker` npm package (`package.json`)
- Enable service worker support in the Angular CLI configuration file (`angular.json`)
- Import and register `ServiceWorkerModule` in the `AppModule` class (`app.module.ts`)
- Update the main app's HTML template file (`index.html`)
- Add a suitable icon file (`icon.ico`)
- Add the manifest file (`manifest.webmanifest`)
- Add the service worker configuration file (`ngsw-config.json`)

For each step, we've mentioned the relevant file that we'll have to update in parentheses.

Adding the @angular/service-worker npm package

The first thing to do is to add the `@angular/service-worker` npm package to our `package.json` file. As we can easily guess, such a package contains Angular's service worker implementation that we were talking about a moment ago.

Open the `/ClientApp/package.json` file and add the following package reference to the `"dependencies"` section, right below the `@angular/router` package:

```
// ...

"@angular/router": "11.0.2",
"@angular/service-worker": "11.0.2",
"aspnet-prerendering": "3.0.1",

// ...
```

As soon as we save the file, the npm package should be downloaded and installed automatically by Visual Studio.

Updating the angular.json file

Open the `/ClientApp/angular.json` configuration file and add the `"serviceWorker"` and `"ngswConfigPath"` keys to the end of the **projects** | **health_check** | **architect** | **build** | **configurations** | **production** section:

```
// ...

"vendorChunk": false,
"buildOptimizer": true,
"serviceWorker": true,
"ngswConfigPath": "ngsw-config.json"

// ...
```

> As always, whenever we have issues while applying these changes, we can check out the source code available from this book's GitHub repository.

The "serviceWorker" flag that we've just set up will cause the production build to include a couple of extra files in the output folder:

- ngsw-worker.js: The main service worker file
- ngsw.json: The Angular service worker's runtime configuration

Both of these files are required for our service worker to perform its job.

Importing ServiceWorkerModule

ServiceWorkerModule provided by the @angular/service-worker npm package library will take care of registering the service worker as well as providing a few services we can use to interact with it.

To install it on our HealthCheck app, open the /ClientApp/src/app/app.module.ts file and add the following lines (the new lines are highlighted):

```
import { BrowserModule } from '@angular/platform-browser';
import { NgModule } from '@angular/core';
import { FormsModule } from '@angular/forms';
import { HttpClientModule, HTTP_INTERCEPTORS } from '@angular/common/http';

import { AppRoutingModule } from './app-routing.module';

import { AppComponent } from './app.component';
import { NavMenuComponent } from './nav-menu/nav-menu.component';
import { HomeComponent } from './home/home.component';
import { HealthCheckComponent } from './health-check/health-check.component';

import { ServiceWorkerModule } from '@angular/service-worker';
import { environment } from '../environments/environment';

// ...

imports: [
  BrowserModule.withServerTransition({ appId: 'ng-cli-universal' }),
  HttpClientModule,
  FormsModule,
  AppRoutingModule,
  ServiceWorkerModule.register(
      'ngsw-worker.js', {
```

```
        enabled: environment.production
      })
  ],

  // ...
```

As we said earlier, the `ngsw-worker.js` file referenced in the preceding code is the main service worker file, which will be auto-generated by the Angular CLI when building the app.

When implemented in this way, the service worker will be enabled only when our Angular app runs in a production environment, which is precisely what we want. Moreover, since we didn't specify a `registrationStrategy`, it will be registered using the default behavior, which is once the application stabilizes (that is, as soon as there are no pending micro- and macro-tasks): this will ensure that the service worker is registered as soon as possible, without affecting the application's first-time load.

> For additional information regarding the service worker registration options and the various `registrationStrategy` settings, visit the following URL: `https://angular.io/api/service-worker/SwRegistrationOptions`

Updating the index.html file

The `/ClientApp/src/index.html` file is the main entry point for our Angular app(s). It contains the `<app-root>` element, which will be replaced by our app's GUI at the end of the bootstrap phase, as well as some resource references and meta tags that describe our application's behavior and configuration settings.

Open that file and add the following code at the end of the `<head>` element (the updated lines are highlighted):

```
<!DOCTYPE html>
<html lang="en">
 <head>
 <meta charset="utf-8" />
 <title>HealthCheck</title>
 <base href="/" />

 <meta name="viewport" content="width=device-width,
 initial-scale=1" />
 <link rel="icon" type="image/x-icon" href="favicon.ico" />

 <!-- PWA required files -->
 <link href="https://fonts.googleapis.com/css?family=Roboto:300,400,
 500&amp;display=swap" rel="stylesheet">
 <link href="https://fonts.googleapis.com/icon?family=Material+Icons"
 rel="stylesheet">
```

```
<link rel="manifest" crossorigin="use-credentials"
  href="manifest.webmanifest">
<meta name="theme-color" content="#1976d2">

  </head>
  <body>
  <app-root>Loading...</app-root>
  </body>
</html>
```

The highlighted lines configure the app's `font`, `theme-color`, and—most importantly—the link to the `manifest.webmanifest` file, which—as its name clearly implies—is the app's manifest file, one of the key requirements for any PWA.

That's great to hear, except it doesn't exist in our app yet: let's fix this gap now.

Adding the Web App Manifest file

Instead of manually creating a *Web App Manifest* file from scratch, we can generate it automatically using one of the various Web App Manifest generators available online.

For the purpose of this book we're going to use the *Web App Manifest Generator* by Samson Amaugo: `https://github.com/sammychinedu2ky/Web-App-Manifest-Generator`

And more specifically, we'll use the instance hosted by Netlify at the following URL: `https://manifest-gen.netlify.app/`

This handy tool will also generate all of the required PNG icon files for us, hence saving us a lot of time. However, we'll require a 512 x 512 image source. If we don't have one, we can easily create one using the *DummyImage* website, another useful free tool that can be used to generate placeholder images of any size, which is available at `https://dummyimage.com/`.

Here's a generated PNG file that we can use to feed the preceding Firebase *Web App Manifest Generator* tool:

Figure 11.1: PNG file generated by DummyImage

As we can easily guess, **HC** stands for **HealthCheck**; we won't likely win a graphic contest with this image, but it will work just fine for our current task.

> The preceding PNG file can be downloaded from: `https://dummyimage.com/512x512/361f47/fff.png&text=HC`
>
> The reader is free to either use it, create another file using that same tool, or provide another image.

The 512 x 512 icon will be used by the Web App Manifest Generator online tool to create all the required icons for our PWA.

> As per Google's recommendations, a valid PWA manifest file will need at least two icons with a respective size of 192 x 192 and 512 x 512 pixels: `https://web.dev/installable-manifest/#recommendations`
>
> The online generator will vastly exceed such minimum requirement by creating eight different icons to accommodate most of the major formats used by different devices.

Once done, go back to the Web App Manifest Generator online tool and configure it using the following parameters:

- **App Name**: `HealthCheck`
- **Short Name**: `HealthCheck`
- **Theme Color**: `#2196f3`
- **Background Color**: `#2196f3`
- **Display Mode**: `Standalone`
- **Orientation**: `Any`
- **Application Scope**: `/`
- **Start Url**: `/`

Then, click to the right of the **UPLOAD** button below the **Upload via Graphql** option and select the HC image that we generated a moment ago, as shown in the following screenshot:

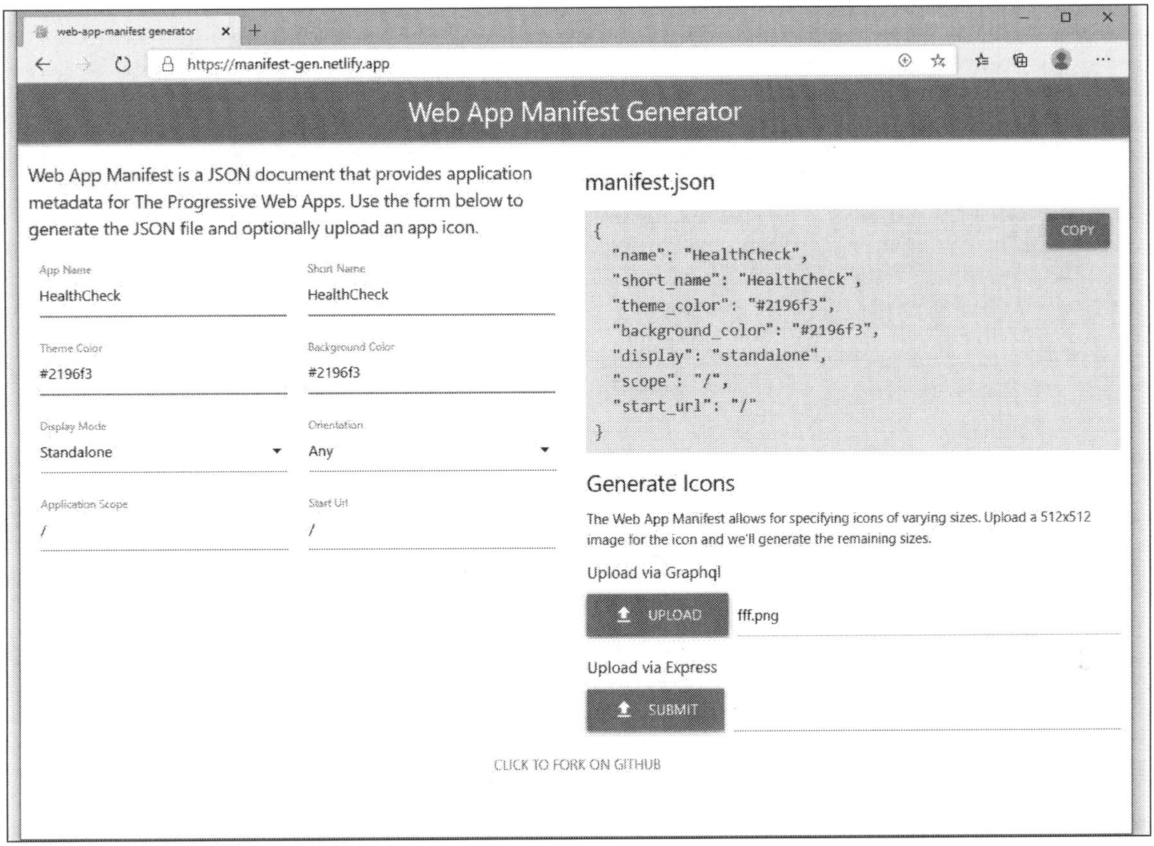

Figure 11.2: Web App Manifest Generator

Generate the archive file by clicking on the **UPLOAD** button, unpack it, and copy the included files in the following way:

- The `manifest.json` file in the `/ClientApp/src/` folder
- The `/icons/` folder, with all of its content, in the `/ClientApp/src/assets/` folder, so that the actual PNG files will be placed in the `/ClientApp/src/assets/icons/` folder

Once done, we need to perform the following changes to the `manifest.json` file:

- Change all of the icon starting paths from `images/icons/` to `assets/icons/`
- Rename it from `manifest.json` to `manifest.webmanifest`, since that's the name defined by the Web App Manifest W3C specs

> Those who want to take a look at the Web App Manifest W3C Working Draft 09 December 2019 can visit the following URL: `https://www.w3.org/TR/appmanifest/`
>
> As a matter of fact, the `.json` and `.webmanifest` extensions will both work, as long as we remember to set the `application/manifest+json` MIME type; however, since most web servers set the MIME type based upon the file extension, opting for the `.webmanifest` choice will arguably make things easier.
>
> Those who want to know more about this `.json` versus `.webmanifest` extension debate should take a look at this interesting discussion in the Web App Manifest GitHub repository: `https://github.com/w3c/manifest/issues/689`

If we prefer to follow the Web App Manifest W3C specs and use the `.webmanifest` extension instead of `.json`, we can rename the file in that way: thanks to the `StaticFilesMiddleware`, our ASP.NET Core app will still be able to properly serve it.

> As a matter of fact, we actually performed this rename in our sample apps: the reader will find a `manifest.webmanifest` file for each one of our apps in the GitHub repository for *Chapter 11* and *Chapter 12*.

Publishing the Web App Manifest file

To have our `/ClientApp/src/manifest.webmanifest` file published together with the rest of our `HealthCheck` Angular app files, we need to add it to the `/ClientApp/angular.json` CLI configuration file.

Open that file and locate all of the following entries:

```
"assets": ["src/assets"]
```

Replace them with the following updated value:

```
"assets": [
  "src/assets",
  "src/manifest.webmanifest"
],
```

There should be two `"asset"` key entries in the `angular.json` file:

- `projects > health_check > architect > build > options`
- `projects > health_check > architect > test > options`

Both of them need to be modified as explained in the preceding code.

With this update, the `manifest.webmanifest` file will be published to the output folder whenever we build the Angular app.

Adding the favicon

A *favicon* (also known as a favorite icon, shortcut icon, website icon, tab icon, URL icon, or bookmark icon) is a file containing one or more small icons that can be used to identify a specific website; whenever we see a small icon in a browser's address bar, history, and/or tab containing a given website, we're looking at that website's *favicon*.

Favicons can be generated manually, but if we're not graphic designers, we might want to use one of the various *favicon online generators* available online, especially considering that most of them are entirely free to use; the only thing that we need is a suitable image, which needs to be provided manually (and uploaded to the service).

> Here's a couple of recommended favicon online generator available nowadays:
>
> **favicon.io** (`https://favicon.io/`)
>
> **Real Favicon Generator** (`https://realfavicongenerator.net/`)

Alternatively, we can download one of the many *loyalty-free* favicon sets available online.

> Here are some websites that offer free favicons to download:
>
> **Icons8** (`https://icons8.com/icons/set/favicon`)
>
> **FreeFavicon** (`https://www.freefavicon.com/freefavicons/icons/`)

As a matter of fact, the ASP.NET Core and Angular Visual Studio template that we used to create our `HealthCheck` project already provided us with a *favicon*: we can find it in our project's `/wwwroot/` folder.

Honestly speaking, this *favicon* is quite ugly, as we can see from the following screenshot:

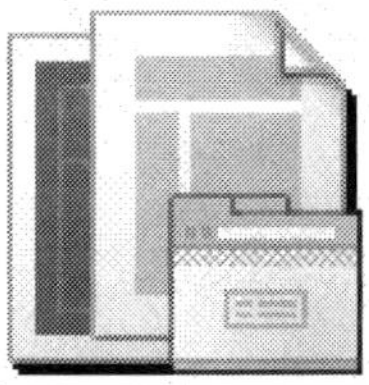

Figure 11.3: The favicon provided by our template

Although not that great, such a favicon won't prevent our app from becoming a PWA; we can either keep it or change it using one of the aforementioned websites.

Adding the ngsw-config.json file

From Solution Explorer, create a new `ngsw-config.json` file in the `HealthCheck` project's `/ClientApp/` folder, and fill its content with the following source code:

```
{
  "$schema": "./node_modules/@angular/service-worker/config/
   schema.json",
  "index": "/index.html",
  "assetGroups": [
    {
      "name": "app",
      "installMode": "prefetch",
      "resources": {
        "files": [
          "/favicon.ico",
          "/index.html",
          "/manifest.webmanifest",
          "/*.css",
          "/*.js"
        ]
      }
    },
    {
      "name": "assets",
      "installMode": "lazy",
      "updateMode": "prefetch",
      "resources": {
        "files": [
          "/assets/**",
          "/*.(eot|svg|cur|jpg|png|webp|gif|otf|ttf|woff|woff2|ani)"
        ]
      }
    }
  ]
}
```

As we can see by looking at the `assetGroup > app` section, the preceding file tells Angular to cache the `favicon.ico` file and the `manifest.webmanifest` file, which we created a short while ago, as well as the main `index.html` file and all of the CSS and JS bundles—in other words, our application's static asset files. Right after that, there is an additional `assetGroup > assets` section, which defines the image files to cache.

The main difference between these two sections is the `installMode` parameter value, which determines how these resources are initially cached:

- `prefetch` tells the service worker to fetch those resources while it's caching the current version of the app; in other words, it will put all of those contents in the cache as soon as they become available, that is, the first time the browser visits the online app. We might call this an **up-front caching strategy**.
- `lazy` tells the service worker to only cache those resources when the browsers explicitly request them for the first time. This could be called an **on-demand caching strategy**.

The preceding settings can be good for generic Angular apps that only rely on the *front-end* (no *back-end* required calls) since *these files basically contain the whole app*; more specifically, an Angular app hosting an HTML5 game—which arguably relies upon a lot of image files—might think about moving some of its image files (or even all of them) from the assets section to the app section, so that the whole application—including the icons, the sprites, and all of the image resources—will be cached upfront and be entirely available even when the app is offline.

However, such a caching strategy would not be enough for our `HealthCheck` and `WorldCities` apps; even if we tell our service worker to cache the whole app files, all of our apps' HTTP calls would still fail whenever the browser is offline, without letting the user know anything about it. As a matter of fact, our *back-end* availability requirement forces us to do some additional work for both of our apps.

However, before doing that, let's bring our `WorldCities` app up to speed.

Automatic installation

All of the steps that we performed manually in the previous section to enable *Service Worker* support for our `HealthCheck` app can be done automatically by using the following CLI command:

```
> ng add @angular/pwa
```

Let's adopt this alternative technique for our `WorldCities` app.

Open Command Prompt and navigate to the `WorldCities` app's `/ClientApp/` folder, then execute the preceding command; the Angular CLI will automatically configure our app by adding the `@angular/service-worker` package and performing the other required steps.

The most relevant information for the whole operation will be written in the console output, as shown in the following screenshot:

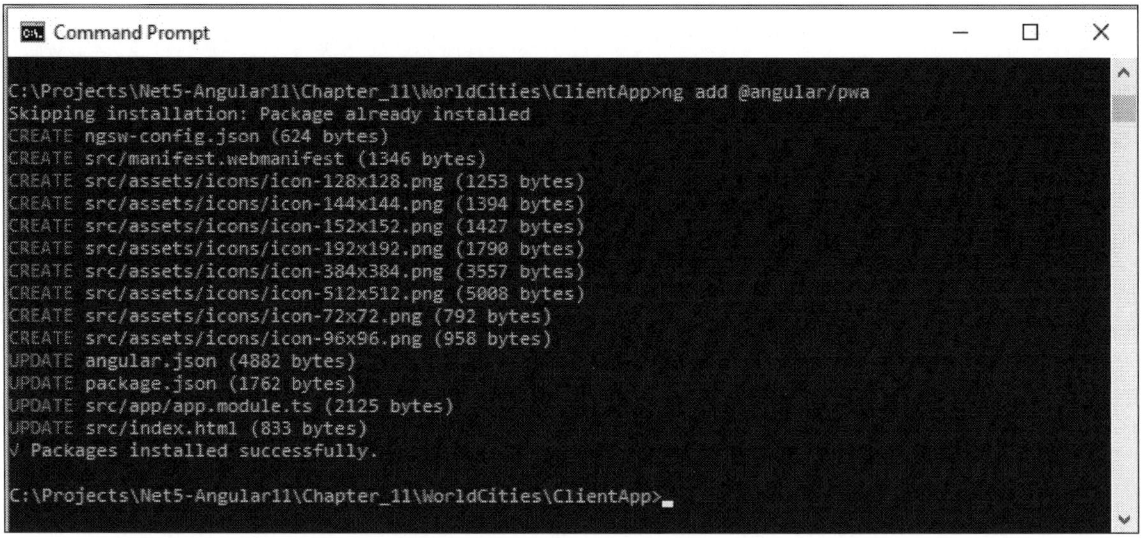

Command Prompt
C:\Projects\Net5-Angular11\Chapter_11\WorldCities\ClientApp>ng add @angular/pwa
Skipping installation: Package already installed
CREATE ngsw-config.json (624 bytes)
CREATE src/manifest.webmanifest (1346 bytes)
CREATE src/assets/icons/icon-128x128.png (1253 bytes)
CREATE src/assets/icons/icon-144x144.png (1394 bytes)
CREATE src/assets/icons/icon-152x152.png (1427 bytes)
CREATE src/assets/icons/icon-192x192.png (1790 bytes)
CREATE src/assets/icons/icon-384x384.png (3557 bytes)
CREATE src/assets/icons/icon-512x512.png (5008 bytes)
CREATE src/assets/icons/icon-72x72.png (792 bytes)
CREATE src/assets/icons/icon-96x96.png (958 bytes)
UPDATE angular.json (4882 bytes)
UPDATE package.json (1762 bytes)
UPDATE src/app/app.module.ts (2125 bytes)
UPDATE src/index.html (833 bytes)
√ Packages installed successfully.
C:\Projects\Net5-Angular11\Chapter_11\WorldCities\ClientApp>

Figure 11.4: Enabling service worker support via Command Prompt

As we can see from the logs, the automatic process performs the same steps that we just applied to the `HealthCheck` app.

The Angular PNG icon set

The PWA automatic setup feature will also provide some PNG icons of various sizes in the `/ClientApp/src/assets/icons/` folder. If we open them with a graphics application, we can see that they all reproduce the Angular logo, as shown in the following figure:

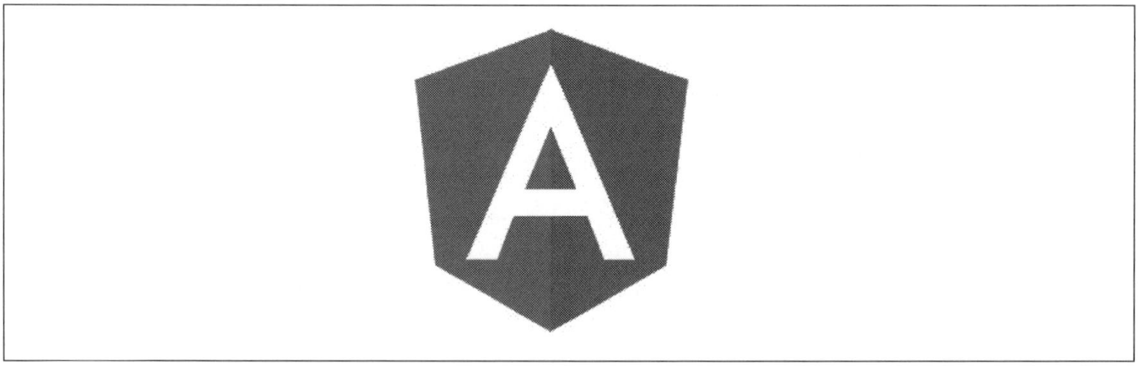

Figure 11.5: The Angular logo provided by the PWA automatic setup

Whenever we want to make our app available to the public, we will likely want to change these icons. However, they are more than enough, at least for the time being; let's keep these files as they are and move on to the last remaining task to transform our SPAs into PWAs.

Handling the offline status

Now that we have configured a service worker in both of our apps, we can think of a way to handle the *offline status* message, so that each one of our components will be able to behave in a different way when the app is offline—such as limiting their features and showing an *offline status* informative message to our users.

To implement these conditional behaviors, we need to find a way to properly determine the browser connectivity status, that is, whether it's online or not; in the following sections, we'll briefly review several different approaches that we can use to do that to make the (arguably) best possible choice. These approaches are:

- The window's `ononline/onoffline` event
- The `Navigator.onLine` property
- The `ng-connection-service` npm package

Option 1 – the window's ononline/onoffline event

If we're willing to accept a pure JavaScript way to handle this, such a task can be easily achieved using the `window.ononline` and `window.onoffline` JavaScript events, which are directly accessible from any Angular class.

Here's how we can use them:

```
window.addEventListener("online", function(e) {
  alert("online");
}, false);

window.addEventListener("offline", function(e) {
  alert("offline");
}, false);
```

However, if we're willing to adopt a pure JavaScript approach, there's an even better way to implement it.

Option 2 – the Navigator.onLine property

Since we don't want to track the network status changes and are just looking for a simple way to determine whether the browser is online or not, we can make things even simpler by just checking the `window.navigator.onLine` property:

```
if (navigator.onLine) {
  alert("online");
}
else {
  alert("offline");
}
```

As we can easily guess from its name, this property returns the online status of the browser. The property returns a Boolean value, with `true` meaning online and `false` meaning offline, and is updated whenever the browser's ability to connect to the network changes.

Thanks to this property, our Angular implementation could be reduced to this:

```
ngOnInit() {
  this.isOnline = navigator.onLine;
}
```

Then, we can use the `isOnline` local variable within our component's template file so that we can show different content to our users using the `ngIf` structural directive. That would be pretty easy, right?

Unfortunately, things are never that simple; let's try to understand why.

Downsides of the JavaScript approaches

Both of the JavaScript-based approaches we've mentioned suffer from a serious drawback caused by the fact that modern browsers implement the `navigator.onLine` property (as well as the `window.ononline` and `window.onoffline` events) in different ways.

More specifically, Chrome and Safari will set that property to `true` whenever the browser can connect to a LAN or a router. This can easily produce a false positive since most home and business connections are connected to the internet through a LAN, which will probably stay up even when the actual internet access is down.

> For additional information regarding the `Navigator.onLine` property and its drawbacks, check out the following URL: `https://developer.mozilla.org/en-US/docs/Web/API/NavigatorOnLine/onLine`

All things considered, this basically means that we cannot use the convenient approaches described earlier to check our browser's online status; as long as we want to seriously deal with this matter, we need to find a better way to do it.

Option 3 – the ng-connection-service npm package

Luckily enough, there's a neat npm package that does precisely what we need: its name is `ng-connection-service` and it's basically an *internet connection monitoring service* that can detect whether the browser has an active internet connection or not.

The online detection task is performed using a (configurable) *heartbeat* system, which will periodically issue *HEAD* requests to a (configurable) URL to determine the internet connection status.

Here are the package default values:

- `enableHeartbeat`: `true`
- `heartbeatUrl`: `//internethealthtest.org`
- `heartbeatInterval`: `1000` (milliseconds)
- `heartbeatRetryInterval`: `1000`
- `requestMethod`: `head`

> For additional information about the `ng-connection-service` npm package, check out the following URL: `https://github.com/ultrasonicsoft/ng-connection-service`

Most of them are good, except for `heartbeatUrl`—for various reasons that we'll explain later on.

Needless to say, with it being an Angular service, we'll be able to configure it in a centralized way and then inject it whenever we need to without having to manually configure it every time: that almost seems too good to be true!

Let's see how we can implement it.

Installing ng-connection-service

Unfortunately, the `ng-connection-service` latest version—which introduced the heartbeat—is not available on npm as of the time of writing: the last updated version is **1.0.4**, which was developed for Angular 6 more than a year ago (as of the time of writing) and was still based upon the `window.ononline` and `window.onoffline` events that we talked about earlier.

At the time of writing, I don't know why the author (Balram Chavan) hasn't updated the npm package yet; however, since he made the latest version's source code available on GitHub under an **MIT** license, we can definitely manually install it to our `HealthCheck` and `WorldCities` apps.

To do this, we need to perform the following steps in both our `HealthCheck` and `WorldCities` projects:

1. Visit the project's GitHub repository at `https://github.com/ultrasonicsoft/ng-connection-service`
2. Clone the project using Git or download the ZIP file locally and unzip it somewhere
3. Create a new `/ClientApp/src/ng-connection-service/` folder and copy the following files there:
    - `connection-service.module.ts`
    - `connection-service.service.spec.ts`
    - `connection-service.service.ts`

The files can be found in the following subfolder of the `ng-connection-service` npm package bundle:

```
ng-connection-service-master\projects\connection-service\src\lib
```

That's it! Now we can implement the service within our apps.

Updating the app.component.ts file

The *offline status* informative message should be shown to our users:

- **As soon as possible**, so that they'll know the app's connectivity status before navigating somewhere
- **Everywhere**, so that they will be warned about it even if they're visiting some internal views

Therefore, a good place to implement it would be the `AppComponent` class, which contains all of our components, regardless of the *front-end* route picked by the user.

Open the `/ClientApp/src/app/app.component.ts` file and modify its class file accordingly (the updated lines are highlighted):

```
import { Component } from '@angular/core';
import { ConnectionService } from '../ng-connection-service/connection-service.
service';

@Component({
  selector: 'app-root',
  templateUrl: './app.component.html'
})
export class AppComponent {
  title = 'app';

  hasNetworkConnection: boolean;
  hasInternetAccess: boolean;
  isConnected: boolean;
  status: string;
  constructor(private connectionService: ConnectionService) {
    this.connectionService.updateOptions({
      heartbeatUrl: "/isOnline.txt"
    });
    this.connectionService.monitor().subscribe(currentState => {
      this.hasNetworkConnection = currentState.hasNetworkConnection;
      this.hasInternetAccess = currentState.hasInternetAccess;
```

```
      if (this.hasNetworkConnection && this.hasInternetAccess) {
        this.isConnected = true;
        this.status = 'ONLINE';
      } else {
        this.isConnected = false;
        this.status = 'OFFLINE';
      }
    });
  }
}
```

As we can see, we took the chance to modify the `heartbeatUrl` value; instead of querying a third-party website, we're going to check a dedicated `isOnline.txt` file that we'll create and properly configure within our app. We've opted for that choice for several good reasons, the most important of them being the following:

- **To avoid being a nuisance** to those third-party hosts
- **To avoid Cross-Origin Resource Sharing (CORS) issues** against third-party resources

> We'll talk more about CORS in a dedicated mini-section in a short while.

Since the aforementioned `isOnline.txt` file doesn't exist yet, we're going to create it now.

From Solution Explorer, right-click on the `HealthCheck` project's `/wwwroot/` folder, then create a new `isOnline.txt` file there and fill its content with the following line:

```
.
```

As a matter of fact, the content is not relevant; since we'll just perform some HEAD requests against it to check for our app's online status, a single dot will suffice.

> **Important**: Remember to perform the preceding changes (and to create the `isOnline.txt` file) for both our projects (`HealthCheck` and `WorldCities`).

Removing the isOnline.txt static file from the cache

The `isOnline.txt` file is, by all means, a static file; therefore, it is subject to the static file caching rules that we set up for our `HealthCheck` app back in *Chapter 2, Looking Around*. However, since that file would be used to periodically check for our app's online status, having it cached on the *back-end* would hardly be a good idea.

To remove it from the global static file caching rule that we've set, open the `Startup.cs` file of `HealthCheck` and update its contents in the following way (the new/updated lines are highlighted):

```
// ...

app.UseStaticFiles(new StaticFileOptions()
{
    ContentTypeProvider = provider,
    OnPrepareResponse = (context) =>
    {
        if (context.File.Name == "isOnline.txt")
        {
            // disable caching for these files
            context.Context.Response.Headers.Add("Cache-Control",
             "no-cache, no-store");
            context.Context.Response.Headers.Add("Expires", "-1");
        }
        else
        {
            // Retrieve cache configuration from appsettings.json
            context.Context.Response.Headers["Cache-Control"] =
                Configuration["StaticFiles:Headers:Cache-Control"];
        }
    }
});

// ...
```

Now that we've excluded the `isOnline.txt` file from the *back-end* cache, we can move to the next step.

> **Important**: Remember to configure the `isOnline.txt` file no-cache features in the `WorldCities` project as well. Even if no caching rules have been defined there, it's definitely a good idea to explicitly keep it outside the cache by adding the above headers.

Installing the ng-connection-service via npm (alternate route)

If we don't want to install `ng-connection-service` manually, we can still use the 1.0.4 version by adding the following highlighted line to the `/ClientApp/package.json` file for both of the preceding projects, at the end of the `"dependencies"` section:

```
// ...
```

```
"zone.js": "0.10.2",
"ng-connection-service": "1.0.4"

// ...
```

And implement it in our `AppComponent`'s file in the following way:

```
import { Component } from '@angular/core';
import { ConnectionService } from 'connection-service';

@Component({
  selector: 'app-root',
  templateUrl: './app.component.html'
})
export class AppComponent {
  title = 'app';
  status = 'ONLINE';
  isConnected = true;

  constructor(private connectionService: ConnectionService) {
    this.connectionService.monitor().subscribe(isConnected => {
      this.isConnected = isConnected;
      if (this.isConnected) {
        this.status = "ONLINE";
      }
      else {
        this.status = "OFFLINE";
      }
    })
  }
}
```

As we can see, the `ConnectionService` interface is slightly different in this version: as a result, we won't be able to rely upon the `hasNetworkConnection` and `hasInternetAccess` variables, as well as the useful info they provide, in the new version.

> However, if we choose that (simplified and less robust) approach, we won't have to configure the `internethealthtest.org` website to our app's CORS policy: we'll talk about that later on.

Updating the app.component.html file

Last but not least, we need to modify the template file of `AppComponent` to show the "offline status" informative message to our users whenever the `isConnected` local variable evaluates to `false`.

Open the `/ClientApp/src/app/app.component.html` file and update its content accordingly:

```
<body>

  <div class="alert alert-warning" *ngIf="!isConnected">
    <strong>WARNING</strong>: the app is currently <i>offline</i>:
    some features that rely upon the back-end might not work as
    expected. This message will automatically disappear as soon
    as the internet connection becomes available again.
  </div>

  <app-nav-menu></app-nav-menu>
  <div class="container">
    <router-outlet></router-outlet>
  </div>
</body>
```

That's it: since our app's *Home view* doesn't directly require a *back-end* HTTP request, we've chosen to just show a warning message to inform the user that some of our app's features might not work while offline. Conversely, we could've entirely shut down the app by putting an additional `ngIf="isConnected"` structural directive to the other elements, so that the *offline status* message would be the only visible output.

Cross-Origin Resource Sharing

As we said earlier, the latest version of `ng-connection-service` allows us to perform a HEAD request over a defined amount of time ("heartbeat") to determine whether we're online or not. However, we have chosen to change the third-party website that was set in the service's default values (`internethealthtest.org`) to a local file (`isOnline.txt`) that we created just for that purpose.

Why did we do that? What's wrong with periodically issuing a HEAD request against a third-party website?

The first reason is rather simple to understand: we don't want to be a nuisance to those websites since they're definitely not meant for us to check their online status. If their system administrators see our requests in their log, they could ban us or take some countermeasures that could prevent our heartbeat check from working or—even worse—compromise its reliability status.

However, there's another important reason for avoiding such a practice.

Allowing our app to issue HTTP requests to *external* websites might violate the default CORS policy settings of those websites; while we're here, it could be useful to spend a couple of words to better understand this concept.

As we might already know, modern browsers have built-in security settings that prevent a web page from making JavaScript requests to a different domain than the one that served the web page: such a restriction is called a **same-origin policy** and is introduced to prevent a malicious third-party website from reading data from another site.

However, most websites might want (or need) to issue some external requests to other websites: for example, the default `heartbeatUrl` configured in `ng-connection-service` would have told our app to issue a HEAD request to the `internethealthtest.org` external website to check its online status.

These requirements, which are rather common in most apps, are called **CORS:** to allow them, the browser expects to receive from the receiving server—the one that hosts the required resources—a suitable **CORS policy** that will allow them to pass. If this policy doesn't come—or doesn't include the requesting origin—the HTTP request will be blocked.

> For additional information about CORS and its settings, visit the following URL: `https://developer.mozilla.org/en-US/docs/Web/HTTP/CORS`

If we were the **remote** server, we could configure such a policy by configuring the .NET CORS middleware, which is part of the `Microsoft.AspNetCore.Cors` NuGet package; unfortunately, the heartbeat mechanism used by the `ng-connection-service` npm package makes our app—and its hostname—the **origin** server, meaning that such a method would only work if the remote server features a CORS policy compatible with us, without ever changing it.

Since this *heartbeat-based* mechanism is now a critical part of our app, we can't take the risk of being blocked by third-party CORS restrictions. Therefore, we've replaced that troublesome *external* reference with a more secure URL pointing to an *internal* resource under our control—and with no CORS policy requirements, since it's being hosted on the same server that serves the Angular app.

> To know more about the `Microsoft.AspNetCore.Cors` NuGet package and how to configure CORS in ASP.NET Core apps, check out the following URL: `https://docs.microsoft.com/en-us/aspnet/core/security/cors`

With this, we've successfully implemented all of the required PWA features. Let's now find a way to properly test out what we did; it won't be easy to do that from within Visual Studio due to the distinctive features of PWAs, yet there are some workarounds we can use to pull it off.

Testing the PWA capabilities

In this section, we'll try to test the service worker registration for our `HealthCheck` app. Unfortunately, doing it from a Visual Studio development environment is a rather complex task for several reasons, including the following:

- `ng serve`, the Angular CLI command that pre-installs the packages and starts the app whenever we run our app in *debug* mode, doesn't support service workers
- The service worker registration tasks that we put in the `AppModule` class a while ago only register it when the app is running in a *production* environment
- The required static files generated by the Angular CLI using the `angular.json` configuration file that we modified earlier on will only be available in *production* environments

However, we can easily work around these limitations by compiling our Angular app for production and then running the generated files within a Visual Studio debug session; this approach will allow us to properly test both our *Web App Manifest* file and *service worker* from within Visual Studio and IIS Express. The actual compilation can be performed with the Angular CLI (using the `ng build` command) or within Visual Studio (by creating a *publish profile*).

If we do not need to test the service worker within a *debug* environment, we can also take a completely different approach, such as publishing our app in a production-like environment or serving the published content with a local HTTP server and then browsing our "locally published" app from the localhost.

In the following sections, we are going to see how we can do all that.

Compiling the app with the Angular CLI

Publishing our app using the Angular CLI is probably the most simple and straightforward approach we can take. To do that, just open Command Prompt, navigate to our project's `/ClientApp/` folder, and type the following command:

```
ng build --prod
```

The CLI will compile our Angular app within a new `/ClientApp/dist/` folder that will contain all the generated files.

Updating the Startup.cs file

Once done, we just need to slightly modify our app's pipeline to ensure that the generated static files will be used even in the development environment.

To do that, open the `Startup.cs` file and comment out the following highlighted lines (around line 73 and 97, respectively):

```
// ...

// if (!env.IsDevelopment())
{
    app.UseSpaStaticFiles();
}

// ...

if (env.IsDevelopment())
{
    // spa.UseAngularCliServer(npmScript: "start");
}
// ...
```

Right after that, we can repeat the preceding tasks for the `WorldCities` app as well.

> It's worth noting that we are going to use this folder (and all its content) to test our service worker only, deleting it afterward; alternatively, we could also exclude it from version control by adding the folder path to the `.gitignore` file.

Now we can choose between starting our tests now (skip to the *Testing out our PWAs* section) or keep reading to learn about an alternative, yet very useful, building method.

Compiling the app with Visual Studio

Instead of compiling our app using the Angular CLI, we can achieve the same result from within Visual Studio; although this approach is slightly more complex than the previous one, learning it will come in very handy in the long run since it will allow us to publish everything at the same time—both the ASP.NET Core back-end and the Angular front-end—with a single click.

> As a matter of fact, this is the method that we are going to use to deploy our web application to a production web server in *Chapter 12, Windows, Linux, and Azure Deployment*.

In a nutshell, here is what we are going to do:

1. Create a publish profile for our `HealthCheck` and `WorldCities` projects and use it to publish our projects in a temporary folder using the *production* environment, which is the default configuration when publishing our app
2. Copy the CLI-generated files from the publishing folder to the `/ClientApp/dist/` folder of our projects
3. Run the two apps in *debug* mode and properly check out their PWA capabilities

> The tweak is to copy the CLI-generated files to the `/wwwroot/` folder so that they will be available to the web browser even if the app is being built and launched from a development environment.

Let's get to work.

Creating a publish profile

As we probably already know, **publish profiles** are a convenient way offered by Visual Studio to deploy our web application projects for production environments. Such a feature allows us to publish our app on the filesystem, over an FTP/FTPS server, on Azure App Service, on Windows or Linux, and so on.

In our specific scenario, we need to publish our ASP.NET Core and Angular web app to a filesystem folder, so that we can serve it with `http-server` from the command line; to do that, we need to perform the following steps:

1. Right-click on the project in **Solution Explorer** and select **Publish**.
2. Select **Folder** from the various options available (see the following screenshot):

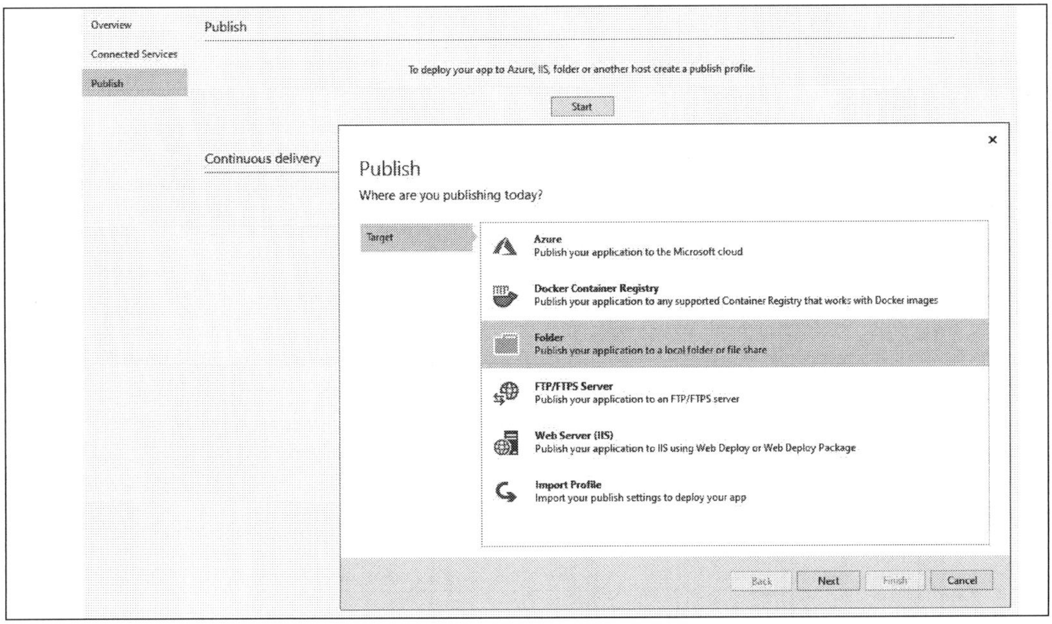
Overview
Connected Services
Publish
Publish
To deploy your app to Azure, IIS, folder or another host create a publish profile.
Start
Continuous delivery
Publish
Where are you publishing today?
Target
Azure
Publish your application to the Microsoft cloud
Docker Container Registry
Publish your application to any supported Container Registry that works with Docker images
Folder
Publish your application to a local folder or file share
FTP/FTPS Server
Publish your application to an FTP/FTPS server
Web Server (IIS)
Publish your application to IIS using Web Deploy or Web Deploy Package
Import Profile
Import your publish settings to deploy your app
Back
Next
Finish
Cancel

Figure 11.6: The Publish modal window

3. Choose a suitable folder path—such as `C:/Temp/HealthCheck/`—then click **Finish** to create the publish profile.
4. The default publishing options should be good enough; however, these are the suggested parameters to use for our test:
    - **Configuration**: **Release**
    - **Target Framework**: **net5.0**
    - **Deployment Mode**: **Framework-Dependent**
    - **Target Runtime**: **Portable**

To check them, click the **Edit** link below the new profile name or one of the pencil icons in the **Settings** panel below:

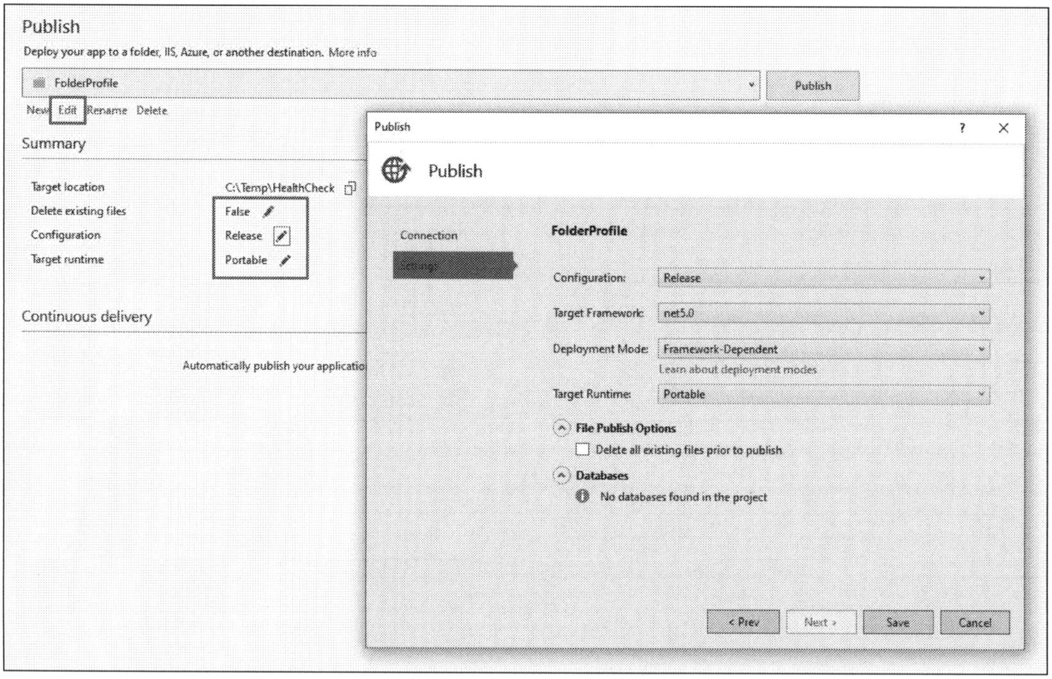

Figure 11.7: Editing the Publish options

5. Once done, click **Save** to save the advanced settings and then **Create Profile** to complete the task. As a result, a new `FolderProfile.pubxml` file will be added to the project's `Properties/PublishProfiles` folder.

Now we can press the **Publish** button to publish the `HealthCheck` app files in the selected folder.

> As we can see by looking at the **Output** | **Build** window, the publishing task will internally call the very same `ng build --prod` command that we've used before to build the Angular app in the target folder.

Once done, we can repeat the same tasks for the `WorldCities` app, changing the target folder accordingly.

Copying the CLI-generated files

Now that we have a production build, we can copy the whole filesystem publishing folder containing all the CLI-generated files—in our example, `C:/Temp/HealthCheck/ClientApp/dist/` and `C:/Temp/WorldCities/ClientApp/dist/`—within the corresponding project's `/ClientApp/` folder, thus creating a "temporary" `/ClientApp/dist/` folder.

> Again, be sure to delete the dist folder (and all its content) after completing the service worker tests below.

Updating the Startup.cs file

Last but not least, we need to modify the `Startup.cs` file, just like we did for the previous approach (the two code lines to comment are highlighted):

```
// ...

// if (!env.IsDevelopment())
{
    app.UseSpaStaticFiles();
}

// ...

if (env.IsDevelopment())
{
    // spa.UseAngularCliServer(npmScript: "start");
}
// ...
```

Now we are ready to properly test the PWA capabilities of our apps.

Testing out our PWAs

For the sake of simplicity, the following screenshots will be all related to `HealthCheck`, but the same checks could be applied to the `WorldCities` app as well since we configured it using the same implementation patterns.

> It's strongly advisable to perform the following tests with a Chromium-based browser, such as Google Chrome or Microsoft Edge, since such engines come with some neat built-in tools to check for Web App Manifest and service worker presence. Also, it's strongly advisable to use the browser's *incognito mode* to ensure that the service worker will always start from scratch, without reading previously built caches or states.

Let's start our test by hitting *F5* to launch the app in debug mode, just like we've always done.

Right after the app's **Home** view is properly loaded, press *Shift* + *Ctrl* + *J* to open the Chrome Developer Tools, as shown in the following screenshot:

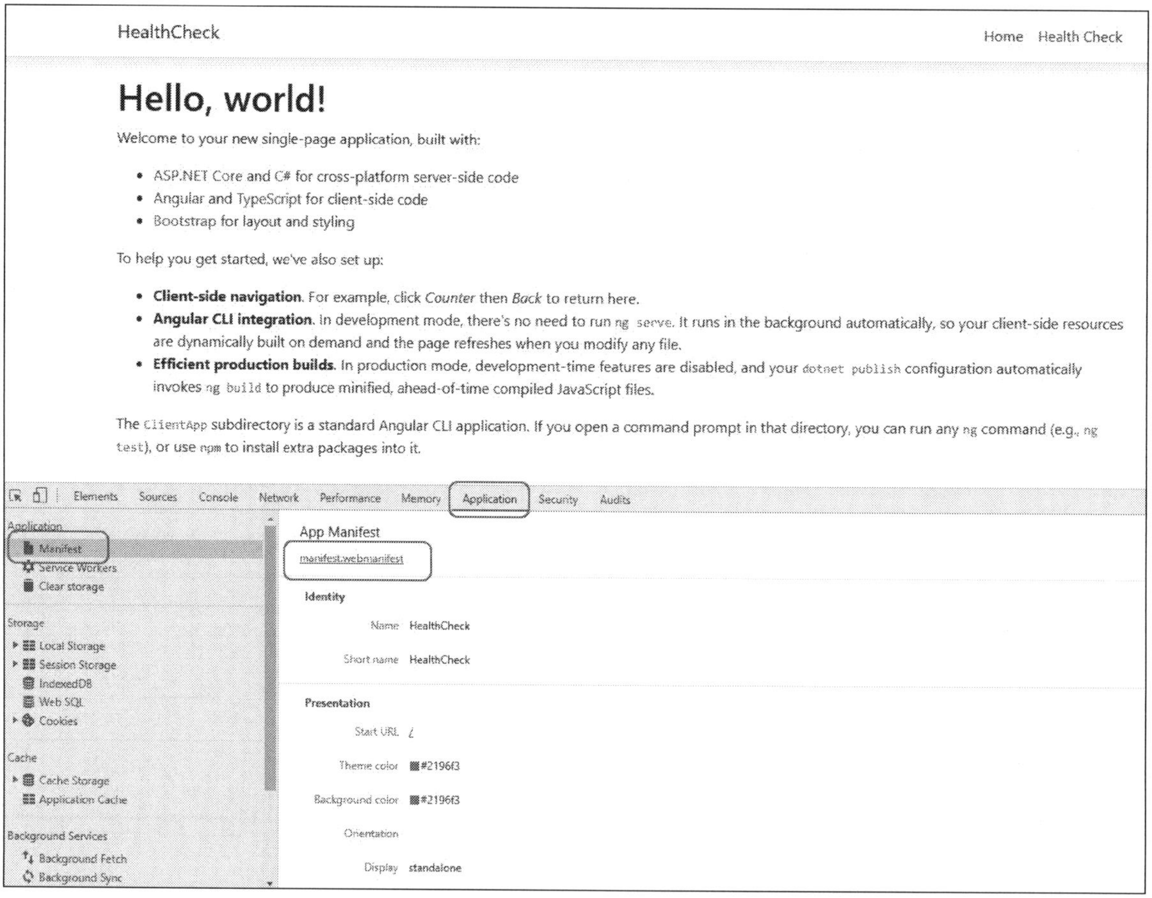
HealthCheck
Home Health Check
Hello, world!
Welcome to your new single-page application, built with:
ASP.NET Core and C# for cross-platform server-side code
Angular and TypeScript for client-side code
Bootstrap for layout and styling
To help you get started, we've also set up:
Client-side navigation. For example, click Counter then Back to return here.
Angular CLI integration. In development mode, there's no need to run ng serve. It runs in the background automatically, so your client-side resources are dynamically built on demand and the page refreshes when you modify any file.
Efficient production builds. In production mode, development-time features are disabled, and your dotnet publish configuration automatically invokes ng build to produce minified, ahead-of-time compiled JavaScript files.
The ClientApp subdirectory is a standard Angular CLI application. If you open a command prompt in that directory, you can run any ng command (e.g., ng test), or use npm to install extra packages into it.
Elements Sources Console Network Performance Memory Application Security Audits
Application
Manifest
Service Workers
Clear storage
Storage
Local Storage
Session Storage
IndexedDB
Web SQL
Cookies
Cache
Cache Storage
Application Cache
Background Services
Background Fetch
Background Sync
App Manifest
manifest.webmanifest
Identity
Name HealthCheck
Short name HealthCheck
Presentation
Start URL /
Theme color #2196f3
Background color #2196f3
Orientation
Display standalone

Figure 11.8: Chrome Developer Tools

As we can see, if we navigate to the developer tools' **Application** tab, we can see that our *Web App Manifest* file has been properly loaded. If we scroll down the **Application** | **Manifest** panel, we'll be able to see our PNG icons as well.

> **Note**: It can take a while (10–20 seconds on a typical development machine) before the service worker actually shows up on the first installation.

The next thing we can check is the **Application** | **Service Workers** panel, which should strongly resemble the one shown in the following screenshot:

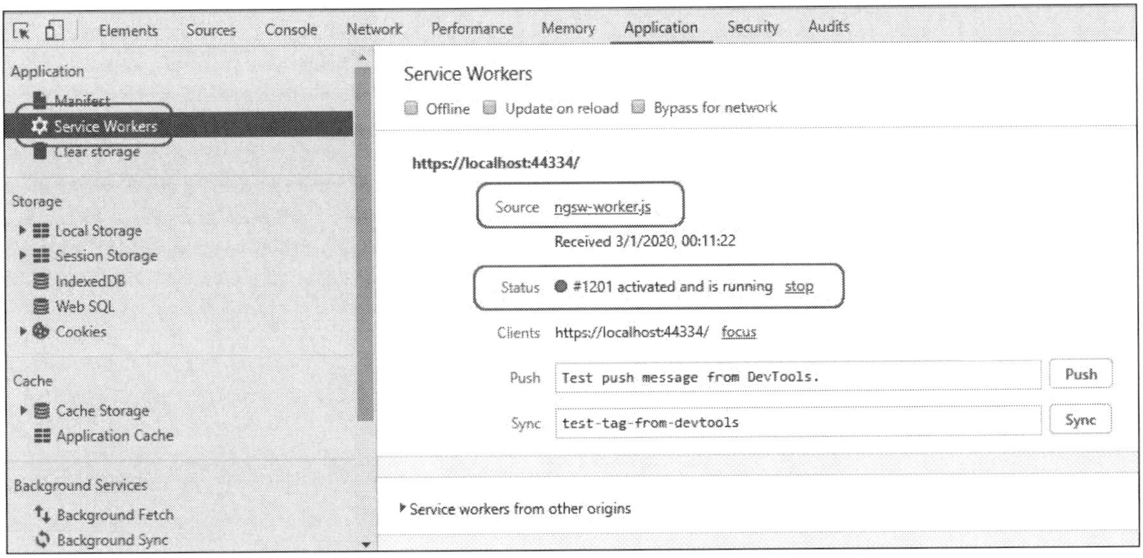

Figure 11.9: The Service Workers panel

The *service worker* JavaScript file should be clearly visible, as well as its registration date and current *up-and-running* status.

Let's now try to put our web browser offline. To do that, activate the **Offline** checkbox in the top-left section of the Chrome Developer Tools' **Application** tab and see what happens:

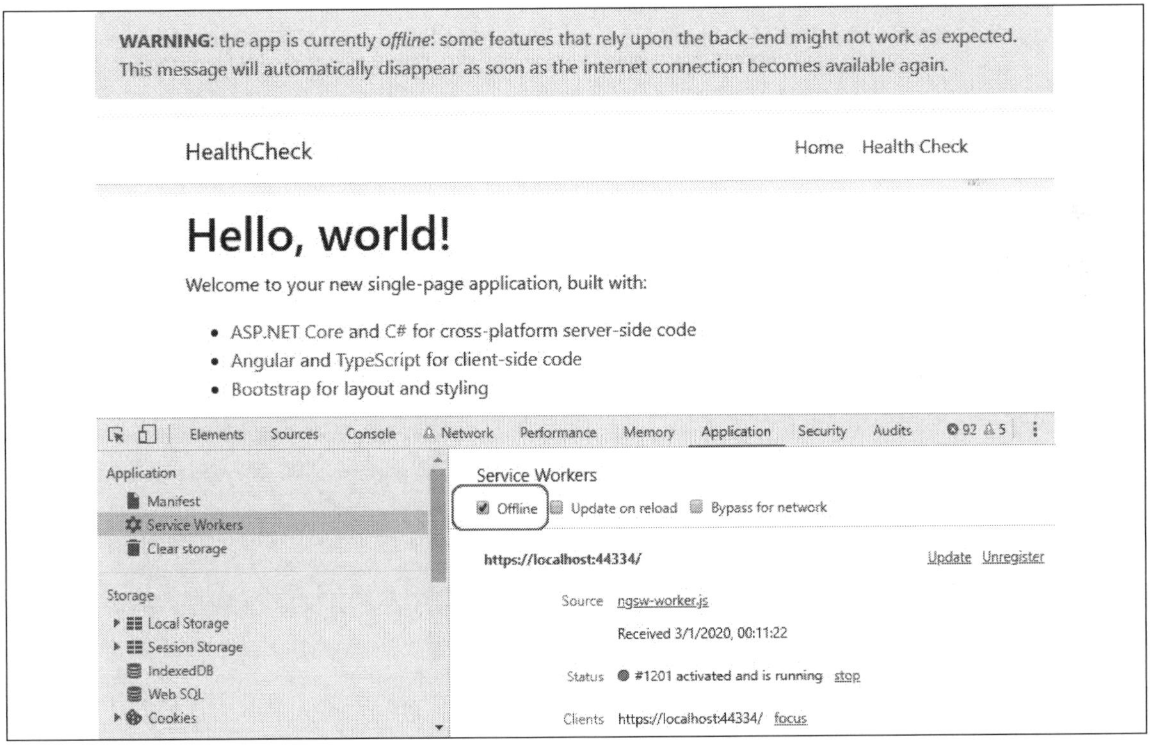

Figure 11.10: View after putting the web browser offline

Our *offline warning* info message should immediately kick in, thanks to our `ng-connected-service` implementation. If we move to the **Network** tab, we can see that the `isOnline.txt` file isn't reachable anymore, meaning that the `isConnected` variable of `AppComponents` now evaluates to `false`.

Now, we can resume the connectivity (by de-selecting the **Offline** checkbox) and check out two more things: the *linkable* and *installable* PWA capabilities. Both of them are clearly shown on the rightmost part of the browser's address bar, as we can see in the following screenshot:

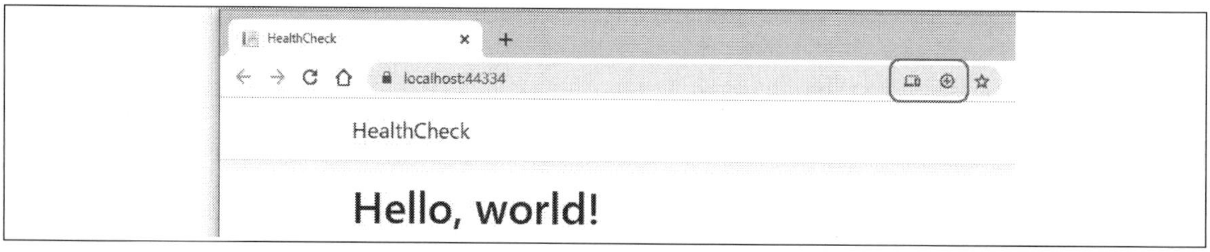
HealthCheck
localhost:44334
HealthCheck
Hello, world!

Figure 11.11: Checking the linkable and installable icons

If we go there with the mouse pointer, we should be able to see the contextual messages asking us to send the app's URL to other devices (left) and install it to the desktop (right).

Installing the PWA

Let's now click the **install** button (the one with the *plus* sign inscribed in a circle) and confirm that we want to locally install the `HealthCheck` PWA.

Within a bunch of seconds we should be able to see the Home view of our newly installed app in a *desktop app-like* window, as shown in the following screenshot:

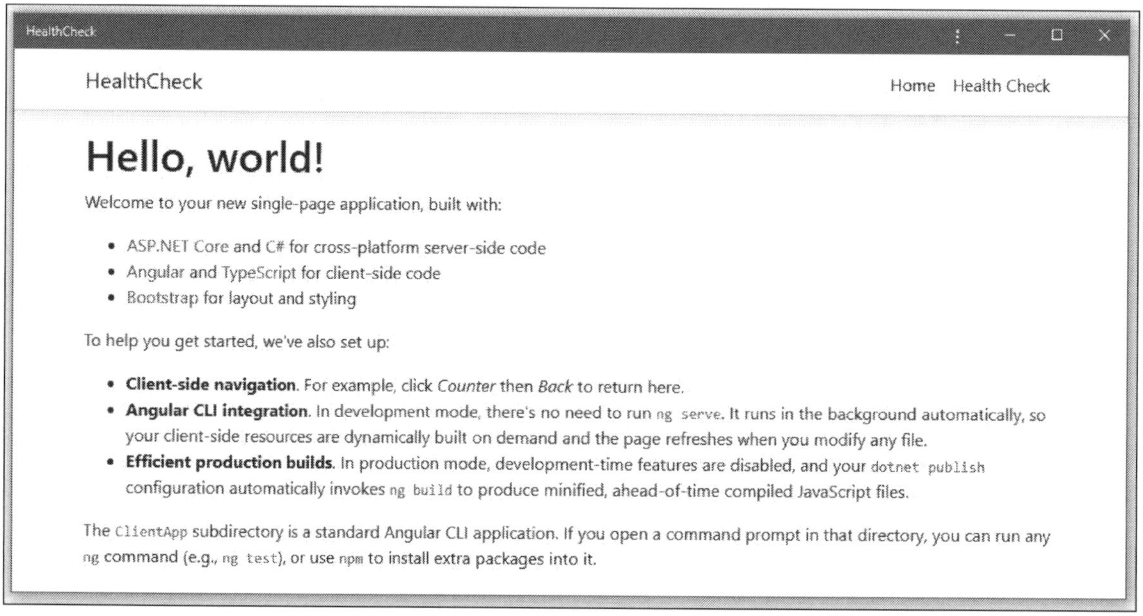
HealthCheck
HealthCheck
Home
Health Check
Hello, world!
Welcome to your new single-page application, built with:
ASP.NET Core and C# for cross-platform server-side code
Angular and TypeScript for client-side code
Bootstrap for layout and styling
To help you get started, we've also set up:
Client-side navigation. For example, click Counter then Back to return here.
Angular CLI integration. In development mode, there's no need to run ng serve. It runs in the background automatically, so your client-side resources are dynamically built on demand and the page refreshes when you modify any file.
Efficient production builds. In production mode, development-time features are disabled, and your dotnet publish configuration automatically invokes ng build to produce minified, ahead-of-time compiled JavaScript files.
The ClientApp subdirectory is a standard Angular CLI application. If you open a command prompt in that directory, you can run any ng command (e.g., ng test), or use npm to install extra packages into it.

Figure 11.12: Home view inside the desktop app

From there, do the following:

1. Press *Shift* + *Ctrl* + *J* to open again the Google Chrome Developer Tools
2. Navigate to the **Application** | **Service Workers** panel
3. Click on the **Offline** checkbox to check/activate it again

The app should again show the *offline warning* information message; once done, try to navigate to the **Health Check** view by clicking on the rightmost link in the app's navigation menu near the top-right corner.

We should be able to see something like this:

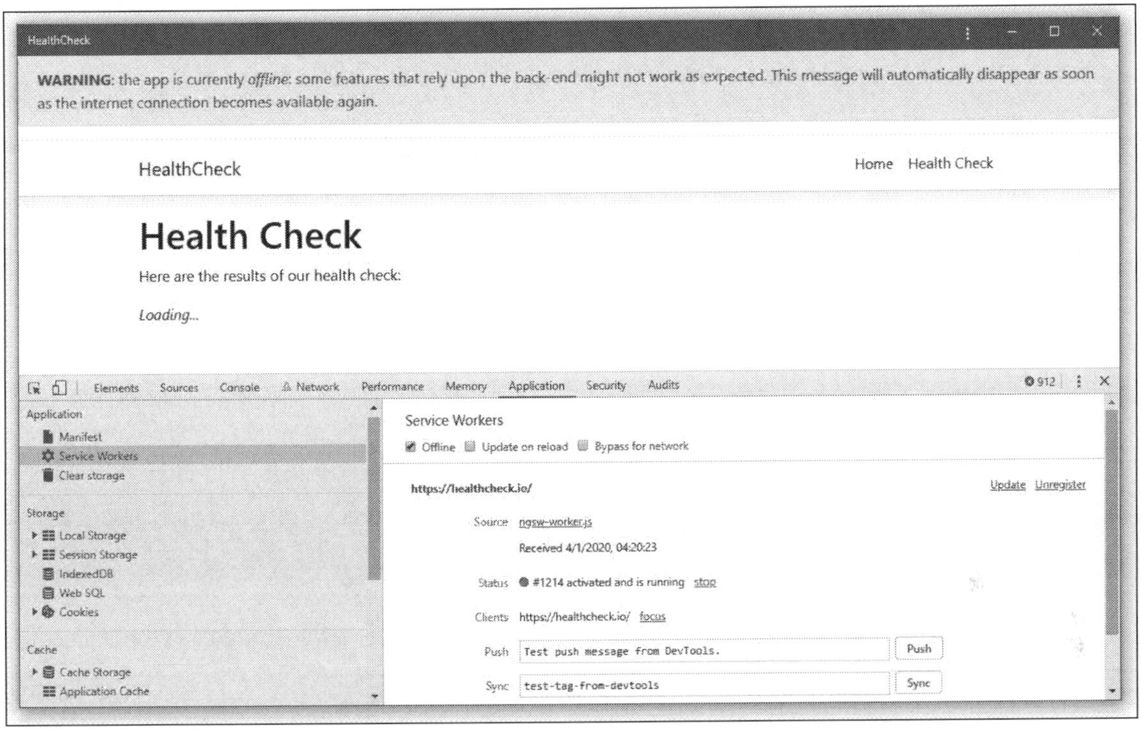

Figure 11.13: Setting our newly installed app to offline

As we can see, our app is working even while offline: the **offline** message is shown to the user.

> The "912" attempts shown in the top-right section of the Google Chrome Developer Tools window also shows that our heartbeat is doing its job, periodically trying to find the `isOnline.txt` file backup.

Needless to say, we won't be able to see our health check results table; however, the *offline warning* information message is enough to make our users aware of the fact that such behavior is perfectly acceptable while the app is offline.

That's it: we have successfully turned our SPAs into PWAs. As a matter of fact, we have just scratched the surface of the many possibilities offered by such a promising deployment approach; however, we've successfully demonstrated that our *front-end* and *back-end* frameworks are fully able to handle their main requirements properly and consistently.

Alternative testing methods

If we don't want to use the preceding workaround, there are various possible options available, such as the following:

- Publishing our app in a production-like environment
- Locally serving the contents of the filesystem folders used to publish our app(s) with an HTTP server that does support service workers

The first option will be extensively covered in *Chapter 12, Windows, Linux, and Azure Deployment*; to implement the second option, we can use `http-server`, a simple and lightweight command-line HTTP server that can be installed and launched within seconds. We'll touch on how to do this below.

Serving our PWA using http-server

`http-server` can be either installed using `npm` or directly launched using `npx`, a tool shipped with Node.js that can be used to execute `npm` package binaries without installing them.

If we want to globally install it before launching it, we can do so with the following commands:

```
> npm install http-server -g
> http-server -p 8080 -c-1 C:\Temp\HealthCheck\ClientApp\dist\
```

If we just want to test out our service worker, we can use the following command instead:

```
> npx http-server -p 8080 -c-1 C:\Temp\HealthCheck\ClientApp\dist\
```

Both commands will launch `http-server` and serve our `HealthCheck` app to the local `8080` TCP port, as shown in the following screenshot:

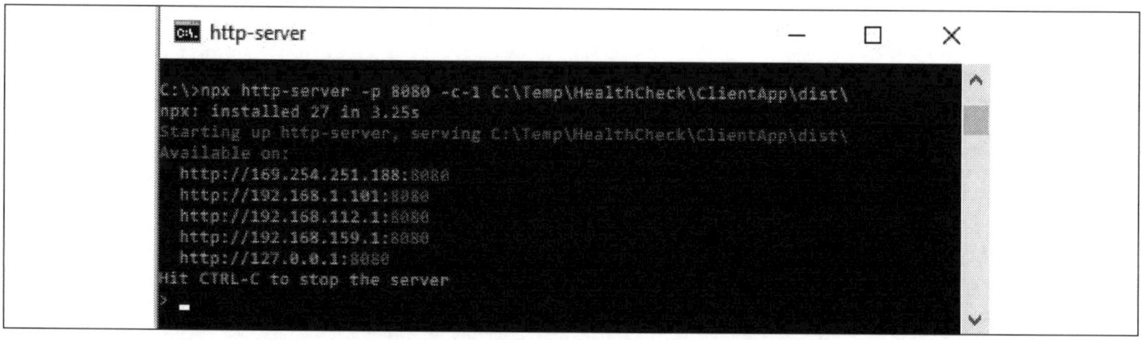

Figure 11.14: Launching http-server and serving the HealthCheck app

As soon as we do that, we can connect to it by opening a browser and typing the following URL in the address bar: `http://localhost:8080`

We can check out the PWA capabilities of our apps just like we did with Visual Studio and IIS Express earlier; however, we won't be able to test the *back-end* HTTP requests since `http-server` won't natively support ASP.NET Core. Luckily enough, we don't need the back-end to run these tests.

Summary

This chapter was all about PWAs: we spent some valuable time better understanding the high-level distinctive features of this modern web development pattern and how to translate them into technical specifications. Right after that, we started implementing them, taking into account the various available options offered by our *front-end* and *back-end* frameworks.

Since the PWA concept is closely related to the *front-end* aspects of our app, we chose to adopt the Angular way of implementing their required capabilities; with that in mind, we chose to take the manual route for our `HealthCheck` app first, then to experience the automatic installation feature powered by the Angular CLI for the `WorldCities` app. In both scenarios, we made good use of the `@angular/service-worker` npm package, a module available since Angular 5 that provides a fully featured service worker implementation that can be easily integrated into our apps.

After we did that, we manually ran some consistency tests to check the brand-new PWA capabilities of our apps using Google Chrome and its developer tools. To do that, we took the chance to learn how to publish our app using Visual Studio's *publish profiles* feature.

At the end of this chapter, we finally saw our service worker in action, as well as the *Web App Manifest* file being able to serve the PNG icons and provide the installing and linking features to our apps.

The various concepts that we learned throughout this chapter have also helped us to focus on some very important issues regarding the differences between *development* and *production* environments, hence making us ready to properly face the final part of our journey: Windows, Linux, and Azure deployment, which will be the main topics of the next chapter.

Suggested topics

Progressive Web Apps (PWAs), @angular/service-worker, secure origin, HTTPS, TLS, Let's Encrypt, service workers, HttpInterceptors, favicons, Web App Manifest file, Microsoft.AspNetCore.Cors, Cross-Origin Resource Sharing (CORS), offline status, window.navigator, ng-connection-service, IIS Express, http-server.

References

- *Progressive Web Apps*: `https://developers.google.com/web/progressive-web-apps`
- *Web Fundamentals*: `https://developers.google.com/web/fundamentals`
- *Progressive Web Apps: Escaping Tabs Without Losing Our Soul*: `https://infrequently.org/2015/06/progressive-apps-escaping-tabs-without-losing-our-soul/`
- *Let's Encrypt*: `https://letsencrypt.org/`
- *The Web App Manifest*: `https://developers.google.com/web/fundamentals/web-app-manifest`
- *Angular Service Workers*: `https://angular.io/guide/service-worker-getting-started`
- *Service worker configuration*: `https://angular.io/guide/service-worker-config`
- *Service Workers – Practical Guided Introduction (several examples)*: `https://blog.angular-university.io/service-workers/`
- *Angular University: Service Worker step-by-step guide*: `https://blog.angular-university.io/angular-service-worker/`
- *favicon.io*: `https://favicon.io/`
- *Real Favicon Generator*: `https://realfavicongenerator.net/`
- *Icons8*: `https://icons8.com/icons/set/favicon`
- *FreeFavicon*: `https://www.freefavicon.com/freefavicons/icons/`
- *Firebase Web App Manifest Generator*: `https://app-manifest.firebaseapp.com`
- *DummyImage – Placeholder Image Generator*: `https://dummyimage.com/`
- *Google Developers recommendation for installability requirements*: `https://web.dev/installable-manifest/#recommendations`
- *Web App Manifest – W3C Working Draft 09 December 2019*: `https://www.w3.org/TR/appmanifest/`
- *Enable Cross-Origin Requests (CORS) in ASP.NET Core*: `https://docs.microsoft.com/en-us/aspnet/core/security/cors`
- *http-server*: `https://www.npmjs.com/package/http-server`
- *npx - execute npm package binaries*: `https://www.npmjs.com/package/npx`
- *ng-serve*: `https://angular.io/cli/serve`
- *Visual Studio publish profiles (.pubxml) for ASP.NET Core app deployment*: `https://docs.microsoft.com/en-us/aspnet/core/host-and-deploy/visual-studio-publish-profiles`
- *Angular – Service Worker registration options*: `https://angular.io/api/service-worker/SwRegistrationOptions`

12

Windows, Linux, and Azure Deployment

Our valuable journey through ASP.NET Core and Angular development is coming to an end. The web applications we've been working on since *Chapter 1, Getting Ready* – `HealthCheck` and `WorldCities` – are now potentially shippable products and mostly ready to be published in a suitable environment for evaluation purposes.

In this chapter, we'll deal with the following topics:

- **Preparing our app for production**, where we'll learn some useful optimization strategies to move our app into a production folder
- **Windows deployment**, where we'll see how we can deploy our `HealthCheck` web application to a Windows Server 2019 virtual machine and publish it over the web using **Internet Information Services** (**IIS**) with the new in-process hosting model
- **Linux deployment**, where we'll deploy our `WorldCities` web application to a Linux CentOS 8 virtual machine and publish it over the web using the Kestrel web server over an Nginx-based proxy
- **Azure App Service deployment**, where we'll deploy our `HealthCheck` web application to an MS Azure web app fully managed instance without the need to set up a VM-based infrastructure.

The ultimate goal of this long and ambitious chapter is to learn the requisite tools and techniques to deploy an ASP.NET Core and Angular app on a production Windows and/or Linux hosting server, as well as within a cloud-based environment: let's embark upon this final effort!

Technical requirements

In this chapter, we're going to need all the previous technical requirements listed in *Chapters 1-11*, together with the following additional packages.

For Windows deployment:

- **Internet Information Services** (**IIS**) (Windows Server)
- **ASP.NET Core Runtime 5 and Windows Hosting Bundle Installer for Win64** (ASP.NET official website)

For Linux deployment:

- **ASP.NET Core Runtime 5 for Linux** (YUM package manager)
- **.NET 5 CLR for Linux** (YUM package manager)
- **Nginx HTTP server** (YUM package manager)

As always, it's advisable to avoid installing them straight away: we're going to bring them in over the course of the chapter to better contextualize their purpose within our project.

The code files for this chapter can be found here: `https://github.com/PacktPublishing/ASP.NET-Core-5-and-Angular/tree/main/Chapter_12`

Getting ready for production

In this section, we'll see how we can further refine our apps' source code in order to get them ready for production usage. We'll mostly deal with server-side and client-side caching, environment configuration, and so on. While we're there, we'll take the chance to learn some useful production optimization tips offered by our *front-end* and *back-end* frameworks.

More specifically, we're going to cover the following:

- **ASP.NET Core deployment tips**, where we'll learn how our *back-end* has been optimized for production usage
- **Angular deployment tips**, where we'll review some strategies used by the Visual Studio template to optimize the *front-end* production building phase

Let's get to work!

ASP.NET Core deployment tips

As we most likely already know, ASP.NET Core allows developers to adjust an application's behavior across many environments: the most common of these are development, staging, and production environments. The currently active environment is identified at runtime by checking an environment variable that can be configured and modified from the project's configuration files.

This variable is called ASPNETCORE_ENVIRONMENT and, while we're running our project on Visual Studio, it can be set by using the /Properties/launchSettings.json file, which controls various settings that will be applied to our local development machine upon our web application's launch.

The launchSettings.json file

If we take a look at the launchSettings.json file, we can see that it contains some specific settings for each execution profile of our app. To look at a quick example of this, here are the contents of the HealthCheck project's /Properties/launchSettings.json file:

```
{
  "iisSettings": {
    "windowsAuthentication": false,
    "anonymousAuthentication": true,
    "iisExpress": {
      "applicationUrl": "http://localhost:53406",
      "sslPort": 44334
    }
  },
  "profiles": {
    "IIS Express": {
      "commandName": "IISExpress",
      "launchBrowser": true,
      "environmentVariables": {
        "ASPNETCORE_ENVIRONMENT": "Development"
      }
    },
    "HealthCheck": {
      "commandName": "Project",
      "launchBrowser": true,
      "applicationUrl":
        "https://localhost:5001;http://localhost:5000",
      "environmentVariables": {
        "ASPNETCORE_ENVIRONMENT": "Development"
      }
    }
  }
}
```

As we can see, there are two execution profiles currently set:

- **The IIS Express profile**, which is related to the IIS Express HTTP server. This profile will be used whenever we launch our project in debug mode, which we can do by pressing *F5* (unless we changed the default debugging behavior)

> The 53046 local port might vary: it's automatically set to a random available port.

- **The HealthCheck profile**, which is related to the application itself. This profile will be used whenever we launch our app using the .NET Core CLI (in other words, the `dotnet run` console command)

For both of them, the `ASPNETCORE_ENVIRONMENT` variable is currently set to the `Development` value, meaning that we're always going to run our apps in *development* mode from Visual Studio, unless we change these values.

Development, staging, and production environments

How do the different environments affect our web application's behavior?

Right after our web application starts, ASP.NET Core reads the `ASPNETCORE_ENVIRONMENT` environment variable and stores its value in the `EnvironmentName` property of our app's `IWebHostEnvironment` instance, which, as its name suggests, provides information about the web hosting environment our application is running in. Once set, this variable can be used programmatically - either directly or with some helper methods - to determine our app's behavior at any moment of our *back-end* life cycle.

We've already seen these methods in action in the `Startup` class of our .NET Core applications—for example, here's what we can find in the `HealthCheck` `Startup.cs` source code:

```
// ...

if (env.IsDevelopment())
{
    app.UseDeveloperExceptionPage();
}
else
{
    app.UseExceptionHandler("/Error");
    // The default HSTS value is 30 days. You may want to change this
    // for production scenarios, see https://aka.ms/aspnetcore-hsts.
    app.UseHsts();
}

// ...
```

In the preceding lines, part of the `Startup` class's `Configure()` method, we're telling our app to conditionally use the following:

- The developer exception pages when running in a development environment
- A custom `ExceptionHandler` middleware on staging and production environments

This basically means that, whenever our ASP.NET Core app crashes, it will conditionally show the following:

- Low-level/detailed error messages (such as the exception info and the stack trace) to developers
- High-level/generic unavailability messages to end users

> The developer exception page includes a detailed series of useful information about the exception and the request, such as exceptions and inner exceptions, stack traces, query string parameters, cookies, and HTTP headers.
>
> For additional information about this, and error handling in ASP.NET Core in general, visit the following URL: `https://docs.microsoft.com/en-us/aspnet/core/fundamentals/error-handling`

From this, we can also see how our app, when executed in a production environment, will set up a 30-day **HTTP Strict Transport Security** (**HSTS**) max-age header value. Such behavior, which complies with some good HTTP security practices and is therefore highly desirable when the app is publicly facing the web, is often useless (and can be a hindrance) during debugging, which is the reason why it's not being set.

A few lines beneath this, we can find the following code:

```
// ...

app.UseSpa(spa =>
{
    // To learn more about options for serving an Angular SPA from ASP.NET Core,
    // see https://go.microsoft.com/fwlink/?linkid=864501

    spa.Options.SourcePath = "ClientApp";

    if (env.IsDevelopment())
    {
        spa.UseAngularCliServer(npmScript: "start");
    }
});

// ...
```

This is another key structural point of our app, which we briefly mentioned back in *Chapter 2*, *Looking Around*, when we were given our first look at ASP.NET Core's `Startup` class and played around with the NG-generated app.

The `UseAngularCliServer()` method will pass through all the requests addressed to the Angular app to an in-memory instance of the Angular CLI server (`ng serve`). Such an approach is definitely the way to go for most development scenarios since it will ensure that our app will serve up-to-date CLI-built resources; however, it's not that great for production scenarios, where those files are not subject to changes and could be served using the static files generated by the Angular CLI (`ng build`) without wasting our server's CPU and memory resources.

Rule(s) of thumb

Now that we've seen how to programmatically determine our web app's execution environment and make our HTTP pipeline act accordingly, we should learn how to properly adopt, and adapt, these conditional practices to best suit those environments.

Since the development environment is only available to developers, it should always favor debugging capabilities over performance. Therefore, it should avoid caching, use in-memory loading strategies to quickly respond to changes, and emit as much diagnostic information as possible (logs, exceptions, and so on) to help the developers promptly understand what's happening.

> If we remember what we said in *Chapter 9, ASP.NET Core and Angular Unit Testing*, regarding **Test-Driven Development** (**TDD**), we should easily understand how the development environment is where the TDD practice mostly shines.

Conversely, while addressing a production environment, a good way to make these decisions is by applying the following rules of thumb:

- **Turn on caching whenever possible** in order to save resources and increase performance
- **Ensure that all the client-side resources** (JavaScript, CSS files, and so on) are bundled, minified, and potentially served from a **Content Delivery Network** (**CDN**)
- **Turn off diagnostic error pages** and/or replace them with friendly, human-readable error pages instead
- **Enable production logging and monitoring** using application performance management tools or other real-time monitoring, auditing, and watchdog strategies
- **Implement the best security practices** made available by the frameworks
- **Implement Open Web Application Security Project** (**OWASP**) methodologies for software development, as well as network, firewall, and server configurations

These are the general guidelines (or good practices) that we should always take into serious consideration while refining the *back-end* part of our web applications for production usage.

What about the staging environment? As a matter of fact, it's mostly used as a preproduction environment where we can perform (or make some testers perform) our *front-end* testing before giving the OK for production deployment. Ideally, its physical characteristics should mirror that of production, so that any issues that may arise in production occur first in the staging environment, where they can be addressed without impacting users.

> Again, if we think back to our behavior-driven development analysis back in *Chapter 9, ASP.NET Core and Angular Unit Testing*, we can definitely acknowledge that the staging environment would be the perfect place to test for the expected behavior of any newly added feature of our apps before releasing them into production.

Setting the environment in production

What happens to the `ASPNETCORE_ENVIRONMENT` variable when we publish our web application for production deployment, just like we did during *Chapter 11, Progressive Web Apps*, when we configured a folder-based publish profile for our `HealthCheck` and `WorldCities` apps?

As we can see by looking inside those folders, the `launchSettings.json` file cannot be found there, since it is not being published. That is certainly to be expected, since it's only meant to be used by Visual Studio and other local development tools.

Whenever we host the app on a production server, we'll have to manually set that value using one of the following approaches:

- A dedicated **environment variable** with the same name
- Specific **platform settings**
- A **command-line** switch

These methods strongly depend on the server's operating system. In the upcoming sections, we'll see how we can perform them on Windows and Linux servers.

> It's important to remember that the environment, once set, can't be changed while the web app is running.

If no environment-related setting is found, the web app will always use the production value as the default, this being the most conservative choice for performance and security, since most debugging features and diagnostic messages will be disabled.

Conversely, if the environment is set multiple times (such as by the environment variable and then a command-line switch), the app will use the last environment setting read, thereby following a cascading rule.

.NET 5 deployment modes

In *Chapter 11*, *Progressive Web Apps*, when we created our first publish profile to deploy our app to a local folder, we didn't change the **deployment mode** settings, leaving them as they were. Truth be told, we did that because it wouldn't have made any difference, since we used that build just to steal some **progressive web app** (**PWA**)-related generated files and used them to register our service worker from a standard Visual Studio debug run.

However, the .NET 5 deployment mode is a very important configuration feature that we definitely need to understand in order to make the right choice whenever we have to deploy our application for production usage.

Let's now try to shed some light on the three different types of deployments available from Visual Studio for .NET 5 applications:

- **Framework-dependent deployment** (**FDD**): As the name implies, such a deployment mode requires the presence of the .NET 5 framework, which must be installed and available on the target system; in other words, we'll build a portable .NET 5 application as long as the hosting server supports it.
- **Self-contained deployment** (**SCD**): This deployment mode doesn't rely on the presence of .NET 5 components on the target system. All components, including the .NET 5 libraries and runtime, will be included in the production build. If the hosting server supports .NET 5, the app will run in isolated mode, separating itself from other .NET 5 applications. SCD builds will include an executable file (a `.exe` file on Windows platforms) as well as a `.dll` file containing the application's runtime.
- **Framework-dependent executable** (**FDE**): This deployment mode will produce an executable file that will run on the hosting server, which must have the .NET 5 and ASP.NET Core runtimes installed. Therefore, such a mode is rather similar to FDD since both of them are framework-dependent.

Let's now try to understand the pros and cons of each deployment mode.

Framework-dependent deployment

Using the FDD mode grants the developer a number of advantages, including the following:

- **Platform independence**: There's no need to define the target operating system since the .NET 5 runtime installed on the hosting server will seamlessly handle the app's execution, regardless of its platform.
- **Small package size**: The deployment bundle will be small since it will only contain the app's runtime and the third-party dependencies. .NET 5 itself won't be there since we expect it to already be present on the target machine by design.
- **Latest version**: As per its default settings, FDD will always use the latest serviced runtime installed on the target system, with all the latest security patches.
- **Better performance in multihosting scenarios**: If the hosting server has multiple .NET 5 apps installed, the shared resources will enable us to save some storage space and, most importantly, obtain reduced memory usage.

However, this deployment mode also has a number of weaknesses, including the following:

- **Reduced compatibility**: Our app will require a .NET 5 runtime with a version compatible with the one used by our app (or later). If the hosting server is stuck to a previous version, our app won't be able to run.
- **Stability issues**: If the .NET 5 runtime and/or libraries were to change their behavior (in other words, if they had breaking changes or reduced compatibility for security or licensing reasons), our app will potentially be impacted by these changes as well.

Self-contained deployment

Using the SCD mode has two big advantages that could easily outweigh the disadvantages regarding some specific scenarios:

- **Full control over the published .NET version**, regardless of what is installed on the hosting server (or what will happen to it in the future).
- **No compatibility issues**, since all the requisite libraries are provided within the bundle.

Unfortunately, there are also some relevant disadvantages:

- **Platform dependency**: Being able to provide the runtime with the production package requires the developer to select the target building platforms in advance.
- **Increased bundle size**: The additional presence of the runtime resources will definitely take its toll in terms of disk space requirements. This can be a heavy hit if we plan to deploy multiple SCD .NET Core apps to a single hosting server, as each one of them will require a significant amount of disk space.

The self-contained deployment bundle size issue was addressed in .NET Core 3.0 with the introduction of the *App Trimming* feature (also called **assembly linker**), which basically trims the unused assemblies. This approach has been further improved in .NET 5, where assemblies get "cracked open" and purged from the types and members not used by the application, further reducing the size.

> For further info about the .NET 5 *App Trimming* feature, check out the following post by Sam Spencer (Program Manager, .NET Core team): `https://devblogs.microsoft.com/dotnet/app-trimming-in-net-5/`

Framework-dependent executable

The FDE deployment mode was introduced in .NET Core 2.2 and, starting from version 3.0, is the default mode for the basic `dotnet publish` command (if no options are specified). This new approach has the following advantages:

- **Small package size**, **latest version**, and **better performance in multihosting scenarios**, just like FDD mode

- **Easy to run**: The deployed executable can be directly launched and executed, without having to invoke the **dotnet** CLI

This approach also has some disadvantages:

- **Reduced compatibility**: Just like FDD, the app requires an ASP.NET Core runtime with a version compatible with the one used by our app (or later)
- **Stability issues**: Again, if the ASP.NET Core runtime and/or libraries were to change their behavior, those changes could break the app or alter its behavior
- **Platform dependency**: As the app is an executable file, it must be published for each different target platform

As we can easily guess, all of these three deployment modes can either be good or bad, depending on a number of factors, such as how much control we have over the deployment server, how many ASP.NET Core apps we plan to publish, and the target system's hardware and software capabilities.

As a general rule, as long as we have the rights to install and update system packages on the deployment server, the FDD modes should work well; conversely, if we host our apps on a cloud-hosting provider that doesn't have our desired .NET runtime, SCD would arguably be the most logical choice. The available disk space and memory size will also play a major role, especially if we plan to publish multiple apps.

> As a matter of fact, the requirement of being able to manually install and update the packages on the server should no longer be a hindrance since all .NET updates will now be released through the regular Microsoft Update channel, as explained in the following post by Jamshed Damkewala (Principal Engineering Manager, .NET): `https://devblogs.microsoft.com/dotnet/net-core-updates-coming-to-microsoft-update/`

That said, we're going to use the FDD (default) deployment mode, since our current scenario requires the publication of two different apps that share the same ASP.NET Core runtime version on the same server.

Angular deployment tips

Let's now turn our gaze to the *front-end* to properly understand how the Visual Studio template that we've used to build our two apps handles Angular's production deployment tasks.

It goes without saying that the same good practices we've determined for the *back-end* retain their value at the *front-end* as well, as we'll see in a short while. In other words, performance and security will still be the principal goals in this regard.

Let's now try to understand how the Angular CLI, powered by Ivy, the new compilation and rendering pipeline, handles our applications' publishing and deployment tasks.

ng serve, ng build, and the package.json file

As we should already know, whenever we hit *F5* in Visual Studio, our Angular app is being served using an in-memory instance of the Angular CLI server. Such a server is launched by Visual Studio using the `ng serve` command.

If we take a look at the Visual Studio **Output** window during the initial debug phase, right before the web browser kicks in, we can see it clearly in the following screenshot:

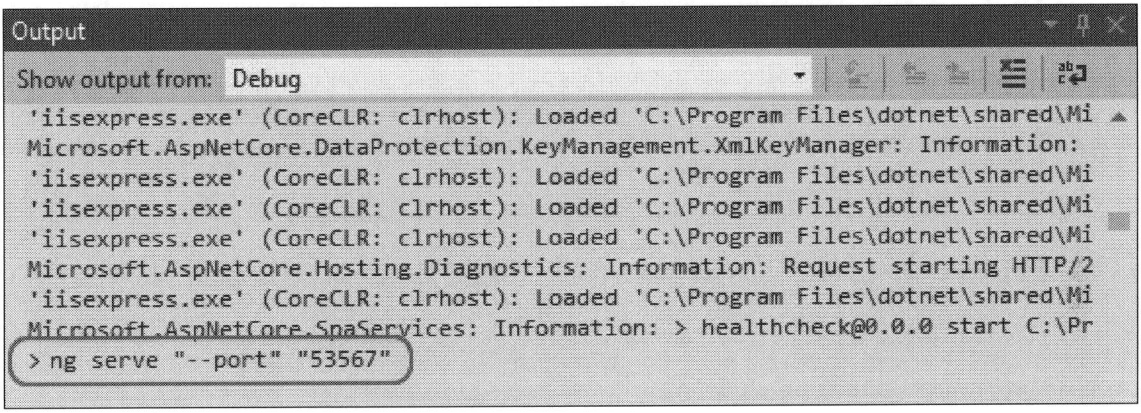

Figure 12.1: Visual Studio Output window during the initial debug phase

Conversely, when we deploy our app for production using a publish profile, Visual Studio uses the `ng build` command with the `--prod` flag instead:

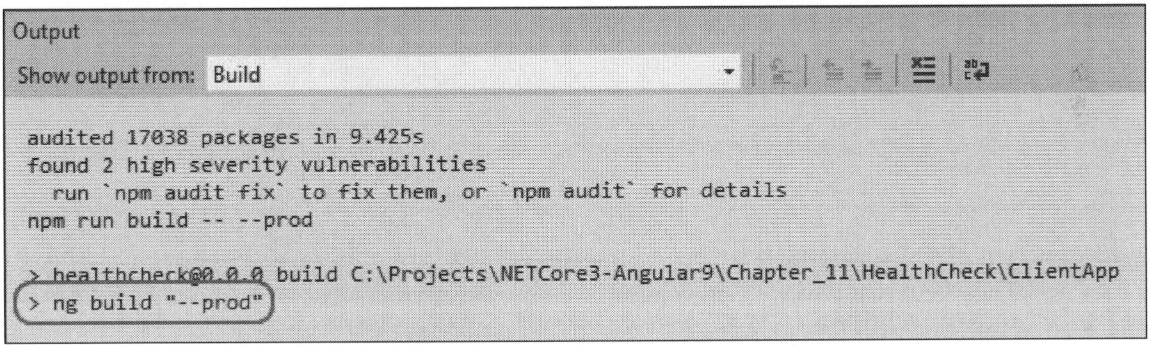

Figure 12.2: Visual Studio Output window during the deployment phase

Both commands can be found in the `/ClientApp/package.json` file, where we can modify or configure them to suit our needs, even if the default settings are already good for both development and production to deploy.

The `--prod` flag that Visual Studio adds to the `ng build` command activates a number of useful optimization features, including the following:

- **Ahead-of-time** (**AOT**) **compilation**: This converts the HTML and TypeScript code into efficient JavaScript code in order to provide a faster rendering in the browser; the default mode (used for `ng serve` and when the `--prod` flag is not enabled), called **just-in-time** (**JIT**) compilation, compiles the app in the browser at runtime and is, therefore, a much slower and less optimized alternative.
- **Production mode**: This makes the app run faster by disabling some development-specific checks, such as the dual change detection cycles.
- **Bundling**: This concatenates the various app and third-party files (NPM packages) into a few bundles.
- **Minification**: This removes whitespaces, comments, optional tokens, and any unnecessary characters and artifacts to HTML, JavaScript, and CSS files.
- **Uglification**: This internally rewrites the JavaScript code to shorten the variable and function names; this will also make our published code less readable, which is often a good thing since it will shield our app against malicious reverse-engineering attempts.
- **Dead code purging**: This removes any unreferenced modules and/or unused code files, snippets, or sections.

As we can see, all of the preceding features aim to increase the performance and security capabilities of our production build.

Differential loading

Another nice feature worth mentioning is differential loading, which was introduced in Angular 8. We haven't added it to the preceding `--prod` switch optimization benefits list because it's there by default, and is therefore not limited to that switch's usage.

Differential loading is Angular's way of overcoming the compatibility issues between the various browsers, especially the older ones; in other words, those that are still based on older versions of JavaScript.

As we can see by looking at the `/ClientApp/tsconfig.json` file, our TypeScript code will be transpiled and bundled into *ES2015*, also known as **ECMAScript 2015**, **ECMAScript version 6**, or **ES6**, a JavaScript syntax that is compatible with the vast majority of modern browsers. However, there are still a number of users with older clients, such as old desktop, laptop, and/or mobile devices, that are still bound to *ES5* and earlier versions.

To work around this, previous versions of Angular, as well as most other *front-end* frameworks, provided a number of support libraries (known as **polyfills**) that would have conditionally implemented the missing features for those browsers that didn't natively support them. Unfortunately, such a workaround massively increased the production bundle, thereby resulting in a performance hit for all users, including those using modern browsers that didn't need those polyfills to begin with.

Differential loading solves this issue by generating two separate bundle sets during the build phase:

- The first bundle contains the app's code, which has been transpiled, minified, and uglified using a modern ES2015 syntax. This bundle ships fewer polyfills and therefore results in a much smaller size.
- The second bundle contains the same code transpiled in the old ES5 syntax, along with all the necessary polyfills. Needless to say, this bundle is much bigger than the first one in terms of file size, but properly supports older browsers.

The differential loading feature can be configured by altering two files:

- The `/ClientApp/browserlist` file, which lists the minimum browsers supported by our application
- The `/ClientApp/tsconfig.json` file, which determines the ECMAScript target version that the code is compiled to

By taking both of these settings into consideration, the Angular CLI will automatically determine whether or not to enable the differential loading functionality.

In our specific scenario, such a feature is enabled, as we can see by looking at the generated `index.html` file's `<body>` section within our app's production deploy folder (the relevant parts are highlighted):

```
<!-- ... -->

<body>
  <app-root>Loading...</app-root>
  <script src="runtime-es2015.e59a6cd8f1b6ab0c3f29.js"
   type="module"></script>
  <script src="runtime-es5.e59a6cd8f1b6ab0c3f29.js" nomodule
   defer></script>
  <script src="polyfills-es5.079443d8bcab7d711023.js" nomodule
   defer></script>
  <script src="polyfills-es2015.58725a5910daef768ca8.js"
   type="module"></script>
  <script src="main-es2015.fc7dc31b264662448f17.js"
   type="module"></script>
  <script src="main-es5.fc7dc31b264662448f17.js" nomodule
   defer></script>
</body>

<!-- ... -->
```

This strategy is very effective since it will allow our Angular apps to support multiple browsers without forcing our *modern* users to retrieve all the unnecessary bundles.

The angular.json configuration file

The most important difference between `npm serve` and `npm build` is that the latter is the only command that actually writes the build-generated artifacts to the output folder: those files are built using the webpack build tool, which can be configured using the `/ClientApp/src/angular.json` configuration file.

The output folder is also set within that file, more precisely, in the **projects** | **[projectName]** | **architect** | **build** | **options** | **outputPath** section. In our sample apps, it's the `dist` folder, meaning that all the build-generated artifacts will be deployed in the `/ClientApp/dist/` folder.

Automatic deployment

Angular 8.3.0 introduced the new `ng deploy` command, which can be used to deploy the Angular app to one of the available production platforms thanks to some third-party builders that can be installed using `ng add`.

Here's a list of the supported builders at the time of writing:

- `@angular/fire` (Firebase)
- `@azure/ng-deploy` (MS Azure)
- `@zeit/ng-deploy` (ZEIT Now)
- `@netlify-builder/deploy` (Netlify)
- `angular-cli-ghpages` (GitHub Pages)
- `ngx-deploy-npm` (NPM)

Although the `ng deploy` CLI option is not yet supported by Visual Studio, it can be very useful to instantly deploy our app using some presets that can be configured in the *deploy* section of the `angular.json` file. Such a section isn't available in the `angular.json` file of our projects, but it will be automatically added as soon as one of the preceding builders is installed using the `ng add` CLI command (with its corresponding default settings).

CORS policy

We've already talked about **Cross-Origin Resource Sharing** (**CORS**) in *Chapter 11, Progressive Web Apps*, when we changed the `ng-connection-service` `heartbeatUrl` default settings by pinging a local `.txt` file hosted by us instead of a third-party URL. Thanks to that modification, neither of our apps will face CORS errors because they will only make HTTP requests to our ASP.NET Core *back-end,* which is likely hosted within the same server and so will have the same IP address/hostname.

However, we might want to either move the *back-end* in the future or add some additional HTTP calls to other remote services (multiple *back-end* systems and/or stores). If we plan to do that, then there's nothing we can do at the client-side level. We would need to implement a suitable CORS policy to the destination server instead.

> For additional information regarding CORS and instructions on how to enable it for specific servers, go to: `https://enable-cors.org`

Luckily enough, we won't need to implement any CORS-specific policy for the Windows, Linux, and Azure deployment scenarios that we're about to introduce.

Windows deployment

In this section, we'll learn how to deploy our `HealthCheck` web application on a Windows 2019 Datacenter edition server hosted on MS Azure.

Here's what we're going to do:

- **Create a new VM on MS Azure** using the Windows 2019 Datacenter Edition template and configure it to accept inbound calls to TCP ports `3389` (for Remote Desktop), `80` (for HTTP), and `443` (for HTTPS)
- **Configure the VM** by downloading and/or installing all the necessary services and runtimes to host the `HealthCheck` app
- **Publish the HealthCheck app** to the web server we've just set up
- **Test the HealthCheck app** from a remote client

Let's get to work!

> In this deployment example, we're going to set up a brand-new VM on the MS Azure platform, which requires some additional work; those users who already have a production-ready Windows server should skip the sections related to the VM setup and go directly to the publishing topics.

Creating a Windows Server VM on MS Azure

If we remember our journey through MS Azure in *Chapter 4, Data Model with Entity Framework Core*, when we deployed an SQL database there, we should already be prepared for what we're going to do:

- **Access the MS Azure portal**
- **Add and configure a new VM**
- **Set the inbound security rules** to access the VM from the internet

Let's do this.

Accessing the MS Azure portal

As usual, let's start by visiting the following URL, which will bring us to the MS Azure website: `https://azure.microsoft.com/`

Again, we can either log in using an already-existing MS Azure account or create a new one (possibly taking the chance to use the free 30-day trial, if we haven't used it already).

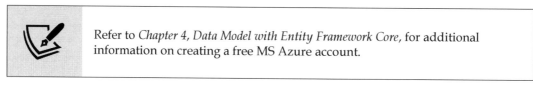

> Refer to *Chapter 4, Data Model with Entity Framework Core*, for additional information on creating a free MS Azure account.

As soon as we have created the account, we can go to `https://portal.azure.com/` to access the MS Azure administration portal, where we can create our new VM.

Adding and configuring a new VM

Once logged in, click on the **Virtual machines** icon (refer to the following screenshot):

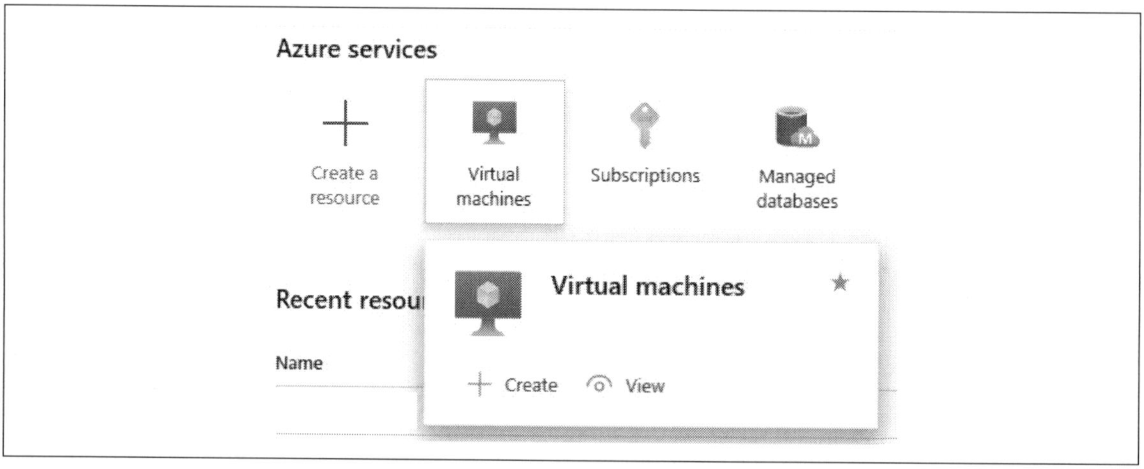

Figure 12.3: Clicking on the Virtual machines icon

From the next page, click **Add** (near the top-left corner of the page) to access the **Create a virtual machine** panel.

The **Create a virtual machine** panel is basically a detailed wizard that allows us to configure a new VM from scratch. The various configuration settings are split into a number of panels, each one dedicated to a specific set of capabilities, as shown in the following screenshot:

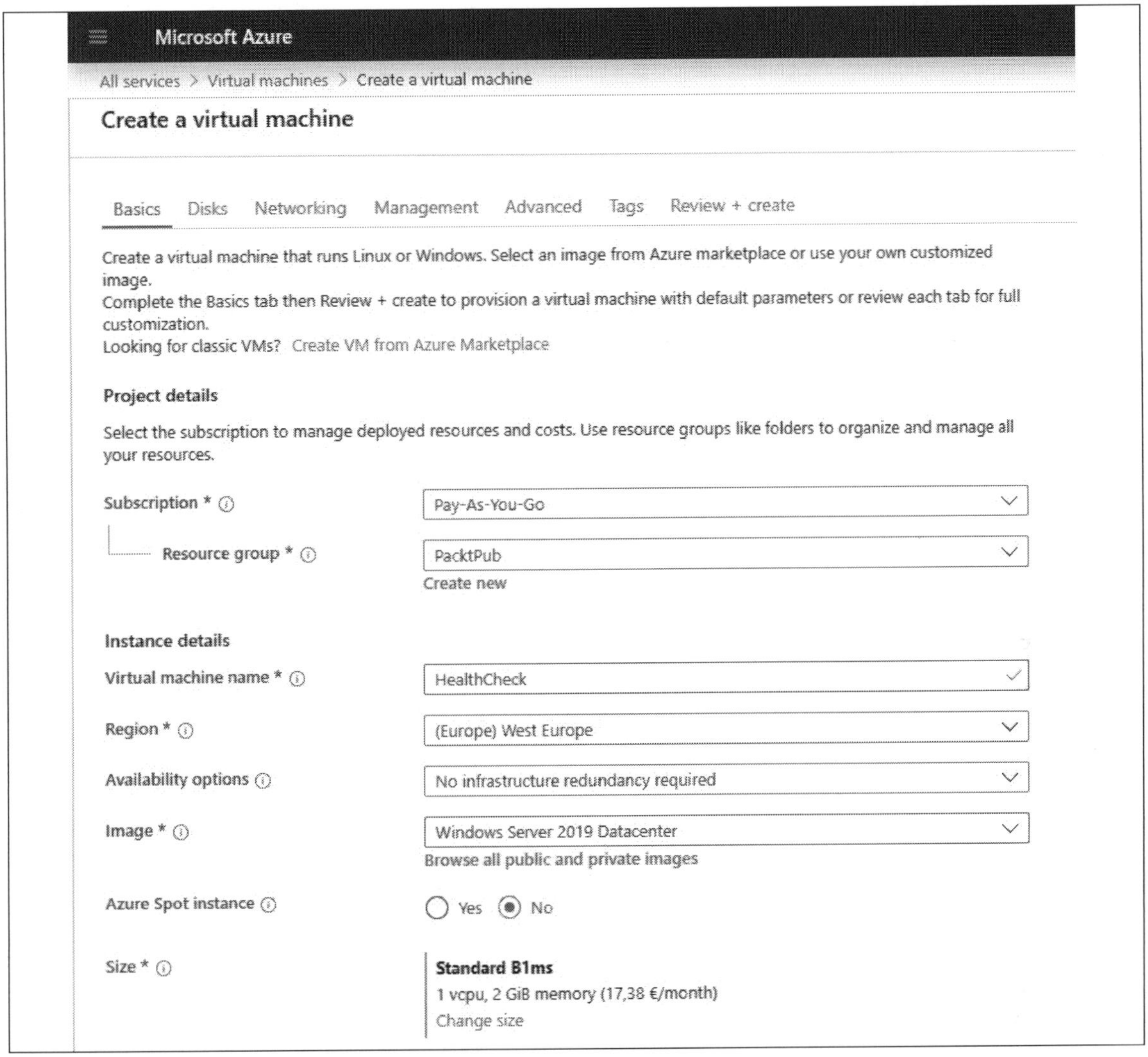

Figure 12.4: The Create a virtual machine panel

Here's a brief summary of the various settings panels:

- **Basics**: Subscription type, VM name, deployment region, image, login credentials, and so on
- **Disks**: The number and capacity of HDDs/SDDs to provide the VM with
- **Networking**: Network-related configuration settings
- **Management**: Monitoring features, auto-shutdown capabilities, backup, and more
- **Advanced**: Additional configuration, agents, scripts, extensions, and the like
- **Tags**: These allow some name-value pairs that can be useful in categorizing the various MS Azure resources to be set

In our current scenario, we just have to slightly modify the first four tabs, leaving the remaining ones as their default settings.

In the **Basics** tab:

- **Resource group**: Use the same resource group used for the SQL database (or create a new one).
- **Virtual machine name**: Use `HealthCheck`, `NET5-Angular11-Windows`, or any other suitable name.
- **Region**: Choose the region closest to our geographical position.
- **Availability options**: No infrastructure redundancy required.
- **Image**: In our example, we're going to use the Windows Server 2019 Datacenter default image; feel free to use it as well or pick another one.
- **Azure Spot instance**: Select **Yes** if we want to create the VM using the Azure Spot feature, which allows us to take advantage of Azure unused capacity at a significant cost saving. However, since these VMs can be evicted at any point in time when Azure needs the capacity back, we should only use this feature for short-term testing purposes: if we want to create a permanent, production-like VM, we should definitely choose **No** and create a standard pay-as-you-go machine.
- **Size**: **Standard B1ms (1 vCPU, 2 GiB memory)**. Feel free to choose a different size if we're willing to spend more: the B1ms is an entry-level machine featuring a very limited set of resources that will suffice for this deployment sample, but won't perform well in production.
- **Administrator account**: Select the **Password authentication** type, and then create a suitable username and password set. Remember to write these down in a secure place, since we'll definitely need these credentials to access our machine in a while.
- **Public inbound ports**: None (for the time being; we're going to set them up later on in a more secure way).

In the **Disk** tab:

- **OS disk type**: Select **Standard HDD**; this is the cheapest available choice
- **Data disks**: Create a new **Standard HDD** (or **Premium SSD**, if we're willing to pay some extra bucks) disk for the OS, with no additional data disks

In the **Network** tab:

- **Virtual Network**: Select the same **VNet** used for the SQL database (or create a new one)

In the **Management** tab:

- **Monitoring** | **Boot diagnostics**: `Off`

> For further info regarding the Azure Spot feature, read the following article: `https://docs.microsoft.com/en-us/azure/virtual-machines/spot-vms`

Once done, click the **Review + create** button to review our configuration settings and initiate the VM deployment process.

At the end of the process, we should see a screen along the lines of the following:

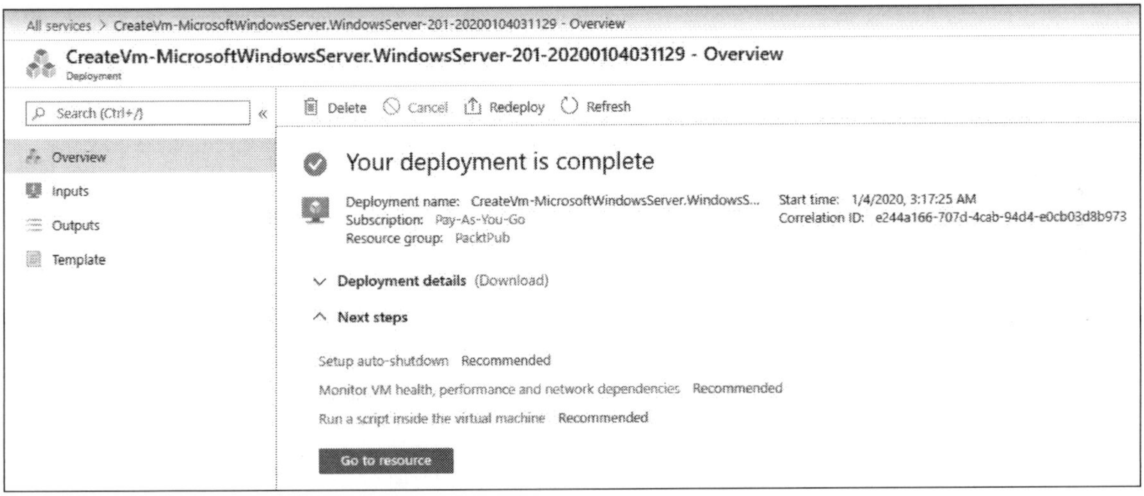

Figure 12.5: Deployment complete screen

From there, we can click the **Go to resource** button to access the VM **Overview** panel.

Configuring a DNS name label

Now we have the chance to add a DNS name label to our VM, which will be used to generate a unique fifth-level domain name in addition to its unique numeric IP address.

To do this, locate the **DNS Name** label in the virtual machine's **Overview** panel and click on the **Configure** link next to it, as shown in the following screenshot:

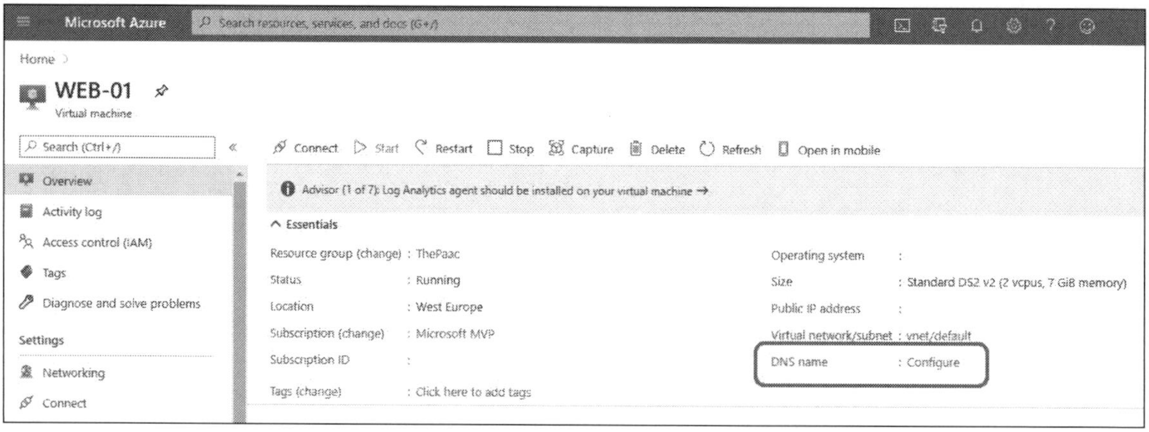

Figure 12.6: Configuring a DNS name label

Once generated, the DNS name will look like this: `your-chosen-name.westeurope.cloudapp.azure.com`

> The DNS name label is basically an A record that will grant a "human-readable" public endpoint to your VM server. It goes without saying that the DNS name must be unique within the chosen Azure region.

Configuring the DNS name label and getting the DNS name can be useful if we don't have a domain name and/or if we want to access our web application from the web without having to configure anything on our end (such as a host mapping to the VM's IP address or something like that). If we've configured a DNS name, or we have our own domain name we want to use, we should use that hostname instead of the `healthcheck.io` sample name mentioned in the following sections.

Setting the inbound security rules

Go to the **Settings** | **Networking** tab and take note of the machine's public IP address; we will need this in a short while. Once done, add the following inbound security rules:

- **TCP port 22**, so that we'll be able to access the machine using the Secure Shell protocol (also known as **SSH**)
- **TCP ports 80 and 443**, to access the HTTP server (and our `HealthCheck` web app) from the internet

For this deployment test, it's strongly advisable to restrict access to these inbound rules to a secure **source IP address** (or address range), which can be set to either our static IP address or our ISP's IP mask. Such a setting will ensure that no third parties will be able to attempt Remote Desktop access or visit our web application.

The following screenshot depicts the **Add inbound security rule** panel in the Azure VM portal, which will open when clicking on the corresponding button:

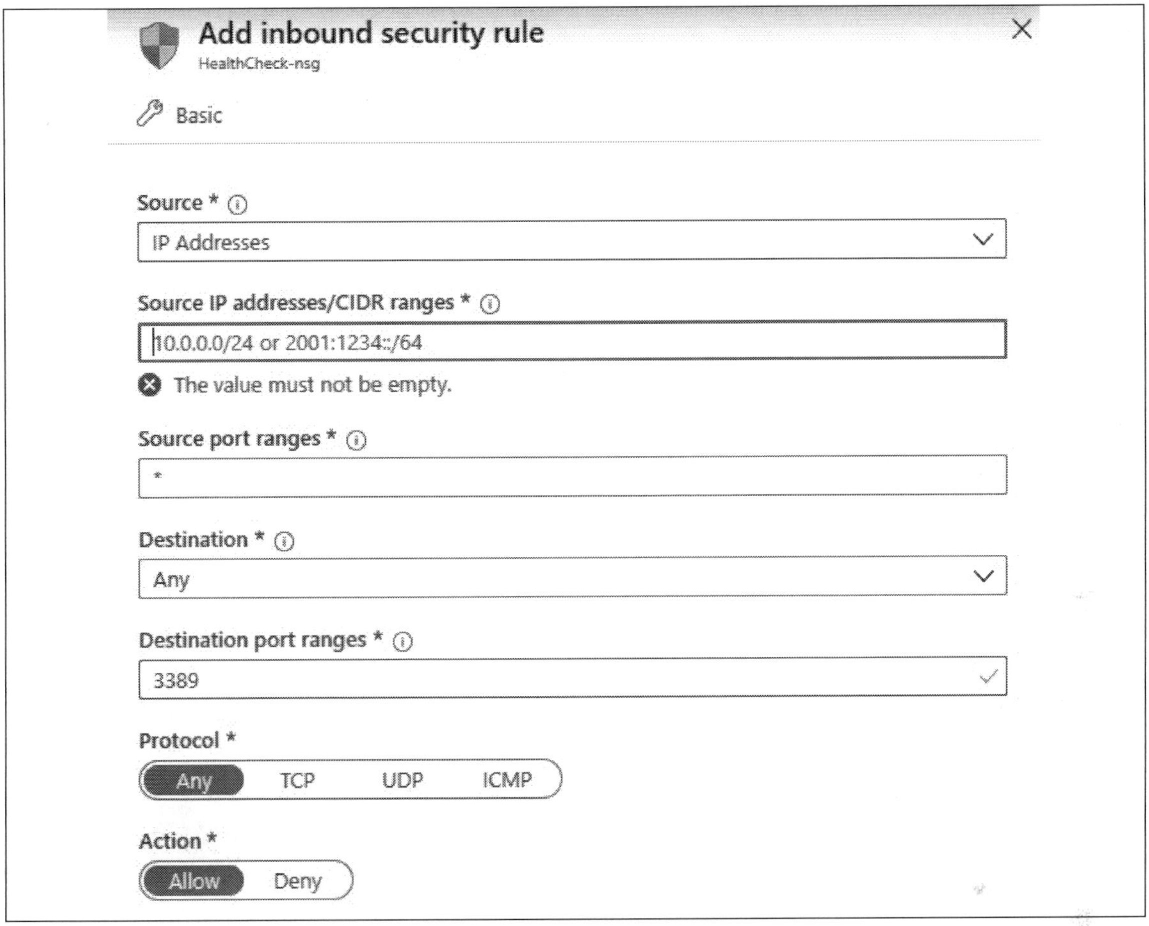

Figure 12.7: Add inbound security rule panel

Now, we should be able to access our new VM with a standard Remote Desktop connection from our development system.

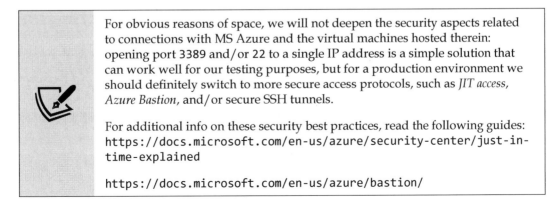

> For obvious reasons of space, we will not deepen the security aspects related to connections with MS Azure and the virtual machines hosted therein: opening port 3389 and/or 22 to a single IP address is a simple solution that can work well for our testing purposes, but for a production environment we should definitely switch to more secure access protocols, such as *JIT access*, *Azure Bastion*, and/or secure SSH tunnels.
>
> For additional info on these security best practices, read the following guides:
> `https://docs.microsoft.com/en-us/azure/security-center/just-in-time-explained`
>
> `https://docs.microsoft.com/en-us/azure/bastion/`

Configuring the VM

With TCP port `3389` open, we can launch the **Remote Desktop Connection** built-in tool from our local Windows-based development machine. Type in the public IP address of the Azure VM and click **Connect** to initiate an RDC session with our remote host:

Figure 12.8: The Remote Desktop Connection tool

If the inbound security rule has been properly configured, we should be able to connect to our new VM's desktop and set up our VM for serving our ASP.NET Core and Angular `HealthCheck` web application. Doing this requires a series of configuration tasks that will be described in the next sections.

The first step, which we'll be dealing with in the following section, will be installing **Internet Information Services** (**IIS**), a flexible, secure, and manageable HTTP server that we'll use to host our ASP.NET Core and Angular application over the web.

> For obvious reasons of space, we're not going to talk about IIS or explore its functionalities. For additional information regarding this, check out the following URL: `https://www.iis.net/overview`

Adding the IIS web server

Once connected via Remote Desktop, we can access **Control Panel** | **Program and Features** | **Turn Windows features on and off** (or the **Add Roles and Features Wizard** from the **Server Manager** dashboard) to install IIS on the VM, as shown in the following screenshot:

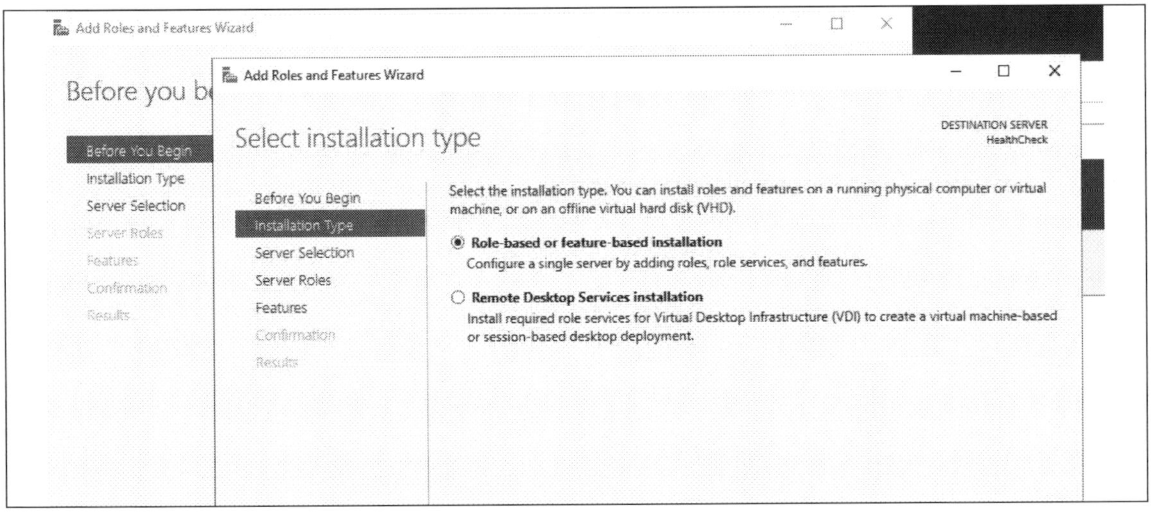

Figure 12.9: The Add Roles and Features Wizard

From the various roles available, select **Web Server (IIS)**, as shown in the following screenshot. Be sure that the **Include management tools** checkbox is checked, and then click **Add Features** to start installing it:

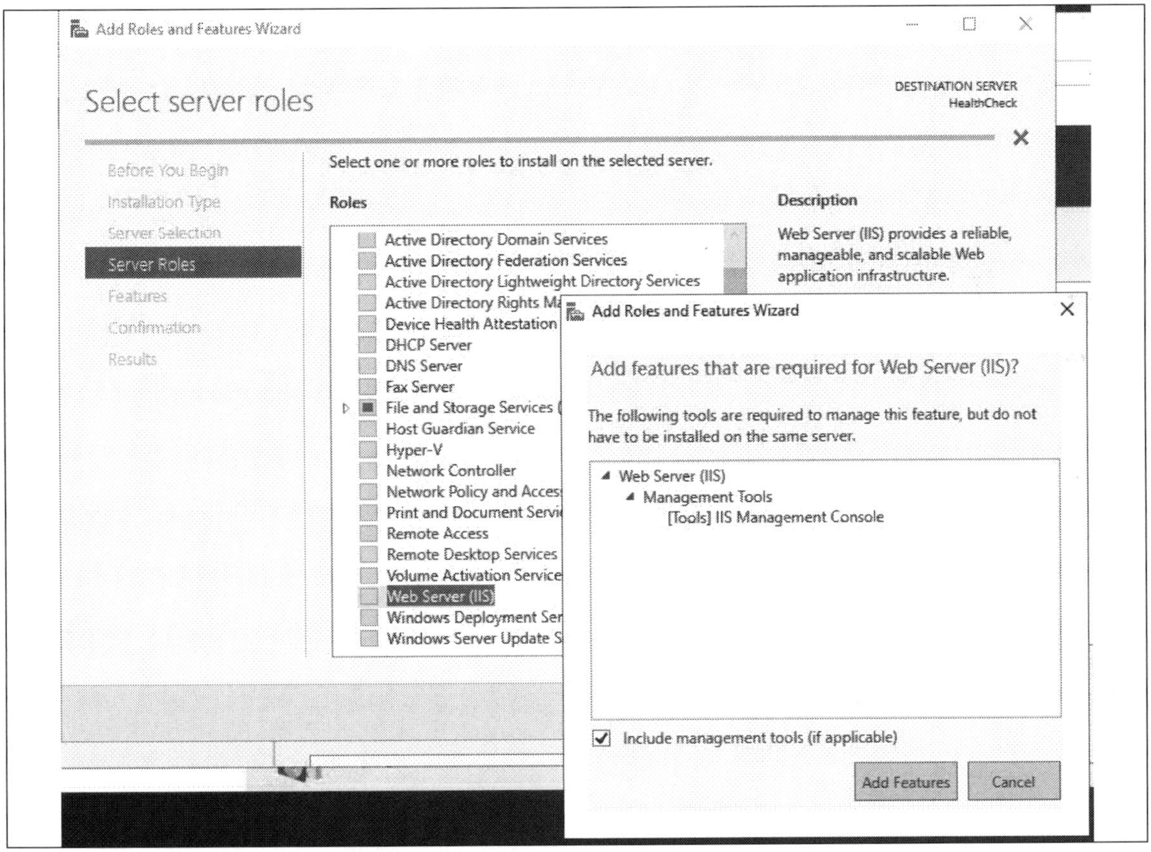

Figure 12.10: Selecting Web Server (IIS)

There's no need to change anything until the end of the installation phase; the default settings will work just fine for our deployment scenario.

Installing the ASP.NET Core Windows hosting bundle

Once IIS has been installed, we can proceed with downloading and installing the **ASP.NET Core runtime**.

> It's strongly advisable to install the .NET 5 runtime after installing IIS because the package bundle will perform some modifications to the IIS default configuration settings.
>
> To download the .NET 5 runtime, visit the following URL: `https://dotnet.microsoft.com/download/dotnet/5.0`

Be sure to pick the **ASP.NET Core 5.0.0 Runtime – Windows Hosting Bundle Installer** package for **Windows x64**, as shown in the following screenshot:

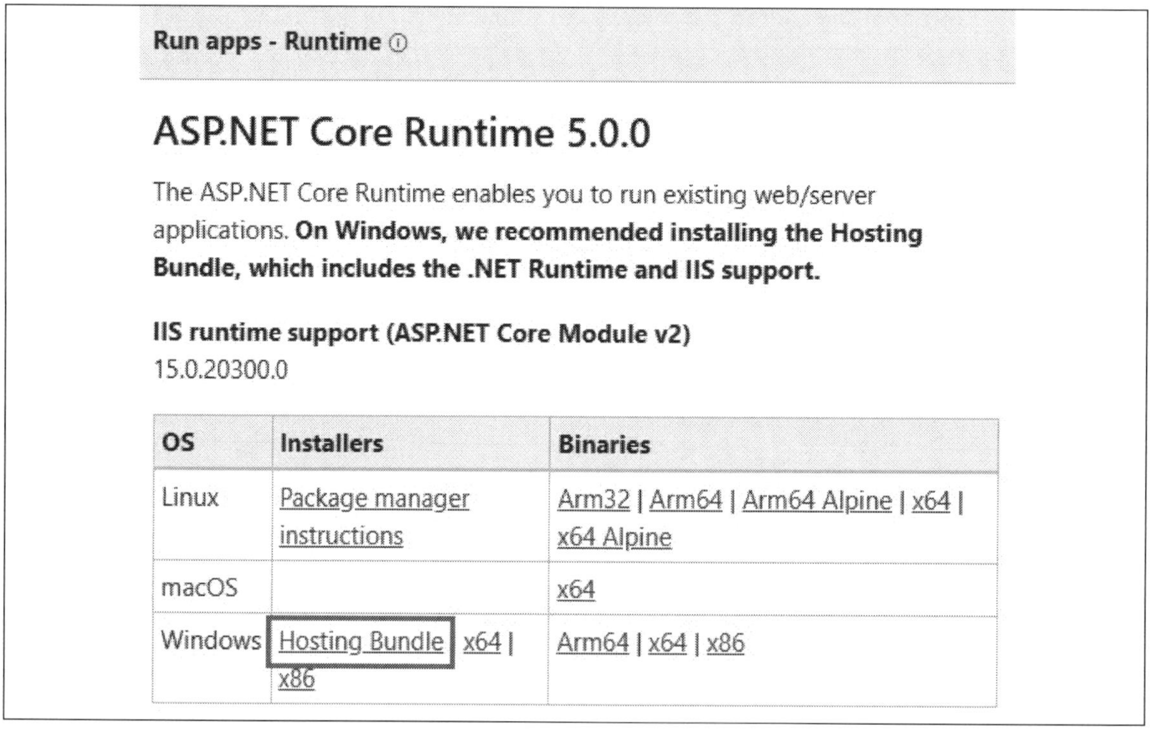

Run apps - Runtime
ASP.NET Core Runtime 5.0.0
The ASP.NET Core Runtime enables you to run existing web/server applications. On Windows, we recommended installing the Hosting Bundle, which includes the .NET Runtime and IIS support.
IIS runtime support (ASP.NET Core Module v2)
15.0.20300.0
OS
Installers
Binaries
Linux
Package manager instructions
Arm32 | Arm64 | Arm64 Alpine | x64 | x64 Alpine
macOS
x64
Windows
Hosting Bundle | x64 | x86
Arm64 | x64 | x86

Figure 12.11: Picking the Windows Hosting Bundle Installer package

A bundle such as this includes the .NET runtime, the ASP.NET Core runtime, and the ASP.NET Core IIS module, everything we need to run our ASP.NET Core and Angular app from our VM.

Restarting IIS following ASP.NET Core runtime installation

Once the ASP.NET Core runtime installation process is complete, it's strongly advisable to issue a stop/start command to restart the IIS service.

To do this, open a Command Prompt window with administrative rights and execute the following console commands:

```
> net stop w3svc /y
> net start w3svc
```

These commands will allow IIS to pick up a change to the system PATH made by the Windows hosting bundle installer.

Publishing and deploying the HealthCheck app

Now, we must find a way to publish the `HealthCheck` app and deploy it to our server. There are a number of alternative options to do this, including the following:

- Use our existing **Folder publish profile** and then copy the files to the web server somehow
- Install an FTP/FTPS server on our web server and then set up an **FTP publish profile**
- Use Visual Studio's **Azure Virtual Machine publish profile**

The third option is arguably the most obvious choice. However, the other alternatives are perfectly fine as well, as long as we can handle them properly. Let's go over all three of them now.

Folder publish profile

Since we created a **Folder publish profile** in *Chapter 11, Progressive Web Apps*, we're going to use it here as well.

If we want to create a new one, here's what we need to do:

1. Select the **Folder** option (or select the previous publishing profile)
2. Specify the path of the folder that will contain the published application
3. Click the **Create Profile** button to create the profile
4. Click the **Publish** button to deploy our `HealthCheck` app to the chosen local folder

> Visual Studio will suggest a path located within the application's `/bin/Release/` subfolder; we can either use this or choose another folder of our choice.

Otherwise, we can just click the **Publish** button for our existing profile to get the job done that way.

When the publishing task is complete, we can copy the whole `HealthCheck` folder inside the `C:\inetpub\` folder of the remote VM. A simple way to do this is by using the Remote Desktop resource-sharing feature, which allows our local HDD to be accessed from a remote instance.

FTP publish profile

If our web server can accept FTP (or FTPS) connections, then a suitable alternative way of publishing our project is to create an FTP-based *publish profile* that will automatically upload our web project to our web server using the FTP/FTPS protocol.

> If we don't want to use the built-in FTP server provided by Windows Server, we can install a third-party FTP server, such as FileZilla FTP Server, a great open source alternative that comes with full FTPS support. You can find FileZilla FTP Server at the following URL:
> `https://filezilla-project.org/download.php?type=server`

To make use of the FTP publish profile, we'll also need to open our VM's TCP port `21` (or another non-default port) by adding another inbound security rule, just like we did with ports `80`, `443`, and `3389`.

All we need to do is link the FTP destination folder to a new website project using IIS, and we'll be able to publish/update our website in a real-time fashion, as everything will be put online as soon as the publishing task is complete.

> As we said earlier, we're doing all this assuming that we have a web server accessible through FTP or that we're willing to install an FTP server. If that's not the case, we might as well skip this paragraph and use a different publishing profile, such as Azure Virtual Machine or Folder.

To set up the FTP publishing profile, select IIS, FTP, and the other icons, wait for the wizard-like modal window to appear, and then select the following options:

- **Publish method**: Select **FTP**.
- **Server**: Specify the FTP server URL (IP address or domain name).
- **Site path**: Insert the target folder from the FTP server root, such as `/HealthCheck/`. We can also avoid the slashes, as the tool will handle them automatically.
- **Passive Mode, Username, Password**: Set these values according to our FTP server settings and given credentials. Activate **Save Password** if we want to let Visual Studio store it, so we won't have to write it with each publishing attempt.

- **Destination URL**: This URL will be automatically launched as soon as the publishing task successfully ends using the default browser. It's often wise to set it to our web application's base domain, such as `www.our-website-url.com`, or to leave it empty.

Once done, click on the **Validate Connection** button to check the preceding settings and ensure that we're able to reach the server through FTP. If we aren't, it might be wise to perform a full-scale network check, looking for firewalls, proxies, antivirus, or other software that can prevent the FTP connection from being established.

Azure Virtual Machine publish profile

The **Azure Virtual Machine** publish profile is a great way to enforce the **continuous integration** and **continuous delivery** (**CI/CD**) DevOps pattern because it will either act as a build system (for producing packages and other build artifacts) or a release management system to deploy our changes.

To use this, select the **Azure Virtual Machine** option, click **Browse**, and then select the VM that we created a moment ago (see the following screenshot):

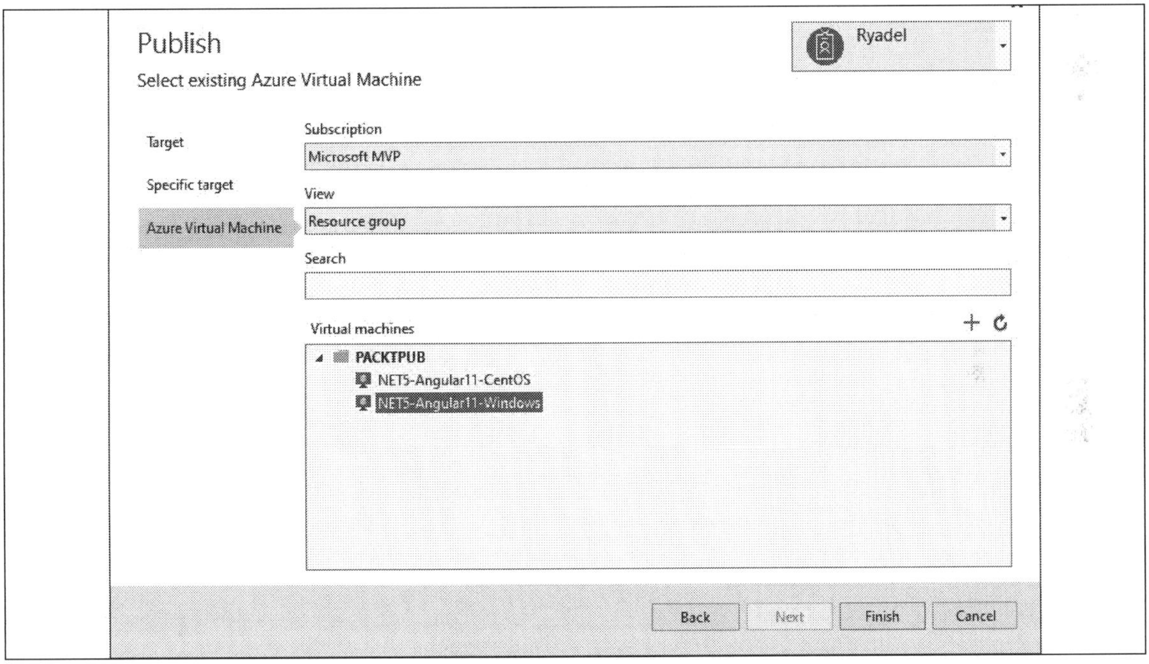

Figure 12.12: Selecting the newly created VM

However, in order to do this, we need to perform some additional configuration changes to our VM, including the following:

- Install the Web Deploy service tool (just like we did with IIS early on)
- Open the `22` and `8172` TCP ports, just like we did with `80`, `443`, and `3389` a while ago
- Set up a globally unique DNS name for the VM (as explained in the *Configuring a DNS name label* section a while ago)

For reasons of space, we won't go through these settings. However, for additional information regarding the preceding tasks, check out the following guide: `https://github.com/MicrosoftDocs/azure-docs/blob/master/articles/virtual-machines/windows/publish-web-app-from-visual-studio.md`.

Once we're done with these settings, we *should* be able to publish our web application to the VM in a seamless and transparent manner.

Unfortunately, this publishing method seems to be broken in the latest versions of Visual Studio 2019. At the time of writing, even if we follow the preceding guide to the letter, trying to generate the publish profile will result in the following error being shown:

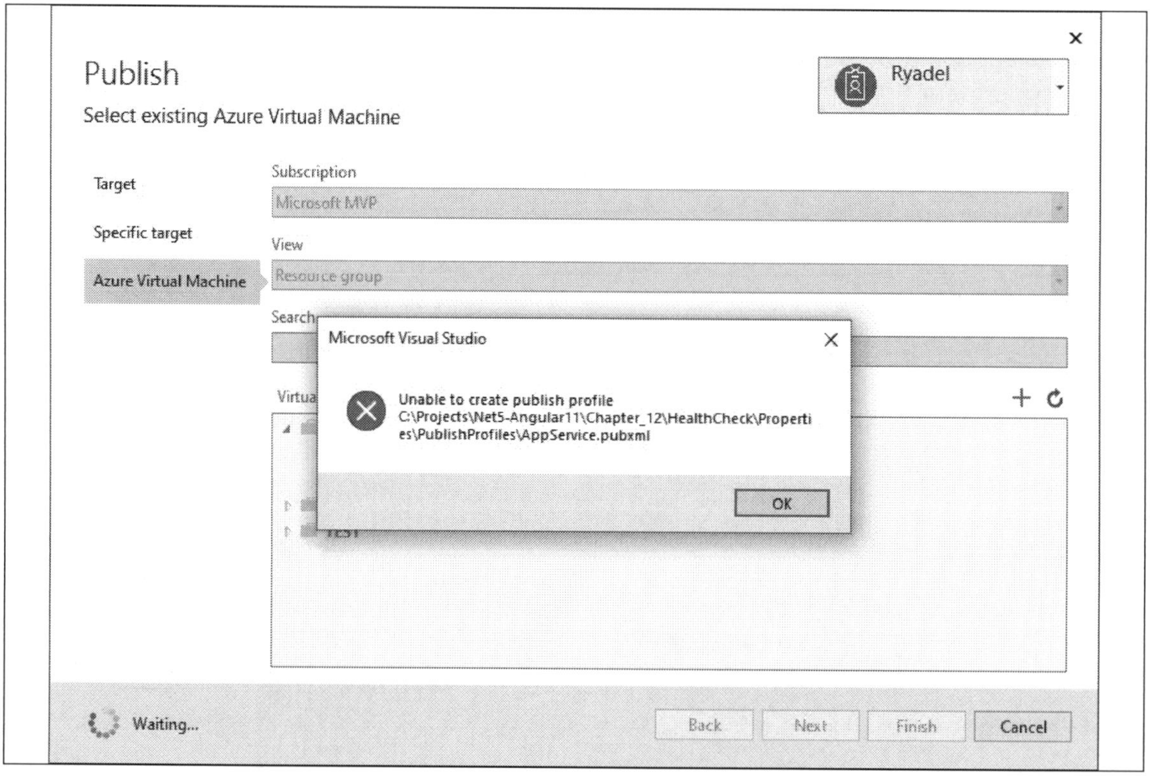

Figure 12.13: Unable to create publish profile error message

The issue has been recently raised in the following Microsoft Q&A thread, and is still without a proper fix as of the time of writing: `https://docs.microsoft.com/en-us/answers/questions/173913/vs2019-unable-to-create-publish-profile-azure-virt.html`

Until the Visual Studio development team fixes this error, there is a viable workaround that we can use to create that publishing profile.

Alternative method using the IIS Web Deploy Publishing feature

Instead of creating the publish profile from within Visual Studio, we can use the **Configure Web Deploy Publishing** feature of IIS directly on the VM and import the IIS-generated publish profile in Visual Studio.

In order to do that we need to do the following:

- Connect to the VM using Remote Desktop (through the `3389` TCP port that we opened a while ago)
- Navigate to **Control Panel | Administrative Tools**
- Launch the **IIS Manager** tool
- Right-click on the **Default Web Site** node
- Select the **Deploy | Configure Web Deploy Publishing** option (see the following screenshot)
- Configure the form in the modal window, adding the VM's hostname generated within the Azure portal a short while ago (DNS name):

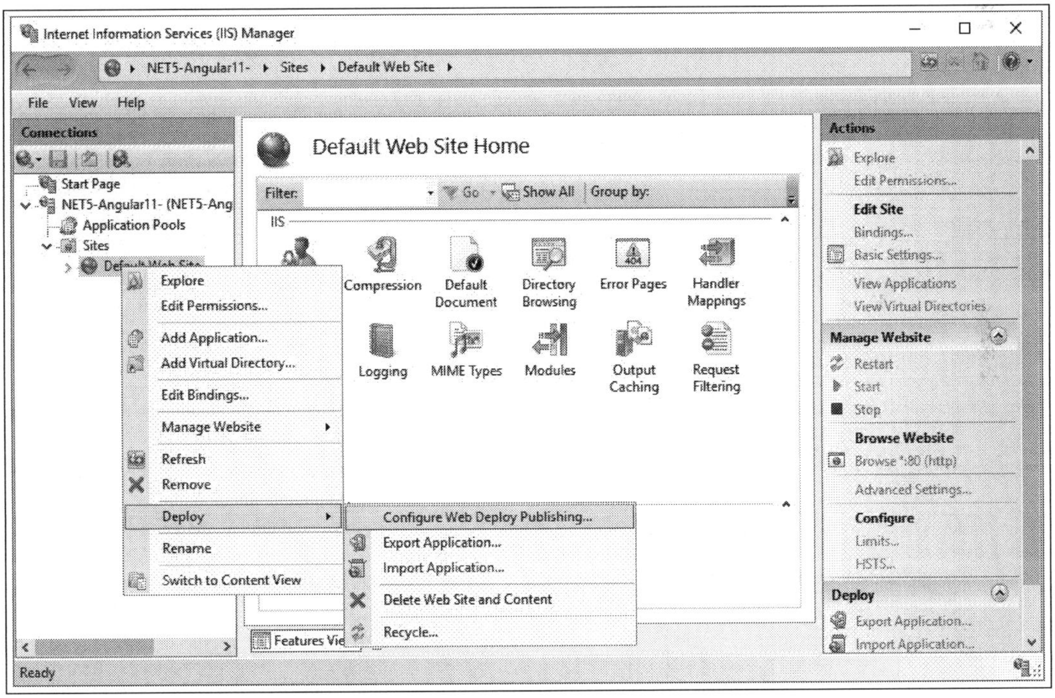

Figure 12.14: Configuring Web Deploy Publishing

The tool will generate a `.PublishSettings` file that we can then copy to our development machine and then import within Visual Studio using the **Import Profile** feature, thus generating a brand-new publish profile:

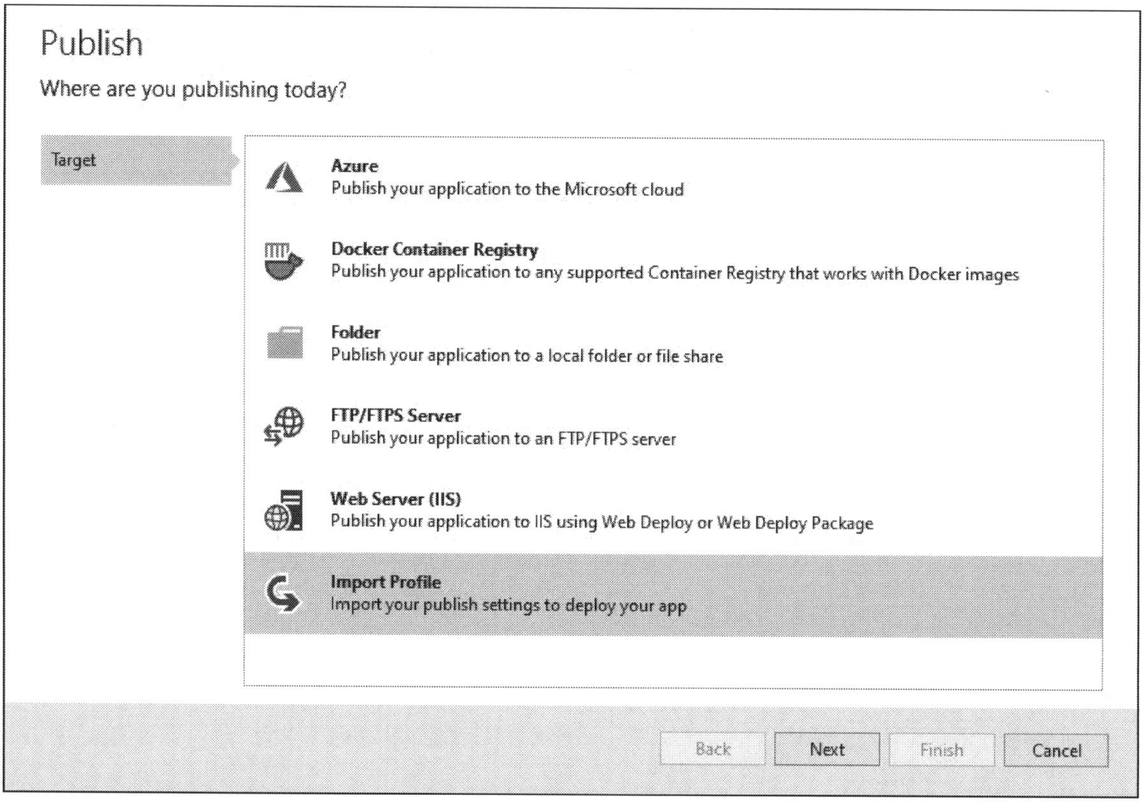
Publish
Where are you publishing today?
Target
Azure
Publish your application to the Microsoft cloud
Docker Container Registry
Publish your application to any supported Container Registry that works with Docker images
Folder
Publish your application to a local folder or file share
FTP/FTPS Server
Publish your application to an FTP/FTPS server
Web Server (IIS)
Publish your application to IIS using Web Deploy or Web Deploy Package
Import Profile
Import your publish settings to deploy your app
Back
Next
Finish
Cancel

Figure 12.15: Selecting Import Profile

Once imported, the new publish profile will allow us to publish our web application to our VM server without issues.

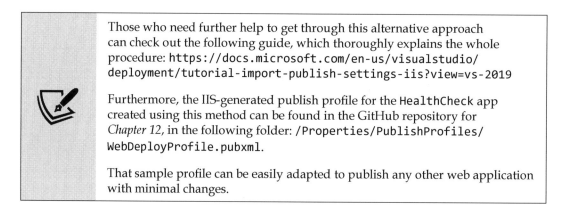

> Those who need further help to get through this alternative approach can check out the following guide, which thoroughly explains the whole procedure: `https://docs.microsoft.com/en-us/visualstudio/deployment/tutorial-import-publish-settings-iis?view=vs-2019`
>
> Furthermore, the IIS-generated publish profile for the `HealthCheck` app created using this method can be found in the GitHub repository for *Chapter 12*, in the following folder: `/Properties/PublishProfiles/WebDeployProfile.pubxml`.
>
> That sample profile can be easily adapted to publish any other web application with minimal changes.

Configuring IIS

Now that our web application's files have been copied to the server, we need to configure IIS to publish it.

In this section, we are going to configure the IIS service to make it serve our `HealthCheck` web app using the in-process hosting model, which has been made available since ASP.NET Core 2.2 and is a significant improvement over the previous out-of-process model.

To quickly summarize the differences between the two hosting models, we can say the following:

- In the **out-of-process** hosting model, IIS proxies the HTTP requests to the ASP.NET Core Kestrel server, which directly serves the app using a different TCP port (for internal use only); in other words, IIS acts as a reverse proxy.
- In the **in-process** hosting model, the ASP.NET Core application is hosted inside an IIS application pool; therefore, all the HTTP requests are directly handled by IIS, without being proxied to an external `dotnet.exe` instance running the ASP.NET Core native Kestrel web server.

As a matter of fact, the in-process model doesn't use Kestrel at all, replacing it with a new web server implementation (`IISHttpServer`) that is hosted directly inside the IIS application pool. Therefore, we could say that this new model is somewhat similar to the classic ASP.NET hosting model that we've been used to since ASP.NET version 1.x (and then 2.x, up to 4.x).

The in-process model is the default method for ASP.NET Core projects, and it's often a better approach when it comes to serving ASP.NET Core web applications, providing us with the following benefits:

- It provides better performances since, instead of using Kestrel, it relies on a custom `IISHttpServer` implementation that directly interfaces with the IIS request pipeline
- It's less resource-intensive, as it avoids the extra network hop between IIS and Kestrel

In the following section, we'll see how to configure it properly.

Adding an SSL certificate

Since our app will be served using HTTPS, we have two choices:

- Purchase and install an SSL certificate from a third-party reseller
- Create a self-signed one

For actual production scenarios, we should definitely follow the former path; however, the self-signed route might be OK when performing the initial deployment tests, because it provides a faster (and no-cost) alternative to achieve our goal. However, this choice will have the following downsides:

- All browsers will raise the typical SSL warnings and not secure messages, which we'll have to manually skip
- We won't be able to properly test most of the PWA features of our app, because the service workers registration will fail

> As we've seen in *Chapter 11, Progressive Web Apps*, a trusted HTTPS connection is one of the requirements for PWAs; unfortunately, a self-signed SSL certificate won't do the trick, unless we create a CA certificate, register it into our Chromium browser, and then use it to sign our own SSL certificate.
>
> Those who want to try that route can follow the instructions explained in this Stack Overflow answer by *JellicleCat*: `https://stackoverflow.com/a/60516812/1233379`
>
> Or check other alternative methods discussed in that thread.

To create a self-signed SSL certificate, connect to the VM using Remote Desktop and perform the following steps:

1. Open the IIS Manager desktop app, select the `HealthCheck` node from the tree view on the left, and then double-click the **Server Certificates** icon, as shown in the following screenshot:

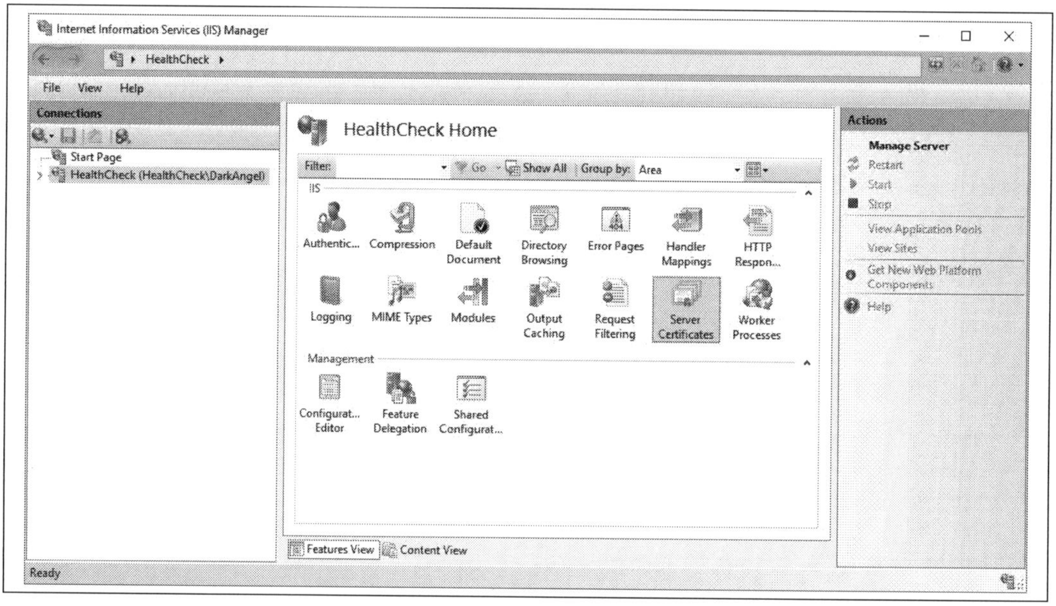

Figure 12.16: HealthCheck home view

2. Once in the **Server Certificates** panel, click the **Create Self-Signed Certificate** link in the **Actions** column on the right.
3. A modal window will appear (see the following screenshot), where we'll be asked to specify a friendly name for the certificate. Choose a friendly name for the certificate (in our example we're using `healthcheck.io`), select the **Personal** certificate store, and then click **OK** to create the self-signed certificate:

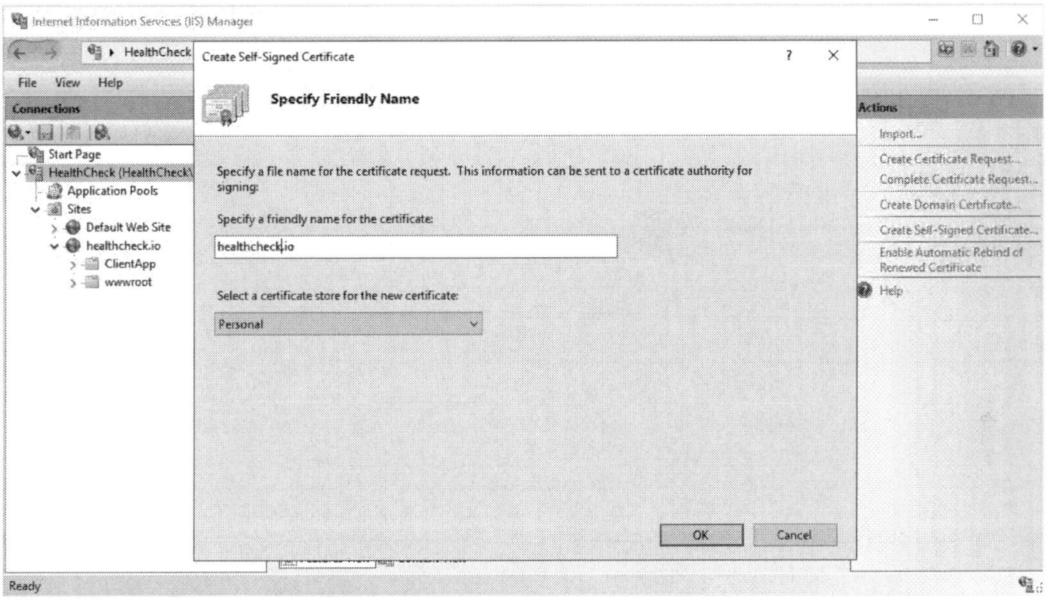

Figure 12.17: Create Self-Signed Certificate modal window

Once done, we can finally add the `HealthCheck` website entry to IIS.

Adding a new IIS website entry

From the IIS Manager main page, right-click on the `HealthCheck` root node and select the **Add Website** option to create a new website.

Fill out the **Add Website** modal window, as shown in the following screenshot:

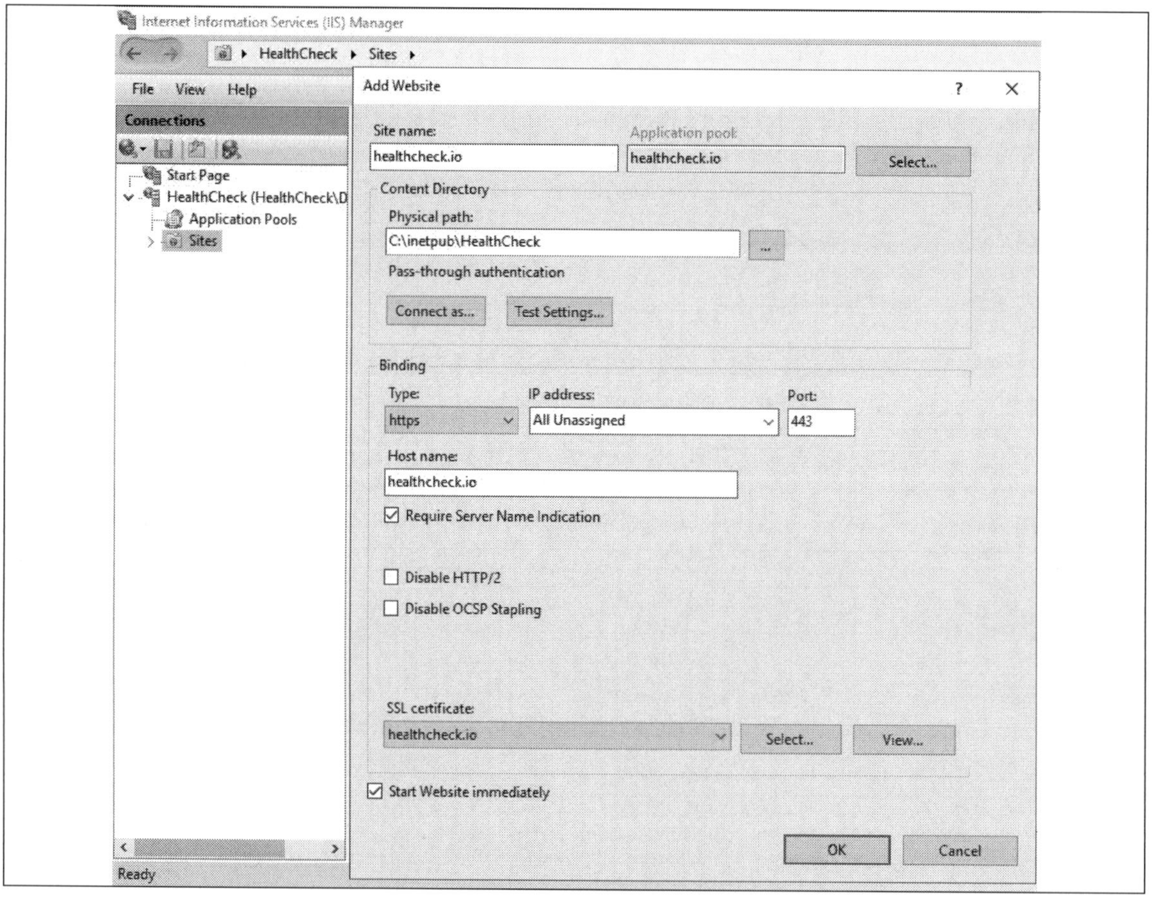

Figure 12.18: Add Website modal window

Here's a summary of the most relevant settings:

- **Site name**: The name you want to give to your website, which typically resembles the application's domain name; in our example we use `healthcheck.io`
- **Physical path**: `C:\inetpub\HealthCheck` (the path where we've copied our development machine's local deployment folder)
- **Binding Type**: **https**
- **IP address**: **All Unassigned**
- **Port**: `443`
- **Host name**: This is the main hostname the website will respond to. If we want to use a domain name in our possession, such as the one created using the MS Azure portal early on, we should definitely use it. If we do not have one, we can just type in `healthcheck.io` and go ahead; we'll explain how to use it to locally connect to the web server in a short while.
- **Require Server Name Indication**: Yes

- **Disable HTTP/2**: No
- **Disable OCSP Stapling**: No
- **SSL certificate**: The self-signed certificate that we created a short while ago – in our example we called it `healthcheck.io`
- **Start Website immediately**: Yes

Once done, click **OK** to add the new website. A new entry will appear in the tree view on the right within the `HealthCheck/Sites` folder.

Configuring the IIS application pool

As you may already know, the IIS service runs the various configured websites under one or more application pools. Each application pool configured will spawn a dedicated `w3wp.exe` Windows process that will be used to serve all the websites that have been configured to use it.

Depending on the publishing requirements of the various websites we need to host, we could run all websites in a few application pools (or even a single one) or each one with its own application pool. Needless to say, all the websites that share the same application pool will also share its various settings, such as memory usage, pipeline mode, identity, and idle timeout.

In our specific scenario, when we created our `healthcheck.io` website in the previous section, we chose to create a dedicated application pool with that same name – which is also the IIS default behavior. Therefore, in order to configure the website's application pool settings, we need to click on the `Application Pools` folder from the tree view on the left and then double-click the website entry from the `Application Pools` list panel, as shown in the following screenshot:

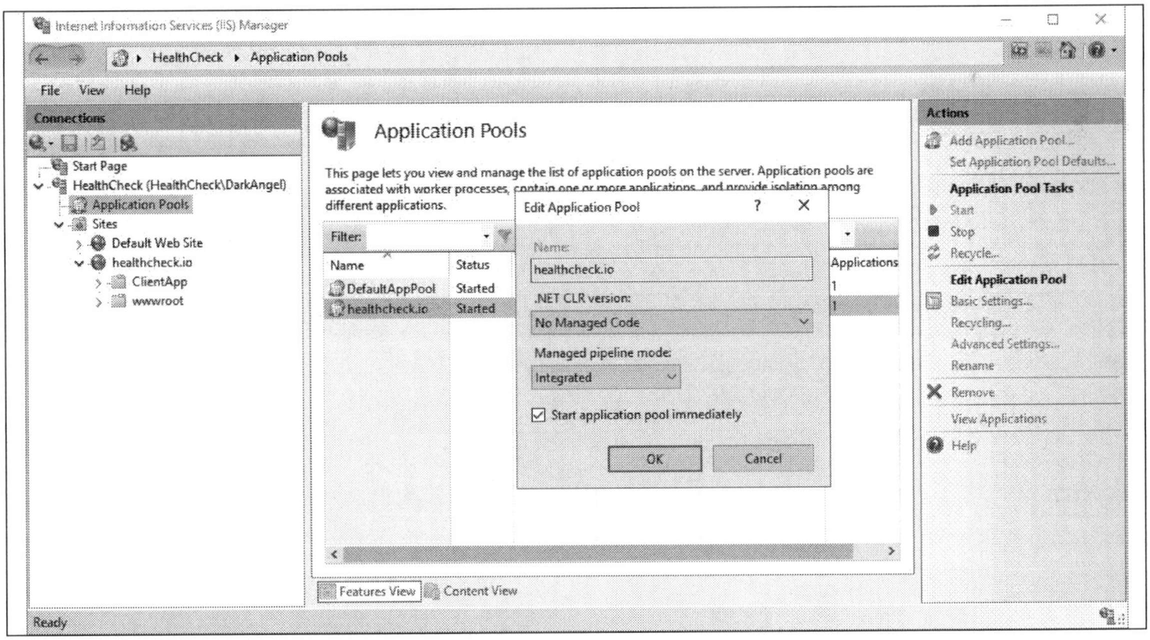

Figure 12.19: The Edit Application Pool modal window

In the **Edit Application Pool** modal window, choose the following settings, as shown in the preceding screenshot:

- **.NET CLR version**: **No Managed Code**
- **Managed pipeline mode**: **Integrated**

We might be wondering why we're choosing **No Managed Code** since we're clearly using the ASP.NET Core CLR. The answer is simple: since ASP.NET Core runs in a separate IIS process, there's no need to set any .NET CLR version on IIS.

> For additional information regarding the ASP.NET Core hosting model on IIS, including the various differences between the in-process and out-of-process hosting models, check out the following URL: `https://docs.microsoft.com/en-us/aspnet/core/host-and-deploy/iis/`

Testing the HealthCheck web application

Our web application should now be ready to receive HTTP requests; we only need to ensure that remote clients will be able to access it, including the machine we'll want to use to perform our first connection test.

More specifically, what we need to do depends on how we have configured our IIS website's hostname:

1. If we have used a domain name under our possession, we just have to set up its *A* record to make it point to the VM server's IP address and wait some time for the DNS records to propagate; once done, we can skip to the following *Testing the app* section.
2. If we have used the hostname generated from the MS Azure portal from our DNS name label, the *A* record is already configured and DNS is already propagated. This means that we don't need to do or wait for anything and we can immediately go to the following *Testing the app* section.
3. If we have used the `healthcheck.io` hostname, we need to map that hostname to the remote VM server's IP address from the Windows-based development machine where we want to perform our tests. The next section will explain how to do that.

Updating the testing machine's HOSTS files

The easiest and most effective way to map a hostname to a given IP address on any Windows system is by editing the `Windows\System32\drivers\etc\hosts` file, which is used by the operating system to ultimately map hostnames to IP addresses before (and instead of) resolving them through the DNS lookup.

> For additional information about the Windows HOSTS file, check out the following URL: `https://en.wikipedia.org/wiki/Hosts_(file)`

To alter the Windows HOSTS file, we need to open the `C:\Windows\System32\drivers\etc\hosts` file with a text editor such as `notepad.exe`.

Then, we need to add the following entry:

```
VM.IP.ADDRESS    healthcheck.io
```

> In order to edit the Windows HOSTS file, we'll need to acquire administrative privileges for it; otherwise, we won't be able to permanently change it on disk.

Replace the preceding `VM.IP.ADDRESS` placeholder with the VM's external IP file so that Windows will map the `healthcheck.io` hostname to it, ignoring the default DNS resolution; in other words, the preceding line will send all HTTP requests addressing the `healthcheck.io` hostname to our VM, even if we don't own that domain name. As a matter of fact, that's an easy and effective way to test our app using a real hostname (instead of a mere IP address) without having to actually purchase a domain.

Testing the app

Now, we can finally launch our favorite Chromium-based web browser and call the web server URL that we configured early on: our own domain name, the Azure-generated DNS name, or `https://healthcheck.io`, depending on what route we've chosen to take.

> A Chromium-based browser, such as Google Chrome or Microsoft Edge, will make us able to immediately check out the Web App Manifest file and the service worker, just like we did with the "local" publishing test that we performed in *Chapter 11, Progressive Web Apps*.

If we did everything correctly, we should be able to see our `HealthCheck` web application in all its glory:

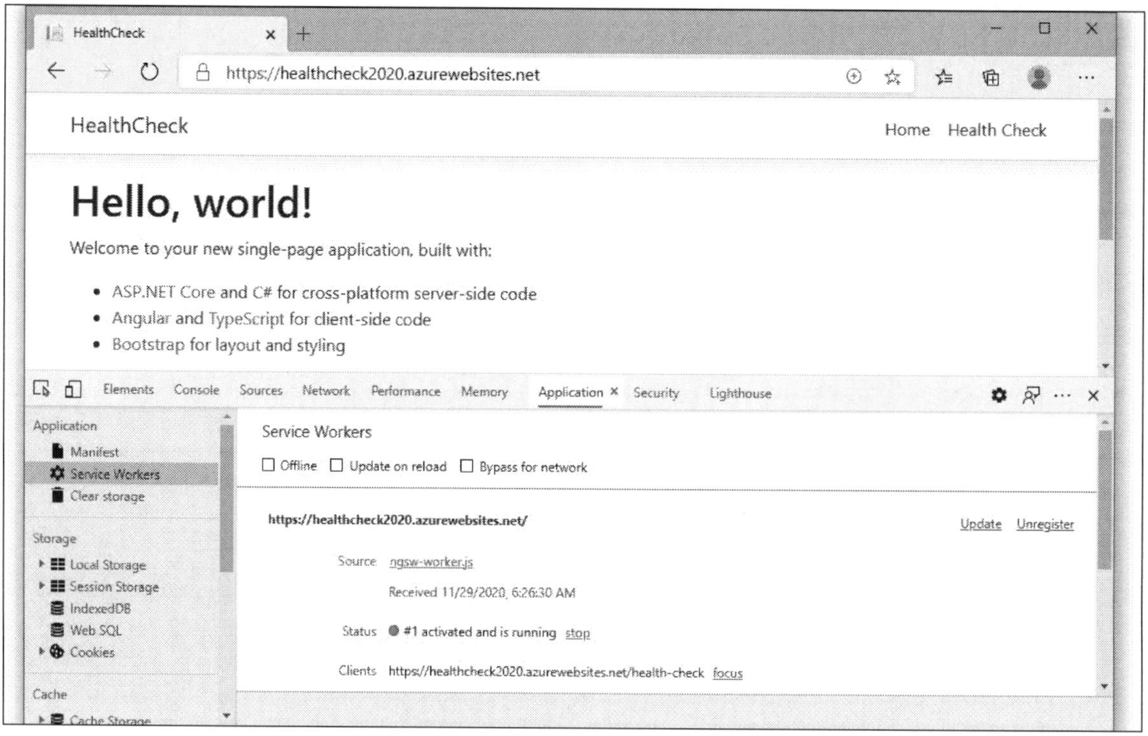

Figure 12.20: Launching our HealthCheck web application

It's worth noting that, in order to perform this test, we've used a real SSL certificate; as we explained early on, a self-signed SSL certificate won't allow the service worker registration, unless we perform a rather complex CA authorization procedure that goes way beyond the scope of this book.

Other than seeing the home view, we should also be able to see the following:

- The app manifest file (with all the *HC* icons) in the **Application** | **Manifest** panel of the Google Chrome development console
- The service worker properly registered in the **Application** | **Service Workers** panel of the Google Chrome development console
- The *send this page* and *install* icons in the rightmost part of the browser's address bar

In order to see those panels, remember to press *Shift* + *Ctrl* + *J* to bring the Google Chrome development console into view.

From there, we can now install the app and check/uncheck its offline status to test the service worker's behavior, just like we did in *Chapter 11, Progressive Web Apps*, when we tested our published app from a standard Visual Studio debug run; if we did everything properly, everything should work and behave in the same way.

With this, we've completed our Windows deployment journey; our `HealthCheck` web app has achieved its ultimate goal.

In the next section, we'll learn how to deploy our `WorldCities` web app to a completely different Linux machine.

Linux deployment

Throughout this section, we'll learn how to deploy our `WorldCities` web application on a Linux CentOS 8 server hosted on MS Azure.

More precisely, here's what we're going to do:

- **Create a new VM on MS Azure** using the CentOS-based 8.2 template
- **Configure the VM to accept inbound calls** to TCP ports `22` (for SSH), `80` (for HTTP), and `443` (for HTTPS)
- **Adapt the WorldCities app** for the Nginx + Kestrel edge-origin hosting model
- **Publish the WorldCities app** to the web server we've just set up
- **Test the WorldCities app** from a remote client

Let's get to work!

> It's worth noting that the CentOS-based template that we're going to use in this deployment sample can be easily replaced – with minor variations – with any other Linux VM template available on MS Azure: as a matter of fact, the ASP.NET Core Linux runtime works well with most Debian-based and RPM-based Linux distributions, with few minor differences mostly related to their package management systems.
>
> Needless to say, those who already have a production-ready Linux server could probably skip the sections related to the VM setup and go directly to the subsequent publishing topics.

Creating a Linux CentOS VM on MS Azure

Once again, we need to perform the following steps:

- **Access the MS Azure portal**
- **Add and configure a new VM**
- **Set the inbound security rules** to access the VM from the internet

However, since we've already explained the MS Azure VM creation process with Windows Server earlier on in this chapter, we're going to briefly summarize all the common tasks and avoid resubmitting the same screenshots.

> Those who require additional explanations regarding the various required steps can check out the *Creating a Windows Server VM on MS Azure* section.

Let's go back to MS Azure once more!

Add and configure the Linux CentOS VM

Once again, we need to log in to MS Azure using our (existing or new) account and access the MS Azure portal administration dashboard.

Right after that, we can click on the **Virtual Machine** icon and click **Add** to access the **Create a virtual machine** panel and enter the following settings.

In the **Basics** tab:

- **Resource group:** Use the same resource group used for the SQL database (this is mandatory unless our database is not there).
- **Virtual machine name**: Use `WorldCities`, `NET5-Angular11-CentOS`, or any other suitable name.
- **Region**: Choose the region closest to our geographical position.
- **Availability options**: No infrastructure redundancy required.
- **Image**: In our example, we're going to use the CentOS-based 8.2 default image; alternatively, we can choose any other Linux-based VM template as long as we're willing, and able, to adapt the following instructions to the (arguably minor) differences between different Linux distributions.
- **Azure Spot instance**: Again, select **Yes** for an Azure Spot instance, or **No** for a standard pay-as-you-go instance.
- **Size**: **Standard B1ms (1 vcpu, 2 GiB memory)**. Feel free to choose a different size if we're willing to spend more; *B1ms* is an entry-level machine featuring a very limited set of resources that will suffice for this deployment sample, but won't perform well in production.
- **Administrator account**: Select the **Password authentication** type, and then create a suitable username and password set. Remember to write these down in a secure place, since we'll definitely need these credentials to access our machine in a while.
- **Public inbound ports**: None (for the time being, we're going to set them up later on in a more secure way).

In the **Disk** tab:

- **OS disk type**: Select **Standard HDD**; this is the cheapest available choice. It goes without saying that those who want to instantiate a production environment (or are willing to pay some extra bucks) should choose a faster choice instead, such as **Standard** or **Premium SSD**.
- **Data disks**: Azure Linux VMs come with a temporary disk and an OS disk, which are good enough for our sample purposes; again, those who want to set up a production environment can (and should) add additional storage here.

In the **Network** tab:

- **Virtual Network**: Select the same VNet used for the SQL database (or create a new one)

In the **Management** tab:

- **Monitoring** | **Boot diagnostics**: Off

Once done, click the **Review + create** button to review our configuration settings and initiate the VM deployment process.

Once deployment is complete, we can click the **Go to Resource** button to access the **Virtual Machine overview** panel.

Configuring a DNS name label

Again, we have the chance to add a DNS name label to our VM and generate a unique fifth-level domain name to conveniently access it. If we choose to do this we need to locate the **DNS Name** label in the virtual machine's **Overview** panel, click on the **Configure** link next to it, and perform the steps already explained for the Windows VM.

Setting the inbound security rules

Go to the **Settings** | **Networking** tab and take note of the machine's public IP address. Then, add the following inbound security rules:

- **TCP port 22**, so that we'll be able to access the machine using the Secure Shell protocol (also known as **SSH**)
- **TCP ports 80 and 443**, to access the HTTP server (and our `WorldCities` web app) from the internet using SSL

Again, be sure to restrict access to these inbound rules to a secure **source IP address** (or address range), which can be set to either our static IP address or our ISP's IP mask.

Configuring the Linux VM

Now, we can use the SSH protocol to access our new Linux VM and perform two different (yet both required) sets of tasks:

- **Set up and configure the VM** by installing the various required packages (the ASP.NET Core runtime, the Nginx HTTP server, and the like)
- **Publish the WorldCities folder** (and the entirety of its contents) generated from the publish profile that we set up in *Chapter 11, Progressive Web Apps*

From the former set of tasks, we're going to use **PuTTy**, a free SSH client for Windows that can be used to remotely access a Linux machine's console. The latter will be handled with Secure Copy (aka **SCP**), a Windows command-line tool that allows files to be copied from a (local) Windows system to a remote Linux machine.

> **PuTTy** can be downloaded and installed from the following URL: `https://www.putty.org/`
>
> The **SCP** command-line tool is already shipped with most Windows versions, including Windows 10; for additional information on it, visit the following URL: `https://docs.microsoft.com/en-us/azure/virtual-machines/linux/copy-files-to-linux-vm-using-scp`

Connecting to the VM

Once installed, launch **PuTTy** and insert the VM public **IP address** (or DNS name), as shown in the following screenshot:

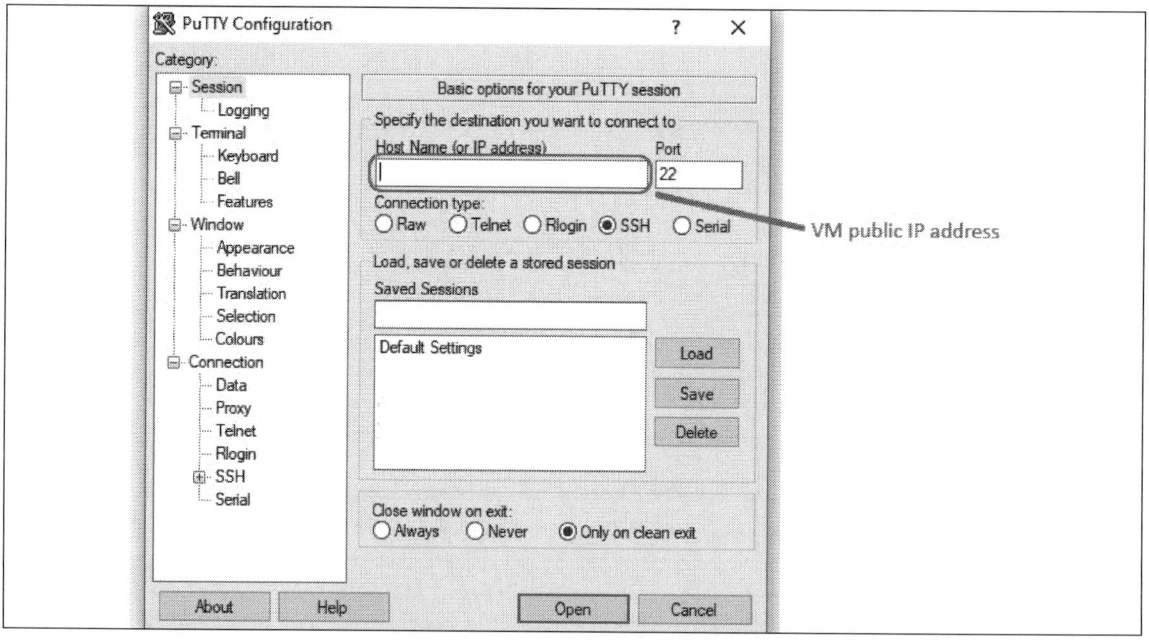

Figure 12.21: PuTTY Configuration window

Once done, click **Open** to launch the remote connection.

We'll be asked to accept the public SSH key. Once accepted, we'll be able to authenticate ourselves with the username and password specified a short time ago in MS Azure portal's virtual machine setup wizard:

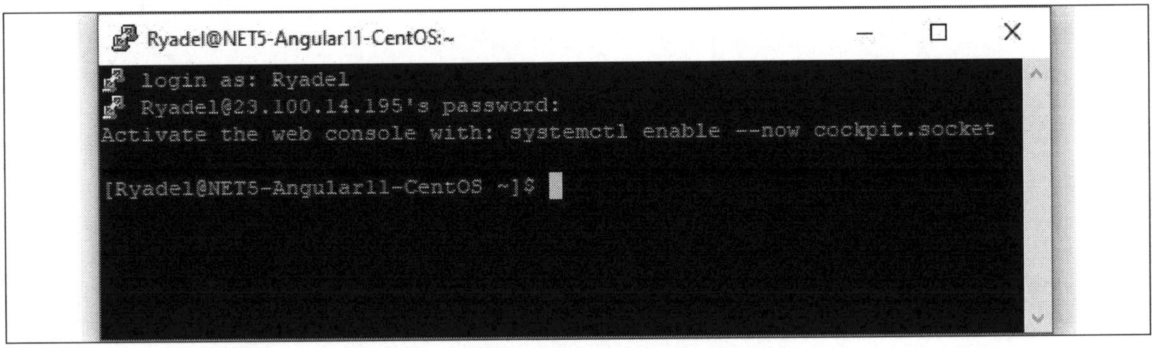

Figure 12.22: Command-line authentication

Once connected, we'll be able to issue terminal commands on the remote VM to set up and configure it according to our needs.

> The preceding steps explained will be OK for the time being, but could change in the future following the release of new versions of .NET 5 and/or CentOS. For up-to-date info, check out the following guide: `https://docs.microsoft.com/en-us/dotnet/core/install/linux-centos`

Installing the ASP.NET Core runtime

Once we've successfully logged in to the Linux VM terminal, we can start to configure the remote system to enable it to run (and host) ASP.NET Core applications. To achieve this, the first thing to do is to download and install the ASP.NET Core runtime.

However, before we can do that, we need to execute the following required steps:

- Register the Microsoft key
- Register the product repository
- Install the required dependencies

These steps need to be done once per Linux machine. Luckily enough, all of them can be done with the following command:

```
$ sudo rpm -Uvh https://packages.microsoft.com/config/centos/8/packages-microsoft-prod.rpm
```

Once this is done, we'll be able to install the ASP.NET Core 5.0 runtime in the following way:

```
$ sudo dnf install aspnetcore-runtime-5.0
```

The preceding command will ask us for confirmation a couple times and will likely take a while to complete.

> Alternatively, if we don't want to install the ASP.NET Core runtime on the Linux server, we could publish the app as a **Self-Contained Deployment** (**SCD**), as explained in the first section of this chapter.

Installing Nginx

The next step involves installing the Nginx server package. For those that don't know it, Nginx is a free and open source high-performance HTTP server, load balancer, and reverse proxy used by millions: this is the HTTP server we're going to use in Linux to serve our web application by reverse-proxying the Kestrel service.

> As of February 2020, Netcraft estimated that Nginx served 36.48 percent of all active websites ranked, ranking it first, above Apache at 24.51 percent: however, according to W3Techs, Apache was ranked first at 40.1 percent and Nginx second at 31.8 percent around that same period. That said, we're going to use Nginx because it features a modular, event-driven, asynchronous, single-threaded architecture that scales well on generic server hardware and across multi-processor systems, thus being an ideal partner for an ASP.NET Core web application hosted on Linux.

In previous versions of CentOS, before being able to do this, we had to add the EPEL repository, which was required for YUM to find the Nginx package to install:

```
$ sudo dnf install epel-release
```

However, starting with CentOS 8, Nginx can be installed without prerequisite steps in the following way:

```
$ sudo dnf install nginx
```

> For additional information about installing an ASP.NET Core web application on Linux with Nginx, check out the following URL: `https://docs.microsoft.com/en-us/aspnet/core/host-and-deploy/linux-nginx`

Starting up Nginx

When we install IIS on Windows, the service will start automatically and will be configured with an automatic startup type by default. Conversely, Nginx does not start on its own and won't be executed automatically upon startup.

To start Nginx, execute the following command:

```
$ sudo systemctl start nginx
```

To set Nginx to run automatically on system startup, use the following command:

```
$ sudo systemctl enable nginx
```

After applying these settings, it would be wise to reboot the Linux machine to be sure that all the configured settings will be applied upon reboot. The reboot can be done with the following command:

```
$ sudo reboot
```

Checking the HTTP connection

The CentOS-based MS Azure VM template that we've used in this deployment scenario doesn't come with a local firewall rule blocking TCP ports `80` and/or `443`. Therefore, as soon as Nginx is up and running, we should be able to connect to it properly by typing the VM's public IP address (or hostname) in the browser's address bar from our development machine.

Again, if we don't have a hostname and we didn't use the DNS name label option provided by Azure, we can add another mapping to the Windows `C:\Windows\System32\drivers\etc\hosts` file:

```
VM.IP.ADDRESS    worldcities.io
```

Here, we replace the preceding `VM.IP.ADDRESS` placeholder with the VM's external IP file so that Windows will map the `worldcities.io` hostname to it (as already explained in the Windows deployment section).

Once done, we should be able to connect to the VM's Nginx HTTP server using the `worldcities.io` hostname address, as shown in the following screenshot:

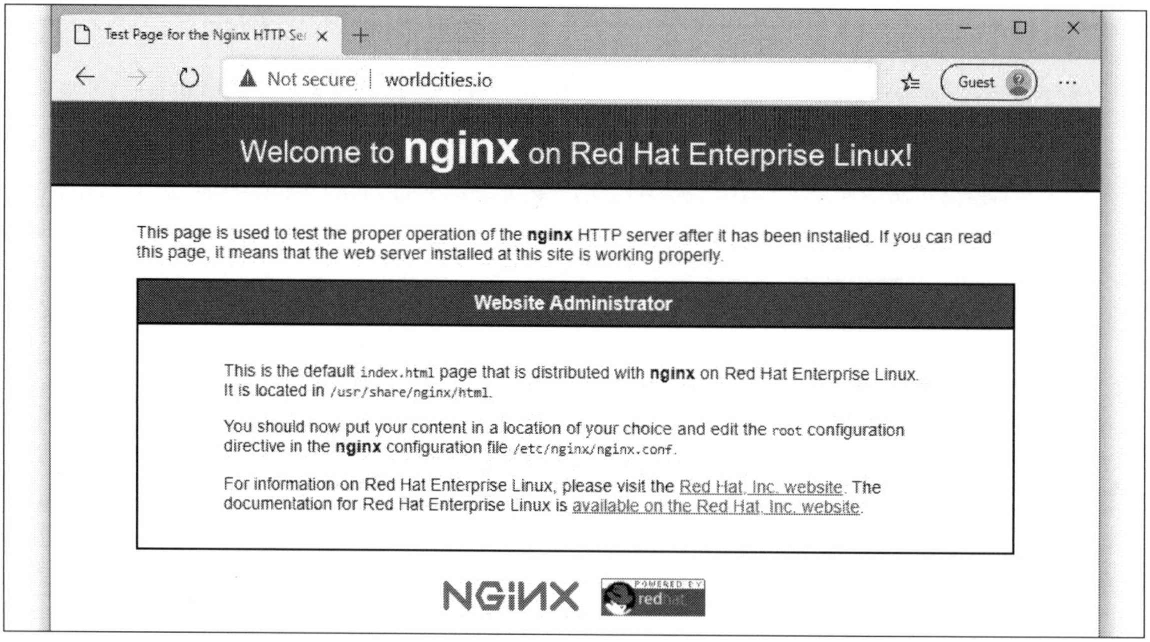

Figure 12.23: Connecting to the VM's Nginx HTTP server

If we can see the preceding response, it means that we likely have no firewall to worry about, therefore we can skip the following paragraph and move on to the next. Conversely, if the connection cannot be established, we might have to perform some additional steps to open the VM's `80` and `443` TCP ports.

> Before altering the VM firewall rules, it might be wise to carefully check for the TCP `80` and `443` inbound security rules that we should have set on the MS Azure portal administration site, as explained in the *Setting the inbound security rules* section.

Opening the 80 and 443 TCP ports

Depending on the Linux template chosen, it could be necessary to change the local firewall settings to allow incoming traffic for the `80` and `443` TCP ports. The commands required to do this might vary, depending on the built-in firewall abstraction layer shipped with the Linux distributions.

In Linux, the Kernel-based firewall is controlled by `iptables`; however, most modern distributions commonly use either the `firewalld` (CentOS, RHEL) or `ufw` (Ubuntu) abstraction layers to configure `iptables` settings.

> In a nutshell, both `firewalld` and `ufw` are firewall-management tools that can be used by the system administrators to configure the firewall features using a managed approach. We can think of them as front-ends for the Linux kernel's networking internals.

In VM Azure's CentOS-based Linux template, `firewalld` is present, but it's usually disabled (although it can be started and/or enabled to have it automatically run on each startup); however, if we're using a different template/VM/Linux distribution, it might be useful to spend a couple of minutes learning how we can properly configure these tools.

firewalld

Here's the command to check whether `firewalld` is installed:

```
$ sudo firewall-cmd --state
```

If the command returns something other than *not running*, this means that the tool is installed and active. Therefore, we need to execute the following `firewalld` commands to open TCP ports `80` and `443`:

```
$ sudo firewall-cmd --permanent --add-port=80/tcp
$ sudo firewall-cmd --permanent --add-port=443/tcp
$ sudo firewall-cmd --reload
```

The `--reload` command is required to immediately apply the `firewalld` settings without having to issue a reboot.

ufw

Here's the command to check whether `ufw` is running:

```
$ sudo ufw status
```

If the preceding command returns something other than *command not found*, this means that the tool is installed and running.

Here's the `ufw` required terminal command to open TCP ports `80` and `443`:

```
$ sudo ufw allow 80/tcp
$ sudo ufw allow 443/tcp
```

After executing these commands, we should be able to connect the Nginx HTTP server from our developer machine and receive the response page shown in the previous screenshot.

Adapting the WorldCities app

Before publishing the `WorldCities` app to the Linux VM, we need to ensure that our web application is properly configured to be served through a reverse proxy and will be able to access the production database.

In order to do this, we need to use the **Forwarded Headers Middleware** from the `Microsoft.AspNetCore.HttpOverrides` package.

> When HTTPS requests are proxied over HTTP using an edge-origin technique, such as the one we're pulling off with Kestrel and Nginx, the originating client IP address, as well as the original scheme (HTTPS), is lost between the two actors. Therefore, we must find a way to forward this information. If we don't do this, we could run into various issues while performing routing redirects, authentication, IP-based restrictions or grants, and so on.
>
> The most convenient way to forward this data is to use the HTTP headers: more specifically, using the `X-Forwarded-For` (client IP), `X-Forwarded-Proto` (originating scheme), and `X-Forwarded-Host` (host header field value). The built-in **Forwarded Headers Middleware** provided by ASP.NET Core performs this task by reading these headers and filling in the corresponding fields on the web application's `HttpContext`.
>
> For additional information regarding forwarded headers middleware and its most common usage scenarios, check out the following URL: `https://docs.microsoft.com/en-us/aspnet/core/host-and-deploy/proxy-load-balancer`

While we're there, we also need to properly check the connection string to the SQL database that we set up in *Chapter 4, Data Model with Entity Framework Core*, to ensure that it will still be reachable by the Linux VM (or change it accordingly). In the following two sections we will deal with both of these issues.

Adding the forwarded headers middleware

To add the forwarded headers middleware, open the `WorldCities` `Startup.cs` file and add the following highlighted lines to the `Configure()` method:

```
using Microsoft.AspNetCore.HttpOverrides;

// ...

app.UseRouting();

// Invoke the UseForwardedHeaders middleware and configure it
// to forward the X-Forwarded-For and X-Forwarded-Proto headers.
```

```
// NOTE: This must be put BEFORE calling UseAuthentication
// and other authentication scheme middlewares.
app.UseForwardedHeaders(new ForwardedHeadersOptions
{
    ForwardedHeaders = ForwardedHeaders.XForwardedFor
    | ForwardedHeaders.XForwardedProto
});

app.UseAuthentication();
app.UseIdentityServer();
app.UseAuthorization();

// ...
```

As we can see, we're telling the middleware to forward the `X-Forwarded-For` and `X-Forwarded-Proto` headers, thereby ensuring that redirected URIs and other security policies will work properly.

> **Important**: As written in the comments, this middleware must be put before calling `UseAuthentication` or other authentication scheme middlewares.

Now, we can move on to the following step.

Checking the database connection string

From Solution Explorer, open the `secrets.json` file and check out the connection string that we set up in *Chapter 4, Data Model with Entity Framework Core*, which has arguably worked flawlessly for our development machine since then. We need to be sure that such a connection string will work on our Linux VM as well.

If the SQL database is hosted on MS Azure or on a publicly accessible server, we won't have to do anything; however, in the case where we've used a local SQL database instance installed on our development machine, we'll need to choose one of the following available options:

1. Move and/or copy the `WorldCities` SQL database to MS Azure
2. Install a local SQL Server Express (or Development) instance on the CentOS VM right after creating it
3. Configure an inbound rule to the custom local (or remote) SQL Server Express (or Development) instance that we set up in *Chapter 4, Data Model with Entity Framework Core*, possibly restricting external access to the new VM's public IP address only

> For option #1, right-click the local SQL Database instance and select **Tasks | Deploy Database to MS Azure SQL Database**; check out *Chapter 4, Data Model with Entity Framework Core,* for additional details.
>
> For option #2, take a look at the following SQL Server Linux installation guide: `https://docs.microsoft.com/en-us/sql/linux/sql-server-linux-setup`
>
> For option #3, check out the following URL: `https://docs.microsoft.com/en-us/sql/sql-server/install/configure-the-windows-firewall-to-allow-sql-server-access`

Regardless of the option we choose to adopt, we won't need to update the connection string within the `secrets.json` file, since the existing settings are already good enough for our development environment; what we need to do instead is publish the updated contents on the production server. Let's see how we can do that.

Creating the appsettings.Production.json file

As explained in *Chapter 4, Data Model with Entity Framework Core,* we have at least a couple of alternatives to bring the *User Secrets* data into production: publishing an `appsettings.Production.json` file or defining some environment variables on the server. In our given scenario we'll adopt the former approach, which is quite easy to pull off.

Here's what we need to do:

1. Publish the `WorldCities` app in a local folder – such as `C:\Temp\WorldCities\` – using the publishing profile that we set in *Chapter 11, Progressive Web Apps*
2. Create a new `appsettings.Production.json` file in that same folder (or in any other temporary folder, as long as it's outside of the Visual Studio project folder)
3. Copy the content of the `secrets.json` file there
4. Update the `ConnectionString` value pointing it to the production database, depending on the option we chose early on

The connection string is not the only value we need to check, add, and/or update in the new `appsettings.Production.json` file. We also need to properly configure the `key` settings of the `IdentityServer`, just like we did in *Chapter 10, Authentication and Authorization,* within the `appsettings.Development.json` file for the *Development* values:

```
"IdentityServer": {
  "Key": {
    "Type": "File",
    "FilePath": "/var/ssl/worldcities.pfx",
    "Password": "<YOUR_OWN_PASSWORD>"
  }
}
```

This will ensure that `IdentityServer` will check for a real SSL certificate while in production. Such a certificate doesn't exist yet, but we'll generate it later from the Linux VM command line. For now, just choose a suitable password, replacing the `<YOUR_OWN_PASSWORD>` placeholder in the preceding code.

Here's how the `appsettings.Production.json` file should look after these changes; needless to say, all the marked placeholders will have to be replaced with our own values and passwords:

```
{
  "ConnectionStrings": {
    "DefaultConnection": "Server=localhost;Database=WorldCities;User
Id=WorldCities;Password=<YOUR_DB_PASSWORD>;Integrated Security=False;MultipleAct
iveResultSets=True"
  },
  "IdentityServer": {
    "Key": {
      "Type": "File",
      "FilePath": "/var/ssl/worldcities.pfx",
      "Password": "<YOUR_OWN_PASSWORD>"
    }
  }
}
```

In the preceding example, we're connecting to a locally hosted SQL Server Express database installed on the same Linux CentOS machine that hosts the web app; it's worth noting that SQL Server on Linux doesn't have an instance name, hence we're using `localhost` instead of `localhost\SQLEXPRESS` like we usually do on Windows machines.

> The preceding sample file has been added – for reference purposes only – in the GitHub repository for *Chapter 12*. Be sure not to do that in your non-sample projects and/or when dealing with actual database credentials, as doing that would negate the whole purpose of the *Visual Studio User Secrets* feature, which we introduced back in *Chapter 4, Data Model with Entity Framework Core*: keeping our credentials away from source control repositories.

It's worth noting that creating and setting up the `appsettings.Production.json` file is not a Linux-specific task; if we had published the `WorldCities` app on a Windows server, we would have had to do the exact same thing.

Publishing and deploying the WorldCities app

Now, we can publish the `WorldCities` app and deploy it to the Linux VM server.

The publishing step can be done in many ways, including the following:

- Use our existing **Folder publish profile** and then copy the files to the web server using the SCP command-line tool
- Use our existing **Folder publish profile** and then copy the files to the web server using a GUI-based SFTP Windows client, such as:
    - **WinSCP**: A free SFTP, SCP, S3, and FTP client for Windows: `https://winscp.net/`
    - **FileZilla FTP Client**: Another free, open source FTP client with FTP over TLS (FTPS) and SFTP support: `https://filezilla-project.org/`
- Install an FTP/FTPS server on our web server and then set up an **FTP publish profile**
- Use Visual Studio's **Azure Virtual Machine publish profile**

In this deployment scenario, we'll go with the first option, which is arguably the easiest one to achieve; as for the other available alternatives, we've already talked about them in the previous section (Windows publishing), so we won't repeat anything there.

Creating the /var/www folder

The first thing we need to do is create a suitable folder to store our application's published files on the Linux VM. For this deployment scenario, we're going to use the `/var/www/<AppName>` folder, thereby following a typical Linux convention.

Since the Azure CentOS-based template doesn't come with an existing `/var/www` folder, we need to create that as well. To do this, execute the following command from the Linux VM console:

```
$ sudo mkdir /var/www
```

This `/var/www/` folder will be our Linux equivalent of the Windows `C:\inetpub\` folder, the directory that will contain our web applications' files.

Right after this, we can create a new `/var/www/WorldCities` subfolder there by means of the following command:

```
$ sudo mkdir /var/www/WorldCities
```

Adding permissions

Now, we need to add the read and write permissions to the `/var/www/WorldCities` folder of the Nginx default user.

In this deployment scenario, we're taking for granted the fact that the Nginx instance is running with its default **Nginx** user and **Nginx** group. In other Linux environments, the username and/or group might vary—for example, in most Linux distributions, the Nginx group is called **www** or **www-data**.

To determine which user Nginx is running in, use the following command:

```
$ ps -eo pid,comm,euser,supgrp | grep nginx
```

To list all available Linux users and/or groups, use the following commands:

```
$ getent passwd
$ getent group
```

Once we retrieve the user and group, we can use them to change the `/var/www` folder permissions. Assuming the default values (`nginx` user and `nginx` group), this can be done in the following way:

```
$ sudo chown -R nginx:nginx /var/www
$ sudo chmod -R 550 /var/www
```

This will make both the `nginx` user and its corresponding `nginx` group able to access it in read and execute mode while blocking any access to every other user/group.

Before moving on, there's still one thing to do. If we aim to publish our app using FTP, FTPS, or SFTP, the above permissions won't be enough; we need to be sure to set them accordingly with our FTP server requirements and/or the account that we plan to use to perform the upload task.

Publishing permissions

The most common way to set up publishing permissions is to use the Linux `setfacl` command to grant read and write permissions to the `/var/www` folder for the publishing account.

If we plan to publish our app with the user account that we set up in MS Azure, we can do that in the following way:

```
$ sudo setfacl -R -m u:<USERNAME>:rwx /var/www
```

Replacing the preceding `<USERNAME>` placeholder with the username that we previously set up on VM Azure (the same one we used to log in to the VM terminal).

> Setting the permissions as explained previously should be enough for most scenarios; however, the server could require additional tweaking depending on the Linux distribution and version, system configuration, and other settings.

Copying the WorldCities publish folder

Once the `/var/www/WorldCities` folder has been properly set up on the Linux VM, we can open Command Prompt (with administrative rights) to our local development machine and issue the following SCP command to copy the local `C:\Temp\WorldCities` folder contents there:

```
> scp -r C:\Temp\WorldCities <USERNAME>@<VM.IP.ADDRESS>:/var/www
```

> Remember to replace the `<USERNAME>` and `<VM.IP.ADDRESS>` placeholders with the actual values.

The SCP command will then ask us whether we want to connect to the remote folder, as shown in the following screenshot:

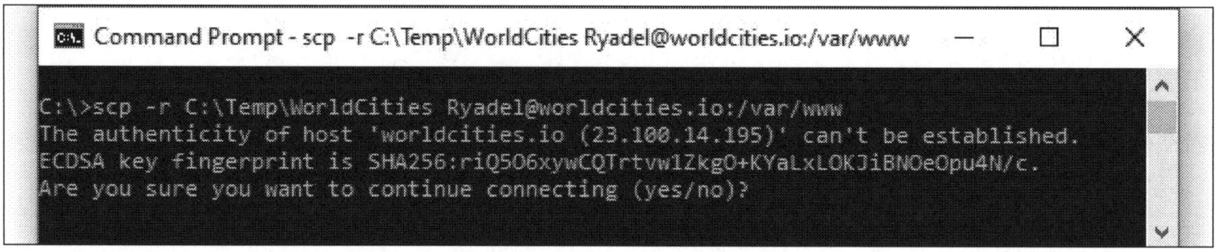

Command Prompt - scp -r C:\Temp\WorldCities Ryadel@worldcities.io:/var/www
C:\>scp -r C:\Temp\WorldCities Ryadel@worldcities.io:/var/www
The authenticity of host 'worldcities.io (23.100.14.195)' can't be established.
ECDSA key fingerprint is SHA256:riQ5O6xywCQTrtvwlZkgO+KYaLxLOKJiBNOeOpu4N/c.
Are you sure you want to continue connecting (yes/no)?

Figure 12.24: Authorizing the connection to the remote folder

Type yes to authorize the connection, and then repeat the command to copy the source folder to its destination. The SCP command will start to copy all the files from the local development machine to the VM folder, as shown in the following screenshot:

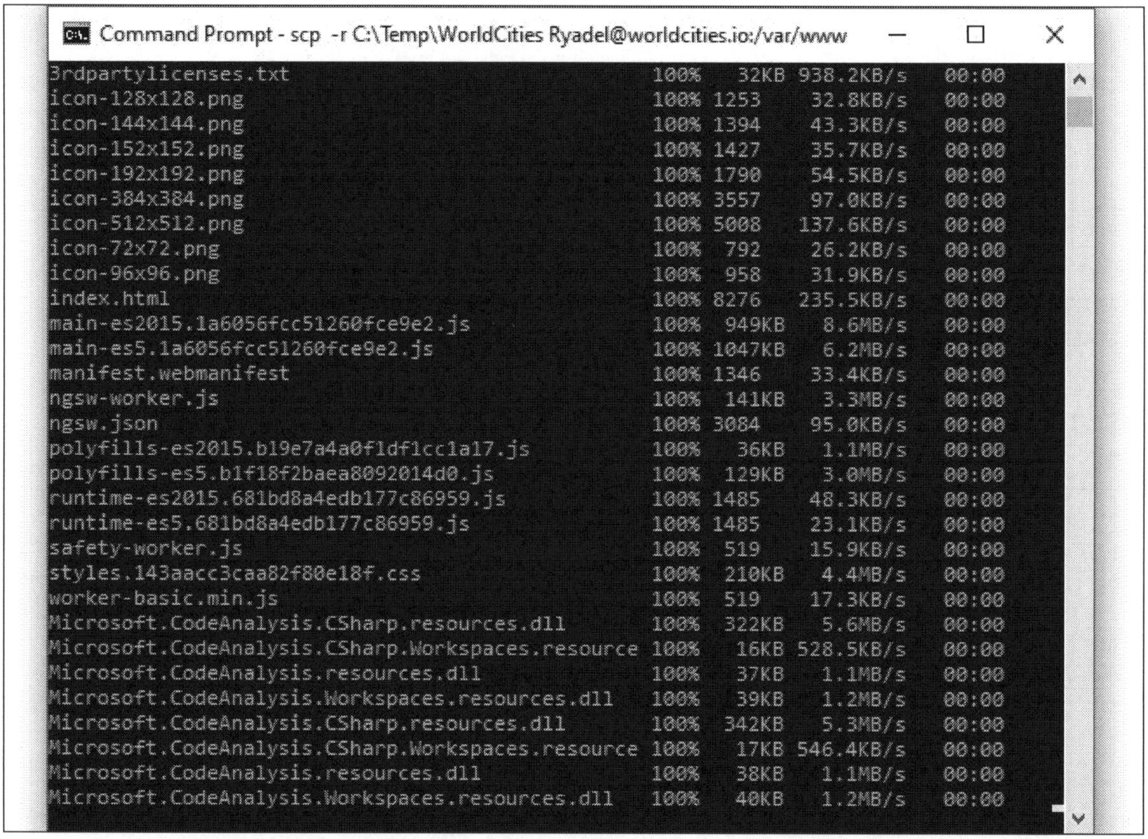

Figure 12.25: Copying all files from the local development machine to the VM folder

If we created the `appsettings.Production.json` file in the `C:\Temp\WorldCities\` folder, we've already published it together with the app; if we've used a different folder, we need to publish it as well in the `/var/www/WorldCities/` remote folder, using the same technique we've just used to deploy the app.

Right after that, we should delete all traces of the `appsettings.Production.json` file from our local server since we don't need them anymore.

> It's worth noting that this file will never be overwritten, even if we're going to publish our app again in the future, because it won't be generated again by the publishing process: it will be kept (and used) by the production server until we choose to update or delete it.

Now that our `WorldCities` app files have been copied to the Linux VM, we just need to configure the Kestrel service and then the Nginx reverse proxy to serve it.

Configuring Kestrel and Nginx

Before starting up, it can be wise to quickly explain how the Kestrel service and the Nginx HTTP server will interact with each other.

The high-level architecture is quite similar to the Windows out-of-process hosting model that has been used since ASP.NET Core 2.2:

- The Kestrel service will serve our web app on TCP port `5000` (or any other TCP port; `5000` is just the default one)
- The Nginx HTTP server will act as a reverse proxy, forwarding all the incoming requests to the Kestrel web server

This pattern is called **edge-origin proxy**, and can briefly be summarized by the following diagram:

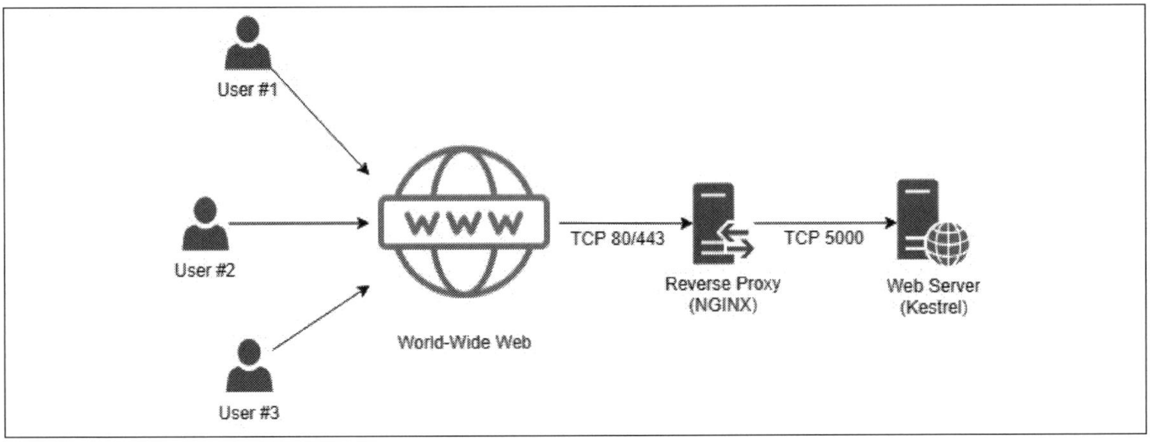

Figure 12.26: The edge-origin proxy

Now that we've understood the general picture, let's do our best to pull it off.

Creating the self-signed SSL certificate

Since our app will be served using HTTPS, we need to either purchase and install an SSL certificate from a third-party reseller or create a self-signed one. For this deployment scenario, we'll stick to the self-signed approach, just like we did with Windows.

In Linux, we can create a self-signed certificate using the `OpenSSL` command-line tool.

To do this, implement the following steps from the Linux VM terminal:

1. Create the `/var/ssl` folder with `sudo mkdir /var/ssl`
2. Create the self-signed SSL certificate (`worldcities.crt`) and the private key file (`worldcities.key`) with the following command:

   ```
   $ sudo openssl req -x509 -newkey rsa:4096 -sha256 -nodes -keyout /var/ssl/worldcities.key -out /var/ssl/worldcities.crt -subj "/CN=worldcities.io" -days 3650
   ```

3. Once done, merge the certificate and the private key into a single `worldcities.pfx` file:

   ```
   $  sudo openssl pkcs12 -export -out /var/ssl/worldcities.pfx -inkey /var/ssl/worldcities.key -in /var/ssl/worldcities.crt
   ```

   When asked for the PFX file password, insert the same password that we specified in the `appSettings.Production.json` file early on. This will ensure that `IdentityServer` will be able to find and use the expected key.

4. Right after that, set the new file and folder permissions to make them accessible from both Nginx and the app:

   ```
   $ sudo chown -R nginx:nginx /var/ssl
   $ sudo chmod -R 550 /var/ssl
   ```

5. Last but not least, we need to change the security context of the `/var/ssl` folder (and all its containing files) so that Nginx will be able to access it:

   ```
   $ sudo chcon -R -v --type=httpd_sys_content_t /var/ssl
   ```

If we don't execute the preceding command, **Security-Enhanced Linux** (**SELinux**) will prevent `httpd` daemons from accessing the `/var/ssl` folder, causing unwanted "permission denied" errors during the Nginx startup phase. It goes without saying that if our Linux system is not running SELinux, or we have permanently disabled it, the preceding command can be skipped. However, since it's active in the MS Azure CentOS-based VM template, we might need to execute it.

> **SELinux** is an access control (MAC) security mechanism implemented in the CentOS 4 kernel. It is quite similar to the Windows UAC mechanism and has strong default values that can be relaxed in case of specific requirements.
>
> To temporarily disable it, run the `sudo setenforce 0` terminal command. Doing this can be useful when we run into permission issues to determine whether the problem may be related to SELinux.
>
> For additional information regarding SELinux and its default security settings, check out the following URLs:
>
> `https://wiki.centos.org/HowTos/SELinux`
>
> `https://wiki.centos.org/TipsAndTricks/SelinuxBooleans`

Now we have a valid self-signed SSL certificate that can be used by both `IdentityServer` and Nginx.

> For additional information regarding the OpenSSL tool, check out the following URL: `https://www.openssl.org/docs/manmaster/man1/openssl.html`

Truth to be told, using the same certificate for signing JWTs and providing HTTPS access is not the best thing we can do in terms of security; it's strongly advisable to use two different key/certificate pairs in any non-sample production scenario.

Configuring the Kestrel service

Let's start by creating the service definition file in the `/etc/systemd/system/` folder.

To do that, we'll use `nano`, an open source text editor for Linux that can be used from a command-line interface (similar to `vim`, but much easier to use). Let's go through the following steps:

1. Execute the following command to create a new `/etc/systemd/system/kestrel-worldcities.service` file:

```
$ sudo nano /etc/systemd/system/kestrel-worldcities.service
```

2. Once done, fill the newly created file with the following content:

```
[Unit]
Description=WorldCities

[Service]
WorkingDirectory=/var/www/WorldCities
ExecStart=/usr/bin/dotnet /var/www/WorldCities/WorldCities.dll
Restart=always
```

```
# Restart service after 10 seconds if the dotnet service crashes:
RestartSec=10

KillSignal=SIGINT
SyslogIdentifier=WorldCities
User=nginx
Environment=ASPNETCORE_ENVIRONMENT=Production
Environment=DOTNET_PRINT_TELEMETRY_MESSAGE=false
Environment=ASPNETCORE_URLS=http://localhost:5000

# How many seconds to wait for the app to shut down after it receives the
initial interrupt signal.
# If the app doesn't shut down in this period, SIGKILL is issued to
terminate the app.
# The default timeout for most distributions is 90 seconds.
TimeoutStopSec=90

[Install]
WantedBy=multi-user.target
```

3. Once done, press *Ctrl* + *X* to exit and then *Y* to save the file on disk.

> The `kestrel-worldcities.service` file is available in the `/_LinuxVM_ConfigFiles/` folder of this book's GitHub repository.

As we can see, this file's contents will be used by Kestrel to configure our app's production values, such as the `ASPNETCORE_ENVIRONMENT` variable, which we talked about earlier on, and the TCP port, which will be used to internally serve the app.

> The preceding settings are OK for our current deployment scenario; however, they should be changed to comply with different usernames, folder names, TCP ports used, the web app's main DLL name, and so on. When hosting a different web application, be sure to update them accordingly.

Now that we have configured the service, we just need to start it, which can be done using the following command:

```
$ sudo systemctl start kestrel-worldcities.service
```

If we also want to make the service automatically run on each VM reboot, add the following command:

```
$ sudo systemctl enable kestrel-worldcities.service
```

Immediately after this, it would be wise to run the following command to check whether the service is running without issues:

```
$ sudo systemctl status kestrel-worldcities.service
```

If we see a green `active (running)` message, such as the one in the following screenshot, this most likely means that our Kestrel web service is up and running.

> To exit from the `systemctl status` command, press *Ctrl* + C and then hit the *Enter* key.

Now, we just need to set up Nginx to reverse proxy it and we're done:

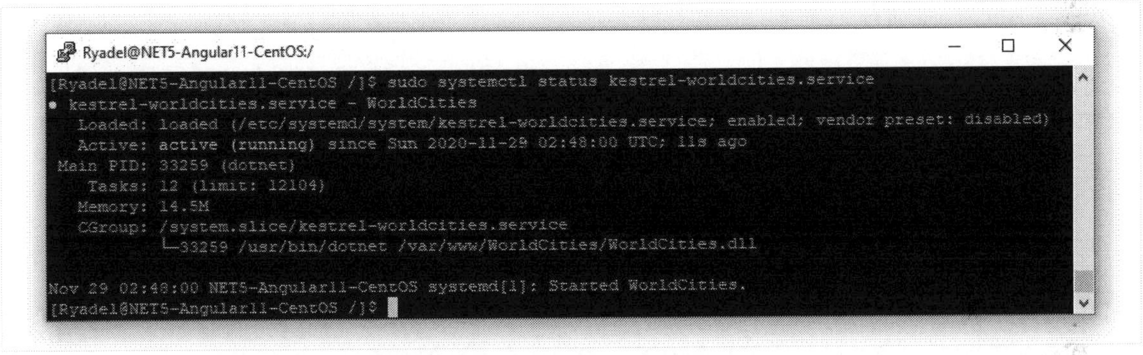

Ryadel@NET5-Angular11-CentOS:/
[Ryadel@NET5-Angular11-CentOS /]$ sudo systemctl status kestrel-worldcities.service
● kestrel-worldcities.service - WorldCities
Loaded: loaded (/etc/systemd/system/kestrel-worldcities.service; enabled; vendor preset: disabled)
Active: active (running) since Sun 2020-11-29 02:48:00 UTC; 11s ago
Main PID: 33259 (dotnet)
Tasks: 12 (limit: 12104)
Memory: 14.5M
CGroup: /system.slice/kestrel-worldcities.service
└─33259 /usr/bin/dotnet /var/www/WorldCities/WorldCities.dll
Nov 29 02:48:00 NET5-Angular11-CentOS systemd[1]: Started WorldCities.
[Ryadel@NET5-Angular11-CentOS /]$

Figure 12.27: Seeing the green active (running) message

If the status command shows that something's off (red lines or advice), we can troubleshoot the issue by looking at the detailed ASP.NET Core application error log with the following command:

```
$ sudo journalctl -u kestrel.worldcities
```

The `-u` parameter will only return messages coming from the `kestrel-worldcities` service, filtering out everything else.

Since the `journalctl` log could easily become very long, even with the preceding filter, it could also be advisable to restrict its timeframe using the `--since` parameter in the following way:

```
$ sudo journalctl -u kestrel-worldcities --since "yyyy-MM-dd HH:mm:ss"
```

Be sure to replace the `yyyy-MM-dd HH:mm:ss` placeholders with a suitable date-time value.

Last but not least, we can just output the last-logged error with the `-xe` switch:

```
$ sudo journalctl -xe
```

These commands should be very useful in troubleshooting most error scenarios on Linux in an effective manner.

> For additional information regarding the `journalctl` tool, check out the following URL: `https://www.freedesktop.org/software/systemd/man/journalctl.html`

Why are we not serving the web app with Kestrel directly?

We could be tempted to just configure the Kestrel web service on TCP port `443` (instead of TCP `5000`) and get the job done now, without having to deal with Nginx, and skipping the whole reverse proxy part.

Despite being 100% possible, we strongly advise against doing this for the same reasons as stated by Microsoft here:

> *Kestrel is great for serving dynamic content from ASP.NET Core. However, the web serving capabilities aren't as feature-rich as servers such as IIS, Apache, or Nginx. A reverse proxy server can offload work such as serving static content, caching requests, compressing requests, and SSL termination from the HTTP server. A reverse proxy server may reside on a dedicated machine or may be deployed alongside an HTTP server.*
>
> *[Source:* `https://docs.microsoft.com/en-us/aspnet/core/host-and-deploy/linux-nginx`*]*

In short, Kestrel is not intended to be used on the front line, at least for the time being; therefore, the correct thing to do is to definitely keep it far from the edge and leave such a task to Nginx.

Configuring the Nginx reverse proxy

The last thing we need to do is to configure the Nginx HTTP server to act as a reverse proxy for our Kestrel service. Observe the following steps:

1. Type the following command to create a dedicated Nginx configuration file for this job:

```
$ sudo nano /etc/nginx/nginx-worldcities.conf
```

2. Then, fill the new file's content with the following configuration settings:

```
server {
    listen        80;
    listen        [::]:80;
```

```
    server_name  worldcities.io;
    return       301 https://worldcities.io$request_uri;
}

server {
  listen 443 ssl http2;
  listen [::]:443 ssl http2;

  ssl_certificate /var/ssl/worldcities.crt;
  ssl_certificate_key /var/ssl/worldcities.key;

  server_name worldcities.io;

  root /var/www/WorldCities/;
  index index.html;
  autoindex off;

  location / {
    proxy_pass http://localhost:5000;
    proxy_http_version 1.1;

    proxy_cache_bypass $http_upgrade;

    proxy_set_header Connection $http_connection;
    proxy_set_header Host $host;
    proxy_set_header Upgrade $http_upgrade;
    proxy_set_header X-Forwarded-For $proxy_add_x_forwarded_for;
    proxy_set_header X-Forwarded-Host $host:$server_port;
    proxy_set_header X-Forwarded-Proto $scheme;
    proxy_set_header X-Forwarded-Server $host;
  }
}
```

3. Once done, press *Ctrl* + *X* to exit and then *Y* to save the file.
4. Right after that, execute the following command to authorize the Nginx service to connect to the network:

```
$ sudo setsebool -P httpd_can_network_connect 1
```

> The preceding command will probably take a while to complete; however, it is required to change the SELinux default settings, which prevents all `httpd` daemons (such as Nginx) from accessing the local network and, hence, the Kestrel service. If our Linux system is not running SELinux, or we have permanently disabled it, we don't need to execute the preceding command.

Updating the nginx.conf file

The `nginx-worldcities.conf` file needs to be referenced within the main Nginx configuration file; otherwise, it won't be read and applied.

To do this, edit the `/etc/nginx/nginx.conf` file with the following command:

```
$ sudo nano /etc/nginx/nginx.conf
```

Then, add the following highlighted line near the end of the file, just before the final closing square bracket:

```
# ...existing code...

      location / {
      }

      error_page 404 /404.html;
        location = /40x.html {
      }

      error_page 500 502 503 504 /50x.html;
        location = /50x.html {
      }
    }

  include nginx-worldcities.conf;

}
```

That single `include` line will ensure that our reverse proxy configuration works properly. The new settings will be applied as soon as Nginx is restarted, which is something that we'll do in a short while.

> The `nginx.conf` and `nginx-worldcities.conf` files are both available in the `/_LinuxVM_ConfigFiles/` folder of this book's GitHub repository.

All the required deployment tasks on Linux have been completed. Now, we just have to properly test the `WorldCities` web application to see whether it works.

Testing the WorldCities application

The testing phase will be very similar to what we did at the end of the Windows deployment section. Observe the following steps:

1. Before leaving the Linux VM terminal, it would be wise to restart both the Kestrel and Nginx services in the following way:

```
$ sudo systemctl restart kestrel-worldcities
$ sudo systemctl restart nginx
```

2. Immediately after this, check for their statuses with the following commands to ensure that they're up and running:

```
$ sudo systemctl status kestrel-worldcities
$ sudo systemctl status nginx
```

> In production environments, it is advisable to test the updated Nginx configuration before restarting Nginx using the following command:
>
> ```
> sudo nginx -t
> ```
>
> That way the production site won't go down if Nginx fails to load due to a configuration error of any kind.

Now, we're ready to switch to our local development machine and start the test.

Update the testing machine's HOSTS files

Just like we did with the `HealthCheck` app early on, if we aren't planning to use the Azure DNS name or a custom hostname, the first thing we have to do is to map the `worldcities.io` hostname to our remote VM's IP address.

If that is the case, observe the following steps:

1. To do this, edit the `C:\Windows\System32\drivers\etc\hosts file` and add the following entry:

```
VM.IP.ADDRESS    worldcities.io
```

2. Replace the preceding `VM.IP.ADDRESS` placeholder with the VM's external IP file so that Windows will map the `worldcities.io` hostname to it.

Now, we can test the app from our development machine using the Google Chrome web browser.

Testing the app

Again, we're going to perform these tests using a Chromium-based browser (Google Chrome or Microsoft Edge) because of their built-in development tools that conveniently allow us to check for Web App Manifest and service worker presence.

Launch Google Chrome and write the following URL in the browser's address bar: `https://worldcities.io`

If we have done everything correctly, we should be able to see the `WorldCities` web application's home view:

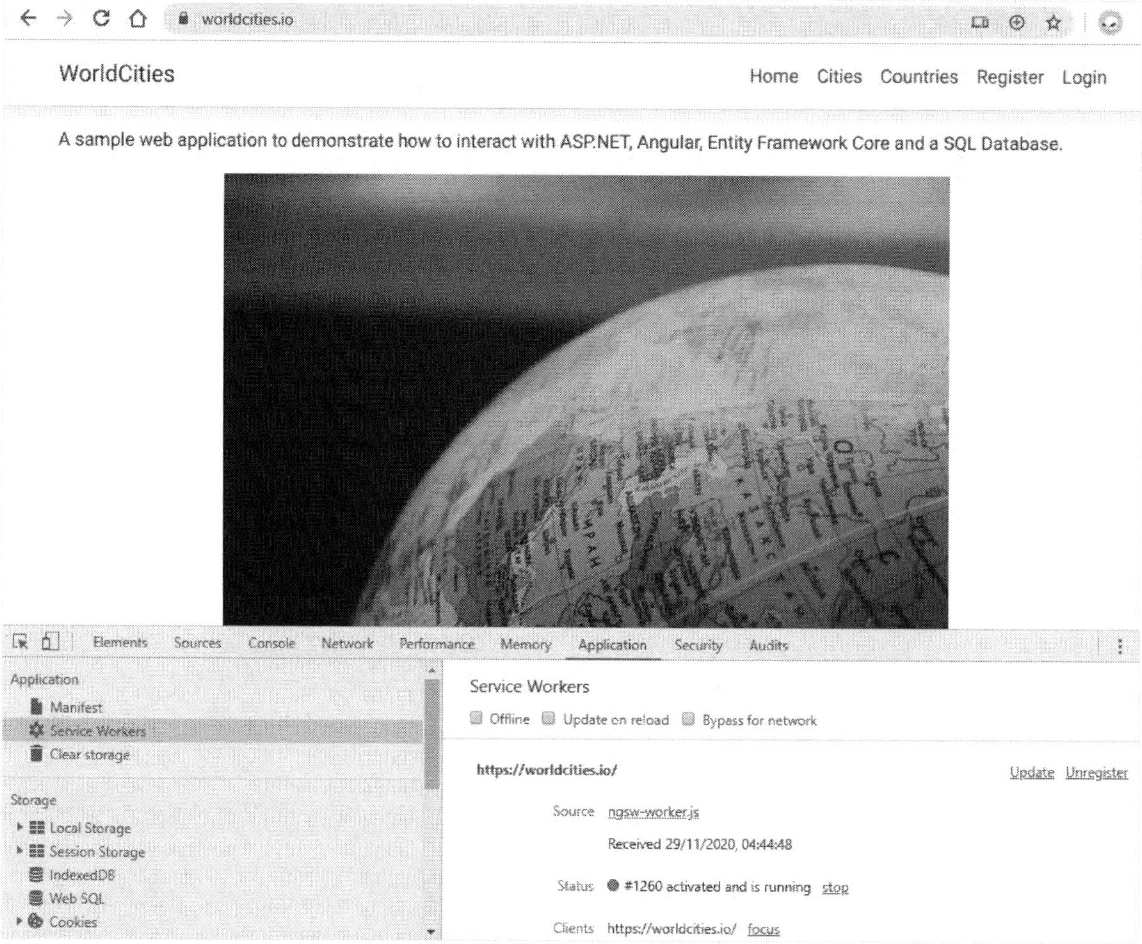

Figure 12.28: The WorldCities home view

> Again, this test has been done using a real SSL certificate; go back to the Windows testing section for further details on that.

From there, we should check for the presence/availability of the following goodies:

- The app manifest file (with all the *HC* icons) in the **Application** | **Manifest** panel of the Google Chrome development console
- The service worker properly registered in the **Application** | **Service Workers** panel of the Google Chrome development console

- The *send this page* and *install* icons in the rightmost part of the browser's address bar
- The service worker behavior when checking and unchecking the offline status to test the service worker's behavior
- Access to the SQL database
- The **Edit City** and **Edit Country** reactive forms
- The login and registration workflows

If everything works as expected, we can say that our Linux deployment journey is over as well.

Troubleshooting

If the web application encounters a runtime error, the production environment won't show any detailed information about the exception to the end user. For this reason, we won't be able to know anything useful about the issue unless we switch to **Development Mode** (refer to the following screenshot):

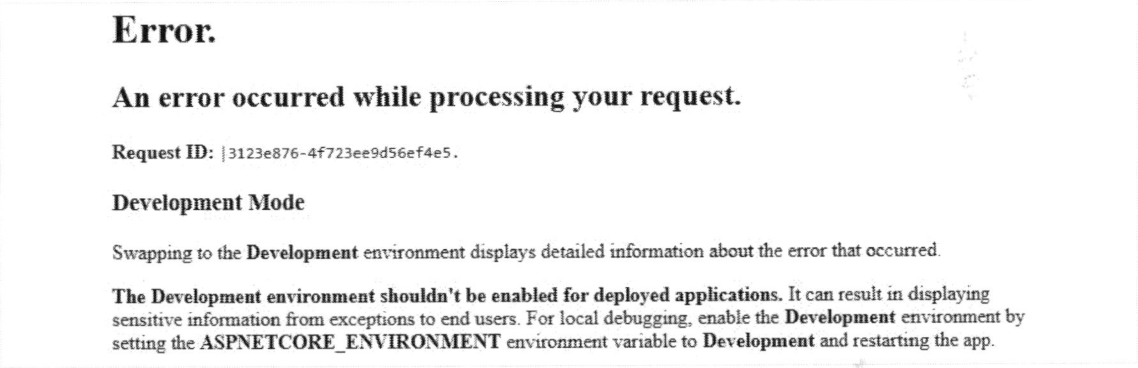

Error.
An error occurred while processing your request.
Request ID: |3123e876-4f723ee9d56ef4e5.
Development Mode
Swapping to the Development environment displays detailed information about the error that occurred.
The Development environment shouldn't be enabled for deployed applications. It can result in displaying sensitive information from exceptions to end users. For local debugging, enable the Development environment by setting the ASPNETCORE_ENVIRONMENT environment variable to Development and restarting the app.

Figure 12.29: Error message in the production environment

This can be done in the following way:

1. Change the `/etc/systemd/system/kestrel-worldcities.service` file's `ASPNETCORE_ENVIRONMENT` variable value to `Development`
2. Restart the Kestrel service (and regenerate the dependency tree afterward) with the following commands:

```
$ sudo systemctl restart kestrel-worldcities
$ sudo systemctl daemon-reload
```

However, you are strongly advised to never do this in real production environments and inspect the Kestrel's journal logs with the following `journalctl` commands instead, as we suggested early on:

```
$ sudo journalctl -u kestrel-worldcities --since "yyyy-MM-dd HH:mm:ss"
$ sudo journalctl -xe
```

Such an approach will give us the same level of information without exposing our errors to the public.

Now that we're done with Linux, we're ready to explore our last - but not least - deployment alternative.

Azure App Service deployment

Throughout this section, we'll learn how to deploy our `HealthCheck` web application on **MS Azure App Service**, a fully managed platform for building, deploying, and scaling web apps.

As we'll be able to see, this deployment will be considerably easier and faster than the previous ones, because we won't need to deploy a virtual machine; App Service's fully managed approach grants a deployment experience similar to the one we experienced back in *Chapter 4, Data Model with Entity Framework Core*, when we created an MS Azure database: we'll just get what we need to publish our app, without the need to perform any hardware and/or software setup. This approach can be a tremendous advantage for most projects, as long as we don't need to perform complex low-level infrastructure configuration tasks.

Here's what we'll do in detail:

- **Create a Web App instance on MS Azure** using the free-tier (F1) pricing plan
- **Publish our HealthCheck app to the Azure App Service** using Visual Studio

This is going to be our last set of tasks: let's get them done!

Creating the Web App instance

Go to `https://portal.azure.com/` and log in with your account. Once done, input `app service` in the search bar and select the **App Services** feature.

Once there, click on the **Add** button in the topmost menu to access the **Create Web App** form, shown in the following screenshot:

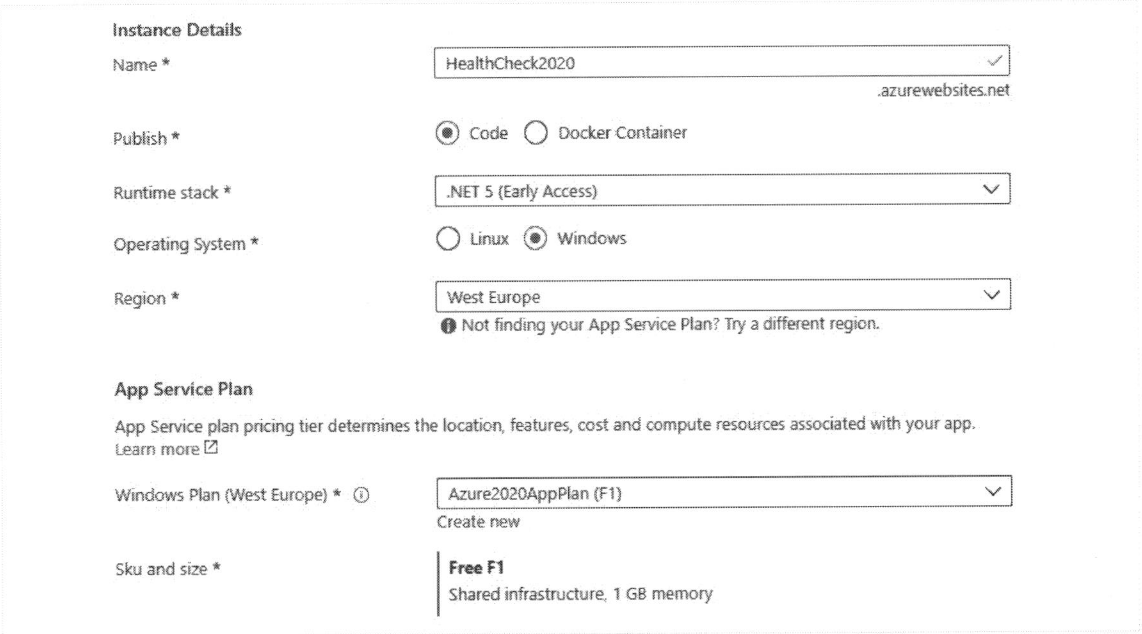

Figure 12.30: The Create Web App form

Fill out the required fields in the following way:

- **Name**: This will be our web app instance's unique name, which will be also used as the public URL's subdomain. In the preceding screenshot, we've used `HealthCheck2020` because `HealthCheck` was already taken, but any suitable name will do.
- **Publish**: Choose **Code**, unless you want to host the app within a managed Docker container.
- **Runtime stack**: Choose **.NET 5**.
- **Operating System**: Choose **Windows**, since we've optimized our `HealthCheck` app for a Windows OS to deploy at the beginning of this chapter.
- **Region**: Choose the region closest to our geographical position.
- **App Service Plan**: Choose a suitable plan, or just pick the free plan (F1) if you only want to test the service – just like we did in the preceding screenshot.
- **Subscription**: Select your MS Azure subscription.
- **Resource group**: Use the same resource group used for the SQL database and/or the VMs (or create a new one).

Once done, click the **Review + Create** button at the bottom left of the page to access the review page. From there, click the **Create** button to start the deployment process. The whole operation will take a bunch of seconds, after which we'll be able to go to our newly created resource:

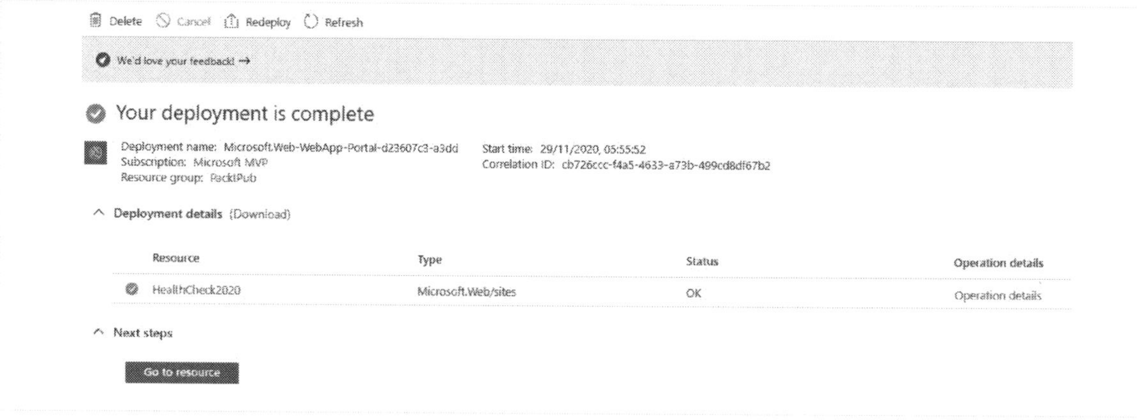

Figure 12.31: Deployment complete screen

If we click on the **Go to resource** button, we'll be taken to the Web App instance's configuration panel, with a bunch of available options:

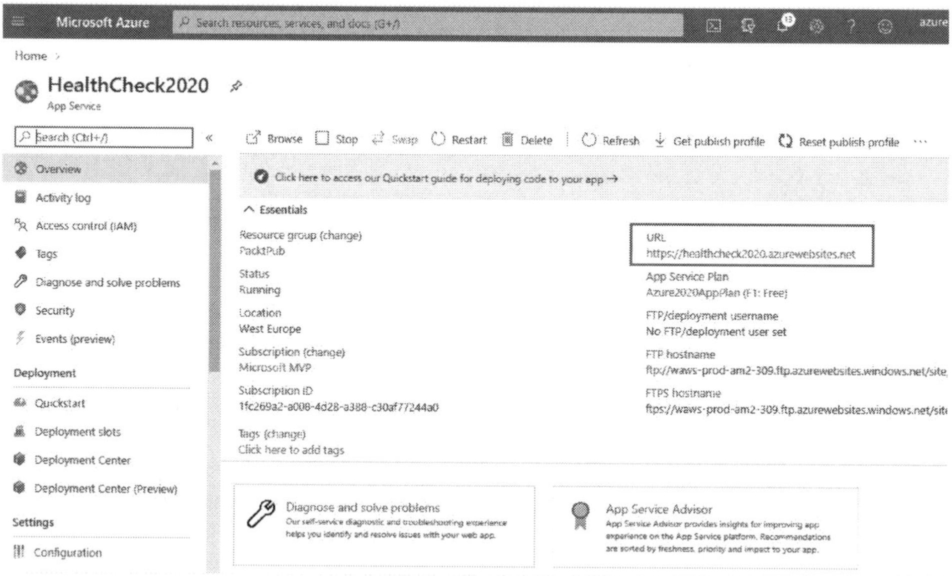

Figure 12.32: HealthCheck2020 configuration panel

However, we don't need any of the settings for now; we just have to retrieve the public URL of our app, which will be in the `https://<appname>.azurewebsites.net/` format.

As we can see in the preceding screenshot, our sample web app instance's public URL is: `https://healthcheck2020.azurewebsites.net/`

If we navigate to that URL, we'll see a welcome screen informing us that the managed instance is ready to host our web app and asking us to deploy our code, which is precisely what we're going to do.

Publishing the Web App

Switch back to Visual Studio. From Solution Explorer, right-click on the `HealthCheck` project's root node and select **Publish** to access the publishing settings.

Once there, select **Azure** and then **Azure App Service (Windows)**, as shown in the following screenshot:

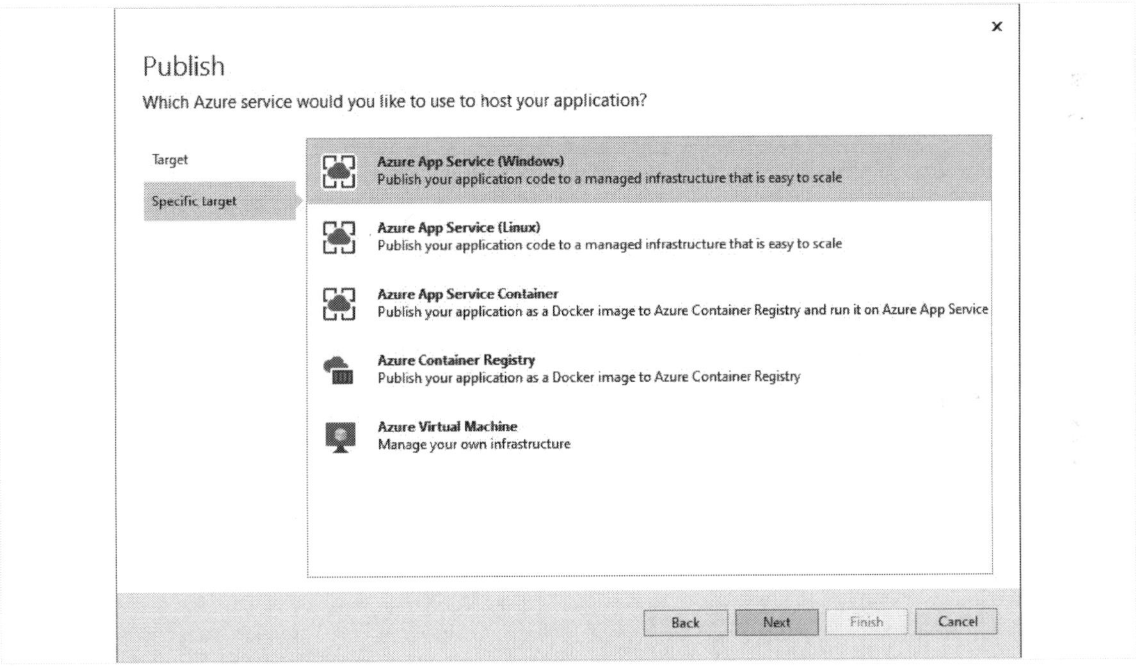

Figure 12.33: Selecting Azure App Service (Windows) in the Publish window

In the next section, we'll be asked to log in to our MS Azure account (unless we've already linked it to Visual Studio); once done, we'll be asked to select a **Resource group** and an **App Service instance** within it:

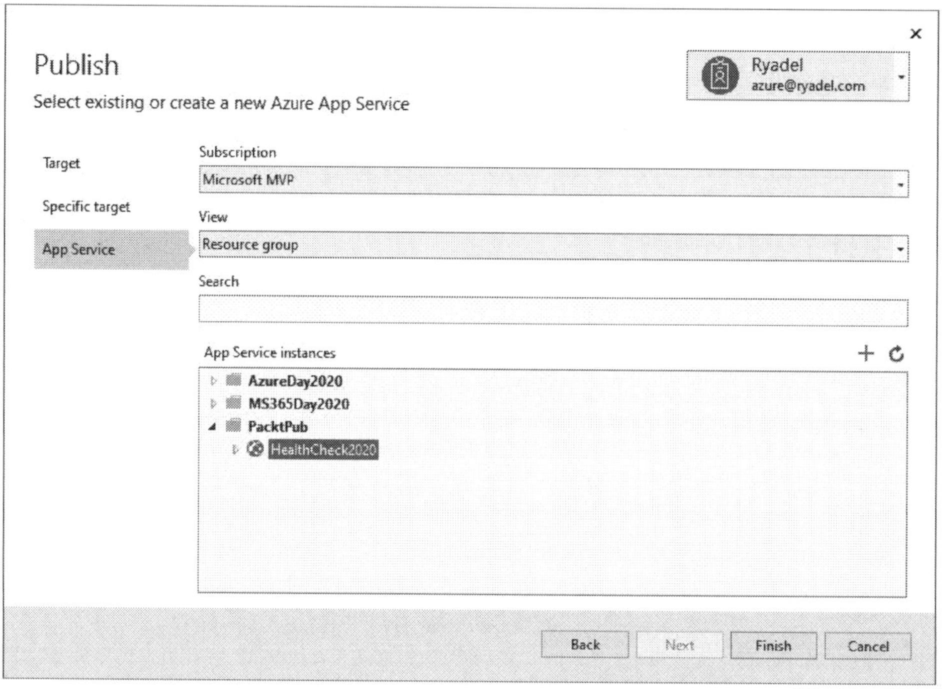

Figure 12.34: Selecting a Resource group and App Service instance

From here we can select the Web App instance we created a short while ago and click **Finish** to save the publish profile.

> `HealthCheck`'s App Service publish profile won't be available in the GitHub project for *Chapter 12* because it contains personal info regarding the Azure subscription: however, it shouldn't be a problem for the reader to create their own profile, it being a very simple and straightforward process.

Right after that, we can hit the **Publish** button and let Visual Studio work its magic on MS Azure; within a bunch of seconds, if we did everything correctly, we should be able to see our `HealthCheck` app publicly available on the web:

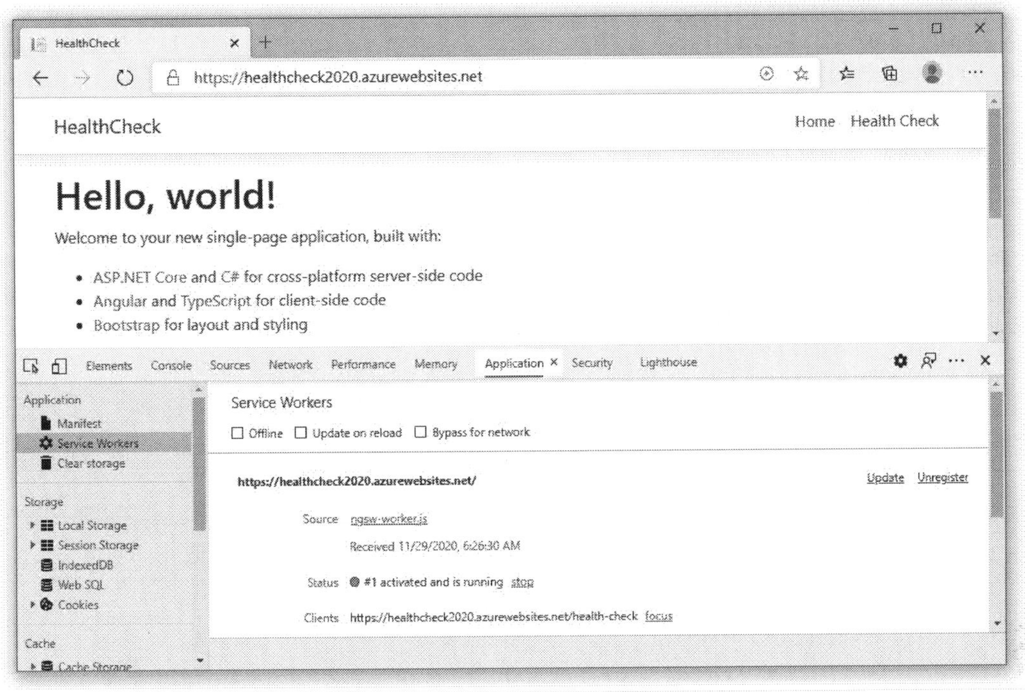

Figure 12.35: Our HealthCheck app on the web

As we can see in the preceding screenshot, the app is served in HTTPS thanks to the built-in wildcard certificate provided by MS Azure, meaning that we'll also be able to test our service worker without having to purchase an SSL certificate on our own.

That's it. Our ASP.NET Core and Angular deployment tasks have come to an end. We sincerely hope you've enjoyed the trip as much as we've enjoyed writing it.

Summary

Finally, our journey through ASP.NET Core and Angular has come to an end. Our final task involved getting our SPAs—now empowered with the most relevant features of PWAs—ready to be published in a suitable production environment.

The first thing we did was to explore some pivotal deployment tips for our *back-end* and *front-end* frameworks. Since the Visual Studio template already implemented the most important optimization tweaks, we took some valuable time to properly learn and understand the various techniques that can be used to increase our web application's performance and security when we need to publish it over the web.

Right after that, we went through Windows deployment with a step-by-step approach. We created a Windows Server 2019 VM on the MS Azure portal, and then we installed the IIS service and properly configured it in order to publish our existing `HealthCheck` app over the web. We did this with the new ASP.NET Core in-process hosting model, which has been the default (and arguably the most recommended) hosting model for Windows-based platforms since ASP.NET Core 2.2.

Then, we switched to Linux, where we learned how to deploy our `WorldCities` app on a CentOS-based VM. After configuring it properly, we took the opportunity to implement the out-of-process hosting model using Kestrel and Nginx, which is the standard approach for serving ASP.NET Core web applications on Linux-based platforms. To achieve this, we had to change some of our `WorldCities` app's *back-end* settings to ensure that they would be properly served behind a reverse proxy.

Once we did all that, we thoroughly tested the result of the preceding deployment efforts with a web browser from our development machine. For both scenarios, instead of purchasing real domain names and SSL certificates, we explained how to use self-signed certificates and host-mapping techniques, which allowed us to achieve the same outcome without spending any money.

The last thing we did was deploy our `HealthCheck` app to MS Azure App Service, a fully managed platform that can be a great fit for most projects that don't require complex low-level configuration settings.

Our adventure with ASP.NET Core and Angular has finally ended. We could have talked much longer about both frameworks, and spent much more time perfecting our apps, that's for sure. Anyhow, we should be satisfied with the results obtained and the lessons learned.

We hope you enjoyed this book. Many thanks for reading it!

Suggested topics

HTTPS, Secure Socket Layer (SSL), ASP.NET Core deploy, HTTP Strict Transport Security (HSTS), General Data Protection Regulation (GDPR), Content Delivery Network (CDN) MS Azure, Open Web Application Security Project (OWASP), SQL Server, SQL Server Management Studio (SSMS), Windows Server, IIS, FTP server, publish profiles, ASP.NET Core In-process Hosting Model, ASP.NET Core Out-of-process Hosting Model, CentOS, Kestrel, Nginx, reverse proxy, Forwarded Headers Middleware, SCP, FileZilla FTP Client, WinSCP, journalctl, nano, HOST mapping, self-signed SSL certificate, openssl, Security-Enhanced Linux (SELinux).

References

- *Host and deploy ASP.NET Core*: https://docs.microsoft.com/en-us/aspnet/core/host-and-deploy/
- *Host ASP.NET Core on Windows with IIS*: https://docs.microsoft.com/en-us/aspnet/core/host-and-deploy/iis/
- *ASP.NET Core Performance Best Practices*: https://docs.microsoft.com/en-us/aspnet/core/performance/performance-best-practices
- *Use multiple environments in ASP.NET Core*: https://docs.microsoft.com/en-us/aspnet/core/fundamentals/environments
- *Handle errors in ASP.NET Core*: https://docs.microsoft.com/en-us/aspnet/core/fundamentals/error-handling
- *Enforce HTTPS in ASP.NET Core*: https://docs.microsoft.com/en-us/aspnet/core/security/enforcing-ssl
- *.NET Core application deployment*: https://docs.microsoft.com/en-us/dotnet/core/deploying/
- *.NET Core 2.1, 3.1, and .NET 5.0 updates are coming to Microsoft Update*: https://devblogs.microsoft.com/dotnet/net-core-updates-coming-to-microsoft-update/
- *App Trimming in .NET 5*: https://devblogs.microsoft.com/dotnet/app-trimming-in-net-5/
- *Angular – Deployment Guide*: https://angular.io/guide/deployment
- *Enable cross-origin resource sharing*: https://enable-cors.org/
- *Angular: The Ahead-of-Time (AOT) compiler*: https://angular.io/guide/aot-compiler
- *Publish an ASP.NET Web App to an Azure VM from Visual Studio*: https://github.com/MicrosoftDocs/azure-docs/blob/master/articles/virtual-machines/windows/publish-web-app-from-visual-studio.md
- *Publish an application to IIS by importing publish settings in Visual Studio*: https://docs.microsoft.com/en-us/visualstudio/deployment/tutorial-import-publish-settings-iis?view=vs-2019
- *Use Spot VMs in Azure*: https://docs.microsoft.com/en-us/azure/virtual-machines/spot-vms
- *Quick reference: IIS Application Pool*: https://blogs.msdn.microsoft.com/rohithrajan/2017/10/08/quick-reference-iis-application-pool/
- *Configure the Windows Firewall to Allow SQL Server Access*: https://docs.microsoft.com/en-us/sql/sql-server/install/configure-the-windows-firewall-to-allow-sql-server-access

- *Configure ASP.NET Core to work with proxy servers and load balancers*: `https://docs.microsoft.com/en-us/aspnet/core/host-and-deploy/proxy-load-balancer`
- *Host ASP.NET Core on Linux with Nginx*: `https://docs.microsoft.com/en-us/aspnet/core/host-and-deploy/linux-nginx`
- *PuTTty: A free SSH and Telnet client for Windows*: `https://www.putty.org/`
- *Move files to and from a Linux VM using SCP*: `https://docs.microsoft.com/en-us/azure/virtual-machines/linux/copy-files-to-linux-vm-using-scp`
- *Install the .NET SDK or the .NET Runtime on CentOS*: `https://docs.microsoft.com/en-us/dotnet/core/install/linux-centos`
- *Installation guidance for SQL Server on Linux*: `https://docs.microsoft.com/en-us/sql/linux/sql-server-linux-setup`
- *Deploy an ASP.NET Core Web Application to Linux CentOS*: `https://www.ryadel.com/en/asp-net-core-2-publish-deploy-web-application-linux-centos-tutorial-guide-nginx/`
- *journalctl – Query the systemd journal*: `https://www.freedesktop.org/software/systemd/man/journalctl.html`
- *openssl – OpenSSL command-line tool*: `https://www.openssl.org/docs/manmaster/man1/openssl.html`

Other Books You May Enjoy

If you enjoyed this book, you may be interested in these other books by Packt:

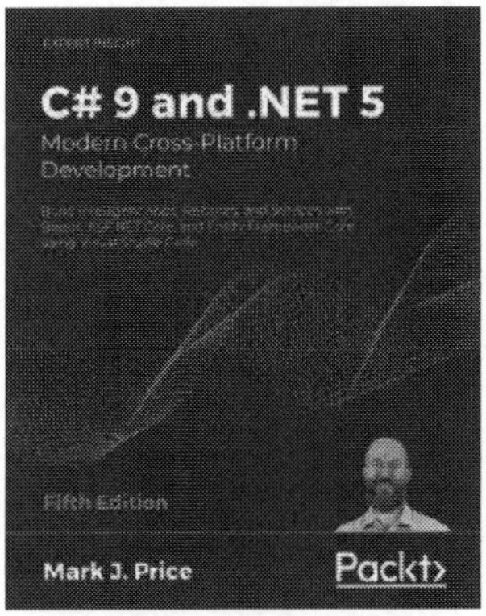

C# 9 and .NET 5 – Modern Cross-Platform Development, Fifth Edition

Mark J. Price

ISBN: 978-1-80056-810-5

- Build your own types with object-oriented programming
- Query and manipulate data using LINQ
- Build websites and services using ASP.NET Core 5
- Create intelligent apps using machine learning
- Use Entity Framework Core and work with relational databases
- Discover Windows app development using the Universal Windows Platform and XAML
- Build rich web experiences using the Blazor framework
- Build mobile applications for iOS and Android using Xamarin.Forms

Software Architecture with C# 9 and .NET 5, Second Edition

Gabriel Baptista, Francesco Abbruzzese

ISBN: 978-1-80056-604-0

- Use different techniques to overcome real-world architectural challenges and solve design consideration issues
- Apply architectural approaches such as layered architecture, service-oriented architecture (SOA), and microservices
- Leverage tools such as containers, Docker, Kubernetes, and Blazor to manage microservices effectively
- Get up to speed with Azure tools and features for delivering global solutions
- Program and maintain Azure Functions using C# 9 and its latest features
- Understand when it is best to use test-driven development (TDD) as an approach for software development
- Write automated functional test cases
- Get the best of DevOps principles to enable CI/CD environments

Index

Symbols

@angular/service-worker 595
#if preprocessor directives
reference link 432
[JsonIgnore] attributes 380, 381
.NET 5 deployment modes 638
framework-dependent deployment (FDD) 638
framework-dependent executable (FDE) 639, 640
self-contained deployment (SCD) 639
.NET 5 SDK
reference link 31
.NET authentication and authorization, for SPAs
reference link 506
.NET console application, debugging with Visual Studio
reference link 419
.NET Core 3
proprietary authentication 501, 502
.NET Core debugging features
reference link 419
[NotMapped] attributes 380, 381

A

abstract methods 395
ADO.NET 140
Amazon Web Services (AWS) 532
Angular 10, 19, 20
AppModule 275
AppRoutingModule 275, 276
countries.component.css 274
countries.component.html 273, 274
CountriesComponent, testing 277
countries.component.ts 271, 273
country.ts 271
implementing 270, 271
NavComponent 276, 277
Angular 2 12
Angular Mobile Toolkit (AMT) 13
command-line interface (CLI) 13
components 13
semantic versioning (SemVer) 12
server-side rendering (SSR) 12
TypeScript 12
Angular 4 13
ahead-of-time (AOT) compilation 13
animations npm package 13
Angular 5 14
HTTP Client API 14
State Transfer API 14
Angular 6 14
Angular 7 15
features 15
Angular 8 16, 17
features 16
Angular 9 17, 18
features 17
Angular 10 18
Angular 11 19
features 19
Angular app
angular-material.module.ts 250
AppModule, adding 124, 125
AppRoutingModule, adding 125
cities.component.html 252-254
cities.component.ts 250, 252
component, adding 124
HealthCheckComponent, adding 126, 127
NavMenuComponent, adding 125
updating 249
Angular app, cities list 212
app.module.ts 216, 217
app-routing.module.ts 217
cities.component.css 216
cities.component.html 214
cities.component.ts 213
city.ts 213
nav-component.html 218, 219

Angular authentication
AuthSample project, creating 534, 535
implementing 534
Angular authorization APIs
authorization components 546
exploring 537-539
Http interceptor 544, 546
registration and login, testing 552
route guards 539
Angular CLI
Angular app, comparing 75
Angular app, creating 73-75
app, creating 72, 73
installing 73
NG Angular app, testing 77
Startup.cs file, updating 76
Angular CLI app
compiling 618
Startup.cs file, updating 618
Angular component
component (.ts) file 110
creating 110
creating, Angular CLI used 110, 111
health-check.component.css 122
health-check.component.html 121
health-check.component.ts 111, 112
heath checks 110
style (.css) file 110
styling 123
template (.html) file 110
Angular deployment tips 632, 640
angular.json configuration file 644
automatic deployment 644
CORS policy 644
differential loading 642
ng build 641
ng serve 641
package.json file 641
Angular deprecations guide
reference link 17
Angular form debugging 439
changes, reacting to 442, 443
Form Model 440, 441
pipe operator 442
Angular form debugging, activity log 443, 444
extending 446, 447
testing 445
Angular forms 282-284
exploring 282
using 284
Angular front-end 53
app, testing 67, 71, 72
/ClientApp/src/ folder 63
workspace 54
Angular HTTP service class
limitations 118
Angular Initialization Cycle 64
Angular.io
URL 120
AngularJS 11
reference link 11
angular.json 54
angular.json configuration file 644
Angular Language Service
reference link 16
Angular Material 219
URL 220
used, for serving data 219-221
Angular Material typography 221
Angular modules 89
Angular's animation system
reference link 221
Angular test suite 482
cities tests, creating 489, 490
component, configuring 488
describe and beforeEach sections 483, 484
fixture, configuring 488
import section 482
mock CityService, adding 484
running 491, 492, 493
title test, creating 489
Angular unit tests 479, 480
concepts 480, 481
Jasmine tests 481
TestBed interface 481
URL 480
Angular Universal Server-Side Rendering (SSR) 65
anonymous types
versus DTO classes 378, 379
anonymous types, in C#
reference link 379
app, Angular front-end
CounterComponent 69, 70
HomeComponent 67
NavMenuComponent 68
application logging 453, 454
application programming interfaces (APIs) 2
AppRoutingModule
adding 89-91
using 91

appSettings.Development.json file
updating 512, 513
appsettings.json file 52, 53, 179
updating 179
Arrange, Act, Assert pattern 469
AsNoTracking extension method
reference link 199
ASP.NET 2, 3, 19, 20, 267
CountriesController 267, 268
features 20
ASP.NET 5 7, 8, 9
reference link 10
ASP.NET back-end 41
configuration files 43
controllers 42
Razor Pages 41, 42
ASP.NET Core previous versions
ASP.NET Core 1.x 3, 4
ASP.NET Core 2.1, 5
ASP.NET Core 2.2,6
ASP.NET Core 3.0,7
ASP.NET Core 3.1, 7
ASP.NET Core 3.x 6, 7
ASP.NET Core deployment tips 632
development environment 634, 635
launchSettings.json file 633, 634
production environment 634, 635
staging environment 634, 635
ASP.NET Core health checks 98
ICMPHealthCheck class, improving 104
Internet Control Message Protocol (ICMP) check, adding 100
middleware, adding 98, 99
ASP.NET Core Identity 503
ApplicationDbContext, extending 506
ApplicationUser, creating 505
async tasks 523, 524
await keyword 523, 524
deadlocks 523, 524
IdentityServer middleware, configuring 511, 512
middleware, configuring 508-511
NuGet packages, adding 505
SeedController, revising 513
setting up 504
unit tests, adjusting 507, 508
ASP.NET Core Identity APIs
reference link 502
ASP.NET Core Identity model 503
entity types 503, 504
ASP.NET Core Identity UI package
customizing 558
installing 558
ASP.NET Core logging 455
ASP.NET Core PWA middleware alternative 596, 597
ASP.NET Core revolution 3
ASP.NET 5 7-9
ASP.NET Core 1.x 3, 4
ASP.NET Core 2.x 4-6
ASP.NET Core 3.x 6, 7
ASP.NET Core solution
overview 40, 41
ASP.NET Core unit tests
Act phase 469
Act phase, implementing 471
Arrange phase 469
Arrange phase, implementing 470
Assert phase 469
Assert phase, implementing 472
Behavior-Driven Development (BDD) 478, 479
building 464, 468, 469, 470
debugging 474, 476
executing, ways 472
executing, with .NETCLI 472, 473
executing, with Visual Studio Test Explorer 473, 474
Test-Driven Development (TDD) 476, 477
WorldCities.Test project, creating 464
ASP.NET Core Windows hosting bundle
installing 654
assembly linker 639
Asynchronous JavaScript and XML (AJAX) 389
authentication 497
implementing 496
authentication methods 529, 530
conclusions 533
sessions 530, 531
signatures 532
tokens 531, 532
Two-Factor Authentication (2FA) 533
authorization 499
implementing 496
authorization API
back-end code, adjusting 557
front-end authorization APIs, importing 554
implementing, in WorldCities app 553
login and registration, testing 561, 563
authorization components, of Angular
LoginComponent 548-551
LoginMenuComponent 546-548

LogoutComponent 551
AuthSample project
creating 534, 535
troubleshooting 535, 536
automatic installation, PWA requisites
Angular PNG icon set 608
Azure
SQL Database, creating on 162, 163
Azure AD Authentication Library (ADAL) 501
Azure App Service deployment 696
Web App instance, creating 696-699
Web App, publishing 699-701
Azure Spot
reference link 649
Azure Virtual Machine publish profile 657, 658

B

back-end action methods
securing 559, 561
back-end debugging 418
in Linux 419
in Windows 419
BaseFormComponent
implementing 362-364
BaseService
creating 394
Behavior-Driven Development (BDD) 478, 479
Bootstrap 214
reference link 215
Bootstrap styling 214
BrowserAnimationsModule
reference link 221
browser developer tools 435-439
bug fixes 366
bug improvements 366
built-in validators
reference link 321

C

caching service 594
calls
debouncing, to back-end 352
calls, updation
CitiesComponent, updating 352-354
CountriesComponent, updating 354
Cascading Style Sheets (CSS) 134
child class 362
CityEditComponent 291, 292
city, adding 301, 302
city button, adding 306
city-edit.component.css 297
city-edit.component.html 296, 297
city-edit.component.ts 293-295
extending 302, 305
implementing 364, 365
MatSelectModule, using 314-316
route, adding 306-308
select statement, using 308-312
CityService
AppModule 399
CitiesComponent 400, 402
CityEditComponent 402, 404
creating 397, 399
implementing 399
IsDupeCity, implementing 404, 406
loadCountries, implementing 404, 406
class inheritance 362
BaseFormComponent, implementing 362-364
CityEditComponent, implementing 364, 365
CountryEditComponent, implementing 365
client app 86
AppModule source code 89
AppRoutingModule, adding 89-91
component list, trimming 86, 88
NavMenu, updating 91-94
client-side debugging 447
client-side debugging, with Google Chrome
reference link 447
client-side paging 226-228
client-side validation 326
code bloat 360
form validation 360, 362
template, improving 360
code debouncing 351, 352
Code-First 144
cons 145
pros 145
used, for creating database 173
code refactoring
reference link 387
code throttling 351, 352
common interface methods
adding 395, 396
generic types 397
Observable types, returning 397
type variables 397
Common Language Runtime (CLR) 504
Component Dev Kit (CDK) 219
conditional breakpoint 420

conditional breakpoint, setting panel 420
Actions 421
Conditions 421
testing 422
configuration files 43
appsettings.json file 52, 53
Program.cs file 44
Startup.cs file 46-52
Configure Web Deploy Publishing feature
using 659, 660
connection string
securing 179, 180
content management systems (CMSes) 22
Continuous Delivery (CD) 12, 657
Continuous Integration (CI) 138, 657
controllers 42
advantages 42
CORS policy 617
CountryEditComponent
AppModule 344
AppRoutingModule 345
countries.component.html 346
country-edit.component.css 343
country-edit.component.html 341, 343
country-edit.component.ts 334-338
creating 334
implementing 365
IsDupeField server-side API 339
testing 347-350
country name
adding 383
Angular front-end, updating 384-387
CitiesController 383, 384
CountryService
CountriesComponent 408, 410
CountryEditComponent 410, 413
creating 406, 408
C# preprocessor directives
reference link 432
Create, Read, Update, and Delete (CRUD) 497
C# regions
using 153, 154
Cross-Origin Resource Sharing (CORS) policy 616, 617, 644
reference link 617
Cross-Site Request Forgery (CSRF) 531
CRUD operations 137
custom async validators
reference link 330

D

data
fetching 210
seeding 528, 529
serving, with Angular Material 219-221
data annotations 174
database
creating 184
creating, with Code-First 173
data, seeding 528, 529
identity migration, adding 525
identity migration, applying 525
populating 191
Startup.cs file, updating 184
updating 524, 525
Database as a Service (DBaaS) 162
Database-First 145
best choice, making 147
cons 146
pros 146
database initialization strategies
choice, making 178
database initializers (DbInitializers) 178
database schema (DB schema) 527
data migration
need for 191
data model 140
Entity Framework Core (EF Core) 140, 141
Entity Framework Core (EF Core), installing 141, 142
SQL Server Data Provider 142
data modeling approaches 144
Code-First 144
Database-First 145
data seeding 191
data service 388
BaseService, creating 394
building 393
CityService, creating 397, 399
CityService, implementing 399
common interface methods, adding 395, 396
CountryService, creating 406, 408
XMLHttpRequest (XHR), versus Fetch API 388
data source 138, 139
Data Transfer Object (DTO) 373
data validation 316
Model-Driven validation 319
server-side validation 326, 327, 328

Template-Driven validation 317, 318
DbContext
setting up 173
DBMS licensing models 143
DBMS structured logging, with Serilog 455
HTTP requests, logging 458
logs, accessing 458-460
NuGet packages, installing 455
Serilog, configuring 456, 457
DB table names
defining 158
debouncing
defining 351
debugging
see Angular form debugging
see back-end debugging
see client-side debugging
see Entity Framework Core (EF Core), debugging
see front-end debugging
see .NET console application, debugging with Visual Studio
see .NET Core debugging features
see Visual Studio JavaScript debugging
Dependency Injection (DI) 115, 504
deployment
see Azure App Service deployment 696
see Linux deployment 669
see Windows deployment 645
developer edition 143
development environment 634, 635
differential loading 642, 643
Digital Equipment Corporation (DEC) 17
DI, in Angular
reference link 115
DI, in ASP.NET Core
reference link 115
Document Object Model (DOM) 116, 216
dotnet CLI
database, updating 188
dotnet ef command 189
using 186-188
DTO classes
entities, securing 379
security consideration 377
separation, considering 377
using 377, 382
versus anonymous types 378, 379
DupeCityValidator
CitiesController 330
city-edit.component.html 331
city-edit.component.ts 328-330
creating 328
observables 332, 333
performance issues 333
RxJS operators 332, 333
testing 331, 332

E

ECMAScript 2015 642
ECMAScript version 6 642
edge-origin proxy 685
Elvis Operator 318
email sending service
adding 563
end-to-end (E2E) tool 10
entities
City entity 149, 151
Country entity 152, 153
creating 147
DB table names, defining 158
defining 148, 149
relationships, defining 155
entity controllers 200
CitiesController 201, 204
CountriesController 204
testing 204, 205
Entity Data Model (EDM) 140
Entity Framework Core (EF Core) 140, 141, 148, 370, 425
approaches 191
EF Core .NET CLI 190
EF Core PMC 190
EF model scaffolding 145
Entity Framework Core migrations 525
Entity Framework Core (EF Core, debugging) 425, 426
GetCountries() SQL query, using 426, 427
Entity type configuration methods 174
choice, making 177
classes 176, 177
data annotations 174
Fluent API 175, 176
EPPlus licensing
reference link 194
ETag response header 81
reference link 81
evaluation edition 143
express edition 143
extension methods
reference link 429

external SMTP server
MailKit, using 582
Startup class 586

F

fake service class 485
feature modules 64
Fetch API 388, 390
advantages 392
reference link 393
versus XMLHttpRequest (XHR) 388
filter behavior
debouncing 351
improving 350
throttling 351
filtering 219
adding 254, 255
AngularMaterialModule 265, 266
ApiResult, extending 255-261
CitiesComponent 262, 263
CitiesComponent CSS style file 264
CitiesComponent HTML template file 264
CitiesController 261
performance considerations 267
firewalld 677
Fluent API 175, 176
FormBuilder 333, 334
CountryEditComponent, creating 334
form model 287
Forwarded Headers Middleware 678
framework-dependent deployment (FDD) 638
advantages 638
disadvantages 639
framework-dependent executable (FDE) 638
advantages 639
disadvantages 640
front-end authorization APIs
api-authorization.constants 554
AppModule 554
AppRoutingModule 555, 556
importing 554
NavMenuComponent 556, 557
front-end debugging 432
Angular form debugging 439
browser developer tools 435-439
client-side debugging 447
Visual Studio JavaScript debugging 433
front-end debugging, observables unsubscription 447
alternatives 451, 452
need for 453
takeUntil() operator 449, 450
unsubscribe() method 448, 449
full-stack approach 21

G

General Data Protection Regulation (GDPR) 5
generic types 397
GetAngular 10
GetCountries() SQL query
#if preprocessor, using 432
SQL code, obtaining programmatically 427, 429
ToParametrizedSql() method, implementing 429-432
using 426, 427
Google identity provider 498
Graphical User Interface (GUI) 453

H

health-check.component.ts 111, 112
constructor 117, 118
dependency injection (DI) 114, 115
HttpClient 118, 119
import and modules 113, 114
interfaces 120
ngOnInit (and other lifecycle hooks) 116, 117
observables 119, 120
HealthCheck profile 634
HealthCheck web application
Azure Virtual Machine publish profile 657, 658
Folder publish profile 655, 656
FTP publish profile 656, 657
HOSTS files, updating of testing machine 667
publishing 655
testing 666, 667, 668
hidden attribute 215, 216
reference link 215
HTTP cache
ETag response header 81
Last-Modified response header 81
working 80, 81
HttpClient 391, 392
advantages 392
HTTP/HTTPS implementation standards 497
Http interceptor 544, 546
reference link 546
HttpInterceptors
versus service workers 595
HTTP requests and responses 210

HTTP Strict Transport Security (HSTS) 635
ICMPHealthCheck class, improving 104
custom output message, implementing 107, 108
health check responses 108
HTTP status codes 108
middleware setup, updating 106
output message, configuring 109
parameters and response messages, adding 104, 105
identity migration, database
data model, dropping from scratch 527, 528
data model, recreating from scratch 527, 528
data model, updating 526, 527
IdentityServer
reference link 502
IEmailSender interface
implementing 571, 583
reference link 563
IEmailSender interface, options
MailKitEmailSender 584, 586
MailKitEmailSenderOptions 583, 584
new sender, creating 574, 575
SendGridEmailSender 572, 573
SendGridEmailSenderOptions 572
Startup class 574
IHost versus web server 44-46
IIS application pool
configuring 665, 666
IIS ASP.NET Core runtime installation
starting 655
IIS, configuring
IIS website entry, adding 663, 664
SSL certificate, adding 661-663
IIS Express profile 633
Infrastructure as a Service (IaaS) 159
inheritance 362
initial migration
adding 186
in-memory Web API package 137
reference link 138
in-process hosting model 661
internal membership provider 501
International Organization for Standardization (ISO) 153
Internet Control Message Protocol (ICMP) 100
check, adding 100
ICMPHealthCheck class, adding to pipeline 103, 104
ICMPHealthCheck class, creating 101, 102
ICMPHealthCheck class, flaws 103
possible outcomes 101
Internet Information Services (IIS) 652
IsDupeField server-side API 339
Linq.Dynamic, using 340, 341
isDupeField validator 338

J

Jasmine 479
URL 480
JavaScript approaches
limitations 610
JavaScript Object Notation (JSON) 210
JavaScript source maps 434, 435
JSON conventions and defaults 210-212
JSON naming issue 268, 269, 270
JSON Web Tokens (JWTs) 497, 533
URL 533
just-in-time (JIT) compilation 642

K

Karma 55, 479
URL 480
Katana
reference link 46
Kestrel 690
Kestrel service
configuring 687-689
Kitchen Sink 382

L

Language-Integrated Query (LINQ) 244, 245
Last-Modified response header 81
reference link 82
lat and lon values
city-edit.component.html 368, 369
city-edit.component.ts 366, 367
validating 366
launchSettings.json file 633, 634
Let's Encrypt
URL 593
Library General Public License (LGPL) 193
lifecycle hooks methods 117
Linq.Dynamic
using 340, 341
Linq.Dynamic.Core
pros and cons 246
LINQ
LINQ, lambda expressions 246

LINQ, query expressions 246
LINQ structured queries 245
Linux 143
back-end debugging 419
Linux CentOS VM
adding 670
configuring 670
Linux CentOS VM, creating on MS Azure 670
DNS name label, configuring 671
inbound security rules, setting 671
Linux deployment 669
Kestrel, configuring 685
Linux CentOS VM, creating on MS Azure 669
Linux VM, configuring 672
Nginx, configuring 685
self-signed SSL certificate, creating 686, 687
WorldCities app, adapting 678
Linux VM
80 and 443 TCP ports, opening 676
ASP.NET Core runtime, installing 673, 674
configuring 672
connecting to 672, 673
Nginx, installing 674
LiteXHealthChecks 127
loading pattern, EF Core
eager loading 157
explicit loading 157
lazy loading 157
local area network (LAN) 100
loop
countries, adding 267

M

MailKit 582
reference link 582
MailKit NuGet package
installing 582
manual installation, PWA requisites
angular.json file, updating 598
@angular/service-worker npm package, adding 598
favicon, adding 605
index.html file, updating 600, 601
ngsw-config.json file, adding 606, 607
ServiceWorkerModule, importing 599, 600
Web App Manifest file, adding 601-604
Material Design 219
purpose 219
MatPaginatorModule
used, for adding pagination 225
MatSortModule
used, for adding sorting 240
MatTableModule 221-225
Microsoft.AspNetCore.Cors NuGet package
reference link 617
Microsoft SQL Database Provider 142
Microsoft XML Core Services (MSXML) 389
migrations 190
minification 435
mock CityService
adding 484
extending 485
fake service class 485
implementing 485, 486, 487
implementing with interface approach 487, 488
interface instance 485
overriding 485
spy feature 485
mocking 466
Model-Driven Forms 287, 288
working 290
Model-Driven validation 319
async validators 319
sync validators 319
validators 319, 321, 323, 324, 325
model-view-controller (MVC) 110
Model-View-ViewModel (MVVM) 110, 377
Moq 466
Moq NuGet package 467
MS Azure
Windows Server VM, creating on 645
Multi-Page Applications (MPAs) 22

N

Native Web Applications (NWAs) 21, 25
navigation link
adding 297
app.module.ts 298
app-routing.module.ts 299
cities.component.html 299-301
Navigator.onLine property 609, 610
reference link 610
NavMenu
updating 91-94
ng build 641
ng-connection-service npm package 610
app.component.html file, updating 616
app.component.ts file, updating 612, 613
isOnline.txt static file, removing from cache 613, 614

ng-connection-service, installing 611, 612
ng-connection-service, installing via NPM 614, 615
reference link 611
Nginx
configuring, Nginx reverse proxy 690, 691
HTTP connection, checking 675, 676
installing 674
starting up 675
nginx.conf file
updating 692
Nginx reverse proxy
configuring 690, 691
NgModules 64, 89
ng serve 641
Node.js 55
Node Package Manager (npm) 55
npmJS syntax 56
npm packages 55
number of cities
adding 369, 370
Angular front-end updates 373-376
CountryDTO class, creating 372, 373
GetCountries() method 370-372

O

OAuth 499
OAuth 2 499
object-oriented programming (OOP) 362
object relational mapper (ORM) 140
observables 119
advantages 119
Observable types
returning 397
offline loading 594
offline mode 594
offline status
handling 609
offline status, options
Navigator.onLine property 609, 610
ng-connection-service npm package 610
window's onoffline event 609
window's ononline event 609
offline warning 594
oidc-client library 537
reference link 537
on-demand caching strategy 607
OpenID 498
OpenID 2.0, to OIDC migration
OpenID Connect (OIDC) 499
Open Web Interface for .NET (OWIN)
reference link 46
Outlook Web Access (OWA) 388
out-of-process hosting model 661

P

package.json 55
Angular code, upgrading 59, 60
Angular, downgrading 56, 57
Angular, upgrading 56, 57
other packages, downgrading 57, 59
other packages, upgrading 57, 59
package.json file 641
Package Manager Console 245
using 190
pagination
adding, with MatPaginatorModule 225
see server-side paging
PING 100
Platform as a Service (PaaS) 159, 162
polyfills 642
polymorphism 362
production environment 632-635
setting in 637
rules of thumb, applying 636, 637
product owner expectations 25, 27
adaptability 27
early release 26
fast completion 27
GUI over back-end 26
Program.cs file 44
IHost versus web server 44-46
Progressive Web Applications (PWAs) 21-24, 638
distinctive features 592, 593
features 23, 24
offline loading 594
reference link 593
secure origin feature, implementing 593
subset 24
Web App Manifest 594
proprietary
versus third-party 500, 501
proprietary authentication
proprietary versus third-party 500, 501
with .NET Core 501, 502
Protractor 480
URL 480
Promise
reference link 393

publish profile 620
PWA capabilities
alternative testing methods 628
Angular CLI app, compiling with 618
installing 626-628
serving, with http-server 628, 629
testing 618-626
Visual Studio app, compiling with 619
PWA requisites
automatic installation 607
implementing 597
manual installation 597

R

Razor Class Library (RCL) 558
Razor Pages 41, 42
advantages 42
mapping, to EndpointMiddleware 559
reference link 41
Reactive Extensions for JavaScript (RxJS) 390
reference link 393
Reactive Forms 285, 290
building 290
CityEditComponent 291, 292
navigation link, adding 297
ReactiveFormsModule 290, 291
ReactiveFormsModule 290, 291
ReactiveX JavaScript (RxJS) library 119
URL 120
Red Hat Enterprise Linux (RHEL) 143
regular expressions (regex) 338
URL 338
relationships, entities
Cities property, adding to Country entity class 156
Country property, adding to City entity class 155, 156
route guards 539
in Angular 540-544
reference link 544
RxJS operators
reference link 355

S

Safe Navigation Operator 318
reference link 319
same-origin policy 617
secrets.json file
adding 181, 182
sharing, between multiple projects 183
working with 184
Secrets Storage 181
secure origin feature 593
Security-Enhanced Linux (SELinux) 686
SeedController
CreateDefaultUsers() method, implementing 519, 522
CreateDefaultUser() unit test, defining 514, 517, 518, 519
excel file, importing 193-200
implementing 192, 193
revising 513
RoleManager, adding through DI 513, 514
unit test, rerunning 522
UserManager, adding through DI 513, 514
self-contained deployment (SCD) 638
advantages 639
disadvantages 639
SELinux 687
URL 687
semantic versioning (SemVer) 12
SendGrid
URL 564
Serilog
DBMS structured, logging with 455
URL 460
server-side paging 229
ApiResult, creating 231-236
CitiesComponent, modifying 236-239
CitiesController, modifying 229-231
server-side validation 326-328
DupeCityValidator, creating 328
service worker
registration options 600
versus HttpInterceptors 595
sessions 530, 531
disadvantages 530
signatures 532
Single-Page Application (SPA) 21-23, 41, 118, 497, 531
features 22
project 27
Hello World! 28
Single Responsibility Principle (SRP) 42, 382
singleton services
URL 399
SMTP Relay method 582
SMTP settings
setting up 583
sorting 219, 239
adding, with MatSortModule 240

Angular app, updating 249
ApiResult, extending 240, 244
CitiesController, updating 249
System.Linq.Dynamic.Core, installing 244
spec.ts file 70
SQL Database 162
creating, on Azure 162, 163
instance, configuring 166-168
setting up 163-166
SQL Injections
preventing 247, 248
reference link 246
SQL Managed Instance 162
SQL Server 159
database, configuring 169, 170
login, mapping to database 172, 173
SQL Server 2019, installing 159-162
SQL Server alternatives 144
SQL Server database, backup performing 526
SQL Server Data Provider 142
SQL Server Express 159
WorldCities database, creating 170
WorldCities login, adding 171
SQL Server installing
Linux 161
Windows 161
SQL Server Management Studio (SSMS) 161
SQL Server Management tools 161
SQL virtual machine 162
SSH access 593
Stack Overflow thread
reference link 49
staging environment 635
Startup.cs file 46-52
updating 184
static file caching 78-80
HTTP cache, working 80, 81
strategy improvement 82
strategy improvements, static file caching
Cache-Control header, implementing 82, 83
configuration model, advantage 83-85
typed approach 85, 86
structural directives
URL 122
subclass 362
SUSE Enterprise Server 143
Swiss Army Knives
limitations 382
System.Reflection
reference link 248

T

Task Asynchronous Programming (TAP) 502
Template-Driven Forms 285, 286
cons 286
pros 286
reference link 287
working 289
Template-Driven validation 317, 318
reference link 318
Safe Navigation Operator 318
template syntax
URL 122
Test-Driven Development (TDD) 476-636
third-party authentication 498
OpenID Connect (OIDC) 499
OpenID, implementing 498
third-party authorization 499, 500
third-party versus proprietary 500, 501
throttling 355
defining 351
Time-Based One-Time Password (TOTP) algorithm 533
reference link 533
tokens 531, 532
transactional email API
email-based account verification, testing 579-582
Identity pages, scaffolding 575-578
IEmailSender interface, implementing 571
integration, verifying 568-570
link-based account verification, disabling 578, 579
SendGrid account, using 564-566
SendGrid NuGet package, installing 568
SendGrid, using 564
Web API key, obtaining 566, 568
tree shaking 400
reference link 400
tsconfig.json 61
reference link 62
TSLint 63
URL 63
Two-Factor Authentication (2FA) 533
reference link 533
TypeScript 3.9 release notes
reference link 18
TypeScript access modifiers 395

TypeScript compiler (TSC) 62
type variables 397

U

Ubuntu 143
ufw command 677
unit testing 463, 493
user interface (UI) 453
using declaration techniques 102
reference link 102

V

variable scoping technique 116
validation
see client-side validation
see data validation
see form validation
see Model-Driven validation
see server-side validation
see Template-Driven validation
Virtual Network (VNet) 162
Visual Studio
debugging features 419
Visual Studio app (VS app) 75
CLI-generated files, copying 622
compiling 619
publish profile, creating 620-622
Startup.cs file, updating 623
Visual Studio Code
download link 419
Visual Studio Container tools, with ASP.NET Core
reference link 419
Visual Studio, debug options
conditional breakpoint 420
Output window 423, 424
Visual Studio Docker container tools, for Windows
installation link 419
Visual Studio JavaScript debugging 433, 434
JavaScript source maps 434, 435

W

waterfall model
reference link 27
WeatherForecastController 43
Web App Manifest 594
file, adding 601-604
file, publishing 604
Web.config approach 180
WebEssentials.AspNetCore.ServiceWorker
reference link 597
WET approach 261
wide area network (WAN) 100
Windows
back-end debugging 419
Windows deployment 645
HealthCheck app, deploying 655
HealthCheck app, publishing 655
IIS, configuring 661
VM, configuring 652
Windows Server VM, creating on MS Azure 645
Windows HOSTS file
reference link 667
window's ononline/onoffline event 609
Windows Presentation Foundation (WPF) 6
Windows Server VM
IIS web server, adding 652, 654
Windows Server VM, creating on MS Azure 645
DNS name label, configuring 649
inbound security rules, setting 650, 651
MS Azure portal, accessing 646
VM, adding 646-648
VM, configuring 646-648
workspace
broken code 29, 30
preparing 28, 29
project, setting up 31
upgrading 30, 31
workspace, Angular front-end
angular.json 54
package.json 55
tsconfig.json 61
workspace-level files 62
workspace-level files 62
workspace, project
Angular project, creating 32
.NET 5 SDK, installing 31, 32
.NET 5 SDK version, checking 32
.NET project, creating 32
test run, performing 34, 35
Visual Studio project, launching 32-34
WorldCities app
adapting 678
appsettings.Production.json file, creating 680, 681
database connection string, checking 679
deploying 682
forwarded headers middleware, adding 678

HOSTS files, updating of testing machine 693
permissions, adding 682, 683
permissions, publishing 683
publishing 681
testing 692-695
troubleshooting 695, 696
/var/www folder, creating 682
WorldCities publish folder, copying 683-685
WorldCities.Test project
creating 464, 466
Microsoft.EntityFramework.InMemory 467
Moq 466
WorldCities dependency reference, adding 468
WorldCities web app 132, 134
CSS basics 134-137
data server, using 137, 138
styling 134-137
World Wide Web Consortium (W3C) 389

X

XMLHttpRequest (XHR) 283-390
reference link 389
versus Fetch API 388

Made in the USA
Middletown, DE
24 September 2021

48995860R00413